The Political Theory of the American Founding

This book provides a complete overview of the American Founders' political theory, covering natural rights, natural law, state of nature, social compact, consent, and the policy implications of these ideas. It is a response to the current scholarly consensus, which holds that the founders' political thought is best understood as an amalgam of liberalism, republicanism, and perhaps other traditions. Against that view, West argues that the foundational documents overwhelmingly point to natural rights and natural law as the lens through which all politics is understood. The book explores in depth how the Founders' supposedly "republican" policies on citizen character formation do not contradict but instead complement their "liberal" policies on property and economics. Additionally, the book shows how the Founders' embrace of other traditions in their politics – such as common law and Protestantism – was always guided and limited by overarching principles derived from the laws of nature.

Thomas G. West holds the Paul Ermine Potter and Dawn Tibbetts Potter Endowed Professorship in Politics at Hillsdale College, Michigan. His research areas include American political thought, natural law and natural right, Aquinas, Hobbes, Locke, and Leo Strauss.

The Political Theory of the American Founding

Natural Rights, Public Policy, and the Moral Conditions of Freedom

THOMAS G. WEST

CAMBRIDGE
UNIVERSITY PRESS

CAMBRIDGE
UNIVERSITY PRESS

University Printing House, Cambridge CB2 8BS, United Kingdom

One Liberty Plaza, 20th Floor, New York, NY 10006, USA

477 Williamstown Road, Port Melbourne, VIC 3207, Australia

314–321, 3rd Floor, Plot 3, Splendor Forum, Jasola District Centre, New Delhi – 110025, India

79 Anson Road, #06-04/06, Singapore 079906

Cambridge University Press is part of the University of Cambridge.

It furthers the University's mission by disseminating knowledge in the pursuit of education, learning and research at the highest international levels of excellence.

www.cambridge.org
Information on this title: www.cambridge.org/9781107140486
DOI: 10.1017/9781316492840

© Thomas G. West 2017

First published 2017
Reprinted 2018

Printed in the United States of America by Sheridan Books, Inc.

A catalog record for this publication is available from the British Library.

ISBN 978-1-107-14048-6 Hardback
ISBN 978-1-316-50603-5 Paperback

For Grace Starry West

6/5/2020

Contents

Acknowledgments

This book grew out of – and eventually went far beyond – five 2002 public lectures presented in the annual Frank M. Covey, Jr., Loyola Lectures in Political Analysis at Loyola University Chicago. Thanks to Thomas S. Engeman for the invitation.

I am grateful to Hillsdale College's President Larry Arnn and Vice-President Douglas Jeffrey for support and encouragement over the years, both at the Claremont Institute and at Hillsdale, for this and other writing projects. I also thank the Earhart Foundation for grants that supported the writing of this book.

Friends and acquaintances who have responded helpfully, sometimes critically, to my arguments over the years include John Alvis, David Azerrad, James Ceaser, Eric Claeys, John Marini, Tiffany Miller, Joseph Postell, Paul Rahe, Kevin Slack, and Michael Zuckert. Especially helpful were John Grant, Charles Kesler, and Phillip Muñoz, who gave the entire book a thorough reading; their recommendations and criticisms made it clearer and better. Bruno Cortes, Robert Fullilove, Emily Runge, and William Zeiser provided valuable and extensive copy-editing. Alyssa Bornhorst prepared the index. Michael Hoffpauir proofread the manuscript. Clayton Cramer helped me track down some early state laws. Regarding Chapter 11 (on government and public opinion), my former University of Dallas colleague Leo Paul S. de Alvarez first kindled my appreciation of the role of patriotic music in the formation of the American character. Thanks to all.

My deepest intellectual debt is to Leo Strauss and Harry Jaffa for their important work in reviving serious intellectual interest in the founders' political theory and its European antecedents. Their writings generated my initial and continuing interest in the founding, although my conclusions often differ from theirs. Many Straussians regard the political theory of the founding as "liberal" in the sense of being based predominantly on Lockean natural rights, in which there is supposedly no significant place for moral duties, for the classical virtues, for religion, or for viewing sex and ethnic differences as politically relevant.[1] As a graduate student, I had absorbed that opinion from Jaffa, Martin Diamond, and others.[2] Jaffa later changed his mind, arguing that the founding "was dominated by an Aristotelian Locke – or a Lockean Aristotle."[3] I accepted Jaffa's modified view – which still assumed that there is something wrong with the unvarnished Locke – in some of my earlier writings.[4] No longer. In the 2000s I revised my view of Locke and other modern philosophers. Although European political thought is not my theme, I will say a little more about Strauss and Locke in Chapter 8. As to the European origins of the founders' political theory, I now believe it is safer to avoid distracting entanglements in that debate – at least until we understand better the founders' views on their own terms. That is my concern in this book.

[1] Catherine and Michael Zuckert, *The Truth about Leo Strauss: Political Philosophy and American Democracy* (Chicago: University of Chicago Press, 2006), 58–79.

[2] Harry V. Jaffa, *Crisis of the House Divided: An Interpretation of the Lincoln-Douglas Debates* (1959; repr. Chicago: University of Chicago Press, 1999); Martin Diamond, *As Far as Republican Principles Will Admit*, ed. William A. Schambra (Washington: AEI Press, 1991); Allan Bloom, *The Closing of the American Mind* (New York: Simon and Schuster, 1987).

[3] Harry V. Jaffa, "Aristotle and Locke in the American Founding," *Claremont Review of Books* 1, No. 2 (Winter 2001), www.claremont.org; Harry V. Jaffa, *A New Birth of Freedom: Abraham Lincoln and the Coming of the Civil War* (Lanham, MD: Rowman & Littlefield, 2000); Thomas G. West, "Jaffa's Lincolnian Defense of the Founding," *Interpretation* 28, No. 3 (Spring 2001): 279–96 (on Jaffa's revised view of the founding).

[4] E.g., Thomas G. West, "Leo Strauss and the American Founding," *Review of Politics* 53 (Winter 1991): 157–72.

Introduction

This book is an account of the political theory of the American founding, with three main parts. Part I is an overview of the main elements of the natural rights theory, including equality, the laws of nature, the social compact, consent, and foreign and domestic policy. One might think such an overview would be unnecessary, but a topic-by-topic treatment of these topics is not readily available in the existing literature. Besides, misunderstandings of the founders' political thought are so pervasive – and I respond to these throughout Part I – that a complete review of the subject is indispensable.

"To secure these rights, governments are instituted among men," says the Declaration of Independence. Parts II and III of the book go into two major policy areas – promotion of citizen virtue and laws concerning property and economics – to show in greater depth how government secures the people's natural rights. This kind of analysis is also rare.

In the course of my argument, I challenge some of the leading interpretations of the founding. These either misunderstand the founders' principles in important ways, or deny their coherence, or understate the extent to which those principles lead to specific policies and laws. (I use the term "founders" to refer to leading government officials between about 1760 and 1800 – the fertile period when principles were being articulated and political institutions established.) In Part II, I show that although some scholars have recognized the connection between natural rights and government promotion of morality, previous accounts have been insufficient. Part III explains how the natural rights theory shapes the founders' surprisingly complex body of policies on property and economics.

I ground my argument, within reason, on documents approved by elected bodies or issued by politicians acting in their official capacity. My concern is with the principles and policies that helped to set in motion the beginnings of a great nation. My aim is to explain the political theory of the founding as the consensus that it was. I discuss opinions of individual founders only as far as they are useful to explain the public documents. The founders were all members of a team. Each had characteristic strengths and weaknesses. As a team, they shared the same understanding of victory: to set up a consent-based political regime that would effectively "secure these rights." They agreed on many of the means – policies, laws, and institutional structures. They quarreled, sometimes bitterly, about others. But their common goal was never in doubt.

Scholars often prefer to emphasize the founders' differences. I have no objection to that approach if one's concern is the distinctiveness of their various contributions. That is not my aim. I want to bring out the agreements on principles and policy that came to prevail in the making of the Revolution and the establishment of the state and federal governments. If I am right about the essential coherence of the founders' political thought, what matters most to later American political development is what was agreed on, not what was disputed. Historian Jack Rakove sensibly argues that there was "a distinction that Americans at every level of politics understood: that between fundamental *principles* of government, on the one hand, and the actual *forms* that any individual government could take. On the principles of government, a broad consensus reigned." Political scientist Gary Jacobsohn agrees: "the differences between Jeffersonians and Hamiltonians, Federalists and Anti-Federalists, are ultimately reconcilable within a broad consensus of agreement on political fundamentals." Illustrating this consensus, political scientist George Thomas notes that the "national university project [supported by the first six presidents] would unite leading Jeffersonians and Federalists even while they disagreed on particulars.... Perpetuating a 'constitutional consensus' with regard to political fundamentals... was a central rationale." Historian Gordon Wood shows that the founders' embrace of republicanism meant that consent rather than family connections and patronage increasingly became the basis of social and political relations. In spite of disagreements on government support of religion, writes political scientist Phillip Muñoz, all leading founders agreed that there is a "natural right to religious freedom" and that government must protect that freedom.[1]

---

[1] Jack N. Rakove, *Original Meanings: Politics and Ideas in the Making of the Constitution* (New York: Vintage Books, 1996), 19; Gary Jeffrey Jacobsohn, *Apple of Gold: Constitutionalism in Israel and the United States* (Princeton: Princeton University Press,

My earlier book, *Vindicating the Founders*, attempted to answer those who disparage the founders as hostile to the rights of blacks, women, and the poor.[2] But *Vindicating* was not limited to polemics. It contained serious analyses of the founders' policies on voting rights, property, the family, welfare, and immigration – analyses which some readers seem not to have noticed. Perhaps the book's partisan frame distracted them. I was originally inclined to write a second book of the same type as *Vindicating*, defending the founders against their conservative detractors – people like political scientists Peter Lawler and Patrick Deneen, who are wary of the founders because they supposedly believed in equality and liberty *too much*.[3]

Instead, I decided that there is a more pressing need for explanation than vindication. Evaluation presupposes knowledge. After I published *Vindicating*, I became increasingly aware that for many people – often including scholars who might be expected to know better – the founders' political theory might as well be buried in some deep and long-forgotten pit. My task, then, has something in common with archaeology – digging up old bones. But these bones, unlike those of long-dead Romans or Chinese, are of interest today because they claim to be living principles based on timeless truth.

The present book does have its polemical side. When it comes to interpreting the founding, my criticisms of other scholars are sometimes pointed – some might say pugnacious. But my intention throughout is to clarify the founders' views by contrasting my reading of the evidence with the views of others. My criticisms have nothing to do with today's partisan disputes about principles of justice. Readers will also see that I am happy to agree with other scholars when I think they are right. Gordon Wood, for example, is an outstanding historian whose insights

1993), 115; George Thomas, *The Founders and the Idea of a National University: Constituting the American Mind* (New York: Cambridge University Press, 2015), 5; Gordon S. Wood, *The Radicalism of the American Revolution* (New York: Knopf, 1992); Vincent Phillip Muñoz, *God and the Founders: Madison, Washington, and Jefferson* (New York: Cambridge University Press, 2009), 7. Also Randy E. Barnett, *Our Republican Constitution: Securing the Liberty and Sovereignty of We the People* (New York: HarperCollins, 2016) (the founders adhered to a unified natural rights consensus).

[2] Thomas G. West, *Vindicating the Founders: Race, Sex, Class, and Justice in the Origins of America* (Lanham, MD: Rowman & Littlefield, 1997).

[3] Peter Augustine Lawler, "Locke, Darwin, and the American Science of Modern Virtue," *Society* 50, No. 5 (Oct. 2013): 447–55. (My response to Lawler is "Locke's Neglected Teaching on Morality and the Family," ibid., 472–6.) Patrick J. Deneen, "Unsustainable Liberalism," *First Things*, August/September 2012, 25–31.

I cite frequently with approval. But he sometimes makes serious errors. I have learned a lot from him and from the many other historians, political scientists, and economists who precede me in writing about the founding. I would be remiss if I did not acknowledge that debt.

An Overview of the Book

The current scholarly consensus, as Alan Gibson correctly describes it, holds "that the Founders' political thought is best understood as an amalgam of liberalism, republicanism, and perhaps other traditions."[4] For Mark Noll, "the multivalent, tumultuous, and often extraordinarily fluid ideas of America's founding era ... [prevent us from] defining a single, dominant ideology for America's early political life."[5] Anticipating Noll, Paul Eidelberg writes, "Compounded of Puritan Christianity and classical patriotism on the one hand, and the rationalism and utilitarianism of the Enlightenment on the other, the founding reveals an age in contradiction with itself."[6]

Contrary to these scholars, I argue that the founders' consensus documents point to natural rights and the laws of nature as the lens through which politics is understood. If I am correct, the founders embraced "other traditions" – common law, Protestantism, etc. – only to the extent they helped to "secure these rights." In this respect, my approach is in general agreement with that of Thomas Pangle, Paul Rahe, William Galston, and Michael Zuckert. Pangle writes that "the gravitational field" of the natural rights theory "drew [the founders] ... into its orbit."

---

4 Alan Gibson, *Understanding the Founding: The Crucial Questions*, 2nd ed. (Lawrence: University Press of Kansas, 2010), 135; Joseph Postell, "Regulation during the American Founding: Achieving Liberalism and Republicanism," *American Political Thought* 5 (Winter 2016): 81–5, 105 (summarizing the "liberal/republican amalgam" consensus).

5 Mark Noll, "The Contingencies of Christian Republicanism: An Alternative Account of Protestantism and the American Founding," in *Protestantism and the American Founding*, ed. Thomas S. Engeman and Michael P. Zuckert (Notre Dame, IN: University of Notre Dame Press, 2004), 226. Noll's full argument is in *America's God: From Jonathan Edwards to Abraham Lincoln* (New York: Oxford University Press, 2002).

6 Paul Eidelberg, *A Discourse on Statesmanship: The Design and Transformation of the American Polity* (Champaign: University of Illinois Press, 1970), 212. See also Bernard Bailyn, *The Ideological Origins of the American Revolution*, enlarged ed. (Cambridge: Harvard University Press, 1992); Gordon S. Wood, *The Creation of the American Republic, 1776–1787* (New York: Norton, 1969); Gibson, *Understanding the Founding*; Forrest McDonald, *Novus Ordo Seclorum: The Intellectual Origins of the Constitution* (Lawrence: University Press of Kansas, 1985); Rogers M. Smith, *Civic Ideals: Conflicting Visions of Citizenship in U.S. History* (New Haven: Yale University Press, 1997).

I diverge from Pangle (and the others) when he, in partial agreement with the dominant scholarly approach, speaks of "the sometimes disharmonious moral categories and commitments our statesmen-founders tried to implement."[7] I say more later about my agreements with, and reservations about, these authors. All of them at some point see inconsistency or tension in the founders' moral vision. But the more I immerse myself in the political thought of the founding, the more I see a theoretically coherent understanding.

In Part I of this book, I explain the logically consistent core ideas expressed in the leading official documents. These ideas are familiar but often misunderstood. For this reason, I have patiently gone through all the main parts of the founders' political theory: the meaning of equality, natural rights, and the laws of nature (Chapter 1); the central role of natural rights – and not an "amalgam" of conflicting traditions (Chapter 2); their response to the typical misunderstandings of equality and natural rights (Chapter 3); the rational basis of their principles (Chapter 4); the "state of nature" as real and not hypothetical (Chapter 5); the multiple meanings of "consent of the governed" (Chapter 6); and how government secures natural rights in domestic and foreign policy (Chapter 7).

In these first seven chapters, we will see that rights and duties always go together for the founders. Natural rights are just claims against others, while the laws of nature are rules of just conduct that all are obliged to obey. From these rights and duties the founders concluded that government has two complementary roles. We may roughly describe these, in terms used by recent scholars, as "liberalism" and "republicanism." By liberalism, scholars mean government protection of individual rights. Republicanism means devotion to the common good and sustenance of a healthy moral consensus.

Scholars often treat "liberalism" and "republicanism" as distinct traditions that may or may not be in tension with each other in the "amalgam" supposedly forged by the founders.[8] Historian Frank Lambert, for example, sees "two powerful sets of secular ideas" in the founding: "liberalism and civic humanism." According to historian William Novak, the founders embraced "the autonomous self [with] its presocial rights" together with a countervailing "legal discourse that took duties, not

---

[7] Thomas L. Pangle, *The Spirit of Modern Republicanism: The Moral Vision of the American Founders and the Philosophy of Locke* (Chicago: University of Chicago Press, 1988), 276, 1.

[8] Gibson, *Understanding the Founding*, 134–5, 165–8, 234–40.

rights, seriously." A variation on this is Wood's well-known thesis that
a democratic "republicanism" – "[i]deally, republicanism obliterated the
individual" – predominated in 1776, supplanted by an anti-democratic
"liberal tradition" initiated by the Constitution of 1787.[9] I argue that
the founders rejected the idea of an individualistic "autonomous self"
with rights and no duties. Rather, they held legal protections of liberty
and promotion of citizen virtue – rights and duties – to be two aspects
of the same political theory. Both are indispensable. Government deters
threats to natural rights by raising armed forces to repel or deter external
aggression; by enforcing criminal laws protecting person and property
against injury from fellow citizens; by defining property ownership; and
by enforcing contracts in courts of law. Government encourages the people to respect and fight for the natural rights of fellow citizens by promoting appropriate moral conduct, including devotion to the common
good.

Parts II and III of the book investigate two policy areas in depth:
sustaining the moral conditions of freedom, and securing property rights
through the right kind of laws and economic policies.

Part II as a whole will show that although the founders were glad to
let private interest have its way in the realm of property, markets, and the
ordinary affairs of daily life, that interest had to be guided by the laws
of nature and defended by patriots who would value their sacred honor
as something higher than mere lives and fortunes. No founder wanted
an extreme Spartan regimen that inculcates morality at the expense of
liberty. However, as I show in Chapter 8, they were confident that without
public respect for the most important citizen virtues, a free society would
not last. The chapters that follow show how government requires or
encourages people to perform their moral duties. Government promotes
civic virtue through laws (Chapter 9), by laws in particular concerning
marriage and family (Chapter 10), and by shaping public opinion through
teaching and example (Chapter 11). Chapters 12 and 13 look at the
specific moral qualities to be promoted, namely, the right blend of the
social and republican virtues of self-restraint (such as justice, moderation,
humanity, and frugality) with the more assertive virtues (such as courage,
prudence, and vigilance).

---

[9] Frank Lambert, *Religion in American Politics: A Short History* (Princeton: Princeton
University Press, 2008), 22. William J. Novak, *The People's Welfare: Law and Regulation
in Nineteenth-Century America* (Chapel Hill: University of North Carolina Press, 1996),
34–5; Wood, *Creation*, 61, 513, 562. Wood modified this position in his later writings;
see the 1998 preface to *Creation*.

Part III turns to property and economics, one major part of the "liberal" side of the founding. (I mean *liberal* not as that term is used in today's politics, but in the "individual rights" sense used by recent scholars.) The theme that runs through this final part of the book is how government can best provide legal protections for the *twofold* right to property: to possess and to acquire. Both are necessary. If the right to acquire is not secured, the "have-nots" will be unable to get what they need. And if the right to possess is not secured, then the property of the "haves" will be at risk. The founders' policies were meant to provide for the common good of both. In Chapter 14, I clarify their conception of property rights. Then I explain the legal framework that defines and protects private ownership (Chapter 15), secures market freedom (Chapter 16), and ensures that money will have a stable value (Chapter 17). Chapter 18 explores the often misunderstood Hamilton-Jefferson quarrel of the 1790s over federal economic policy.

The founders' principles provide real guidelines to political life, but principles do not dictate answers to all questions of policy, law, and government structure. Far from it. What James Madison called "inventions of prudence"[10] had to be found not only in regard to matters like separation of powers but also in every policy area. For example, all agreed that government should be involved somehow in promoting the basic virtues needed for a free society, and that the right to acquire property must be protected. But what policies should government enact to those ends? On some points there was universal agreement, such as laws encouraging honest and peaceable behavior by punishing attacks on persons or property. They also agreed on laws prohibiting no-fault divorce. But the terms on which divorce should be granted were more controversial. And the details of property law and taxation varied from state to state. The more one descends from the laws of nature and natural rights into policy details, the more the prudence of politicians will be needed. Readers of Chapter 10 will immediately see that a politician today who believes that lasting marriage is important would be stark mad to try to bring back all the founders' policies on that subject. They would be too harsh for our time. The practical question – what encouragements government should offer to marriage – would and should be answered differently today.

---

[10] James Madison, *Federalist* 51, in Alexander Hamilton, Madison, and John Jay, *The Federalist Papers*, ed. Clinton Rossiter (New York: Signet Classics, 2003), 319. Throughout the book I have modernized capitalization, spelling, and punctuation in quotations from older documents.

I said earlier that few scholars address the policy consequences of the natural rights theory. Some, such as James Ceaser, come close to denying any connection whatever. Ceaser rightly acknowledges the centrality of natural rights and natural law in the founding. However, he writes that "deductions from nature could not provide direct guidance on...most policies relating to governing."[11] If "direct guidance" is taken to mean that natural rights lead to an a priori set of detailed laws, then Ceaser is correct. However, "deductions from nature" – from natural right – *did* provide "direct guidance" in the form of principles that helped to shape all of the founders' policies. For example, in the chapters on property and economics, we will see that the founders agreed that there are certain minimal legal conditions for securing the natural right to property. Many scholars understand that natural rights have definite implications for slavery, religious liberty, and freedom of speech.[12] That is a good start. But what about the rest of what government is supposed to do? Why are investigations of the connection between natural rights and policy so often limited merely to these three and perhaps a few other topics? It is true that important studies of the founders' policies on finance, property, education, and foreign affairs have been published. I make extensive use of them in this book. However, these topics tend to be analyzed without much attention to how they relate to government's main task – protecting rights.

Two things especially surprised me while I was writing this book. First, I was struck by the seriousness of the founders' concern with citizen character. Scholars have mostly overlooked this. I had already known in a general way of the importance of virtue in the founders' minds. I now understand far better how robust, sophisticated, and coherent their policies were in this regard.

My second surprise was to discover how complicated the panoply of laws and policies must be to secure the right to possess and acquire property. I had previously been inclined toward the common view that in the founding, property rights are protected by getting government out of the way and upheld by institutional restraints such as separation

---

[11] James W. Ceaser, *Nature and History in American Political Development: A Debate* (Cambridge: Harvard University Press, 2006), 25.

[12] For example, Harry V. Jaffa, *How to Think about the American Revolution* (Durham: Carolina Academic Press, 1978), 34–48, 64–6 (slavery); Gary B. Nash, *Race and Revolution* (Lanham, MD: Rowman & Littlefield, 1990) (slavery); Muñoz, *God and the Founders* (religion); Philip A. Hamburger, "Natural Rights, Natural Law, and American Constitutions," *Yale Law Journal* 102 (Jan. 1993): 907–61 (freedom of speech).

of powers. On the contrary: protection of individual rights, including property rights, requires a substantial legal infrastructure.

A Word on Method

First, as I mentioned earlier, to understand the founders' consensus, it is best to begin with the Declaration of Independence and other leading official documents, supplemented by other public documents and laws. Private opinions found in sermons, newspaper articles, pamphlets, or letters can also be useful, but only to illuminate, not to contradict or correct, the all-important public record. Scholars often stress personal or private documents which may or may not reflect the founders' consensus on principles and policies. In Gordon Wood's massive *Creation of the American Republic*, extensive use is made of letters, sermons, and pamphlets. Yet there is no sustained discussion of the natural rights theory that is so prominent in the founders' many official statements of principle. Another example is political scientist Barry Shain, who argues that the founding was animated not by a concern for individual rights but rather by "a Protestant communal understanding of the good."[13] In order to reach that conclusion, he relies largely on a tendentious selection of sermons and other private sources, while excluding or distorting the statements of principle found again and again in public and private documents.

The same problem sometimes arises in studies of particular founders. Immersion in the writings and careers of individual men often leads scholars to highlight things on which the founders differed – e.g., Jefferson's preference for farming versus Hamilton's for manufacturing – while neglecting the fundamentals on which they agreed. Legal historian Philip Hamburger is helpful: "[One] cannot simply examine the writings of Madison, Jefferson, and the half-dozen others whose views are the focus of so much historical study. Although the writings of these eminent Americans are of great importance and deserve the careful study they have received, they constitute only part of the evidence.... To learn more generally about late eighteenth-century American natural rights theory, we will have to reconstruct the common assumptions of a much larger

---

[13] Barry Alan Shain, *The Myth of American Individualism: The Protestant Origins of American Political Thought* (Princeton: Princeton University Press, 1994), 16. Shain continues to minimize the role of natural rights in *The Declaration of Independence in Historical Context: American State Papers, Petitions, Proclamations, and Letters of the Delegates to the First National Congresses*, ed. Shain (Indianapolis: Liberty Fund, 2014), 1–20, 525.

number of Americans." In my approach, those "common assumptions" are most reliably to be found in the official documents. [14]

A variation on this theme is the "great man" approach of Ralph Lerner and others. Lerner devotes a chapter of *The Thinking Revolutionary* to showing how "'liberty and the rights of mankind' had to be reflected in and secured by appropriate laws."[15] This is also a major theme of my book. The difference between Lerner and me, however, is that he is guided by his thesis that the founding was created by "thinking revolutionaries," as he calls the most thoughtful founders. To understand the founding, he argues, "one must listen to those historical actors who seem to have considered what they were about and who . . . were most intent on reshaping" the "presuppositions of their age."[16] Agreeing with Lerner on this point is Thomas Pangle: one should study the "small minority of geniuses who . . . [saw] further into . . . the philosophic roots and the distant goals of the new political culture being generated."[17] Following this approach, Lerner limits his discussion of how rights are "secured by appropriate laws" to a single set of documents by a leading "thinking revolutionary," Jefferson. Lerner's chapter on Jefferson's proposed revisions of Virginia's laws is informative and insightful. My project, however, broadens the scope to include a wide range of documents, whether written by geniuses or not.

Lerner's approach partially overlaps with mine, since many of these consensus documents were authored by the best of the "thinking revolutionaries." The Massachusetts Constitution, mostly written by John Adams, is a rich source for my arguments. Jefferson wrote the Declaration of Independence. Besides, I too make significant use of private writings of founding "geniuses" in elaborating on the meaning of some of the official documents. It is even possible, as Hamburger argues, to reach an adequate understanding of the founders' consensus on the basis of private writings if they are selected with a view to the "shared assumptions" that appear

---

[14] Hamburger, "Natural Rights, Natural Law," 914. Barry A. Shain, "Rights Natural and Civil in the Declaration of Independence," in *The Nature of Rights at the American Founding and Beyond*, ed. Shain (Charlottesville: University of Virginia Press, 2007), 147, chides scholars who "have difficulty in discriminating between the public work of a representative body and the private philosophical views of an individual." Unfortunately, Shain often fails to follow the trail of his own correct method. See also John P. Reid, "The Authority of Rights," in ibid., 97 ("resolutions passed by representative bodies" are a more reliable guide than "pamphlets and anonymous newspaper articles").

[15] Ralph Lerner, *The Thinking Revolutionary: Principle and Practice in the New Republic* (Ithaca: Cornell University Press, 1987), 64–5.

[16] Ibid., 18.   [17] Pangle, *Spirit of Modern Republicanism*, 2.

in the official documents: "Congregationalists and Baptists, Federalists and Anti-Federalists, Southerners and Northerners, all could use the natural rights analysis and, even while developing different versions of that analysis, they appear to have drawn upon certain shared assumptions. It is this foundation of shared assumptions about natural rights and natural law that will be examined here." When I quote individual founders in this book, I try to do it in the spirit recommended by Hamburger.[18]

A second methodological point: scholars often become preoccupied with the origins of the founders' political thought. Are they found in European philosophy, Christianity, English common law, "the larger Atlantic or imperial world out of which the Revolution came," or in other traditions?[19] As fascinating as that question is, provenance is not my concern here. Besides, it is distracting as well as risky to turn to the question of sources and influence before we have adequately understood what was said and done on the American side of the Atlantic between 1760 and 1800. For example, Zuckert turns to John Locke instead of American documents to "make clear what the Declaration meant by 'consent.'"[20] Although the colonists quoted Locke more often than any other political writer during the fertile period of political thought leading up to the break with Britain, from 1760 to 1775,[21] they cannot be presumed to have agreed with everything Locke said. The founders' views must be accessed first through their own words. Only after we have permitted the founders to speak for themselves are we entitled to consider the European background and the question of sources. From time to time I bring up the views of both ancient and modern philosophers. Generally, my purpose is not to make claims about the founders' sources, but rather to shed light on their views by comparing them with accounts of political and moral principles found in outstanding European thinkers.

A third feature of my method is that I give state government documents and policies their due. Scholars often write on the founding as if the federal government is of such paramount importance that nothing much

---

[18] Ibid.

[19] Gibson, *Understanding the Founding*, ch. 4 and 6 (summarizing the passionate scholarly debates on this theme). The quoted phrase is from Craig Yirush, *Settlers, Liberty, and Empire: The Roots of Early American Political Theory, 1675–1775* (New York: Cambridge University Press, 2011), 7.

[20] Michael P. Zuckert, *The Natural Rights Republic* (Notre Dame, IN: University of Notre Dame Press, 1996), 29.

[21] Donald S. Lutz, "The Relative Influence of European Writers on Late Eighteenth-Century American Political Thought," *American Political Science Review* 78, No. 1 (Mar. 1984): 193.

needs to be said about the states. I agree that documents like the Declaration, the Constitution, and *The Federalist* are indispensable. But if taken by themselves, they are misleading as a guide to the political thought of the founding as a whole. Jefferson correctly describes the division of labor between the state and national governments in his First Annual Message to Congress: the federal government "is charged with the external and mutual relations only of these states; . . . the states themselves have principal care of our persons, our property, and our reputation, constituting the great field of human concerns."[22] Because of its focus on domestic policy, this book concerns itself more with the states than the federal government, although both had a hand in the policies that I examine.

Finally, my book treats the founders' political theory as if it might be true. I say *might be* because an adequate assessment of that theory requires an inquiry whose conclusion must remain open until we have considered all the relevant arguments and facts. I do not claim to have reached that point in this book, although I believe I will bring readers into a better position to make that judgment. Most writers on the founding, in contrast, do not take seriously the founders' claim that there really are natural rights and laws of nature that ought to govern human action.

My stance in this regard is so unusual that it deserves a brief elaboration. Most scholars presume that the founders' ideas belong to a "world that is dead and gone," in the dismissive phrase of former Supreme Court justice William Brennan.[23] However, if one is convinced in advance that their ideas do not have to be taken seriously, what is the incentive to analyze them without distorting them? It is safer to approach the founders with an open mind, with the view that they might be right after all, and that *we* might be wrong. I do not ask for blind worship. I do ask for us to listen before we reject them – or agree with them.

To illustrate: in a review of my *Vindicating the Founders*, historian Joseph Ellis mocks the view "that ideas are like migratory birds that can take off in the eighteenth century and land intact in our time." Ellis's witty characterization of my position is correct, if I may change his word "are" to "might be." I do believe that some ideas that were accepted as true in 1776 might also be true today. Ellis is so sure that I am wrong that he does not even bother to attempt to disprove my claim. He substitutes ridicule

---

[22] Thomas Jefferson, First Annual Message to Congress, December 8, 1801, Avalon Project of Yale Law School, http://avalon.law.yale.edu.

[23] William Brennan, "To the Text and Teaching Symposium," October 12, 1985, Federalist Society website, www.fed-soc.org.

("migratory birds") for argument. He accepts as gospel truth the claim that the principles and policies of the founding could not possibly be valid now. One may call his unspoken premise *historicism*. Historian James Kloppenberg helpfully explains: "By historicism I mean the conviction that all human values and practices are products of historical processes and must be interpreted within historical frameworks. All principles and social patterns change; none stands outside the flow of history."[24] As a devout believer in the historicist faith, Ellis concludes that those (like me) who argue that the founders' understanding might be relevant to our own time are guilty of "presentist sins."[25]

Ellis's theological language ("sins") suggests that heretics who refuse to accept the orthodoxy established by the authorities of the modern university should be excommunicated. Ellis unconsciously echoes the Progressive intellectual John Dewey, who called the founders' belief in permanent standards of justice in political life "evil": "Ideas that at one time are means of producing social change assume another guise when they are used as means of preventing further social change," Dewey writes. "This fact is itself an illustration of historic relativity, and an evidence of the *evil* that lay in the assertion by earlier liberalism of the immutable and eternal character of their ideas." In another place, he asserts, "Changes in knowledge have *outlawed* the signification of the words they commonly used."[26] In response to Dewey, Ceaser quite reasonably quips, "Historical shifts by this account can criminalize past concepts. The philosopher's task is to play sheriff, deputize a posse of polemicists, and round up any stray rustlers who persist in using outmoded terms."[27] Ellis belongs to the polemicist posse. I am a stray rustler.

Ellis's unproven assumption is itself an example of the "presentism" that he claims to condemn. He imposes on the past a framework derived from present-day academic fashion. This allows him to dismiss the founders' most important claim: that there are certain truths that can reliably guide political life in all times and places. Ellis's presentist

---

[24] James T. Kloppenberg, *Reading Obama* (Princeton: Princeton University Press, 2011), 79–80.

[25] Joseph J. Ellis, "Who Owns the Eighteenth Century?" *William and Mary Quarterly* 57 (Apr. 2000): 418, reviewing West, *Vindicating the Founders*.

[26] John Dewey, "The Future of Liberalism," 1935, in *New Deal Thought*, ed. Howard Zinn (Indianapolis, IN: Bobbs-Merrill, 1966), 30–1; Dewey, *Freedom and Culture*, 1939, in *The Later Works, 1925–1953*, ed. Jo Ann Boydston (Carbondale: Southern Illinois University Press, 2008), 13:155 (my emphasis).

[27] James Ceaser, "Progressivism and the Doctrine of Natural Rights," *Social Philosophy and Policy* 29, No. 2 (Summer 2012): 190.

orientation is shared by Gordon Wood, who writes that truth "may not be eternal, but...[some truths] cut across a decade or two or across several cultures at the same time."[28] Unfortunately, what follows all too often from these blasé dismissals of enduring standards is blind embrace of whatever ideology, liberal or conservative, feels most comfortable.

This is the incoherent position that philosopher Richard Rorty cheerfully labels "liberal irony." On the one hand, for Rorty all ideas are a product of "historical contingency."[29] There is absolutely no foundation for deciding what is right or wrong, for preferring democracy over Nazism. If some future fascists take over, says Rorty (quoting Sartre), "[a]t that moment, fascism will be the truth of man, and so much the worse for us." Rorty explains: "there is nothing deep down inside us except what we have put there ourselves, no criterion that we have not created..., no standard of rationality that is not an appeal to such a criterion."[30] On the other hand, nothing prevents us from cooking up "narratives" that will persuade people to commit themselves to liberalism. But we must do so ironically, knowing that our commitment is groundless. "For liberal ironists, there is no answer to the question, 'Why not be cruel?'"[31] It is an arbitrary personal preference, nothing more.

Ellis, Wood, and Rorty may be right. But they may be wrong. The present book presupposes neither view.

Conclusion

The United States today is governed nominally under the same Constitution, as amended, that it adopted in 1788. Yet in practice, government policies are increasingly shaped by an understanding of justice very

---

[28] Gordon S. Wood, "The Fundamentalists and the Constitution," *New York Review of Books* 35, No. 2 (February 18, 1988): 34. Wood states the same opinion in *The Purpose of the Past: Reflections on the Uses of History* (New York: Penguin Books, 2008), 162–3. Wood's presentist historical methodology is not to be confused with the very different ideological presentism of "many historians," who, Wood writes, "have become obsessed with inequality and white privilege." He adds, "It's as if academics have given up trying to recover an honest picture of the past and have decided that their history-writing should become simply an instrument of moral hand-wringing." Wood, "History in Context: The American Vision of Bernard Bailyn," *Weekly Standard*, February 23, 2015, www.weeklystandard.com.

[29] Richard Rorty, *Contingency, Irony, and Solidarity* (New York: Cambridge University Press, 1989), 50.

[30] Richard Rorty, *The Consequences of Pragmatism: Essays, 1972–1980* (Minneapolis: University of Minnesota Press, 1982), xlii.

[31] Rorty, *Contingency*, xv–xvi.

different from that of the founders. That new understanding has led to a departure from many if not most of the founders' guidelines on policy explained in this book. To evaluate whether the change from then to now was on balance good or bad, one must first know not only *why* the founders set up the regime they did – what government is *for* – but also *how* their political order worked, or was intended to work, in practice. This book is a contribution to that end.

PART I

THE POLITICAL THEORY OF THE FOUNDING

An Overview

I

Equality, Natural Rights, and the Laws of Nature

The natural rights doctrine – including the concepts of equality, the laws of nature, and the social compact basis of government – is the core of the founders' political theory. This doctrine guided them on the way to independence and in the creation of the state and national governments. I do not mean to imply that a mere shared opinion about abstract truths caused the American Revolution. The manly "don't tread on me" spirit[1] of the English colonists – which existed long before anyone had heard of natural rights – also partly explains their conviction that Americans, not the British Parliament, should decide how they were governed. Both of these things – the colonial spirit of liberty, and the political theory of liberty – were part of the American experience for six decades before the founding.

The Colonial Turn to Natural Rights

Throughout the eighteenth century, legislatures in most colonies frequently contended with their British-appointed governors and royal vetoes – but with the advantage increasingly on the side of the people.[2] As early as 1732, Massachusetts governor Jonathan Belcher complained that "the House of Representatives of this province are continually running

---

[1] The phrase "manly spirit" appears frequently in the founding, e.g., in Alexander Hamilton, James Madison, and John Jay, *The Federalist Papers*, ed. Clinton Rossiter (New York: Signet Classics, 2003), *Federalist* 14, p. 99, and *Federalist* 57, p. 350.

[2] Jack P. Greene, *The Quest for Power: The Lower Houses of Assembly in the Southern Royal Colonies, 1689–1776* (Chapel Hill: University of North Carolina Press, 1963).

wild, nor are their attempts for assuming (in a manner) the whole legislative as well as the executive part of the government into their hands, to be endured with honor to his Majesty."[3] British authorities were equally exasperated by the recalcitrance of the locals in South Carolina, New Jersey, and other colonies.[4]

The French and Indian War ended in 1763 with the expulsion of France from Canada. From the British point of view, there was no longer a need to tread lightly in their dealings with the colonies. With the French threat eliminated, the British decided to govern with a firmer hand. For the first time Parliament levied taxes on the colonists. When protests throughout the colonies prevented the Stamp Tax from being collected, Parliament repealed it but insisted in the Declaratory Act of 1766 on its power "to bind the colonies in all cases whatsoever."[5]

On the American side, the colonists, no longer fearing the French, could afford to become more confrontational with Britain. They felt free to insist ever more explicitly on a right to self-government through their elected legislatures. By 1773, British aggressiveness provoked outright defiance of the law, such as the Boston Tea Party (bundles of taxable tea were thrown into the harbor) and similar incidents in other colonies. The British responded in 1774 with what the Americans labeled "the Intolerable Acts," a series of laws regarded as unconstitutional and oppressive. Parliament abolished representative government in Canada. It extended the Canadian border down to the Ohio River, hemming in the British colonies from the West. Many elected officials of the government of Massachusetts would henceforth be appointed by the royal governor, and no meetings of citizens were permitted without his consent. The port of Boston was closed. British troops were to be forcibly quartered "where[ver] their presence may be necessary and required." All of these

---

[3] Jonathan Belcher, To the Lords of Trade, Jan. 5, 1732, *The Belcher Papers,* in *Collections of the Massachusetts Historical Society,* 6th series (Boston: Massachusetts Historical Society, 1893), 6:241.

[4] Claude H. Van Tyne, *The Causes of the War of Independence* (Boston: Houghton Mifflin, 1922), 47 (quoting Governor Glen of SC, 1743); Representation of the Lords, in *Documents Relating to the Colonial History of New Jersey,* 1st series, ed. William A. Whitehead (Newark, NJ: Daily Advertiser Printing House, 1883), 7:521.

[5] William W. Crosskey, *Politics and the Constitution in the History of the United States* (Chicago: University of Chicago Press, 1953–80), 1:139–46 (summarizing the facts presented in this and the next paragraphs); also Bernhard Knollenberg, *Growth of the American Revolution, 1766–1775,* ed. Bernard W. Sheehan (Indianapolis: Liberty Fund, 2003). The "Intolerable Acts": *Colonies to Nation, 1763–1789: A Documentary History of the American Revolution,* ed. Jack P. Greene (New York: Norton, 1975), 202–11.

and other "wicked and oppressive measures"[6] appeared to be aiming at what legal historian William Crosskey calls "a firm intention everywhere to use force."[7] They were detailed in a multitude of indignant colonial protests, culminating in the list of grievances in the Declaration of Independence.[8]

In the decades leading up to independence, the colonists had adopted a body of political ideas that justified and promoted the American drive toward self-rule. At the foundation of these ideas was the claim that all men are created equal. Some scholars wrongly believe "the principle of human equality" was only discovered in the 1770s. Historian Edmund Morgan states that it was not until Thomas Paine published *Common Sense* in 1776 that Americans were "propelled . . . into the great discovery of human equality toward which they had been moving *unwittingly* ever since they first denied Parliament's right to tax."[9] "Unwittingly"? Contra Morgan, equality had been discussed and embraced quite wittingly in America for more than fifty years.

A 1717 book by Massachusetts minister John Wise was perhaps the first American publication to discuss what Wise called "the principle of equality in a natural state."[10] This "principle of equality," along with other ideas that later became the founders' political theory, spread rapidly.[11] Connecticut minister John Bulkley published the first American overview of John Locke's political theory in 1725.[12] Three years later, the same ideas were featured in a Daniel Dulany pamphlet endorsed by the

---

[6] Town of Boston, Suffolk Resolves, Sept. 9, 1774, Massachusetts Historical Society, www.masshist.org/revolution/congress1.php.

[7] Crosskey, *Politics*, 1:143.

[8] These protests were summed up in Continental Congress, Declaration and Resolves, Oct. 14, 1774, in *The Founders' Constitution*, ed. Philip B. Kurland and Ralph Lerner (Chicago: University of Chicago Press, 1987), 1:1. An earlier list is Boston, Instructions to their Representatives, May 15, 1770, in Thomas Hutchinson, *The History of the Colony and Province of Massachusetts-Bay*, 1828 (Cambridge: Harvard University Press, 1936), 3:370.

[9] Edmund S. Morgan, *The Birth of the Republic, 1763–89*, 2nd ed. (Chicago: University of Chicago Press, 1977), 75, my emphasis. See also 66.

[10] John Wise, *A Vindication of the Government of New England Churches* (Boston: J. Allen, 1717), 42. Wise's account of the natural rights theory follows the German philosopher Samuel Pufendorf, a precursor of John Locke.

[11] Strangely, Morgan himself provides plenty of evidence for this in *Puritan Political Ideas, 1558–1794*, ed. Edmund S. Morgan (Indianapolis: Bobbs-Merrill, 1965).

[12] John Bulkley, Preface to Roger Wolcott, *Poetical Meditations* (New London, CT: T. Green, 1725), xi–xxiv.

Maryland Assembly.[13] Elisha Williams of Connecticut discussed Locke extensively in a 1744 treatise pleading for religious toleration.[14] In 1747, a group of New Jerseyans, in a dispute over property titles, argued (quoting Locke) that government "cannot take from any man, any part of his property, without his own consent."[15] Educated Americans in every colony, including the clergy, adopted the natural rights theory in their own thinking and writing.[16] Alice Baldwin writes that "every church-going New Englander long before 1763" was familiar with "the doctrines of natural right, the social contract, and the right of resistance."[17]

In the 1760s, Americans applied these ideas with increasing boldness to the colonial political order. The British constitution was interpreted everywhere as informed by the political theory of natural rights.[18] As the Massachusetts Assembly put it in 1765, the people "have a just value for those inestimable rights, which are derived to all men from nature, and are happily interwoven in the British constitution."[19] When it became

---

[13] Daniel Dulany, *The Right of the Inhabitants of Maryland to the Benefit of English Laws* (Annapolis, MD: W. Parks, 1728), 2–3, 9, 13–14, 30.

[14] Elisha Williams, *The Essential Rights and Liberties of Protestants*, 1744, in *Political Sermons of the American Founding Era, 1730–1805*, ed. Ellis Sandoz (Indianapolis: Liberty Fund, 1990), 51–118.

[15] Answer of the Rioters to the Publication of the Proprietors, Aug. 1747, in *Documents . . . of New Jersey*, ed. Whitehead, 7:42. See Brendan McConville, *These Daring Disturbers of the Public Peace: The Struggle for Property and Power in Early New Jersey* (Ithaca: Cornell University Press, 1999), ch. 8 (detailing the NJ dispute and citing additional documents appealing to Locke's doctrine).

[16] David Ramsay, *The History of the American Revolution, 1789* (Indianapolis: Liberty Classics, 1990), 29–30 (on the popularity of such natural rights writings as *Cato's Letters* and the *Independent Whig*); Craig Yirush, *Settlers, Liberty, and Empire: The Roots of Early American Political Theory, 1675–1775* (New York: Cambridge University Press, 2011) (spread of the natural rights theory in the 1700s).

[17] Alice M. Baldwin, *The New England Clergy and the American Revolution* (1928; repr. New York: Frederick Ungar, 1958), xii.

[18] New York Petition to the House of Commons, Oct. 18, 1764, in *Prologue to Revolution: Sources and Documents on the Stamp Act Crisis, 1764–1766*, ed. Edmund S. Morgan (New York: Norton, 1973), 9; a Virginia example of this view of the British constitution is Richard Bland, *An Inquiry into the Rights of British America*, 1766, in *American Political Writing during the Founding Era, 1760–1805*, ed. Charles S. Hyneman and Donald S. Lutz (Indianapolis: Liberty Press, 1983), 1:73. On the positive-law (as opposed to natural-law) constitutional arguments on both sides, see the editor's remarks in *The Briefs of the American Revolution*, ed. John P. Reid (New York: New York University Press, 1981); also Jack P. Greene, *The Constitutional Origins of the American Revolution* (New York: Cambridge University Press, 2011).

[19] Massachusetts Assembly, Answer to Governor Hutchinson, Oct. 25, 1765, in Hutchinson, *History of the Colony*, 3:340. See also Resolutions of the House of Representatives of Massachusetts, Oct. 29, 1765, in *Founders' Constitution*, 1:629. For the Virginia

clear that the British government totally rejected that interpretation – that is, when Parliament insisted on a right to absolute rule over the colonists "in all cases whatsoever" and began to act on that claim – the Americans declared independence with the natural rights theory as their justification.

Some historians accept Pennsylvania loyalist William Smith's 1776 claim that American Whig leaders had "been constantly enlarging their views, and stretching them beyond their first bounds, till at length they have wholly changed their ground."[20] It is certainly true that few Americans saw at first the full implications of their natural rights principles. But they did not "change their ground." Rather, the implacable logic of their principles, in the face of aggressive British attempts to govern the colonies and the restless colonial impulse for freedom, drove the Americans to an increasingly spirited insistence on their right to live under laws made by their own representatives. "In the end," writes Rakove, "independence emerged as a logical conclusion flowing from principles and opinions that most delegates [to the First Continental Congress] shared and as a response to events they could neither control nor evade."[21]

How to Proceed

With this historical context in mind, I turn now to the political theory of natural rights. That is the theme of the rest of this chapter and of all of Part I of this book. The last chapter of Part I – on how natural rights and natural law guide public policy – will bring us to the discussion of two central policy issues: the moral conditions of a free society, and property and economics. Parts II and III will investigate these two in detail.

To avoid misunderstanding, I quickly add this qualification: although natural rights guided the founding, the leading officials were unable to create a government fully in accord with their principles. The most obvious example of this is slavery, to which we will return in Chapter 3.

I start with the Declaration of Independence, because it is America's original official founding document. Congress formally approved it to justify the break with Britain at the moment when the United States declared itself "one people" independent of Britain. The language of the

view, Thomas Jefferson, *A Summary View of the Rights of British America*, 1774, in *Writings*, ed. Merrill D. Peterson (New York: Library of America, 1984), 105–22.

[20] Greene, *Quest for Power*, 449 (citing the Smith quotation with approval).

[21] Jack N. Rakove, *The Beginnings of National Politics: An Interpretative History of the Continental Congress* (Baltimore: Johns Hopkins University Press, 1979), 102.

Declaration is familiar: "created equal," "life, liberty, and the pursuit of happiness," "consent of the governed." But few people today understand those phrases in the founders' sense. Nor do they have access to the reasoning that led the founders from abstract principles to the policies and laws they adopted. The theoretical statements at the beginning of the Declaration are too brief to spell out the meaning of its key terms. Fortunately, it is not hard to clarify the Declaration, to fill out the picture that it only sketches, by consulting other official documents.

Equality

The second paragraph of the Declaration begins, "All men are created equal." Equal in what sense? The poet Robert Frost was simply puzzled:

> [T]he principle
> That all men are created free and equal . . .
> That's a hard mystery of Jefferson's.
> What did he mean? . . .
> But never mind, the Welshman got it planted
> Where it will trouble us a thousand years.
> Each age will have to reconsider it.[22]

Even sophisticated scholars such as historian Eric Foner share Frost's view that equality is a "hard mystery." Foner writes, "the notion of equality, like many slogans of the revolutionary era, was an idea whose meaning lay in the eye of the beholder."[23] In other words, equality in the founders' core document has no clear meaning at all.

But the necessary clarification lies before us in plain sight. The state constitutions, writes political scientist Donald Lutz, "are generally ignored by those writing in American political theory, . . . and are almost always viewed as historical documents rather than as expressions of

---

[22] Robert Frost, "The Black Cottage," in *North of Boston* (New York: Henry Holt, 1914), 52–3. Donald S. Lutz, "The Theory of Consent in the Early State Constitutions," *Publius* 9, No. 2 (Spring 1979): 11–12.

[23] Eric Foner, "Tom Paine's Republic: Radical Ideology and Social Change," in *The American Revolution: Explorations in the History of American Radicalism*, ed. Alfred F. Young (DeKalb: Northern Illinois University Press, 1976), 207. Equally mystified is John Ferling, *Whirlwind: The American Revolution and the War That Won It* (New York: Bloomsbury Press, 2015), 161. Other scholars, cited in this and other chapters, have no difficulty understanding the equality idea, e.g., Ronald Hamowy, "Declaration of Independence," in *Encyclopedia of American Political History*, ed. Jack P. Greene (New York: Scribner's, 1984), 457–9.

political theory."[24] Yet these and other important documents contain some of the best statements of the founders' principles. In nine of these early constitutions, the equality idea is restated in different words, always with the same basic meaning. Virginia says, "All men are by nature equally free and independent." Pennsylvania, Vermont, New Hampshire, and Ohio declare, "All men are born equally free and independent." In Massachusetts, "All men are born free and equal." Kentucky and Connecticut have "all men, when they form a social compact, are equal." New York's preamble quotes the Declaration of Independence, including "all men are created equal."[25]

In these documents, "created," "born," and "by nature" are equivalent terms. "By nature" means *as they really are*, independent of customs and traditions. What human beings really are – with respect to freedom – is individuals who are neither the masters nor the slaves of other people. They own themselves. They can of course be deprived of that equality by being forced to submit to the will of another, but that does not make slavery right. My claim that "equality" means primarily "not ruled by another" is made clear by two variations on "equal" in the state bills of rights: "equally free and independent" and "free and equal." In both phrases, "equal" is tied to "free." The phrase "equally free and independent" (Virginia) makes especially clear what is meant by "created equal": it means being free from the domination of others, being independent of their control or rule. Even more explicitly, the Town of Northampton, Massachusetts, declares: "all men are naturally equal with respect to a right of dominion, government, and jurisdiction, over each other."[26] The same idea appears in similar formulations, e.g., "All men are born equally free" (the Massachusetts town of Essex).[27]

Natural Rights: The Moral Meaning of Equality

To clarify the moral meaning of equality, the founders proceeded to name the rights that exist even before the formation of civil society.

---

[24] Lutz, "Theory of Consent," 11–12.
[25] Declarations of Rights of VA, 1776, art. 1; MA, 1780, art. 1; PA, 1776, art. 1; VT, 1777, art. 1; NH, 1784, art. 2; Constitution of KY, 1792, art. 12, §1; OH, 1803, art. 8, §1; CT, 1818, art. 1. Also NY Constitution, 1777, Preamble. In the notes in this book, I generally use abbreviations for the names of states.
[26] Return of Northampton, MA, May 22, 1780, in *Founders' Constitution*, 1:528–31.
[27] *The Essex Result*, 1778, in ibid., 1:114.

The tie between natural equality and equal natural rights is evident in several state constitutions, in which the affirmation of the equality of "all men" is immediately followed by a statement of equal rights. The Massachusetts Bill of Rights states, "All men are born free and equal, and have certain natural, essential, and unalienable rights." The Declaration of Independence has the same twofold formulation: "that all men are created equal, that they are endowed by their creator with certain inalienable rights." By adding the language of rights to that of "born free and equal," these documents affirm that the original equality is not only a fact, but a fact pregnant with moral weight. All men are born free, but they also, as Boston says, "have a right to remain in a state of nature as long as they please."[28] And this right to equal freedom exists not only outside of civil society, but after its establishment. That is why the rights are called "inalienable" (Declaration of Independence), "inherent" (Virginia Bill of Rights), "natural" (Massachusetts Bill of Rights), or "natural, inherent, and inalienable" (Pennsylvania, Vermont, New Hampshire, and Ohio bills of rights). Another variant, "the indelible rights of mankind," is found in the Georgia resolutions of 1774, and in the Virginia Bill of Rights, there is "an indubitable, inalienable, and indefeasible right to reform, alter, or abolish" government.[29] Finally, although nine early state constitutions affirm human equality, sixteen out of seventeen constitutions or fundamental state documents contain natural rights language or the equivalent.[30] This numerical disparity suggests that statements of natural rights are practically more important than statements of equality. That is because the idea of natural rights makes explicit the significance of equality as a moral guide.

Michael Zuckert rightly states that "created equal" means that "[b]y nature, or in nature, human beings are equal, that is, not subject to

---

[28] Boston, Rights of the Colonists, 1772, in *The Writings of Samuel Adams*, ed. Harry A. Cushing (1904–8; repr. New York: Octagon, 1968), 2:351.

[29] Declarations of Rights of MA, 1780, art. 1; VA, 1776, art. 1 and 3; PA, 1776, art. 1; VT, 1777, art. 1; NH, 1784, art. 2; OH, 1803, art. 8, §1; NY Constitution, 1777, Preamble. GA Resolutions, Aug. 10, 1774, in *American Archives: Fourth Series*, ed. Peter Force (Washington: M. St. Clare Clarke, 1837–53), 1:700.

[30] Preambles of PA, 1776; MA, 1780; NY, 1777; DE, 1792. Bills of Rights of MD, 1776, art. 33; VA, 1776, art. 1; VT, 1777, art. 1; NH, 1784, art. 2; OH, 1803, art. 8, §1; CT, 1818, art. 1. Constitutions of SC, 1790, art. 8, §1; GA, 1798, §10; KY, 1792, §2, 3 and 7; TN, 1796, art. 11, §3 and 19. Federal declarations of rights proposed by ratifying conventions of NC, Aug 1, 1788, and RI, May 29, 1790, in *Documents Illustrative of the Formation of the Union of the American States*, ed. Charles C. Tansill (Washington: Government Printing Office, 1927), 1044, 1052. Only NJ, which does speak of "the inestimable privilege" of religious freedom (art. 18), is missing from this list.

the rightful authority of any other human being," "whatever the many inequalities among human beings may be." But Zuckert muddies the water by saying that "there is little foundation for the suggestion often made that 'created equal' means 'possessing equal rights.'"[31] Zuckert thereby implies that Abraham Lincoln was wrong when he argued that the authors of the Declaration of Independence "defined with tolerable distinctness, in what respects they did consider all men created equal – equal in 'certain inalienable rights, among which are life, liberty, and the pursuit of happiness.'"[32] However, Zuckert draws a distinction without a difference. For if, as he says, all are equal in the sense that no one is by nature "subject to the rightful authority of any other," then Lincoln is right. Not being "subject to the rightful authority" means the same thing as "equal in 'certain inalienable rights'" or "equal in rights" (Connecticut's Bill of Rights). James Wilson anticipates Lincoln when he writes that there is "one aspect in which all men in society, previous to civil government, are equal. With regard to all, there is an equality in rights and in obligations."[33]

Zuckert might respond that "equal in rights" includes several rights besides the basic liberty we are born with. Yet all the natural rights can easily be understood as implicit in "equally free and independent." Philip Hamburger explains: "Eighteenth-century Americans . . . tended to discuss their natural rights as portions of their natural liberty – as portions of the general freedom of individuals in the state of nature. The freedom of individuals in the absence of government was what Americans generically described as 'life, liberty, and property,' or 'life, liberty, and the pursuit of happiness.'" Harry Jaffa agrees: natural rights "form a continuum of inferences from man's natural equality."[34]

There are quite a few variations in the founders' many lists of natural rights. In the leading documents, the most frequently mentioned are life, liberty, property, religious liberty, and seeking and obtaining happiness (or happiness and safety). Other rights sometimes mentioned include

[31] Michael P. Zuckert, *The Natural Rights Republic* (South Bend, IN: University of Notre Dame Press, 1996), 18–20.

[32] Lincoln, speech on *Dred Scott*, June 26, 1857, in *The Collected Works of Abraham Lincoln*, ed. Roy T. Basler (New Brunswick: Rutgers University Press, 1953), 2:405–6.

[33] CT Constitution, 1818, art. 1; James Wilson, *Lectures on Law*, 1791, in *Collected Works of James Wilson*, ed. Kermit L. Hall and Mark David Hall (Indianapolis: Liberty Fund, 2007), 1:638.

[34] Philip A. Hamburger, "Trivial Rights," *Notre Dame Law Review* 70, No. 1 (1994): 6; Harry V. Jaffa, *How to Think about the American Revolution* (Durham: Carolina Academic Press, 1978), 111.

reputation, keeping and bearing arms, freedom of speech and press, and assembly. This variety might make one wonder whether there was any real consensus on the subject. Furthermore, scholars sometimes claim that the meaning of the natural rights doctrine is unclear. Historian Douglas Bradburn speaks of "the vague logic of natural rights," and in Rakove's overview of the state bills of rights, he asserts that there were "uncertainties surrounding the entire subject."[35] I agree that the *political application* of natural rights is not clear in every situation. For example, there can be reasonable disagreement on how exactly the law should define the permissible use of violence in defense of one's life and property. However, the founders' consensus on the broad meaning of natural rights was both clear and firm. Historian Marc Kruman rightly observes that the state bills of rights, "though sometimes treated as hodgepodges of principles and rights, represented strikingly coherent statements of principles."[36] I will now show how Kruman is right.

The Natural Rights to Life, Liberty, and Property

If all are "born free and equal," and if no one is entitled to take that freedom away, that means everyone is rightfully free of the violence of others. Murder being the worst kind of violence, life is the first or most urgent natural right. Expressed in the law of nature language that the founders sometimes used, "the law of self-preservation . . . is the first law of nature."[37] The right to life – along with all the other natural rights – includes the right to self-defense, if necessary by using force to resist force. The right to own firearms would follow.

Second, although equal freedom by nature may be said to be the foundation of all the other natural rights, the founders also treated liberty as a particular right among the other rights. Liberty means being left alone, not being coerced by others. Being born free, all may do as they

---

[35] Douglas Bradburn, *The Citizenship Revolution: Politics and the Creation of the American Union, 1774–1804* (Charlottesville: University of Virginia Press, 2009), 42; Jack N. Rakove, *Original Meanings: Politics and Ideas in the Making of the Constitution* (New York: Vintage Books, 1996), 309.

[36] Marc W. Kruman, *Between Authority and Liberty: State Constitution Making in Revolutionary America* (Chapel Hill: University of North Carolina Press, 1997), 40; for the "hodgepodge" view, see Wood, *Creation*, 271.

[37] Samuel West, *On the Right to Rebel against Governors*, 1776, in *American Political Writing*, 1:417. "Election sermons" such as this are quasi-official documents, typically solicited and published by a colony or state legislature. "Law of self-preservation" also appears in Boston, Rights of the Colonists, 2:351.

please, without interference from other people, subject only (as we will see later in the chapter) to the laws of nature. Liberty in daily life therefore means that people are free to organize their affairs as they see fit. The First Amendment mentions the "right of the people peaceably to assemble." This natural right to get together with others is not limited to political assemblies or protests, as it is often narrowly understood today. Congressman Theodore Sedgwick "criticized the proposed [First Amendment] right of assembly as redundant in light of the freedom of speech: 'If people freely converse together, they must assemble for that purpose; *it is a self-evident, unalienable right* which the people possesses; it is certainly a thing that never would be called in question; it is derogatory to the dignity of the House to descend to such minutiae.'"[38] Six state constitutions mention freedom of assembly for political purposes, but none specifies that the same right extends to a general freedom of association for all lawful purposes.[39] This right was so "self-evident" to everyone that it was rarely mentioned. No one ever questioned it. On the few occasions when it was made explicit, it was typically in connection with religion. President Jefferson, addressing a group of New Orleans nuns after the purchase of Louisiana, wrote: "the principles of the constitution and government of the United States are a sure guarantee... that your institution will be permitted to govern itself according to its own voluntary rules, without interference from the civil authority."[40] But this freedom was not limited to religious associations. Liberty includes the right of any self-selected group to "converse together," to assemble, and to "govern itself according to its own voluntary rules" for any other noninjurious purpose.

Liberty in Sedgwick's sense of "a self-evident, unalienable right" means that no one may disrupt a free association because of disapproval of its purpose, unless that purpose is to harm the equal rights of others. In the founding it was taken for granted that an employer and an employee generally have a natural right to exchange money for labor on any mutually agreeable terms, and that private clubs and schools may establish

---

[38] John D. Inazu, *Liberty's Refuge: The Forgotten Freedom of Assembly* (New Haven: Yale University Press, 2012), 24 (my emphasis).

[39] Bills of Rights of NH, 1784, art. 31; VT, 1777, art. 18; PA, 1776, art. 16; NC, 1776, art. 18; KY, 1792, art. 10, §22; TN, 1796, art. 11, §22.

[40] Bills of Rights of NH, 1784, art. 31; VT, 1777, art. 18; PA, 1776, art. 16; NC, 1776, art. 18; KY, 1792, art. 10, §22; TN, 1796, art. 11, §22. Jefferson to Ursuline Nuns of New Orleans, July 13, 1804, Founding Era Collection, University of Virginia, http://rotunda.upress.virginia.edu/founders.

any criteria of membership they like. In chapters 11 and 15, we will see how the founders established laws enabling easy formation of private associations for business, educational, or other purposes. In *Federalist* 10, Madison even defends the liberty of forming factions, i.e., private associations that promote their own interest at the expense of others. Although it is an unfortunate fact, he writes, that "liberty . . . nourishes faction," it would be "folly to abolish liberty, which is essential to political life." To take away the right to form private associations (clubs, businesses, private schools, churches, and so on) in the name of eliminating selfishness, bigotry, or superstition would mean the end of liberty.[41] Stating a widely shared opinion of our time, Linda Chavez writes, "The principles contained in our founding document, the Declaration of Independence, took nearly 200 years to find their fulfillment in the Civil Rights Act."[42] Whatever may be said of other parts of that act, it is not true of Title VII. There is no evidence that the founders would have approved of government-mandated nondiscrimination by race, sex, or religion in privately owned businesses – to say nothing of affirmative action.

Third, the right "of acquiring, possessing, and protecting property"[43] also follows from equal freedom. Some scholars have wrongly claimed that the Declaration's omission of the right to property means that it was not one of the founding principles. Vernon Parrington wrote in 1927 that the "substitution of 'pursuit of happiness' for 'property' marks a complete break with the Whiggish doctrine of property rights that Locke had bequeathed. . . . [I]t was this substitution that gave to the document the note of idealism which was to make its appeal so perennially human and vital." Garry Wills agrees: the omission means Jefferson "was not a Lockean individualist, basing the social contract on property rights."[44]

---

[41] Madison, *Federalist* 10, p. 73.

[42] Linda Chavez, "The Landmark Struggle to Pass the 1964 Civil Rights Act," *New York Post*, July 6, 2014, nypost.com.

[43] MA Bill of Rights, art. 1.

[44] Vernon L. Parrington, *Main Currents in American Thought* (1927; repr. New York: Harvest Books, Harcourt, Brace, 1954), 1:350; Garry Wills, *Inventing America: Jefferson's Declaration of Independence* (Garden City, NY: Doubleday, 1978), 255. Agreeing: Richard K. Matthews, *The Radical Politics of Thomas Jefferson: A Revisionist View* (Lawrence: University Press of Kansas, 1978), 27. Disagreeing: Willi Paul Adams, *The First American Constitutions: Republican Ideology and the Making of the State Constitutions in the Revolutionary Era* (Chapel Hill: University of North Carolina Press, 1980), 191 ("New Left historians in search of an American tradition of radicalism were disappointed in their search for confirmation of Parrington's view"); Jean Yarbrough, "Jefferson and Property Rights," in *Liberty, Property, and the Foundations of the American Constitution*, ed. Ellen Frankel Paul and Howard Dickman (Albany: SUNY Press,

Yet Jefferson affirms the natural right to property in the strongest terms again and again. Contradicting Parrington and Wills, Jefferson writes that "the first principle of association [is] 'the guarantee to everyone of a free exercise of his industry, and the fruits acquired by it.'" In another letter, Jefferson states, "The true foundation of republican government is the equal right of every citizen in his person and property, and in their management."[45]

The connection between liberty and property is obvious. If we are "born free and equal," we own ourselves, and our liberty necessarily includes the "free exercise of [one's] industry, and the fruits acquired by it" – to acquire things useful or enjoyable for life. Madison explains in *Federalist* 10: there is a "diversity in the faculties of men, from which the rights of property originate." Such "faculties" include ambition, intelligence, experience, and strength. These lead people into different jobs and professions, and they partly explain why people acquire different amounts of wealth.[46]

Jefferson's 1774 *Summary View of the Rights of British America* treats the right to property as part of the right to liberty: "Still less let it be proposed that our *properties* within our own territories shall be taxed or regulated by any power on earth but our own. The God who gave us life gave us *liberty* at the same time; the hand of force may destroy, but cannot disjoin them."[47] When government takes your property without your consent, it thereby takes away your liberty to use your talents to acquire the property you need for life and happiness.

Religious Liberty

A fourth natural right held by "every individual," in New Hampshire's wording, is "a natural and inalienable right to worship Almighty God

1988), 70, 81; Ronald Hamowy, "Jefferson and the Scottish Enlightenment: A Critique of Garry Wills's *Inventing America*," *William and Mary Quarterly* 36, No. 4 (Oct. 1979): 503–23; Harry V. Jaffa, "Inventing the Past: Garry Wills's *Inventing America* and the Pathology of Ideological Scholarship," in *American Conservatism and the American Founding* (Claremont, CA: Claremont Institute, 2002), 76–108; Luigi Marco Bassani, *Liberty, State, and Union: The Political Theory of Thomas Jefferson* (Macon, GA: Mercer University Press, 2010).

45 Jefferson to Milligan, Apr. 6, 1816, in *Writings of Thomas Jefferson*, ed. Albert E. Bergh (Washington: Thomas Jefferson Memorial Association, 1904), 14:466; Jefferson to Kercheval, July 12, 1816, in *Writings*, ed. Peterson, 1398.

46 Madison, *Federalist* 10, p. 73.

47 Jefferson, *Summary View*, in *Writings*, ed. Peterson, 121–2 (my emphasis).

according to the dictates of his own conscience and reason." Other favorite formulations of this right include "the rights of conscience," "free exercise of religious worship," or simply "religious liberty."[48] The First Amendment of the U.S. Constitution similarly affirms the "free exercise of religion." These phrases all mean the same thing. Maryland gives the fullest statement of the right: "no person ought by any law to be molested in his person or estate on account of his religious persuasion or profession, or for his religious practice."[49] Prior to 1776, there was a widely shared view that government should forbid or discourage religious opinions or religiously motivated actions that were not in conformity with the religion approved by the government. Michael McConnell writes, "As late as 1775, [in Virginia] Baptist ministers . . . were jailed and sometimes horsewhipped for preaching the gospel." Even after 1776, Connecticut Baptists and Methodists were occasionally fined and even imprisoned for failing to obtain an approved government certificate of attendance at an approved church. Not every state granted full religious freedom immediately after 1776, but historian Chris Beneke rightly remarks that "[t]he toleration that prevailed by the 1780s made almost all previous tolerationist regimes in the Western world, as well as in colonial North America, look halting and limited."[50]

The founders' conception of religious liberty has two main elements. First, not only may all persons worship God in the way they think best, but they are also permitted to follow what they believe to be God's will in their daily life outside of church. If I believe God wants me to sacrifice animals or drink wine in the course of a religious ceremony, I

---

[48] NH Bill of Rights, 1784, art. 4. Seven states have "free exercise of religion": Bills of Rights of VT, 1777, art. 3; PA, 1776, art. 2; DE, 1776, §2; VA, 1776, §16; and in constitutions of NY, 1777, art. 38; SC, 1790, art. 8; GA, 1777, art. 56. Eleven states mention the right to "worship" and include the term "conscience": NH, pt. 1, art. 4; VT, ch. 1, art. 3; MA, 1780, pt. 1, art. 2; PA, 1776, ch. 1, art. 2; DE, Bill of Rights, §2; NC, 1776, art. 19; SC, art. 8; GA, 1798, art. 4, §10; KY, 1792, art. 12, §3; TN, 1796, art. 11, §3; OH, 1803, art. 8, §3. "Conscience" also occurs in RI's proposed constitutional amendments, 1790. Vincent Phillip Muñoz, "Church and State in the Founding-Era State Constitutions," *American Political Thought* 4, No. 1 (Winter 2015): 1–38, describes in detail the religious provisions of state constitutions.

[49] MD Declaration of Rights, art. 33.

[50] Michael W. McConnell, "The Supreme Court's Earliest Church-State Cases: Windows on Religious-Cultural-Political Conflict in the Early Republic," *Tulsa Law Review* 37, No. 1 (2001): 8–9; M. Louise Greene, *The Development of Religious Liberty in Connecticut* (Boston: Houghton, Mifflin, 1905), 338, 359, 377; Chris Beneke, "The 'Catholic Spirit Prevailing in Our Country': America's Moderate Religious Revolution," in *The First Prejudice: Religious Tolerance and Intolerance in Early America*, ed. Beneke and Christopher S. Grenda (Philadelphia: University of Pennsylvania Press, 2011), 266.

am permitted to do so. If I believe God requires me to close my business or refuse to work on Saturday or Sunday, I may do that too. Of course, religious liberty does not give me a right to be paid if I refuse to work for religious reasons at the times my employer needs me, or if I refuse to follow the employer's dress code or policy regarding proselytizing at work.

But free exercise of religion has limits. In most founding documents, religious liberty is hedged in with qualifications. Take the 1780 Massachusetts Bill of Rights: "no subject shall be hurt... or restrained for worshipping God in the manner... most agreeable to the dictates of his own conscience;... provided he doth not disturb the public peace." This formulation is typical. Everyone has religious liberty, but no one may abuse that liberty by "disturbing the public peace." The same is true in Maryland's Constitution: "religious liberty" is guaranteed "unless, under color of religion, any man shall... infringe the laws of morality, or injure others, in their natural, civil, or religious rights."[51] In other words, religious liberty must be exercised without harming others – without disobeying the laws that protect the life, liberty, and property of others or sustain the moral basis of society. No one has a natural right to sacrifice children as was done in the religion of the Aztecs and of the biblical Canaanites.[52] Nor may one murder "infidels" or incite others to murder.[53] When people talk about religious freedom today, these limits are often forgotten.

Pursuit of Happiness and Other Natural Rights

Besides the natural rights to life, liberty, property, and free exercise of religion, a fifth natural right can be inferred from the fact that human beings are "by nature free and equal." That right is to seek what we care about most deeply: happiness. Besides the Declaration of Independence, eight early state constitutions, and constitutional amendments proposed by two other states, speak of a right to pursue happiness.[54] In New Hampshire's Bill of Rights, this right sums up all the rest; after listing life, liberty, and property, it concludes, "in a word, of seeking and obtaining happiness."[55]

---

[51] MD Declaration of Rights, art. 33.   [52] Psalms 106:38.
[53] I will say more about religious liberty in ch. 9, "Promotion of Belief in Religion."
[54] Constitutions of NH, 1784, pt. 1, art. 2; VT, 1777, ch. 1, art. 1; MA, 1780. pt. 1, art. 1; NY, 1777, preamble; PA, ch. 1, art. 1; VA Declaration of Rights, 1776, art. 1; KY, 1799, preamble; OH, 1803, art. 8, §1; NC and RI, Declarations of Rights published by Ratifying Conventions, 1788.
[55] NH Constitution, 1784, pt. 1, art. 2.

When the Declaration of Independence discusses the right to revolution, it takes "safety and happiness" to be the sum of government's purpose. "Safety" summarizes security of life, liberty, and property, while "happiness" is the goal of human life. Harry Jaffa rightly remarks that "safety and happiness are the alpha and omega of political life. . . . [S]afety is the first of the ends or purposes of political life, but happiness is the end for which life, liberty, and property are wanted."[56]

From statements like this, one might be tempted to conclude that government's job would therefore be to define happiness and to make sure that every citizen pursues the correct way of life to that end, including government-supervised religious doctrines and practice. That was arguably Plato's logic, and Aristotle's, but the founders followed Locke and other modern philosophers in turning away from this kind of politics. Rather, they thought the best way to promote public happiness was "to secure these rights," i.e., to limit "the design and end of government" to "freedom and security" (as Thomas Paine phrased it in *Common Sense*).[57] Government's primary duty is to protect citizens against predatory violence or other interference with their liberty, whether from fellow citizens or from foreign attack.

The bills of rights of six states speak of a right to "obtaining happiness."[58] This phrase must be understood in the same sense as the right to "acquire and possess property." It does not mean government guarantees a certain amount of happiness and property to everyone, but only that government will protect the right to pursue happiness and the right to keep the fruits of one's labor. Perhaps that is why, when Pennsylvania revised its Bill of Rights in 1790, the right of "obtaining happiness" was replaced with a more precise formulation: "pursuing their own happiness."[59] No one would have dreamed of claiming that his fellow citizens have a duty to make him happy.

As a sixth natural right, some founding documents add the right to reputation (or the "right to character"), as in Delaware's Constitution of 1792, which includes "acquiring and protecting reputation" in its

---

[56] Harry V. Jaffa, *A New Birth of Freedom: Abraham Lincoln and the Coming of the Civil War* (Lanham, MD: Rowman & Littlefield, 2000), 50.

[57] Thomas Paine, *Common Sense*, 1776, ed. Isaac Kramnick (New York: Penguin, 1976), 68.

[58] VA, 1776, art. 1; PA, 1776, art. 1; VT, 1777, art. 1; MA, 1780, art. 1; NH, 1784, art. 2; OH, 1803, art. 8, §1.

[59] PA Constitution, 1790, art. 9, §1.

list of natural rights.⁶⁰ A 1788 Pennsylvania court case explains why reputation must be a natural right: "injuries which are done to character and reputation seldom can be cured, and the most innocent man may, in a moment, be deprived of his good name, upon which, perhaps, he depends for all the prosperity, and all the happiness of his life."⁶¹

I have already mentioned other important natural rights, such as freedom of speech and press, and the right to own and use firearms. These and all natural rights are instances of the equal liberty of all human beings by nature. One right that all founders accepted, but which was rarely mentioned because no one questioned it, is the natural right to marry. I will say more about that in Chapter 10.

The list of natural rights is potentially infinite. As mentioned above, Sedgwick ridiculed mentioning a constitutional right of assembly during a debate in Congress on what later became the First Amendment. He argued that the Constitution "might have gone into a very lengthy enumeration of rights; they might have declared that a man should have a right to wear his hat if he pleased, that he might get up when he pleased, and go to bed when he thought proper.... [Was] it necessary to list these trifles in a declaration of rights, under a government where none of them were intended to be infringed"?⁶²

Rights and Duties

The first sentence of the Declaration of Independence shows that rights and duties go together in the founding. The "laws of nature and of nature's God" entitle the United States to "a separate and equal station" "among the powers of the earth." America has a *right* to national independence. But that means Britain has a corresponding *duty* not to trespass on the "separate and equal station" of other nations.

Some scholars argue that the founders' philosophy of natural rights has no place in it for moral duties. In his *Closing of the American Mind*, political theorist Allan Bloom writes, "Hobbes and Locke, and the American Founders following them," point "in the direction of indiscriminate freedom." Later he explains: "In fact, rights are nothing

---

⁶⁰ DE Constitution, 1792, Preamble.
⁶¹ *Respublica v. Oswald*, 1 Dall. 319 (PA, 1788), in *Founders' Constitution*, 5:126.
⁶² Statement of Congressman Theodore Sedgwick, Aug. 15, 1789, quoted in Hamburger, "Trivial Rights," 1.

other than the fundamental passions, experienced by all men.... Civil society then sets as its sole goal that satisfaction [of these passions] – life, liberty, and the pursuit of property – and men consent to obey the civil authority because it reflects their wants. Government becomes more solid and surer, now based on passions rather than virtues, rights rather than duties."[63]

If Bloom is correct, if rights are nothing but "the fundamental passions," then everyone would have a natural right to licentiousness and the pursuit of happiness by predatory domination of others. In Bloom's argument, the founders believed that the only thing that can restrain the passions is long-term self-interest, but certainly no moral principle.

Going beyond Bloom but drawing a possible conclusion from Bloom's view of natural rights, political theorist Wilson Carey McWilliams writes, "Human beings, in the framers' creed, are by nature free, morally independent without obligations to nature or their fellows." The founders' principles, he continues, lead to the conclusion that the "really desirable regime is not democracy, but a tyranny in which I am the tyrant, able to command the bodies and resources of others to 'live as I like.'"[64] This claim might seem bizarre in light of the founders' actual views, but McWilliams is simply stating one possible consequence of the error about the natural rights doctrine that he shares with Bloom and others. Political scientist Patrick Deneen holds a similar opinion: the "founding philosophy" of America "bases politics on a conception of an idealized autonomous individual for whom all social and communal relationships are the result of contract, or 'voluntarism.'"[65] For Bloom, McWilliams, and Deneen, the founders' approach was, if I may exaggerate for the sake of clarity, *all rights, no duties.*

Historian Michal Jan Rozbicki has a simple but correct rejoinder to these scholars. "We tend to focus on rights as such," he writes, "but contemporaries emphasized duties as inseparable from rights." Bradburn agrees: "We should be careful about employing 'liberal,' in a nineteenth-century sense, to describe the political use of natural rights in the eighteenth century.... Natural and common law bound people together with

---

[63] Allan Bloom, *The Closing of the American Mind* (New York: Simon and Schuster, 1987), 28, 287.

[64] Wilson Carey McWilliams, "Democracy and the Citizen," in *Redeeming Democracy in America*, ed. Patrick J. Deneen and Susan J. McWilliams (Lawrence: University Press of Kansas, 2011), 15.

[65] Patrick J. Deneen, "A House Divided: Peter Lawler's America Rightly Understood," *Perspectives on Political Science* 3, No. 37 (Summer 2008): 147.

natural *duties* as well as rights."[66] Rozbicki's and Bradburn's claim is confirmed in Jefferson's preface to a proposed revision of Virginia's criminal law, where he speaks of the need to restrain "wicked and dissolute men resigning themselves to the dominion of inordinate passions."[67] This phrase contradicts Bloom's view of "rights as fundamental passions" as well as Deneen's "autonomous individual." For Jefferson, some men are "wicked," some passions "inordinate." We have a duty to restrain those passions independently of any contracts we might make. In his First Inaugural, Washington states, "the foundation of our national policy [should] be laid in the pure and immutable principles of private morality . . . : since there exists in the economy and course of nature an indissoluble union between virtue and happiness; between duty and advantage."[68] Pursuit of happiness and advantage is permitted, but it must be in accordance with the "principles of private morality." In the context of its discussion of natural rights, the Massachusetts town of Essex states: "We have duties, for the discharge of which we are accountable to our Creator and benefactor, which no human power can cancel. What those duties are, is determinable by right reason."[69]

The Laws of Nature

The inseparability of rights from duties can also be seen in the founders' understanding of the *laws of nature* (or *natural law*). This term appears frequently in founding documents. I find two predominant political uses of the term: natural law as the ground of natural rights (without any explicit mention of duties), and natural law as defining the moral limits of the natural right to liberty.

First, founding documents frequently recognize the laws of nature as the ground of natural rights. However, how natural law leads to the rights of individuals is never clearly spelled out. As Benjamin Wright remarks,

---

[66] Michal Jan Rozbicki, *Culture and Liberty in the Age of the American Revolution* (Charlottesville: University of Virginia Press, 2011), 150; Bradburn, *Citizenship Revolution*, 29. However, I do not accept Rozbicki's characterization of the founders' natural law as "inherent elitism." He speaks of "an unequal scope of freedom befitting each rank" for which I find no convincing evidence; I explain the founders' view of slavery and voting rights later.

[67] Thomas Jefferson, Bill for Proportioning Crimes and Punishments, 1778, in *Founders' Constitution*, 5:374.

[68] George Washington, First Inaugural Address, in *Writings*, ed. John Rhodehamel (New York: Library of America, 1997), 732–3.

[69] *Essex Result*, 1778, in *American Political Writing*, 1:487.

"in American political thought, the natural law concept is extensively used but never carefully analyzed."[70] In this usage of the term, the emphasis is not on the laws of nature as creating obligations, but rather as justifying the assertion of our rights against others.

We see this frequently in official documents. In response to the Stamp Act crisis of 1765, the Massachusetts Assembly resolved that "there are certain essential rights... which are founded in the law of God and nature, and are the common rights of mankind" and that "no law of society can, consistent with the law of God and nature, divest [the people] of those rights."[71] Congress's 1774 Declarations and Resolves repeat that claim: "By the immutable laws of nature," the colonists "are entitled to life, liberty and property" and "to participate in their legislative council."[72] The Georgia Constitution of 1777 refers to "the common rights of mankind" which Americans "are entitled to by the laws of nature and reason."[73] Although duties are not explicit in this use of the expression, they are implied, since a right is a just claim that others have a duty to respect.

The same view is also found in important unofficial documents, for example in a widely read 1766 pamphlet by Richard Bland: "As then we can receive no light from the laws of the kingdom, or from ancient history, to direct us in our inquiry, we must have recourse to the law of nature, and those rights of mankind which flow from it."[74] In Jefferson's 1774 *Summary View*, Americans are "a free people, claiming their rights as derived from the laws of nature, and not as the gift of their chief magistrate.... [They] are asserting the rights of human nature."[75]

Second, the laws of nature were also often treated as the basis of moral duties. An early example is the Massachusetts Assembly's 1762 instructions to its agent in London: "The natural rights of the colonists

---

[70] Benjamin Fletcher Wright, Jr., *American Interpretations of Natural Law: A Study in the History of Political Thought* (New York: Russell & Russell, 1962), 70. The founders mostly used the expression *law* or *laws of nature*, although occasionally the term *natural law* appears, e.g., Samuel West, *On the Right to Rebel against Governors*, 1776, in *American Political Writing*, 1:413; John Witherspoon, "Queries, and Answers Thereto, Respecting Marriage," in *The American Museum, or Repository*, vol. 4 (Philadelphia: Mathew Carey, 1788), 315. Scholars of the founding prefer the term *natural law*.

[71] Resolutions of the House of Representatives of Massachusetts, Oct. 29, 1765, in *Founders' Constitution*, 1:629.

[72] Continental Congress, Declarations and Resolves, Oct. 14, 1774, in *Founders' Constitution*, 1:2.

[73] Preamble, GA Constitution, 1777.

[74] Bland, *An Inquiry*, in *American Political Writing*, 1:73.

[75] Jefferson, *Summary View*, in *Writings*, ed. Peterson, 121.

we humbly conceive to be the same with those of all other British subjects, and indeed of all mankind. The . . . principal of these rights is to be
'free from any superior power on earth, and not to be under the will or
legislative authority of man, but to have only the law of nature for his
rule.'"[76] In other words, natural liberty exists only within the moral limits
of the law of nature. In another document approved by the Massachusetts
Assembly, James Otis repeats this view: "Nature has placed all such in
a state of equality and perfect freedom to act within the bounds of the
laws of nature and reason without consulting the will or regarding the
humor, the passions, or whims of any other man. . . . The law of nature
was not of man's making. . . . He can only perform and keep, or disobey
and break it."[77] William Whiting, on behalf of the Massachusetts legislature in 1778, writes, "In a state of nature, each individual has a right . . . to
dispose of, order, and direct, his property, his person, and all his own
actions, within the bounds of the law of nature, as he thinks fit."[78] James
Wilson states: "selfishness and injury are as little countenanced by the law
of nature as by the law of man. . . . In a state of natural liberty, everyone
is allowed to act according to his own inclination, provided he transgress
not those limits, which are assigned to him by the law of nature."[79]

This second "moral duties" usage of the term was applied to both
foreign and domestic policy. Secretary of State Jefferson, in an official
1793 statement, says that foreign policy should be guided by "the moral
law of our nature." That is "the moral law to which man has been
subjected by his creator. . . . The moral duties which exist between individual and individual in a state of nature, accompany them into a state of
society."[80] Jefferson repeats this point in a letter written later: the "people
in mass . . . are inherently independent of all but moral law."[81] In his legal
treatise, Zephaniah Swift says the "duties of parents consist in affording
their children maintenance, protection, and education. These duties are
all founded in nature."[82] In Chapter 10, we will see that Swift's use of

---

[76] Massachusetts Assembly, Instructions to Jasper Mauduit, 1762, in Massachusetts Historical Society, *Collections*, 74:39 (quoting Locke, *Second Treatise*, §22).

[77] James Otis, *The Rights of the British Colonies Asserted and Proved*, 1764, in *Pamphlets
of the American Revolution*, ed. Bernard Bailyn (Cambridge: Harvard University Press,
1965), 1:438–41.

[78] William Whiting, Address to the Inhabitants of Berkshire County, 1778, in *American
Political Writing*, 466.

[79] Wilson, *Lectures on Law*, 2:1056.

[80] Jefferson, Opinion on the French Treaties, 1793, in *Writings*, ed. Peterson, 423, 428.

[81] Jefferson to Spencer Roane, Sept. 6, 1819, in ibid., 1426.

[82] Zephaniah Swift, *A System of the Laws of the State of Connecticut* (Windham, CT:
John Byrne, 1795), 204.

natural law arguments as a foundation of marriage and parental duties was quite common.

Protestant sermons also referred to the laws of nature in the duties sense, as in a quasi-official 1762 Massachusetts election sermon of Abraham Williams: "The law of nature (or, those rules of behavior, which the Nature God has given men...) is the law and will of the God of nature, which all men are obliged to obey. Almighty God, as head of the system, and supreme governor of the universe, will suitably animadvert upon every violation.... The law of nature, which is the constitution of the God of nature, is universally obliging."[83]

Sometimes these two typical usages of natural law – duties and source of rights – appear together, as in Hamilton's 1775 *Farmer Refuted*. Hamilton writes that the law of nature "is indispensably obligatory upon all mankind, prior to any human institution whatever.... Hence, in a state of nature, no man had any *moral* power to deprive another of his life, limbs, property, or liberty." But in the same passage Hamilton says: "Upon this law, depend the natural rights of mankind." Levi Hart, a Connecticut preacher, uses the term in the same way: "to enslave men... is a most atrocious violation of one of the first laws of nature."[84] Slaves have rights under the laws of nature, and others have a natural-law duty not to violate those rights. Natural law, then, is both the source of natural rights and a statement of our duties.

Philip Hamburger correctly sums up the founders' consensus in this way: "Natural law implied that individuals should restrain themselves in the exercise of their physical natural liberty, and it defined an individual's noninjurious or more broadly moral natural liberty."[85]

Natural Rights in Conflict

In the founders' theory, it is possible for one person to have a natural right to violate the natural rights of another. In an 1810 letter, Jefferson illustrates the tension with this example: "A ship at sea in distress for provisions, meets another having abundance, yet refusing a supply; the law of self-preservation authorizes the distressed to take a supply by

---

[83] Abraham Williams, *An Election Sermon*, 1762, in *American Political Writing*, 1:7–8, 15. Also West, *On the Right to Rebel*, in ibid., 1:413;

[84] Hamilton, *Farmer Refuted*, in *The Papers of Alexander Hamilton*, ed. Harold C. Syrett (New York: Columbia University Press, 1961–79), 1:87–8; Levi Hart, *Liberty Described and Recommended*, 1775, in *American Political Writing*, 1:312.

[85] Philip A. Hamburger, "Natural Rights, Natural Law, and American Constitutions," *Yale Law Journal* 102 (Jan. 1993): 930.

force."[86] Here we see a conflict between the right of self-preservation on one side, and the right to possess property on the other. It can be resolved only by force.

Slavery presents another, more controversial example. Discussing the reasons why immediate emancipation was the wrong policy, Jefferson writes, "we have the wolf by the ears, and we can neither hold him, nor safely let him go. Justice is in one scale, and self-preservation in the other." By *justice* he means the slaves' natural right to liberty, and by *self-preservation* he means, quite literally, the lives of the slave owners. "Deep rooted prejudices entertained by the whites; ten thousand recollections by the blacks of the injuries they have sustained; new provocations; the real distinctions which nature has made; and many other circumstances, will divide us into parties, and produce convulsions which will probably never end but in the extermination of the one or the other race."[87] If Jefferson's description of the situation were accurate, slavery would have been justified, but only as a necessary evil to be ended as quickly as possible in a way compatible with both justice *and* self-preservation. Jefferson thought that would be most likely to happen if the former slaves could be sent to live in another country. Otherwise relations between the races would be murderous. Nicholas Guyatt argues that the founders attempted to reconcile the natural right to liberty with security of Americans' rights and with consent-based citizenship by having Indians live apart from American citizens and by the idea of colonization of blacks to another country.[88] Although most people today would say that Jefferson was wrong to fear "the extermination of the one or the other race," it is a fact that whites and blacks have inflicted terrible crimes on each other ever since the founding, including many thousands of murders.[89]

---

[86] Jefferson to John B. Colvin, Sept. 20, 1810, in *Founders' Constitution*, 4:127. Another example: Hamilton, *A Full Vindication of the Measures of Congress*, 1774, in *Papers*, 1:51.

[87] Jefferson to Holmes, Apr. 22, 1820, in *Writings*, 1434. Jefferson, *Notes on Virginia*, Query 14, in *Writings*, 264.

[88] Nicholas Guyatt, *Bind Us Apart: How Enlightened Americans Invented Racial Segregation* (New York: Basic Books, 2016).

[89] In his heated attack on my *Vindicating the Founders*, Alan Gibson incorrectly claims that I "apotheosize" and "sanitize" the founders and treat their arguments against immediate abolition of slavery as "simply correct." In fact, as Gibson should have admitted, I frankly acknowledge that their motives were mixed, and that they included "selfishness," "avarice," and "interest," along with a recognition of slavery's injustice and "not altogether unreasonable" fears of race war. See Alan Gibson, *Understanding the Founding: The Crucial Questions*, 2nd ed. (Lawrence: University Press of Kansas, 2010), 217–19; West, *Vindicating*, 21–3.

Some might wonder whether this conflict of natural rights is a problem that is tied to the supposedly selfish basis of the founders' modern natural rights doctrine. "[T]he problem lies rather in the principles themselves," writes Herbert Storing. "There is a tendency," he continues, "under the principles of the Declaration of Independence itself, for justice to be reduced to self-preservation, for self-preservation to be defined as self-interest, and for self-interest to be defined as what is convenient and achievable."[90]

However, there is nothing in any important founding document that would support such an interpretation of natural rights. Criticizing the doctrine "that the interest of the majority is the political standard of right and wrong," Madison writes: "Taking the word 'interest' as synonymous with 'ultimate happiness,' in which sense it is qualified with every necessary moral ingredient, the proposition is no doubt true. But taking it in the popular sense, as referring to the immediate augmentation of property and wealth, nothing can be more false. In the latter sense it would be the interest of the majority in every community to despoil and enslave the minority."[91]

The difficulty under consideration – the possible conflict between justice and self-preservation – is not unique to the natural rights doctrine. The problem arises from reality itself. All philosophers who have seriously considered the subject recognize this sort of unfortunate, but hopefully rare, conflict of just claims. Even Thomas Aquinas, whom everyone would admit to be a serious moralist, admits that law – including the usual rules of morality – can be suspended in emergencies, because, as he writes, "necessity is not subject to law."[92]

---

[90] Herbert J. Storing, "Slavery and the Moral Foundations of the American Republic," in *The Moral Foundations of the American Republic*, ed. Robert J. Horwitz, 3rd ed. (Charlottesville: University Press of Virginia, 1986), 325. Thomas Merrill makes a similar error in "The Later Jefferson and the Problem of Natural Rights," *Perspectives on Political Science* 44, No. 2 (Apr. 2015): 126–9 (slavery "revealed the implicit egoism of the natural rights doctrine").

[91] Madison to Monroe, Oct. 5, 1786, in Founders Online, National Archives, founders .archives.gov.

[92] Thomas Aquinas, *Summa Theologiae*, pt. 1–2, q.96, a.6, www.corpusthomisticum.org (my translation). Also Leo Strauss, *Natural Right and History* (Chicago: University of Chicago Press, 1953), 160–1 (general rules of natural right may be suspended in urgent circumstances).

2

The Case Against the Natural Rights Founding

The argument in the previous chapter is opposed to the view of scholars who hold that the founding was not guided primarily by the natural rights philosophy, but rather by a blend or "amalgam" of disparate elements, only one of which is natural rights.[1] I agree that there is a sense in which the amalgam thesis is correct. Jefferson writes, "Every species of government has its specific principles. Ours perhaps are more peculiar than those of any other in the universe. It is a composition of the freest principles of the English constitution, with others derived from natural right and natural reason."[2] Jefferson is making the obvious point that some of the specific institutions incorporated into the state constitutions (and later the federal one) were inherited from colonial times and were of English origin. But when he adds that some American principles are "derived from natural right and natural reason," he means that the English tradition had to be modified or even thrown out wherever it stood in conflict with the equal rights of the individual.

The amalgam thesis goes well beyond Jefferson's view. An early version of that approach is found in Alexis de Tocqueville. Writing in 1835, he famously asserts that there is no logical connection between the founders' concern with morality and their concern with liberty: "Anglo-American civilization . . . is the product . . . of two perfectly distinct elements, . . . the *spirit of religion* and the *spirit of freedom*. . . . Thus in the moral world,

---

[1] Alan Gibson, *Interpreting the Founding: Guide to the Enduring Debates over the Origins and Foundations of the American Republic* (Lawrence: University Press of Kansas, 2006), 53, has multiple examples.

[2] Thomas Jefferson, Query 8, *Notes on the State of Virginia*, 1787, in *Writings*, ed. Merrill D. Peterson (New York: Library of America, 1984), 211.

everything is classified, coordinated, foreseen, decided in advance. In the political world, everything is agitated, contested, uncertain."[3] When Tocqueville says that the spirit of religion and the spirit of freedom are "perfectly distinct" and that "the spirit of freedom" lacks moral content, he anticipates some scholars' view of the individual rights doctrine. Like Tocqueville, the recent literature tends to treat the political theory of the founding as an amalgam of distinct traditions. However, a more accurate understanding of the founding shows that conclusion to be a mistake.

The Amalgam Thesis in Recent Scholarship

Among more recent writers, Michael Sandel gives us a secularized version of the Tocqueville thesis. He calls the founders' supposedly separate traditions *liberalism* and *republicanism*. He argues that the idea of individual rights belongs to a tradition of liberalism "that runs from John Locke, Immanuel Kant, and John Stuart Mill to John Rawls." "Liberal" thinkers, Sandel says, believe that government should be "neutral on the question of the good life." Sandel rejects "liberalism" for this very reason: if government is "neutral on moral and religious questions," it cannot "secure the liberty it promises, because it cannot sustain the kind of political community and civic engagement that liberty requires." Sandel thinks that the founding was partly based on this liberal neutrality, but that it was combined with a countervailing and initially more powerful doctrine of "republicanism." "The republican conception of freedom," writes Sandel, "unlike the liberal conception, requires a formative politics, a politics that cultivates in citizens the qualities of character self-government requires."[4]

Isaac Kramnick agrees with Sandel's argument that the founding is a blend of opposing traditions. He sees a tension between the founders' liberalism – a "modern, self-interested, competitive, individualistic ideology emphasizing private rights" – and a competing republican "ideology emphasizing selfless duty-based participation in the communal pursuit of the virtuous public good." Kramnick differs from Sandel by arguing

---

[3] Alexis de Tocqueville, *Democracy in America*, 1835, 1840, trans. Harvey C. Mansfield and Delba Winthrop (Chicago: University of Chicago Press, 2000), vol. 1, pt. 1, ch. 2, p. 43.

[4] Michael Sandel, *Democracy's Discontent* (Cambridge: Harvard University Press, 1996), 4–7, 24. Cf. Howard Gillman, *The Constitution Besieged: The Rise and Demise of Lochner Era Police Powers Jurisprudence* (Durham: Duke University Press, 1993), 23 ("rich and diverse language of liberalism and republicanism"), 218 ("four idioms: republicanism, Locke, work ethic, and state theory").

that the founding was predominantly "liberal," while Sandel says it was predominantly "republican."[5]

Largely agreeing with Sandel, William Galston accepts the view – a view that few founders would have found intelligible – that the origin of today's problems lies partly in what he too calls the liberalism of the founding principles: "The . . . founding set in motion a new political order based to an unprecedented . . . extent on individual rights, personal choice, and democratic/egalitarian social relations. . . . [W]hat has happened to the American family in the past two generations is in important respects a consequence of the unfolding logic of authoritative, deeply American moral-political principles."[6] For Galston, like Sandel, the "unfolding logic" of natural rights was restrained by a "long-standing balance between juridical liberal principles and a complex of traditional moral beliefs." This balance, Galston continues, was made possible by the founders' "amalgam" of "the essentially secular principles of democratic liberalism; the moral maxims derived from Christianity; and the mores of Protestant Americans."[7] Galston differs from most scholars because he correctly states that the founders held that a moral foundation is necessary for security of rights. However, Galston believes that in spite of that commitment, their acceptance of "juridical liberal principles" eventually proved destructive of their own best intentions.

Michael Zuckert's account is at first glance similar to mine in Chapter 1. He agrees that the founders' concern with morality belongs to their natural rights orientation. He says that the founders saw the need to promote a "rights infrastructure," the "social institutions and traits of character that make rights-securing possible."[8] Zuckert appears to be

---

[5] Isaac Kramnick, *Republicanism and Bourgeois Radicalism: Political Ideology in Late Eighteenth-Century England and America* (Ithaca: Cornell University Press, 1990), 35. Cf. Robert P. Kraynak, *Christian Faith and Modern Democracy: God and Politics in the Fallen World* (Notre Dame, IN: University of Notre Dame Press, 2001), xii (there is a univocal liberal tradition "from Locke and Kant to Rorty and Rawls," and the founding was mostly "liberal").

[6] William A. Galston, "The Reinstitutionalization of Marriage: Political Theory and Public Policy," in *Promises to Keep: Decline and Renewal of Marriage in America*, ed. David Popenoe, Jean Bethke Elshtain, and David Blankenhorn (Lanham, MD: Rowman & Littlefield, 1996), 281–2. Galston's view on this topic is similar to Patrick J. Deneen, "A House Divided: Peter Lawler's America Rightly Understood," *Perspectives on Political Science* 3, No. 37 (Summer 2008): 147–51.

[7] William A. Galston, *Liberal Purposes: Goods, Virtues, and Diversity in the Liberal State* (New York: Cambridge University Press, 1991), 269, 267.

[8] Michael P. Zuckert, *Launching Liberalism: On Lockean Political Philosophy* (Lawrence: University Press of Kansas, 2002), 226, 361.

saying that there is no tension between individual rights and the elements of this "rights infrastructure." While he correctly writes that "the other [elements] could enter the amalgam only so far as they were compatible, or could be made so, with natural rights," he then asserts that there is some tension, perhaps even a contradiction, in the mix. Like Galston, Zuckert therefore speaks of an American amalgam of British constitutionalism, Christianity, "republicanism," and natural rights. This amalgam, he says, "led America . . . to a particularly tense existence as these four different, and, *in some dimensions, incompatible* elements fell in and out of harmony with each other."[9] Zuckert's position is close to that of Thomas Pangle, who writes that although the leading element in the American amalgam is natural rights, there were "competing moral visions that came together to generate the liberal-democratic polity."[10]

In disagreement with Zuckert, Pangle, and other "amalgam" scholars, I argue that the important tensions that arise in later American history come either from disagreements over the practical meaning of the founding principles (such as the fight over the federal Sedition Act of 1798) or outright rejection of the founding principles, as in the Southern attack on natural rights starting in the 1830s, repeated in a different form by Progressive writers after 1880. Those inclined to blame the founders' principles for those features of contemporary liberalism to which they object should pay greater attention to the loud and explicit *rejection* of the founding principles by leading intellectuals after the Civil War and continuing to the present day.[11]

---

[9] Michael P. Zuckert, *The Natural Rights Republic: Studies in the Foundation of the American Political Tradition* (Notre Dame, IN: University of Notre Dame Press, 1996), 95 (my emphasis).

[10] Thomas L. Pangle, *The Spirit of Modern Republicanism: The Moral Vision of the American Founders and the Philosophy of Locke* (Chicago: University of Chicago Press, 1988), 1. Unlike most scholars, Randy E. Barnett, *Our Republican Constitution: Securing the Liberty and Sovereignty of We the People* (New York: HarperCollins, 2016), ch. 1, argues that the Declaration was wholly based on the political theory of natural rights. However, Barnett's libertarian reading is silent on the founders' concern with the people's moral character. See also Harry V. Jaffa, *How to Think about the American Revolution* (Durham: Carolina Academic Press, 1978) (the predominance of the natural rights theory); Edward J. Erler, "The Political Philosophy of the Constitution," in *To Form a More Perfect Union: The Critical Ideas of the Constitution*, ed. Herman Belz, Ronald Hoffman, and Peter J. Albert (Charlottesville: University Press of Virginia, 1992), 134–65 (applying Jaffa's argument to the Constitution).

[11] Thomas G. West, "Progressivism and the Transformation of American Government," in *The Progressive Revolution in Politics and Political Science: Transforming the American Regime*, ed. John Marini and Ken Masugi (Lanham, MD: Rowman & Littlefield, 2005), 13–33; Charles R. Kesler, *I Am the Change: Barack Obama and the Crisis of Liberalism* (New York: Broadside Books, HarperCollins, 2012).

The founders did not separate rights from duties. They believed that the laws of nature and of nature's God impose moral obligations on human beings in their dealings with other people. They also oblige nations in their dealings with each other. The founders believed, as Virginia's Bill of Rights states, that "no free government, or the blessings of liberty, can be preserved to any people but by a firm adherence to justice, moderation, temperance, frugality, and virtue."[12] The evidence presented throughout this book lends support to the view that the rejection of the founders' moral concerns came about not through the unfolding logic of the natural rights principles of the founding, but rather through their repudiation.

The Founders' Understanding of Rights versus Post-1960s Rights

The amalgam approach arises in part because scholars often fail to distinguish sufficiently between the founders' conception of rights and the view that prevails today. Political theorist Harvey Mansfield speaks for many when he writes that Locke's *Two Treatises of Government* is "still the greatest philosophic statement of the liberalism by which we live."[13] In reality, the post-1960s "liberalism by which we live" repudiates the doctrines of Locke and the founders.

To clarify the difference between the founders' "liberalism" – which really deserves a different label – and the liberalism with which we are familiar today, one can begin with the post-1960s understanding of the fundamental right to "equal concern and respect," to use legal philosopher Ronald Dworkin's term. He understands this to mean "the right to equal treatment, that is, to the same distribution of goods or opportunities." This requires not only transfer of material benefits from the more advantaged to the less but also public esteem and respect for any manner of life however degraded (from the founders' point of view). That is because it is wrong for anyone's "conception of a proper or desirable life [to be] despised by others."[14] As Alan Ryan explains, liberalism means "that individuals are self-creating, that no single good defines successful self-creation," so that every person's "projects" deserve "moral respect." Charles Taylor agrees: "the withholding of recognition can be

---

[12] VA Declaration of Rights, 1776, art. 15.

[13] Harvey C. Mansfield, *Manliness* (New Haven: Yale University Press, 2006), 177. David Wootton agrees, in *Political Writings of John Locke*, ed. Wootton (New York: Penguin, 1993), 9.

[14] Ronald Dworkin, *Taking Rights Seriously* (Cambridge: Harvard University Press, 1977), 73, 276.

a form of oppression."[15] In recent liberal theory, speech and publications that disparage or harm the self-esteem of the "disadvantaged" should be discouraged or punished.[16]

In a 2009 speech, Secretary of State Hillary Clinton summarizes the new view. "Human rights," she says, "have both negative and positive requirements." The negative ones are based on the idea that people "should be free from tyranny in whatever form." These are rights the founders would have agreed with, except for her addition of the freedom "to love in the way they choose" – an allusion to the gay and transgender rights agenda promoted by the Barack Obama administration. Clinton's "positive" rights also go beyond the founding and contradict it: "Human development must be part of our human rights agenda," and development means being "free from the oppression of want," above all from the "want of equality in law and in fact." In other words, we must transfer resources and opportunity from those who have more to those who have less, so that there will be "equality...in fact." Thus in Louis Fisher's recent book on how Congress protects individual rights, there are chapters on the rights of blacks, women, children, religious minorities, and Indians, but nothing on the rights of Americans who do not belong to these groups.[17]

In spite of these principles, contemporary liberalism permits and even encourages inequality. Philosopher John Rawls explains: the "difference principle" is that "social and economic inequalities, for example... [in] wealth and authority, are just only if they result in compensating benefits for everyone, and in particular for the least advantaged."[18] Although Rawls does not say so explicitly, this principle implies that professors at prestige universities, important government officials, and leaders of major

[15] Alan Ryan, *The Making of Modern Liberalism* (Princeton: Princeton University Press, 2012), 35, 95; Charles Taylor, "The Politics of Recognition," in *Multiculturalism: Examining the Politics of Recognition*, ed. Amy Gutmann (Princeton: Princeton University Press, 1994), 36 (the context is "race relations" and "feminism"; Taylor does not explicitly address sexual self-expression here).

[16] Thomas G. West, "Free Speech in the American Founding and in Modern Liberalism," in *Freedom of Speech*, ed. Ellen Frankel Paul, Fred D. Miller, Jr., and Jeffrey Paul (New York: Cambridge University Press, 2004), 356–71. John Rawls, *A Theory of Justice* (Cambridge: Harvard University Press, 1972), 520, 523, 526–7, explicitly states that although many ways of life are permissible and should be celebrated, everyone must agree with the sole permissible view of justice – namely, Rawls's view.

[17] Hillary Clinton, Remarks on the Human Rights Agenda for the 21st Century, December 14, 2009, www.state.gov; Louis Fisher, *Congress: Protecting Individual Rights* (Lawrence: University Press of Kansas, 2016).

[18] Rawls, *Theory of Justice*, 14–15.

foundations which promote liberal social programs – as well as their corporate sponsors – deserve the unequal wealth, privileges, and honors they enjoy, because they are working to transfer honor and resources to the disadvantaged. Rawls's approach thereby requires redistribution of income and prestige from the more advantaged not only to those who are less advantaged but also to those at the top who are promoting social justice.

For the founders, the "want of equality in fact" does not create a rightful claim against others to provide them with resources – except in extreme circumstances such as disability, orphanhood, insanity, destitution, and the like. Political scientist Jennifer Nedelsky rightly contrasts the post-1960s view with the founders': "once we acknowledge that some basic rights can only be enjoyed with state economic support, we have left the boundary of [the founders'] negative liberty behind (and, of course, further redistributive incursions on property are likely to follow)."[19] The founders did not think liberty includes a right to demand "state economic support" from others. Instead, natural rights are based on what human beings are and have by nature – their life, liberty, and talents – which give them the ability to acquire property, worship God, and pursue happiness. Modern liberal rights are not natural rights because no one possesses food, transportation, respect, and access to medical care by nature. In the book's final chapter, I will explain how the founders' principles lead to a very limited right to welfare.

Unlike Nedelsky, who is helpfully clear about the difference, some scholars try to assimilate the founders' political theory to one or another version of current liberalism. For example, political scientist James Flynn writes, "Since the inception of our nation, we have had a noble public philosophy" whose promise can be "actualized" only through "a robust welfare state."[20] Nedelsky and I see no support for that view in the founding. The founders believed that people are usually capable of taking care of themselves, if only the artificial weights of hereditary privilege and legal restrictions – the legacy of medieval times – are removed. Mansfield sensibly observes, "The political philosophy behind limited government affirms that nature is more important than nurture: that humans have

---

[19] Jennifer Nedelsky, *Private Property and the Limits of American Constitutionalism: The Madisonian Framework and Its Legacy* (Chicago: University of Chicago Press, 1990), 263.

[20] James R. Flynn, *Where Have All the Liberals Gone? Race, Class, and Ideals in America* (New York: Cambridge University Press, 2008), 298–9.

a fixed nature enabling them to overcome a background of poverty and deprivation."[21]

The promiscuous application of the term *liberal* to such disparate people as Locke, Jefferson, Kant, Dewey, the Roosevelts, Rawls, Dworkin, Obama, and the Clintons is evidence of an underestimation of the distance between the founders and their Progressive and liberal opponents in the past century. The word *liberalism* was unknown in the founding. The founders did call themselves *liberal*, meaning generous or respectful of the rights of others. They were devoted to liberty – but not "self-creation" contrary to the laws of nature. They prized the virtue of liberality (generosity). But they were emphatically not liberals in the post-1960s sense of Rawls, Dworkin, Obama, or Clinton.[22]

Natural Rights: The "Form" Shaping the American "Matter"

If the founders' political theory is not an amalgam in the sense in which some scholars describe it, what then is the relation between their natural rights principles and the other colonial traditions that were partially incorporated into the founding, such as government support of Protestantism and other parts of the English common law? Borrowing a remark of Leo Strauss made in a different context, I suggest that natural rights and the laws of nature are the *form* of the founding, and the facts of colonial America are the *matter*. Both of them together – matter shaped by form – produced the American regime. I use these terms not in their technical, Aristotelian, sense, but as rough analogies. "The classics held the view," Strauss writes, "that the form [of a thing] is higher in dignity than the matter.... The Jewish equivalent of this relation might be said to be the relation between the Torah and Israel."[23] The Torah, God's law revealed at Sinai, was supposed to govern the Jewish people. America's "Torah," the "form" that is supposed to animate and shape it, is its principles: the laws of nature and of nature's God. In the political sphere (as opposed to private life), nothing should be higher than the laws of nature – not Christianity, not the English tradition, not "republicanism," not race or sex or class. The "matter" – the conditions and traditions

---

[21] Harvey Mansfield, *America's Constitutional Soul* (Baltimore: Johns Hopkins University Press, 1991), 94.

[22] Philip Hamburger, "Liberality," *Texas Law Review* 78 (May 2000): 1215–85 (on the founders' understanding of *liberal*).

[23] Leo Strauss, *What Is Political Philosophy? And Other Studies* (Glencoe, IL: Free Press, 1959), 35–6.

of colonial America before 1776 – was honed and shaped by the form.

The *matter* that existed in 1776 was a brute fact, which included the universal features of human nature. But it also included the particular geography, laws, racial stock, popular sentiments, moral habits, and religion of colonial America. The *form*, the natural rights theory, animated the politicians elected to public office. It determined, more than anything else, which traditions would continue and which would be discarded as the new regime took shape under the ruling guidance of natural rights.

The right to liberty and the laws of nature are universal. They are permanent truths, valid for every human being everywhere. But it is difficult and therefore rare for such a form to shape and govern recalcitrant human matter – to establish a political order that secures life and liberty on the basis of consent. Most people lack the necessary qualities of character and mind, due to prejudices, habits, dispositions, or ignorance. In some nations, people do not have the intelligence to see their long-term interest. In others, there is a defect in the necessary self-assertiveness to acquire and defend liberty, or the self-restraint to enjoy it in tranquility. And of course there will always be people who insist that heretics or unbelievers have no natural right to liberty, that it is God's will that they be suppressed or persecuted.

Hamilton understood this difficulty perfectly: "I hold with Montesquieu that a government must be fitted to a nation as much as a coat to the individual, and consequently that what may be good at Philadelphia may be bad at Paris and ridiculous at Petersburg." In other words, political freedom is not possible for everyone. Commenting on the recent slave rebellion in the French colony of St. Domingo (later Haiti), Hamilton wrote that a republican form of government would fail there: "No regular system of liberty will at present suit St. Domingo. The government, if independent, must be military – partaking of the feudal system."[24] Jefferson too knew that well-governed societies require a rare combination of qualities: "if a nation expects to be ignorant and free, in a state of civilization, it expects what never was and never will be."[25] In 1823 Jefferson laments, "Whether the state of society in Europe can bear a republican

---

[24] Alexander Hamilton to Marquis de Lafayette, January 6, 1799, in *The Papers of Alexander Hamilton*, ed. Harold C. Syrett (New York: Columbia University Press, 1961–79), 22:404. Hamilton to Timothy Pickering, February 21, 1799, ibid., 492.

[25] Jefferson to Charles Yancey, January 6, 1816, in *The Writings of Thomas Jefferson*, ed. Andrew A. Lipscomb and Albert E. Bergh (Washington: Thomas Jefferson Memorial Association, 1903), 14:384.

government, I doubted [at the time of the French Revolution] . . . and still do now." For Jefferson, as Jaffa remarks, "Not consent as mere acquiescence of the will, but consent as enlightened by full consciousness of natural rights, and by the aptness of governments to secure those rights, is consent in the full or proper meaning of the term."[26] Strauss explains, in language that these founders would have agreed with, that only the philosopher in his study, and not the real-world statesman, is "free to choose the most favorable conditions that are possible [for the best political order] – ethnic, climatic, economic, and other . . . : a given community may be so rude or so depraved that only a very inferior type of order can 'keep it going.'"[27]

The American "matter," while far from perfect, was about as good (in the founders' understanding) as could be found at any time or place. The people warmly supported their colonial tradition of English law, Protestant Christianity, and republican political institutions. As explained in Chapter 1, preachers and politicians, and then the people, increasingly embraced the natural rights teaching throughout the eighteenth century.[28] It is unlikely that the American Revolution could have succeeded without something like the Anglo-American people with their distinctive ethnic character, religion, and legal heritage – the healthy and intelligent "matter." To that extent the amalgam thesis is correct: natural rights are not enough. But the Revolution would not have taken the direction it did without the leading role of the natural rights theory to give it its distinctive shape.

One of the most important differences between the several early American declarations of rights and the 1789 French Declaration of the Rights of Man and of the Citizen is the absence of the laws of nature – the idea of moral obligation and self-restraint – in the latter. An even more telling difference is the complete lack of recognition in the French Declaration of the importance of prudence in establishing a regime of temperate liberty, and of the limits imposed on politics by the "matter" – the moral, religious, and ethnic state of the people. This second point is illustrated in the absurd assertion – i.e., absurd from the American point of view – in the Preamble to the French Declaration that "ignorance, neglect, or contempt of the rights of man are the *sole* causes of public calamities

---

[26] Jefferson to Marquis de Lafayette, Nov. 4, 1823, in ibid., 15:491; Jaffa, *How to Think*, 116.

[27] Strauss, *What Is Political Philosophy?* 87.

[28] This development is summarized at the beginning of Chapter 1.

and of the corruption of governments"[29] – as if national character and a people's traditions have nothing to do with the success or failure of political liberty.

In *Federalist* 2, John Jay exemplifies the founders' quite different approach in his discussion of whether the thirteen states should "be one nation, under one federal government," or "divide themselves into separate confederacies." Jay starts out logically, with universal principles. "[T]he people must cede to [government] some of their natural rights, in order to vest it with requisite powers," i.e., powers to secure the rest of their natural rights. This is the "form," the template for good government. However, these true but abstract principles do not answer the particular question of who should be included in a nation that will effectively secure the people's rights. So Jay proceeds to discuss whether the people of the thirteen states – the "matter" – are suited to liberty and political unity. He concludes that they are, for several reasons: "Providence has been pleased to give this one connected country to one united people, a people descended from the same ancestors, speaking the same language, professing the same religion, attached to the same principles of government, very similar in their manners and customs, and who, by their joint counsels, arms and efforts, fighting side by side throughout a long and bloody war, have nobly established their general liberty and independence.... [Americans are] a band of brethren, united to each other by the strongest ties."[30] Jay is saying that Americans are already partly united into one people by the accidents of geography (one connected country), religion (a widely shared Protestantism), common ancestry (most Americans being whites from northwestern Europe), "manners and customs" (things that foster mutual trust, such as common festivals, holidays, and sports, and especially shared ideas of good and evil), and, last but not least, what I am calling the "form," the "same principles of government" (the natural rights theory). Having fought a successful war for independence together, Americans are, in an important sense, friends, "a band of brethren."[31] This compatibility of matter and form throughout the thirteen states points to the reasonableness of a single federal union.

[29] National Assembly of France, Declaration of the Rights of Man, 1789, Avalon Project of Yale Law School, http://avalon.law.yale.edu (my emphasis).
[30] Jay, *Federalist* 2, pp. 31–3.
[31] Jay echoes, probably without knowing it, some of Aristotle's criteria (*Politics*, bk. 3, ch. 3) for a genuine political community as opposed to a mere contract to avoid mutual injury (discussed below near the end of Chapter 11).

Some today think that the founders' America is (or should have been) a "proposition nation," a country defined solely by its form, the idea of equal rights, without any need to pay attention to its matter, the citizens. Jay rejects that view. He implies that a nation that is serious about securing the natural rights of its citizens should be composed of people from nations and cultures that will become and remain one people, "a band of brethren," to the greatest extent possible. And in fact that was the founders' consensus. As I will discuss in Chapter 11, they believed future citizens should be predominantly Europeans.

Natural Rights and the British Constitution

To clarify my form-and-matter analogy, I will contrast my argument with that of legal historian John Reid. My view is summarized well by Douglas Bradburn: "the notion of natural rights...was absolutely fundamental to the meaning and experience of the American Revolution, as it was to American understandings of the British Constitution.... Natural rights language...was ubiquitous and transformative."[32] Reid disagrees. He admits that a multitude of documents in the pre-1776 period appeal to natural law and natural rights, but he insists on the "irrelevancy of natural rights." "Nature," he claims, "was mentioned either as alternative authority or as rhetorical flourish" during the 1760s and early '70s, but the real source of the rights fought for in the Revolution was "British constitutional theory or common law." To illustrate, Reid quotes Congress's 1774 Declaration and Resolves, which appeal to "the immutable laws of nature, the principles of the English constitution, and the several [colonial] charters or compacts." In that document, Reid writes, "not one right is asserted that was not either a constitutional right or a right derived from the authority of custom" or law.[33]

Reid is correct to quote the 1774 declaration as an important statement of American principles. He is also correct that prior to 1776, the

---

[32] Douglas Bradburn, *The Citizenship Revolution: Politics and the Creation of the American Union, 1774–1804* (Charlottesville: University of Virginia Press, 1994), 27. See also J. C. D. Clark, *The Language of Liberty, 1660–1832: Political Discourse and Social Dynamics in the Anglo-American World* (New York: Cambridge University Press, 1994), 108 ("By 1774, natural law arguments took precedence over all others").

[33] John Phillip Reid, *Constitutional History of the American Revolution: The Authority of Rights* (Madison: University of Wisconsin Press, 1986), 90, 92. In broad agreement with Reid is Daniel Boorstin, *The Genius of American Politics* (Chicago: University of Chicago Press, 1953), 66–98. Zuckert responds well to Reid in *Natural Rights Republic*, 108–17.

Americans were careful to appeal to both the laws of nature *and* English tradition. They had good reason to do so. The American strategy was to argue that colonial government was grounded in both natural and positive law – "the immutable laws of nature" as well as "the principles of the English constitution," as Reid admits Congress said in 1774. As long as any hope remained that England would be willing to respect its own constitutional tradition *as the Americans understood that tradition* (i.e., as guided by the laws of nature), the colonies were willing to continue as formally subordinated to the king – but only as long as he was willing to uphold the colonies' right to self-government. Against those historians who dismiss the growing American concerns as "extravagant, seemingly paranoiac fears" (to quote Bernard Bailyn),[34] William Crosskey provides a lively account of the Americans' frightened and angry reaction to various British encroachments in the decade after 1763. By the time of the Coercive Acts of 1774, most Americans were convinced that a British plan was well underway "to fasten upon Americans the arbitrary type of government that Parliament seemed to prefer."[35] "It was no longer of any importance to them," writes historian Samuel Williams in 1794, "what were the powers and prerogatives of the crown, or what was the origin or extent of liberty under the British constitution. One question only remained to be decided; and that was whether for the future they were to be conquered provinces, or free and independent states."[36] A principle of right higher than mere human law was the only recourse: "the laws of nature and of nature's God." That means the true American standard was *never* British tradition (the "matter") but rather natural law – in the American understanding, the "form" that shaped, or should have shaped, the British constitution.

Even so, what I have said does not discount the importance of prudence in the application of principle. John Adams counseled in 1773 that it would be dangerous at that time to appeal solely to "principles which are founded in nature, and eternal unchangeable truth." As long as there was a prospect of reconciliation with Britain, he said, it was wise to avoid

---

[34] Bernard Bailyn, *The Ideological Origins of the American Revolution*, enlarged ed. (Cambridge: Harvard University Press, 1967), 158. Ralph Lerner collects similar dismissive remarks by Gordon Wood and other historians in *The Thinking Revolutionary: Principle and Practice in the New Republic* (Ithaca: Cornell University Press, 1987), 6–7.

[35] William Crosskey, *Politics and the Constitution in the History of the United States* (Chicago: University of Chicago Press, 1953), 1:139–46; the quotation is on 146.

[36] Samuel Williams, *The Natural and Civil History of Vermont* (Walpole, NH: I. Thomas and D. Carlisle, 1794), 229–30.

appeals to "the *ratio ultima rerum* [the ultimate ground of things], – resort to club law and the force of arms."[37] Should anyone object that Adams was a "conservative" who had reservations about the equality principle, I answer that he was the author of the 1780 Massachusetts Bill of Rights, whose first words are "all men are born free and equal." By "resort to club law" Adams meant that an effective appeal to the law of nature against an existing political authority – an outright conflict of "form" and "matter" – is in effect an appeal to the use of violence. Adams therefore proposed leaving out those "principles which I loved as well as any of the people," and "discussing the question . . . upon principles more especially legal and constitutional."[38] Three years earlier, the Massachusetts Assembly had anticipated Adams's concern: "We beg leave to recite to your honor what the great Mr. Locke has advanced in his treatise of civil government. . . . '[If] either the executive or legislative . . . design or go about to enslave or destroy . . . [t]he people, [they] have no other remedy in this as in all other cases, where they have no judge on earth, but to appeal to heaven. . . .' We would, however, by no means be understood to suggest, that this people have occasion at present to proceed to such extremity."[39] In "Mr. Locke," the phrase "appeal to heaven" means "to use violence."[40] For these reasons, most pre-1776 documents protesting British misconduct emphasized the legal and constitutional argument. But when the time came for the break with Britain in 1776, the "eternal unchangeable truth," not "British constitutional theory or common law," became the explicit foundation of the new nation. In sum, Reid neglects the tactical reasons that led the Americans to conceal, or distract attention from, the fact that their ultimate standard all along was the laws of nature, not anything specifically British at all.

In the 1760s and '70s, this American understanding of the English constitution was shared by few in England itself. For Americans, the true English constitution was the body of English law and custom that conformed to the principles of natural law. In other words, far from being "irrelevant," as Reid argues, the natural rights theory determined for the

---

[37] Adams, Diary, 1773, in *Works of John Adams*, ed. Charles Francis Adams (Boston: Little, Brown, 1854), 2:312.

[38] Adams, Diary, in *Works*, 2:312–13.

[39] Massachusetts House of Representatives, Reply to a speech of Lt.-Gov. Hutchinson, July 31, 1770, in Thomas Hutchinson, *The History of the Province of Massachusetts Bay, from 1749 to 1774* (London: John Murray, 1828), 527.

[40] John Locke, *Two Treatises of Government*, 1690, ed. Peter Laslett (Cambridge: Cambridge University Press, 1960), *Second Treatise*, §20–21.

colonists the very meaning of the British constitution. An illustration may be seen in Richard Bland's pamphlet discussing voting rights in Britain. Noting that "nine-tenths of the people of Britain" are not eligible to vote because voters have to own a large amount of land, he concludes in all seriousness that the structure of Parliament itself is "contrary to the fundamental principles of the English Constitution," which is "founded upon the principles of the law of nature."[41] In the American mind, the genuine "English constitution" existed in perfect conformity with the principles of natural right, which require that the people be adequately represented in the legislative body. Thus the English constitution did not fully exist even in England! The "form" – the law of nature that grounded the constitution – was more real to the colonists than the "matter," the way Britain was actually governed. This idealized "English constitution" became for the Americans a kind of higher-law standard that could be appealed to without obvious disloyalty as long as they remained part of the British Empire.

Similarly, in his 1774 *Summary View*, Jefferson denounced the actual royal practice of vetoing colonial legislation. Contrary to any actual experience in British history, he defined the constitutional role of the British king as limited to protecting the self-governing American colonies against Parliament.[42] "[T]he great office of his majesty . . . [is] to prevent the passage of laws by any one legislature of the empire, which might bear injuriously on the rights and interests of another." In other words, the Americans' understanding of the role of the British monarch was similar to what later became the practice in the British Commonwealth of Nations. The monarch was recognized as a nominal sovereign, while former colonies, such as Australia and Canada, governed themselves through locally elected legislatures.

---

[41] Richard Bland, *An Inquiry into the Rights of the British Colonies*, 1766, in *American Political Writing during the Founding Era*, ed. Charles S. Hyneman and Donald S. Lutz (Indianapolis: Liberty Press, 1983), 1:69–70.

[42] Jefferson, *A Summary View of the Rights of British America*, 1774, in *Writings*, ed. Peterson, 115. Eric Nelson, *The Royalist Revolution: Monarchy and the American Founding* (Cambridge: Harvard University Press, 2014), 2, argues that "for many of its participants" the Revolution was a "rebellion in favor of royal power." He defends this apparently bizarre claim by qualifying it ("royalism" predominated only in "the early 1770s" and "the later 1780s") (9), but even then he understates the fierce American commitment, before and after 1776, to government by consent. Nelson calls Jefferson's *Summary View* "idiosyncratic" (58), yet its broad popularity led to his selection as author of the Declaration of Independence. See Gordon S. Wood, "Revolutionary Royalism: A New Paradigm?" *American Political Thought* 5 (Winter 2016): 132–46 (refuting Nelson).

New York's constitution of 1777, quoted earlier, similarly states that "all such parts of the said common law [of England]...[that] are repugnant to this constitution...are abrogated and rejected."[43] Since "this constitution" begins with a quotation of the natural rights language of the Declaration of Independence, we may conclude that the authority of the English tradition in America, no less before than after 1776, was strictly limited by a higher law. Bradburn speaks of a "republicanization of the common law" in the Revolution, through which the common law, understood as "ultimately derived from the 'natural rights of mankind,'" "had evolved...as a jurisprudence...that protected free people from arbitrary power." Bailyn shows at length how "the Contagion of Liberty" unleashed after 1776 transformed Americans' views and laws on slavery, religion, elections, and the whole social hierarchy inherited from British colonial customs.[44] Natural rights were in charge.

[43] NY Constitution, 1777, §35. Similar provisions in DE 1776, art. 25; MD 1776, Bill of Rights, art. 3; NJ 1776, art. 22; MA 1780, ch. 6, art. 6; NH 1784.

[44] Bradburn, *Citizenship Revolution*, 43–4; Bailyn, "The Contagion of Liberty," ch. 6 of *Ideological Origins*, 230–319.

3

Equality and Natural Rights Misunderstood

This chapter will explain equality and natural rights more fully by discussing some common misconceptions about them. It is impossible to understand the founders' political theory without getting past these errors.

Is There a Conflict between Equality and Liberty?

Political scientist Samuel Huntington writes, "The basic ideas of the American Creed – equality, liberty, individualism, constitutionalism, democracy – clearly do not constitute a systematic ideology, and they do not necessarily have any logical consistency. At some point, liberty and equality may clash."[1] This sort of error is quite common. It can be easily avoided by reading more carefully the documents quoted in the previous two chapters. In the founders' understanding, equality as a political principle cannot conflict with liberty because equality and liberty mean the same thing. Human beings are born equal in the sense that they are born "equally free and independent."[2]

Joseph Ellis, commenting on the second paragraph of the Declaration of Independence, makes the same mistake: "Perfect freedom doesn't lead to perfect equality. It usually leads to inequality. But Jefferson's genius is to assert [the principles of liberty and equality] at a level of abstraction where they have a kind of rhapsodic, inspirational quality. And we all

---

[1] Samuel P. Huntington, *American Politics: The Promise of Disharmony* (Cambridge: Belknap Press of Harvard, 1981), 33.
[2] VA Declaration of Rights, 1776, art. 1.

agree not to notice that they are unattainable, and not to notice that they are mutually exclusive or contradictory."[3] Ellis is so sure that equality and liberty are "mutually exclusive" that he is able to praise Jefferson's words only by in effect denying that they mean what they say. Ellis is of course correct to say that liberty in the founders' sense leads to *some* inequality of income, of success, of happiness, and misery. But as we saw in Chapter 1, what they meant by equality *as a political principle* is that "all men are naturally equal with respect to a right of dominion . . . over each other,"[4] not that all are (or should be) equal in intellect or property or happiness. Adults have a right to relate to others without being coerced. We may associate with those we choose to, on terms mutually agreeable, as long as we leave others alone.

When Huntington and Ellis assert that "liberty and equality may clash," they agree with Tocqueville: the "taste that men have for freedom and the one they feel for equality are in fact two distinct things," and that their love of equality endangers their liberty. "[T]hey want equality in freedom, and, if they cannot get it, they will still want it in slavery." But what Tocqueville means by equality here is something altogether different from what the founders meant in their fundamental documents. He is thinking instead of equality as a fact – he calls it "the equality of conditions" – meaning that Americans are "more equal in their fortunes . . . than they are in any country in the world."[5]

A minor but unusually thoughtful figure among the founders, Nathaniel Chipman, published the first American overview of the principles of political science in 1793. He agrees with Ellis (and me) that "equality of property" conflicts with equality in the sense of equal liberty. Equality of results can be achieved only by coercion – by taking away the equal liberty of some by violence in order to make others "equal." Chipman explains: "If we make equality of property necessary in a society, we must employ force against both the industrious and the indolent.

---

[3] Joseph Ellis, in Ken Burns, director, *Thomas Jefferson* (film), Part 1, PBS, 1997, at 39:30; Ellis makes the same argument in *American Sphinx: The Character of Thomas Jefferson* (New York: Vintage, 1998), 10–11.

[4] Return of Northampton, MA, May 22, 1780, in *The Founders' Constitution*, ed. Philip B. Kurland and Ralph Lerner (Chicago: University of Chicago Press, 1987), 1:528–31.

[5] Alexis de Tocqueville, *Democracy in America*, 1835, 1840, trans. Harvey C. Mansfield and Delba Winthrop (Chicago: University of Chicago Press, 2000); Introduction, p. 3, and vol. 1, pt. 1, ch. 3 (equality of conditions); vol. 2, pt. 2, ch. 1 (liberty versus equality). Thomas G. West, "Misunderstanding the American Founding," in *Interpreting Tocqueville's Democracy in America*, ed. Ken Masugi (Lanham, MD: Rowman & Littlefield, 1991), 155–77.

On the one hand, the industrious must be restrained from every exertion which may exceed the power or inclination of common capacities; on the other hand, the indolent must be forcibly stimulated to common exertions. This would be acting the fable of Procrustes, who, by stretching, or lopping to his iron bedstead, would reduce every man to his own standard length."[6]

Gordon Wood is therefore mistaken when he writes, "A republic presumed, as the Virginia declaration of rights put it, that men in the new republic would be 'equally free and independent,' and property would make them so" because property was regarded "as a source of personal authority or independence."[7] Wood is correct to say that the founders wanted property ownership to be as widespread as possible. But he confuses Virginia's "by nature equally free and independent" – something true of all human beings everywhere – with the rough equality in material possessions praised by Tocqueville.

Are Blacks Excluded?

Another misconception about the equality principle is that it applies to white males only, not to women or blacks. Some prominent historians, such as Forrest McDonald, support that view: "the words *equal* and *equality*, as used in the eighteenth century, did not necessarily imply a conflict with the institution of slavery." Conor Cruise O'Brien adds, "the words 'all men are created equal' do not, in their literal meaning, apply to women, and were not intended by the Founding Fathers (collectively) to apply to slaves.... They are for whites only." According to Jon Meacham, Jefferson "basically meant all white men, especially propertied, ones." Gordon Wood also believes that the Declaration of Independence "did not mean that blacks... were created equal to white men."[8]

---

[6] Nathaniel Chipman, *Sketches of the Principles of Government*, 1793, in *Founders' Constitution*, 1:557.

[7] Gordon S. Wood, *The Radicalism of the American Revolution* (New York: Knopf, 1992), 178.

[8] Forrest McDonald, *Novus Ordo Seclorum: The Intellectual Origins of the Constitution* (Lawrence: University Press of Kansas, 1985), 53; Conor Cruise O'Brien, *The Long Affair: Thomas Jefferson and the French Revolution, 1785–1800* (Chicago: University of Chicago Press, 1996), 319; Jon Meacham, *Thomas Jefferson: The Art of Power* (New York: Random House, 2012), 107; Gordon S. Wood, "Equality and Social Conflict in the American Revolution," *William and Mary Quarterly* 51 (1994): 707.

Not all scholars accept this view. Bernard Bailyn speaks for many when he writes, "the contradiction between the proclaimed principles of freedom and . . . [slavery] in America became generally recognized."[9] Bailyn complains about the typical misunderstanding of the founders' opposition to slavery: "What is significant in the historical context of the time is not that the liberty-loving Revolutionaries allowed slavery to survive, but that they – even those who profited directly from the institution – went so far in condemning it, confining it, and setting in motion the forces that would ultimately destroy it."[10]

St. George Tucker, a Virginia law professor writing in 1796, provides a good example of what Bailyn has in mind: "whilst [in 1775] we adjured the God of Hosts to witness our resolution to live free or die, . . . we were imposing upon our fellow men who differ in complexion from us a *slavery* ten thousand times more cruel than the utmost extremity of those grievances and oppressions of which we complained." Describing the slavery laws of Virginia, he notes "how frequently the laws of nature have been set aside in favor of institutions [that are] the pure result of prejudice, usurpation, and tyranny."[11] James Otis, in a pamphlet endorsed by the Massachusetts colony legislature, writes: "The colonists are by the law of nature freeborn, as indeed all men are, white or black."[12]

The language of founding documents did not exclude either blacks or women from equal natural rights. Congress's 1774 Declarations and Resolves state, "the inhabitants [i.e., not only white male property owners] of the English colonies in North-America . . . have the following rights, . . . life, liberty and property." In 1776, Congress published an

---

[9] Bernard Bailyn, *The Ideological Origins of the American Revolution*, enlarged ed. (Cambridge: Harvard University Press, 1992), 235. The arguments of this section are based on or supported by Thomas G. West, *Vindicating the Founders: Race, Sex, Class, and Justice in the Origins of America* (Lanham, MD: Rowman & Littlefield, 1997), ch. 1; Herbert J. Storing, "Slavery and the Moral Foundations of the American Republic," in *The Moral Foundations of the American Republic*, 3rd ed., ed. Robert H. Horwitz (Charlottesville: University Press of Virginia, 1986), 313–32; Paul Rahe, *Republics Ancient and Modern* (Chapel Hill: University of North Carolina Press, 1992), 617–41; Douglas Bradburn, *The Citizenship Revolution: Politics and the Creation of the American Union, 1774–1804* (Charlottesville: University of Virginia Press, 2009), 241–2.

[10] Bernard Bailyn, *Faces of Revolution: Personalities and Themes in the Struggle for American Independence* (New York: Knopf, 1990), 222–3.

[11] St. George Tucker, "On the State of Slavery in Virginia," 1796, in *View of the Constitution of the United States, with Selected Writings* (Indianapolis: Liberty Fund, 1999), 428.

[12] James Otis, *The Rights of the British Colonies Asserted and Proved*, 1764, in *Pamphlets of the American Revolution*, ed. Bernard Bailyn (Cambridge: Harvard University Press, 1965), 1:439.

address to foreigners fighting for the British, saying that among them "there may be many of liberal minds, possessing just sentiments of the rights of human nature," meaning not only of whites, males, or property owners. Georgia's 1776 Constitution states that "the common rights of mankind" (not "of white males") are the basis of independence from Britain. In 1777 Congress again affirmed "the common rights and privileges of human nature."[13]

Slavery was legal and practiced in every state in 1776. Few questioned it before the 1760s. That attitude was transformed by the Revolution. For example, emancipation laws in two states made explicit the connection between "created equal" and people of all races. First is Pennsylvania's 1780 Act for the Gradual Abolition of Slavery: "we conceive that it is our duty...to extend a portion of that freedom to others, which hath been extended to us, and release them from that thralldom, to which we ourselves were tyrannically doomed.... It is not for us to inquire why, in the creation of mankind, the inhabitants of the several parts of the earth were distinguished by a difference in feature or complexion. It is sufficient to know that all are the work of the Almighty hand."[14] Rhode Island's abolition law states: "Whereas all men are entitled to life, liberty, and the pursuit of happiness, yet the holding mankind in a state of slavery, as private property,...is repugnant to this principle,...be it therefore enacted...that no person or persons...born within the limits of this state, on or after the first day of March AD 1784, shall be deemed or considered as servants for life or slaves."[15]

By 1810, more than a hundred thousand slaves had been freed, either by legal actions that began the process of emancipation in eight states, or by individual acts of manumission.[16] However, the early movement

---

[13] Continental Congress, Declaration and Resolves, October 14, 1774, in *Founders' Constitution*, 1:2; Resolution of Congress, Inviting Foreigners Fighting for the British to Join the American Side, August 27, 1776, *Journals of the Continental Congress, 1774–89*, ed. Worthington C. Ford (Washington: Government Printing Office, 1904–37), 5:707; Preamble, GA Constitution, 1776; Resolution of Congress, Nov. 22, 1777, *Journals*, 9:953.

[14] An Act for the Gradual Abolition of Slavery, March 1, 1780, Preamble, in *Writings of Thomas Paine*, ed. Moncure Conway (1902; repr. New York: Burt Franklin, 1969), 2:29.

[15] An Act authorizing the Manumission of Negroes, Mulattoes, and others, and for the gradual Abolition of Slavery, 1784, Rhode Island State Archives, Secretary of State, http://sos.ri.gov/virtualarchives/items/show/71. CT (1784), NY (1799), and NJ (1804) adopted similar laws, but without the natural rights language.

[16] Arthur Zilversmit, *The First Emancipation: The Abolition of Slavery in the North* (Chicago: University of Chicago Press, 1967).

toward ending slavery in America came to a halt, for four main reasons: sheer selfishness – the convenience of having slaves and the expense of emancipation; fears of the possible violent consequences of emancipation; sincere concerns that the ex-slaves would be unfit for citizenship in a free society; and a vague faith in progress that took the edge off the firmness needed to overcome these powerful anti-abolition concerns.[17] Scholars today generally find these reasons unconvincing – except for selfish interest, to which they often add blind prejudice.[18] Be that as it may, by establishing the equality principle at the center of the American polity, the founders laid the ground for the eventual total abolition of slavery. Abraham Lincoln and other opponents of its expansion appealed to that principle when they built the Republican Party, whose victory in 1860 eventually led to the end of slavery in America.

Strong evidence of the founders' anti-slavery consensus is also found in the frequent denunciations of the founders by Southerners after 1830, such as by Senator John C. Calhoun in 1848:

[The doctrine] that all men are born free and equal... [is] the most dangerous of all political errors.... We now begin to experience the danger of admitting so great an error to have a place in the declaration of our independence. For a long time it lay dormant; but in the process of time it began to germinate, and produce its poisonous fruits. It had strong hold on the mind of Mr. Jefferson, the author of that document, which caused him to take an utterly false view of the subordinate relation of the black to the white race in the South; and to hold, in consequence, that the former, though utterly unqualified to possess liberty, were as fully entitled to both liberty and equality as the latter; and that to deprive them of it was unjust and immoral. To this error, his proposition to exclude slavery from the territory northwest of the Ohio may be traced, and to that of the ordinance of '87.[19]

Calhoun's complaint, so different from what one often hears today, is that Jefferson and the other founders believed in equality too much. Calhoun's last sentence alludes to Jefferson's unsuccessful 1784 proposal to ban slavery from all the territory west of the original thirteen states, a proposal partially incorporated in the Northwest "ordinance of '87," forbidding

[17] West, *Vindicating*, 21–32 (discussing each of these four causes).

[18] Alan Gibson, *Understanding the Founding: The Crucial Questions*, 2nd ed. (Lawrence: University Press of Kansas, 2010), 211–19; Paul Finkelman, *Slavery and the Founders: Race and Liberty in the Age of Jefferson*, 3rd ed. (New York: Routledge, 2014).

[19] John C. Calhoun, Senate speech on the Oregon Bill, June 27, 1848, in *Union and Liberty: The Political Philosophy of John C. Calhoun*, ed. Ross M. Lence (Indianapolis: Liberty Fund, 1992), 569–70. Jefferson's plan for a temporary government of the Western territory. Apr. 1784, in *Journals of the Continental Congress*, 26:274–9; Northwest Ordinance, art. 6, 1787, in *Founders' Constitution*, 1:29.

slavery north of the Ohio River. The founders' belief in equality, Calhoun laments, threatens the existence of slavery in the South. He was right.

Lincoln was correct to say that from the beginning, the nation was "dedicated to the proposition that all men are created equal," but he was also right that only "a new birth of freedom" could finally rid the nation of the injustice of slavery.[20] A suggestion of Leo Strauss explains how the founders could live with slavery while believing in equality. He writes, "Every human being and every society is what it is by virtue of the highest to which it looks up."[21] The founders (and Lincoln) looked up to the laws of nature and of nature's God. In this sense, the founders' America was defined in 1776 by its anti-slavery principles, in spite of the fact that slavery was then legal in every state. Even in the South, where slavery persisted until the Civil War, few defended slavery in principle before 1830. "[I]f the South was accommodating itself [in the founding era] to slavery in practice," writes historian Matthew Mason, "its spokesmen . . . continued to defend slavery as a necessary evil rather than embracing it as a positive good."[22] In a famous passage lamenting the existence of slavery in Virginia, slaveholder Thomas Jefferson exclaimed, "I tremble for my country when I reflect that God is just, that his justice cannot sleep forever."[23]

Whether ex-slaves or immigrant blacks had a natural right to become citizens – the founders believed they did not – is a question entirely different from slavery, which almost everyone regarded as contrary to natural right. Immigration and citizenship will be discussed in Chapters 6 and 11.

Are Women Excluded?

Writing in 1764, James Otis asks, "Are not women born as free as men? Would it not be infamous to assert that the ladies are all slaves by nature? . . . [H]ad not every one of them a natural and equitable right to be consulted in . . . the formation of a new original compact or

[20] Abraham Lincoln, Gettysburg Address, November 19, 1863.
[21] Leo Strauss, *The City and Man* (Chicago: Rand McNally, 1964), 153.
[22] Matthew Mason, *Slavery and Politics in the Early American Republic* (Chapel Hill: University of North Carolina Press, 2006), 21. Also Lacy K. Ford, *Deliver Us from Evil: The Slavery Question in the Old South* (New York: Oxford University Press, 2009), 5, 23.
[23] Thomas Jefferson, *Notes on the State of Virginia*, 1787, Query 18, in *Writings*, ed. Merrill D. Peterson (New York: Library of America, 1984), 289.

government?"[24] No one in the founding denied that women are "born equally free and independent." Yet many scholars claim that the founders believed that women do not have the same natural rights as men. Gordon Wood flatly claims that the Declaration of Independence "did not mean that... women were created equal to white men."[25] Historian Linda Kerber writes, "There had been a blind spot in the Revolutionary vision.... [The founders failed] to ask what the Declaration of Independence might have been like had women's private and public demands been included."[26] Morton White asserts that the founders believed women "lacked... rationality."[27]

These scholars are incorrect. Every leading statement of principle in the founding refers to all human beings – not only males – as "men." One can see this in other pronouncements of Congress from the same period in which parallel phrases were used, such as "humanity" and "mankind." Congress's 1774 Declarations and Resolves state, "the inhabitants [i.e., not only the males] of the English colonies in North America, by the immutable laws of nature, ... have the following rights."[28] A report published by the Pennsylvania convention of 1774 speaks of "all," i.e., all human beings of whatever sex and race: "Nature has made all of the same species, all equal, all free and independent of each other."[29] Therefore, their principles were always open to the possibility of voting rights for both sexes. In New Jersey, women voted in elections routinely during the 1790s and early 1800s, for the first time anywhere in world history.[30]

The equality principle changed the way people understood family relations. Women and men were increasingly understood to have equal importance, but different roles, in the family and society.[31] Historian Jan Lewis notes that "Revolutionary-era writers held up the loving

---

24 Otis, *Rights of the British Colonies*, 420–1.
25 Wood, "Equality and Social Conflict," 707.
26 Linda S. Kerber, *Women of the Republic: Intellect and Ideology in Revolutionary America* (Chapel Hill: University of North Carolina Press, 1980), xii.
27 Morton White, *The Philosophy of the American Revolution* (New York: Oxford University Press, 1978), 261.
28 Continental Congress, Declaration and Resolves, October 14, 1774, in *Founders' Constitution*, 1:2.
29 Instructions from the Committee for the Province of Pennsylvania to the Representatives in Assembly met, July 21, 1774, in *American Archives: Fourth Series*, ed. Peter Force (Washington: M. St. Clare Clarke, 1837–53), 1:558.
30 West, *Vindicating*, ch. 3.
31 Wood, *Radicalism*, 147, 183–4; Michael Grossberg, *Governing the Hearth: Law and the Family in Nineteenth-Century America* (Chapel Hill: University of North Carolina Press, 1985), 4–9.

partnership of man and wife in opposition to patriarchal dominion as the republican model for social and political relationships." Abigail Adams expressed the new view when she wrote: "I will never consent to have our sex considered in an inferior point of light. Let each planet shine in their own orbit. God and nature designed it so – if man is Lord, woman is *Lordess* – that is what I contend for."[32] Mary Beth Norton explains: "In the 1780s and 1790s, by contrast, numerous authors proclaimed the importance of America's female citizens. At times it even seemed as though republican theorists believed that the fate of the republic rested squarely, perhaps solely, upon the shoulders of its womenfolk."[33]

This "republican" understanding of marriage, in which the rights and duties of husband and wife are different but complementary, was widely accepted because in the minds of both sexes, the best protection of the natural rights of women and children was found not in voting rights, but in the integrity of the family, which they regarded as the core institution of a free and civilized society. Rightly or wrongly, they thought laws giving males a more prominent role in positions of formal leadership, both inside and outside the family, would strengthen it. Internally, the husband was legally the head of the family, which meant that he would have the final word on where the family would live and on major expenditures. In the political world outside the family, men mostly – though not always – had the exclusive right to vote, to serve on juries, and to be appointed to public office.

The founders may have been wrong, but their judgments were not based on the idea that women are created unequal. Jefferson boasted that Americans did in fact fully recognize and protect women's equality: "The [Indian] women are submitted to unjust drudgery. This I believe is the case with every barbarous people. With such, force is law.... It is civilization alone which replaces women in the enjoyment of their natural equality." Jefferson says "replaces" because in his view barbarism deprives women of the natural equality that they are born with. He explains: civilization "first teaches us to subdue the selfish passions, and to respect those rights in others which we value in ourselves. Were we in equal barbarism, our females would be equal drudges." Jefferson implies that women are restored to their "natural equality" when men and women

---

[32] Jan Lewis, "The Republican Wife: Virtue and Seduction in the Early Republic," *William and Mary Quarterly* 44 (1987): 689. Abigail Adams to Elizabeth Peabody, July 19, 1799, in Page Smith, *John Adams* (Garden City: Doubleday, 1962), 2:1006.

[33] Mary Beth Norton, *Liberty's Daughters: The Revolutionary Experience of American Women, 1750–1800* (Ithaca: Cornell University Press, 1980), 243.

become civilized. Men "subdue the[ir] selfish passions" by taking the lead within the family and doing the hardest work while treating their wives as honored companions, not subjecting them to arbitrary dictatorship and arduous physical labor inappropriate to their sex. Gordon Wood reports that Jefferson's view was widely shared in the early republic: "civilizations were now being ranked by the way they treated women (did not 'savages' regard their women as 'beasts of burden'?)."[34] What Jefferson had in mind is something like an observation about Indians once made by the French explorer Champlain, "their women were their mules." One is reminded of Aristotle's dictum that "among the barbarians the female and the slave have the same rank."[35]

Chapter 10 will examine more fully the founders' view of the family along with the laws that were meant to sustain it.

Equality and Racial Difference

Another common misunderstanding of the idea that all men are created equal is that it must mean all races and both sexes have by nature the same average intelligence and the same capacity for acquiring skills and other kinds of excellence. Any observable differences among the different races and sexes must therefore be explained entirely by outside factors, such as diet, discrimination, the legacy of slavery and oppression, white privilege, or other historically contingent factors. Rogers Smith holds this view: "the Declaration of Independence's doctrine of human equality" must mean that "African-Americans were inferior only because of environmental factors."[36] Smith complains that Jefferson "provided the most intellectually prestigious statement of inherent black inferiority, even as he strongly condemned slavery." He accuses Jefferson of writing "the cornerstone statement of American scientific racism." Smith is referring to *Notes on the State of Virginia*, where Jefferson concludes from personal observation that blacks "are inferior in the faculties of reason and imagination." Smith admits that Jefferson advances this opinion "as a suspicion only," and that he says it "must be hazarded with great diffidence." Jefferson acknowledges there that "their condition of life" as

---

[34] Wood, *Radicalism*, 356.

[35] Jefferson, *Notes on Virginia*, Query 6, in *Writings*, 185–6; Francis Parkman, *France and England in North America* (1865–92; repr. New York: Library of America, 1983), 1:358; Aristotle, *Politics*, bk. 1, ch. 2 (my translation).

[36] Rogers M. Smith, *Civic Ideals: Conflicting Visions of Citizenship in U.S. History* (New Haven: Yale University Press, 1997), 174.

uneducated slaves, not their nature, is at least partly responsible for their lesser accomplishments. However, Smith has no patience for Jefferson's cautious qualifications. He simply condemns his "racism."

In evaluating Jefferson's suspicion about the average level of black intelligence, one must first note that other founders held views closer to those we hear most often today. After a visit to a school for black children, Benjamin Franklin wrote: "[I] have conceived a higher opinion of the natural capacities of the black race than I had ever before entertained. Their apprehension seems as quick, their memory as strong, and their docility in every respect equal to that of white children."[37] Alexander Hamilton's judgment was the same: "their natural faculties are probably as good as ours.... The contempt we have been taught to entertain for the blacks, makes us fancy many things that are founded neither in reason nor experience."[38] St. George Tucker admitted that the belief in black inferiority might turn out to be based on "prejudices [that have] have taken... deep root in our minds."[39]

However, the important point is not whether this or that founder thought blacks were inferior or equal in native intelligence, but that the relative intelligence of blacks and whites is irrelevant to whether human beings are "by nature equally free and independent." Jefferson explains: "whatever may be the degree of talent [of blacks], it is no measure of their rights. Because Sir Isaac Newton was superior to others in understanding, he was not therefore lord of the person or property of others."[40] In other words, intelligence does not create a natural right to rule. If it did, then the more intelligent members of any race, such as Newton, would have a natural right to rule the less intelligent without their consent. Benjamin Rush, a Pennsylvania signer of the Declaration of Independence, responded to a slavery advocate in the same way: "But supposing our author had proved the Africans to be inferior...: will his cause derive any strength from it? Would it avail a man to plead in a court of justice that he defrauded his neighbor, because he was inferior to him in genius

[37] Benjamin Franklin to Waring, Dec. 17, 1763, in *Writings*, ed. J. A. Leo Lemay (New York: Library of America, 1987), 800. Founder Benjamin Rush agrees: *Address... upon Slave-Keeping*, 1773, in *Am I Not a Man and a Brother: The Antislavery Crusades of Revolutionary America, 1688–1788*, ed. Roger Bruns (New York: Chelsea House, 1977), 224–5.

[38] Hamilton to Jay, March 14, 1779, in *The Papers of Alexander Hamilton*, ed. Harold C. Syrett (New York: Columbia University Press, 1961–79), 2:18.

[39] Tucker, "On the State of Slavery," 439.

[40] Jefferson to Gregoire, February 25, 1809, in *Writings*, 1202.

or knowledge?"[41] If greater intelligence does not give one individual the right to rule another, then it also does not give one race the right to rule another race. The decisive point here is that blacks are human beings – that they are not, as Madison says, "irrational animals" like dogs and cows, who are ruled without their consent and who are not prosecuted for injuries they commit.[42] That is enough to establish that blacks are "created equal" in the founders' sense.

Yet Rogers Smith's erroneous view – that Jefferson's belief in natural equality was in conflict with his belief that blacks are intellectually inferior – is widely shared. James Ceaser writes that Jefferson's views "are an anathema to human equality."[43] Aristide Tessitore agrees that Jefferson's "speculations" on black intelligence "could only work against the cause of emancipation" of slaves.[44] The founders themselves rejected this logic. The puzzle is why Ceaser and Tessitore accept it. Do they really want to agree with Smith that if the members of one race have greater average intelligence than the members of another, then human beings are *not* born "equally free and independent"? Do these scholars mean to say that a more intelligent race – if there is one – may justly deprive a less intelligent one of its freedom? They would probably deny it. But their insistence that there is a conflict between the founders' idea of equality and possible differences in native intelligence inevitably suggests that conclusion.

The founders, as this chapter shows, would have had contempt for this line of argument. In our time it could lead to the absurd result that both the black *and* the white races may justly be enslaved by East Asians. That, at least, would seem to follow on the basis of Smith's and Ceaser's premise, if one may trust recent research on racial differences. Summarizing these studies, Charles Murray concludes that whites as a group are more intelligent than blacks, and that East Asians are more intelligent than whites. Almost all scholars acknowledge a genetic component to this difference, although its extent is of course highly controversial. My point is not to agree or disagree with research. I am no expert on racial differences. I merely note that Jefferson's account of the black–white

---

[41] Rush, *Vindication of the Address*, 1773, in *Am I Not a Man*, ed. Bruns, 240.
[42] Madison, *Federalist* 54, in Alexander Hamilton, Madison, and John Jay, *The Federalist Papers*, ed. Clinton Rossiter (New York: Signet Classics, 2003), 334.
[43] James W. Ceaser, *Reconstructing America: The Symbol of America in Modern Thought* (New Haven: Yale University Press, 1997), 50.
[44] Aristide Tessitore, "Legitimate Government, Religion, and Education: The Political Philosophy of Thomas Jefferson," in *History of American Political Thought*, ed. Bryan-Paul Frost and Jeffrey Sikkenga (Lanham, MD: Lexington Books, 2003), 148.

intelligence difference is supported by a number of social scientists who work in this field today. In any event, I repeat that the founders' notion of natural equality has nothing to do with differences in intelligence – or in beauty, ambition, athletic ability, physical strength, capacity for self-restraint, or other characteristics. "Born free and equal" means only that no one is by nature the ruler of any other person.[45]

Smith also believes the Declaration is inconsistent when it denounces "the merciless Indian savages, whose known rule of warfare is an undistinguished destruction of all ages, sexes, and conditions." Smith writes, "The universalist, egalitarian claims of inalienable rights with which the Declaration began rested uncomfortably with the denunciation of Indian 'savages.'"[46] But Smith misses the point. The Declaration denounces Indians not because of their race but because they were savages. Historian Patrick Griffin argues that the white settlers "did not view Indians as an alien race and did not refer to Indians by their physical features.... [T]he templates that they used for making sense of human difference remained cultural," not racial.[47] As quoted earlier in this chapter, Jefferson denounces Indians as "barbarous" because they force their women to undertake "unjust drudgery." Therefore, when the Declaration referred to merciless Indian savages, it affirms the superiority of civilized manners and morals over barbarism and criticizes the British for unleashing these savages "on the inhabitants of our frontiers."

In fact, Indians often did fight by means of indiscriminate and merciless killing of all ages, sexes, and conditions. And the British really did have a policy of encouraging Indian attacks on frontier Americans. In a 1777 speech in the British Parliament, William Pitt criticized his government's policy of setting "the savages of America loose...upon the weak, the aged, and defenseless;...on the very babes upon the breast; to be cut, mangled, sacrificed, broiled, roasted; nay, to be literally eaten." Tellingly, the British government did not deny these charges. Instead, it claimed, first, that "the Americans endeavored to raise them [the Indians] on their side"; and second, that it was "perfectly justifiable to use every means

---

[45] Gibson, *Understanding the Founding,* 211–19, denounces my treatment of slavery in *Vindicating the Founders,* partly on the ground that I fail to call Jefferson a "racist" for his views on racial differences. I thought I sufficiently defined racism in that book as "believing that some races are destined to be rightfully enslaved by other races" (169), but that is not good enough for Gibson.

[46] Smith, *Civic Ideals,* 81.

[47] Patrick Griffin, *American Leviathan: Empire, Nation, and Revolutionary Frontier* (New York: Hill and Wang, 2007), 65.

that God and nature put into our hands" to put down the American rebellion.[48] Historian William Nester notes that the first British excuse was factually incorrect: "The American policy from the beginning was to promote neutrality rather than alliance with the Indians."[49] As for Indian savagery, Griffin states that during the French and Indian War – less than two decades before 1776 – "[p]eople did not just die or children simply vanish; rather, they did so in appalling ways. . . . [For example,] a raiding party . . . killed a number of women 'in such a brutal manner that decency forbids the mentioning.' Thomas Cresap witnessed an Indian raider stabbing his neighbor in the back before tearing 'his ribs from the backbone.' . . . [N]ear Fort Pitt alone . . . were two boys . . . who were 'killed and scalped'; a man beheaded; a family, including mother, father, grandfather, five sons, and one daughter, 'killed'; and the two Delong sisters, who were scalped but not killed."[50]

The founders' experience with Indian tribes and free blacks led them to treat them mostly as separate peoples, not as potential fellow citizens. Equality in natural rights does not mean that all people in the world, or even those physically present in America, have a right to become citizens. I will return to this point in the chapter on consent.

Equality and Inequality

In a widely quoted remark, Harvey Mansfield writes, "a regime based on the self-evident half-truth that all men are created equal will eventually founder because of its disregard of the many ways in which men are created unequal."[51] This is not Mansfield's final word on the Declaration of Independence.[52] Still, this mischaracterization of the equality principle is heard often from conservatives. In reality, the doctrine of equality was meant to respect what the founders regarded as true equality – the understanding that there are no natural masters or natural slaves – while acknowledging the natural and legitimate inequality in the human condition. James Wilson explains in his *Lectures on Law*: "When we say

---

[48] William Pitt, speech in Parliament, 1777, quoted in William R. Nester, *The Frontier War for American Independence* (Mechanicsburg, PA: Stackpole Books, 2004), 187.

[49] Ibid.   [50] Griffin, *American Leviathan*, 62–3.

[51] Harvey C. Mansfield, "Returning to the Founders," *New Criterion* 12 (Sept. 1993): 50.

[52] On the complexity of Mansfield's actual view, see Thomas G. West, "Jaffa versus Mansfield: Does America Have a Constitutional or a 'Declaration of Independence' Soul?" *Perspectives on Political Science* 31, No. 4 (Fall 2002): 235–46. Nevertheless, I conclude in this article that Mansfield misunderstands the principles of the founding.

that all men are equal, we mean not to apply this equality to their virtues, their talents, their dispositions, or their acquirements. In all these respects, there is, and it is fit for the great purposes of society that there should be, great inequality among men.... That social happiness, which arises from the friendly intercourse of good offices, could not be enjoyed, unless men were so framed and so disposed, as mutually to afford and to stand in need of service and assistance. Hence the necessity not only of great variety, but even of great inequality in the talents of men, bodily as well as mental."[53]

No founder denied that human beings are unequal in all sorts of politically relevant ways. Pennsylvania's and Vermont's constitutions state, "The house of representatives... shall consist of persons most noted for wisdom and virtue, to be chosen by the freemen." The constitutions of Maryland and Kentucky similarly instruct their "electors of the Senate" to choose "men of the most wisdom, experience and virtue." Maryland adds that "a person of wisdom, experience, and virtue, shall be chosen Governor."[54] Whether stated explicitly or not, these views were accepted everywhere, for the reason stated by Madison in *Federalist* 57: "The aim of every political constitution is, or ought to be, first, to obtain for rulers men who possess most wisdom to discern, and most virtue to pursue, the common good of the society."[55]

Against Mansfield, the founders' idea of equality was meant to allow genuine as opposed to sham inequality to shine forth and receive the recognition it deserves. The state constitutions just quoted show that elections were supposed to be based on the ability of the candidate to perform the duties of his office, not on family pedigree or hereditary privilege. Long before the colonists' quarrel with Britain became serious, George Washington denounced the British custom of filling places in the military through connections and patronage. His honor was bruised when he found himself commanded and passed over for promotion by men less capable than himself. He held that "the strictest justice" required appointment by merit alone. This was not only Washington's pride speaking. Most Americans shared his view. According to Paul Longmire, when Washington became head of the American armies in 1775, he did his best to ensure that appointments would go, unequally, to those best qualified.

---

[53] James Wilson, *Lectures on Law*, 1791, in *Collected Works of James Wilson*, ed. Kermit L. Hall and Mark David Hall (Indianapolis: Liberty Fund, 2007), 1:637.
[54] Constitutions of PA, 1776, ch. 2, §7; VT, 1777, ch. 2, §7; MD, 1776, §15 and 25; KY, 1792, art. 1, §12.
[55] Madison, *Federalist* 57, p. 348.

This practice he thought was characteristically American.[56] Gordon Wood writes: "To eliminate these clusters of personal and familial influence and transform the society became the idealistic goal of the revolutionaries.... [They thought of] republicanism [as] a vindication of frustrated talent at the expense of birth and blood. For too long, they felt, merit had been denied."[57] Many years after the Revolution Jefferson famously wrote to John Adams, "I agree with you that there is a natural aristocracy among men. The grounds of this are virtue and talents.... May we not even say that that form of government is the best which provides the most effectually for a pure selection of these natural aristoi into the offices of government?"[58]

This understanding of equality is not only compatible with but requires recognition of the profound natural and artificial inequality among human beings, insofar as that inequality relates to important aspects of human life. David Ramsay, a South Carolina founder, explains the American view in this way: "It is the happiness of our present constitution, that all offices lie open to men of merit, of whatever rank or condition; and that even the reins of state may be held by the son of the poorest man, if possessed of abilities equal to the important station. We are no more to look up for the blessings of government to hungry courtiers, or the needy dependents of British nobility; but must educate our own children for these exalted purposes."[59] John Adams also believed in the equal rights of mankind, but he was well aware of the reality and necessity of human inequality: "Nature... has ordained that no two objects shall be perfectly alike, and no two creatures perfectly equal. Although, among men, all are subject by nature to *equal laws* of morality, and in society have a right to *equal laws* for their government, yet no two men are perfectly equal in person, property, understanding, activity, and virtue, or ever can be made so by any power less than that which created them."[60] The "equal laws of morality" mentioned by Adams are the laws of nature.

---

[56] Paul K. Longmore, *The Invention of George Washington* (Berkeley: University of California Press, 1988), 46–7, 188.

[57] Wood, *Radicalism*, 177, 180.

[58] Jefferson to Adams, October 28, 1813, in *Writings*, ed. Peterson, 1305–6.

[59] David Ramsay, Oration on the Advantages of Independence, Charleston, SC, July 4, 1778, in *Principles and Acts of the Revolution in America*, ed. Hezekiah Niles (New York: A. S. Barnes, 1876), 375.

[60] John Adams, *Discourses on Davila*, No. 15, in *Works of John Adams*, ed. Charles Francis Adams (Boston: Little, Brown, 1854), 6:285.

Equality and the Parental Rule of Children

Another obvious misunderstanding of the equality principle has a long pedigree. In an 1848 Senate speech, speaking of the Massachusetts Bill of Rights' statement that "all men are born free and equal," John C. Calhoun ridicules the doctrine: "Taking the proposition literally (it is in that sense it is understood), there is not a word of truth in it. It begins with 'all men are born,' which is utterly untrue. Men are not born. Infants are born.... While infants they are incapable of freedom, being destitute alike of the capacity of thinking and acting, without which there can be no freedom. Besides, they are necessarily born subject to their parents."[61] Calhoun is correct that infants need adult caretakers if they are to survive. But the founders thought that children are "born equal" in two senses: first, they are not born the property or the slaves of their parents to be used and disposed of at will; and second, they are to be given their full liberty when they have reached the age when they are old enough to take care of their own affairs. When Calhoun mentions that children lack "the capacity of thinking and acting," he implies that once they develop that capacity, they are no longer rightfully ruled without their consent. But that is exactly what the founders meant.

This view was widely shared but rarely made explicit.[62] The town of Northampton did so in its explanation of why children have no natural right to vote: "As to what may be replied by way of answer in behalf of infants, that is, persons under the age of twenty-one years, we ask leave to refer to what Mr. Locke has most judiciously said on that head, in the sixth chapter of the second book of his treatise of Government, entitled paternal power." In that chapter, Locke explains that "we are born free, as we are born rational; not that we have actually the exercise of either [at birth]: age that brings one, brings with it the other too."[63] An anonymous 1775 pamphlet makes the same point: "A parent has a natural right to govern his children during their minority and continuance in his family, but has no such authority over them when they arrive at full age." Thomas Paine sums it up: "To know whether it be the interest of the

---

[61] Calhoun, on the Oregon Bill, 1848, in *Union and Liberty*, 565. Meacham, *Thomas Jefferson*, 107, makes the same mistake as Calhoun: "the essential American view," says Meacham, was "that a child, at the moment of his birth, has the same quantity of natural power as the parent."

[62] Wood, *Radicalism*, 147–61.

[63] Return of Northampton, MA, May 22, 1780, in *Founders' Constitution*, 1:529; John Locke, *Two Treatises of Government*, 1690, ed. Peter Laslett (Cambridge: Cambridge University Press, 1960), *Second Treatise*, §61.

continent to be independent, we need only ask this easy, simple question: Is it the interest of a man to be a boy all his life?"[64] Only children, not adults, may rightfully be governed without their consent.

[64] Anonymous, "Some Thoughts on the Constitution of the British Empire," June 12, 1775, in *American Archives*, ed. Force, 2:964; Paine, *The America Crisis*, 1777, in *Writings*, 1:203. For similar statements, see Richard Wells, *A Few Political Reflections*, 1774, quoted in Edwin G. Burrows and Michael Wallace, "The American Revolution: The Ideology and Psychology of National Liberation," *Perspectives in American History* 6 (1972): 212; Moses Mather, *America's Appeal to the Impartial World* (Hartford, CT, 1775), in *Political Sermons of the American Founding Era: 1730–1805*, ed. Ellis Sandoz (Indianapolis: Liberty Fund, 1990), 452; Jacob Duche, *The Duty of Standing Fast in Our Spiritual and Temporal Liberties* (Philadelphia, 1775), in *Patriot Preachers of the American Revolution*, ed. Frank Moore (New York: Charles T. Evans, 1862), 83–4.

4

The Founders' Arguments for Equality, Natural Rights, and Natural Law

The three previous chapters have described what the founders meant by equality, natural rights, and the laws of nature. This chapter is about their arguments for the truth of these doctrines.

The founders made three main arguments for the obligatory character of moral law. Thomas Reese, a South Carolina Presbyterian minister, lists them in a 1788 essay: "It is well known three different opinions have been advanced on this head: some founding it on the moral sense, others on the essential difference of things, others on the will of God."[1] The "moral sense" is a supposed innate sense of right and wrong; the "essential difference of things" was also sometimes called "the natural fitness of things."

Before turning to these three lines of argument, I want to state and reject the views of political scientists Harvey Mansfield and Walter Berns, who contradict the statement just quoted. Mansfield asserts that the founders followed Hobbes and his successors, who believed that by "turning to the passions that allegedly precede opinions, above all to the passion of fear, we can discover a universal, non-partisan foundation for politics." Berns expresses the same point in the language of rights: "In the teachings of Hobbes and Locke" – which, he says, the founders followed – "the laws of nature are merely deductions from the rights of nature and ultimately from the rights of self-preservation."[2] In fact, I have found only

---

[1] Thomas Reese, *An Essay on the Influence of Religion in Civil Society* (Charleston: Markland & M'Iver, 1788), 19.

[2] Walter F. Berns, "The Constitution as Bill of Rights," in *How Does the Constitution Secure Rights?* ed. Robert A. Goldwin and William A. Schambra (Washington: AEI Press, 1985), 55. Harvey C. Mansfield, "Returning to the Founders: The Debate on the

one official founding document that deduces the rights of nature from self-preservation. That is Boston's Rights of the Colonists, which states, "natural rights . . . are evident branches of, rather than deductions from, the duty of self-preservation, commonly called the first law of nature."[3] Self-preservation is indeed fundamental in Boston's statement, but, contrary to Berns, it is called a *duty*, not a right. And contrary to Mansfield, this and later chapters will show that in almost all important documents, the founders had their eyes on something higher than mere life or the fear of death as the basis of natural right.

However, before I discuss the founders' arguments for natural law, there are three points that need to be clarified. First is the mistaken claim that they had no need of arguments because, as the Declaration of Independence says, "we hold these truths to be self-evident." Second, there is a question as to why nature should be a standard at all. Third is the claim that the founders were explicitly or implicitly appealing to belief in divine revelation as the basis of their doctrine. When I conclude these preliminaries, I will turn to the founders' arguments.

Self-Evident Truths

On the first point, James Wilson writes: "In the sciences, truths, if self-evident, are instantly known. If their evidence depends on their connections with other truths, it is evinced by tracing and discovering those connections."[4] If "created equal" and "endowed with inalienable rights" are *self-evident* in Wilson's sense, it must mean that as soon as one understands what a human being is, one sees "instantly" that all men are created equal in the sense of participating in a common human nature where no one is so superior as to justify ruling another without consent. But this claim is not "instantly known." It is a conclusion from a series of observations. This conclusion requires, in Wilson's words, "tracing and discovering" the connection between the facts of human nature and the conclusion that no one is a natural slave. Therefore, the truths of the Declaration cannot be "self-evident" in Wilson's sense.

There is a different meaning of the term "self-evident" that is more apt here. In common speech, we use it as a synonym for *obvious*, as in

---

Constitution," *New Criterion* 12, No. 1 (Sept. 1993): 51. I also disagree with Berns's and Mansfield's statements on Hobbes and Locke, but that is not our concern here.

3 Boston, Rights of the Colonists, 1772, in *The Writings of Samuel Adams*, ed. Harry A. Cushing (1904–8; repr. New York: Octagon, 1968), 2:351.

4 James Wilson, *Lectures on Law*, 1791, in *Collected Works of James Wilson*, ed. Kermit L. Hall and Mark David Hall (Indianapolis: Liberty Fund, 2007), pt. 2, ch. 6, 2:957.

this quotation from a political science journal: "*Self-evident* truths are frequently invoked when scholars and policymakers proposed political reforms. We often hear: 'It is *obvious* that X is true, therefore we need to do Y.'"[5] For the purpose of the Declaration of Independence – a political document, not a philosophic treatise – an unsupported assertion of something strongly believed is sufficient. This Declaration starts with a quick summary of principles, not an explanation of the rational ground of human equality. It is what Americans hold to be obvious – or, as Jefferson wrote in his first draft of the Declaration, "sacred and undeniable."[6]

Michael Zuckert argues that when the signers of the Declaration say "we hold these truths to be self-evident" – as opposed to saying "these are self-evident truths" – they are "insinuat[ing] a doubt as to the status of the truths," introducing "an element of hesitation." These truths, Zuckert writes, "are not affirmed to be in themselves self-evident, only to be held as such by the Americans."[7] In this claim, Zuckert misses how unlikely it is that serious political men, in the midst of a Revolution and risking their lives and fortunes, would be expressing "doubt" and "hesitation" regarding the momentous step they were about to take. David J. Hill, American ambassador to Germany a century ago, comes closer than Zuckert to what the Declaration means by "we hold these truths": "the natural and divine foundation of the rights of man," Hill writes, "is self-evident to all Americans."[8] By this he means that Americans have no doubts as to its truth, just as Rev. Samuel Cooper of Massachusetts had no doubts in a 1780 address: "We want not, indeed, a special revelation from heaven to teach us that men are born equal and free.... These are the plain dictates of that reason and common sense with which the common parent of men has informed the human bosom."[9]

But if equality is not self-evident in Wilson's strict sense, then there must be a chain of reasoning that leads to equality as a conclusion. In

---

[5] Elinor Ostrom, "The Danger of Self-Evident Truths," *PS: Political Science and Politics* 33, No. 1 (Mar. 2000): 33 (my emphasis).

[6] Jefferson, Original Rough Draught of the Declaration of Independence, in *The Papers of Thomas Jefferson*, ed. Julian P. Boyd et al. (Princeton: Princeton University Press, 1950-), 1:423.

[7] Michael P. Zuckert, *The Natural Rights Republic* (South Bend: University of Notre Dame Press, 1996), 45–6.

[8] Quoted in Ernst Troeltsch, "The Ideas of Natural Law and Humanity in World Politics," in *Natural Law and the Theory of Society* ed. Otto Gierke (Cambridge: Cambridge University Press, 1934), 209.

[9] Samuel Cooper, *A Sermon Preached before his Excellency John Hancock*, 1780, in *Political Sermons of the American Founding Era, 1730–1805*, ed. Ellis Sandoz (Indianapolis: Liberty Fund, 1990), 637.

fact, the founders sometimes provide arguments "tracing and discovering...connections" between equal natural rights and "other truths." Although most founders were acting on the basis of convictions deeply felt, not philosophic arguments, they did provide evidence for their core conviction in various documents, even if only briefly.

Why Should Nature Be a Standard for Human Life?

Before we turn to the founders' arguments from nature, it is reasonable to ask why they thought that nature should be a standard for political life. For the founders, "natural" meant two things: first, that which occurs spontaneously, not as a product of human making (e.g., sexual desire and reproduction); and second, a standard of right and wrong, discovered by human reason, based on the constant features of human nature, and true for all human beings in all times and places. The first meaning of nature is indicated by Madison's remark in *Federalist* 55: "As there is a degree of depravity in mankind which requires a certain degree of circumspection and distrust, so there are other qualities in human nature which justify a certain portion of esteem and confidence."[10] Human nature spontaneously contains the capacity for both depravity and nobility. Second, nature can denote what is by nature good or right, i.e., what people should do – not on the basis of a religious teaching or other authority imposed on them by others, but on the basis of human nature itself. This is the ground of the idea of natural right. It was first advanced by Greek philosophers around 2500 years ago.[11]

Natural right is not the same as merely conventional or customary right. When different beings have natures – characteristics that recur in all circumstances – there will likely be things that are enduringly good for them, that they *ought* to do. Few would deny that food and water will always be naturally good for human beings, assuming that life is better than death. The question then is not whether there is something that is only a permanent natural *good* (like food) but whether there is also something that is always naturally *right*. The founders thought there is.

Hamilton alludes to the difference between natural and conventional right in his *Farmer Refuted*: "The sacred rights of mankind are not to be rummaged for among old parchments or musty records. They are

[10] James Madison, *Federalist* 55, in Alexander Hamilton, Madison, and John Jay, *The Federalist Papers*, ed. Clinton Rossiter (New York: Signet Classics, 2003), 343.
[11] *The Republic of Plato*, trans. Allan Bloom (New York: Basic Books, 1968), 501b2.

written, as with a sunbeam, in the whole volume of human nature, by the hand of the divinity itself; and can never be erased or obscured by mortal power."[12] A right that is natural belongs to every human being because they are human. A right that is based on "old parchments and musty records" (such as the charter allowing a particular group of men to set up a colony in Massachusetts and granting them specified privileges) is a merely legal right. A legal right is granted by government and can be taken away by government. What is naturally right comes from human nature and "can never be erased," no matter what laws a government may pass. It is inalienable.

Many today find the idea of natural right quaint and unconvincing. Law professor Sanford Levinson captures the current mood when he writes, "to believe in Jefferson's Declaration of Independence... would require a leap of faith indeed."[13] Levinson says *faith* because he accepts the postmodern view, as Richard Rorty explains it, that "socialization, and thus historical circumstance, goes all the way down – that there is nothing 'beneath' socialization or prior to history which is definatory of the human."[14] For both Rorty and Levinson, society and history, not nature, make us what we are. Nature therefore cannot be a guide to how we should live and govern ourselves. European philosophers began to adopt this view not long after the founding: "About two hundred years ago," writes Rorty – and here he is right – "the idea that truth was made rather than found began to take hold of the imagination of Europe."[15] In other words, for more than two centuries, people have increasingly believed that human reasoning cannot lead to universally true principles of natural right, but only to an awareness of the historical contingency of all claims to truth.

In contrast to Rorty, the idea of natural right in the founders' sense rests on the possibility of political philosophy, which may be defined as "the conscious, coherent and relentless effort to replace opinions about the political fundamentals by knowledge regarding them."[16]

---

[12] Alexander Hamilton, *The Farmer Refuted*, 1775, in *The Papers of Alexander Hamilton*, ed. Harold C. Syrett (New York: Columbia University Press, 1961), 1:122.

[13] Sanford Levinson, "Self-Evident Truths in the Declaration of Independence," *Texas Law Review* 57 (1979): 858.

[14] Richard Rorty, *Contingency, Irony, and Solidarity* (New York: Cambridge University Press, 1989), xiii.

[15] Ibid., 3. The same premise animates Jack M. Balkin, *Constitutional Redemption: Political Faith in an Unjust World* (Cambridge: Harvard University Press, 2011).

[16] Leo Strauss, *What Is Political Philosophy? And Other Studies* (Glencoe, IL: Free Press, 1959), 12.

The fundamentals in question are the principles of the good society – principles that are naturally right or just. The founders were confident that the European thinkers they admired had succeeded in this task.

The God of Nature

How then are we to understand the fact that God is mentioned as the ground of rights almost as often as nature, or at least in the same breath as nature? The Declaration of Independence speaks of "the laws of nature and of nature's God." One might wonder whether the frequent appeals to God in these and other founding documents indicate that the colonists' appeals are not to reason at all, but instead to divine revelation.

That this is incorrect can be seen in the theology of the founding era, in which God was understood from two perspectives: reason *and* revelation. In the Bible, God issues commands, such as "love God with all your heart" and "do unto others as you would be done by." But independently of the Bible, the founders believed that human reason is also able to grasp that a first principle animates the world. This principle they called the God of nature – by which they meant God insofar as he is known by reason's inferences from the orderly structure of nature, including human nature. Believers and unbelievers alike could accept this understanding of God. Vermont's Ethan Allen is an example of a non-Christian who believes in a God of nature.[17]

Matthew Stewart incorrectly states that "'Nature's God' properly belongs to the radical philosophical religion of deism," which he takes to be "heretical" from a Christian point of view.[18] Stewart is correct that deists like Ethan Allen – who may be defined as believers in a God but not in divine revelation – found the term "God of nature" acceptable. But so too did many Christians during the century leading up to the founding. In 1679, Puritan minister James Fitch writes, "Nature is in all creatures, and God as a God of nature overruleth [i.e., rules over] them." Rev. Ebenezer Pemberton, another Massachusetts Puritan, says in a 1707 eulogy, "The God of nature was pleased with a liberal hand to bestow on him those

---

[17] Ethan Allen, *Reason the Only Oracle of Man* (Bennington, VT: Haswell & Russell, 1784), vii, 275.

[18] Matthew Stewart, *Nature's God: The Heretical Origins of the American Republic* (New York: Norton, 2014), 7. Catherine L. Albanese, *Sons of the Fathers: The Civil Religion of the American Revolution* (Philadelphia: Temple University Press, 1976), ch. 4, understands "God of nature" more accurately.

natural intellectual endowments." In 1762, Rev. Abraham Williams calls the law of nature "the constitution of the God of nature."[19] In a 1774 sermon, Nathaniel Niles writes, "We are all stewards, to whom the God of nature has committed this talent." On the eve of independence in 1776, Rev. Samuel West sermonizes that the British "are robbing us of the inalienable rights that the God of nature has given us as men and rational beings."[20] As these and many other Christian examples show, the God of nature is not necessarily "deistic."

Eighteenth-century Christians often made a distinction between Christianity and "natural religion" – a distinction that does not necessarily imply a conflict. By natural religion they meant truths about the world and its divine basis – the "God of nature" – that can be known by mere reason. Thomas Reese writes: "Christianity is a very important confirmation of natural religion. Here the conclusions of reason are corroborated and rendered more certain by the additional evidence of divine testimony. Those miracles and prophecies which were designed as a proof of the Christian dispensation are also a proof of the truth of natural religion. Thus the dictates of natural light are ratified, if I may so express it, by the stamp of divine authority, and their truth proclaimed by a voice from heaven."[21]

Like Stewart, Harvey Mansfield argues for an outright opposition between the God of nature and Christianity: "'Nature's God' was intended in contrast to a revealed god; so the Declaration (at least in Jefferson's understanding) seems hostile to revealed religion. Revealed religion is revealed only to the godly, and from what Jefferson said in many places against priests, one may suppose that the godly will take advantage of the favor of revelation to demand political power.... Revelation in its nature, and not merely by its abuse, is

---

[19] Abraham Williams, *An Election Sermon*, 1762, in *American Political Writing during the Founding Era*, ed. Charles S. Hyneman and Donald S. Lutz (Indianapolis: Liberty Press, 1983), 1:7–8, 15.

[20] James Fitch, *The First Principles of the Doctrine of Christ*, 1679, quoted in Perry Miller, *The New England Mind: The Seventeenth Century* (Cambridge: Harvard University Press, 1939), 515; Ebenezer Pemberton, *A Funeral Sermon on the Death of... Samuel Willard* (Boston: B. Green, 1707), 63; Williams, *Election Sermon*, in *American Political Writing*, 1:15; Nathaniel Niles, *Two Discourses on Liberty*, 1774, in ibid., 1:271; Samuel West, *On the Right to Rebel against Governors*, 1776, in ibid., 1:437. Stewart, in *Nature's God*, 183, guesses incorrectly when he writes, "'Nature's God' appears in American print for possibly the first time in... 1747."

[21] Thomas Reese, *An Essay on the Influence of Religion in Civil Society* (Charleston: Markland & M'Iver, 1788), 41.

opposed to the equality of men."[22] This conclusion would be correct if the teaching of the Bible contradicted the teaching of reason on human freedom. But American Christians believed that superstition, not the Bible, taught that the mass of mankind are "born with saddles on their backs," while "a favored few" ("the godly") are born "booted and spurred, ready to ride them legitimately, by the grace of God."[23] John Adams, denouncing the "cruel tyranny" of the Middle Ages, asserts that it was "framed by the Romish clergy for the aggrandizement of their own order."[24] In the founding, believers and unbelievers agreed that God's law denies them the right to rule others without consent. Therefore Walter Berns is wrong when he concludes, on the basis of Mansfield's argument, that "*any* revealed religion is incompatible with modern natural right."[25]

Believers of all sects supported what John Carroll, the first Catholic bishop of the United States, called "the luminous principles on which the rights of conscience and liberty of religion depend."[26] The Jews of Newport, Rhode Island, addressing President Washington, celebrated the new federal government, which protects "liberty of conscience" and secures "the blessings of civil and religious liberty."[27] And almost all Protestants agreed with this statement of Rev. Nathaniel Niles: "liberty secures the rights of conscience by protecting every member of the state in the free exercise of his religion, unless it be such a religion as is inconsistent with the good of the state."[28]

---

[22] Harvey C. Mansfield, "Thomas Jefferson," in *American Political Thought: The Philosophic Dimensions of American Statesmanship*, ed. Morton J. Frisch and Richard G. Stevens (New York: Scribner's, 1971), 28.

[23] Jefferson to Roger Weightman, June 24, 1826, in *Writings*, ed. Merrill D. Peterson (New York: Library of America, 1984), 1517; Wilson uses the same metaphor in *Lectures on Law*, 1:477.

[24] Adams, *Dissertation on the Canon and Feudal Law*, 1765, in *Works of John Adams*, 3:448–9.

[25] Walter F. Berns, *The First Amendment and the Future of American Democracy* (Chicago: Gateway Editions, 1985), 22 (my emphasis). In support of my argument is Alice M. Baldwin, *The New England Clergy and the American Revolution* (1928; repr. New York: Frederick Ungar, 1958).

[26] John Carroll, "To John Fenno of the Gazette of the United States," June 10, 1789, in *The John Carroll Papers*, ed. Thomas O. Hanley (Notre Dame, IN: University of Notre Dame Press, 1976), 1:365.

[27] Address of the Hebrew congregation in Newport to Washington, 1790, in Anson P. Stokes, *Church and State in the United States* (New York: Harper, 1950), 1:861. See also the similar Address of the Hebrew Congregations of Philadelphia, New York, Charleston, and Richmond to the President, December 19, 1790, in *The Occident and American Jewish Advocate* 2, No. 4 (July 1844), www.jewish-history.com.

[28] Niles, *Two Discourses on Liberty*, 1774, in *American Political Writing*, 1:268.

God and the Laws of Nature

"The religious language of the Declaration has made some later commentators uncomfortable," writes Professor Eric Slauter.[29] This indicates a major difference between then and now: instead of looking for divine support for our ideas of justice, politicians and intellectuals today tend to be wary of or repulsed by such appeals. In contrast, the consensus of the founders was favorable to religious language. Indeed, of the three main arguments for the obligatory character of moral law, the most prominent is the argument from divine authority: the claim that the laws of nature are binding because they come from God's will. In the Declaration of Independence, we see this in the four references to God: as the author of "the laws of nature and of nature's God"; as the "creator" who endows us with inalienable rights; as "divine providence," involving himself in human affairs; and as "the supreme judge of the world" who – it is implied – enforces his judgments with rewards and punishments. Some of that religious language – the references to divine providence and to God as supreme judge – was absent from Jefferson's original draft but was added by Congress.[30] One might surmise that the skeptical Jefferson was less concerned than the majority of Congress (i.e., the consensus of the founders) to emphasize the divine foundations of human rights.

Accordingly, the assertion that the laws of nature are also the laws of God appears frequently in founding documents. An early example is the reference to "the laws of God and nature" in the Resolves on the Stamp Act published by the Massachusetts Assembly in 1765.[31] The young Hamilton explains it in this way: "there is a supreme intelligence who rules the world, and has established laws to regulate the actions of his creatures.... This is what is called the law of nature.... Upon this law, depend the natural rights of mankind."[32] James Wilson concurs: "properly speaking, there is only one general source of superiority and obligation. God is our creator: in him we live, and move, and have our being.... [H]e, as master of his own work, can prescribe to it

[29] Eric Slauter, "The Declaration of Independence and the New Nation," in *The Cambridge Companion to Thomas Jefferson*, ed. Frank Shuffelton (New York: Cambridge University Press, 2009), 22.

[30] Jefferson, *Autobiography*, in *Writings*, 23–4.

[31] Resolutions of the House of Representatives of Massachusetts, October 29, 1765, in *The Founders' Constitution*, ed. Philip B. Kurland and Ralph Lerner (Chicago: University of Chicago Press, 1987), 1:629.

[32] Hamilton, *Farmer Refuted*, in *Papers*, 1:87.

whatever rules to him shall seem meet.... This is the true source of all authority."[33]

It is striking how little evidence is provided for these assertions in the official documents. How do we know that God has issued moral commandments that we are obliged to obey? Christians and Jews can answer that question by appealing to the Bible, but the laws of nature and of nature's God are supposed to be discoverable by reason alone.

In a quasi-official Massachusetts election sermon in 1770, Rev. Samuel Cooke acknowledges this difficulty by speaking of belief, not reason, as the basis of moral obligations: "without a true fear of God, justice will be found to be but an empty name. Though reason may in some degree investigate the relation and fitness of things, yet I think it evident that moral obligations are founded wholly in a belief of God and his superintending providence."[34] When Cooke says that reason can discover "the fitness of things," he probably has in mind something like the "fitness" of the prohibition against murder as a means to promote peace. But he doubts that "moral obligations" can be established without the existence of a God who issues moral commands and enforces them through his "superintending providence." Thomas Reese agrees: "Strictly speaking, perhaps this last only [the will of God] can properly oblige men.... The will of God, or what comes nearly to the same thing, religion, ... is indeed the only proper and stable foundation of morality.... Take away the belief of a deity; a providence and future state, and there is an end of all oaths at once."[35]

Most founders spoke as if such a God exists, either from sincerity or from the opinion that belief in a law-giving God is good for liberty and happiness.[36] For one or the other of these reasons, they favored government promotion of religion. Jefferson spoke for many when he asked, "can the liberties of a nation be thought secure when we have removed their only firm basis, a conviction in the minds of the people that these liberties are of the gift of God? That they are not to be violated

---

[33] James Wilson, *Lectures on Law*, in *Works*, 1:501, quoting Jean-Jacques Burlamaqui, *The Principles of Natural and Politic Law*, 1763, ed. Peter Korkman (Indianapolis: Liberty Fund, 2006), pt. 1, ch. 9, §6, p. 96.

[34] Samuel Cooke, *A Sermon*, 1770, in *The Pulpit of the American Revolution: Political Sermons of the Period of 1776*, ed. John W. Thornton (1860; repr. New York: Da Capo Press, 1970), 168.

[35] Reese, *Essay*, 19, 21.

[36] This point will be further discussed in the section on "The Natural Fitness of Things" later in this chapter, and in the religion section of Chapter 9.

but with His wrath?"[37] This is a statement of belief and conviction, not knowledge. The idea that natural law comes as a commandment from God is not so much an argument as an unsupported assertion. This difficulty perhaps helps to explain why the founders spoke of other foundations for the laws of nature.

That does not diminish the importance of genuine belief in God – whether the God of nature or of the Bible – so widely shared at the time of the founding. It is hard to deny Jefferson's and Reese's doubt that the founding would have succeeded without widespread belief in a religion that supports the main features of the laws of nature. However, belief is not knowledge. Our question concerns the founders' implicit claim that reason alone, unaided by faith, can know moral truth.

The Moral Sense

A second claim concerning the ground of natural right is that human beings are endowed by nature with a moral sense, a conscience, an inborn awareness of right and wrong. Jefferson (with some other founders) frequently appeals to this awareness, for example in his Opinion on the French Treaties, written in his capacity as secretary of state in 1793. Jefferson says there is a "moral law to which man has been subjected by his Creator, and of which his feelings or conscience, as it is sometimes called, are the evidence with which his Creator has furnished him."[38] Much later, Jefferson continues to affirm this view: "we appealed to those [laws] of nature, and found them engraved on our hearts."[39] James Wilson gives an elaborate defense of this position in his *Lectures on Law*: "If I am asked – why do you obey the will of God? I answer – because it is my duty so to do. If I am asked again – how do you know this to be your duty? I answer again – because I am told so by my moral sense or conscience. If I am asked a third time – how do you know that you ought to do that, of which your conscience enjoins the performance? I can only say, I feel that such is my duty." Wilson is aware that "moral sentiment is different in different countries, in different ages, and under different forms of government and religion." He answers that "it is but candid to consider human nature in her improved, and not in her most rude or depraved forms. 'The good experienced man,' says Aristotle, 'is the last

---

[37] Jefferson, *Notes on the State of Virginia*, 1787, Query 18, in *Writings*, 289.
[38] Jefferson, Opinion on the French Treaties, 1793, in *Writings*, 423–4.
[39] Jefferson to Cartwright, June 5, 1824, ibid., 1491.

measure of all things.' To ascertain moral principles, we appeal not to the common sense of savages, but of men in their most perfect state."[40] Other founders seem to have believed in something like a moral sense. Human beings, writes John Adams, "have all what Dr. Rush calls a moral faculty; Dr. Hutcheson, a moral sense; and the Bible and the generality of the world, a conscience. They are all, therefore, under moral obligations to do to others as they would have others do to them."[41]

As shown earlier, the existence of a God who imposes a moral obligation to obey his laws is asserted rather than proven. The same problem afflicts the moral sense argument. Jefferson cannot show that the inborn sense of right really represents a divine command. He admits that in this sentence: "For the reality of these principles I appeal to the true fountains of evidence, the head and heart of *every rational and honest* man."[42] In other words, the moral sense will not be felt in irrational and dishonest men. Here Jefferson is tacitly appealing to reason even while speaking of feelings or conscience. Wilson is also compelled to admit that the moral sense is a feeling and that he is excluding those who do not experience that feeling on the ground that one must consider only "men in their most perfect state." The difficulty here is that someone raised in civilization will be disposed to "feel that such is my duty" insofar as he has been habituated to think that way. As Locke cynically observes, "Murders in duels, when fashion has made them honorable, are committed without remorse of conscience."[43] Therefore, when Wilson says that we must consider "the common sense of . . . men in their most perfect state," he begs the question of how we know what state of man is perfect and what state imperfect. Like Jefferson, Wilson is tacitly using reason to determine whose moral sense should be regarded as correct and whose should be considered false. I conclude that even those founders who spoke of the

---

[40] Wilson, *Lectures on Law*, 1791, in *Collected Works of James Wilson*, ed. Kermit L. Hall and Mark David Hall (Indianapolis: Liberty Fund, 2007), 1:508, 515–16. Wilson was paraphrasing British philosopher Thomas Reid: Mark David Hall, *the Political and Legal Philosophy of James Wilson*, *1742–1798* (Columbia: University of Missouri Press, 1997), 68 ("Wilson often borrowed from Reid in his law lectures, frequently neglecting to cite him").

[41] Adams to John Taylor, April 15, 1814, in *Works of John Adams*, ed. Charles Francis Adams (Boston: Little, Brown, 1854), 6:449. "Dr. Rush" is founder Benjamin Rush, author of *An Inquiry into the Influence of Physical Causes on the Moral Faculty*, 1786. "Dr. Hutcheson" is Scottish philosopher Francis Hutcheson.

[42] Jefferson, French Treaties, in *Writings*, 423 (my emphasis).

[43] John Locke, *An Essay concerning Human Understanding*, 1690, ed. Peter H. Nidditch (New York: Oxford University Press, 1979), bk. 1, ch. 3, §9.

moral sense were half-consciously aware of the insufficiency of their own argument.

The Natural Fitness of Things

Given these difficulties with claims about God or an inborn sense as the source of moral principles, the founders relied most heavily on a third consideration, which the Massachusetts Assembly calls "the natural fitness of things."[44] Samuel Cooke, quoted earlier, speaks of "the relation and fitness of things"; Reese's expression is "the essential difference of things."[45] Similar expressions recur frequently, for example in *Federalist* 78: "the nature and reason of the thing." It appears again in William Johnston's dissent in an 1810 Supreme Court case: there is "a general principle, . . . the reason and nature of things: a principle which will impose laws even on the deity."[46] Arguments on this ground were often brought forward to prove that all men are created equal and that the laws of nature require mutual respect for the equal rights of all. Several considerations were mentioned, all of them plausible.

Same Species and Faculties

First is the argument from the fact that human beings are very much alike. John Dickinson writes on behalf of Pennsylvania: "Nature has made us all of the same species, all equal, all free and independent of each other; and was willing that those, on whom she has bestowed the same faculties, should have all the same rights. It is therefore beyond doubt that in this primitive state of nature, no man has of himself an original right of commanding others, or any title to sovereignty."[47] This argument was sometimes formulated in the manner of Locke's *Second Treatise*. In a 1764 publication of the Massachusetts Assembly, James Otis writes, "In order to form an idea of the *natural rights* of the colonists, I presume it will be granted that they are men, the common children of the same

---

[44] Proclamation of the Massachusetts General Court, January 23, 1776, in *Principles and Acts of the Revolution in America*, ed. Hezekiah Niles (New York: A. S. Barnes, 1876), 142.

[45] Cooke, *Sermon*, 168; Reese, *Essay*, 19.

[46] Hamilton, *Federalist* 78, p. 467; *Fletcher v. Peck*, 10 U.S. 87 (1810), 143, dissent by William Johnston.

[47] John Dickinson, Instructions from the Committee for the Province of Pennsylvania, July 21, 1774, in *American Archives: Fourth Series*, ed. Peter Force (Washington: M. St. Clare Clarke, 1837–53), 1:558, quoting Burlamaqui, *Principles*, pt. 1, ch. 6, §3, p. 301.

Creator with their brethren of Great Britain." Two pages later he explains: "There is nothing more evident, says Mr. Locke, than 'that creatures of the same species and rank, promiscuously born to all the same advantages of nature and the use of the same faculties, should also be equal one among another without subordination and subjection, unless the master of them all should . . . set one above another and confer on him . . . dominion and sovereignty.'"[48]

There is an obvious difficulty with this same-species argument. Locke himself was aware of it. He well knew that human beings are not "born to all the same advantages of nature." In the end Locke's argument for equal natural rights does not depend on equal talents, because, as Locke writes, "there is a greater distance between some men and others in this respect [namely, men's understandings, apprehensions, and reasonings], than between some men and some beasts."[49] Consider the case of bees.[50] They are all members of the same species, but some are born queen bees, some worker bees, and some drones. The same-species argument for equal rights only works if human beings are not like bees. But that is precisely the question: does the greater ability or virtue of some people make them natural rulers of others? There must be a further explanation of why the wise and virtuous among us – our "queen bees" – do not deserve to rule us without our consent.

Divine Perfection versus Human Imperfection; or, Men are Not Angels

The insufficiency of the same-species argument often led to the addition of an account of the differences between God and man. Again, I quote Dickinson: "There is none but God alone that has of himself, and in consequence of his nature and perfections, a natural . . . right of . . . absolute sovereignty. . . . This liberty and independence is therefore a right naturally belonging to man."[51] The same distinction between divine perfection and human imperfection is made in a 1773 Massachusetts

---

[48] James Otis, *The Rights of the British Colonies Asserted and Proved* (Boston, 1764), in *Pamphlets of the American Revolution, 1750–1776*, ed. Bernard Bailyn (Cambridge: Harvard University Press, 1965), 1:438, 440, quoting Locke, *Two Treatises of Government*, 1690, ed. Peter Laslett (Cambridge: Cambridge University Press, 1960), *Second Treatise*, §4.

[49] Locke, *Essay*, bk. 4, ch. 20, §5; Thomas G. West, "The Ground of Locke's Law of Nature," *Social Philosophy and Policy* 29, No. 2 (Summer 2012): 3–5 (discussing Locke's awareness of this difficulty).

[50] See Edward J. Erler, *The American Polity* (New York: Crane Russak, 1991), 10.

[51] Dickinson, Instructions from the Committee, 558.

document: "Supreme or unlimited authority can with *fitness* belong only to the sovereign of the universe: And that *fitness* is derived from the perfection of his nature. – To such authority, directed by infinite wisdom and infinite goodness, is due both active and passive obedience: Which, as it constitutes the happiness of rational creatures, should with cheerfulness and from choice be unlimitedly paid by them."[52] The *Essex Result* has the same argument: "The reason why the supreme governor of the world is a rightful and just governor... is because he is infinitely good, wise, and powerful. His goodness prompts him to the best measures, his wisdom qualifies him to discern them, and his power to effect them." Massachusetts and Essex both add that we cannot expect these qualities from human beings.[53]

The purpose of these contrasts between divine perfection and human deficiency is not theological; the argument does not depend on whether or not God exists. The comparison is meant to show that if there is any being who has a right to rule human beings without their consent, that being must be infinitely good, wise, and powerful. Since no human has such qualities, there must be a natural right to liberty, i.e., a right not to be compelled to submit to another person's rule without consent. When Madison restates the point in *Federalist* 51, he substitutes angels (presumably beings of superior justice and wisdom) for God: "If angels were to govern men, neither external nor internal controls on government would be necessary."[54]

This argument from "the relation and fitness of things" appeals to the implicit premise that no one would reasonably agree to be ruled by someone else unless there is good evidence that the ruler will act for the good of the person ruled. But as Madison says, "the philosophical race of kings wished for by Plato" does not exist.[55] It therefore makes no sense for any person to submit blindly to the absolute power of another. The phrase "all men are created equal" does not claim that we are all the same. Rather, it means that whatever our differences may be, none of them is great enough to justify absolute rule without consent.[56] Aristotle

---

[52] Answer of the Council of Massachusetts to Governor Thomas Hutchinson, 1773, in *The Briefs of the American Revolution*, ed. John P. Reid (New York: New York University Press, 1981), 35 (authored by James Bowdoin) (my emphasis).

[53] *The Essex Result*, 1778, in *American Political Writing*, 1:489–90.

[54] Madison, *Federalist* 51, p. 319.   [55] Madison, *Federalist* 49, p. 312.

[56] Harry V. Jaffa, *How to Think about the American Revolution* (Durham: Carolina Academic Press, 1978), 41–3.

said that some men are born natural slaves.[57] He meant that some men are born so inferior, and others so superior, that no consent to the rule of the superior is necessary. Responding to Aristotle's suggestion that a man of perfect virtue deserves to be given absolute kingship,[58] James Wilson writes, "Aristotle, it seems, has said that if a man *could* be found, excelling in *all* virtues, such a one would have a *fair title* to be king. . . . Excellence in every virtue furnished the strongest recommendation, in favor of its happy possessor, *to be elected* for the exercise of authority." By adding the need for election, Wilson refuses to grant Aristotle's suggestion that a man of outstanding virtue deserves absolute obedience. Such perfection is beyond the human. Wilson adds: there are no "distinct and superior species among men, in the same manner as men are a distinct and superior species among animals."[59]

Happiness

The third and final line of argument from the "natural fitness of things" is probably the one that appears most often: the direct connection between natural rights and human well-being. John Dickinson makes happiness the explicit ground of natural rights: "The infinitely great, wise, and good Being, who gave us our existence, certainly formed us for a state of society, as would be productive of happiness. Liberty is essential to the happiness of a society, and therefore is our right."[60] Official documents frequently speak of a connection between happiness and liberty, misery and slavery. The Declaration of Independence speaks of security of natural rights – "to secure these rights" – as a condition of "safety and happiness." As early as 1764, the New York Assembly stated that if they are deprived of their natural and other rights, it "will dispirit the people, abate their industry, discourage trade, introduce discord, poverty, and slavery; or, by depopulating the colonies, turn a vast, fertile, prosperous region into a dreary wilderness."[61] The Continental Congress summarizes the point: "These are the rights, without which a people cannot be free and happy, and under the protecting and encouraging influence of which,

---

[57] Aristotle, *Politics*, trans. Carnes Lord (Chicago: University of Chicago Press, 1984), bk. 1, ch. 5.

[58] Ibid., bk. 3, ch. 17.   [59] Wilson, *Lectures on Law*, 1:476, 478.

[60] John Dickinson, To the Inhabitants of the British Colonies in America, 1774, Letter IV, in *The Writings of John Dickinson*, vol. 1: *Political Writings, 1764–1774*, ed. Paul L. Ford (Philadelphia: Historical Society of Pennsylvania, 1895), 494.

[61] NY Petition to the House of Commons, October 18, 1764, in *Prologue to Revolution*, ed. Morgan, 13.

these colonies have hitherto so amazingly flourished and increased."[62] In 1774, Charleston, South Carolina, argued that in the absence of liberty, "[w]here gay fields now smile, bedecked in the yellow robe of full eared harvest, soon would desolation frown over the uncultivated earth. Suns would in vain arise, and in vain would showers descend; for who would be industrious when others would reap the fruit of his labor?"[63] My final quotation comes from Jonathan Mayhew's 1750 sermon, which was, according to John Adams, "read by everybody, celebrated by friends, and abused by enemies": "Tyranny brings *ignorance* and *brutality* along with it. It degrades men from their just rank into the class of brutes. It damps their spirits. It suppresses arts. It extinguishes every spark of noble ardor and generosity in the breasts of those who are enslaved by it. It makes naturally strong and great minds feeble and little, and triumphs over the ruins of virtue and humanity.... For which reason it becomes every friend to truth and humankind, every lover of God and the Christian religion, to bear a part in opposing this hateful monster."[64] All these statements convey the same idea: without liberty, there will be only poverty, slavery, and misery. Liberty is good – it is a natural right – because it is indispensable for happiness.

These quotations name two considerations pointing to that conclusion. First is a merely material one: no one will have an incentive to produce the things useful for life if they can be taken arbitrarily by the will of a superior. The second consideration is higher: slavery and oppression are bad also because of the offense to human pride – it "degrades men" – and to "virtue," including "noble ardor and generosity." Without liberty, the higher things in life will suffer no less than the needs of the body. So for reasons both low and high, liberty is good and must therefore be regarded as a natural right.

All these quotations defend natural rights on the ground that they serve a purpose beyond themselves. James Wilson writes, "Property, highly deserving security, is, however, not an end but a means. How miserable, and how contemptible, is that man who inverts the order of nature, and makes his property not a means but an end!"[65] For the founders, liberty is not an end. Who would want to be free if freedom led to misery and death? Liberty is valuable for its consequences. For this reason the federal

[62] Continental Congress to ... Quebec, October 26, 1774, in *Founders' Constitution*, 5:63.
[63] Resolution of Charlestown, SC, June 4, 1774, in *American Archives*, ed. Force, 1:383–4.
[64] Jonathan Mayhew, *A Discourse Concerning Unlimited Submission*, 1750, in *Pamphlets*, ed. Bailyn, 1: 209, 214.
[65] Wilson, *Lectures on Law*, pt.1, ch. 1, in *Collected Works*, 1:449.

Constitution speaks not merely of liberty but of "the blessings of liberty." So too do the early constitutions of five states. A sixth, Massachusetts, has "the blessings of life."[66] In a 1787 sermon before the elected officials of Connecticut, Elizur Goodrich summarizes, "The principles of society are the laws which Almighty God has established in the moral world, and made necessary to be observed by mankind, in order to promote their true happiness.... [B]y the knowledge of them, we discover those rules of conduct which direct mankind to the highest perfection and supreme happiness of their nature."[67] Liberty is a right because it is a condition of human happiness.

Although Locke is not our concern here, it may be worth mentioning (since it is not generally known) that there is a sentence in his *Second Treatise* that provides a similar explanation of law: "Law, in its true notion, is...the direction of a free and intelligent agent to his proper interest.... [C]ould they be happier without it, the law, as a useless thing, would of itself vanish."[68] In this formulation, happiness – not mere life, liberty, or estate – is the end and foundation of all law, including the law of nature.

To clarify the founders' position, I compare it briefly with the classical and medieval tradition of political philosophy. What that older tradition said – here I deliberately exaggerate for the sake of clarity – was that all men are created unequal, and that the wise and the virtuous ought to rule the unwise without their consent. For Plato and Aristotle, the best regime is aristocracy or kingship, where the rulers are the philosophers, or at least the most virtuous.[69] Why did Locke and the founders reject that claim? Actually, they did not. As shown earlier, the founders held that "God alone...has of himself, and in consequence of his nature and perfections, a natural, essential, and inherent right of giving laws to mankind." And "if angels were to govern men," no constraints on government would be needed. In principle the founders agreed that the best form of government is an absolute monarchy or aristocracy of the wise and good – a government of "angels." They spoke cheerfully of their readiness to submit to such a government.

[66] Constitutions of NH, 1784, pt. 1, art. 38; VT, 1777, ch. 1, art. 16; PA, 1776, ch. 1, art. 14; VA, 1776, Declaration of Rights, art. 15; NC, 1776, Declaration of Rights, art. 21; OH, 1803, Preamble; MA, 1780, Preamble.

[67] Elizur Goodrich, *The Principles of Civil Union and Happiness*, 1787, in *Political Sermons*, ed. Sandoz, 914.

[68] Locke, *Second Treatise*, §57.

[69] *Republic of Plato*, 473d; Aristotle, *Politics*, bk. 3, ch. 17–18.

But from the time of antiquity through the Middle Ages and into modern times, what became clear, at least to the founders, is that the argument for aristocratic or monarchical politics had proved to be wrong in theory and bad in practice. No mere human being has perfect wisdom and virtue. And more to the point, past attempts to create aristocracy – "rule of the best" – rarely led to the rule of the wise and the virtuous. Instead, all too often they degenerated, John Adams writes, into "tyranny, cruelty, and lust."[70] The kings, priests, ministers, and aristocrats of the Middle Ages of course claimed to be wise and virtuous, but they typically ruled in their own perceived self-interest.

The advantage of arguing that human well-being is the foundation of natural rights is that there is manifest evidence in favor of that claim. If people really are better off when government protects their life, liberty, and property, then it is obviously reasonable to conclude that natural rights are a sound basis of society. The disadvantage of this argument is that it turns on considerations of usefulness that are not morally binding. In Kantian language, it leads to a hypothetical imperative (if you want to be happy, obey the laws of nature) rather than a categorical one (it is your moral duty to obey the laws of nature). The laws of nature, founded in reason's judgment of what is useful for human life and happiness, become morally obligatory only when they take on a juridical or legal character. If moral laws are not commands, they are only suggestions. Thus the founders presented rational arguments regarding the usefulness of natural rights while supporting teachings like divine will and the moral sense to give their arguments moral weight. If we could ask them whether their arguments are ultimately grounded in the sacred or in the useful, in virtue or advantage, they would probably reply "both." I do not doubt that the founders believed in the sacredness of the rights of mankind. However, we must acknowledge that reason does not lead to moral absolutes, even if political life depends in some sense on the belief in moral absolutes.

[70] Adams, *Dissertation on the Canon and Feudal Law*, 1765, in *Works of John Adams*, 3: 450.

5

The State of Nature

The idea of natural equality is logically tied to the idea of the state of nature. Yet scholars sometimes treat the state of nature as if it were some sort of weird leap of faith. Rogers Smith regards the founders' "stories of social compacts created in a state of nature" as "quasi-religious creation myths, easily adapted to confer legitimacy on American constitutions."[1] Historian Bernard Bailyn scarcely mentions the topic in his well-known book on the founding.[2] That is odd, because it is an essential part of the founders' political theory. Not only is the state of nature not a fiction; it is a condition that some if not all Americans lived in during the transition between British and American rule.

The phrase *state of nature* was common in the founding. Washington's Circular to State Governments, written when he retired from the Army in 1783, warns that "dissolution of the Union . . . [would leave us] nearly in a state of nature." James Madison mentions the term in *Federalist* 51: "In a society under the forms of which the stronger faction can readily unite and oppress the weaker, anarchy may as truly be said to reign, as in a state of nature where the weaker individual is not secured against the violence of the stronger."[3] James Hutson writes,

---

[1] Rogers M. Smith, *Civic Ideals: Conflicting Visions of Citizenship in U.S. History* (New Haven: Yale University Press, 1997), 36.

[2] Bernard Bailyn, *The Ideological Origins of the American Revolution*, enlarged ed. (Cambridge: Harvard University Press, 1992).

[3] George Washington, *Writings*, ed. John Rhodehamel (New York: Library of America, 1997), 520; James Madison, *Federalist* 51, in Alexander Hamilton, Madison, and John Jay, *The Federalist Papers*, ed. Clinton Rossiter (New York: Signet Classics, 2003), 321.

Many Americans regarded the British Parliament's passage of the Intolerable Acts in 1774 as an act of aggression that converted the fictional state of nature into fact. This was the view of Patrick Henry, who, at the First Continental Congress in September 1774, declared: "Government is dissolved.... We are in a State of Nature."... Massachusetts Whig leader James Warren wrote John Adams on 16 October 1774 that "It can be no longer a question whether any People ever subsisted in a State of Nature. We have been and still remain in that Situation." And on 21 January 1775 John Adams wrote a British correspondent that in the province "four hundred thousand people are in a state of nature."[4]

The idea of the state of nature is implicit in the language of the Declaration of Independence. After "all men are created equal," it adds, "to secure these rights, governments are instituted among men." This implies that there is a condition before "governments are instituted" (or after they collapse) in which rights are not "secure." That condition is the state of nature. Michael Zuckert helpfully suggests that the Declaration of Independence tells "a kind of mini-historical narrative of the political experience of the human race. It begins with a pre-political condition, that is, the condition before governments are 'instituted among men'... and then tells of the post-institution phase (... an altering or abolishing that culminates in a new institution)."[5]

Vermont was created quite unambiguously from a state of nature. Samuel Williams' 1794 history of that state explains that even before 1776, the people living in the area that later became Vermont had rejected the authority of the colony of New York. "By the dissolution of all connection with the crown of Great Britain, they concluded they were no longer subject to the claims of New York, founded on the arbitrary decisions of that crown. The period was now come when, as they expressed it, they were reduced to a *state of nature*." For several years, a "large number of people were scattered over a large tract of country, in small settlements, at a great distance from each other, without any form of government, any established laws, or civil officers.... Some form of government must be adopted. They had the same right to assume the powers

---

4 James H. Hutson, "The Bill of Rights and American Revolutionary Experience," in *A Culture of Rights: The Bill of Rights in Philosophy, Politics, and Law, 1791–1991*, ed. Michael J. Lacey and Knud Haakonssen (New York: Cambridge University Press, 1992), 72.

5 Michael P. Zuckert, *The Natural Rights Republic* (Notre Dame, IN: University of Notre Dame Press, 1996), 18. Zuckert's suggestion is very helpful, superior to that of most scholars. The present account differs from his by providing additional evidence from founding documents; he relies too heavily on Locke (18–20, 23–4). Zuckert is also too reticent with historical examples of the state of nature in the breakdown of British authority.

of government that the Congress had. The step seemed to be absolutely necessary for the immediate safety and protection of the people."[6]

The situation in Massachusetts was more ambiguous. The inhabitants of several counties in the western part of the state refused to allow state courts to function for several years. Political power, writes Douglas Bradburn, was "effectively in the hands of ad hoc Committees of Public Safety, county conventions, and crowds"[7] – in effect, a state of nature. The men of Berkshire pointed out that Massachusetts after 1774 no longer had a constitution approved by the people; that no one is obliged to submit to a government to which he has not consented; that Massachusetts therefore ought to create a new constitution; and that if it did not, then they preferred to "remain so far as we have done for some time past, in a state of nature." In answer to this argument, William Whiting argued that Massachusetts was not in fact in a state of nature, because the Declaration of Independence "did not annihilate or materially affect the union or compact existing among the people," and the majority of the people had in fact consented to "rules and orders prescribed by the major part of the society," i.e., through a de facto legislative assembly elected by the people of the state.[8] By 1778, the Berkshire protesters had modified their earlier position: "We do not consider this state in all respects in a state of nature, though destitute of such fundamental constitution."[9] Unlike many scholars today, Whiting and the Berkshire protesters both took for granted that the state of nature is a real condition that comes into existence whenever the "compact," i.e., the agreement to live together in a political society, is broken.

Even where there was a smooth transition from the old colonial governments to new ones in each state approved by the people's representatives, there was arguably a return, however brief, to a state of nature.

---

[6] Samuel Williams, *The Natural and Civil History of Vermont* (Walpole, NH: Isaiah Thomas and David Carlyle, 1794), 233, 227–8; Peter S. Onuf, *The Origins of the Federal Republic: Jurisdictional Controversies in the United States, 1775–1787* (Philadelphia: University of Pennsylvania Press, 1983), 127–45.

[7] Douglas Bradburn, *The Citizenship Revolution: Politics and the Creation of the American Union, 1774–1804* (Charlottesville: University of Virginia Press, 2009), 38.

[8] Pittsfield Memorial, December 26, 1775, in *The Popular Sources of Political Authority: Documents on the Massachusetts Constitution of 1780*, ed. Oscar and Mary Handlin (Cambridge: Harvard University Press, 1966), 63; William Whiting, An Address to the Inhabitants of Berkshire County, Mass., 1778, in *American Political Writing during the Founding Era*, ed. Charles S. Hyneman and Donald S. Lutz (Indianapolis: Liberty Press, 1983), 1:467.

[9] Statement of Berkshire County Representatives, November 17, 1778, in ibid., 1:459.

The nation as a whole went through the same change, as Randy Barnett explains: The first sentence of the Declaration of Independence "revokes the 'social compact' that existed between the Americans and the rest of the people of the British commonwealth, reinstates the 'state of nature' between Americans and the government of Great Britain, and makes 'the laws of nature' the standard by which this dissolution and whatever government is to follow are judged."[10]

The state of nature idea is implicit in the statement that human beings "enter into a state of society" (New Hampshire and Virginia Bills of Rights).[11] "Enter into" implies that they were previously not in a "state of [political] society" but rather in another state – the state of nature. Kentucky's Bill of Rights likewise states that "all men, when they form a social compact, are equal."[12] In other words, in a state of nature, at the moment when people found a political society ("form a social compact"), they are equals in the sense that no one has political authority over anyone else. Virginia and North Carolina both use similar language in their ratifications of the Constitution of 1787: "there are certain natural rights of which men, *when they form a social compact*, cannot deprive or divest their posterity."[13] The phrase "entering into society" is also used by the Constitutional Convention of 1787 in its letter transmitting the proposed Constitution to the Confederation Congress: "Individuals entering into society must give up a share of liberty to preserve the rest."[14] The phrase "[m]ankind being in a state of nature equal" (Boston's 1772 Rights of the Colonists) therefore means the same thing as "all men are created equal" (Declaration of Independence).[15]

Historian Daniel Rogers argues that the state of nature concept fell into disuse and even disrepute shortly after 1776 because "the centrifugal impulses in the language of Natural Rights became a liability." Politicians, he says, worried that appeals to the state of nature would "pull

---

[10] Randy E. Barnett, *Our Republican Constitution: Securing the Liberty and Sovereignty of We the People* (New York: HarperCollins, 2016), 36.

[11] Bill of Rights of NH, 1784 and 1792, pt. 1, art. 1; of VA, 1776, art. 1.

[12] KY Constitution, 1792, art. 12, §1, repeated in CT, 1818, art. 1, §1 (with "equal" changed to "equal in rights").

[13] Ratification of the Constitution by VA, June 26, 1788, and by NC; November 21, 1789, Avalon Project of Yale Law School, avalon.law.yale.edu (my emphasis).

[14] Letter of the Convention to the President of Congress, September 17, 1787, in *The Founders' Constitution*, ed. Philip B. Kurland and Ralph Lerner (Chicago: University of Chicago Press, 1987), 1:195.

[15] Boston, Rights of the Colonists, 1772, in *The Writings of Samuel Adams*, ed. Harry A. Cushing (1904–8; repr. New York: Octagon, 1968), 2:351.

their polities apart."[16] That is incorrect. I have just quoted the Constitutional Convention of 1787 using the familiar language of "giv[ing] up a share of liberty" and "enter[ing] into society" without discomfort. The same language continued to appear in some nineteenth-century state constitutions. Ohio's 1803 Bill of Rights and Indiana's in 1816 repeat the language of Pennsylvania's in 1776: "all men are born equally free and independent." Connecticut's 1818 constitution states, "All men when they form a social compact [i.e., while they are still in a state of nature], are equal in rights."[17]

The Madison remark quoted earlier from *Federalist* 51 points to an important defect of the state of nature. Although it is our natural condition in the sense that all are born free, it is not desirable for us to live together for long without government. Boston's Rights of the Colonists explains: "In the state of nature, every man is, under God, judge and sole judge of his own rights and the injuries done him."[18] But when everyone is "sole judge," everyone must look out for himself. The weaker are vulnerable, as Madison says, to "the violence of the stronger."

The potential nastiness of the state of nature teaches a harsh but necessary lesson about the human condition. Leo Strauss writes, "At the beginning there is Terror, not Harmony, or Love."[19] Strauss applies this phrase to Niccolò Machiavelli, but Machiavelli and the founders are in full agreement on the need for government to control the destructive passions. The Massachusetts legislature proclaimed in 1776 the view that all Americans held: "The frailty of human nature, the wants of individuals, and the numerous dangers which surround them through the course of life, have, in all ages and in every country, impelled them to form societies and establish governments."[20]

It is sometimes incorrectly said that the state of nature is an amoral state, that in it there are no standards of right and wrong. This at any rate is a common view of Hobbes's state of nature, which is sometimes taken to be the same as the view of Locke and the founders. Yet the founders universally rejected this view. The Massachusetts Assembly states in 1762

[16]   Daniel T. Rogers, *Contested Truths: Keywords in American Politics since Independence* (Cambridge: Harvard University Press, 1987), 57.
[17]   Bill of Rights of OH, 1803, art. 8, §1; of IN 1816, art. 1, §1; of CT, 1818, art. 1, §1 (repeating Bill of Rights of KY, 1796).
[18]   Boston, Rights of the Colonists, 351.
[19]   Leo Strauss, *Studies in Platonic Political Philosophy* (Chicago: University of Chicago Press, 1983), 215.
[20]   Proclamation of the General Court, January 23, 1776, in Handlin, *Popular Sources*, 65.

that the most important natural right is "'not to be under the will or legislative authority of man, but to have only the law of nature for his
rule.'"[21] The teenaged Alexander Hamilton also rejected the amoral state
of nature in a 1775 pamphlet, *The Farmer Refuted*. A Tory critic of the
American colonists had written, "Man in a state of nature may be considered as perfectly free from all restraints of *law* and *government*, and
then the weak must submit to the strong." Hamilton responds that "the
deity... has constituted an eternal and immutable law, which is indispensably obligatory upon all mankind, prior to any human institution
whatever. This is what is called the law of nature."[22]

Therefore, political theorist Charles Taylor misunderstands the state
of nature when he argues that in this state, "people stand outside all
relations of superiority and inferiority." In the founders' understanding,
there can be many relations of "superiority and inferiority" in the state
of nature, such as employers over employees and parents over children. A
marriage contract might include a provision that the husband will be the
head of the household. Hamilton remarks in *The Farmer Refuted*: "in a
state of nature, no man had... the least authority to command, or exact
obedience from... [another person], *except that which arose from the ties
of consanguinity*." Here Hamilton refers to the rule of parents over their
children. That is, it is *political* power alone that is by definition totally
excluded from the natural state. And there is certainly no obligation in a
state of nature to treat others equally in regard to honor or "recognition,"
as Taylor seems to think, or to refrain from discriminating in favor of
those whose company one prefers in the selection of friends or employees.
Taylor is wrong when he says the idea of the state of nature leads to "equal
treatment or nondiscrimination provisions" in modern law.[23]

The Critique of the State of Nature

A little over a century ago, it became fashionable to argue, as political
scientist Charles Merriam reports in 1903, that "the 'state of nature' has

---

[21] Massachusetts Assembly, Instructions to Jasper Mauduit, 1762, in Massachusetts Historical Society, *Collections*, 74:39, quoting John Locke, *Two Treatises of Government*,
1690, ed. Peter Laslett (Cambridge: Cambridge University Press, 1960), *Second Treatise*,
§22.

[22] Hamilton, *The Farmer Refuted*, 1775, in *The Papers of Alexander Hamilton*, ed. Harold
C. Syrett (New York: Columbia University Press, 1961–79), 1:87 (my emphasis).

[23] Charles Taylor, *Modern Social Imaginaries* (Durham, NC: Duke University Press, 2004),
5; Hamilton, *Farmer Refuted*, 1:88.

no basis in fact. Man is essentially a social creature, and hence no artificial means for bringing him into society need be devised." Consequently, "liberty is not a natural right." Merriam admits that he is repeating the view of John C. Calhoun, the most prominent defender of slavery in the pre-Civil War South. For Calhoun, since man in the state of nature "liv[es] by himself apart from the rest of his species," it is "clear that man cannot exist in such a state; that he is by nature social, and that society is necessary, not only to the proper development of all his faculties, moral and intellectual, but to the very existence of his race."[24]

The state of nature is often treated by scholars today with the same disdain we see in Merriam and Calhoun. Daniel Rogers argues that given the existing stock of "political slogans available to the colonists in the 1760s," there was no reason to expect "that the Americans would end up talking seriously, heatedly, of rights passed down unimpaired from something so fantastic as a state of nature." This state, he writes, is a "palpable abstraction" based on "imagined historical facts." It led to "the fiction of a reservoir of rights retrievable from the past."[25] Historian Edmund Morgan agrees: "Locke's state of nature was purely hypothetical."[26] Pierre Manent, a French political theorist, describes the state of nature as "the condition that the modern political philosophers situated only in a distant past or hypothetical space."[27] Merriam and Calhoun, like Rogers, Manent, and many others, misunderstand both the founders and Locke. The widespread acceptance of this misunderstanding may be seen in popular sources such as Wikipedia: "The state of nature...denote[s] the hypothetical conditions of what the lives of people might have been like before societies came into existence."[28] As a matter of fact, the claim that the state of nature is purely "hypothetical," belonging to a "distant" and "imagined" past, is more applicable to Rousseau's 1755 *Discourse on Inequality* than to the founders.[29] Rousseau's state of nature really

---

[24] C. Edward Merriam, *A History of American Political Theories* (New York: Macmillan, 1903), 307, 312–13. John C. Calhoun, on the Oregon Bill, June 27, 1848, in *Union and Liberty: The Political Philosophy of John C. Calhoun*, ed. Ross M. Lence (Indianapolis: Liberty Fund, 1992), 567.

[25] Rogers, *Contested Truths*, 52–3, 57, 51.

[26] Edmund S. Morgan, *The Birth of the Republic, 1763–1789*, 3rd ed. (Chicago: University of Chicago Press, 1992), 95.

[27] Pierre Manent, *A World beyond Politics? A Defense of the Nation-State*, trans. Marc A. LePain (Princeton: Princeton University Press, 2006), 120.

[28] "State of Nature," http://wikipedia.org, 2017.

[29] Jean-Jacques Rousseau, *Discourse on the Origins and Foundations of Inequality*, 1755, in *The First and Second Discourses*, ed. Roger D. Masters (New York: Bedford/St. Martin's, 1964).

did belong to a prehistoric past. The founders held an entirely different conception.

Not all scholars make this mistake. Forrest McDonald writes, "it should be obvious" that the state of nature is not "a situation in which autonomous individuals live outside of society, as critics have misrepresented. . . . Rather, it meant the absence of organized *political* society and of government."[30]

For the founders, human beings are naturally sociable. Whether there is an established government or not, people will have friends and live together in families. John Adams' view was shared by all the founders: "Men, in their primitive conditions, however savage, were undoubtedly gregarious; and they continue to be social . . . in every possible situation in which they can be placed. . . . [N]ature intended them for society."[31] In a later letter to Adams, Benjamin Rush writes, "I grant that man is naturally a domestic, a social, and a political or rational animal, and that Horace's line is in general true, 'naturam expellas furca, tamen usque recurret' [you may expel nature with a pitchfork, but it always returns]." Washington's Circular, quoted earlier, warns that America might return to a state of nature. He does not mean that friendships and families would dissolve and that people would live as isolated individuals. He means that there might be a breakdown in government to the point of anarchy or war. The founders' state of nature is not, as Manent writes, a state where human beings are "independent, without ties" to other people.[32]

Since Locke is so often dragged into this argument, I cannot refrain from mentioning that his state of nature, like the founders', is a social state. He defines it as "[m]en *living together* according to reason, without a common superior on earth." In other words, man is by nature social but not political. Further, "God having designed man for a sociable creature, made him not only with an inclination, and under a necessity, to have fellowship with those of his own kind."[33]

---

[30] Forrest McDonald, *Novus Ordo Seclorum: The Intellectual Origins of the Constitution* (Lawrence: University Press of Kansas, 1985), 62. Zuckert (*Natural Rights Republic*, 24) and Bradburn (*Citizenship Revolution*, 20–21, 38–42) are among those who also understand the founders' view correctly.

[31] John Adams, *Discourses on Davila*, 1790, in *Works of John Adams*, ed. Charles Francis Adams (Boston: Little, Brown, 1854), 6:232. Compare Benjamin Rush to John Adams, September 6, 1809, in *The Spur of Fame: Dialogues of John Adams and Benjamin Rush, 1805–1813*, ed. John Schutz and Douglass Adair (San Marino, CA: Huntington Library, 1966), 154 (my translation).

[32] Manent, *World beyond Politics?*, 120.

[33] Locke, *Second Treatise*, §19 (my emphasis); Locke, *An Essay concerning Human Understanding*, 1690, ed. Peter H. Nidditch (New York: Oxford University Press, 1979), bk. 3, ch. 1, §1.

The Reality of the State of Nature – Past, Present, and Future

As mentioned earlier, the breakdown of a previously existing government can also create a state of nature. In Russia during the 1990s, the nominal post-Soviet government was so weak that criminal enterprises successfully competed for power with the formal authorities. Business owners had to hire their own private armed forces.[34] In Mexico, drug cartels created a state of nature when their violent tactics neutralized the central government in many areas during the 2000s.[35] In Germany, Chief Police Commissioner Bernhard Witthaut was asked in a 2011 interview, "Are there urban areas...that are 'no-go areas,' meaning that they can no longer be secured by the police?" Witthaut replied: "Every police chief and every interior minister will deny it. But...[w]e know that these areas exist. Even worse: in these areas crimes are no longer prosecuted. People take care of everything 'among themselves.'...The power of the state is completely out of the picture." These "no-go zones," says Witthaut, are inhabited by "immigrants."[36] In France, writes Vincent Trémolet, there are "multiple [Muslim] neighborhoods where police and gendarmerie cannot uphold the laws of the republic or even enter without risking confrontation, projectiles, or even a fatal shooting."[37] Even if Witthaut and Trémolet are mistaken, as most German and French officials would claim publicly, this is one way the state of nature can come into being.

Calhoun argued in an 1848 speech attacking the founding principles that the political state is always to be preferred to the state of nature. The founders disagreed. Theophilus Parsons, speaking for the town of Essex in 1778, writes, "Surely the state of nature is more excellent than that in which men are meanly submissive to the haughty will of an imperious

---

34 Stephen Handelman, *Comrade Criminal: Russia's New Mafiya* (New Haven: Yale University Press, 1995); Vadim Volkov, *Violent Entrepreneurs: The Use of Force in the Making of Russian Capitalism* (Ithaca: Cornell University Press, 2002).

35 Mark Stevenson, "Drug Lords Go after Mexican Police Officers," Associated Press, May 18, 2008, http://news.yahoo.com (Ciudad Juarez taken over by drug cartels).

36 Interview with Bernhard Witthaut, "In Problemvierteln fürchtet sich sogar die Polizei" [In Problem Areas, Even the Police Are Frightened], Aug. 1, 2011, *Der Westen*, www.derwesten.de (my translation).

37 Vincent Trémolet, "'Les Zones de Non-Droit' dans le République Française, Mythe ou Réalité?" ["No-Law Zones" in the French Republic: Myth or Reality?], 2002, Département de Recherche sur les Menaces Criminelles Contemporaines, Université Panthéon-Assas – Paris II, Institut De Criminologie De Paris, www.drmcc.org/spip.php?article326, p. 6 (my translation). For an update, Soeren Kern, "European 'No-Go' Zones: Fact or Fiction? Part 1: France," Jan. 20, 2015, Gatestone Institute, www.gatestoneinstitute.org.

tyrant, whose savage passions are not bounded by the laws of reason, religion, honor, or a regard to his subjects."[38] In its 1772 statement, the town of Boston states, "All men have a right to remain in a state of nature as long as they please."[39] Somalia lacked any formal government at all from 1991 until well into the 2000s, and economist Peter Leeson argues that Somalia was "better off stateless."[40]

The founders saw clearly that the state of nature can be either bad or good. It is bad in the sense that without civil law, as Madison says, "the weaker individual is not secured against the violence of the stronger." The founders would agree completely with Calhoun and Merriam that "[i]t is the state that makes liberty possible, determines what its limits shall be, guarantees and protects it." After all, government is instituted "to secure these rights." Again, the founders would not have objected to Progressive political scientist John Burgess's assertion that the conditions of establishing a free state "never exist in the beginning of the political development of a people, but are attained only after the state has made several periods of its history."[41]

But the state of nature is also good because it gives us, through our capacity for reason, access to facts (for example, that we are born free) and standards (the law of nature) that can and should guide political life.[42] The founders would ask the Progressives and other critics of the state of nature how they know that civilization is better than the primitive state of nature. Is it not because the state of nature provides us with freedom and the capacity for reason, so that we can know that all men are created equal and therefore what principles ought to govern political society?

Historian Carl Becker persuasively suggests that the founders thought about nature in two ways: "The eighteenth century had to appeal, as it were, from nature drunk to nature sober. Now the test or standard by which this appeal could be validly made was found in nature itself – in reason and conscience; for reason and conscience were parts of man's nature too.... Natural law, as a basis for good government, could never be found in the undifferentiated nature of man, but only in human reason

---

[38] *Essex Result*, 1778, in *American Political Writing*, 1:484.

[39] Boston, Rights of the Colonists, 351.

[40] Peter T. Leeson, "Better Off Stateless: Somalia before and after Government Collapse," *Journal of Comparative Economics* 35 (2007): 689–710.

[41] Merriam, *History of American Political Theories*, 313; John W. Burgess, *Political Science and Comparative Constitutional Law* (Boston: Ginn & Co., 1893), 1:62.

[42] Michael Zuckert, *Natural Rights Republic*, 24, correctly characterizes the state of nature as both bad and good.

applying the test of good and bad to human conduct."[43] The savage and violent state of nature is "nature drunk." The state of nature as presided over by the laws of nature and reason, providing a reliable standard for political life, is "nature sober." Nature guided by reason is good for human life, but outside of civil society nature sober will eventually fall into drunkenness.

How "Natural" Is the State of Nature?

For the founders, the state of civilization is more "natural" than the state of nature in the sense that it is more in accord with human nature – "nature sober" – for people to live in political societies. "The infinitely great, wise, and good Being, who gave us our existence, certainly formed us for a state of society, as would be productive of happiness," writes John Dickinson.[44] It is probably with this sort of thought in mind that Jefferson writes, "the *bellum omnium in omnia* [war of all against all things], which some philosophers observing to be so general in this world, have mistaken it for the natural, instead of the abusive state of man."[45] Government is necessary "to secure these rights," as the Declaration of Independence says. By providing security, government restores the natural equality we have a right to in the state of nature, but which we are deprived of in the savage existence that too often prevails there. From this point of view, living in a well-governed political society is more in accord with human nature than living in a nasty and brutish state of nature.

John Witherspoon, a signer of the Declaration, was also president of the College of New Jersey (later Princeton) and a Presbyterian clergyman. In one of his Princeton lectures, he asks whether "the state of nature is a state of society" or "a state of war" that arises when people live outside of political society. He answers that it is both. On the one hand, "[t]hat the principles of our nature lead to society – that our happiness and the improvement of our powers are only to be had in society – is of the most undoubted certainty.... But on the other hand, that our nature as it is now when free and independent is prone to injury, and consequently to

---

43 Carl L. Becker, *The Declaration of Independence: A Study in the History of Political Ideas* (New York: Knopf, 1948), 60–61.

44 Dickinson, Letters to the Inhabitants of the British Colonies, 1774, in *The Political Writings of John Dickinson*, ed. Paul Leicester Ford (1895; repr. New York: Da Capo, 1970), Letter 4, 494.

45 Thomas Jefferson to Samuel Kercheval, July 12, 1816, in *Writings*, ed. Merrill D. Peterson (New York: Library of America, 1984), 1401.

war, is equally manifest, and that in a state of natural liberty there is no other way but force for preserving security and repelling injury. The inconveniences of the natural state are very many."[46]

The founders' position must not be confused with Aristotle's, with which there is some common ground. Aristotle did not argue for the equal natural liberty of human beings or a state of nature. For Aristotle, one might say, all men are created unequal. Therefore Aristotle never says that the "just powers" of government are derived "from the consent of the governed." However, the founders (and Locke) agree with Aristotle that "man is by nature a political animal" – but only in the sense that human beings cannot live well outside of a political community. That at any rate seems to be Aristotle's point, for immediately after making that remark he writes, "when a human being is perfected, he is the best of the animals, but separated from law and just punishment he is worst of all." Aristotle's dictum that "man is by nature political" is sometimes mistakenly taken to mean that human beings automatically form cities that are independent political communities. Aristotle indeed writes that "by nature there is an impulse in everyone for such a community," but unlike the sexual union of man and woman, the impulse is not strong enough for the spontaneous emergence of the *polis*. He agrees with the founders that the political community needs human effort to get it started. That is implied in Aristotle's remark that the "first one who founded [a *polis*] was the cause of great goods."[47]

How "All Men" Can Naturally Be in the State of Nature

So far I have treated the state of nature as a condition that exists in the absence of established human government. But some founders understood that term in a second sense, as the state which, to quote Locke, "*all* men are naturally in." To emphasize the point, Locke quotes Richard Hooker's view that the condition of human beings living outside of government ends once governments are formed. Disagreeing with Hooker, Locke writes, "But I moreover affirm that *all* men are naturally in that state [of nature], and remain so, till by their own consents they make themselves members

---

[46] John Witherspoon, *Lectures on Moral Philosophy*, 1772–94, in *The Selected Writings of John Witherspoon*, ed. Thomas Miller (Carbondale: Southern Illinois University Press, 1990), Lecture 10, 189.

[47] Aristotle, *Politics*, bk. 1, ch. 2 (my translation). On the complexity of Aristotle's view of the naturalness of political life: Wayne Ambler, "Aristotle's Understanding of the Naturalness of the City," *Review of Politics* 47, No. 2 (Apr. 1985): 163–85.

of some politic society."[48] That is an inescapable implication of all men being "created equal" or "born equally free and independent." In this sense of the term, children are in the state of nature until they reach what the founders called "full age" or "years of discretion." At this moment, they are no longer wards of their parents, but they have not yet given their adult – and therefore rational – consent to become members of a political society. Samuel Adams explains:

> Mr. Locke...shows that express consent alone makes any one a member of any commonwealth. He holds that submission to the laws of any country, and living quietly and enjoying privileges and protection under them, does not make a man a member of that society...any more than it would make a man subject to another, in whose family he found it convenient to abide for some time, tho' while he continued under it, he were obliged to comply with the laws and submit to the government he found there. Every man was born naturally free; nothing can make a man a subject of any commonwealth, but his actually entering into it by positive engagement, and express promise and compact.... Every man being born free, says another distinguished writer, the son of a citizen, arrived at the years of discretion, may examine whether it be convenient for him to join in the society for which he was destined by birth. If he finds that it will be no advantage for him to remain in it, he is at liberty to leave it, preserving, as much as his new engagements will allow him, the love and gratitude he owes it.[49]

Massachusetts founder James Otis anticipates Adams in a 1764 document published by order of the Massachusetts Assembly. At first glance, Otis seems to say that the state of nature is merely hypothetical and that no one is born outside of society: "Nature has placed all such in a state of equality and perfect freedom.... This it must be confessed is rather an abstract way of considering men than agreeable to the real and general course of nature. The truth is, as has been shown, men come into the world and into society at the same instant." But unlike Calhoun and Merriam, Otis adds that this consideration is not at all "abstract" in the decisive respect: "Yet it is left to every man as he comes of age to choose what society he will continue to belong to."[50] If, on reaching adulthood, people are free to decide whether or not to become a member of a political society,

---

[48] Locke, *Second Treatise*, §4, §15 (my emphasis).

[49] Adams, "Valerius Poplicola," *Boston Gazette*, Oct. 28, 1771, in *Writings of Samuel Adams*, 2:257–8. Adams paraphrases Locke, *Second Treatise*, §122; at the end of the passage he paraphrases and footnotes Emer de Vattel, *The Law of Nations; or, Principles of the Law of Nature*, 1758 (Indianapolis: Liberty Fund, 2008), 220.

[50] James Otis, *The Rights of the British Colonies*, 1764, in *Pamphlets of the American Revolution: 1750–1776*, ed. Bernard Bailyn (Cambridge: Harvard University Press, 1965), 1:439, 425.

they are not yet full members of any society. As long as they are children, ruled without their consent, they are in a state of nature in relation to the country they happen to be born in.

The state of nature can therefore be understood individually or collectively. Collectively, it is a condition without civil law, in which people are free to establish a new government or reinstate a failed one. Individually, it is what every person experiences (usually without noticing it) upon reaching adulthood. He or she is – or at least ought to be – free to leave the society of his birth and live elsewhere. People who refuse to be citizens of the society in which they reside, and who prefer not to leave, might remain nonmembers, but only as long as the society permits them to remain as resident aliens. In practice, of course, people who grow up in a particular society are automatically regarded as citizens of that society, because most are content to live in the country of their birth.

Since no one is bound to become a subject of the country that his parents happen to reside in, the bills of rights of Pennsylvania and Vermont therefore state that "all people have a natural inherent right to emigrate from one state to another, that will receive them; or to form a new state in vacant countries, or in such countries as they can purchase, whenever they think that thereby they can promote their own happiness."[51] In other words, there is a natural right for a grown-up child to remain in, or for an adult to return to, the state of nature. Jefferson's *Summary View* affirms the "right, which nature has given to all men, of departing from the country in which chance, not choice has placed them, of going in quest of new habitations, and of there establishing new societies, under such laws and regulations as to them shall seem most likely to promote public happiness."[52] A 1775 Philadelphia sermon elaborates the same thought: "I am not insensible that it is a doctrine of antiquity, patronized by many, that natural allegiance is universal and perpetual;... but notwithstanding, I beg leave to suggest a few considerations on this point. The place of a man's birth, in respect to himself, is a matter of accident and necessity, and not of choice; and is a man so bound by accident and necessity, as to the place of his birth, that when he arrives to the age of discretion, he cannot remove into another kingdom and country, and become the subject of another prince? Doth not the obligation of subjection and obedience

[51] PA Bill of Rights, art. 15; repeated with insignificant variation in the Bill of Rights of VT, 1777, art. 17 (and VT, 1786, art. 21, and 1793, art. 19). KY's constitution, 1790, art. 12, §27, affirms a right to emigrate without calling it a natural right.
[52] Jefferson, *A Summary View of the Rights of British America*, 1774, in *Writings*, 105–6.

to parents cease with our childhood and state of dependence, although that of respect and reverence ever remains?"[53]

Conclusion

God and nature provide us with the capacity for reason by which we can know the moral law, but not with the political order to enforce that law. Allan Bloom misunderstands the founders' position when he writes, "[In the state of nature of Hobbes, Locke, and the founders, man's] current state is not a result of sin, but of nature's miserliness. He is on his own. God neither looks after him nor punishes him. Nature's indifference to justice is a terrible bereavement for man." Bloom sees well one side of the founders' argument: the state of nature is not a place that is fit for lasting human habitation. But he misses the positive side: in the state of nature we are all equal, meaning that no one has any natural title to rule another person without that person's consent. As Zuckert rightly says, "[n]obody is merely born into moral subjection to political power."[54] In this way, nature and nature's God provide a guide that is both negative (because dangerous) and positive (because in it we are free). These two points suggest that although civil society is needed to make life less dangerous, society should, as much as possible, protect the freedom enjoyed in the natural state.

In a 1773 sermon, Simeon Howard, a Massachusetts preacher, gives a particularly clear overview of the state of nature and the need for civil society:

In a state of nature... God has given to everyone liberty to pursue his own happiness..., provided he keeps within the bounds of the law of nature.... This however is not a state of licentiousness, for the law of nature, which bounds this liberty, forbids all injustice and wickedness, allows no man to injure another in his person or property, or to destroy his own life. But experience soon taught that, either through ignorance of this law, or the influence of unruly passions, some were disposed to violate it, by encroaching upon the liberty of others; so that the *weak* were liable to be greatly injured by the superior power of bad men, without any means of redress. This gave birth to civil society, and induced a number of individuals to combine together for mutual defense and security; to give up a part of their natural liberty for the sake of enjoying the remainder in greater safety; to

---

[53] Jacob Duche, *The Duty of Standing Fast in Our Spiritual and Temporal Liberties* (Philadelphia, 1775), in *Patriot Preachers of the American Revolution*, ed. Frank Moore (New York: Charles T. Evans, 1862), 83–4.

[54] Zuckert, *Natural Rights Republic*, 23.

agree upon certain laws among themselves to regulate the social conduct of each individual.[55]

The state of nature helps us to understand several important truths about political life. First, if all are born free in a state of nature, then government is an artificial construct, made by human beings and not by God or nature. Second, given our original natural freedom, the only noncoercive way to initiate government is by a "social compact" entered into voluntarily by each individual. Third, the state of nature is not a good place for human beings to live in indefinitely. Its defects point to the need for civil society. Finally, the state of nature is not a state where everything is permitted; there is a moral law to govern it – the law of nature – and this law should be the basis of political society.[56]

[55] Simeon Howard, *A Sermon Preached to the...Artillery Company in Boston*, 1773, in *American Political Writing*, 1:187.

[56] Clinton Rossiter, *Seedtime of the Republic: The Origin of the American Tradition of Political Liberty* (New York: Harcourt, Brace, 1953), 365, has a similar list of implications of the state of nature.

6

The Social Compact and Consent of the Governed

The defects of the state of nature show why government is needed. "Brutus" provides an overview in a 1787 article: "In a state of nature...the weak were a prey to the strong....[E]very individual was insecure; common interest therefore directed that government should be established, in which the force of the whole community should be collected, and under such directions as to protect and defend everyone who composed it."[1] More succinctly, the Declaration of Independence states, "to secure these rights, governments are instituted among men."

But before government can "protect and defend," it has to be established. The statement by "Brutus" on that is also helpful: "all men are by nature free. No one man, therefore, or any class of men, have a right, by the law of nature or of God, to assume or exercise authority over their fellows. The origin of society then is to be sought...in the united consent of those who associate."[2] James Wilson agrees: "All men are, by nature, equal and free: no one has a right to any authority over another without his consent: all lawful government is founded on the consent of those who are subject to it."[3] The Declaration of Independence simply states that governments "deriv[e] their just powers from the consent of the governed."

[1] Brutus, No. 2, *New York Journal*, November 1, 1787, in *The Documentary History of the Ratification of the Constitution*, ed. Merrill Jensen (Madison: State Historical Society of Wisconsin, 1976–), 13:525. "Brutus," an Antifederalist, held the same natural rights principles as the Federalists.

[2] Ibid.

[3] James Wilson, *Considerations on the Nature and Extent of the Legislative Authority of the British Parliament*, 1774, in *Collected Works of James Wilson*, ed. Kermit L. Hall and Mark David Hall (Indianapolis: Liberty Fund, 2007), 1:4.

These two criteria of just government will be the theme of this chapter and the next: Chapter 6 explains consent, and Chapter 7 sketches the policies and institutional arrangements that "protect and defend" life, liberty, and property.

Not all scholars recognize the extent to which natural rights provide guidelines for just government. "[F]or most of the delegates who supported the Declaration," writes Barry Shain, "natural law and rights described a condition outside of civil society, and . . . this meant for most of them that such claims played a limited role in shaping the specific moral and political contours within society."[4] Historian Pauline Maier agrees: the Declaration was "a peculiar document to be cited by those [such as Abraham Lincoln] who championed the cause of equality [for slaves]. Not only did its reference to men's equal creation concern people in a state of nature before government was established, but the document's original function was to end the previous regime, not to lay down principles to guide and limit its successor."[5] These two scholars incorrectly argue that the founders thought human beings are equal only outside of civil society, and that once they become members of a political community, their original equality has little significance for how government is instituted and what it does.

The list of complaints in the Declaration of Independence illustrates how natural rights are supposed to shape "the specific . . . political contours within society," although many scholars fail to recognize that connection. Rakove notes that for some historians, there is a "perceived tension . . . between the preambular invocation of natural rights and the legalist appeal to specific English rights in the body of the text."[6] Daniel Boorstin, for example, mistakenly believes that "specific list of grievances" in the Declaration of Independence is "historical . . . or

---

[4] Barry Alan Shain and Rogers Smith, introduction to *The Nature of Rights at the American Founding and Beyond*, ed. Shain (Charlottesville: University of Virginia Press, 2007), 8.

[5] Pauline Maier, *American Scripture: Making the Declaration of Independence* (New York: Knopf, 1997), 192. It is true that Maier contradicts the statement quoted in the text on 136 and 146: "equality meant simply that no one held authority over others by right of birth or as a gift of God. . . . Some people recognized the contradiction [between slavery and equality] and were ready to move toward greater consistency between principle and practice." In these passages, it seems that equality does indeed "lay down principles to guide and limit" government. She nowhere resolves this contradiction.

[6] Jack N. Rakove, *Original Meanings: Politics and Ideas in the Making of the Constitution* (New York: Vintage Books, 1996), 293 (Rakove himself disagrees with that "perceived tension").

narrowly constitutional," as does John Reid.[7] But the Declaration's logical structure shows that the complaints cannot be about "specific English rights" alone. It begins with a statement of the two basic requirements of just politics (securing rights and consent). It asserts the right to revolution "whenever any form of government becomes destructive of these ends." Then it provides eighteen examples of the king's "long train of abuses" whose "object [is] the establishment of an absolute tyranny over these states." The conclusion is that "all political connection" between America and Britain "is totally dissolved."

The structure of the Declaration – an initial statement of principles, followed by evidence of their repeated violation – implies that every single grievance describes a trespass against one or both of the two criteria of just government: consent and securing rights. Once this is understood (and there are few scholars who state this simple but essential point), the grievances become understandable as well. For example, the eighth – "He has obstructed the administration of justice by refusing his assent to laws for establishing judiciary powers" – refers to both criteria. "Refusing his assent" is a denial of consent, while "judiciary powers" – for trials of murderers and thieves – are necessary for criminal prosecutions that protect life, liberty, and property.

Why is consent a fundamental principle? The Declaration of Independence does not give reasons for its claim that consent is the source of the "just powers" of government. But many state constitutions do, anticipating the explanation already quoted from "Brutus." Vermont's is typical: "all power [is] originally inherent in, and consequently derived from, the people." All of the first sixteen states affirm that the people's right to political authority is fundamental. Most succinct is Maryland's Bill of Rights: "all government of right originates from the people."[8]

---

[7] Daniel J. Boorstin, *The Americans: The National Experience* (New York: Vintage, 1965), 399; John Phillip Reid, *Constitutional History of the American Revolution: The Authority of Rights* (Madison: University of Wisconsin Press, 1986), 5.

[8] Bill of Rights of VA, 1776, §2; of PA, 1776, art. 4; of DE, 1776, art. 1; of NC, 1776, art. 1; of VT, 1777, art. 5; of MD, 1776, art. 1; of MA, 1780, art. 5; of NH, 1784, art. 8; CT Constitution, 1776, Preamble; NJ Constitution, 1776, Preamble; GA Constitution, 1776, Preamble; NY Constitution, 1777, Preamble; KY Constitution, 1792, art. 12, §2; TN Constitution, 1796, art. 11, §1. RI, proposed Bill of Rights, art. 2, published by Ratifying Convention, 1790, in *Documents Illustrative of the Formation of the Union of the American States*, ed. Charles C. Tansill (Washington: Government Printing Office, 1927), 1052. SC Constitution, 1776 (taxation without representation is "the most abject slavery").

But what sort of consent is required? The founders speak of three distinct objects of consent. First, the people must agree to form a political society – the "social compact" – or to join one already existing. Second, the form of government must be agreed on. Third, there should be periodic elections of part or all of the legislative body. Fourth – if negative consent may be counted as a form of consent – the people may also withdraw their consent if the government fails to meet the two minimal standards of just government. This is the right to revolution.

Scholars who write on consent often are only partly or vaguely aware of these distinct kinds of consent. John Reid writes at length about consent but mostly limits it to the third kind just mentioned – consent as representation, meaning lawmaking through elected officials.[9] Better are Gordon Wood and Willi Adams, who have separate discussions of legislation, constitution-making, and revolution.[10] Nathan Tarcov mentions all four kinds of consent, but without explicitly distinguishing them as such.[11] When it comes to consent in the lawmaking process, scholars sometimes simply get it wrong, as shown later in this chapter.

There is the additional question of how consent is to be registered. For example, the founders chose to tie representation to localities, as opposed to today's Germany (for example), where voting is for representatives on party lists who have no connections to a particular geographical region. The size of districts and lengths of terms for elected officials were also much discussed in the founding.[12] This book does not investigate these topics because they are of subordinate importance to the fundamental principle that there must be an opportunity for periodic elections of leading government officials. However, the end of the chapter treats

[9] John Phillip Reid, *The Concept of Representation in the Age of the American Revolution* (Chicago: University of Chicago Press, 1989).

[10] Gordon S. Wood, *The Creation of the American Republic, 1776–1787* (New York: Norton, 1969); Willi Paul Adams, *The First American Constitutions: Republican Ideology and the Making of the State Constitutions in the Revolutionary Era* (Chapel Hill: University of North Carolina Press, 1980). See also Donald S. Lutz, "The Theory of Consent in the Early State Constitutions," *Publius* 9, No. 2 (Spring 1979): 11–42; Marc W. Kruman, *Between Authority and Liberty: State Constitution Making in Revolutionary America* (Chapel Hill: University of North Carolina Press, 1997), ch. 2–5.

[11] Nathan Tarcov, "Popular Sovereignty in Democratic Political Theory," in *Encyclopedia of the American Constitution*, 2nd ed., ed. Leonard W. Levy and Kenneth L. Karst (New York: Macmillan, 2000), 4:1962–4.

[12] Adams, *First American Constitutions*, 234–43; Kruman, *Between Authority and Liberty*, 64–86.

the matter of voting rights briefly, because it would seem that the natural rights principle is violated to the extent that anyone is excluded from the franchise.

The Social Compact

The first kind of consent is to the formation of a social compact, or to joining a compact after it has been established. The Preamble to the Massachusetts Constitution explains: "The body politic is formed by a voluntary association of individuals: It is a social compact, by which the whole people covenants with each citizen, and each citizen with the whole people, that all shall be governed by certain laws for the common good." If political society does not yet exist, this kind of consent should precede the setting up of a government and laws. As Massachusetts says, the compacters agree "that all shall be governed by certain laws," but the method of lawmaking is not yet settled by the mere agreement to form a compact. The idea of the social compact is evident in one of the common formulations of the founding: that men retain their natural rights when they "enter into society."[13] To "enter into" society means that you join a society of which you were not previously a member, by which you become part of a social compact with the others who have "enter[ed] into" the same society.

The founders' critics sometimes assume that the social compact is meant to be a factual description of how every political society comes into existence out of a state of nature. Charles Merriam writes in 1903, "The hypothesis of an original contract to form the state is...wholly contrary to our knowledge of the historical development of political institutions."[14] The founders would agree with that statement. However, they would add that the contract theory is not meant to be a description of how political societies have evolved historically. They knew well that most have been founded, as Hamilton says, by "accident and force," not "from reflection and choice." The compact theory is rather about how political societies *should* be founded and continued at all times – by consent. As Michael Zuckert explains, "the Lockean contract cannot be a once and for all event in the distant past but must be...made and

---

[13]   VA Bill of Rights, art. 1.
[14]   C. Edward Merriam, *A History of American Political Theories* (New York: Macmillan, 1903), 308.

accepted by each individual as he or she comes to accept the legitimacy of political authority."[15]

This most foundational kind of consent determines citizenship. Wilson writes, "The individuals who are not parties to [the social compact] are not members of the society." David Ramsay distinguishes between citizens and subjects in this way: citizens are "a mass of free people who collectively possess sovereignty," while a subject is simply "one who is under the power of another." Before 1776, Britain treated everyone living in its colonies as subjects, including Indians and slaves. After 1776, Americans distinguished between citizens, who "collectively possess sovereignty," and noncitizens such as Indians and slaves who reside on American soil but are not consenting members of the political community. Although some states treated free blacks as citizens in the early years after 1776, writes Douglas Bradburn, "the vast majority of non-enslaved blacks...lived within the bounds of the law, but not as accepted citizens of the United States." Citizens are those who consent to be members, and whom the existing members consent to accept as fellow citizens.[16] As one lawyer argued before the Supreme Court in 1795, "citizenship is the effect of compact," and the compact, as Hamilton writes, is "made between the society at large and each individual."[17] There must be consent on both sides – between the whole society and every person who wants to be a member. Boston's Rights of the Colonists explains the point in this way: "All men have a right to remain in a state of nature as long as they please.... When men enter into society, it is by voluntary consent."[18]

[15] Alexander Hamilton, *Federalist* 1, in Hamilton, James Madison, and John Jay, *The Federalist Papers*, ed. Clinton Rossiter (New York: Signet Classics, 2003), 27; Michael P. Zuckert, *Launching Liberalism: On Lockean Political Philosophy* (Lawrence: University Press of Kansas, 2002), 257.

[16] Wilson, *Lectures on Law*, 1:636; David Ramsay, *A Dissertation on the Manner of Acquiring the Character and Privileges of a Citizen*, 1789; Douglas Bradburn, *The Citizenship Revolution: Politics and the Creation of the American Union*, 1774–1804 (Charlottesville: University of Virginia Press, 2009), 10–11 (quoting Ramsay), 237; Alexander Keyssar, *The Right to Vote: The Contested History of Democracy in the United States* (New York: Basic Books, 2000), 20 (free blacks "were tacitly enfranchised" in six states).

[17] *Talbot v. Janson*, 3 U.S. 133, at 141 (1795); Alexander Hamilton, Phocion No. 2, 1784, in *Founders' Constitution*, 1:644.

[18] Boston, Rights of the Colonists, 1772, in *Writings of Samuel Adams*, ed. Harry A. Cushing (1904; repr. New York: Octagon, 1968), 2:351.

If membership is determined by the unanimous consent of "each individual," there should be a natural right to depart from a society, at least when the society has no immediate need of a person's presence or services. Earlier I quoted Jefferson: there is a "right, which nature has given to all men, of departing from the country in which chance, not choice has placed them."[19] Children of citizens are automatically offered citizenship, but they do not have to accept the offer. Pennsylvania and Vermont codified the right of expatriation in their Bills of Rights: "all men have a natural inherent right to emigrate."[20] A 1779 Virginia law affirms a "natural right which all men have of relinquishing the country in which birth or other accident may have thrown them."[21] Douglas Bradburn notes that these laws were "a direct rejection of the British practice," which regarded subjectship as a permanent condition. Although expatriation proved difficult to regularize by law, and the right was disputed by some, everyone acknowledged the principle that citizenship should be consensual.[22]

However, people have a right to become a citizen of another country only when, as Pennsylvania states, there is "another [country] that will receive them." In other words, although there is a natural right to reject your current society, there is no natural right to become a citizen of a society that refuses to accept you. Since "citizenship is the effect of compact," there can be no right to immigrate unless there is consent on both sides: the would-be immigrants and the country "that will receive them." Rogers Smith believes that limiting immigration by race or national origin is "quite obviously illiberal, inconsistent with the ideals of liberty and equality professed in...the nation's 'Creed.'" On the contrary, Gouverneur Morris observed at the Constitutional Convention of 1787 that "every society from a great nation down to a club had the right of declaring the conditions on which new members should be admitted."[23]

---

[19] Thomas Jefferson, *A Summary View of the Rights of British America*, 1774, in *Writings*, ed. Merrill D. Peterson (New York: Library of America, 1984), 105. See also Samuel Adams, "Valerius Poplicola," *Boston Gazette*, October 28, 1771, in *Writings of Samuel Adams*, 2:257–8, quoted above, near the end of ch. 5.

[20] Bill of Rights of PA, 1776, art. 15; of VT, 1777, art. 17.

[21] An Act Declaring Who Shall Be Deemed Citizens, 1779, in *Statutes at Large... of Virginia*, ed. William Hening (Richmond: George Cochran, 1822), 10:129.

[22] Bradburn, *Citizenship Revolution*, ch. 3 (expatriation as a natural right and its role in early federal and state law; quotation on 106).

[23] Rogers M. Smith, "The 'American Creed' and American Identity: The Limits of Liberal Citizenship in the United States," *Western Political Quarterly* 41, No. 2 (June 1988):

In this case, the right to discriminate is nothing more than the right to liberty itself.

In the Massachusetts Preamble, a political society is formed "to furnish *the individuals who compose it,* with the power of enjoying, in safety and tranquility, their natural rights, and the blessings of life." The compact is to protect the rights of the citizens only, not of people elsewhere in the world. Americans are no more responsible for securing the rights of Mexicans and Canadians than Mexicans and Canadians are for securing the rights of Americans. Each of these peoples must undertake that task by and for itself. Therefore citizens also have a duty to obey only the government of the nation they belong to and no other. Today's custom of allowing dual citizenship makes no sense in the founders' political theory, because the compact requires exclusive loyalty to the laws of one's own community. Therefore the 1795 Naturalization Act required new citizens "to renounce forever all allegiance and fidelity to any foreign prince, potentate, state, or sovereignty whatever."[24]

The term social contract or compact has sometimes been used in a second sense, to name an agreement between the rulers and the people. Franklin Roosevelt attributes this understanding to the founders in a 1932 speech: "The Declaration of Independence discusses the problem of government in terms of a contract.... Under such a contract, rulers were accorded power, and the people consented to that power on consideration that they be accorded certain rights."[25] Ramsay's 1789 history of the Revolution anticipates and rejects Roosevelt's error: "The far-famed social compact between the people and their rulers did not apply in the United States. The sovereignty was in the people."[26] As Massachusetts says, the social compact is formed when "the whole people covenants with each citizen, and each citizen with the whole people" to establish a government. The compact precedes the government; the people then delegate powers to the government they establish. Government is the people's trustee, but it is not part of the compact.

---

245. Gouverneur Morris, speech on Aug. 9, in *The Records of the Federal Convention of 1787,* ed. Max Farrand (New Haven: Yale University Press, 1937), 2:238.

[24] Naturalization Act, January 29, 1795, in *Public Statutes at Large,* ed. Richard Peters (Boston: Little and Brown, 1845), 1:414.

[25] Franklin D. Roosevelt, Commonwealth Club Address, 1932.

[26] David Ramsay, *The History of the American Revolution,* 1789 (Indianapolis: Liberty Classics, 1990), 1:330; Wood, *Creation,* 268–73, 282–91 (more evidence that the social compact is created solely by the people, not by a contract between the people and government).

Nor is the social compact an agreement among groups or classes. That is because individuals, not societies, are "born free and equal." There is no room in the founders' political theory for an "organic" society whose authority takes the place of the free choice of individuals. Societies are – or should be – formed by individuals. Whatever rights government possesses derive from the free grant of the individuals who constitute the people. The rights of society begin from, and are guided and limited by, the rights of individuals.

The Declaration speaks of the necessity for "one people," the Americans, to separate itself from another people, the British. What makes the American people distinct from the British? Choice alone. In the original rough draft of the Declaration, Jefferson writes, "we [British and Americans] might have been *a* free and *a* great *people* together."[27] The Declaration's text as adopted speaks of "our British brethren" and our "consanguinity" (belonging to the same race) with them. Race or ethnicity may of course be an accidental reason why a particular group of people agree to a social compact. "Consanguinity" is often correlated with similarity in intelligence, religion, habits, and tastes. But it is the choice, not the common race or ethnicity or religion, that is decisive. In 1776, one people largely of the same race and religion became two when the people of the United States chose to secede from the British Empire. Americans would have become one people with the Canadians, most of whom were Catholics and of French ancestry, if they had accepted the invitation of Congress to join the United States in 1774.[28]

Donald Lutz mistakenly believes that the founders were communitarians, not individualists. He claims that when the Declaration says that "one people" is dissolving "the political bands which have connected them with another," the "people are acting, not a collection of individuals." He adds: "Communitarianism, not individualism, permeates the list of abuses" in the Declaration.[29] But Lutz fails to ask how a people becomes "one people" – a community – in the first place. The only answer given in the founding is *consent*, a voluntary agreement of individuals.

---

[27] Thomas Jefferson, Original Rough Draught of the Declaration, in *The Papers of Thomas Jefferson*, ed. Julian P. Boyd et al. (Princeton: Princeton University Press, 1950-), 1:427 (my emphasis).

[28] Continental Congress, Appeal to the Inhabitants of Quebec, 1774, in *American Political Writing during the Founding Era*, ed. Charles S. Hyneman and Donald S. Lutz (Indianapolis: Liberty Press, 1983), 1:231–9.

[29] Donald S. Lutz, "Consent," in *A Companion to the American Revolution*, ed. Jack P. Greene and J. R. Pole (Malden, MA: Blackwell, 2000), 654.

It is true that many of the grievances in the Declaration are about injuries to the community. But what makes these things injuries? Why is it wrong for the king to dissolve legislative bodies and veto colonial laws? Ultimately it is because no *individual* may be ruled without his or her consent. Further, the reason the king is wrong to "destroy the lives of our people" is that the right to life belongs to every individual. The founders are indeed communitarians in the sense that once one enters the compact and becomes a citizen, contributing to the preservation and liberty of the community becomes a contractual moral obligation. The founders' communitarianism is based on an underlying individualism – the individual natural rights to life, liberty, and property.

Because of the existence of both state and national governments, America was formed and sustained by multiple social compacts. Many of the passages quoted in this chapter come from state constitutions and refer to the compact of that particular state. But there was another compact in which the people of the several states formed the nation, which led first to the adoption of the Articles of Confederation, then to the 1788 Constitution. Madison writes in *Federalist* 33: "If a number of political societies enter into a larger political society, the laws which the latter may enact ... must necessarily be supreme over those societies and the individuals of whom they are composed." In this way Americans typically belong to two political societies, the state and the nation, the one inside of, and a part of, the other. These two compacts can coexist – there can be dual citizenship in one's home state as well as the nation – because there is a division of political responsibility between state and national governments, with roles defined by the constitutions of each. This is not to deny that there was a certain ambiguity regarding this question in the founding, with many jurisdictional controversies between the state and national governments. The Declaration says that Americans are "one people," but it declares independence on behalf of "free and independent states," plural.[30]

Consent in the Formation of a Constitution

In the initial social compact, the agreement to be a citizen of a particular society can and ought to be unanimous. In principle, this original consent

---

[30] Madison, *Federalist* 33, p. 200; No. 39, pp. 239–43; Peter S. Onuf, *The Origins of the Federal Republic: Jurisdictional Controversies in the United States, 1775–1787* (Philadelphia: University of Pennsylvania Press, 1983).

of each person should be unanimous, as James Wilson writes in his *Lectures on Law:* "each individual engages with the whole collectively, and the whole collectively engage with each individual."[31] Every natural-born or naturalized citizen can agree on whether to remain an American, as long as there is a right to depart. So too in an altogether new founding when there is no government currently in place, everyone can either join or depart. (Historian R. R. Palmer reports that "the number of émigré loyalists who went to Canada or England during the American Revolution is set as high as 100,000," at least five times the number of émigrés per capita than in the French Revolution.) But once the compact is formed, the form of government should be determined by the majority or their representatives.[32]

However, consent to become a member of society is just the beginning. Once a self-selected group of people unanimously decides to leave the state of nature, the majority has a right to consent to the form of government they will live under. The Declaration of Independence recognizes this right to determine the constitution: if a government "becomes destructive of these ends, it is the right of the people to alter or to abolish it, and to institute new government, . . . organizing its powers in such form as to them shall seem most likely to effect their safety and happiness." Referring to the consent requirement for the adoption of constitutions, Hamilton writes, "The fabric of American empire ought to rest on the solid basis of the consent of the people. The streams of national power ought to flow from that pure, original fountain of all legitimate authority."[33]

But how should the people express that consent to their form of government? The first state constitutions were mostly written by elected bodies that became the state legislatures, with no provision for amendment. The general assumption seemed to be that the same representatives who pass ordinary statute laws should also make the fundamental law establishing the form of government. That view was questioned during the 1770s and '80s, however, until a consensus emerged to separate ordinary legislation from constitution-making. Thomas Tucker of South Carolina writes, "The constitution should be the avowed act of the people at large. . . .

---

[31] Wilson, *Lectures on Law*, in *Collected Works*, 1:636.

[32] Wood, *Creation*, 283–91 (distinguishing the social compact from "the formation of a fundamental constitution"); however, Wood is not quite clear on the unanimity requirement in the original compact; R. R. Palmer, *The Age of the Democratic Revolution: A Political History of Europe and America, 1760–1800* (Princeton: Princeton University Press, 1959), 1:188.

[33] Hamilton, *Federalist* 22, p. 148.

It should be declared to be paramount to all acts of the legislature, and irrepealable and unalterable by any authority but the express consent of a majority." The idea, as Concord, Massachusetts, stated as early as 1776, was that "a constitution alterable by the supreme legislative is no security at all to the subject against any encroachment of the governing part on any, or on all of their rights and privileges." Consequently, Concord recommended that a "convention, or congress, be immediately chosen, to form and establish a constitution," subject to public ratification.[34] With this in view, the states began to adopt the idea of temporary conventions to amend or rewrite their constitutions. The federal Constitution was proposed in the same manner, with elected ratifying conventions in each state to approve or reject it. Explaining that method, Madison argued that the Articles of Confederation had never received a proper approval because "in many of the states it had received no higher sanction than a mere legislative ratification."[35]

Consent in the Legislative Body: Does Natural Rights Theory Require It?

Some scholars deny that the Declaration requires democratic institutions. Martin Diamond asserts that the Declaration "was *not* a democratic document" because it allows the people to select whatever "forms, as to them shall seem most likely to effect their safety and happiness." Diamond concludes that the British king is condemned "not because he was a king, but because he was a *tyrannical* king. Had the British monarchy continued to secure to the colonists their rights, . . . the colonists would not have been entitled to rebel." Other than that, says Diamond, the Declaration provides "no guidance whatsoever" as to the form of government.[36] Edmund Morgan agrees: "The Declaration . . . was directed only against the 'present' king of Great Britain and would not have precluded a monarchical form of government for the United States." Morgan adds that the Declaration meant nothing more than that America is entitled

---

[34] Lutz, "Theory of Consent," 33–6; Wood, *Creation*, 273–82 (quoting Tucker on 281); Concord Town Meeting Resolutions, October 21, 1776, in *Founders' Constitution*, 1:637.

[35] Madison, *Federalist* 43, p. 276.

[36] Martin Diamond, "The American Idea of Equality," in *As Far as Republican Principles Will Admit*, ed. William A. Schambra (Washington: AEI Press, 1991), 243–6; Diamond, "The Revolution of Sober Expectations," in ibid., 214. Harry V. Jaffa, *How to Think about the American Revolution* (Durham: Carolina Academic Press, 1978), has a powerful response to Diamond.

to a "separate and *equal* station" among the nations of the earth.[37] Michael Zuckert concurs: "That a government derives its powers from the consent of the governed does not mean, however, that governments necessarily operate democratically or through representative assemblies." The Declaration has "no inherent antipathy to monarchy."[38]

But later passages in the Declaration show otherwise. The British king has prevented some American colonial legislatures from being elected on a regular basis, "whereby the legislative powers, incapable of annihilation, have returned to the people at large for their exercise." The town of Stoughton, Massachusetts, illustrates this idea: "the majority of the people [is where] the supreme power is vested.... [A]ll persons entrusted with any of the delegated powers of the state are servants of the people and as such are elected by them and accountable to them and removable for breach of trust, incapacity, or misbehavior."[39] "Consent" in this context means periodic elections of government officials.

The Declaration uses the term consent in two other places. As in the statements just quoted, these other instances imply the need for consent not only in joining a society and making its constitution, but also in government's operation once founded: "He has kept among us, in times of peace, standing armies, without the *consent* of our legislatures." And the king has approved of Parliament's "pretended legislation... imposing taxes on us without our *consent*." The raising of armies and the imposition of taxes are major acts of government. The Declaration implies that no such act should be undertaken without the consent of "our legislatures." What is meant by "legislatures" is clear from the second quotation: when the Declaration says taxes have been imposed without our consent, it means without the consent of our elected representatives. These two statements explain why the Declaration speaks of a people's "right of representation in the legislature, a right inestimable to them and formidable to tyrants only."[40]

---

[37] Edmund S. Morgan, *The Birth of the Republic, 1763–89*, 2nd ed. (Chicago: University of Chicago Press, 1977), 75–6. Agreeing with Morgan: Lee Ward, *The Politics of Liberty in England and Revolutionary America* (New York: Cambridge University Press, 2004), 397.

[38] Michael P. Zuckert, *The Natural Rights Republic* (Notre Dame, IN: University of Notre Dame Press, 1996), 29, 206.

[39] Instructions from Stoughton to its delegates, 1779, in *Massachusetts, Colony to Commonwealth*, ed. Robert P. Taylor (Chapel Hill: University of North Carolina Press, 1961), 121–2.

[40] Jaffa, *How to Think*, 122–6 (the Declaration requires consent not only to the institution but also to the operation of government). The American view of the king's lack of authority in the colonies is explained in the final section of Chapter 2, above.

Although the founders thought there may be circumstances when an unrestrained people would be unable to sustain a free government, it was generally accepted that the government most consistent with equal liberty is government by elected representatives. Hamilton calls the latter form of government "representative democracy." Madison calls it a "republic" in *Federalist* 10. Some, such as the *Providence Gazette*, simply used the term democracy, as we do today: "By a *democracy* is meant that form of government where the highest power of making laws is lodged in the common people, or persons chosen out from them. This is what by some is called a republic, a commonwealth, or free state, and seems to be most agreeable to *natural right and liberty*."[41] Jefferson writes, "the republican is the only form of government which is not eternally at open or secret war with the rights of mankind."[42] Thus the idea of *democratic* government, no less than *limited* government, arises from equal natural liberty.

It is not the Declaration alone that testifies to the founders' consensus that equal natural liberty requires democracy. Already in 1765, in response to the Stamp Act, the Massachusetts Assembly resolved that "there are certain essential rights . . . which are founded in the law of God and nature, and are the common rights of mankind" – one of which is that "no man can justly take the property of another without his consent; and that upon this original principle the right of representation in the same body, which exercises the power of making laws for levying taxes, . . . is evidently founded."[43] In the documents of the 1760s, the emphasis was on taxation. If property is to be given to government, we ourselves – meaning, practically speaking, a majority of our representatives – must make that grant. In the debate over the Stamp Act, Americans returned again and again to the same point, here expressed by John Dickinson in his widely read *Letters from a Farmer*: "If they have any right to tax us – then . . . 'There is nothing which' we can call our own; or, to use the words of Mr. Locke – 'What property have we in that which another may, by right, take when he pleases to himself?' . . . Those who are taxed without their own consent, expressed by themselves or their representatives,

[41] Hamilton to Gouverneur Morris, May 19, 1777, in *The Papers of Alexander Hamilton*, ed. Harold C. Syrett (New York: Columbia University Press, 1961–79), 1:255; Madison, *Federalist* 10, p. 75; *Providence Gazette*, August 9, 1777, in Adams, *First American Constitutions*, 96.

[42] Jefferson, Response to the Address of Welcome from the Mayor of Alexandria, March 11, 1790, in *Papers*, ed. Boyd, 16:225.

[43] Resolutions of the House of Representatives of Massachusetts, October 29, 1765, in *Founders' Constitution*, 1:629.

are slaves."[44] Slavery, of course, is a violation of the natural right to liberty.

This argument establishes that the people have a right to participate in the part of government that raises taxes. But the colonists went further. The link between taxation and representation was seen, by the same logic, as a link between representation and all lawmaking. If the meaning of slavery is to be subject to the will of another, then forcing someone to do something against his will deprives him of his freedom no less than taking his property for taxes against his will. All laws for the governance of society are commands, telling people what they must do on pain of punishment if they refuse. Accordingly, Virginia's 1764 protest against the Stamp Act states that the "natural and civil rights" of Virginians are violated "if laws respecting the internal government and taxation of themselves are imposed upon them by any other power than that derived from their own consent."[45] Not only taxation but also all "internal government" must be by consent. The elected part of the legislative body must give its approval to *all* laws. Thus, contrary to Diamond, Morgan, and Zuckert, government by elected representatives is not optional in the founding. It is required by "the law of God and nature," according to which all humans possess an equal right to liberty.

Therefore the Preamble to the Georgia Constitution of 1777 states: Britain's pretension "to make laws to bind them in all cases whatsoever, without their consent...[is] repugnant to the common rights of mankind...[and] the rights and privileges they are entitled to by the laws of nature and reason." New Jersey's 1774 Resolutions mention "the common principles of humanity and justice" as one reason that the consent of the governed must inform the making of laws.[46] In a 1776 sermon, Samuel West says, "this ought to be looked upon as a sacred and inalienable right,... viz., that no one be obliged to submit to any law except such as are made either by himself or by his representative."[47]

---

[44] John Dickinson, *Letters from a Farmer*, 1768, Letter 7, in *The Political Writings of John Dickinson, 1764–1774*, ed. Paul L. Ford (New York: Da Capo, 1970), 356.

[45] Resolution of the Virginia House of Burgesses, November 14, 1764, in *Great Issues in American History: From Settlement to Revolution, 1584–1776*, ed. Clarence L. Ver Steeg and Richard Hofstadter (New York: Vintage, 1969), 321.

[46] New Jersey Resolutions, July 21, 1774, in *American Archives: Fourth Series*, ed. Peter Force (Washington: M. St. Clare Clarke, 1837–53), 1:624.

[47] Samuel West, *On the Right to Rebel against Governors* (Boston, 1776), in *American Political Writing*, 1:438.

Even so, the argument for popular *participation* in the lawmaking body would still leave open the possibility of mixed government, in which elements based on wealth could share political power with the popular element. The founders' partial acceptance of this view is visible in their property ownership requirements for voters and for elected officials. The *Essex Result* argues that one house of the legislative body should be selected by owners of substantial amounts of property. That advice was followed in the Massachusetts Constitution of 1780: state senators had to own three times the amount of property as the representatives. Most states required elected officials to be property owners, and most had higher requirements for senators and governors. New York required voters for state senators and governor to possess a 100-pound freehold, but only 20 pounds for voters for the state Assembly. As it became evident that these requirements did not much affect the kinds of people who were elected, they were dropped or went unenforced.[48]

Clearly, the king of Britain was a tyrant, according to the founders, not only because his policies were harmful to life, liberty, and property, but also because *anything* he did, if contrary to the consent of America's elected legislatures, was unjust. Of the eighteen grievances listed in the Declaration of Independence, the first thirteen contain instances of the king denying the colonists' right to self-government. The culminating item in this first list is that the king combined with "others" (Parliament), "suspending our own legislatures, and declaring themselves invested with power to legislate for us in all cases whatsoever." The logic of the equality principle necessarily leads to the right of the people to rule themselves in person or through elected representatives.

Consent Withdrawn, or the Right to Revolution

The fourth and final kind of consent in the founding is the withdrawal of consent – the right to revolution. The Declaration of Independence concludes its list of self-evident truths by announcing that right: "That whenever any form of government becomes destructive of these ends, it is the right of the people to alter or abolish it, and to institute new government." This right follows logically from the consent principle.

---

[48] *Essex Result*, in *American Political Writing*, 1:491; MA Constitution, ch. 1, §2.5, §3.3; NY Constitution, art. 7, 10. On property requirements for voters and elected officials, see Lutz, "Theory of Consent," 21–30. Wood, *Creation*, 197–255 (the initial partial acceptance of "mixed government," followed by its rejection).

If government is not doing its job, it loses its legitimate claim on the people.[49]

New Hampshire's constitution explicitly affirms the right of revolution: "whenever the ends of government are perverted, and public liberty manifestly endangered, and all other means of redress are ineffectual, the people may, and of right ought, to reform the old, or establish a new government. The doctrine of nonresistance against arbitrary power and oppression is absurd, slavish, and destructive of the good and happiness of mankind." The Preamble to the 1776 New Jersey Constitution declares, "allegiance and protection are, in the nature of things, reciprocal ties, each equally depending upon the other, and liable to be dissolved by the others being refused or withdrawn."[50] When government fails to protect its citizens, their duty of allegiance has ended.

Plainly, the right to revolution does not mean that a minority may overthrow any government, however good and democratic, whenever it dislikes the results of an election or the policies established by elected officials. That would justify the Southern secession of 1861, which was undertaken to protect and expand slavery and the Southern way of life based in part upon that institution.[51] Lincoln rightly argued that if the right to revolution could be exercised whenever a part of the society was dissatisfied with the laws, anarchy would result.[52] The solution to the insecurity of the state of nature requires that people be compelled to obey the government once they have established it. But if, in New Hampshire's words, "the ends of government are perverted, and public liberty manifestly endangered," revolution is justified.

Still, these simple and inspiring formulas harbor a tremendous difficulty. The right to revolution, in plain words, is a right to set force against force – ultimately a right to kill members of the existing government and those who support it, if necessary. Revolution is not to be undertaken lightly. John Adams exposed this harsh reality when he called revolution "club law."[53] Revolution returns people to the state of nature during the

49 Adams, *First American Constitutions*, 134–42.
50 NH Bill of Rights, art. 10; NJ's Preamble is repeated in NC Constitution, 1776. The right to revolution is also in PA, MD, VA, VT, and MA.
51 See the Declarations of Secession of SC, GA, MS, and TX, Avalon Project of Yale Law School, http://avalon.law.yale.edu.
52 Lincoln, First Inaugural Address, March 4, 1861, in *The Collected Works of Abraham Lincoln*, ed. Roy T. Basler (New Brunswick: Rutgers University Press, 1953), 4:256.
53 Adams to William Tudor, March 8, 1817, in *Works*, 2:312; discussed in *The Briefs of the American Revolution*, ed. John P. Reid (New York: New York University Press, 1981), 45–8.

transition from the old regime to the new. In such a state, the hoped-for security for life and liberty may be shattered by passions unleashed and violence uncontrolled.

Prior to the Declaration's affirmation of the right to revolution, the principles of government are affirmed as "abstract truth, applicable to all men and all times."[54] But at this point the Declaration hesitates, acknowledging the need for caution and patience. "Prudence indeed will dictate that governments long established should not be changed for light and transient causes. And accordingly all experience hath shown that mankind are more disposed to suffer, while evils are sufferable, than to right themselves by abolishing the forms to which they are accustomed." Whether or when to undertake a revolution is not something that principle alone can decide. Only prudence can judge how far "evils are sufferable" in the unique circumstances of a particular time and place.

In 1776, when the Continental Congress debated whether to declare independence, several delegates who were warmly attached to the rights of mankind nevertheless opposed the break with Britain. The dispute was not about the principles of natural right, on which most delegates were heartily agreed, but concerned the prudence of undertaking a revolution at that particular time. The most respected of those delegates opposed to independence was Dickinson. He had explained in the *Letters from a Farmer* why revolution ought to be resorted to only with great reluctance: "When the appeal is made to the sword, highly probable is it, that the punishment will exceed the offence; and the calamities attending on war outweigh those preceding it.... Anger produces anger; and differences that might be accommodated by kind and respectful behavior may, by imprudence, be enlarged to an incurable rage.... [A]ll considerations of reason and equity vanish; and a blind fury governs, or rather confounds all things."[55] However, the consensus in July 1776 held that defeating the British threat to colonial freedom was worth the bloodshed that everyone knew would follow.

Consent and Voting Rights

Can there be genuine consent if women and the poor are excluded? It is not necessary to investigate this long and complicated question here.[56] In

---

[54] Lincoln to Henry Pierce and others, April 6, 1859, in *Collected Works*, 3:376.
[55] Dickinson, *Letters from a Farmer*, Letter 3, 325–7.
[56] See Thomas G. West, *Vindicating the Founders: Race, Sex, Class, and Justice in the Origins of America* (Lanham, MD: Rowman & Littlefield, 1997), ch. 3 and 5.

the founders' theory of natural rights, it is not important for every citizen to vote. Madison defines a republic as "a government which derives all its powers directly or indirectly from the great body of the people." As long as most are voting – meaning, as we will see, most adult males – the sentiments of the majority will generally determine the broad direction of laws and policy. In the founders' view, that was enough to satisfy the consent principle.

In accordance with that principle, the franchise was significantly expanded during and after the Revolution. Bradburn reports that in comparison with colonial practice, "the new legislatures became much larger, more popularly elected, more geographically representative and substantially more powerful."[57] Even in the colonial period, Morgan writes, "the size of the electorate ... [already] included the great majority of free adult males."[58] Most states limited voting rights to property owners or taxpayers, but these small property requirements were gradually reduced or not enforced. By the 1790s, about 85 to 90 percent of adult male citizens had the right to vote. By the early 1800s, says Marc Kruman, "white manhood suffrage would sweep the land."[59] Still, the leading founders generally believed, as Dickinson put it, that property qualifications for voters are "a necessary defense against the dangerous influence of those multitudes without property and without principle."[60] As the years went by, actual experience with republican government led Americans to put more trust in the people, including the poorest. The reasonable hope of acquiring property – to be explained at length in Part III of this book – proved to be sufficient to reconcile the poor to a regime protecting property rights. In most states, this mildly oligarchic element

[57] Bradburn, *Citizenship Revolution*, 47.
[58] Edmund S. Morgan, *Inventing the People: The Rise of Popular Sovereignty in England and America* (New York: Norton, 1988), 175.
[59] West, *Vindicating*, 114; Donald S. Lutz, "Political Participation in Eighteenth-Century America," in *Toward a Usable Past: Liberty under State Constitutions*, ed. Paul Finkelman and Stephen E. Gottlieb (Athens: University of Georgia Press, 1991), 24 (65–75% of adult male citizens qualified to vote in the 1780s, i.e., ten years before my estimate – although Lutz admits that property requirements "were frequently ignored"); Adams, *First American Constitutions*, 197 ("at least a quarter ... of white male adults" could not vote in the 1770s). Kruman, *Between Authority and Liberty*, 107.
[60] John Dickinson, speech of August 7, 1787, in *Records of the Federal Convention*, 2:202; also Address of the Convention, March 1780, in *The Popular Sources of Political Authority: Documents on the Massachusetts Constitution of 1780*, ed. Oscar and Mary Handlin (Cambridge: Harvard University Press, 1966), 437.

in the regime – as Aristotle would have called it – was soon abandoned as unnecessary.[61]

Women were mostly excluded from voting in the founding. John Adams offers this explanation: "why exclude women? You will say, because their delicacy renders them unfit for practice and experience in the great businesses of life, and the hardy enterprises of war, as well as the arduous cares of state. Besides, their attention is so much engaged with the necessary nurture of children, that nature has made them fittest for domestic cares."[62] Similarly, the *Essex Result* claims that women lack "sufficient acquired discretion; not from a deficiency in their mental powers, but from the natural tenderness and delicacy of their minds, their retired mode of life, and various domestic duties." In other words, although men and women are equal in "mental powers," the natural differences between the sexes in other respects, sharpened by their customary social roles, make it unsuitable for women to vote. Finally, Essex argues that most women, like the poor, are "so situated as to have no wills of their own," being dependent on their husbands for their livelihood.[63]

There is evidence that women's "acquired discretion" – their knowledge of political affairs – was then, and continues to be now, less than that of men. "Women Know Less about Politics than Men Worldwide" is the title of an article summarizing a 2013 survey. It is also true that women are generally less capable of "the hardy enterprises of war." One study, summarizing the consensus of recent research, found that men on average have "60% more total lean muscle mass than women..., 80% greater arm muscle mass and... 90% greater upper-body strength.... The average man is stronger than 99.9% of women." And married women continue to be largely "dependent on their husbands for their livelihood."[64]

---

[61] Aristotle, *Politics*, trans. Carnes Lord (Chicago: University of Chicago Press, 1984), bk. 4, ch. 9; Keyssar, *Right to Vote*, ch. 2.

[62] Adams to Sullivan, May 26, 1776, in *Works of John Adams*, 9:375–6.

[63] *Essex Result*, 497.

[64] Michael X. Delli Carpini and Scott Keeter, *What Americans Know about Politics and Why It Matters* (New Haven: Yale University Press, 1996), 183; "Women Know Less about Politics than Men Worldwide," *The Guardian*, July 11, 2013, www.theguardian .com (in a survey by the Economic and Social Research Council, women in ten countries know much less than men about national and international politics); Kingsley Browne, *Co-Ed Combat: The New Evidence that Women Shouldn't Fight the Nation's Wars* (New York: Sentinel, 2007), 19–20, 65, 209 (much lower military training standards for women); David A. Puts, "Beauty and the Beast: Mechanisms of Sexual Selection in

Nevertheless, few today would find these or any other arguments sufficient to reject voting rights for women. Recent research, summed up in books by David Geary and Bobbi Low, supports Adams's opinion about sex differences, but neither of these psychologists would endorse Adams's view of voting rights.[65]

Even from the founders' own point of view, denial of suffrage to half of the adult population would be compatible with human equality only if male voters could generally be counted on to look out for women's best interests. In other words, the founders' implicit assumption is that men and women, on average, have the same basic interests with regard to government policy. In fact, both sexes seem to have thought that women were sufficiently represented by the votes of their husbands, brothers, fathers, and sons, whom they loved and who loved them. The reasons for this belief are given in the discussion of the rights and duties of husbands and wives at the end of Chapter 10. If women had thought of themselves as unfree or oppressed because of the absence of voting rights, they would not have equated the American Revolution with the cause of liberty so enthusiastically – as they did.[66]

However, the founders' political theory – as they understood it – neither requires nor prohibits female suffrage, as we see in the case of New Jersey. Without anyone paying much attention, that state went against the grain by giving "inhabitants" the vote in its 1776 Constitution. Kruman argues that this inclusion of women was likely deliberate. Women voted in that state until 1807, when the Jeffersonian party took the right away because female voters were giving Federalists an electoral advantage. Apparently it was easier for Federalist women, who tended to live in the towns and not on farms, to get to the polling places, which were closer to their homes. Six decades later, when women again began to be

---

Humans," *Evolution and Human Behavior* 31 (2010): 161 (male versus female body strength); "Percentages of Household Income Earned by Married Men and by Married Women," June 5, 2016, Audacious Epigone, http://anepigone.blogspot.com (in the General Social Survey, between 2008 and 2014, married men earned 65 percent and women 35 percent of household income). I thank Derek Clopton for researching this at my request.

[65] David C. Geary, *Male, Female: The Evolution of Human Sex Differences*, 2nd ed. (Washington: American Psychological Association, 2010); Bobbi S. Low, *Why Sex Matters: A Darwinian Look at Human Behavior*, 2nd ed. (Princeton: Princeton University Press, 2015). See also Stephen Rhoads, *Taking Sex Differences Seriously* (New York: Encounter Books, 2005).

[66] Wood, *Creation*, 178–9 (women were thought to be virtually represented by those elected by men); Mary Beth Norton, *Liberty's Daughters: The Revolutionary Experience of American Women, 1750–1800* (Ithaca, NY: Cornell University Press, 1980), ch. 6.

granted the right to vote – in 1869 Wyoming – nothing in the text of the Constitution, or in its political theory, had to be changed.[67]

The Priority of Protection over Consent

The two criteria of just government – consent and security of natural rights – are not necessarily in harmony. What happens if the majority consents to policies that betray the rights of the minority? This is the problem of majority faction discussed in *Federalist* 10 and 51. Jefferson addresses the problem in his First Inaugural, where he affirms "this sacred principle, that though the will of the majority is in all cases to prevail, that will, to be rightful, must be reasonable; that the minority possess their equal rights, which equal laws must protect, and to violate would be oppression."[68] The founders never stopped thinking about ways to make it more likely, in Madison's phrase, that "the reason of the public" – and not their "passions" – would "control and regulate the government."[69] One such device is representation itself, which, unlike a democracy in which the people rule in person, filters public opinion through elections that can be expected to "refine and enlarge the public view," as Madison puts it. He and others expected that elected officials will be more likely than the people themselves to understand what laws will best secure the people's rights. Another device is a bill of rights that would restrain government. In *The Federalist*, governmental structure is a major theme, justified in part by this same concern. Properly designed offices, modes of election and appointment, and other institutional constraints to be discussed in the next chapter were meant to refute the claim that "republican government ... [is] inconsistent with the order of society."[70] The founders' laws regarding property and citizen virtue – to be discussed in Parts II and III of this book – were partly intended to prevent or mitigate injustices supported by popular majorities.

The fundamental difficulty with any political order resting on consent is that although institutional devices and good laws can help, the wishes of the sovereign people will eventually prevail. In some circumstances, it may prove impossible to reconcile majority rule with protection of rights. Since the purpose of government is "to secure these rights," consent

[67] Kruman, *Between Authority and Liberty*, 105–6; West, *Vindicating*, 75–7.
[68] Jefferson, First Inaugural Address, in *Writings*, 494.
[69] Madison, *Federalist* 49, p. 314.
[70] These themes are discussed throughout *The Federalist*, e.g., in 9, 10, 35, 51, 62, and 72.

must then be sacrificed to security. Protection of life and property comes first. The founders' attachment to democracy was therefore conditional, not absolute. As Jaffa says, consent in the founding must be "just or enlightened consent" in order to be legitimate.[71] Accordingly, in 1787 Madison observed that "if the state of Rhode Island were separated from the Confederacy and left to itself, the insecurity of rights under the popular form of government within such narrow limits would be displayed by such reiterated oppressions of factious majorities that some power altogether independent of the people would soon be called for."[72] Americans of the founding period frequently spoke of "the genius of the people of America,"[73] by which they meant their intelligence and enlightenment, their moral restraint, and their spirited republican character. This "genius," the founders knew, was not shared by all peoples. In some times and places, a despotism to secure life and property may be the best option available. Madison hints that such might be the fate of Rhode Island. Gouverneur Morris, the American ambassador to France during the French Revolution, saw clearly that the success of the American Revolution, and the failure of the French, could be explained by the differences in the characters of the two peoples.[74]

This possible need to turn away from consent would obviously be a diminution of liberty, a falling short of what is fully consistent with natural rights. In the recorded history of the world, republican government has rarely been successful, and the founders knew it. They did their best to establish a popular government that would act rightfully and reasonably as much as possible. The policies and laws needed by such a government are the theme of the next chapter.

---

[71] Jaffa, *How to Think*, 115.

[72] Madison, *Federalist* 51, p. 293.   [73] Ibid., No. 39, p. 208.

[74] Gouverneur Morris, *A Diary of the French Revolution*, ed. Beatrix C. Davenport (Boston: Houghton Mifflin, 1939), 1:2, 61, 136, 266; 2:283, 333–4, 387, 452, 581, quoted and discussed in West, *Vindicating*, 163–5. See also Hamilton's low opinion (in ch. 3 of the present study) regarding the prospects of liberty in Haiti.

7

Natural Rights and Public Policy

The last chapter showed that consent of the governed is the necessary foundation for a government constructed in accord with the natural equality of mankind. That is the first criterion of just government in the Declaration of Independence. The second is explained by the town of Lexington, Massachusetts: "in emerging from a state of nature into a state of well-regulated society, mankind gave up some of their natural rights in order that others of greater importance to their well-being, safety, and happiness, both as societies and individuals, might be the better enjoyed, secured, and defended."[1] Contrary to the views of James Ceaser, Barry Shain, and Pauline Maier discussed earlier, the state of nature provides guidelines for government in both of these two ways. The second way specifies the purpose of government – securing and defending natural rights – which is the theme of this chapter.

Securing rights may be said to be the sole purpose of government. At least that is the constant refrain in the fundamental documents. Vermont's Constitution is typical: government is instituted "for the security and protection of the community as such, and to enable the individuals who compose it, to enjoy their natural rights, and the other blessings which the Author of existence has bestowed upon man." Besides Vermont, eight other states explicitly state or clearly imply in fundamental documents that government's purpose is to secure the natural rights of citizens.[2]

---

[1] Return of Lexington, MA, June 1778, in Alice M. Baldwin, *The New England Clergy and the American Revolution* (1928; repr. New York: Frederick Ungar, 1958).

[2] Preambles of PA, 1776; NY, 1777; MA, 1780; Constitutions of VA, 1776, art. 1; NH, 1784; DE, 1792, Preamble; NC and RI, Declarations of Rights published by Ratifying Conventions, in *Documents Illustrative of the Formation of the Union of the American*

Scholars are well aware that securing rights is the purpose of government, so it is surprising how little attention has been given to the subject. One example: in an encyclopedia on the Revolution, its 90 articles include "Liberty," "Equality," "Consent," "Property," and "Rights," but none on how government secures rights.[3]

Natural Rights: Alienable and Inalienable

Before we turn to the question of policy, we must consider how it can make sense to say that government protects life, liberty, and property while threatening punishments – depriving us of life, liberty, or property – when we disobey its commands. Can government really "secure our rights" if we have to give up some of the liberty we enjoy in the state of nature? Can this be justified? And were the founders even consistent on this subject? The Declaration of Independence and several states claim that natural rights are "inalienable" (or some equivalent term, such as "indefeasible").[4] Conservative public intellectual Robert Bork therefore ridicules the founders for their supposed inconsistency: "The 'inalienable Rights' of the Declaration turned out, of course, frequently to be alienable. The Fifth Amendment to the Constitution, for example, explicitly assumes that a criminal may be punished by depriving him of life or liberty, which certainly tends to interfere with his pursuit of happiness."[5] Bork's criticism was anticipated over two centuries earlier, when a British critic of the Declaration triumphantly pointed out, "Every law is an abridgement of man's liberty."[6] But Bork and the anonymous critic are incorrect when they accuse the founders of inconsistency. Liberty is in one sense inalienable, and in another sense alienable.[7]

States, ed. Charles C. Tansill (Washington: Government Printing Office, 1927), 1044 (NC, August 1, 1788), 1052 (RI, May 29, 1790).

3   Jack P. Greene and J. R. Pole, ed., *A Companion to the American Revolution* (Malden, MA: Blackwell, 2000).

4   E.g., Bill of Rights of VA, art. 1; PA, art. 1; MA, art. 1.

5   Robert Bork, *Slouching towards Gomorrah: Modern Liberalism and American Decline* (New York: Regan Books, Harper Collins, 1996), 57.

6   "Thoughts on the Late Declaration," *Gentleman's Magazine*, 1776, quoted in John Phillip Reid, *The Concept of Liberty in the Age of the American Revolution* (Chicago: University of Chicago Press, 1988), 31.

7   Philip A. Hamburger, "Natural Rights, Natural Law, and American Constitutions," *Yale Law Journal* 102 (Jan. 1993): 956–8; Hamburger, "Equality and Diversity: The Eighteenth-Century Debate about Equal Protection and Equal Civil Rights," *Supreme Court Review* (1992): 302–13 (in both, there is a helpful discussion of alienable and inalienable).

According to an official statement of the Constitutional Convention of 1787, "Individuals entering into society must give up a share of liberty to preserve the rest."[8] Alienation of some rights is the price paid to escape the violence of the state of nature. The author of the Declaration of Independence – in which the fundamental rights are "inalienable" – writes in another place, "Our rulers can have authority over such natural rights only as we have submitted to them."[9] So even Jefferson admits that we submit or alienate some of our rights. Yet this partial alienation is always conditional, as the *Essex Result* explains: "the equivalent every man receives, as a consideration for the rights he has surrendered, ... consists principally in the security of his person and property.... [F]or if the equivalent is taken back, those natural rights which were parted with to purchase it, return to the original proprietor." We retain control over the government to which we alienate some of our rights by "reserving a control over the supreme power, or a right to resume in certain cases." The "control" is exercised through periodic elections, and the "right to resume" is the right to revolution. In the latter case, all natural rights "return to the original proprietor," the individual.[10] Shain argues that the alienability of some natural rights means that the Declaration has "corporate rather than individualistic intentions" and therefore that Lincoln's "expansive view of the inalienable individual rights of all human beings" was a "noble but creative act of mythmaking at Gettysburg."[11] In fact, the founders rejected Shain's view, as Boston makes explicit: "the right to freedom being the gift of God Almighty, it is not in the power of man to alienate this gift and voluntarily become a slave."[12] Thus natural rights are from one point of view partly alienable and from another wholly inalienable.

[8] Letter from the Convention to the President of Congress, September 17, 1787, in *The Founders' Constitution*, ed. Philip B. Kurland and Ralph Lerner (Chicago: University of Chicago Press, 1987), 1:195.

[9] Thomas Jefferson, *Notes on the State of Virginia*, 1787, in *Writings*, ed. Merrill D. Peterson (New York: Library of America, 1984), 285.

[10] *Essex Result*, 1778, in *American Political Writing during the Founding Era*, ed. Charles S. Hyneman and Donald S. Lutz (Indianapolis: Liberty Press, 1983), 1:489.

[11] Barry A. Shain, "Rights Natural and Civil in the Declaration of Independence," in *The Nature of Rights at the American Founding and Beyond*, ed. Shain (Charlottesville: University of Virginia Press, 2007), 144. Craig Yirush, *Settlers, Liberty, and Empire: The Roots of Early American Political Theory, 1675–1775* (New York: Cambridge University Press, 2011), 265 (responding to Shain: "the rights individuals enjoy in civil society" are in fact "derived from" "natural rights").

[12] Boston, Rights of the Colonists, 1772, in *Writings of Samuel Adams*, ed. Harry A. Cushing (1904; repr. New York: Octagon, 1968), 2:351.

Not all natural rights can be alienated even conditionally. The New Hampshire Bill of Rights states: "When men enter into a state of society, they surrender up some of their natural rights to that society, in order to insure the protection of others.... Among the natural rights, some are in their very nature inalienable, because no equivalent can be given or received for them. Of this kind are the rights of conscience."[13] Jefferson too writes, in the passage already quoted in part, "But our rulers can have authority over such natural rights only as we have submitted to them. The rights of conscience we never submitted, we could not submit."[14] As for freedom of speech and press, Elisha Williams remarks in a 1744 treatise: "The members of a civil state or society do retain their natural liberty in all such cases as have no relation to the ends of such a society. In a state of nature men had a right to read Milton or Locke for their instruction or amusement: and why they do not retain this liberty under a government that is instituted for the preservation of their persons and properties, is inconceivable."[15] For this reason Madison considered freedom of speech to be one of the "natural rights retained."[16]

Insufficiency of Limits on Government to Secure Rights

Let us return to our subject: how government secures the "natural rights retained." When the topic of securing rights is discussed at all, scholars often frame their answer in terms of limits on government. Take the case of the rights of conscience. It is typically assumed that government secures the free exercise of religion by holding itself back: by refraining from persecution, from forcibly imposing a religious orthodoxy on society. But that is only one side of the picture. Governmental inaction can also lead to violations of religious liberty. In 2014 an Anglican bishop in Pakistan reported, "When a Christian is accused of blasphemy, the people of a neighborhood gather to punish the culprit, burning him alive or lynching him. The police and the government have never punished such

---

[13] NH Bill of Rights, 1784, art. 3–4. Similar statements appear in many other documents, e.g., Instructions from the town of Stoughton to its delegates, 1779, in *Massachusetts, Colony to Commonwealth*, ed. Robert P. Taylor (Chapel Hill: University of North Carolina Press, 1961), 120.

[14] Jefferson, *Notes on Virginia*, 285.

[15] Elisha Williams, *The Essential Rights and Liberties of Protestants*, 1744, in *Political Sermons of the American Founding Era, 1730–1805*, ed. Ellis Sandoz (Indianapolis: Liberty Fund, 1990), 61.

[16] James Madison, Notes for Speech in Congress, 1789, in *The Bill of Rights: A Documentary History*, ed. Bernard Schwartz et al. (New York: Chelsea House, 1971), 2:1042.

acts."[17] In cases like this, the problem is not government persecution but rather government passivity in the face of private anti-religious violence.

It is certainly true that a government which secures the rights of its citizens must restrain itself from violating those rights. Jack Rakove correctly refers to "the belief that separation of powers was essential to the protection of rights."[18] To this extent the limited-government approach, discussed later in this chapter, is right. The question remains: what rules must government lay down to secure rights?

An example of the view that security of rights comes from limitations on government is Robert Rutland's "How the Constitution Protects Our Rights."[19] His title promises an answer to our question. Disappointingly, however, the essay equates "protecting our rights" with a federal Bill of Rights enforced by the judiciary – as if government secures rights solely by having judges forbid government actions opposed to the Bill of Rights. In the book in which Rutland's essay appears – *How Does the Constitution Secure Rights?* – none of the authors discusses the question asked in the book's title in terms of the laws needed to secure rights, at least not for more than a few sentences. Once again, the assumption throughout tends to be that government protects rights by limiting itself.[20]

Many political scientists rely heavily on *The Federalist* when they teach the political theory of the founding. There is nothing wrong with that, as long as students understand two important caveats: first, that much of this document focuses on the question of government structure as opposed to government policy, and second, that its scope is limited to the federal government. The role of state governments is mentioned, but only in passing. Its discussion of securing rights in domestic politics tends to emphasize institutional means of preventing government from misbehaving. *Federalist* 10 argues that in a large republic, with its "greater variety of parties and interests, you make it less probable that a majority of the

---

[17] "The Anglican Bishop of Karachi: 'Christians in Danger, Police and Judiciary in Lethargy,'" February 13, 2014, Agenzia Fides: Information Service of the Pontifical Mission Societies, www.fides.org.

[18] Jack N. Rakove, *Original Meanings: Politics and Ideas in the Making of the Constitution* (New York: Vintage Books, 1996), 19.

[19] Robert A. Rutland, "How the Constitution Protects Our Rights," in *How Does the Constitution Secure Rights?* ed. Robert A. Goldwin and William A. Schambra (Washington: AEI Press, 1985).

[20] Some of my own earlier publications also lack an adequate discussion of this topic, e.g., Thomas G. West, "The Political Theory of the Declaration of Independence," in *The American Founding and the Social Compact*, ed. Ronald J. Pestritto and Thomas G. West (Lanham, MD: Lexington Books, 2003), 95–145.

whole will have a common motive to invade the rights of other citizens."
Federalist 51 shows that government is more likely to "control itself"
through a "dependence on the people" by means of periodic elections,
together with an effective separation of powers in a "federal system"
consisting of both state and national governments. Other papers show
how the various ways the offices are constructed will likely lead to higher
quality government officials than had been customary under the Articles
of Confederation.[21]

Securing rights by institutional arrangements that make government
misconduct less likely is of course essential. But this is only part of
the solution, and not even the first part. As *Federalist* 51 says, "you
must *first* enable the government to control the governed; and in
the next place, oblige it to control itself."[22] In what ways should
government "control the governed" so as to prevent people from
violating each other's rights? Our answer can be found in the founders'
statements on foreign and domestic policy in important state and federal
documents.

Few if any scholars, or sources in the founding itself, put together,
simply and coherently, the main laws and policies needed to secure the
natural rights of citizens. I will provide it here. In both foreign and domestic affairs, government's purpose is to protect people against "the violence
of the stronger" – the condition, as Madison says, of the state of nature.
Government in America today has an unlimited scope, ranging from
global climate management to methods of child rearing to detailed mandates for employers regarding hiring and promotion. The founders had
a much more limited understanding of the end of government: protection. This sole purpose is supposed to inform everything that government
does. In an early legal treatise, Zephaniah Swift writes: it is "a maxim
in legislation, that the rule to be adopted in enacting laws must be to
restrain no acts but those which tend to the injury of individuals and
the dissolution of government. Every law that deviates from this rule is
arbitrary and unjust, and reduces the people to political slavery."[23] Or,
as Thomas Reese asserts: "the security of life, liberty, and property is

---

[21] *Federalist* 10, p. 78; No. 51, pp. 319–20; Nos. 62–63, 68, and 72, in Alexander Hamilton, Madison, and John Jay, *The Federalist Papers*, ed. Clinton Rossiter (New York:
Signet Classics, 2003).

[22] *Federalist* 51, p. 319 (my emphasis).

[23] Ibid., 320; Zephaniah Swift, *A System of the Laws of the State of Connecticut* (Windham,
CT: John Byrne, 1795), 13.

the precise and specific end of the social compact."[24] Potential or actual violence from foreign nations is the primary concern of foreign policy, while domestic policy protects the people against injuries committed by their fellow citizens.

Foreign Policy: Protection against Injuries from Abroad

Protection from foreign enemies is government's most urgent task. There are two main principles that guide government in this task, both stated at the beginning of the Declaration of Independence. One is the familiar formulation that government must "secure these rights." The second is the nonintervention principle: all nations have a right to "the separate and equal station to which the laws of nature and of nature's God entitle them." Taking these principles together, the Declaration is saying that government's main job in foreign policy is to defend the nation while refraining from interference in other nations.

Protection of the political community is sometimes described as a precondition to securing individual rights, as in the Preamble to the Massachusetts Constitution: "The end of ... government is to secure the existence of the body politic; to protect it; and to furnish the individuals who compose it, with the power of enjoying ... their natural rights, and the blessings of life." The "existence of the body politic" – its territorial integrity and safety – comes first, because the people cannot "enjoy ... their natural rights" if the society is invaded by foreigners. There is no such thing as a nation without borders. Armed forces therefore must protect the border and deter or defeat foreign intrusion, whether violent or nonviolent. In the Massachusetts Constitution, the purpose of war is vividly described: "to kill, slay, and destroy, if necessary, and conquer, ... such person and persons as shall, at any time hereafter, in a hostile manner, attempt or enterprise the destruction, invasion, detriment, or annoyance of this Commonwealth." In *Federalist* 41, the purpose of the foreign policy provisions of the Constitution is simply "security against foreign danger," which is "one of the primitive objects of civil society."[25] In the Preamble of the U.S. Constitution, "the common defense" – of the lives and liberties of all Americans – is one of the purposes of the union.

---

[24] Thomas Reese, *An Essay on the Influence of Religion in Civil Society* (Charleston: Markland & M'Iver, 1788), 5–6.

[25] MA Constitution, pt. 2, ch. 2, §1, art. 7 (duties of the governor regarding war); Madison, *Federalist* 41, p. 252.

Under the principles of the social compact, only one government can be responsible for foreign as well as all other policies, and that is the one consented to by the people. Today, that view is called *unilateralism*. Some believe foreign policy should not be conducted unilaterally but multilaterally, in conjunction with other nations in organizations like the United Nations and NATO. For the founders, that approach means giving up national sovereignty. The founders were glad to form alliances when they were needed for national defense, such as the French alliance that enabled them to establish independence during the Revolutionary War, or the alliance with Sicily during the First Barbary War. However, all agreed with Washington that the "great rule of conduct for us in regard to foreign nations is...to have with them as little *political* connection as possible.... [W]e may safely trust to temporary alliances for extraordinary emergencies."[26]

As I said earlier, the fundamental duty of government – to protect its citizens against external attacks – corresponds to a parallel duty to refrain from attacking or interfering with other nations unless it is necessary for survival. Because every nation has a right to a "separate and equal station," government must not make war against other nations for any reason except defense of the body politic – the protection of the life, liberty, and property of its own citizens. For the same reason that no individual may rule another without his or her consent – namely, because everyone has a natural right to liberty – so also no nation may rule another without its consent. Imperialistic acquisition of territory for the sake of glory or greed is therefore a violation of the laws of nature.[27] The nonintervention requirement even applies when other nations are governed undemocratically, mistreating their own citizens, or making war on their neighbors. America's stance toward all nations is the same: because each has a right to a "separate and equal station," America will treat them all, in the Declaration's words, as "enemies in war, in peace friends." Its

---

[26] George Washington, Farewell Address, 1796, in *Founders' Constitution*, 1:685.

[27] There are a few studies that discuss the relation between the founders' principles and their foreign policy, but even these fail to make clear that the unifying thread was security of the people's natural rights and respect for the equal natural rights of other nations. See, e.g., Robert W. Smith, *Keeping the Republic: Ideology and Early American Diplomacy* (DeKalb: Northern Illinois Press, 2004); David C. Hendrickson, *Peace Pact: The Lost World of the American Founding* (Lawrence: University Press of Kansas, 2003). Patrick J. Garrity, in *In Search of Monsters to Destroy? American Foreign Policy and Regime Change, 1776–1900* (Fairfax, VA: National Institute Press, 2012), 18–27, is much better than most, although he underemphasizes the specific and limited primary task of foreign policy that flows from the terms of the social compact: national defense.

duty to other nations is to leave them alone or, in any commercial or other dealings, to honor private and public contracts (such as treaties). Madison acknowledges these limited moral obligations between nations in *Federalist* 43: "the claims of justice, both on one side and on the other, must be fulfilled; the rights of humanity must in all cases be duly and mutually respected."[28] There is a second reason that a nation has an obligation to noninterference. That is the nature of the social compact, which limits government's duty to preserving the natural rights of its own citizens. Interference in other nations' affairs to protect foreigners will involve an expenditure of taxpayer money and may lead to the deaths of citizens. Government may intrude on the alienable natural rights of its citizens – taking their money or endangering their lives – only to the extent needed to protect them.

Hamilton showed the practical meaning of this approach when he criticized the French Revolutionary government's policy of offering "fraternity and assistance to every people who wish to recover their liberty." Hamilton called this "little short of a declaration of war against all nations having princes and privileged classes, . . . repugnant to the general rights of nations [and] to the true principles of liberty." Jefferson was far more sympathetic to the French, yet he too denounced them for "endeavoring to force liberty on their neighbors in their own form."[29] Secretary of State John Quincy Adams memorably echoed the Declaration when he said in 1821 that America "goes not abroad in search of monsters to destroy." Two years later, President James Monroe expanded on this idea in his Monroe Doctrine speech: our policy toward Europe is "not to interfere in the internal concerns of any of its powers; to consider the government de facto as the legitimate government for us; to cultivate friendly relations with it."[30] In other words, as long as European nations do not attack or threaten our near abroad by increasing their interference in the Western Hemisphere, we will leave them alone.

By 1893, Progressive-era political scientists such as John Burgess were complaining that Americans "are far too much inclined to regard" the

---

[28] Madison, *Federalist* 43, pp. 276–7.

[29] Hamilton, Pacificus No. 2, July 1793, in Founders Online, National Archives, http://founders.archives.gov; Jefferson to Thomas Randolph, June 24, 1793, ibid.

[30] James Monroe, Seventh Annual Message, December 2, 1823, millercenter.org; John Quincy Adams, An Address, July 4, 1821, http://teachingamericanhistory.org. On the founders' foreign policy generally, see Washington, Farewell Address, in *Founders' Constitution*, 1:681–5; George C. Herring, *From Colony to Superpower: U.S. Foreign Relations since 1776* (New York: Oxford University Press, 2008), ch. 1–3.

policy of carrying "the political civilization of the modern world into those parts of the world inhabited by unpolitical and barbaric races as unwarrantable interference in the affairs of other states." Burgess advocated, and America soon adopted, a "colonial policy" that would reverse the founders' orientation. Although President George W. Bush did not explicitly advocate colonialism, he did proclaim that America's policy is "to seek and support the growth of democratic movements and institutions in every nation..., with the ultimate goal of ending tyranny in our world." Bush's democratization agenda led to American "proconsuls" being sent to govern places like Iraq. A few years later, the Obama administration endorsed the same approach, promoting the overthrow of governments in Libya and Syria.[31]

The most important partial exception to the nonintervention principle was American expansion into the territories that later became parts of the United States. To be sure, that expansion was due in part to unjustifiable territorial greed or even a desire for the expansion of slavery. Yet considerations of national defense – security of Americans' natural rights – were never absent in the acquisition of Louisiana, Florida, Oregon, Texas, California, and northern Mexico. The same considerations were also at work in American dealings with Indian tribes. Here was a clash of natural rights: the Indians' right to be left alone versus the Americans' right to safety. The moral judgment in question here would include taking into account the usual Indian insistence on retaining their own often violent way of life and their unwillingness to adopt American standards of citizenship, grounded in natural rights. There was also a question of whether any people have a natural right to occupy a large expanse of territory excluding all others, if there is no clear allocation of property ownership and a regular system of agriculture. Certainly many Americans opposed the Mexican War on moral grounds, and many believed that America's treatment of the Indians was profoundly unjust.[32] The

---

[31] John W. Burgess, *Political Science and Comparative Constitutional Law* (Boston: Ginn & Co., 1893), 1:45; George W. Bush, Second Inaugural Address, 2005, National Public Radio, www.npr.org; Carnes Lord, *Proconsuls: Delegated Political-Military Leadership from Rome to America Today* (New York: Cambridge University Press, 2012), ch. 9–10; Hillary Clinton, Remarks on the Human Rights Agenda for the 21st Century, December 14, 2009, www.state.gov.

[32] The best treatment of the mixed motives behind America's pre-Civil War territorial expansion is Harry V. Jaffa, *Crisis of the House Divided: An Interpretation of the Lincoln-Douglas Debates* (1959; repr. Chicago: University of Chicago Press, 1999), ch. 4 ("Manifest Destiny"). See also Walter A. McDougall, *Promised Land, Crusader State: The American Encounter with the World since 1776* (Boston: Houghton Mifflin, 1997),

question of American motives regarding expansion and Indians does not affect my explanation of the founders' view of the moral basis of foreign policy. The question of whether they always lived up to their own standards is not of concern here. It is also important to add that Americans never had any idea of ruling these territories despotically. They eventually became self-governing states on a legal par with the other states. Had these mostly empty territories been heavily populated with people who would have had difficulties assimilating to the Anglo-American majority, it is doubtful that these acquisitions would have been pursued.

Protecting citizens from foreign violence requires more than deterring attacks on American soil and paying attention to great-power involvement in nearby territory and nations. It also includes protecting citizens' lives and property on the high seas. The war against the Barbary pirates, who were preying on American commerce in the Mediterranean, is an early example. The founders were not isolationists in the sense of avoiding foreign policy action outside the homeland. But the purpose of foreign policy was always the defense of the lives and property of Americans, whether at home or abroad. This requires maximum freedom of action in America's near abroad – Hamilton anticipates the Monroe Doctrine in *Federalist* 11 – and the protection of Americans engaged in legitimate activities far from home.[33]

Jefferson and Hamilton quarreled passionately in the 1790s over American treaties with Britain and France, but both sides agreed on the basic principles. Historians Stanley Elkins and Eric McKitrick write, "[There] appeared to be two violently conflicting versions of foreign policy as advocated by [Hamilton and Jefferson] . . . , the one partial to England, the other to France. . . . Actually these divisions, bitter though they may have been, were hardly as wide as they seemed. . . . Jefferson was no more

ch. 4; John Lewis Gaddis, *Surprise, Security, and the American Experience* (Cambridge: Harvard University Press, 2004), 15–19; Herring, *From Colony*, ch. 3-5; Jeremy Rabkin, "American Founding Principles and American Foreign Policy," in *Modern America and the Legacy of the Founding*, ed. Ronald J. Pestritto and Thomas G. West (Lanham, MD: Lexington, 2007), 313–15. There is an even-handed treatment of Indian policy in Ralph Lerner, *The Thinking Revolutionary: Principle and Practice in the New Republic* (Ithaca: Cornell University Press, 1987), ch. 4–5; but many scholars would disagree, e.g., Gordon S. Wood, *Empire of Liberty: A History of the Early Republic, 1789–1815* (New York: Oxford University Press, 2009), 4, 9. On the Indians and land rights, see Rev. Mr. [John] Bulkley, Preface to Roger Wolcott, *Poetical Meditations, Being the Improvement of Some Warant Hours* (New London, CT: T. Green, 1725), xv-xxx (using Locke to argue that Indians, who live in a state of nature, have no natural right to exclusive use of uncultivated land).

[33] Hamilton, *Federalist* 11, pp. 85–6.

prepared than Hamilton to be bound by them [the French treaties] in any way that might endanger the external security of the United States."[34] Walter LaFeber confirms this judgment: "the Jeffersonian belief in isolationism, in maximum freedom of action, has [long] been at the center of the nation's debate over foreign affairs... [in] the Washington administration's stance in the 1790's toward the French Revolution [and in] Jefferson's non-entangling alliances pledge of his first Inaugural."[35] LaFeber's statement is unobjectionable, except for the pejorative term "isolationism."

Although Elkins, McKitrick, and LaFeber describe the founders' consensus accurately enough, neither they nor most other scholars try to explain the connection between the founders' principles, which provided the moral basis of their foreign policy, and the actual policies that they pursued. An exception is John Grant, whose study of William Howard Taft accurately contrasts the natural rights principles animating the founders' foreign policies with the quite different principles of that Progressive president.[36]

Trade policy – regulation of commerce with other nations – was also one of the founders' foreign policy tools. Although Congress promised Americans in 1778 "a free commerce with every part of the earth" at the conclusion of the war, this goal was always qualified by considerations of America's prosperity and national defense. The first substantive law passed under the new federal Constitution was the 1789 Tariff Act, which states that taxes on imports are "necessary for the support of government, for the discharge of the debts of the United States, and the encouragement and protection of manufactures." Prosperity for Americans and the economic independence required for national defense were both supported

---

[34] Stanley Elkins and Eric McKitrick, *The Age of Federalism* (New York: Oxford University Press, 1993), 336.

[35] Walter LaFeber, "Jefferson and an American Foreign Policy," in *Jeffersonian Legacies*, ed. Peter S. Onuf (Charlottesville: University Press of Virginia, 1993), 375; Carson Holloway, *Hamilton versus Jefferson in the Washington Administration: Completing the Founding or Betraying the Founding?* (New York: Cambridge University Press, 2015), 332 ("both [Hamilton and Jefferson] were committed to the same fundamental principles").

[36] John W. Grant, "William Howard Taft on America and the Philippines: Equality, Natural Rights, and Imperialism," in *Toward an American Conservatism: Constitutional Conservatism during the Progressive Era*, ed. Joseph Postell and Johnathan O'Neill (New York: Palgrave Macmillan, 2013), 121–9. Also useful are Rabkin, "American Founding Principles," 310–24; Nathan Tarcov, "Principle and Prudence in Foreign Policy: The Founders' Perspective," *The Public Interest* 76 (1984): 45–60; McDougall, *Promised Land, Crusader State.*

by domestic manufactures, to be aided by a protective tariff. From 1807 to 1809, Congress outlawed all exports to retaliate against British and French acts of war against American shipping.[37]

Immigration and naturalization policy are directly related to national defense. One of the complaints of the Declaration of Independence is that Britain "has endeavored to prevent the population of these states; for that purpose obstructing the laws for naturalization of foreigners." A thinly populated nation of three million needed immigrants to produce enough future soldiers and wealth to defend itself. But the founders also thought it important to limit immigration if necessary, also for the defense of liberty. Jefferson explains that immigrants "will bring with them the principles of the governments they leave, imbibed in their early youth," and consequently "will infuse into [our legislation] their spirit, warp and bias its direction."[38] Immigrants of the wrong sort, or in numbers too great to assimilate easily, would endanger the rights of Americans. Washington, Adams, Hamilton, and other founders agreed.[39]

Although Rogers Smith argues that the political theory of natural rights obliges a nation to open its borders to people of every race and nation, the founders disagreed. Accordingly, both naturalization and immigration have been restricted from the start, although "throughout the first two thirds of the nineteenth century, the seaboard states, rather than the federal government, exercised primary authority over the landing of immigrants."[40] Walter Lippmann accurately describes the ethnic and non-imperial character of the nation the founders were building: "Americans had always regarded it as self-evident that any territory they acquired

---

[37] Address of Congress, May 8, 1778, in *Journals of the Continental Congress, 1774–1789*, ed. Worthington C. Ford (Washington: Government Printing Office, 1904–37), 11:481; An Act for Laying a Duty on Goods, July 4, 1789, in *Public Statutes at Large*, ed. Richard Peters (Boston: Little and Brown, 1845), 1:24. See also Patrick J. Garrity, "Foreign Policy and *The Federalist*," in *Saving the Revolution: The Federalist Papers and the American Founding*, ed. Charles R. Kesler (New York: Free Press, 1987), 92 ("trade as the preferred tool of American diplomacy"); Garrity, *In Search*, 22-7. In contrast, David C. Hendrickson, *Peace Pact: The Lost World of the American Founding* (Lawrence: University Press of Kansas, 2003), 164–6, argues that the founders were unreservedly committed to free trade with all nations. That is only partly correct.

[38] Jefferson, *Notes on the State of Virginia*, 1787, Query 8, in *Writings*, 211.

[39] Thomas G. West, *Vindicating the Founders: Race, Sex, Class, and Justice in the Origins of America* (Lanham, MD: Rowman & Littlefield, 1997), 149–73.

[40] Rogers M. Smith, *Civic Ideals: Conflicting Visions of Citizenship in U.S. History* (New Haven: Yale University Press, 1997), 2; Matthew J. Lindsay, "Immigration as Invasion: Sovereignty, Security, and the Origins of the Federal Immigration Power," *Harvard Civil Rights-Civil Liberties Law Review* 45, No. 1 (2010): 13.

would be organized into states and would be admitted into the Union, and that the inhabitants – who would be predominantly of European stock – would then be assimilated into equal American citizenship."[41]

Domestic Policy: Protection against Injuries from Fellow Citizens

Government's purpose is "to secure these rights," which means, in the phrase quoted at the beginning of the last chapter, to "protect and defend" the people.[42] Today those words are often applied to police departments, but in the founding they refer to the whole of what government is supposed to do.

The founders sometimes used the expression "civil and religious liberty" (Northwest Ordinance) or "civil rights" (Virginia's Act for Religious Freedom) as a summation of the most important legal rights that "protect and defend" people against injuries from their fellow citizens. There are two main categories of civil rights: the indispensable legal rights of all persons, citizens as well as noncitizens, for basic protection of person and property; and the civil rights of citizens, sometimes called privileges and immunities of citizenship. These civil rights of persons and of citizens are sketched in the various bills of rights in the founding, such as the first eight amendments to the federal Constitution and the state bills of rights.

The civil rights belonging to all persons are the minimal legal protection of the basic natural rights. The most important of these is the right to equal protection, i.e., equal enforcement, of criminal and civil laws that protect person and property. In addition to the right to equal protection is a corresponding right, as the Massachusetts Bill of Rights states, to "an impartial interpretation of the laws and administration of justice"[43] so that the guilty may be punished while the innocent are protected. Most importantly, this requires procedural judicial rights when government seeks to deprive someone of life, liberty, or property, such as the right to confront witnesses, to hire legal counsel, to a jury trial in criminal and sometimes also in civil cases, and to immunity from cruel and unusual punishment.

[41] Walter Lippmann, *Isolation and Alliances: An American Speaks to the British* (Boston: Little, Brown, 1952), 18–19.
[42] Brutus, No. 2, *New York Journal*, November 1, 1787, in *The Documentary History of the Ratification of the Constitution*, ed. Merrill Jensen (Madison: State Historical Society of Wisconsin, 1976-), 13:525.
[43] MA Bill of Rights, art. 29.

Besides these rights of all persons, the founders also spoke of the civil rights of citizens. In a 1797 Maryland case, these "privileges and immunities of citizenship" include "any civil right which a man as a member of civil society must enjoy." Foreigners would enjoy the civil rights of persons just mentioned, but not necessarily the "general rights of citizenship." Such citizen rights include, as a later case states, "the right of a citizen of one state to pass through, or to reside in any other state, for purposes of trade, agriculture, professional pursuits, or otherwise; to claim the benefit of the writ of habeas corpus; to institute and maintain actions of any kind in the courts of the state; to take, hold and dispose of property, either real or personal." To this list we can add other civil rights that belong, according to the founders, to "the people," such as the right to keep and bear arms, to freedom from unreasonable searches, and freedom of assembly for political purposes – rights that would not necessarily be available to noncitizens.[44] We still maintain this distinction between civil rights of persons and citizens in the requirement of a "green card" to get a job, as well as the requirement for foreigners to receive permission if they want to come to America and travel here. Noncitizens – nonmembers of the society – do not automatically have a right to travel and to work for a living in America.

To return to the civil rights belonging to everyone: the Massachusetts Bill of Rights makes protection of the laws a civil right: "Each individual of the society has a right to be protected by it in the enjoyment of his life, liberty, and property, according to standing laws." Philip Hamburger rightly comments, "The natural rights context of equal protection is apparent in article ten of the Massachusetts Bill of Rights."[45] Hamburger is referring to the natural rights of life, liberty, and property mentioned there. The right to protection by the laws is repeated in the Bills of Rights of Delaware and Pennsylvania.[46] In the Declaration of Independence, British withdrawal of protection was one of the grievances demonstrating the king's failure "to secure these rights" to his American

---

44 Samuel Chase's opinion, *Campbell v. Morris*, 3 H. & McH. 535, 553–4 (Md. 1797), in *Founders' Constitution*, 4:490; *Corfield v. Coryell*, 6 F. Cas. 546, 551–2 (C.C.E.D. Pa. 1823), in ibid., 4:503; U.S. Constitution, Amendments 1, 2, and 4; *Dred Scott v. Sandford*, 60 U.S. 393, 417 (1857) (if blacks were citizens – which they are not – they would have the "liberty . . . to hold public meetings upon political affairs, and to keep and carry arms wherever they went").

45 Philip A. Hamburger, "Equality and Diversity: The Eighteenth-Century Debate about Equal Protection and Equal Civil Rights," *Supreme Court Review* (1992): 332.

46 Declaration of Rights of DE, 1776, §10; of PA, 1776, §8. of NH, 1792, art. 12.

subjects: "He has abdicated government here, withdrawing his governors, and declaring us out of his protection and waging war against us."

Government provides this protection of the laws in several ways. A crime is defined by James Wilson as "an injury, so atrocious in its nature, or so dangerous in its example, that... it affects... the interest, the peace, the dignity, or the security of the public."[47] Examples are murder, rape, robbery, and assault. Jefferson explains the connection to security of rights in his preface to a proposed revision of Virginia's criminal law: "[Bad men] commit violations on the lives, liberties, and property of others.... [G]overnment would be defective in *its principal purpose* were it not to restrain such criminal acts, by inflicting due punishments on those who perpetrate them."[48] In an early textbook for schools, Noah Webster begins his discussion of the "Principles of Government" with a simple explanation of natural rights and social contract theory: "All mankind are by nature free, and have a right to enjoy life, liberty, and property.... [E]very society must have a government to prevent one man from hurting another, and to punish such as commit crimes.... [I]f one man may do harm without suffering punishment, every man has the same right, and no person can be safe. It is necessary therefore that there should be laws to control every man."[49] It is characteristic of the founders' view that in the list of crimes in Wilson's *Lectures on Law*, all are either "crimes against the rights of individuals" – which rights he traces back to natural rights – or else "against the community," i.e., crimes endangering government's ability to protect its citizens.[50] Deterrence of future crime, not the evil of the original act, was supposed to determine the character and duration of the punishment.[51]

Today, we tend to think of "the police" as the principal arm of law enforcement and of federal courts as the principal protectors of civil rights. But there were no police departments in early America, and the federal judiciary had almost nothing to do with law enforcement. For the

---

[47] James Wilson, *Lectures on Law*, 1791, in *Collected Works of James Wilson*, ed. Kermit L. Hall and Mark David Hall (Indianapolis: Liberty Fund, 2007), 2:1088.

[48] Jefferson, Bill for Proportioning Crimes and Punishments, 1778, in *Founders' Constitution*, 5:374 (my emphasis).

[49] Noah Webster, *The Little Reader's Assistant*, 4th ed. (Northampton, MA: William Butler, 1798), 116–7.

[50] Wilson, *Lectures on Law*, 1:vii.

[51] Jefferson, Bill for Proportioning Crimes, in *Founders' Constitution*, 5:374; Ronald J. Pestritto, *Founding the Criminal Law: Punishment and Political Thought in the Origins of America* (DeKalb: Northern Illinois Press, 2000) (documenting the growing focus in the founding on deterrence rather than retribution based on just deserts).

founders, criminal law enforcement involved all three branches of state government. First, a law is approved by the lawmaking body. Next, a judicial officer typically issues a warrant for the arrest of a suspect; the arrest is done either by a public officer in the executive (such as a sheriff) or by deputized citizens. This is followed by executive-branch indictment and judicial trial (usually by jury). For the guilty, the executive carries out the punishment, whether by fine, imprisonment, or death.[52] Here we see the foundation of the distinct roles of the legislative, judicial, and executive, all of which are necessary for protection of the laws. Criminal law enforcement was mostly undertaken by the states, because they were primarily responsible for protection of rights domestically.

The founders' belief that punishment of intentional injuries to life, liberty, and property is government's single most important domestic policy may be contrasted with the much lower priority of enforcement of such laws in America today, in spite of the huge growth of tax revenues. In Houston, "a report revealed that some 20,000 burglary, theft, assault and hit-and-run cases with workable leads were not investigated in 2013."[53] Texas judges have often punished first-degree murder with probation and no prison time.[54] In 2014, "nearly five years after the discovery of 11,000 abandoned rape evidence kits in a Detroit police warehouse sparked outrage, only about 2,000 of the kits have undergone DNA testing, allowing serial rapists to remain free and in some cases commit more attacks." Memphis, Tennessee, had a "backlog of 12,000 untested rape kits" in 2014.[55] These lapses represent a tacit rejection of the founders' view that government's principal purpose is protection of persons and property.

A second feature of the founders' domestic policy is civil laws that protect people against smaller injuries to person, property, or reputation by allowing the injured party to sue for damages. These would be cases such as car accidents, personal libel, or using property in a way that harms others. The Massachusetts Bill of Rights accordingly provides, "Every subject of the Commonwealth ought to find a certain remedy,

---

[52] Wilson, *Lectures on Law*, 2:1175–1204 (law enforcement at the founding).

[53] James Pinkerton and Mike Morris, "20,000 Criminal Cases Not Investigated in 2013 by Houston Police Department," *Houston Chronicle*, June 2, 2014, www.houstonchronicle.com.

[54] Stefanie Thomas, "Family of Humble Murder Victim Secures Legislative Victory," *The Observer*, Humble, TX, May 25, 2011, www.yourhoustonnews.com.

[55] "Detroit Rape Kit Testing Backlog Lingers," *Detroit Free Press*, April 21, 2014, www.usatoday.com; Bill Dries, "Ongoing Rape Kit Backlog Fallout Expands," *Daily News*, Memphis, TN, April 21, 2014, www.memphisdailynews.com.

by having recourse to the laws, for all injuries or wrongs which he may receive in his person, property, or character."

Third, the civil law of property and contract must establish the terms of property ownership, use, and exchange. Government must also ensure that money is legally defined in a way that makes it a reliable medium of exchange of goods and services. Part III of this book, on property and economics, shows how all of these are necessary for citizens to be protected in their right to possess and acquire property.

Fourth, security of rights requires – at least to some extent – public virtue. Virginia's Bill of Rights states, "no free government, or the blessings of liberty, can be preserved to any people but by a firm adherence to justice, moderation, temperance, frugality, and virtue." This sort of language is found everywhere in the constitutions, laws, and other official documents of the states and in the federal Northwest Ordinance.[56] The conviction that security of natural rights is impossible without public morality led to government support of cultivation of mind and character through religion, education, and other means. Government's involvement with the moral formation of citizens is the theme of Part II of this book.

Fifth, there must be civil laws concerning the family – to be discussed in Chapter 10. Because children are temporarily ruled without their consent, government cannot be indifferent to the circumstances in which this takes place. Therefore, in this unique area, the law suspends its usual presumption that adults can manage their own affairs by voluntary agreements with other adults. Sex generates children, who need adult care after they are born. The founders believed that their married biological parents are most likely to have both the incentive (parental love) and the resources (money and protection) that promote children's well-being. Children's security therefore requires a body of family law, specifying the mutual rights and duties of parents and children.

Sixth, government must make some minimal provision for its poor – those who are really destitute. Although the founders did not provide natural-law reasoning to explain their welfare policies, we can infer it from the basic terms of the social compact. People join political society for greater security of life. For most, life is sustained by the protection of the laws, enabling daily needs to be provided by one's own labor or the support of one's family. But there may be circumstances that pose an immediate threat to life, such as unemployment, disability, or the death of a child's parents. In this case, government should provide a safety net

---

[56] VA Declaration of Rights, 1776, art. 15.

of last resort. There is a right – not a natural right, but a civil right derived from the purpose of the social compact – to minimal support in extreme cases. The founders' welfare policies are discussed in the last chapter of this book.

The founders' idea of limited government did not mean weak government. Instead, government was supposed to be strong in its proper sphere, and not involved at all anywhere else. The intention was the greatest possible degree of personal liberty for each citizen consistent with the security of everyone else.

Protection against Injuries from Government: The Rule of Law

In order to implement its foreign and domestic policies, government must have adequate power to coerce its own citizens and repel foreign attacks. There are limits on those powers – stated in various declarations of rights and other documents, as we have seen – but there is an obvious danger here that government might use its powers to harm its own citizens. After all, *The Federalist* reminds us that "power is of an encroaching nature."[57] Earlier I criticized the view that government secures our rights mainly by putting limits on itself. The founders favored strong government – in its proper sphere. It must be able to act energetically in law enforcement and foreign affairs. But practical limits on government are also indispensable for security of rights.

Given that government needs extensive powers, the question is how it should exercise them. There are two ways by which it can punish wrongdoers. First, it can treat each injury on an ad hoc basis, judging each case without reference to a standing legal rule. This is the way preferred by despotic governments generally, and by Governor John Winthrop of Massachusetts in the early days of Puritanism in America. Winthrop found to his dismay that his fellow Puritans did not agree with his presumption that he could be trusted with unlimited power over them. They compelled him to agree to the adoption of a code of laws.[58] The founders followed the example of Winthrop's constituents. Without the rule of law, government will violate the people's natural rights. James Wilson clarifies the distinction between a law and a decision on the spot regarding a particular case: "Law is called a rule, in order to distinguish it from a sudden, a transient,

---

[57] *Federalist* 48, p. 305.
[58] John Winthrop, *Journal*, 1639, in *Puritan Political Ideas, 1558–1794*, ed. Edmund S. Morgan (Indianapolis: Bobbs-Merrill, 1965), 114–15.

or a particular order: uniformity, permanency, stability characterize a law."[59]

There are two kinds of laws that government can implement. The first prescribes in detail the course of everyday life, regulating people's choices and actions so minutely that injury can be anticipated and stopped before it happens. This is the approach of much recent American law. It is based on the assumption that people are better protected by limiting their liberty in advance so that they are less likely to harm themselves or others. Today there are detailed requirements for almost every possible activity, including elaborate housing and construction codes, mandatory designs for baby seats in cars, and much more. Restraining orders, which became common after 1970, deprive people (usually men) of liberty (the right to associate with and help raise their own children) and property (the right to live in their own house) because of something they might do but have not actually done.[60]

This recent way of protecting against injury was rejected by the founders. In their view, when government forbids conduct that is only *potentially* injurious, it may protect the liberty and property of some, but it does so at the expense of the liberty and property of others. In *Federalist* 10, Madison argues that the right to liberty entails the acceptance of misconduct and prejudice. Removing liberty in order to prevent men from acting in ways that may eventually harm the rights of others is like annihilating air in order to prevent fire. Just as air is "essential to animal life," he says, so also is liberty "essential to political life." It is essential because our "faculties" – our minds and talents – are our own, and the "protection of these faculties is the first object of government." Concisely put, liberty is the free, noninjurious use of our unequal "faculties."[61]

Rather than forbidding conduct that may be potentially injurious, the founders followed a second approach: to punish criminals or compensate injuries only after the deed has been done. That is, no one may be deprived of his liberty unless it is proved that he has done, or is conspiring to do, something that is actually injurious. This was not an absolute rule, but it was the presumption. Any "prior restraint" on freedom was viewed with suspicion, and the exceptions were few. Major injuries were handled by criminal prosecutions and punishments; minor ones through lawsuits

---

[59] Wilson, *Lectures on Law*, 1:468.

[60] Carolyn N. Ko, "Civil Restraining Orders for Domestic Violence," *Southern California Interdisciplinary Law Journal* 11 (2002): 362.

[61] Madison, *Federalist* 10, p. 73.

followed by monetary damages or injunctions against future injurious conduct.[62]

Today, "the rule of law" is a platitude that has lost its force by constant repetition. We tend to think the "law" is violated whenever a ruling by some authorized government authority is disobeyed. In fact "law" is a term of distinction. Not everything that government does is by law. In *The Federalist*, laws are "rules for the regulation of the society."[63] In the 1780s, some state legislatures acted lawlessly by condemning or rewarding particular individuals outside of or against the written or common laws. A speaker at the Virginia ratifying convention complained that a man was arbitrarily deprived of his life without trial by the Virginia legislature during the 1780s. But more typically, without rules publicly agreed upon that apply equally to all persons similarly situated, nothing prevents the whims, passions, or private interests of the rulers from having their way. Without laws that have a reasonable degree of stability and clarity, no one would know in advance what is forbidden or permitted. Madison illustrates this point in *Federalist* 62: "Law is defined to be a rule of action; but how can that be a rule, which is little known and less fixed?"[64]

Most important, the rule of law helps government do something that would otherwise be difficult if not impossible: to control the passions of the people when the people themselves elect the government. In *The Federalist* Hamilton asks: "Why has government been instituted at all? Because the passions of men will not conform to the dictates of reason without constraint."[65] Madison states the problem as it affects republican government: "it is the reason alone of the public that ought to control and regulate the government. The passions ought to be controlled and regulated by the government."[66] Under the rule of law, the people's *reason* is more likely to prevail over and constrain the people's *passions*. For instance, an assembly may wish to exempt themselves, their friends, and their donors from taxes, but a general tax law requires all with the same

---

[62] On the minimal reach of early American regulation of property, Eric R. Claeys, "Takings, Regulation, and Natural Property Rights," *Cornell Law Review* 88, No. 6 (Sept. 2003): 1549–1671.

[63] Hamilton, *Federalist* 75, p. 418.

[64] *The Debates in the Several State Conventions*, ed. Jonathan Elliot (Philadelphia: Lippincott, 1836), 3:66; Madison, *Federalist* 62, p. 379.

[65] Hamilton, *Federalist* 15, p. 78; also *Federalist* 9, pp. 66–7, on the difficulty of reconciling free government and public order (security of rights).

[66] Madison, *Federalist* 49, p. 275.

income or property to pay the same taxes. Applying equally to all similarly situated, law inhibits action based on the favoritism or hatred that a government official might have for a friend, relative, political opponent, or personal enemy. Madison explains in *Federalist* 57: one important circumstance "restraining them [the legislative body] from oppressive measures, [is] that they can make no law which will not have its full operation on themselves and their friends, as well as on the great mass of the society."[67] In recent times, Congress has made it a systematic practice to exempt "themselves and their friends" from many laws which they impose on the rest of society, including the Civil Rights Act of 1964 and the Americans with Disabilities Act of 1990.[68] Boston's Rights of the Colonists states that laws should be rules that are truly general, so that there is "one rule for rich and poor, for the favorite at court, and the country man at plow."[69] A 1779 Virginia law required every judge to "swear . . . that you will do equal right to all manner of people, great and small, high and low, rich and poor, without respect of persons."[70]

Daniel Webster explained the difference between genuine law and arbitrary enactments in an 1819 argument before the Supreme Court: "every citizen shall hold his life, liberty, property, and immunities under the protection of the general rules which govern society. Everything which may pass under the form of an enactment is not, therefore, to be considered the law of the land. If this were so, . . . acts of confiscation, acts reversing judgments, and acts directly transferring one man's estate to another, legislative judgments, decrees, and forfeitures, in all possible forms, would be the law of the land."[71]

Much of what government does today violates the founders' understanding of law. Today's "law" concerning child abuse is a striking example. In most states, the law does not define abuse. Child Protective

---

[67] Madison, *Federalist* 57, p. 350.

[68] Congress exempted itself completely from these two laws up to 1995, after which it nominally required itself to obey them. However, enforcement is entrusted by Congress to Congress's own enforcement agency. In other words, Congress continues to exempt itself from accountability to normal law enforcement by the executive. See U.S. Congress Office of Compliance, *Congressional Accountability Act of 1995*, www.compliance.gov. Congress continues to exempt itself entirely from other laws, such as the Whistleblower Protection Act of 1989, according to the Office of Compliance, *Recommendations for Improvements to the Congressional Accountability Act*, 2010, www.compliance.gov.

[69] Boston, Rights of the Colonists, 2:351, quoting Locke.

[70] An Act Constituting the Court of Appeals, 1779, in *Statutes at Large . . . of Virginia*, ed. William Hening (Richmond: George Cochran, 1822), 10:90.

[71] *Dartmouth College v. Woodward*, 4 Wheat. (17 U.S.) 518 (1819), 581.

Services workers are authorized to remove children from the home of the parent at their own discretion. Hearings before a judicial official typically do not provide for the kind of trial procedure available to murderers and rapists, who enjoy full legal counsel, the right to hear and answer the specific charges, and the right to confront witnesses. Family court judges almost always follow the recommendation of the case workers. There is little parents can do to get their children back, except to submit to whatever demands the CPS makes and hope for the best.[72]

Even so, the founders did not regard the rule of law as an absolute requirement. Both federal and state constitutions allow for suspension of the writ of habeas corpus in some circumstances, enabling the government to imprison people without trial. The federal exception – "when in cases of rebellion or invasion the public safety may require it" – shows that the suspension of the rule of law would take place only in emergencies threatening the very existence of the body politic.[73]

Finally, the rule of law requires certain minimal procedural protections to people accused of crimes or personal injuries. This is summarized in the Fifth Amendment's provision that no person may "be deprived of life, liberty, or property, without due process of law." The due process (or "law of the land") requirement typically includes at least two things. First, no one can be convicted of a crime unless it can be shown that he or she has violated a law – that is, a general rule approved by an elected legislative body. Second, the determination must be through a trial with appropriate safeguards to promote impartial judgment. Virginia's Bill of Rights sums these up: the accused has "a right to demand the cause and nature of his accusation, to be confronted with the accusers and witnesses, to call for evidence in his favor, and to a speedy trial by an impartial jury of his vicinage, without whose unanimous consent he cannot be found guilty."[74] The same requirement of a trial or at least a full opportunity to present evidence in one's favor is required in civil cases, where the question is whether someone's legal rights have been violated. The state and federal constitutions contain numerous provisions to this end. All of these aim at the goal specified in the Massachusetts Bill of Rights: "It

---

[72] Richard Wexler, *Wounded Innocents: The Real Victims of the War against Child Abuse* (Buffalo: Prometheus Press, 1990); Julian J. Dominguez and Melinda Murphy, *A Culture of Fear: An Inside Look at Los Angeles County's Department of Children and Family Services* (Houston: Strategic Book Publishing, 2014).

[73] U.S. Constitution, art. 1, §9.

[74] VA Declaration of Rights, 1776, art. 8. MA has a more elaborate list of rights of the accused in art. 10–15.

is essential to the preservation of the rights of every individual, his life, liberty, property and character, that there be an impartial interpretation of the laws, and administration of justice. It is the right of every citizen to be tried by judges as free, impartial and independent as the lot of humanity will admit."[75]

Perhaps the most obvious contemporary repudiation of the older due process standard is found in family law. As mentioned earlier, children can be arbitrarily removed from their parents' home on the mere suspicion of child abuse, without any real opportunity for the parents to hear and respond to the charges against them. Equally arbitrary are protective orders. A former president of the Massachusetts Bar Association writes, "The facts have become irrelevant. Everyone knows that restraining orders and orders to vacate . . . are granted to virtually all who apply. . . . In virtually all cases, no notice, meaningful hearing, or impartial weighing of evidence is to be had."[76] According to an article published by the California Bar, protective orders are "almost routinely issued by the court in family law proceedings even when there is relatively meager evidence." In cases like this, a man is deprived of liberty and property without being charged with any crime and without any opportunity to present evidence in his own defense.[77]

Why Religious Liberty Does Not Require Exemptions from the Laws

Religious liberty deserves a separate discussion because the founders' approach is so often misunderstood today. It is commonly believed that the natural right to religious liberty requires government to grant exemptions from laws that contradict a person's religious opinions or practice, but in fact, the founders consistently rejected that view. It is true that exemptions were sometimes granted in the founding, notably for Quakers, who refused to serve as soldiers on religious grounds. President George Washington wrote a letter to the Quakers in which he indicated with perfect clarity what religious liberty means in their case. He begins with an affirmation of the right: "The liberty enjoyed by the people of these states of worshipping Almighty God agreeably to their consciences, is . . . among the choicest of their . . . rights." But he adds this condition:

---

[75] MA Declaration of Rights, art. 29.

[76] Elaine M. Epstein, "Speaking the Unspeakable," *Massachusetts Bar Association Newsletter* 33, No. 7 (June/July 1993): 9.

[77] Lynette Berg Robe and Melvyn Jay Ross, "Extending the Impact of Domestic Violence Protective Orders," *Family Law News* 27, No. 4 (2005), http://familylaw.calbar.ca.gov.

"While men perform their social duties faithfully, they do all that society or the state can with propriety demand or expect." Washington then says that the Quakers do not meet this condition: "[Except for Quakers'] declining to share with others the burden of the common defense, there is no denomination among us, who are more exemplary and useful citizens."[78] Washington is being polite but firm. Yes, Quakers have a right to religious liberty, but only if they "perform their social duties faithfully." Quakers are "exemplary and useful citizens," says Washington, except for one big thing: they refuse to share "the burden of the common defense." Washington implies that this refusal is not justified by the right to religious liberty.

To understand why the founders denied a religious right to exemptions from assisting in the common defense, or from any other laws, we have to remember two things: first, the terms of the social compact – the unanimous agreement "that all shall be governed by certain laws for the common good" – and second, the meaning of the common good: "enjoying, in safety and tranquility, their natural rights." As equal members of the social compact, Quakers too have made a covenant to obey the laws protecting those rights. Madison writes in *Federalist* 33: "If individuals enter into a state of society, the laws of that society must be the supreme regulator of their conduct."[79] One of those laws may require citizens to fight in time of war, when the lives and liberties of the people are threatened from abroad. The Quakers' refusal to fight is therefore a violation of the terms of the compact. They are liable to punishment for that refusal.

However, Washington does not leave it at that. He adds a final, conciliatory paragraph to his letter. He now adopts a personal tone. He speaks of "my wish and desire" and "my opinion," as opposed to the strict requirements of the social compact: "I assure you very explicitly, that in my opinion the conscientious scruples of all men should be treated with great delicacy and tenderness; and it is my wish and desire, that the laws may always be as extensively accommodated to them, as a due regard to the protection and essential interests of the nation may justify and permit." Washington makes this final paragraph his personal "wish and desire" because although there can be no religious liberty to disobey the laws that protect the citizens' natural rights, there might be good reason to make an exception in some cases. However, if the Quakers are to be

---

[78] George Washington to the Annual Meeting of Quakers, 1789, in Washington, *A Collection*, ed. W. B. Allen (Indianapolis: Liberty Fund, 1988), 533–4.

[79] MA Constitution, Preamble; Madison, *Federalist* 33, p. 200.

exempted from the duties of national defense, it has to be as a favor to them, not as a matter of natural or constitutional right. Washington adds – again reminding the Quakers that an exemption from the law is not their right – that the accommodation would be made only if "the protection and essential interests of the nation" permit it. When Washington says "the laws" would be accommodated to the Quakers, he means that this decision will be made not by himself as president, but by Congress, the lawmaking body.

Washington's view of religious liberty is evident in numerous official documents. The Northwest Ordinance is representative: "No person, demeaning himself in a peaceable and orderly manner, shall ever be molested on account of his mode of worship, or religious sentiments."[80] Religious liberty extends only to people who conduct themselves in a "peaceable and orderly manner." That is, they have to obey the laws.

Of course, if the laws exceed their proper scope – securing natural rights – then they violate the right to liberty, which is alienated only to the extent necessary for the government "to secure these rights." So if government denies to a religious school the right to require that its teachers and staff adhere to the church's teachings, it violates not only the religious liberty of the school but also the natural right to freedom of association that government is required to protect for all citizens.

Protection against Injuries from Government: Separation of Powers, Federalism, and Consent

To establish the rule of law, the three principal ways government acts – making laws, adjudicating violations of law, and managing the day-to-day operation of government as well as organizing and deploying force to punish criminals and to repel foreign attacks – are assigned in the founding to three different bodies of men. Although separation of powers is not absolutely required by natural rights theory, having one body to make the rules and two others to enforce them increases the likelihood that the government will govern through general laws, not by the ad hoc

---

[80] Northwest Ordinance, art. 1, 1787, in *Founders' Constitution*, 1:28. An able defense of the view that the founders' religious liberty requires exemptions is Michael W. McConnell, "The Origins and Historical Understanding of Free Exercise of Religion," *Harvard Law Review* 103 (May 1990): 1409–1517; answered convincingly by Philip A. Hamburger, "A Constitutional Right of Religious Exemption: An Historical Perspective," *George Washington Law Review* 60 (1992): 915–48.

commands of an arbitrary sovereign.[81] Both the federal and state constitutions adopted this device. As an additional check to the lawmaking branch, which will necessarily be predominant in a society ruled by laws, the federal government and most states added "legislative checks and balances" in the form of a two-house legislature and a qualified executive veto. Hamilton saw an additional check in judicial overturning of unconstitutional laws.[82] Other structural features of American constitutions, such as indirect elections to the federal and to some state senates, and moderate property requirements for voting in some states, were meant to contribute to the same end.

Nor does the natural rights theory require federalism, a division of authority between the federal and state governments. It was the accident that the United States was formed out of multiple colonies that made possible this additional restraint on government. Madison explains in *Federalist* 51: "In the compound republic of America, the power surrendered by the people, is first divided between two distinct governments [i.e., federal and state], and then the portion allotted to each, subdivided among distinct and separate departments. Hence a double security arises to the rights of the people. The different governments will control each other, at the same time that each will be controlled by itself [through the separation of powers]." The sheer size of the nation can also help, as Madison famously observes in *Federalist* 10: "In a free government, the security for civil rights must be the same as for religious rights. It consists in the one case in the multiplicity of interests, and in the other, in the multiplicity of sects." This "multiplicity," which will make it hard for a single religion or faction to control the government through elections, will be present only in a large republic.[83]

Other restraints on government include verbal guarantees of freedom of religion and the press, the prohibition of favored classes or monopolies, prohibition of "unreasonable" searches and seizures, and more. Madison mocks such merely written restraints in *Federalist* 51 as "parchment barriers." All of these written limitations on government amount to very little, Hamilton notes in *Federalist* 84, if "public opinion" and "the general spirit of the people, and of the government" are defective.[84] If public officials have wrong opinions about justice, nothing can be done, whether

---

[81] Madison, *Federalist* 51, pp. 317–19.
[82] Hamilton, *Federalist* 9, p. 67; No. 78; Madison, *Federalist* 48, pp. 306–7; No. 51, pp. 319–20.
[83] Madison, *Federalist* 51, p. 320–21; No. 10.
[84] *Federalist* 51, p. 305; Hamilton, *Federalist* 84, pp. 513–14.

by institutional arrangements or by written restraints on government, to prevent the government from violating the natural rights of citizens.

The "parchment barriers" of bills of rights, together with concepts such as "natural justice" and "the law of nature," were not altogether ineffectual as long as politicians and judges took seriously the political theory of the founding. Law professor Suzanna Sherry demonstrates that judges in Virginia's state courts made frequent and genuine use of these and like expressions in their judicial opinions in the first decades after the Revolution. She also shows that courts in Massachusetts, New York, Virginia, and South Carolina made significant use of natural law and natural rights analysis in deciding constitutional cases from 1788 to 1830. Federal courts followed a similar pattern.[85]

As discussed earlier, the consent principle does not by itself secure people's rights against predatory behavior. But it can contribute to making it less likely that government will threaten natural rights. As Madison writes in *Federalist* 51, "A dependence on the people is no doubt the primary control on the government."[86] The Massachusetts Council explains Madison's thought in greater detail: "Life, liberty, property, and the disposal of that property with our own consent, are natural rights.... The preservation of these rights is the great end of government: but is it probable they will be effectually secured by a government, which the proprietors of them have no part in the direction of, and over which they have no power or influence whatever? Hence is deducible, representation: which being necessary to preserve these invaluable rights of nature, is itself, for that reason, a natural right, coinciding with, and running into, that great law of nature, self-preservation."[87]

---

[85] Suzanna Sherry, "The Early Virginia Tradition of Extratextual Interpretation," in *Toward a Usable Past: Liberty under State Constitutions*, ed. Paul Finkelman and Stephen E. Gottlieb (Athens: University of Georgia Press, 1991), 157–88; Sherry, "Natural Law in the States," *University of Cincinnati Law Review* 61 (1992): 171–222; Sherry, "The Founders' Unwritten Constitution," *University of Chicago Law Review* 54 (1987): 1127–77. Sherry's claims are challenged (in my view not convincingly) by Gary L. McDowell, *The Language of Law and the Foundations of American Constitutionalism* (New York: Cambridge University Press, 2010).

[86] Madison, *Federalist* 51, p. 319.

[87] Answer of the Council of Massachusetts to Governor Thomas Hutchinson, 1773, in *The Briefs of the American Revolution*, ed. John P. Reid (New York: New York University Press, 1981), 35.

PART II

THE MORAL CONDITIONS OF FREEDOM

8

Why Government Should Support Morality

Earlier I explained how the founders' political theory of natural law and natural rights includes both an individual-rights dimension and a moral-formation dimension. Individual rights will be most prominent in the chapters in Part III on property and economics. The moral-religious or communitarian element predominates in this chapter and in the rest of Part II. I will show that the founders shared a serious concern for morality, and that they wanted government to promote it – insofar as it is integral to establishing and sustaining political liberty – securing the people's natural rights on the basis of consent.

To introduce the founders' consensus, I quote three early laws. First, in a 1789 law providing for public education, Massachusetts declares, "a general dissemination of knowledge and virtue is necessary to the prosperity of every state, and the very existence of a commonwealth. . . . [Virtue is] the basis upon which the republican constitution is structured: And . . . [the teachers shall] endeavor to lead those under their care . . . into a particular understanding of the tendency of the aforementioned virtues to preserve and perfect a republican constitution, and to secure the blessings of liberty as well as to promote their future happiness; and the tendency of the opposite vices to slavery and ruin."[1]

Second, a 1785 Georgia law establishing a state university states, "As it is the distinguishing happiness of free governments that civil order should be the result of choice and not necessity, and the common wishes of the

[1] An Act to Provide for the Instruction of Youth, June 25, 1789, in *The Perpetual Laws of the Commonwealth of Massachusetts, 1780–1800* (Boston: I. Thomas and E. T. Andrews, 1801), 2:39–41.

people become the laws of the land, their public prosperity and even existence very much depends upon suitably forming the minds and morals of their citizens. When the minds of people in general are viciously disposed and unprincipled and their conduct disorderly, a free government will be attended with greater confusions and with evils more horrid than the wild, uncultivated state of nature."[2]

Finally, North Carolina's charter for its university puts it concisely: "it is the indispensable duty of every legislature to consult the happiness of a rising generation, and endeavor to fit them for an honorable discharge of the social duties of life, by paying the strictest attention to their education."[3]

Notably, the word "happiness" appears in all three quotations. For the founders – as also for philosophers as diverse as Aristotle, Cicero, Aquinas, and Locke – the goal of human life is happiness, for which virtue is an indispensable condition. The founders might have been amused by, but they would ultimately have disagreed with, Ogden Nash's lament: "O Duty,/ Why hast thou not the visage of a sweetie or a cutie?" President George Washington expressed the consensus of the day in his First Inaugural: "there exists in the economy and course of nature an indissoluble union between virtue and happiness, between duty and advantage, between the genuine maxims of an honest and magnanimous policy and the solid rewards of public prosperity and felicity."[4]

The Supposed Tension between "Republicanism" and "Liberalism"

It may seem strange that a government whose purpose is to secure life, liberty, and property should concern itself with citizen character. Harvey Mansfield formulates the paradox nicely: "Liberty and virtue are not a likely pair. At first sight they seem to be contraries, for liberty appears to mean living as you please and virtue appears to mean living not as you

---

[2] University of Georgia Charter, 1785, in An Act for the More Full and Complete Establishment of a Public Seat of Learning in this State, January 27, 1785, in *A Digest of the Statute Laws of the State of Georgia*, ed. Thomas R. R. Cobb (Athens, GA: Christy, Kelsea, and Burke, 1851), 1083.

[3] An Act to Establish a University in This State, December 11, 1789, in *Laws of the State of North Carolina*, ed. Henry Potter (Raleigh: J. Gales, 1821), 1:606, 610.

[4] George Washington, First Inaugural Address, 1789, in *Writings*, ed. John Rhodehamel (New York: Library of America, 1997), 732–3.

please but as you ought."[5] Some therefore argue that the founders had
no concern for virtue at all, because "liberalism" – a common scholarly
label for their natural rights theory – by definition excludes considerations
of character from the legitimate scope of politics. Yet it takes only a
passing acquaintance with the founders to notice that they had plenty
to say about the need for virtue. This fact has led other scholars to
deny the relevance of the natural rights language that appears in the
founding documents, and to emphasize instead the supposedly "non-
liberal" traditions present in the founding era, which are sometimes called
"republicanism" or "civic humanism."[6] In sum, scholars on all sides tend
to posit a disjunction between individual rights on the one hand and virtue
and "republicanism" on the other. But the principles these scholars see
as opposed were inextricably connected in the founding.

In recent decades, unable to ignore the presence of both "republican"
and "liberal" elements, scholars have increasingly adopted the view that
the founding is a blend of distinct, perhaps contradictory, traditions of
political discourse. Earlier I quoted Alan Gibson: "the political thought
of the founders is best understood as an amalgam of liberalism, republicanism, and perhaps other traditions of political thought."[7] To this list,

---

[5] Harvey C. Mansfield, "Liberty and Virtue in the American Founding," in *Never a Matter
of Indifference: Sustaining Virtue in a Free Republic*, ed. Peter Berkowitz (Stanford:
Hoover Institution Press, 2003), 3.

[6] Advocates of the "republicanism" thesis: Gordon S. Wood, *The Creation of the American
Republic, 1776–1787* (New York: Norton, 1969) (partially recanted in the 1998 Preface);
Michael Sandel, *Democracy's Discontent* (Cambridge: Harvard University Press, 1996)
(discussed in ch. 1 above); Robert E. Shalhope, "Toward a Republican Synthesis: The
Emergence of an Understanding of Republicanism in American Historiography," *William
and Mary Quarterly* 29, No. 1 (Jan. 1972): 49–80; Bernard Bailyn, *The Ideological
Origins of the American Revolution*, enlarged ed. (Cambridge: Harvard University Press,
1992). Critics of the "republicanism" thesis: Thomas L. Pangle, *The Spirit of Modern
Republicanism: The Moral Vision of the American Founders and the Philosophy of
Locke* (Chicago: University of Chicago Press, 1988); Paul A. Rahe, *Republics Ancient and
Modern: Classical Republicanism and the American Revolution* (Chapel Hill: University
of North Carolina Press, 1992); Michael P. Zuckert, *The Natural Rights Republic: Studies
in the Foundation of the American Political Tradition* (Notre Dame, IN: University of
Notre Dame Press, 1996); Jean Yarbrough, "Republicanism Revisited: Some Thoughts
on the Foundation and Preservation of the American Republic," *Review of Politics* 41
(Jan. 1979): 61–95; Lance Banning, "Some Second Thoughts on Virtue and the Course
of Revolutionary Thinking," in *Conceptual Change and the Constitution*, ed. Terence
Ball and J. G. A. Pocock (Lawrence: University Press of Kansas, 1988), 194–212.

[7] Alan Gibson, *Understanding the Founding: The Crucial Questions*, 2nd ed. (Lawrence:
University Press of Kansas, 2010), 135. See also his *Interpreting the Founding: Guide
to the Enduring Debates over the Origins and Foundations of the American Republic*

Rogers Smith, who is especially interested in what he regards as anti-liberal elements in the founding, adds "ascriptivism," by which he means racism, sexism, and anti-homosexuality.[8]

Another scholar, Paul Rahe, argues that the founders' aspiration to greatness and their devotion to "political liberty" were learned not from Locke and the moderns, but from the Greek and Roman classics. This was supposedly part of a "restricted appropriation of the classical heritage" in the founding. He also writes that "no community can long endure ... unless it is animated by something transcending the [modern natural rights tradition, with its] narrow, prosaic concern with 'security and well-being,' 'commodious living,' and 'comfortable preservation.'"[9] In short, Rahe argues that the founders' amalgam of virtue and natural rights was effective but incoherent, because virtue aims high while the natural rights theory aims at "narrow" and "prosaic" goals.

Philip Hamburger rightly observes that these approaches lead to the conclusion that the founding is intellectually incoherent: "Republicanism has been described as an attachment to government – an intense identification with the state that has seemed to thrive mostly in small, homogenous societies. In contrast, liberalism has been treated by historians as the individualistic pursuit of self-interest – as the sort of selfishness common in large, diverse and individuated populations. Thus, the concepts of republicanism and liberalism seem to define two opposite types of society, and they thereby offer modern scholars a bold dichotomy within which to understand the late eighteenth century. Yet these ideas, whether considered alone or coupled together, tend to reduce eighteenth-century political thought to a pair of extremes or some muddled compromise between them."[10]

The amalgam approach tends to assume that we already know the answer to a question that must be asked at the outset: Why treat "liberalism" and "republicanism" as distinct traditions at all? Perhaps scholars have imagined difference where there is unity. What if individualistic "liberalism" and communitarian "republicanism" are not opposed at all,

(Lawrence: University Press of Kansas, 2006); and Robert E. Shalhope, "Republicanism and Early American Historiography," *William and Mary Quarterly* 39, No. 2 (Apr. 1982): 334–56.

8   Rogers M. Smith, *Civic Ideals: Conflicting Visions of Citizenship in U.S. History* (New Haven: Yale University Press, 1997), ch. 1.

9   Rahe, *Republics Ancient and Modern*, 570–71, 772.

10 Philip Hamburger, "Liberality," *Texas Law Review* 78 (May 2000): 1217.

but rather complementary aspects of the founders' political theory? Or, to put it another way, if "liberalism" is our label for the founders' natural law theory, including its political implications, then "republicanism" might prove to be an indispensable feature of "liberalism."

The founders certainly thought of themselves as "liberal," i.e., generous and respectful of the natural rights of all human beings. But they were not liberals in today's sense. Nor did they call their political theory "liberalism." They embraced natural rights and natural law, not as an affirmation of self-interest, but as a theory that would generously ("liberally") treat all citizens in accord with equal natural rights. President Washington illustrates nicely the founders' conception of "liberal" in his 1790 letter to American Catholics: "As mankind become more *liberal*, they will be more apt to allow that all those who conduct themselves as worthy members of the community are equally entitled to the protection of civil government. I hope ever to see America among the foremost nations in examples of justice and *liberality*."[11]

The founders' concern with natural rights and their concern with virtue did not belong to distinct categories of thought. Instead, they thought of virtue as a condition of freedom and a requirement of the laws of nature. In the Virginia Bill of Rights, as elsewhere, we are told that "no free government, or the blessings of liberty, can be preserved...but by a firm adherence to...virtue."[12] In other words, the founders thought of what is now called "republicanism" (devotion to the common good and cultivation of citizen virtues) as a necessary feature of a political order based on the premise that all men are created equal. It was not until the 1960s – after the founders' arguments had been long forgotten – that scholars began the debate over whether the founding is "liberal," "republican," Christian, or some sort of amalgam.

Morality, *The Federalist*, and Martin Diamond

Some scholars simply deny that the founders thought government should concern itself with forming the moral character of its citizens. One of the most influential statements of that position appeared in an article by Martin Diamond published over half a century ago. He argues that the

---

[11] Washington to the Roman Catholics of the United States, March 12, 1790, in *Documents of Catholic History*, ed. John Tracy Ellis (Milwaukee: Bruce Publishing, 1956), 176 (my emphasis).

[12] VA Constitution, 1776, Declaration of Rights, art. 15.

American Constitution is based on a deliberate choice to remove government from the business of promoting or even caring about morality.[13] With respect to "courage, civic-spiritedness, moderation, or individual excellence in the virtues, . . . *The Federalist* is either silent, or has in mind only pallid versions of the originals, or even seems to speak with contempt." According to Diamond, the Constitution solves the problem of "faction" (the organized pursuit of selfish interest at other people's expense) by means of properly channeled self-interest and not by virtue. Quoting Madison, who writes, "neither moral nor religious motives can be relied on as an adequate control" of factions,[14] Diamond concludes that Madison abandons any concern with such motives and replaces them with purely selfish ones. In this Madisonian scheme, says Diamond, government ignores qualities like civic spirit and moderation. Not only is virtue dispensed with, but Diamond goes further: "All men must be free – and even encouraged – to seek their immediate profit." He concludes, "The Madisonian solution involved a fundamental reliance on ceaseless striving after immediate interest."[15] The strategy, in other words, is to unleash selfishness so as to maximize the number of factions, which will keep each other in check.

Diamond is correct to say that Madison feared a situation in which one big majority faction – the poor against the rich – would determine government policy and violate the rights of the minority. It is also true that Madison favored a "multiplicity of interests," because that multiplicity would make it harder for a single faction, hostile to the security of individual rights, to dominate. Institutional devices are certainly needed to make up for the absence of what he called "better motives,"[16] but Madison never for a moment believed that "striving after immediate interest" would lead to good government. (Similarly, Ralph Lerner observes that Jefferson's proposed 1778 Virginia legal code "does not eschew using private interest to further a public purpose, . . . but it would hardly mistake such support for the bedrock of a self-governing society. More is

---

[13] Martin Diamond, "Democracy and *The Federalist*," 1959, in *As Far as Republican Principles Will Admit* (Washington: AEI Press, 1991), 17–36 (quotations on 31–6). In "Ethics and Politics: The American Way," 1977 (in ibid., 337–68), Diamond substantially revises his earlier argument. He admits there that the founders did care about citizen virtue, although he continues to underrate the extent.

[14] James Madison, *Federalist* 10, in Alexander Hamilton, Madison, and John Jay, *The Federalist Papers*, ed. Clinton Rossiter (New York: Signet Classics, 2003), 75.

[15] Diamond, "Democracy and *The Federalist*," 34.

[16] Madison uses these phrases in *Federalist* 51, pp. 319, 321.

needed.")[17] Later in *The Federalist*, Madison is explicit: without virtue, republican government will fail. "As there is a degree of depravity in mankind which requires a certain degree of circumspection and distrust," he writes, "so there are other qualities in human nature which justify a certain portion of esteem and confidence. Republican government presupposes the existence of these qualities in a higher degree than any other form." Madison continues: if people were as incapable of self-restraint as some critics of the Constitution imply, "the inference would be that there is not sufficient virtue among men for self-government; and that nothing less than the chains of despotism can restrain them from destroying and devouring one another."[18]

Madison's view of separation of powers is similar. He does suggest relying on selfish motives in one respect: "Ambition must be made to counteract ambition. The interest of the man must be connected with the constitutional rights of the place."[19] Madison means that the ambition of the representative or president must be connected to maintaining the rightful power of his own branch of the government. If the ambition takes the form of "immediate interest" – for example, acquiring money and positions for oneself and one's children by serving the interests of corporate clients of the state who are in bed with the bureaucracy – then the separation of powers will fail to prevent government oppression. In other words, the ambition must be an honorable one – tied to defending the "constitutional rights of the place," whether it be Congress, the presidency, or the judiciary – in order for Madison's argument to work.

Contrary to Diamond, Madison's point in *Federalist* 10 and 51 is not to forgo virtue, but to show how institutional constraints and the large size of the nation can help make selfishness less dangerous to the security of individual rights. In *Federalist* 10, Madison argues that it is "impracticable" in a free society for everyone to have "the same opinions, the same passions, and the same interests."[20] But this is not Madison's last word. Although it is impossible to create perfect uniformity, there can and must be a considerable degree of agreement. In the 1790s, Madison argued that it is desirable "that a consolidation should prevail in their [the people's] interests and affections" and in their "sentiments." The reason is that "the less the supposed difference of interests, and the greater the concord and confidence throughout the great body of the people, the

---

[17] Cf. Ralph Lerner, *The Thinking Revolutionary: Principle and Practice in the New Republic* (Ithaca: Cornell University Press, 1987), 90.

[18] *Federalist* 55, p. 343.   [19] *Federalist* 51, p. 319.   [20] *Federalist* 10, p. 73.

more readily must they sympathize with each other," and "the more effectually will they consolidate their defense of the public liberty." For Madison, the Republican Party of the '90s was a vehicle to promote that consolidation in public opinion, with the goal of "erect[ing] over the whole, one paramount empire of reason, benevolence, and brotherly affection."[21] While perfect devotion to the common good, to liberty, to justice will never be attained, most must share "the same opinions" about justice and right, and "the same passions" in regard to a disposition of "benevolence" to follow those principles.[22]

In fact, this point is one of the foundations of the argument of *Federalist* 10 itself. Madison contends that a large nation governed by elected representatives is less likely than a small nation to be dominated by a single faction that controls the government. "Besides other impediments," he writes, "it may be remarked that, where there is a *consciousness of unjust or dishonorable purposes*, communication is always checked by distrust in proportion to the number whose concurrence is necessary" (emphasis mine). That is, in a large republic, those with bad motives will worry that their unjust design will be found out if they communicate their plan to too many people. Madison clearly assumes the existence of what one might call a moral majority that will be alarmed at any open attempt to promote injustice.[23]

Strauss's Exaggerated Account of the Moderns

When Diamond argues that the founders had no concern for morality, he reads the founding through a Straussian lens. Leo Strauss was one of the

---

[21] Madison, "Consolidation," *National Gazette*, 1791, in *Writings*, ed. Jack N. Rakove (New York: Library of America, 1999), 499–500. Also Tiffany Jones Miller, "James Madison's Republic of 'Mean Extent' Theory: Avoiding The Scylla and Charybdis of Republican Government," *Polity* 39, No. 4 (Oct. 2007): 545–69 (arguing for the consistency of Madison's position on public opinion and political parties); Colleen A. Sheehan, *James Madison and the Spirit of Republican Self-Government* (New York: Cambridge University Press, 2009); Sheehan, *The Mind of James Madison: The Legacy of Classical Republicanism* (New York: Cambridge University Press, 2015).

[22] I return to the theme of the founders' moral consensus toward the end of Chapter 11.

[23] This point is elaborated by Charles R. Kesler, "Federalist 10 and American Republicanism," in *Saving the Revolution: The Federalist Papers and the American Founding*, ed. Kesler (New York: Free Press, 1987), 13–39; and by Sanderson Schaub, "Justice and Honor, the Surest Foundation of Liberty: The Natural Law Doctrine in The Federalist No. 10," in *Constitutionalism in America*, vol. 1: *To Secure the Blessings of Liberty: First Principles of the Constitution*, ed. Sarah B. Thurow (Lanham, MD: University Press of America, 1988), 2–30.

most insightful philosophers of the last half of the twentieth century. The influence of his interpretations of the great authors grows by the decade. Although Strauss had little to say about the founders, his statements on modern political philosophy have shaped scholarship on the founding so deeply that they deserve a brief response here.

Strauss's teaching, on the surface, argues that the political project of early modern political thought was to abandon government's traditional concern with moral formation. Strauss summarizes and apparently accepts Montesquieu's characterization of the modern state: "The ancient republics based on virtue, needed pure manners; the modern system...replaces virtue by trade." In another place, Strauss writes, "Machiavelli [together with]...Bacon, Hobbes and other Englishmen...conceive[d] of the social order as based not on piety and virtue but on socially useful passions or vices."[24]

However, Strauss (followed by Diamond and many others) grossly exaggerates the extent to which English political thought had jettisoned any concern with "piety and virtue." (I leave aside in this book the question of how far English political thought affected the founding.) Strauss's exaggeration was arguably deliberate. In his book *Liberalism Ancient and Modern*, he says something quite different from the passages just quoted: "In the light of the original conception of modern republicanism [i.e., in Locke]," Strauss writes, "our present predicament appears to be caused by the decay of the religious education of the people and by the decay of liberal education of the representatives of the people."[25] In this statement of Strauss, Locke emphatically does *not* "conceive of the social order as based not on piety and virtue but on socially useful passions or vices." Strauss was probably thinking of Locke's affirmation of the need for religious education of "the greatest part of mankind" in his *Reasonableness of Christianity*.[26]

Strauss may have thought the exaggeration in question (treating the early modern philosophers as if they thought morality was superfluous) was necessary in order to highlight the extent to which the early moderns had broken with the Greek and Roman classics – a point that scholars tended to deny when Strauss was writing over half a century ago. I have

[24] Leo Strauss, *What Is Political Philosophy? And Other Studies* (Glencoe, IL: Free Press, 1959), 50; and Strauss, "Comment," *Church History* 30, No. 1 (Mar. 1961): 102.

[25] Strauss, *Liberalism: Ancient and Modern* (New York: Free Press, 1968), 18.

[26] John Locke, *The Reasonableness of Christianity*, 1695, ed. John C. Higgins-Biddle (Oxford: Clarendon Press, 1999), ch. 14, 264–79 (using the marginal pagination).

suggested elsewhere that Strauss may have chosen to present an immoral-
ist caricature of Locke (and other moderns) as a fishhook to his readers,
to help reel some of them in to become serious students of premodern
philosophy. Disgust with modernity – with Locke – would make them
more open to the classics.[27] Richard Velkley agrees: "For philosophical-
pedagogical purposes Strauss engages at times in one-sided accounts of
modern philosophy as 'fallen.'...One suspects that Strauss's unqualified preference for the ancients and his assessment of modern thought
as unnatural involve some deliberate rhetorical overstatement....[I]t was
necessary to create doubts about modernity as a whole and thereby a sense
of urgency about a theoretical return to the beginnings."[28] In "What Is
Political Philosophy?" Strauss presents modernity as one long slippery
slope from Machiavelli, supposedly in the grip of "anti-theological ire,"
to Heidegger and Hitler.[29] Strauss's intentional distortions of Locke in
particular are almost comically obvious. For instance, Strauss claims that
Locke believed government has no need for morality because he had
found "an immoral or amoral substitute for morality" in "acquisitiveness[,]...an utterly selfish passion."[30] But as Strauss well knew, Locke
explicitly repudiates this view in his *Letter on Toleration*: "Rectitude
of morals...concerns political life, and in it is involved the safety...of
the commonwealth; moral actions, therefore...are subject to the government....No doctrines adverse...to the good morals that are necessary to
the preservation of civil society are to be tolerated by the government."[31]

---

[27] Thomas G. West, "The Ground of Locke's Law of Nature," *Social Philosophy and Policy* 29, No. 2 (Summer 2012): 23–5.

[28] Richard L. Velkley, *Heidegger, Strauss, and the Premises of Philosophy: On Original Forgetting* (Chicago: University of Chicago Press, 2011), 19, 135.

[29] Strauss, *What Is Political Philosophy?* 27, 40–55.   [30] Ibid., 49.

[31] John Locke, *Epistola de Tolerantia [Letter on Toleration]* (Gouda, Netherlands: Justum ab Hoeve, 1689), 66, 73 (my translation). Scholars who agree that Locke thought moral character important to good government include: Nathan Tarcov, "A 'Non-Lockean' Locke and the Character of Liberalism," in *Liberalism Reconsidered*, ed. Douglas MacLean and Claudia Mills (Totowa, NJ: Rowman & Allanheld, 1983); Tarcov, *Locke's Education for Liberty* (Chicago: University of Chicago Press, 1984); Richard C. Sinopoli, *The Foundations of American Citizenship: Liberalism, the Constitution, and Civic Virtue* (New York: Oxford University Press, 1992), 39–52; Steven Forde, "Natural Law, Theology, and Morality in Locke," *American Journal of Political Science* 45, No. 2 (Apr. 2001): 396 ("philosophically, he provided for a social morality more robust than his critics have perceived"); William A. Galston, *Liberal Purposes: Goods, Virtues, and Diversity in the Liberal State* (New York: Cambridge University Press, 1991), 262; Peter C. Myers, *Our Only Star and Compass: Locke and the Struggle for Political Rationality* (Lanham, MD: Rowman & Littlefield, 1998), 198–208 ("The Lockean Family");

That statement could have been made by any of the founders, all of whom agreed that there are moral conditions of a free society. If I am right about Strauss's rhetorical agenda in this regard, he would also have expected his careful readers to realize that his over-the-top denunciations of Locke and other moderns must be left behind, and that the best of these philosophers should be reconsidered *sine ira et studio*, without the anger or bias induced in the unwary by these overstatements. As Peter Berkowitz writes, "Strauss may sometimes have exaggerated the . . . disagreements between ancient and modern thought. . . . Strauss, on occasion, melodramatically emphasized the radical nature of the break."[32] It is high time to leave Straussian *niaiseries* behind and learn from Strauss's example rather than blindly submit to his exoteric doctrine.

Morality in State Constitutions and Other Foundational Documents

Besides Madison's statements from *The Federalist*, already quoted, even stronger evidence can be found in the laws and constitutions of every state. These documents represent the most authoritative expression of the consensus of the founding generation. The 1776 Virginia Declaration of Rights affirms that "no free government, or the blessings of liberty, can be preserved to any people but by a firm adherence to justice, moderation, temperance, frugality, and virtue, and by frequent recurrence to fundamental principles." This strong language was repeated, with minor variations, in the Constitutions of Pennsylvania, Vermont, Massachusetts, and New Hampshire.[33] Pennsylvania and Vermont added this: "Laws for the encouragement of virtue, and prevention of vice and immorality, shall be made and constantly kept in force."[34] The Massachusetts, North Carolina, and Georgia laws quoted at the beginning of this chapter provide further evidence of this universal consensus.

The constitutions of two states express their concern with morality in the context of limits on religious liberty. In Maryland's, no one is

---

Mark E. Button, *Contract, Culture, and Citizenship: Transformative Liberalism from Hobbes to Rawls* (University Park: Pennsylvania State University Press, 2008), ch. 2–3. Peter Berkowitz, *Virtue and the Making of Modern Liberalism* (Princeton: Princeton University Press, 1999), ch. 2.

[32] Berkowitz, *Virtue and the Making of Modern Liberalism*, 21.
[33] Bills of Rights of VA, 1776, art. 15; PA, 1776, art. 14; VT, 1777, art. 16; MA, 1780, art. 18; NH, 1784, art. 38.
[34] Constitutions of PA, 1776, §45; VT, 1777, §41.

permitted to "infringe the laws of morality" in the name of religious liberty, and in New York's, religion cannot "excuse acts of licentiousness."[35] Although New Jersey had no similar constitutional provision, its legislature instructed its congressional delegates to "neglect nothing . . . for promoting piety and good morals among the people at large."[36] Ohio's 1803 constitution says, "religion, morality, and knowledge being essentially necessary to good government and the happiness of mankind, schools and the means of instruction shall forever be encouraged by legislative provision not inconsistent with the rights of conscience."[37]

The federal government supported the same view, as one can see in the 1776 resolution of the Continental Congress advising the states to establish governments free of British authority, passed less than a month before the Declaration of Independence: "[I]t is necessary that the exercise of every kind of authority under the said crown should be totally suppressed, and all the powers of government exerted, under the authority of the people of the colonies, for the *preservation of internal peace, virtue, and good order*, as well as for the defense of their lives, liberties, and properties, against the hostile invasions and cruel depredations of their enemies."[38] In this quotation Congress distinguishes between domestic and foreign policy. The purpose of foreign policy is simply "defense of . . . lives, liberties, and properties" (i.e., defense of natural rights) against external enemies. Domestic policy, however, aims to "preserve" three things: "peace, virtue, and good order." "Peace" is the same security of life, liberty, and property that is the goal of foreign policy. "Virtue, and good order," however, are added. Their preservation is one of the principal tasks of government.

Someone might object that these are documents of the period around 1776, and that the post-1787 national government was animated by different principles. Gordon Wood argues that the 1776-era founders were "republicans" who cared deeply about virtue, but by 1787, those elites who thought of themselves as "the wise and good" had created

---

[35] MD Declaration of Rights, 1776, art. 33. NY Constitution, 1777, art. 38.

[36] Instructions of the New Jersey legislature to its delegates in Congress, December 4, 1777, in *Principles and Acts of the Revolution in America*, ed. Hezekiah Niles (1822; repr. New York: Burt Franklin, 1971), 461–2.

[37] OH Bill of Rights, 1803, art. 8, §3 (paraphrasing the Northwest Ordinance). Examples of additional legislative provisions will appear throughout the rest of Part II.

[38] Continental Congress, Resolution to Establish Governments Free of British Authority, May 15, 1776, in *Journals of the Continental Congress, 1774–1789*, ed. Worthington C. Ford (Washington: Government Printing Office, 1904–37), 4:358 (my emphasis).

a new ideology. The authors of the Constitution, Wood writes, "hoped to create an entirely new and original sort of republican government – a republic which did not require a virtuous people for its sustenance." Wood partially recants this assertion later in the book, when he admits that Madison thought that "the people will at least have sufficient 'virtue and intelligence to select men of virtue and wisdom.'"[39] In fact, the Constitution's framers rejected Wood's thesis no less than the men of 1776. This can easily be seen in the Northwest Ordinance, first passed by Congress in 1787, and again after the Constitution went into effect in 1789. This law is especially revealing of the founders' consensus because it lays out the basic structure and policies of republican governance. Federal territories that were not yet states were required to adhere to this law. Echoing the state constitutions of the 1770s and '80s, article 3 of this law states, "Religion, morality, and knowledge, being necessary to good government and the happiness of mankind, schools and the means of education shall forever be encouraged."[40] In the next few chapters we will see that the founders' concern with moral formation continued long after 1787.

Enforcement of Moral Law as the Purpose of Government

Although there is a sense in which individual rights and moral character can be treated as separate topics, it is also true that morality is not something that government can choose either to address or ignore. Nor is the moral law in tension with, or supplemental to, the founders' natural rights theory. It is its foundation.

This can be seen in the fact that the founders tended to equate the moral law with the laws of nature. In an official paper written in 1793, Secretary of State Jefferson asks what standard a nation should follow in foreign policy. Besides international agreements and customs, his answer is "the moral law of our nature," which is "the moral law to which man has been subjected by his creator." Jefferson adds: "The moral duties which exist between individual and individual in a state of nature accompany them into a state of society.... Questions of natural right are triable by their

---

[39] Gordon S. Wood, *The Creation of the American Republic* (New York: Norton, 1969), 475, 544.

[40] Northwest Ordinance, 1787, art. 3, in *The Founders' Constitution*, ed. Philip B. Kurland and Ralph Lerner (Chicago: University of Chicago Press, 1987), 1:28.

conformity with the moral sense and reason of man."[41] In a private letter written much later, Jefferson repeats this view: the "people in mass . . . are inherently independent of all but moral law."[42]

Alexander Hamilton agrees: "the established rules of morality and justice are applicable to nations as well as to individuals; that the former as well as the latter are bound to keep their promises, to fulfill their engagements, to respect the rights of property which others have acquired under contracts with them. Without this, there is an end of all distinct ideas of right or wrong, justice or injustice, in relation to society or government. There can be no such thing as rights – no such thing as property or liberty."[43]

Both Jefferson and Hamilton speak of "moral law" or the "rules of morality" as binding on all human beings, whether considered as individuals or collectively as nations. Both men have in mind such requirements of the natural law as refraining from murdering or enslaving others, "respect[ing] the rights of property," and the like. Rights presuppose duties. Explaining the law of nature in *The Farmer Refuted*, the young Hamilton writes, "Hence, in a state of nature, no man had any *moral* power to deprive another of his life, limbs, property, or liberty; nor the least authority to command, or exact obedience from him; except that which arose from the ties of consanguinity," i.e., common blood, meaning parental rule of minor children.[44]

In his 1793 treatise, Nathaniel Chipman further explains this understanding of moral law: "Man has a natural, that is, a mere physical power, to injure both himself and others," writes Chipman. "But is a liberty to do this accorded to him by the laws of nature? that is, a right to do wrong[?] . . . [L]iberty of action . . . is limited . . . by the obligations of morality, in a word, by the laws of their whole nature. . . . Man, as a being, sociable by the laws of his nature, has no right to pursue his own interest, or happiness, to the exclusion of that of his fellow men. . . . Beyond this, nature may have given power, but she has accorded no liberty, no right to man."[45] The Massachusetts Assembly, instructing its agent in London

---

[41] Thomas Jefferson, Opinion on the French Treaties, 1793, in *Writings*, ed. Merrill D. Peterson (New York: Library of America, 1984), 423, 428.

[42] Jefferson to Spencer Roane, September 6, 1819, in *Writings*, 1426.

[43] Alexander Hamilton, The Vindication, No. III, 1792, in *The Papers of Alexander Hamilton*, ed. Harold C. Syrett (New York: Columbia University Press, 1961–79), 11:470.

[44] Hamilton, *The Farmer Refuted*, 1775, in *Papers*, 1:88.

[45] Nathaniel Chipman, *Sketches of the Principles of Government* (Rutland, VT: J. Lyon, 1793), 74–5.

in 1762, states: "The natural rights of the colonists we humbly conceive to be the same with... all mankind. The principal of these rights is to be 'free from any superior power on earth, and not to be under the will or legislative authority of man, but to have only the law of nature for his rule.'"[46] Human beings are by nature free and equal with respect to other people, but never free of the law of nature.

Madison discusses in *Federalist* 43 what will happen if any of the thirteen states refuse to ratify the Constitution. His answer: they will become independent states without any political connection to the other states, but "the moral relations will remain uncancelled. The claims of justice... must be fulfilled; the rights of humanity must in all cases be duly and mutually respected."[47] Madison, like Jefferson and Hamilton, includes under "moral relations" both the "claims of justice" and the "rights of humanity." We see from these quotations that "the moral law" or "the rules of morality" are the obligations imposed on us by the laws of nature, including respect for the natural rights ("rights of humanity") that are grounded in those laws. Whether one is living in a political community or stranded with a group of plane-crash survivors on a South Pacific island, one always has moral obligations to others.

The view of Jefferson, Hamilton, and Chipman is also found in the Declaration of Independence, where the purpose of government is "to secure these rights" to "life, liberty, and the pursuit of happiness." Translated into the language of moral obligation, this means that government exists to make sure that "the moral duties which exist between individual and individual" are observed.[48] In his preface to a proposed revision of the Virginia criminal code, Jefferson writes, "wicked and dissolute men... commit violations on the lives, liberties, and property, of others.... [T]he secure enjoyment of these having principally induced men to enter into society, government would be defective in its principal purpose were it not to restrain such criminal acts."[49] Government's "principal purpose" (security of person and property) is achieved by restraining the "wicked" who would otherwise violate the moral law. Morality in this

---

[46] Massachusetts Assembly, Instructions to Jasper Mauduit, 1762, in *Massachusetts Historical Society, Collections* 74 (1918): 39, quoting John Locke, *Two Treatises of Government*, 1690, ed. Peter Laslett (Cambridge: Cambridge University Press, 1960), *Second Treatise*, §22.

[47] Madison, *Federalist* 43, pp. 276–7.

[48] Jefferson, Opinion on the French Treaties, 423.

[49] Jefferson, A Bill for Proportioning Crimes and Punishments, 1778, in *Founders' Constitution*, 5:374.

sense is the basis of government because it is its purpose, its reason for being. Scholars who debate the place of "liberalism" and "republicanism" in the founding tend to overlook the fact that morality, moral virtue and vice, upright behavior and "wicked and dissolute" behavior, are the central concern of a government whose purpose is to secure natural rights.[50]

This conclusion seems so obvious that we must ask why it is so seldom noticed. The first obstacle is that when people think of the term *morality*, especially in connection with government, they do not typically think of laws against murder, assault, rape, theft, and other violations of the rights of others. David Flaherty writes, "the sexual code... is at the heart of morality for most persons."[51] Lawrence Friedman adds, "rape, murder, [etc.,]... are, of course, immoral acts; but 'moral crimes' is used here and in the literature in a more restricted sense," referring to such things as sexual misconduct and gambling.[52] In Robert George's *Making Men Moral*, many of the examples discussed are sexual. Index entries include bestiality, homosexuality, pornography, polygamy, and prostitution.[53] Yet when the founders spoke of the "rules of morality," they did not generally have in mind sexual offenses – although they were certainly concerned about those too, as Chapter 10 demonstrates.

It is true that the narrower contemporary understanding of morality does sometimes seem to appear in the founding. Maryland's Declaration of Rights says, "no person ought by any law to be molested [on account of religion]... unless... [he] shall disturb the good order, peace or safety of the State, or shall infringe the laws of morality, or injure others, in their natural, civil, or religious rights." Maryland seems to draw a distinction between infringing the (unspecified) laws of morality and violating the rights of others. It is possible that Maryland was equating infringing "the laws of morality" with the "acts of licentiousness" mentioned in the New York Constitution of 1777 ("the liberty of conscience, hereby granted, shall not be so construed as to excuse acts of licentiousness").[54]

50 Philip A. Hamburger, "Natural Rights, Natural Law, and American Constitutions," *Yale Law Journal* 102 (Jan. 1993): 924–30 (the founders' natural law sets moral limits on natural liberty).
51 David H. Flaherty, "Law and the Enforcement of Morals in Early America," in *Law in American History*, ed. Donald Fleming and Bernard Bailyn (Boston: Little, Brown, 1971), 205.
52 Lawrence M. Friedman, *Crime and Punishment in American History* (New York: Basic Books, 1993), 126.
53 Robert P. George, *Making Men Moral: Civil Liberties and Public Morality* (Oxford: Clarendon Press, 1993).
54 MD Declaration of Rights, 1776, art. 33. NY Constitution, 1777, art. 38.

However this may be, the term "moral law(s)" in the founding generally meant rules concerning any actions permitted or forbidden by the laws of nature, sexual or otherwise.

A second obstacle to the founders' understanding of moral law is the distinction between actions freely chosen and actions performed under threat of punishment. Martin Luther King writes, "Morality cannot be legislated, but behavior can be regulated. Judicial decrees may not change the heart, but they can restrain the heartless."[55] Similarly, George writes, "Laws cannot make men moral. Only men can do that; and they can do it only by freely choosing to do the morally right thing for the right reason." King and George think of morality as an internal disposition that habitually leads to certain actions designated as moral. The founders also acknowledged this distinction. They agreed with King that laws can "restrain the heartless." In Jefferson's words, laws can "restrain... [the] criminal acts" of "wicked and dissolute men." But the moral law is obeyed whether the motivation comes freely from within or from an external threat of punishment. Laws can form character in both ways, as we will see in the next three chapters.

Twofold Purpose of Government's Concern with Morality

In the Northwest Ordinance, "morality" is spoken of in the context of education and is said to be "necessary to good government and the happiness of mankind." This formulation, repeated in many other official pronouncements in the founding, indicates a twofold purpose of morality, one public ("good government"), and one private ("happiness"). Ultimately, of course, good government serves happiness. Chief Justice Theophilus Parsons elaborates in an 1810 Massachusetts Supreme Court case:

The object of a free civil government is the promotion and security of the happiness of the citizens. These effects cannot be produced, but by the knowledge and practice of our moral duties, which comprehend all the social and civil obligations of man to man, and of the citizen to the state.... To obtain that perfection, it is not enough for the magistrate to define the rights of the several citizens, as they are related to life, liberty, property, and reputation, and to punish those by whom they may be invaded.... Human laws cannot oblige to the performance of the duties of imperfect obligation; as the duties of charity and hospitality,

[55] Martin Luther King, Jr., *Strength to Love* (Philadelphia: Fortress Press, 1981), 37. George, *Making Men Moral*, 1.

benevolence and good neighborhood; as the duties resulting from the relation of husband and wife, parent and child; of man to man, as children of a common parent; and of real patriotism, by influencing every citizen to love his country, and to obey all its laws. These are moral duties, flowing from the disposition of the heart, and not subject to the control of human legislation.[56]

Parsons is saying that the *happiness* of individuals is promoted not only by enforcement of criminal law "to punish those by whom [the natural rights of others] may be invaded" but also by shaping the "disposition of the heart" that enables people to deal appropriately with their husbands, wives, children, and neighbors. And *good government* is promoted when every citizen "love[s] his country, and . . . obey[s] all its laws."

Regarding happiness and private life, a free government allows people wide latitude in regard to personal liberty. It presumes that the people will be able to take care of their ordinary affairs without having to be watched and micromanaged by government. A people without a minimum of self-control cannot be trusted to raise children, deal with family quarrels, and own firearms. A society will be free in name only if its government is constantly second-guessing parental decisions regarding discipline and medical care, interfering in marital quarrels, making it difficult to acquire licenses or permits for ordinary activities, forbidding all but a favored few to own guns, and so on – policies that have become increasingly common in America over the past century. Therefore, as John Adams wrote, "Education is more indispensable, and must be more general, under a free government than any other."[57]

With respect to public life ("good government"), Madison explains in a passage from *The Federalist* quoted earlier that "Republican government presupposes the existence of these qualities [i.e., virtues] in a higher degree than any other form [of government]." Otherwise, "nothing less than the chains of despotism can restrain them from destroying and devouring one another."[58] Benjamin Franklin sums up the point: "only a virtuous people are capable of freedom. As nations become corrupt and vicious, they have more need of masters."[59]

---

[56] *Barnes v. First Parish in Falmouth*, 6 Mass. 401 (1810).
[57] John Adams, *Defence of the Constitutions*, 1787, in *Works of John Adams*, 6:198.
[58] Madison, *Federalist* 55, p. 343.
[59] Franklin to the Abbés Chalet and Arnaud, April 17, 1787, in *The Works of Benjamin Franklin*, ed. John Bigelow (New York: G.P. Putnam's Sons, 1904), 11:326.

The Limits of Virtue

So far I have shown that the founders were unquestionably concerned with morality. However, it is also true that the founders opposed the view that mankind can be preached into obedience to moral law. This is stated with particular clarity by John Adams in a 1790 exchange of letters with his cousin Samuel Adams. Samuel writes that "divines and philosophers, statesmen and patriots" could "renovate the age, by impressing the minds of men with the importance of educating their little boys and girls; of inculcating in the minds of youth the fear and love of the Deity and universal philanthropy, and... the love of their country;... in short, of leading them in the study and practice of the exalted virtues of the Christian system, which will happily tend to subdue the turbulent passions of men, and introduce that golden age, beautifully described in figurative language, – when the wolf shall dwell with the lamb."

John Adams spoke for most founders in his response: "[Y]ou seem to place all your hopes in the universal, or at least more general, prevalence of knowledge and benevolence. I think with you, that knowledge and benevolence ought to be promoted as much as possible; but, despairing of ever seeing them sufficiently general for the security of society, I am for seeking institutions which may supply in some degree the defect. If there were no ignorance, error, or vice, there would be neither principles nor systems of civil or political government."[60] The founders, then, were not naive enough to believe that government could rely on cultivation of virtue as a sufficient basis of obedience to moral law.

Thomas Paine agrees with John Adams on the weakness of what he calls "moral virtue" by itself. "Society is produced by our wants, and government by our wickedness; the former promotes our happiness positively by uniting our affections, the latter negatively by restraining our vices.... Government, like dress, is the badge of lost innocence.... For were the impulses of conscience clear, uniform, and irresistibly obeyed, man would need no other lawgiver.... [However, there is a] necessity, of establishing some form of government to supply the defect of moral

---

[60] Samuel Adams to John Adams, October 4, 1790, in *Works of John Adams*, ed. Charles Francis Adams (Boston: Little, Brown, 1854), 6:414. John Adams to Samuel Adams, in ibid., 6:415. Paul A. Rahe comments sensibly on this John Adams letter in *Republics Ancient and Modern* (Chapel Hill: University of North Carolina Press, 1992), 587 and 1059n63.

virtue. . . . [G]overnment [is] rendered necessary by the inability of moral virtue to govern the world."[61]

Philosophers both ancient and modern have agreed on the need for strong laws to "supply the defect of moral virtue." They have also agreed that no government can rely wholly on citizen virtue. Laws protecting persons and property are indispensable. Martin Diamond correctly remarks, "Aristotle and ancient political science had no illusions about the quantity of better motives available; Aristotle thought them to be in as short supply as is supposed by modern political thought."[62] Shortly before he died, Diamond sent me a letter in which he wrote that he has "one last lecture to give somewhere when I retire. It is to be entitled 'The Ancients versus the Moderns: Or, the Sissies versus the Swine.' In short, I am arguing against the view of the ancients versus the moderns which makes the former all sweetness and light, relying innocently on virtue and education and piety, with the moderns nothing but a bunch of swine determined to lower men wholly to the level of beasts" by relying on law alone and rejecting any concern with virtue.[63] I wish Diamond had lived to give that lecture. The moderns as "swine" is a view one continues to hear with surprising frequency.

If the founders were sensible enough to realize that "moral virtue" cannot "govern the world," they also did not make the opposite error. They did not believe that "socially useful passions or vices" – Strauss's expression – could do away with the need for public-spiritedness and self-restraint. Richard Sinopoli writes, "they realized that institutional and/or social checks and balances were insufficient though necessary guarantees of stability. . . . [B]oth Federalists and Anti-Federalists were concerned with the problem of fostering a *sentiment* of allegiance from which a disposition to undertake civic duties would emerge."[64] In *Common Sense* Paine had said we need law to "supply the defect of moral virtue." Adams's letter quoted above clarifies this (and Paine would probably not have disagreed) by adding that the law can only "supply *in some degree* the defect." The founders unanimously acted on the presumption that the rules of morality will not be observed from legal punishments alone, i.e., from baser motives of self-interest. We noted earlier that almost

---

[61] Thomas Paine, *Common Sense*, 1776, ed. Isaac Kramnick (New York: Penguin, 1976), 65–6, 68.
[62] Diamond, "Ethics and Politics: The American Way," 354.
[63] Diamond, letter to the author, January 18, 1977.
[64] Sinopoli, *Foundations of American Citizenship*, 6.

every state, along with the federal government, affirmed the need for citizen virtue. At least to some extent, these qualities had to be, in Samuel
Adams's phrase, "inculcated" so as to become a habitual moral disposition. The next three chapters will show how the founders thought that
should be done.

9

How Government Supports Morality

The previous chapter showed the pervasive concern of the founders with the moral character of citizens. The next question is what government should do about it.

This chapter, and the rest of Part II of this book, are a response to scholars like Alan Gibson, who argues that "few of the Founders believed that the formation of belief and opinion or the development of a common character among the citizenry was the province of the government." In response to the claim that state governments were expected to provide for "the education of statesmen and citizens," Gibson writes, "As far as I know, no study has proved this to be the case."[1] Gibson cites Peter Onuf, who writes, "by 1787 the states had effectively withdrawn from any active effort to shape character."[2] In partial agreement with Gibson and Onuf, Gordon Wood argues that many founders trusted in the "natural sociality of people" as a "modern substitute for the ascetic classical virtue of antiquity." While Wood agrees with me that the founders believed that government needs virtue, he says that "for many American thinkers," this virtue would arise more or less spontaneously from "the modern willingness to get along with others for the sake of peace and prosperity." Wood calls this a "radical belief in the capacity of affection

---

[1] Alan Gibson, *Understanding the Founding: The Crucial Questions*, 2nd ed. (Lawrence: University Press of Kansas, 2010), 149, 342.
[2] Peter Onuf, "State Politics and Republican Virtue: Religion, Education, and Morality in Early American Federalism," in *Toward a Usable Past: Liberty under State Constitutions*, ed. Paul Finkelman and Stephen E. Gottlieb (Athens: University of Georgia Press, 1991), 91–116.

and benevolence to hold republican societies together."[3] Like Gibson, Onuf, and Wood, Thomas Pangle thinks the founders cared about virtue but did little to promote or sustain it. "The founders certainly restate, at important junctures, some of the principles of the classical republicanism political teaching," writes Pangle. "They are concerned with recruiting men of virtue for public office.... They appeal to the proud, watchful, and fair-minded spirit of the people as the final bulwark against tyranny.... But they integrate these classical or quasi-classical elements into a framework that makes very little provision for the inculcation, or fostering, or even preservation of these crucial excellences of character."[4] Robert Bork has brought this same erroneous view to a larger public: "The signers of the Declaration took the moral order they had inherited for granted."[5] Contrary to all these writers, I argue that the founders held that republican virtue requires the help of human institutions, both public and private.

Other scholars agree with me. Political theorist Jean Yarbrough argues that "the states took the question of character seriously indeed, providing in different ways for religion, education, and political participation." Michael Zuckert was quoted earlier on the founders' approval of government promotion of a "rights infrastructure" which included public education. Historian Thomas James shows that "moral education... in support of republican political institutions" was a leading purpose of government-funded primary education in the early republic. According to Paul Rahe, Jefferson wanted Virginia's legislature to "support... those laws of morality which are necessary for public and private happiness." Rahe continues, "Few in the founding generation were inclined to take

---

[3] Gordon S. Wood, *Empire of Liberty: A History of the Early Republic, 1789–1815* (New York: Oxford University Press, 2009), 12–13.

[4] Thomas L. Pangle, "Republicanism and Rights," in *The Framers and Fundamental Rights*, ed. Robert A. Licht (Washington: AEI Press, 1991), 117. A better presentation, recognizing that many founders advocated government involvement in moral education, is Lorraine Smith Pangle and Thomas L. Pangle, *The Learning of Liberty: The Educational Ideas of the American Founders* (Lawrence: University Press of Kansas, 1993). Also Herbert J. Storing, *What the Anti-Federalists Were For* (Chicago: University of Chicago Press, 1981), 73 (they "took for granted a certain kind of public-spirited leadership" and "the republican genius of the people"); Richard Vetterli and Gary C. Bryner, *In Search of the Republic: Public Virtue and the Roots of American Government*, 2nd ed. (Lanham, MD: Rowman & Littlefield, 1996), xiii (the founders held that virtue "cannot be compelled through the coercive power of government" and therefore relied almost entirely on private institutions).

[5] Robert Bork, *Slouching towards Gomorrah: Modern Liberalism and American Decline* (New York: Regan Books, Harper Collins, 1996), 57–8 (quoting Robert Nisbet).

exception to the [opinion that] . . . 'the civil power . . . has a right to prohibit and punish gross immoralities and impieties because the open practice of these is of evil example and public detriment.'" Mark Kann states that government regulation of morals was thought "necessary for ensuring sufficient public order to host, defend, and extend individual liberty." Leo Paul de Alvarez writes, "there is no doubt that the States were primarily given the task of forming the morals of the people"; the 1787 Northwest Ordinance in particular shows that "the Federal Government accepted a duty from the very beginning to form the people's morality, religion, and knowledge."⁶ Although these and others are in general agreement with my argument in Part II, no one has gone into the matter as thoroughly as I do here. Nor do the scholars mentioned go far enough in showing the connection between the natural rights theory and policies to promote citizen virtues.

To support this claim, I will present an account of the various ways in which the founders promoted civic virtue. The present chapter contains an overview, followed by a chapter on the founders' policies on sex and marriage and one on government's role in forming a public opinion favorable to morality.

The Four Kinds of Moral Law

To clarify the founders' approach, I will make use of John Locke's analysis of moral law and its enforcement in his *Essay concerning Human Understanding*.⁷ I know of no evidence that the founders knew of Locke's

---

⁶ Jean Yarbrough, "The Constitution and Character: The Missing Critical Principle?" in *To Form a More Perfect Union: The Critical Ideas of the Constitution*, ed. Herman Belz, Ronald Hoffman, and Peter J. Albert (Charlottesville: University Press of Virginia, 1992), 237; Michael P. Zuckert, *Launching Liberalism: On Lockean Political Philosophy* (Lawrence: University Press of Kansas, 2002), 226; Thomas James, "Rights of Conscience and State School Systems in Nineteenth-Century America," in ibid., 123–4; Paul A. Rahe, *Republics Ancient and Modern: Classical Republicanism and the American Revolution* (Chapel Hill: University of North Carolina Press, 1992), 762 (quoting Ellsworth in *Connecticut Courant*, December 17, 1787); Mark E. Kann, *Taming Passion for the Public Good: Policing Sex in the Early Republic* (New York: New York University Press, 2013), 21; Leo Paul S. de Alvarez, "The Constitution and American Character: The Framers' Views," in *Constitutionalism in Perspective: The United States Constitution in Twentieth Century Politics*, ed. Sarah B. Thurow (Lanham, MD: University Press of America, 1988), 258.

⁷ John Locke, *An Essay concerning Human Understanding*, 4th ed., 1700, ed. Peter H. Nidditch (Oxford: Clarendon Press, 1975), bk. 2, ch. 28, §4–§13, 350–7.

analysis, although some were familiar with the *Essay*.[8] I mention Locke only because his distinction between the four kinds of moral law helps us to clarify the founders' approach. They are:

1. divine revelation (e.g., the Ten Commandments, given by God directly to human beings)
2. the law of nature (discovered by human reason)
3. civil law (set down by government)
4. "the law of fashion or private censure," also called "the law of opinion or reputation"[9]

If the first kind of moral law is genuine, then God "has power to enforce it by rewards and punishments... in another life." Locke calls the second, the law of nature, the "true touchstone" of morality. It is taught by God through human reason, although mere reason cannot prove that God will enforce it. The third kind of moral law, the civil law, "nobody overlooks," says Locke, for the "rewards and punishments that enforce it [are] ready at hand" in fines, prison, or execution. The fourth, the "law of fashion or private censure," is created by a "tacit consent" in one's group. This can be one's family, friends, classmates, club, church, business, school, or nation. This law is enforced by praise or blame, honor or disgrace, acceptance or exclusion from the group. The power of the law of opinion lies in the fact that "no man escapes the punishment of their censure and dislike, who offends against the fashion and opinion of the company he keeps." Consequently, "the greatest part" of mankind "govern themselves chiefly, if not solely, by this law of fashion."[10]

Jefferson saw the need for all four kinds of moral law, which I will point out in bracketed interpolations in this excerpt from an 1814 letter:

When [the moral sense] is wanting, we endeavor to supply the defect by education, by appeals to reason and calculation, by presenting to the being so unhappily

---

8　Benjamin Franklin, *Autobiography*, in *Writings*, ed. J. A. Leo Lemay (New York: Library of America, 1987), 1321; Philip A. Hamburger, "The Constitution's Accommodation of Social Change," *Michigan Law Review* 88, No. 2 (Nov. 1989): 304–5 (Madison paraphrases Locke's *Essay* in *Federalist* 37); John Adams to Jonathan Sewall, Feb. 1760, in Founders Online, National Archives, founders.archives.gov (praising Locke's "metaphysics" – presumably his *Essay*).

9　Locke actually lists only three kinds of moral law: divine, civil, and the law of opinion. But he distinguishes two sources of divine law: reason and revelation. To avoid confusion, I do not speak of a single "divine law" with two parts, but instead of the law of revelation and the law of reason or nature as two distinct kinds of moral law.

10　Locke, *Essay*, bk. 2, ch. 28, §8–12; bk. 4, ch. 10 (mere reason cannot prove the existence of a God who punishes).

conformed, other motives to do good and to eschew evil, such as [1] the love, or the hatred, or the rejection of those among whom he lives, and whose society is necessary to his happiness and even existence [i.e., the law of opinion]; [2] demonstrations by sound calculation that honesty promotes interest in the long run [reason proves that private interest is served by obedience to natural law]; [3] the rewards and penalties established by the laws [political laws]; and [4] ultimately the prospects of a future state of retribution for the evil as well as the good done while here [the law of divine revelation]. These are the correctives which are supplied by education, and which exercise the functions of the moralist, the preacher, and legislator; and they lead into a course of correct action all those whose depravity is not too profound to be eradicated.[11]

We find the same four kinds of moral law in the constitutions and laws of the founding. The Northwest Ordinance of 1787 sums up "the fundamental principles of civil and religious liberty, which form the basis whereon these republics [i.e., the existing states], their laws and constitutions, are erected." Political law is mentioned: "For the prevention of crimes, and injuries,... laws [are] to be adopted... [both] criminal and civil." The Northwest Ordinance then alludes to the other three kinds of moral law: "Religion, morality, and knowledge being necessary..., schools and the means of education shall forever be encouraged."[12] "Religion" is based on divine revelation. "Morality" is what people privately and sincerely believe to be right, which, if Locke and Jefferson are right, is largely produced by the law of private censure within one's group (and supported by what we learn in "schools"). Through "knowledge" we have access to the law of nature. Although governmental laws, strictly speaking, are only one of the four kinds of moral law, government can affect the other three, as we will see.

John Adams treats the four kinds of moral law in *Discourses on Davila*, written while he was vice-president. On the first, divine revelation, Adams writes that atheists, who believe "that men are but fireflies, and that this all [i.e., the universe] is without a father," will conclude that human life is not sacred and that "murder itself [is] as indifferent as shooting a plover [a bird], and the extermination of the Rohilla nation as innocent as the swallowing of mites on a morsel of cheese."[13] Elsewhere Adams mentions

[11] Jefferson to Thomas Law, June 13, 1814, in *Writings*, ed. Merrill D. Peterson (New York: Library of America, 1984), 1338.

[12] Northwest Ordinance, 1787, in *Founders' Constitution*, 1:27–8.

[13] Adams, *Discourses on Davila*, 1790, end of ch. 13, in *Works of John Adams*, ed. Charles Francis Adams (Boston: Little, Brown, 1854), 6:281. The "Rohilla nation" was an Afghan tribe slaughtered or banished with British assistance in the 1770s. Edmund Burke called this an instance of "the rights of men cruelly violated": speech on Fox's

the need for belief in divine rewards and punishments. Because of the insufficiency of reason as a moral guide, "the joys of heaven are prepared, and the horrors of hell in a future state, to render the moral government of the universe perfect and complete."[14] Jefferson agrees: "And can the liberties of a nation be thought secure when we have removed their only firm basis, a conviction in the minds of the people that these liberties are of the gift of God? That they are not to be violated but with his wrath?"[15]

On reason, the second source of moral law, Adams writes, "Nature has sanctioned the law of self-preservation by rewards and punishments [i.e., natural consequences of misbehavior that are knowable to human reason]. The rewards of selfish activity are life and health; the punishments of negligence and indolence are want, disease, and death. Each individual, it is true, should consider that nature has enjoined the same law on his neighbor, and therefore a respect for the authority of nature would oblige him to respect the rights of others as much as his own." Recognizing the weakness of mere reason, Adams adds: "reasoning as abstruse, though as simple as this, would not occur to all men." Besides, as Adams remarks in his diary, there is a need for an additional source of moral law because "many exceptions to this rule take place upon earth."[16]

On the need for the third kind of moral law, the legal commands of government, Adams says: "government is intended to set bounds to passions which nature has not limited; and to assist reason, conscience, justice, and truth, in controlling interests, which, without it, would be as unjust as uncontrollable."[17]

On the fourth kind of moral law, the law of fashion, Adams writes, "nature therefore has imposed [a] law of promoting the good as well as respecting the rights of mankind, and has sanctioned it by other rewards and punishments. The rewards in this case, in this life, are *esteem* and *admiration* of others; the punishments are *neglect* and *contempt*."[18] This kind of honoring and dishonoring is indispensable in a republic, as Adams also states: "The freedom of censure is a matter of great consequence under our government. There are certain vices and follies, certain

East India Bill, December 1, 1783, in *Select Works of Edmund Burke: Miscellaneous Writings* (Indianapolis: Liberty Fund, 1999), 103, 111–12.
[14] Adams, Diary, August 22, 1770, in *Works of John Adams*, 2:250.
[15] Jefferson, *Notes on the State of Virginia*, 1787, Query 18, in *Writings*, 289.
[16] Adams, *Davila*, ch. 2, 6:234. Diary, August 22, 1770, ibid., 2:250.
[17] Adams, *Davila*, ch. 13, 6:276.
[18] Ibid., ch. 2, 6:234.

indecencies of behavior, beneath the inspection and censure of law and magistracy, which must be restrained and corrected by satire."[19]

Government was expected to be involved in the promotion or enforcement of all four kinds of moral law. First, regarding divine revelation, all the leading founders, including the oft-claimed exceptions of Jefferson and Madison, agreed that government should promote sound religious opinions. There was disagreement on the methods to be used, but at a minimum all accepted the use of official government pronouncements supportive of religion. These include public prayers and invocations of God, the use of religious language in addresses of public officials, and the affirmation of theological claims in formal documents such as state constitutions, which typically begin with religious language. Government-supported religious opinions were always expected to be consistent with, or explicitly supportive of, natural law, natural rights, and the virtues that sustain both.

Second, natural law was to be taught through formal as well as informal instruction.

Third, political laws – the civil and criminal law, and the use of armed forces to punish foreign violations of natural law – were obviously a major concern of government.

Fourth, as explained more fully in Chapter 11, government indirectly contributes to the formation of the law of opinion through its criminal and civil laws, its teaching, its persuasion through speeches and publications, its subsidies and tax breaks, and through the characteristic features of the political regime itself, such as property rights, gun rights, and the absence of hereditary aristocracy. In doing so, it shapes public opinion toward virtue and liberty and turns it away from vice.

Public Education

I will begin with public education, which promotes three of the four kinds of moral law – religion, knowledge of the law of nature, and formation of moral opinion. Government promotes knowledge of the natural law by instruction in the rational arguments that support it. It promotes obedience to the natural law by putting students together in classrooms where the law of fashion will exert its power over them, and by promoting belief in a God whose commands support the same law of nature.

---

[19] Adams to the *Boston Gazette* (draft), May 1761, in *Diary and Autobiography of John Adams*, ed. L. H. Butterfield (Cambridge: Harvard University Press, 1961), 1:215.

According to a report by Jefferson commissioned by the state of Virginia, the purpose of pre-university education is to "instruct the mass of our citizens in these, their rights, interests, and duties, as men and citizens."[20] Washington provides a fuller account in his First Annual Message to Congress:

Knowledge is, in every country, the surest basis of public happiness. . . . To the security of a free constitution it contributes in various ways: by convincing those who are entrusted with the public administration, that every valuable end of government is best answered by the enlightened confidence of the people; and by teaching the people themselves to know and to value their own rights; to discern and provide against invasions of them; to distinguish between oppression and the necessary exercise of lawful authority; between burdens proceeding from a disregard to their convenience, and those resulting from the inevitable exigencies of society; to discriminate the spirit of liberty from that of licentiousness – cherishing the first, avoiding the last; and uniting a speedy but temperate vigilance against encroachments, with an inviolable respect to the laws.[21]

The things that Washington speaks of – such as "vigilance" and "respect to the laws" – are nonrational habitual qualities of character. But he also speaks of real insight, using words like "knowledge," "enlightened," "discern," and "distinguish." He concludes with this advice to Congress: "Whether this desirable object will be best promoted by affording aids to seminaries of learning already established; by the institution of a national university; or by any other expedients, will be well worthy of a place in the deliberations of the Legislature."[22]

Washington's view was shared by Madison, who writes: "Learned institutions ought to be the favorite objects with every free people. They throw that light over the public mind which is the best security against crafty and dangerous encroachments on the public liberty. . . . What spectacle can be more edifying than that of liberty and learning, each leaning on the other for their mutual and surest support?"[23]

The views of Jefferson, Washington, and Madison concerning the importance of instructing and habituating the people in their rights and

---

[20] Report of the Commissioners for the University of Virginia, August 4, 1818, in Jefferson, *Writings*, 459. His discussion of public education in *Notes on the State of Virginia* is in Query 14, in ibid., 272–5.

[21] Washington, First Annual Message to Congress, 1790, in *Writings*, ed. John Rhodehamel (New York: Library of America, 1997), 750.

[22] Ibid. In the founding, "seminaries" were educational institutions, usually advanced ones, and not necessarily places for religious instruction.

[23] Madison to William Barry, August 4, 1822, in *Writings*, ed. Jack N. Rakove (New York: Library of America, 1999), 791, 793.

duties were widely shared. Seven of the twelve states that adopted constitutions by 1790 had provisions for education. Massachusetts provided for
"public schools and grammar schools in the towns," since "wisdom and
knowledge, as well as virtue, diffused generally among the body of the
people [are] necessary for the preservation of their rights and liberties."[24]
Provisions for primary education in the other six state constitutions are
as follows:

> North Carolina: "a school or schools shall be established by the legis-
> lature, for the convenient instruction of youth."
> Georgia: "Schools shall be erected in each county."
> New Hampshire: "Knowledge, and learning, generally diffused
> through a community, being essential to the preservation of a free
> government;...the legislators...[shall] cherish the interest of lit-
> erature and the sciences, and all seminaries and public schools."
> Vermont: "a competent number of schools ought to be maintained in
> each town for the convenient instruction of youth."
> Pennsylvania: "The legislature shall...provide by law for the estab-
> lishment of schools throughout the state, in such manner that the
> poor may be taught gratis."
> Delaware: "The legislature shall...provide by law...for establishing
> schools, and promoting arts and sciences."[25]

Education was not a constitutional power of Congress, except for the federal territories. There, Congress possessed and asserted plenary authority.
The Land Ordinance of 1785 reserved one lot "of every township, for
the maintenance of public schools." The Northwest Ordinance stated,
"schools and the means of education shall forever be encouraged" to
promote "religion, morality, and knowledge."[26]

States both with and without these constitutional provisions gradually began to set up free public education. By 1802 all Northern states
except Rhode Island and New Jersey passed laws for public funding of
elementary schools, sometimes limited to schools for the poor. The District of Columbia opened public schools in 1806. Most of these states
also provided some taxpayer support to privately owned "academies"

---

[24] MA Constitution, 1780, ch. 5, §2.
[25] Constitutions of NC, 1776, §41; GA, 1776, §54; NH, 1784, Part II; VT, 1786, §38;
PA, 1790, art. 7, §1; DE, 1792, art. 8, §12.
[26] Ordinance for the Sale of Western Lands, 1785, in *The Documentary History of the
Ratification of the Constitution*, ed. Merrill Jensen (Madison: State Historical Society of
Wisconsin, 1976), 1:160. Northwest Ordinance, 1787, art. 4, in ibid., 1:173.

(high schools). In the South, much less was done, in spite of requirements for public education in the North Carolina and Georgia constitutions.[27] Historian Charles Dabney explains: "There were long contests in these states between the planters and the small farmers who owned no slaves. The planters generally refused to be taxed for schools, with the result that North Carolina and Kentucky were the only states in the South which had anything approaching a system of public schools before 1860."[28] Legal historian John Eastman notes that the language of some state constitutions was adjusted in light of the slowness of the actual implementation of public education: "Before the end of the century, Pennsylvania, Vermont, and Georgia had all moved away from the obligatory language [of their first constitutions] and adopted more hortatory provisions. Thus, the Vermont Constitutions of 1786 and 1793 simply state that 'schools *ought* to be maintained in each town,' and the Pennsylvania and Georgia Constitutions of 1790 and 1798 ... [use] the phrase, 'as soon as conveniently may be,' a phrase which is also found in the Delaware Constitution of 1792."[29] Nevertheless, most states (with the exceptions noted) developed a system of public education well before the Civil War.

Regarding higher education, the constitutions of Pennsylvania, North Carolina, Vermont, Massachusetts, and Georgia provided for universities.[30] Virginia and Maryland established universities by law. Other states provided some public support to private colleges. Jefferson's official report on the University of Virginia provides a good overview of the purpose of higher education. The main intent is "to form the statesmen, legislators, and judges, on whom public prosperity and individual happiness are so much to depend." Cultivating public officials involved studies in "the principles and structure of government" as well as "political economy" to promote public industry. Students are also to learn "mathematical and physical sciences, which advance the arts, and

---

[27] Ellwood Patterson Cubberley, *Public Education in the United States: A Study and Interpretation of American Educational History* (Boston: Houghton Mifflin, 1919), 61–71; Edwin Grant Dexter, *A History of Education in the United States* (New York: Macmillan, 1906), 73–96; Lawrence A. Cremin, *American Education: The National Experience, 1783–1876* (New York: Harper & Row, 1980), 148–81.

[28] Charles William Dabney, *Universal Education in the South*, vol. 1: *From the Beginning to 1900* (Chapel Hill: University of North Carolina Press, 1936), viii.

[29] John C. Eastman, "When Did Education Become a Civil Right? An Assessment of State Constitutional Provisions for Education, 1776–1900," *American Journal of Legal History* 42 (Jan. 1998): 9.

[30] NC Constitution, 1776, ch. II, §41; PA, 1776, ch. II, §44; PA, 1790, art. 7, §2; VT, 1777, §40; MA, 1780, ch. 5, §2; GA, 1798, art. 4, §13.

administer to the health, the subsistence, and comforts of human life."
Ultimately, the university is to "develop their reasoning faculties" and
"enlarge their minds, cultivate their morals, and instill into them the precepts of virtue and order," in order "to form them to habits of reflection
and correct actions, rendering them examples of virtue to others, and of
happiness within themselves."[31] We may sum up by saying that Jefferson
wanted his graduates to understand the principles of politics, to know
one or more of the sciences, and to be formed in "virtue and order."[32]
Two of the four moral laws are promoted here: knowledge of the law of
nature, and cultivation of the law of fashion in support of suitable moral
qualities.

Maryland's 1784 act funding the state university alludes to these same
two moral laws: "institutions for the education of youth, under the care
and patronage of the state, have ever been encouraged by the wisest
nations, as the most effectual means of dissemination of the principles of
religious and civil liberty, private and public virtue, and those liberal arts
and sciences, which are at once the greatest ornament of a free republic,
and the surest basis of its stability and glory."[33] In another Maryland law
passed two years earlier: "institutions for the liberal education of youth
in the principles of virtue, knowledge, and useful literature are of the
highest benefit to society, in order to raise up and perpetuate a succession
of able and honest men, for discharging the various offices and duties
of the community, both civil and religious."[34] The political and moral
purpose of liberal education is unmistakable.

Thomas Pangle laments that the founders' university education was
limited to "training of sober and eminently practical public servants
of a commercial and agricultural society" shaped by "a relatively narrow, shared moral horizon – the horizon of modern democracy."[35]
The founders would have had two responses. First, nothing can justify

---

[31] Report of the Commissioners for the University of Virginia, August 4, 1818, in Jefferson,
Writings, 459–60.

[32] Eugene F. Miller, "On the American Founders' Defense of Liberal Education in a Republic," *Review of Politics* 46, No. 1 (Jan. 1984): 65–90 (presenting several founders'
opinions, all in general agreement with Jefferson).

[33] An Act to Provide a Permanent Fund for . . . Washington College, 1784, *Hanson's Laws
of Maryland*, vol. 203, p. 374, http://aomol.msa.maryland.gov/000001/000203/html/
index.html.

[34] An Act for Founding a College at Chester-Town, 1782, in ibid., 203:307.

[35] Thomas L. Pangle, *The Spirit of Modern Republicanism: The Moral Vision of the
American Founders and the Philosophy of Locke* (Chicago: University of Chicago Press,
1988), 77.

taxpayer funding of higher education (or of anything at all) other than service to the public. For that reason, government-supported education of course had to be useful to the community. As the Massachusetts and other state constitutions stress, under the terms of the social compact, "all shall be governed by certain laws for the common good," and no one has "any other title to obtain... particular and exclusive privileges... than what arises from the consideration of services rendered to the public."[36] Second, the founders' higher education included more than "eminently practical" training within a "narrow, shared moral horizon." For example, instruction in Maryland's state university was supposed to be "not only in the learned languages, but in philosophy, divinity, law, physic, and other useful *and ornamental* arts and sciences."[37] Maryland implies that a truly useful liberal education requires more than what is useful in any narrow sense.

Anna Haddow demonstrates that during the founding era, instruction in the laws of nature and related subjects was provided at every American college and university that she studied. Virginia's William and Mary College required of all graduates knowledge of "natural law, laws of nations, and the general principles of politics." At Columbia, the professor of moral philosophy taught "the first principles and laws resulting from the nature of man, and his natural relations to God and his fellow creatures, by which human conduct ought to be regulated.... This constitutes the law of nature." Yale's seniors studied "Vattel's *Law of Nature and Nations.*" Harvard's were "examined in the elements of natural and political law."[38] Mark Bailey shows that moral, religious, and natural law themes also prevailed in early American legal education.[39]

Besides teaching and inculcating in children their rights and duties, elementary schools focused on arithmetic, reading, and writing. But it is characteristic of early American education that the best-selling textbook for teaching English was Noah Webster's *Grammatical Institute of the English Language,* one purpose of which was to "furnish schools with... essays containing the history, geography, and transactions of the United States," to better "form the morals as well as improve the

---

[36] MA Constitution, 1780, Preamble; Declaration of Rights, art. 6.

[37] Act for Founding a College, 1782, in *Hanson's Laws*, 203:307 (my emphasis).

[38] Anna Haddow, *Political Science in American Colleges and Universities, 1636–1900* (1939; repr. New York: Octagon Books, 1969), 45, 51, 54, 56.

[39] Mark Warren Bailey, *Guardians of the Legal Order: The Legal Philosophy of the Supreme Court, 1860–1910* (DeKalb: Northern Illinois Press, 2004), 24–84.

knowledge of youth."[40] This text comports with Jefferson's recommendation that primary education should enable every citizen to "improve, by reading, his morals and faculties; . . . understand his duties to his neighbors and country . . . ; [and] know his rights."[41]

The Limits of Enlightenment

One might wonder how much the founders trusted in the power of reason to support liberty. Did they, in Leo Strauss's formulation, think that "the kingdom of darkness could be replaced by the republic of universal light"?[42] For the most part, the founders' stance toward the Enlightenment was sober and cautious, even if they did at times express strong hopes for a more general diffusion of knowledge.

Some of the state constitutions and laws already quoted do appear to presume that the moral law can be inculcated merely by instruction. The Declaration of Independence asserts that the rights of mankind are "self-evident." Does this mean that knowledge of the moral law is easily acquired? In his last letter, Jefferson seems to suggest that moral knowledge is available to everyone: "All eyes are opened, or opening, to the rights of man. The general spread of the light of science has already laid open to every view that the mass of mankind has not been born with saddles on their backs, nor a favored few booted and spurred, ready to ride them legitimately, by the grace of God."[43]

But this impression is misleading. Most founders were aware of the limits of popular enlightenment. Jefferson himself worried that after the Revolutionary War, the American people "will forget themselves, but in the sole faculty of making money, and will never think of uniting to effect a due respect for their rights."[44] In the Virginia report quoted earlier, he

---

[40] Noah Webster, *An American Selection of Lessons in Reading and Speaking, Calculated to Improve the Minds and Refine the Taste of Youth:. . . Being the Third Part of A Grammatical Institute of the English Language*, 3rd ed. (Boston: Isaiah Thomas and Ebenezer T. Andrews, 1793), 5; Pangle and Pangle, *Learning of Liberty*, 133 (Webster's popularity); James, "Rights of Conscience," 123–4 (role of early public schools in forming character). On Webster's huge influence, see also Harry R. Warfel, *Noah Webster: Schoolmaster to America* (1936; repr. New York: Octagon, 1966); Joshua Kendall, *The Forgotten Founding Father: Noah Webster's Obsession and the Creation of an American Culture* (New York: Berkley Books, 2010).

[41] Jefferson, Report of the Commissioners for the University, in *Writings*, 459.

[42] Strauss, *Persecution and the Art of Writing* (Glencoe, IL: Free Press, 1952), 33.

[43] Jefferson to Roger C. Weightman, June 24, 1826, in *Writings*, 1517.

[44] Jefferson, *Notes on Virginia*, Query 17, in ibid., 287.

admits that in addition to "develop[ing] the reasoning faculties of our youth," the university will need to "cultivate their morals, and instill into them the precepts of virtue and order," so that they will be formed "to habits of reflection and correct action." If there is need to "cultivate" and "instill" certain "habits," the implication is that morality cannot be acquired by reason alone. Comparing these remarks with Jefferson's "all eyes are opening" letter, we may conclude that even if "the general spread of the light of science" is sufficient to teach men that they have a natural right to be ruled with their consent, that "light" will not be enough to "cultivate their morals" or inculcate "habits of . . . correct action."

Founders like John Adams went further. Contemplating the failure of the French Revolution, he began to mock openly the belief in enlightenment. He now worried that there might be an opposite danger: "the more knowledge is diffused, the more the passions are extended, and the more furious they grow."[45]

In *Federalist* 49, Madison states bluntly that all forms of government, including "the wisest and freest," depend on "prejudice." Only in "a nation of philosophers" would "reverence for the laws . . . be sufficiently inculcated by the voice of an enlightened reason. But a nation of philosophers is as little to be expected as the philosophical race of kings wished for by Plato." Explaining his reasoning in a letter to Jefferson on "accidental differences in political, religious, or other opinions," Madison writes, "However erroneous or ridiculous these grounds of dissension and faction may appear to the enlightened statesman or the benevolent philosopher, the bulk of mankind, who are neither statesmen nor philosophers, will continue to view them in a different light."[46] He means that the "bulk of mankind" will never be able to transcend the dimension of "political, religious, or other opinions" and achieve the "genuine knowledge" of the "enlightened statesman."

Madison's remarks toward the end of *Federalist* 43 touch on the same difficulty. He writes, "The time has been when it was incumbent on us all to veil" the fact that the Articles of Confederation, having been approved only by the state legislatures, was never ratified in a way that properly expresses the consent of the people.[47] The premature exposure of this truth would have endangered the fragile American republic during the

---

[45] Adams, *Discourses on Davila*, ch. 13, in *Works of John Adams*, 6:275.

[46] Madison, *Federalist* 49, p. 312. Madison to Jefferson, October 24, 1787, in *The Founders' Constitution*, ed. Philip B. Kurland and Ralph Lerner (Chicago: University of Chicago Press, 1987), 1:646.

[47] Madison, *Federalist* 43, p. 276.

Revolutionary War. The fact that the Articles had been set up in partial violation of the principles of natural right had to be concealed because it was the best that could be achieved in the circumstances. It is not always possible or even desirable that the public be enlightened.

Perhaps the clearest statement of the problem is found in Washington's Farewell Address: "Whatever may be conceded to the influence of refined education on minds of peculiar structure, reason and experience both forbid us to expect that national morality can prevail in exclusion of religious principle."[48] Washington distinguishes here between two ways of making men moral. One is "religion," i.e., divine revelation, which is of course inaccessible to mere reason. The other way is "refined education," which is effective only with "minds of peculiar structure" that can discover and obey moral law through reason unassisted by faith. But this will not work for most people and will therefore be insufficient for "national morality." Enlightened statesmen might know through reason alone that it is in everyone's interest (for the security of life and property) for people to pay their debts and refrain from theft and lying, but others would not likely make that connection.

In agreement with Washington, James Wilson also speaks of the weakness of human reason: "If the rules of virtue were left to be discovered by reasoning, . . . unhappy would be the condition of the far greater part of men, who have not the means of cultivating the power of reasoning to any high degree."[49] Hamilton concurs, writing that people are generally "governed more by passion and prejudice than by an enlightened sense of their interests. A degree of illusion mixes itself in all the affairs of society. The opinion of objects has more influence than their real nature."[50] Michael Zuckert shows that the language of the Declaration of Independence itself illustrates the statements just quoted in the expression "we hold these truths to be self-evident." He argues that the Declaration's position is "between that of Socrates and that associated with the Enlightenment," because Socrates says the citizens must "hold" a noble lie to be true, while the Declaration says that Americans "hold" certain truths to be true.[51] Either way, most citizens will believe rather than know the self-evident truths of the founding.

---

[48] Washington, Farewell Address, 1796, in *Writings*, ed. Rhodehamel, 971.

[49] Wilson, *Lectures on Law*, 1:513.

[50] Hamilton to unknown, Dec. 1779, in *The Papers of Alexander Hamilton*, ed. Harold C. Syrett (New York: Columbia University Press, 1961–79), 2:242.

[51] Zuckert, *Natural Rights Republic*, 45–7.

I conclude that although the founders thought that the cultivation of reason contributes to citizen virtue, reason alone is not enough. Some of the founders (and perhaps all the preeminent ones) accepted the view, attributed by Leo Strauss to premodern philosophers, "that the gulf separating 'the wise' and 'the vulgar' was a basic fact of human nature which could not be influenced by any progress of popular education: philosophy, or science, was essentially a privilege of the few."[52] "The great Mr. Locke" (as the founders sometimes called him)[53] held the same view. He writes, "'tis too hard a task for unassisted reason to establish morality in all its parts on its true foundations.... [The] mass of mankind,... [will be unable to follow] the long and sometimes intricate deductions of reason.... And you may as soon hope to have all the day-laborers and tradesmen, the spinsters and dairy maids, perfect mathematicians, as to have them perfect in ethics this way. Hearing plain commands is the sure and only course to bring them to obedience and practice. The greatest part cannot know, and therefore they must believe."[54]

Promotion of Belief in Religion

Almost all founders thought that government has a duty to promote religion – consistently with the rights of conscience, of course. The connection between religion and the moral foundations of liberty was obvious. In his Farewell Address Washington writes, "Let it simply be asked where is the security for property, for reputation, for life, if the sense of religious obligation *desert* the oaths, which are the instruments of investigation in courts of justice?" He immediately adds: "And let us with caution indulge the supposition that morality can be maintained without religion."[55] Washington of course meant not just any religion, such as that practiced by the Indians, but one such as Christianity or Judaism, whose commandments – "Thou shalt not kill," "Thou shalt not steal," "Thou shalt not bear false witness"[56] – make everyone's rights to life and property more secure. The Massachusetts Bill of Rights,

---

[52] Strauss, *Persecution and the Art of Writing*, 34.

[53] Reply of the Massachusetts House of Representatives to the Speech of Governor Hutchinson, July 31, 1770, in Thomas Hutchinson, *The History of the Colony and Province of Massachusetts-Bay* (Cambridge: Harvard University Press, 1936), 3:338.

[54] Locke, *The Reasonableness of Christianity*, 1695, ed. John C. Higgins-Biddle (Oxford: Clarendon Press, 1999), ch. 14, 265–6, 279 (pagination of the first edition, in the margin).

[55] Washington, Farewell Address, 971.   [56] Exodus 20:13–16.

therefore, does not say that government supports Protestantism because it is the true religion, but rather because "the happiness of a people, and the good order and preservation of civil government, essentially depend upon piety, religion and morality." The Continental Congress recommended that the states encourage "true religion and good morals" because these "are the only solid foundations of public liberty and happiness."[57]

Washington goes so far as to justify government support even if the religion is believed to be false: "Of all the dispositions and habits which lead to political prosperity, religion and morality are indispensable supports.... [They are the] great pillars of human happiness, these firmest props of the duties of men and citizens. The mere politician, equally with the pious man ought to respect and to cherish them."[58] Even a nonbeliever – a "mere politician" – will approve of religion if he is thinking clearly. Government favors religion not for personal salvation – security of natural rights has nothing to do with that – but rather for "political prosperity" and to inculcate "the duties of men and citizens." Benjamin Franklin, perhaps speaking as a "mere politician," once advised a young man who had authored a critique of religion not to publish it: "do you imagine any good would be done by it? ... [T]hink how great a proportion of mankind consists of weak and ignorant men and women ... who have need of the motive of religion to restrain them from vice, to support their virtue, and retain them in the practice of it till it becomes *habitual*."[59]

John Adams, writing thirty years before Washington's Farewell Address, anticipates and clarifies Washington's argument by explicitly tying the law of nature to the teachings of Christianity: "One great advantage of the Christian religion is that it brings the great principle of the law of nature and nations, love your neighbor as yourself, and do to others as you would that others should do to you, to the knowledge, belief and veneration of the whole people.... The duties and rights of the man and the citizen are thus taught from early infancy to every creature. The

[57] Continental Congress, Resolution for True Religion and Good Morals, 1778, in *The Founding Fathers and the Debate over Religion in Revolutionary America: A History in Documents*, ed. Matthew L. Harris and Thomas S. Kidd (New York: Oxford University Press, 2012), 32.

[58] Washington, Farewell Address, 971.

[59] Franklin to unknown, December 13, 1757, in *Writings* (New York: Library of America, 1987), 748.

sanctions of a future life are thus added to the observance of civil and political as well as domestic and private duties."[60]

Christianity teaches that God's commandments cannot be disobeyed without consequences. Through this teaching, religion also shapes the law of fashion and thereby the people's habits. In Georgia's law establishing its first state university, "a free government ... can only be happy where the public principles and opinions are properly directed and their manners regulated. This is an influence beyond the stretch of laws and punishments and can be claimed only by religion and education. It should therefore be among the first objects of those who wish well to the national prosperity to encourage and support the principles of religion and morality."[61] John Adams, in his official capacity as president, presents a similar view: "we have no government armed with power capable of contending with human passions unbridled by morality and religion. Avarice, ambition, revenge, or gallantry, would break the strongest cords of our Constitution as a whale goes through a net. Our Constitution was made only for a moral and religious people. It is wholly inadequate to the government of any other."[62]

Finally, Alexis de Tocqueville observed: "There is no country in the world in which the boldest political theories of the eighteenth-century philosophers are put so effectively into practice as in America. Only their anti-religious doctrines have never made headway in that country."[63] Although church and state authority are separated in the founding, writes John Thornton, the "true alliance between politics and religion is the lesson" taught in the political sermons of the founding and in the founders' public policies.[64]

Does Religious Liberty Prohibit Government Support?
Many scholars believe that government support of religion necessarily conflicts with the right to free exercise. For example, political theorist

[60] Adams, Diary, August 14, 1756, in Massachusetts Historical Society, Electronic Archive, www.masshist.org/digitaladams/archive/doc?id=D46.
[61] University of Georgia Charter, 1785, in *A Digest of the Statute Laws*, 1083.
[62] Adams to the Officers ... of the Militia of Massachusetts, October 11, 1798, in *Works of John Adams*, 9:229.
[63] Alexis de Tocqueville, *The Old Regime and the French Revolution* (Garden City, NY: Doubleday Anchor, 1955), 153.
[64] John Wingate Thornton, ed., *The Pulpit of the American Revolution: Political Sermons of the Period of 1776* (1860; repr. New York: Da Capo, 1970), iii.

Lee Ward asserts, "Even the 'sacred' right of individual conscience was qualified in some states, such as Massachusetts and Maryland, by affirmations of the legitimacy of public support for religion."[65] Thomas James thinks it obvious that teaching religion in nineteenth-century public schools violated the individual-liberty principle of the founding: "the natural rights posited by Thomas Jefferson... were more admired than observed during the expansion of the educational system." Thomas Pangle agrees, writing that passages in early state constitutions requiring government support "were intermingled with other passages guaranteeing toleration and religious liberty that seemed, *and indeed were*, at odds with them." For Pangle, provisions for public support of religion were "strong carryovers from the Christian heritage" that were inconsistent with the founding principles.[66]

Jefferson's Virginia bill for religious freedom supports the three scholars just quoted. It states that taxpayer support for religion violates natural right: "to compel a man to furnish contributions of money for the propagation of opinions which he disbelieves and abhors, is sinful and tyrannical." And in conclusion: "the rights hereby asserted are of the natural rights of mankind." Madison was one of the few who endorsed Jefferson's extreme position, asserting in his Memorial and Remonstrance that government support or even "cognizance" of religion is a violation of the right to "free exercise of religion."[67] This would mean government may never support any religion at any time or in any manner, even if everyone's right to worship is left entirely untouched. Thomas and Lorraine Pangle rightly remark that this argument is "one of the least satisfactory from the perspective of theoretical or even logical coherence that Madison ever allowed himself to state in public."[68] Jefferson and Madison may have made these intemperate claims under the influence of their strong anticlerical bias.[69]

---

[65] Lee Ward, *The Politics of Liberty in England and Revolutionary America* (New York: Cambridge University Press, 2004), 405.

[66] Thomas James, "Rights of Conscience and State School Systems in Nineteenth-Century America," in *Toward a Usable Past*, ed. Finkelman, 127. Pangle, *Spirit of Modern Republicanism*, 81 (my emphasis).

[67] Jefferson, A Bill for Establishing Religious Freedom, in *Writings*, 346, 348; James Madison, Memorial and Remonstrance against Religious Assessments, 1785, in *Writings*, ed. Jack N. Rakove (New York: Library of America, 1999), 30–31.

[68] Pangle and Pangle, *Learning of Liberty*, 189.

[69] Vincent Phillip Muñoz, *God and the Founders: Madison, Washington, and Jefferson* (New York: Cambridge University Press, 2009), 70–72; Philip Hamburger, *Separation of Church and State* (Cambridge: Harvard University Press, 2002), 181.

In the Virginia bill, one of Jefferson's arguments against government support of religion is that "our civil rights have no dependence on our religious opinions, any more than our opinions in physics or geometry." In a similar passage in *Notes on Virginia*, Jefferson writes, "it does me no injury for my neighbor to say there are twenty gods or no god. It neither picks my pocket nor breaks my leg."[70] Political theorist Robert Bartlett correctly states that "Aristotle would never have been able" to agree with this view.[71] Bartlett could have added – but did not – that on this point almost every leading founder would have agreed with Aristotle, not Jefferson.

Jefferson sometimes contradicted himself on this important question. In the same *Notes on Virginia*, four pages after the "twenty gods" passage, Jefferson asks, "Can the liberties of a nation be thought secure when we have removed their *only* firm basis, a conviction in the minds of the people that these liberties are of the gift of God?"[72] Here Jefferson in effect acknowledges the doubtfulness of what he had earlier asserted so absolutely. If too many of my neighbors say "there is no god," the liberties of the people, no longer having a "firm basis," will be lost. My atheist neighbors will do me an "injury" after all. However grudgingly, Jefferson is compelled to admit that government has an interest in promoting religious opinions that favor liberty. Consequently, in his First Inaugural, he praises the Christianity then prevailing in America, calling it "a benign religion, professed, indeed, and practiced in various forms, yet all of them inculcating honesty, truth, temperance, gratitude, and the love of man."[73]

It would therefore be incorrect to follow Aristide Tessitore in treating Jefferson as "uniquely authoritative – albeit controversial – in fashioning the American response to this issue," namely, government support of religion. It would also be incorrect to say that by opposing Virginia's proposed taxpayer support of religion, "Jefferson (and Madison) worked to bring this vestige of the old regime into line with the principled basis of

---

[70] Jefferson, Bill for Establishing Religious Freedom, 346, 348; *Notes on Virginia*, Query 17, in *Writings*, 285.

[71] Robert C. Bartlett, "Religion und Politik in der klassischen politischen Wissenschaft," in *Politik und Religion: Zur Diagnose der Gegenwart*, ed. Friedrich W. Graf and Heinrich Meier (Munich: C. H. Beck, 2013), 174 (my translation).

[72] Jefferson, *Notes on Virginia*, in *Writings*, Query 18, p. 289 (my emphasis).

[73] Jefferson, First Inaugural Address, 1801, in *Writings*, 494. On Jefferson's self-contradictions, see Muñoz, *God and the Founders*, 72–3, 92–7; Pangle and Pangle, *Learning of Liberty*, 193.

American government articulated in the Declaration."[74] These statements improperly assume that Jefferson was right and that the statements quoted earlier of the Continental Congress, Massachusetts, Georgia, and Washington were in conflict with religious liberty. As we will see, although many state constitutions forbade laws favoring one sect over another, every state had policies and practices favoring religion, as did the federal government.

In a Massachusetts Supreme Court case, Theophilus Parsons makes perhaps the strongest founding-era argument for the harmony of natural rights and government support of religion. He first states Jefferson's and Madison's argument "that when a man disapproves of any religion, . . . to compel him by law to contribute money for public instruction in such religion or doctrine is an infraction of his liberty of conscience." Then Parsons answers:

When it is remembered that no man is compellable to attend on any religious instruction which he conscientiously disapproves, and that he is absolutely protected . . . in his religious opinions and worship, [this] objection seems to mistake a man's conscience for his money. . . . And if any individual can lawfully withhold his contribution because he dislikes the appropriation, the authority of the state to levy taxes would be annihilated. . . . The great error lies in not distinguishing between liberty of conscience in religious opinions and worship, and the right of appropriating money by the state. The former is an unalienable right; the latter is surrendered to the state, as the price of protection.[75]

Parsons' opinion in this case defends the Massachusetts establishment of religion, i.e., taxpayer funding of ministers and churches in private society. Outside of New England, most states rejected this policy, sometimes on the Jeffersonian ground that it conflicts with natural right. Pennsylvania, for example, states that "all men have a natural and inalienable right to worship Almighty God according to the dictates of their own consciences and understanding, and that no man ought, or of right can be compelled to attend any religious worship, or erect or support any place of worship, or maintain any ministry, contrary to or against his own free will and consent."[76] But however hated taxpayer funding of particular denominations may have been, Parsons' unanswerable distinction between paying taxes and the right to worship shows that in point

---

[74] Aristide Tessitore, "Legitimate Government, Religion, and Education: The Political Philosophy of Thomas Jefferson," in *History of American Political Thought*, ed. Bryan-Paul Frost and Jeffrey Sikkenga (Lanham, MD: Lexington Books, 2003), 137.

[75] *Barnes v. First Parish in Falmouth*, 6 Mass. 401 (1810).

[76] PA Declaration of Rights, 1776, art. 2.

of strict logic, this supposed conflict between free exercise and government support of religion does not exist in this context.[77] An earlier New Hampshire case explains Parsons' point in this way: The situation of the taxpayer who resents funding someone else's religion "is precisely the same as it is in other civil concerns of the state. The minority are compelled to pay for instruction in learning, though they may be of opinion that the schoolmaster chosen by the majority neither promotes learning nor good manners, but the contrary."[78]

Just as Jefferson never really believed that people's religious views are irrelevant to the preservation of liberty, he also knew well that this statement of his from the Virginia Statute is false: "that truth is great and will prevail if left to herself; that she is the proper and sufficient antagonist to error, and has nothing to fear from the conflict unless by human interposition disarmed of her natural weapons, free argument and debate; errors ceasing to be dangerous when it is permitted freely to contradict them." Otherwise he would not have praised the use of "salutary coercions of the law" to punish "false and defamatory publications," as he did in his Second Inaugural.[79]

I conclude that there is no conflict between government support and natural rights as long as people are left free – within the confines of laws protecting person and property – to organize their own religious associations and worship as they like. I quote again the Ohio Bill of Rights: "religion ... being essentially necessary to good government ... , schools and the means of instruction shall forever be encouraged by legislative provision *not inconsistent with the rights of conscience.*"[80] However, this compatibility does not answer the practical question of whether and how government should support religion. Many founders were concerned about real practical dangers of government involvement with religion or the resentment it can cause. Madison has a competent list of those prudential concerns in his Memorial and Remonstrance, which I criticized earlier for its theoretical defects. Most religious policy disputes in the founding were resolved without any need to recur to natural rights.

---

[77] Vincent Phillip Muñoz, "Church and State in the Founding-Era State Constitutions," *American Political Thought* 4, No. 1 (Winter 2015): 33–4 ("the founders ... agreed that individuals should not be coerced to support a religion with which they disagreed"). This statement is true for most founders, but not for those who predominated in MA and NH.

[78] *Muzzy v. Wilkins*, 1 Smith's (N.H.) 1 (1803) (NH Supreme Court).

[79] Jefferson, Second Inaugural Address, in *Writings*, 522.

[80] OH Bill of Rights, 1803, art. 8, §3 (my emphasis).

Means of Support

State governments had primary responsibility for forming public morals, so they had the most to do with promotion of religion. First, some means of support were already contentious in the founding and were mostly abandoned soon afterwards. Taxpayer funding of specific denominations, widely practiced throughout the colonies prior to independence, was so controversial that only four New England states continued the practice after the Revolution: Vermont, New Hampshire, Massachusetts, and Connecticut. Between 1807 and 1833, all four dropped this policy.[81] After 1776 there was a sharp decline in legislation of any kind that treated different sects of Protestants differently.[82]

Second, churches in most states were supported by exemptions from property taxes.[83] State laws have continued this policy up to the present.

Third, many state governments supported the teaching of a sort of generic Protestantism in schools through prayers, Bible readings, and religious themes in the curriculum, which lasted to the 1960s.[84] Even Jefferson approved of religious instruction in public schools, with this caveat: "no religious reading, instruction, or exercise shall be prescribed or practiced inconsistent with the tenets of any religious sect or denomination."[85]

Fourth, public respect for religion was encouraged by anti-blasphemy laws. Mark McGarvie reports that these laws "were generally ignored as anachronisms of an earlier age."[86] Still, there are a few reported

---

[81] Thomas J. Curry, *The First Freedoms: Church and State in America to the Passage of the First Amendment* (New York: Oxford University Press, 1986), 159–92; Jon Butler, "Why Revolutionary America Wasn't a 'Christian Nation,'" in *Religion and the New Republic: Faith in the Founding of America*, ed. James H. Hutson (Lanham, MD: Rowman & Littlefield, 2000), 195 (decline of taxpayer aid to churches after 1776); James Kabala, *Church-State Relations in the Early American Republic, 1787–1846* (Brookfield, VT: Pickering & Chatto, 2013), 3–4.

[82] Chris Beneke, *Beyond Toleration: The Religious Origins of American Pluralism* (New York: Oxford University Press, 2006), ch. 4 and 5.

[83] *Walz v. Tax Commission*, 397 U.S. 664 (1970) (William Brennan's concurrence, listing tax exemptions granted in the founding and after).

[84] Mark Douglas McGarvie, *One Nation under Law: America's Early National Struggles to Separate Church and State* (DeKalb: Northern Illinois University Press, 2004), 60–66; *Engel v. Vitale*, 370 U.S. 421 (1962), and *Abington v. Schempp*, 374 U.S. 203 (1963) (public school prayers and Bible readings declared unconstitutional).

[85] Jefferson to Joseph Cabell, September 9, 1817, in *The Writings of Thomas Jefferson*, ed. Andrew A. Lipscomb and Albert E. Bergh (Washington: Thomas Jefferson Memorial Association, 1903), 17:425 (proposing an act to establish elementary schools).

[86] McGarvie, *One Nation*, 122.

cases.[87] In *People v. Ruggles*, an 1811 New York case, James Kent defines blasphemy as "maliciously reviling God or religion."[88] Kent defends these laws by noting that Christianity is thought to be "the foundation of moral obligation, and the efficacy of oaths." The "reviling" of Christianity is therefore "an offence, because it tends to corrupt the morals of the people, and to destroy good order." In other words, blasphemy laws, like all the founders' religion policies, are not concerned with the truth of Christianity but rather with the moral basis of freedom. We are "in need," Kent writes, "of all the moral discipline, and of those principles of virtue, which help to bind society together." To emphasize the purely nonsectarian basis of his argument, Kent quotes the skeptical English philosopher Francis Bacon and the skeptical pre-Christian Roman philosopher Cicero. In a later Pennsylvania blasphemy case the court quotes with approval another philosophic rationalist from pagan times, Plutarch, who "declares" that religion is "the cement of social union and the essential support of legislation."[89]

Kent argues that prohibiting blasphemy is in no way meant to interfere with "the free exercise and enjoyment of religious profession and worship." He insists that "the free, equal, and undisturbed enjoyment of religious opinion, whatever it may be, and free and decent discussions on any religious subject, is granted and secured; but to revile, with malicious and blasphemous contempt, the religion professed by almost the whole community, is an abuse of that right." In *Ruggles*, the defendant "utter[ed] . . . these false, feigned, scandalous, malicious, wicked and blasphemous words, to wit, 'Jesus Christ was a bastard, and his mother must be a whore.'" Kent's distinction between "decent discussion" and "revil[ing] with malicious . . . contempt" explains why Thomas Paine's *Age of Reason* (1796), a scholarly critique of the Bible, circulated freely throughout America, while in England, with its much stricter blasphemy laws, that book was banned as soon as it was published.[90]

[87] Kabala, *Church-State Relations*, 124; 124–8 (early American blasphemy law).

[88] *People v. Ruggles*, 8 Johns. R. 290 (1811), in *Founders' Constitution*, 5:101–2.

[89] *Updegraph v. Commonwealth*, 11 Serg. and Rawle 394 (PA Supreme Court, 1824), in *Founders' Constitution*, 5:173.

[90] Chris Beneke, "The Myth of American Religious Coercion," *Common-place: The Interactive Journal of Early American Life* 15, No. 3 (Spring 2015), www.common-place .org, responding to David Sehat, *The Myth of American Religious Freedom* (New York: Oxford University Press, 2011) (Sehat argues that blasphemy laws and other post-1776 policies greatly limited religious liberty).

Fifth, all state constitutions except Virginia and New York had some sort of religious test for public office, usually by a required oath.[91] Members of the Pennsylvania state legislature had to declare, "I do believe in one God, the creator and governor of the universe, the rewarder of the good and punisher of the wicked, and I do acknowledge the scriptures of the Old and New Testament to be given by divine inspiration."[92] The argument for religious tests was the same as for other forms of government support: that religion supports morality. A speaker at the Massachusetts ratifying convention explains: the absence of religious tests "would admit deists, atheists, etc., into the general government; and, people being apt to imitate the examples of the court, these principles would be disseminated, and, of course, a corruption of morals ensue."[93]

These religious tests are based on the founders' consensus that certain "civil rights as a citizen" may be limited on many grounds, including religion.[94] For instance, every citizen has an equal right to protection of the laws, but not every citizen has the right to serve in public office. Jury duty was limited to males in the founding and long afterwards. Atheists were sometimes denied the right to testify in court.[95] Children could not vote. Elective office was constitutionally limited in other ways as well, such as the federal constitution's age and citizenship requirements. Subordinate government officials have always been subjected to various legally mandated job requirements. None of these limitations were regarded as violations of natural rights because there is no natural right to a government job, to serve on a jury, or to vote.

In spite of their broad early acceptance, religious tests were already in process of abandonment during the founding. "By 1836," writes James Kabala, "a general consensus had developed that formal religious tests were undesirable."[96] The U.S. Constitution outlaws all religious tests for federal office. Their technical compatibility with natural rights is one thing, but Chris Beneke rightly notes that in "founding

---

[91] Muñoz, "Church and State," 28–9.   [92] PA Constitution, 1776, ch. 2, §9.

[93] Speech of Dr. Jarvis, MA Ratifying Convention, January 30, 1788, in *Founders' Constitution*, 4:642.

[94] PA Bill of Rights, art. 2 ("nor can any man who acknowledges the being of a God be justly deprived or abridged of any civil right as a citizen on account of [religion]"); Muñoz, "Church and State," 31–2.

[95] Kabala, *Church-State Relations*, 133–47.

[96] Ibid., 118; see 87–120 (religious tests in the early republic).

era America . . . libertarian principles . . . repeatedly triumphed over local prejudices and discriminatory laws."[97]

Sixth, both state and federal government supported religion in their own internal organization. Legislative and military chaplains were provided for from the start.[98] Government buildings were sometimes used for religious purposes. President Jefferson famously attended worship services in the House of Representatives.[99]

The federal government also funded religious instruction for Indian tribes. President Jefferson approved a treaty providing for a government-paid Catholic missionary to the Kaskaskia Indians, "who will engage to perform for said tribe the duties of his office, and also to instruct as many of their children as possible in the rudiments of literature."[100] An 1819 law authorized the president to employ "capable persons of good moral character" to instruct the Cherokees in "the habits and arts of civilization." A Protestant missionary, Samuel Worcester, used his appointment to preach the Gospel, with the later approval of the Supreme Court.[101]

Seventh, states often had laws requiring most businesses to close on Sundays, and sometimes prohibiting other activities. These laws rarely generated much controversy and therefore continued up to the 1960s.[102]

Finally, government officials made use of religious themes and prayers in their official proclamations and at solemn ceremonies such as inaugurations and state funerals. Congress and the president have frequently called for national days of prayer and thanksgiving. The House of Representatives voted to issue the first such call on September 24, 1789, the same day that it passed the First Amendment, which states that "Congress shall make no law respecting an establishment of religion."[103] Few regarded

97 Chris Beneke, "The 'Catholic Spirit Prevailing in Our Country': America's Moderate Religious Revolution," in *The First Prejudice: Religious Tolerance and Intolerance in Early America*, ed. Beneke and Christopher S. Grenda (Philadelphia: University of Pennsylvania Press, 2011), 284.
98 Kabala, *Church-State Relations*, 25–35, 151–78.
99 James H. Hutson, *Religion and the Founding of the American Republic* (Washington: Library of Congress, 1998), 84.
100 Treaty between the United States and the Kaskaskia Tribe of Indians, August 13, 1803, in *Laws, Treaties, and Other Documents*, ed. Albert Gallatin (Washington: Roger Weightman, 1811), 78–81.
101 *Worcester v. Georgia*, 31 U.S. 515 (1832).
102 *McGowan v. Maryland*, 366 U.S. 420 (1961) (discussing the history of Sunday closing laws).
103 *Annals of Congress* (Washington: Gales and Seaton, 1834), 1:948–50.

mere verbal support of religion as "establishment." Every president has invoked God's name or the equivalent in a prayerful manner in his inaugural address.[104]

What Religion to Support?

Law professor Michael McConnell gives an able scholarly defense of the view that the founders believed government may promote "religion in general," but "must not favor one form of religious belief over another."[105] This position has been called "nonpreferentialism."[106] It is true that some founders occasionally spoke of "religion in general," as Richard Henry Lee did: "The [Virginia] declaration of rights... [does not prohibit] compelling contribution for the support of religion in general."[107] But in the context, Lee means "Protestantism in general." He is talking about a proposed tax that would require each member of a Protestant sect to support his own sect.

There is no evidence that the founders ever had in mind equal support for every possible religion, biblical or otherwise. Equal *protection* of free exercise for all religions was certainly their policy, but not equal *support* for all religions.[108] There were only three religious positions supported by government in the founding: first, a specific Protestant denomination; second, what Adams called "the general principles of Christianity"; third, the God of liberty who endows all men with inalienable rights, who is identified neither as biblical nor anti-biblical.

I mentioned earlier the first example, namely, the New England practice of funding congregational churches through direct taxpayer support. As for the second, the general principles of Christianity were promoted mainly through the nonsectarian Protestantism that came to be taught in public schools, as well as in other ways mentioned above. The third

---

[104] Charles E. Rice, *The Supreme Court and Public Prayer: The Need for Restraint* (New York: Fordham University Press, 1964), 177–93. I return to government promotion of a religious "law of fashion" in Chapter 11.

[105] Michael W. McConnell, "Accommodation of Religion," *Supreme Court Review* (1985): 21, 39; McConnell, "The Origins and Historical Understanding of Free Exercise of Religion," *Harvard Law Review* 103 (May 1990): 1409–1517.

[106] Leonard W. Levy, *The Establishment Clause: Religion and the First Amendment* (New York: Macmillan, 1986), 91–119; Rahe, *Republics Ancient and Modern*, 749–54 (founders favored nonpreferential encouragement of religion).

[107] Richard Henry Lee to Madison, November 26, 1784, in Pangle and Pangle, *Learning of Liberty*, 190.

[108] Philip A. Hamburger, "Equality and Diversity: The Eighteenth-Century Debate about Equal Protection and Equal Civil Rights," *Supreme Court Review* (1992): 295–392.

object of support, the judgmental and providential God of Liberty, was a theme of the Declaration of Independence and the Great Seal of the United States,[109] taught frequently in official pronouncements, such as Washington's Thanksgiving proclamation:

I do recommend and assign Thursday the 26th day of November next to be devoted by the people of these states to the service of that great and glorious Being, who is the beneficent Author of all the good that was, that is, or that will be – That we may then all unite in rendering unto him our sincere and humble thanks – for his kind care and protection of the people of this country previous to their becoming a nation – for the signal and manifold mercies, and the favorable interpositions of his Providence . . . which we have since enjoyed – . . . for the civil and religious liberty with which we are blessed. . . . And also that we may . . . beseech him to pardon our national and other transgressions – to enable us all . . . to perform our several and relative duties properly and punctually – to render our national government a blessing to all the people, by constantly being a government of wise, just, and constitutional laws – . . . To promote the knowledge and practice of true religion and virtue, and the increase of science.[110]

Even this third kind of nonsectarian religious support is far from "non-preferentialist" in the modern sense of "not favoring one form of religious belief over another." The Thanksgiving Proclamation has a definite theological teaching, which has sometimes incorrectly been called *deism*. In the eighteenth-century sense, writes Gregg Frazer, deism was the belief that "God has withdrawn his active presence from the universe and remains completely aloof while it functions in strict accordance with the natural laws with which he originally endowed it. . . . [God] assumed the aloof character of an absentee landlord." Frazer calls the teaching of the Thanksgiving Proclamation "theistic rationalism" in contrast to deism.[111] Catherine Albanese describes this understanding, which, as she rightly observes, can also be found in the Declaration of Independence, as "mingling perceptions of God as an actor in human history and God as the inactive ground of being."[112] The God of the Thanksgiving Proclamation and of the Declaration is monotheistic as well as providential, helping America achieve "civil and religious liberty." He favors "the increase of

[109] The theology of the Great Seal is explained in ch. 11.

[110] Washington, Thanksgiving Proclamation, October 3, 1789, in http://founders.archives .gov.

[111] Gregg L. Frazer, *The Religious Beliefs of America's Founders: Reason, Revelation, and Revolution* (Lawrence: University Press of Kansas, 2012), 14–20 (quotation on 16, internal quotation marks omitted).

[112] Catherine L. Albanese, *Sons of the Fathers: The Civil Religion of the American Revolution* (Philadelphia: Temple University Press, 1976), 140–41.

science." As judge of our "transgressions," God can also "pardon" them. In Chapter 11 we will explore this theology of theistic rationalism more fully by analyzing the Great Seal printed on the dollar bill.

The state governments tended to favor promotion of "Christianity in general" and not merely theistic rationalism. "By the 1840s," writes James Kabala, a "non-sectarian Protestant consensus underlay the existence of legislative and military chaplains, the proclamation of thanksgiving and fast days by state governors, state blasphemy and Sabbath laws, and restrictions on who could testify in court." By then, "religion had not been purged from public life, but had become organized around a broadly tolerant non-denominational Protestant Christianity that had pushed aside both belief in a confessional Christian state and open 'infidelity.'"[113]

Legal Prohibitions and Punishments

This brings us to Locke's third kind of moral law, governmental laws enforced with penalties or rewards. The Massachusetts Declaration of Rights stated the founders' consensus: "Each individual of the society has a right to be protected by it in the enjoyment of his life, liberty and property, according to standing laws."[114] Those "standing laws" enforce the natural moral law – which requires respect for the life, liberty, and property of others – by punishing the immorality of the "wicked and dissolute." That is how Jefferson justifies the criminal law in his preamble to a proposed Virginia Bill on Crimes, quoted earlier: "wicked and dissolute men, resigning themselves to the dominion of inordinate passions, commit violations on the lives, liberties, and property of others, and, the secure enjoyment of these having principally induced men to enter into society, government would be defective in its principal purpose were it not to restrain such criminal acts, by inflicting due punishments on those who perpetrate them."[115] Fear of losing one's own life, liberty, or property is the incentive to obey governmental moral law, which forbids murder, assault, rape, kidnapping, robbery, stealing, and the like. Obviously, punishments cannot stop crimes already committed, but government can deter future crime if its threats of painful consequences are credible.

---

[113] Kabala, *Church-State Relations*, 179, 2; see Beneke, "Catholic Spirit," 271–3.
[114] MA Declaration of Rights, 1780, art. 10.
[115] Jefferson, A Bill for Proportioning Crimes and Punishments, 1778, in *Founders' Constitution*, 5:374.

Foreign policy, correctly pursued, also enforces the moral law. It too does so by violence, or threat of violence, not against "wicked and dissolute [individual] men," but against wicked leaders of other nations whose "inordinate passions" might tempt them into aggression against America. As Hamilton remarks bluntly in *Federalist* 6, wars will never cease, because "men are ambitious, vindictive, and rapacious."[116] In *Federalist* 11 Hamilton speaks explicitly of America as an enforcer of morality. He advocates a policy of curbing the "arrogant pretensions of the European" by limiting the imperial ambitions of European nations in the Western Hemisphere. Such a policy would teach Europe the moral virtue of "moderation,"[117] leading to greater security of natural rights in the Americas (the right of every nation, under the "laws of nature and of nature's God," to a "separate and equal station").

Government also provides for deterrence of personal injuries – called *torts* in American law – that are not serious enough to be treated as crimes. Citizens are allowed to sue for reparation of damages. An example is a civil lawsuit for monetary compensation when a driver fails to stop at a red light, causing bodily injury or damage to property. Another example is a personal libel lawsuit to recover damages done to one's reputation. Lawsuits are also permitted for breach of contract (failure to pay a debt). Government allows some civil suits to provide for punitive damages. Again, the Massachusetts Declaration of Rights states the principle behind civil lawsuits: "Every subject of the Commonwealth ought to find a certain remedy, by having recourse to the laws, for all injuries or wrongs which he may receive in his person, property, or character."[118] Civil suits (at least those not involving punitive damages) aim at *reparation*; they are meant to compensate someone for an injury suffered. Criminal prosecutions aim at *restraint*, as Jefferson states in the quotation above. However, both forms of punishment have a restraining effect by taking property from the person responsible for the injury or crime.

Other Laws Promoting Good Morals

Because of their importance and complexity, I will discuss the founders' laws promoting marriage in a separate chapter.

Anti-gambling laws deserve a mention. They were probably considered appropriate because they discourage temptations undermining the work ethic necessary for a free society. Pennsylvania's 1779 Act for the

---

[116] Hamilton, *Federalist* 6, p. 48.   [117] Hamilton, *Federalist* 11, pp. 85–6.
[118] MA Declaration of Rights, 1780, art. 11.

Suppression of Vice and Immorality has this vague but forceful explanation: "profane swearing, cursing, drunkenness, cock fighting, bullet playing, horse racing, shooting matches, and the playing or gaming for money or other valuable things, fighting of duels . . . [are] evil practices which tend greatly to debauch the minds and corrupt the morals of the subjects of this commonwealth."[119]

There was a positive requirement in some states to own guns and serve in the militia. John Adams regarded Massachusetts's militia law as one of four decisive institutions "which have produced the American Revolution," in this case by fostering "military valor and ability": "[E]very male inhabitant between sixteen and sixty years of age is enrolled in a company [of the militia]. . . . He is enjoined to keep always in his house, and at his own expense, a firelock in good order, a powder horn, a pound of powder, twelve flints, four-and-twenty balls of lead, a cartridge box, and a knapsack; so that the whole country is ready to march for its own defense upon the first signal of alarm. These companies and regiments are obliged to assemble at certain times in every year, under the orders of their officers, for the inspection of their arms and ammunition, and to perform their exercises and maneuvers."[120]

Whether required by government or not, America was a land of widespread gun ownership. Madison remarks on this in *Federalist* 46: "Americans possess over the people of almost every other nation" the "advantage of being armed."[121] Jefferson argues that gun ownership builds character: "A strong body makes the mind strong. As to the species of exercise, I advise the gun. While this gives a moderate exercise to the body, it gives boldness, enterprise, and independence to the mind. . . . Let your gun therefore be the constant companion of your walks."[122] Guns are power, and power in the hands of a private citizen inspires confidence and a spirit of independence.

The laws also promoted morality through monetary incentives. Tax exemptions for religion have already been mentioned. In *Federalist* 12,

---

[119] Act for the Suppression of Vice and Immorality, 1779, in *The Statutes at Large of Pennsylvania, 1682 to 1801* (n.p.: Wm. Stanley Ray, State Printer of Pennsylvania, 1902), 9:333.

[120] Adams to the Abbé de Mably, 1782, in *Works of John Adams*, 5:495.

[121] Madison, *Federalist* 46, p. 296. Contradicted by Michael A. Bellesiles, *Arming America: The Origins of a National Gun Culture* (New York: Alfred A. Knopf, 2000), 110 ("the vast majority . . . had no use for firearms"). James Lindgren refutes Bellesiles in "Fall from Grace: *Arming America* and the Bellesiles Scandal," *Yale Law Journal* 111 (June 2002): 2195–249.

[122] Jefferson to Peter Carr, August 19, 1785, in *Writings*, 816.

Hamilton proposes a federal tax on the importation of "ardent spirits." If this alcohol tax "should tend to diminish the consumption of it, such an effect would be equally favorable to the agriculture, to the economy, to the morals and to the health of the society."[123]

Objections

I conclude with a brief response to two widely read public intellectuals. In *One Nation, Two Cultures*, historian Gertrude Himmelfarb complains that America's founders failed "to give the government any positive role in promoting the morals of the citizenry. They simply assumed that there was, as the *Federalist Papers* put it, 'sufficient virtue' in the people to sustain self-government."[124] Besides the evidence already presented in this chapter disproving Himmelfarb's claim, I add here that *The Federalist* concludes with Hamilton's reference to "practices on the part of the State governments which . . . have occasioned an almost universal prostration of morals." He was thinking of their abuses of property rights, to be discussed in Part III of this book. These abuses – Madison calls them "wicked" – have "undermined the foundations of property and credit" and "planted mistrust in the breasts of all classes of citizens." Madison argues that the new Constitution's prohibition of ex post facto laws and of laws impairing the obligation of contract will "inspire a general prudence and industry." He also deplores "the pestilent effects of paper money . . . on the industry and morals of the people."[125]

A second writer, Harvard Law professor Mary Ann Glendon, speaks of the Constitution's framers' "apparent unconcern about where they would find citizens with the qualities of character their innovative design for self-government demanded." Glendon believes "they relied on the small structures of civil society – families and tight-knit communities – to inculcate the republican virtues of self-restraint and care for the common good." State governments would also help. "The laws of the states," she writes, "were informed by more capacious notions of personhood, influenced in countless ways by biblical and classical understandings of human nature." Her argument assumes a tension between the Constitution, based on "vivid [Lockean] pictures of man as free and solitary in an imaginary

[123] *Federalist* 12, p. 90.
[124] Gertrude Himmelfarb, *One Nation, Two Cultures* (New York: Vintage Books, 2001), 7.
[125] *Federalist* 85, p. 521; *Federalist* 44, pp. 279, 278. See also my discussion of Diamond and *The Federalist* near the beginning of ch. 7.

'state of nature,'" and the "biblical and classical understandings" present in policies of the states. But the state and local communities which she mentions were based on the same political theory of natural law and individual rights as the federal government. No government that expects to provide security of natural rights can "simply assume" that there is sufficient virtue, or "take the necessary cultural conditions for granted," as she mistakenly says the authors of *The Federalist* did.[126] Although the founders were not Aristotelians, they would have agreed with this statement of Aristotle: "by habituating citizens, lawmakers make them good, and this is the wish of every lawgiver; all who do not do this well are in error."[127]

---

[126] Mary Ann Glendon, "Looking for 'Persons' in the Law," *First Things*, Dec. 2006, www.firstthings.com.

[127] Aristotle, *Nicomachean Ethics*, trans. Robert C. Bartlett and Susan D. Collins (Chicago: University of Chicago Press, 2011), bk. 2., ch. 1.

Sex and Marriage in Political Theory and Policy

Scholarship on the founders' political theory rarely covers one of the most important topics: sex and marriage. Michael Zuckert is among the few who even touch on it, but he does so only glancingly. He refers to the need for a "'rights infrastructure' – the social institutions and traits of character that make rights-securing possible."[1] Marriage, he says, "is arguably an institution that is necessary to the rights infrastructure and prostitution can legitimately be seen as a threat to the health of the family," since it disrupts the attempt "to channel sexual relations into the exclusive channels of marriage."[2] Beyond these brief references, Zuckert has little to say about the founders' conception of government's role in sustaining the family. Better is Paul Rahe, who states that Jefferson and other founders "support[ed] the enforcement of traditional Judeo-Christian morality." He then summarizes some of the laws directed to that end.[3] But neither of these two scholars nor most others go very far into the founders' actual policies and their connection to the natural rights theory. This chapter remedies that by showing that the founders held marriage to be not "arguably" but indispensably necessary for the securing of natural rights.

---

[1] Michael P. Zuckert, "Founder of the Natural Rights Republic," in *Thomas Jefferson and the Politics of Nature*, ed. Thomas S. Engeman (Notre Dame, IN: University of Notre Dame Press, 2000), 22.

[2] Michael P. Zuckert, *Launching Liberalism: On Lockean Political Philosophy* (Lawrence: University Press of Kansas, 2002), 228.

[3] Paul A. Rahe, *Republics Ancient and Modern: Classical Republicanism and the American Revolution* (Chapel Hill: University of North Carolina Press, 1992), 762.

Historian Mark Kann provides an unusually comprehensive treatment of the founders' policies, and he does attempt to show how they relate to their principles. However, his account of that relation is incoherent. On the one hand, he writes, people "guilty of sexual transgressions... were deemed incapable of the autonomy, rationality, and self-control expected of mature adults, liberal consenters, and republican citizens." Kann correctly implies that the natural rights theory requires self-restraint in the realm of sex and marriage. But Kann contradicts this when he writes, "For the founding elites..., the theory of liberalism overemphasized liberty" and was therefore supplemented by "patriarchal authority over the sex lives" of the people. Apparently the founders' "theory of liberalism" both requires and opposes government involvement in sex and marriage. Kann's view is a variant on the amalgam thesis discussed earlier, according to which "republicanism" blends together uneasily with "liberalism." For Kann, "patriarchalism," the extreme version of which is defended in Robert Filmer's *Patriarcha* (1680), replaces other scholars' "republicanism."[4]

Our topic could have been included in the previous chapter, but in view of its complexity and its relative neglect, I give it a chapter of its own. I will start with the founders' understanding of the connection between the family, natural rights, and the laws of nature, and then discuss their policies on sex and marriage.

Marriage as Grounded in Natural Law and Natural Right

It takes some effort to dig up the founders' understanding because it was completely uncontroversial at the time and therefore rarely discussed. But marriage – defined by the Massachusetts Supreme Court in 1810 as "an engagement, by which a single man and a single woman, of sufficient discretion, take each other for husband and wife"[5] – was of the highest importance for the founders, for two main reasons. First, as the Vermont Supreme Court states in 1829, "To marry is one of the natural rights of human nature."[6] During the 1787 ratification debate, Connecticut

---

[4] Mark E. Kann, *Taming Passion for the Public Good: Policing Sex in the Early Republic* (New York: New York University Press, 2013), 1–2, 8, 17, 161.

[5] Opinion of Chief Justice Theophilus Parsons, MA Supreme Judicial Court, *Town of Milford v. Town of Worcester*, 7 Mass. 48 (1810). Thanks to Adam Carrington for the reference.

[6] Vermont Supreme Court, *Newbury v. New Brunswick*, 2 Vt. 151, 159 (1829), quoted in Michael Grossberg, *Governing the Hearth: Law and the Family in Nineteenth-Century*

Federalist Oliver Ellsworth ridiculed the claim that a federal bill of rights was needed to guarantee the freedom of the press, on the ground that the Constitution also omits "liberty of conscience, or of matrimony, or of burial of the dead; it is enough that Congress have no power to prohibit either."[7] Ellsworth implies that the right to marry is no less fundamental than freedom of religion and of the press.

Why was marriage a natural right? It was considered an important component of human happiness, if not for everyone, then certainly for the great majority. Since the pursuit of happiness is a natural right, marriage is therefore part of that right. The connection between marriage and happiness was frequently noted. Historian Jan Lewis has shown that popular magazines of that day were full of praises of "Matrimonial Felicity" (the title of a 1784 article).[8] Expressing the general view, Zephaniah Swift's *Laws of Connecticut* (1795) states: "The connection between husband and wife... when founded on a mutual attachment and the ardor of youthful passions, is productive of the purest joys and tenderest transports that gladden the heart."[9] The pleasures of marriage also come from children who love and are loved by their parents. In a letter to his daughter Mary, Thomas Jefferson writes: "I turn to your situation with pleasure in the midst of a good family which loves you, and merits all your love.... The circle of our nearest connections is the only one in which a faithful and lasting affection can be found." In a later letter he wrote, "it is in the love of one's family only that heartfelt happiness is known."[10]

A second reason for the founders' regard for marriage is its importance to the social compact, formed for the security of natural rights.

America (Chapel Hill: University of North Carolina Press, 1985), 73. Steven G. Calabresi and Sofía M. Vickery, "On Liberty and the Fourteenth Amendment: The Original Understanding of the Lockean Natural Rights Guarantees," *Texas Law Review* 93 (2015): 1366–8 (on the connection between this Vermont case and the natural rights provisions of early state constitutions).

7 "A Landholder" [Oliver Ellsworth], No. 6, *Connecticut Courant*, December 10, 1787, quoted in Philip A. Hamburger, "Trivial Rights," *Notre Dame Law Review* 70, No. 1 (1994): 26.

8 Jan Lewis, "The Republican Wife: Virtue and Seduction in the Early Republic," *William and Mary Quarterly* 44, No. 4 (Oct. 1987): 709, quoting *The Gentleman and Lady's Town and Country Magazine*, 1784.

9 Zephaniah Swift, *A System of the Laws of the State of Connecticut* (Windham, CT: John Byrne, 1795), 183.

10 Jefferson to Mary Eppes, January 1, 1799, and October 26, 1801, *The Family Letters of Thomas Jefferson*, ed. Edwin M. Betts and James A. Bear, Jr. (Columbia: University of Missouri Press, 1966), 170, 210. Jan Lewis, "The Blessings of Domestic Society," in *Jeffersonian Legacies*, ed. Peter S. Onuf (Charlottesville: University Press of Virginia, 1993), 109–46 (Jefferson's view of the family).

Founder John Witherspoon writes, "besides its being part of natural law, [marriage] holds a place of the first importance in the social compact."[11] The 1786 Massachusetts Act against Adultery explains how marriage contributes to the ends of the social compact: "chastity of behavior, and the due observance of the marriage covenant, are highly conducive to the peace, welfare, and good order of the community, and the violation of them productive of great evils to individuals and the public."[12] The Massachusetts Supreme Court opinion quoted above – authored by the ever-insightful Theophilus Parsons – also speaks of the connection between marriage, children, virtue, preservation, and peace (the latter two being the explicit purpose of the social compact):

> Marriage is unquestionably a civil contract, founded in the social nature of man, and intended to regulate, chasten, and refine the intercourse between the sexes; and to multiply, preserve, and improve the species.... Marriage being essential to the peace and harmony, and to the virtues and improvements, of civil society, it has been, in all well-regulated governments, among the first attentions of the civil magistrate to regulate marriages; ... by defining the characters and relations of parties who may marry, so as to prevent a conflict of duties, and to preserve the purity of families; by describing the solemnities, by which the contract shall be executed, so as to guard against fraud, surprise, and seduction; by annexing civil rights to the parties and their issue, to encourage marriage, and to discountenance wanton and lascivious cohabitation, which, if not checked, is followed by prostration of morals, and a dissolution of manners.[13]

I will have more to say later in this chapter about the laws alluded to in this quotation, along with the "civil rights" of man and wife. For now, one might wonder how "multiply[ing] ... the species" contributes to the social compact. The answer is that a lasting community needs children who will become the next generation of citizens. As the Constitution's Preamble says, government exists not only "for ourselves" but also "our posterity."[14]

Parsons says marriages not only "multiply" the species, they also "preserve" and "improve" it. Zephaniah Swift gives part of the explanation:

[11] John Witherspoon, "Queries, and Answers Thereto, Respecting Marriage," in *The American Museum, or Repository*, vol. 4 (Philadelphia: Mathew Carey, 1788), 315–16. Thanks to Kevin Slack for the reference.

[12] Act against Adultery, Polygamy, and Lewdness, March 16, 1786, in *The Perpetual Laws of the Commonwealth of Massachusetts, 1780 to 1800* (Boston: I. Thomas and E. T. Andrews, 1801), 1:217.

[13] Parsons, Massachusetts Supreme Court, *Milford v. Worcester*.

[14] George Washington, General Orders, July 2, 1776, in *Writings*, ed. John Rhodehamel (New York: Library of America, 1997), 225.

not only is a married couple most likely to generate children but also to preserve and improve them, because of "that ardent affection toward their offspring which is implanted in the bosom of parents."[15] In a 1775 magazine article, Witherspoon speaks of the "absolute necessity of marriage for the service of the state."[16] He seems to mean that the state always stands in need of future citizens who will willingly defend their rights and perform their duties, and that a family constituted by a married mother and father with their biological offspring (for whom they will usually have more "ardent affection" than for stepchildren) is the best institution to that end.

Marriage, by limiting sex to husband and wife, "preserve[s] the purity of families." First, the faithfulness of wives gives men confidence that they really are the fathers of their wives' children. Without that confidence, the "ardent affection" that leads fathers to care for their children and teach them their rights and duties will be reduced or destroyed. Further, an unfaithful spouse of either sex will be resented or hated, disrupting the marital harmony that promotes the mutual comfort of the spouses as well as the care of the children. If separation or divorce follows, the children will be deprived of a mother or father.

As for Parsons' worry about "prostration of morals and a dissolution of manners," he probably refers to the founders' belief that marriage has a civilizing effect not only on children but also on adults. Witherspoon writes that the single life "narrows the mind and closes the heart."[17] Other early magazine articles reinforce this view. A 1791 essay states that "while other passions concentrate man on himself, love makes him live in another, subdues selfishness.... The lover becomes a husband, a parent, a citizen." Jan Lewis adds: "Numerous articles attacked bachelors while pitying spinsters."[18] In another article, the "marriage institution" is said to be "the first to produce moral order."[19]

Illustrating this point, John Adams writes, in a diary entry complaining about the absence of the purity of families in France, "The foundations of national morality must be laid in private families.... How is it possible that children can have any just sense of the sacred obligations of morality

---

[15] Swift, *Laws of Connecticut*, 204.
[16] Witherspoon, writing as "Epaminondas," "Reflections on Marriage," *Pennsylvania Magazine*, September 1775, 408, quoted in Lewis, "Republican Wife," 709.
[17] Ibid., 411, in Lewis, "Republican Wife," 709.
[18] "On Love," *New-York Magazine*, June 1791, 311, quoted in ibid., 709.
[19] "A Second Vindication of the Rights of Woman," *Ladies' Monitor*, August 15, 1801, 12, quoted in ibid., 709.

or religion if, from their earliest infancy, they learn that their mothers live in habitual infidelity to their fathers, and their fathers in as constant infidelity to their mothers[?]"[20]

One of the few scholars who report accurately the founders' view of marriage as a natural right is historian Nancy Cott, who writes, "the founders had a political theory of marriage. So deeply embedded in political assumptions that it was rarely voiced as a theory, it was all the more important.... Moral and political philosophy... incorporated and purveyed monogamous morality no less than religion did. Learned knowledge deemed monogamy a God-given but also a civilized practice, a natural right that stemmed from a subterranean basis in natural law."[21] While Cott correctly notes the connection between marriage and natural law, she does not explain how the founders understood that connection.

Four early American legal treatises touch on the political theory of the family. In his *Laws of Connecticut*, quoted earlier, Swift writes in natural law terms throughout his treatment of family law. Incest is "repugnant to the *law of nature*," in part because this sexual connection "destroys the *natural duties* between parents and children." These parental duties "are *all founded in nature*, and result from... [parents'] affection toward their offspring."[22]

Similarly, Tapping Reeve's 1816 treatise traces parental duties to the law of nature: "By the common law, it is the duty of parents to support their minor children. This duty is founded on *the law of nature*. Whoever has been the instrument of giving life to a being incapable of supporting itself, is bound by *the law of morality* to support such being, during such incapacity."[23]

James Wilson's *Lectures on Law* treats family law in his chapter "Of the Natural Rights of Individuals." His chapter title suggests that children and spouses have "natural rights" corresponding to duties prescribed to spouses and parents by the law of nature. Unlike Swift, Witherspoon, and Reeve, Wilson's account is rather vague on the connection between natural right and the "peculiar rights" and "peculiar duties" of spouses, parents, and children. However, he discusses the mutual obligations and

[20] John Adams, Diary, June 2, 1778, in *Works of John Adams*, ed. Charles Francis Adams (Boston: Little, Brown, 1854), 3:171.

[21] Nancy F. Cott, *Public Vows: A History of Marriage and the Nation* (Cambridge: Harvard University Press, 2000), 9.

[22] Swift, *Laws of Connecticut*, 183–4, 186, 204 (my emphasis).

[23] Tapping Reeve, *The Law of Baron and Femme; of Parent and Child* (New Haven, CT: Oliver Steele, 1816), 283 (my emphasis).

rights of family members in the same way as the other legal writers, affirming that the family is the "great foundation of society." He discusses the duties of parents to children ("to maintain,... to protect,... and to educate them"), and of children to parents ("obedience, and subjection to their parents are due from them during their minority; honor and reverence... ever afterwards"), but without reference to the laws of nature.[24]

James Kent, writing two decades after the founding, focuses his argument on the needs of children: "The wants and weaknesses of children render it necessary that some person maintain them, and the *voice of nature* has pointed out the parent as the most fit and proper person. The laws and customs of all nations have enforced this plain *precept of universal law.*... The *obligation of parental duty* is so well secured by the strength of *natural affection*, that it seldom requires to be enforced by human laws."[25]

In the 1788 magazine article quoted earlier, Witherspoon makes two claims: that marriage is "part of natural law" and that it "holds a place of the first importance in the social compact." In his *Lectures on Moral Philosophy*, Witherspoon spells out the reasoning, "drawn from the public good," that would support these claims: "Human creatures at their birth are in a state weaker and more helpless than any other animals. They also arrive much more slowly at maturity and need by far the most assistance and cultivation. Therefore a particular union of the parents is absolutely necessary, and that upon such powerful principles as will secure their common care.... Marriage is a relation expressly founded upon this necessity."[26] From the perspective of the social compact, the main purpose of the "union of the parents" is the "common care" of the children.

Marriage, understood as a requirement of natural law, builds on the natural inclinations of parents, first in their erotic attraction for each other, then in their love for their children and in the affection and friendship seen in couples long married. But since these passions cannot always be counted on, marriage must be sustained also by human laws, even

---

[24] James Wilson, *Lectures on Law*, 1791, in *Collected Works of James Wilson*, ed. Kermit L. Hall and Mark David Hall (Indianapolis: Liberty Fund, 2007), 2:1070, 1076.

[25] James Kent, *Commentaries on American Law* (1826–30; repr. New York: Da Capo, 1971), 2:159–60 (my emphasis).

[26] Witherspoon, Lecture 11, in *Lectures on Moral Philosophy*, 1772–94, in *The Selected Writings of John Witherspoon*, ed. Thomas Miller (Carbondale: Southern Illinois University Press, 1990), 195.

if "contrariety of temper"[27] or annoyance at the burden of raising children would make one of the parents prefer to separate. Kent says this duty "seldom requires to be enforced by human laws";[28] he means that sometimes laws do have to intervene.

William Paley's *Principles of Moral and Political Philosophy* (1785) mentions nature and the law of nature frequently in its discussion of marriage and related subjects. Although written by an Englishman, this book was widely used by American liberal arts colleges starting in the 1790s and continuing through the next two decades and beyond. Paley's book was taught at the University of Pennsylvania, William and Mary, Yale, Harvard, Brown, Dartmouth, Williams, and other colleges. William Blackstone, who was also widely read in the 1780s and '90s, also ties family law to natural law. He speaks of parental duties to children as based on "natural law" and "natural justice," and of children's "natural right" to "a necessary maintenance."[29]

Parsons, Witherspoon, and Swift emphasize two reasons for marriage: to "refine the intercourse between the sexes" and to produce and raise children. Paley explains that "refining" sexual relations promotes the "peace of human society" by "cutting off a principal source of contention by assigning one [woman] to one man, and protecting his exclusive right by sanctions of morality and law." Quarrels from sexual jealousy arise less often when women and men do not cheat on each other. Besides producing "the greatest number of healthy children," marriage, says Paley, also tends to promote the "private comfort of individuals, especially of the female sex" (presumably by guaranteeing that she will be provided for when she becomes a mother).[30] An 1836 essay by Supreme Court Justice Joseph Story appears to plagiarize Paley on marriage.[31]

I have seen little evidence that Locke's understanding of the family influenced the founders. However, I will comment briefly on this because many scholars believe, with Mary Ann Glendon, that the founders "followed Locke and his forerunner Hobbes" in this and in other

---

[27] Ibid., 196.   [28] Kent, *Commentaries*, 2:160.

[29] William Paley, *The Principles of Moral and Political Philosophy* (1785; repr. Indianapolis: Liberty Fund, 2002), pt. 3. Anna Haddow, *Political Science in American Colleges and Universities, 1636–1900* (1939; repr. New York: Octagon, 1969), 44, 49, 54, 57, 60–3 (colleges in which Paley was taught); William Blackstone, *Commentaries on the Laws of England* (1765; repr. Chicago: University of Chicago Press, 1979), 1:435–9.

[30] Paley, *Principles*, 167–8.

[31] Joseph Story, "Natural Law," *Encyclopedia Americana*, ed. Francis Lieber (Philadelphia: Desilver, Thomas, 1836), 9:152.

ways. "Family life," she writes, is "scarcely visible in their accounts."[32] Glendon seems unaware that Locke devotes one whole chapter of the *Two Treatises* and parts of two others to the mutual duties of parents, children, and spouses.[33] From the beginning, Locke states, "all parents were, by the law of nature, under an obligation to preserve, nourish, and educate the children they had begotten." This leads Locke to rule out no-fault divorce. The "conjunction betwixt male and female ought to last even after procreation, so long as is necessary to the nourishment and support of the young ones." In reality, Blackstone and Paley rather than Locke seem to have been more important authors for writers on marriage law.[34]

Although the purpose of marriage in the founding was mainly about producing and raising children, the initial love of husband and wife and their lifelong mutual support were also regarded as important features of the institution. Perhaps for this reason, as well as the prevailing Christianity of the American people, the founders never adopted Locke's minimalist view that the obligation of the marriage tie ends when the children are old enough to "shift for themselves." Locke himself acknowledges that "positive law [in England] ordains all such contracts to be perpetual."[35] Locke's natural law outlines the basic conditions for the family, but civil society may and in the founders' view should add to this minimum.

High regard for marriage persisted long after the founding, as one can see in this 1847 statement of the Pennsylvania Supreme Court: "The great end of matrimony is not the comfort and convenience of the immediate parties, though these are necessarily embarked in it, but the procreation of a progeny having a legal title to maintenance by the father.... [T]he reciprocal taking for better, for worse,... to love and cherish till death, are important, but... no more than ancillary to the principal purpose of [marriage].... [T]he paramount purposes... [are] the procreation and protection of legitimate children, the institution of families, and the creation of natural relations among mankind; from which proceed all the civilization, virtue, and happiness to be found in the world."[36]

---

32 Mary Ann Glendon, "Looking for 'Persons' in the Law," *First Things*, Dec. 2006, www .firstthings.com.

33 John Locke, *Two Treatises of Government*, 1690, ed. Peter Laslett (Cambridge: Cambridge University Press, 1960), *First Treatise*, ch. 9; *Second Treatise*, ch. 6 and 7.

34 Locke, *Second Treatise*, §56, §79. See also Thomas G. West, "Locke's Neglected Teaching on Morality and the Family," *Society* 50, No. 5 (Oct. 2013): 472–6.

35 Locke, *Second Treatise*, §60, §81.

36 Opinion of the Court by Chief Justice John Gibson, *Matchin v. Matchin*, 6 Pa. St. 332 (1847), quoted in *The American and English Encyclopedia of Law*, ed. John Houston

When Paul Rahe says Jefferson supported "Judeo-Christian morality," he is correct. Jews and Christians held monogamous, heterosexual marriage to be a central part of God's requirements for society. However, as we have seen in the previous pages, the founders' case for marriage was built predominantly on arguments from reason, not on appeals to divine authority.

Laws on Sex Outside of Marriage

I will now sketch some of the most important legal supports for marriage. Laws regulating sexual conduct were an inheritance from colonial times, when sex outside marriage was seen not only as injurious to the community, but as a sin against God. After 1776, patterns of criminal prosecutions changed in accord with the new understanding of the purpose of government, and law was brought into conformity with the idea that government exists for the security of natural rights. "The aims of the criminal law," writes David Flaherty, "had now consciously become the preservation of order in society without reference to the saving of souls or the building of God's kingdom on earth." There was a "continuance of prosecutions," continues Flaherty, "for the public offense of bastardy, while fornication came more and more to be viewed as a private act. Many continued to view adultery in particular as a serious public threat . . . , [so] it remained on the statute books in most jurisdictions."[37]

Sex between an Unmarried Man and Woman

Fornication (sex between an unmarried man and woman) tended to be taken less seriously after 1776 because it was not the act itself that was injurious to the family, but only its possible consequence – a fatherless child. Bastardy and adultery, which continued to be prosecuted after 1790, both threaten the community. Bastardy means the birth of a child who will not be provided for by two parents living together in the same household.[38] A wife's adultery threatens to saddle a cuckolded husband

---

Merrill (Northport, NY: Edward Thompson Co., 1890), s.v. "Insanity," 11:142. Thanks to attorney Robert S. Driscoll for the reference.

[37] David H. Flaherty, "Law and the Enforcement of Morals in Early America," in *Law in American History*, ed. Donald Fleming and Bernard Bailyn (Boston: Little, Brown, 1971), 248.

[38] William E. Nelson, *Americanization of the Common Law: The Impact of Legal Change on Massachusetts Society, 1760–1830* (Cambridge: Harvard University Press, 1975), 110–11. Also Robert V. Wells, "Illegitimacy and Bridal Pregnancy in

with the expense and annoyance of raising a child of another man, and adultery of a husband or wife often leads to the abandonment or divorce of a spouse. Richard Godbeer sums up the change: "The judicial system's shift in priorities [during the founding era] led not to the deregulation of sex but to the metamorphosis of sexual regulation."[39]

A 1781 Maryland law embodies the founding orientation. The law allows the government to require "any female person having an illegitimate child" to pay "security to indemnify the county from any charge that may accrue by means of such child," and upon her refusal or failure, to be committed "to the custody of the sheriff of the county." However, if she were willing to name the father, he, not she, would be required "to give security in the sum of thirty pounds current money." The supposed father had a right to a jury trial "as in other criminal cases" if he disputed fatherhood, but if he was found guilty, he would be "committed to the custody of the sheriff [i.e., imprisoned] until he comply."[40] In this law, the cost of welfare for single mothers is the sole concern, not the act of fornication itself. The immorality that is subject to legal penalties is not the indiscretion of the individual, but harming the rights of others by bearing a child without adequate means of support.

Between 1761 and 1800, it is estimated that 33 percent of first births to married women occurred before the ninth month of marriage. Yet the proportion of nonmarital births was probably less than 2 percent. It remained below 4 percent until 1950.[41] This means that although many unmarried women got pregnant, they usually married before the child was born. Fornication, while illegal, was mostly ignored as long as marriage preceded childbirth.

Colonial America," in *Bastardy and its Comparative History: Studies in the History of Illegitimacy*, ed. Peter Laslett et al. (Cambridge: Harvard University Press, 1980), 355–61.

[39] Richard Godbeer, *Sexual Revolution in Early America* (Baltimore: Johns Hopkins University Press, 2002), 228.

[40] An Act Directing the Proceedings against Persons Guilty of Fornication, 1781, *Hanson's Laws of Maryland*, 1763–1784, 203:294, aomol.msa.maryland.gov. VA's law of December 19, 1805, was similar; the father was released from child support if he declared bankruptcy: *Statutes at Large of Virginia*, ed. Samuel Shepherd (Richmond: Samuel Shepherd, 1836), 3:213.

[41] Daniel Scott Smith and Michael S. Hindus, "Premarital Pregnancy in America 1640–1971," *Journal of Interdisciplinary History* 5 (1975): 561; John D'Emilio and Estelle B. Freedman, *Intimate Matters: A History of Sexuality in America*, 3rd ed. (Chicago: University of Chicago Press, 2012), 43; Wells, "Illegitimacy," 354; Daniel Scott Smith, "The Long Cycle in American Illegitimacy and Prenuptial Pregnancy," in *Bastardy*, ed. Laslett, 368 (illegitimacy below 4%, 1920–1950).

Adultery

This contrast between the founders' strict laws and relaxed enforcement characterized all their sex and marriage policies. It also appears in the shocking Vermont adultery statute of 1779, reminiscent of Nathaniel Hawthorne's *Scarlet Letter*: "whosoever shall commit adultery... shall be severely punished by whipping on the naked body not exceeding thirty-nine stripes, and stigmatized, or burnt on the forehead with the letter A, on a hot iron; and each of them shall wear the capital letter A, on the back of their outside garment, of a different color, in fair view, during their abode in this state."[42] I have found no evidence that anyone was ever punished under this law. In other words, the harsh punishments officially prescribed went unenforced, while the prevailing consensus on what is honorable and dishonorable tended to take their place. Historian Karen Weyler writes that the lax enforcement of laws like this "is an indication of how states began deliberately turning a blind eye toward so-called 'domestic' crimes during the late eighteenth century."[43]

The Massachusetts adultery law of 1786 was milder, although still extreme by later standards: "if any man or woman shall commit adultery,... [he or she] shall be set upon the gallows... for the space of one hour, be publicly whipped, not exceeding thirty-nine stripes, [and] imprisoned or fined."[44] William E. Nelson reports zero harsh penalties imposed on adulterers in Massachusetts in his study of this period.[45]

Sodomy and Bestiality

Anti-sodomy and anti-bestiality laws, like all the sexual regulations discussed in this section, forbade sexual activities that deviate from the norm of sex within marriage. Sodomy and bestiality, however, deviate much more from that norm because neither produces offspring. Thus adultery and fornication were not said to be against nature, but sodomy was. Jefferson defines sodomy as "carnal copulation against nature, to wit, of

---

[42] Act against and for the Punishment of Adultery, February 18, 1779, in *Laws of Vermont, 1777–1780*, ed. Allen Soule, vol. 12 of *State Papers of Vermont* (Montpelier: Secretary of State, 1964), 38.

[43] Karen A. Weyler, "The Fruit of Unlawful Embraces," in *Sex and Sexuality in Early America*, ed. Merril D. Smith (New York: New York University Press, 1998), 310.

[44] MA, Act against Adultery, Polygamy, and Lewdness, 217. Similar was NH's Act for the Punishment of Lewdness, Adultery, and Polygamy, February 15, 1791, in *Laws of New Hampshire*, ed. Henry H. Metcalf (Concord, NH: Rumford Press, 1916), 5:706.

[45] Nelson, *Americanization*, 110–11; Wells, "Illegitimacy," 355–61 (transformation of colonial laws against fornication and bastardy).

man or woman in the same sex."[46] Sodomy was punishable – sometimes by death – under the laws of every colony before 1776.[47] Jefferson's proposed revision of Virginia's criminal laws reduced the penalty, although it was still draconian: "Whosoever shall be guilty of rape, polygamy, or sodomy with man or woman shall be punished, if a man, by castration; if a woman, by cutting through the cartilage of her nose a hole of one-half inch diameter at the least."[48] Pennsylvania had a maximum ten-year prison sentence plus a fine. Georgia prescribed lifetime imprisonment.[49] Some states retained the death penalty. In general, writes Mark Kann, "After the Revolution, ... reformers and politicians successfully reduced the penalties for many sex crimes."[50]

As with other sex regulations, it appears that enforcement of these laws was lax. Kann writes, "Despite contrary sexual norms and punitive laws, ... men conducted discreet same-sex relationships without necessarily suffering abuse from their neighbors or prosecution by magistrates."[51] Scholars have found only one reported death-penalty case during the founding era that was unambiguously about sex between males. In this Maryland case, the perpetrator was found guilty of assault with intent to commit sodomy on a nineteen-year-old boy.[52] In other words, the prosecution was not for consensual sex between two people of the same sex, but for attempted homosexual rape of a minor. It is possible that there were prosecutions in the founding era for consensual same-sex copulation, but there is little evidence of it. There is a 1786 instance of a man executed in Pennsylvania for "buggery" (anal intercourse).[53] But the records do not indicate whether the "buggery" was with another man or with an animal, or whether force was involved, as it was in the

---

[46] Jefferson, A Bill for Proportioning Crimes and Punishments, 1779, in *The Papers of Thomas Jefferson*, ed. Julian P. Boyd et al. (Princeton: Princeton University Press, 1950-), 2:497.

[47] *Bowers v. Hardwick*, 478 U.S. 186 (1986), 192 (anti-sodomy laws in force in 1791).

[48] Ibid.

[49] An Act to Reform the Penal Laws, April 5, 1790, in *The Statutes at Large of Pennsylvania, 1682 to 1801*, vol. 13, *1787–1790*, ed. James T. Mitchell and Henry Flanders (Harrisburg: Harrisburg Printing Co., 1906), 511–2; Crimes and Offences against Citizens, in *A Digest of the Statute Laws of the State of Georgia*, ed. Thomas R. R. Cobb (Athens, GA: Christy, Kelsea, and Burke, 1851), 783.

[50] Kann, *Taming Passion*, 165.   [51] Ibid., 72.

[52] *Davis v. The State*, Court of Appeals of MD, 3 H. & J. 154 (1810).

[53] Jack D. Marietta and Gail Stuart Rowe, *Troubled Experiment: Crime and Justice in Pennsylvania, 1682–1800* (Philadelphia: University of Pennsylvania Press, 2006), 89.

Maryland case. (According to Jefferson's comments on his proposed Virginia law, "Buggery is twofold: 1. with mankind, 2. with beasts."[54])

Rogers Smith, who argues that the founders were insufficiently "liberal," strongly objects to their approach to sodomy. "[L]egal systems that automatically subordinate . . . homosexuals," he writes, "are . . . presumptively invalid" in a political regime based on natural rights.[55] However, the founders believed that discouraging sex outside of marriage (both heterosexual and homosexual) promotes the integrity of marriage, which they regarded as a fundamental condition of the social compact required by natural rights theory.

Prostitution, Public Indecency, Obscenity

The founders' approach to public displays or sale of sex is explained in James Wilson's *Lectures on Law*: "[There are some] crimes and offenses which attack several of those natural rights [of individuals. They are] a collection of personal injuries, which annoy the citizens generally and indiscriminately. . . . [P]ublic peace, and order, and tranquility, and safety require them to be punished or abated. . . . Disorderly houses are public nuisances. . . . Indecency, public and grossly scandalous, may well be considered as a species of common nuisance. . . . Profaneness and blasphemy are offences, punished by fine and by imprisonment."[56] My explanation for Wilson's list is that "disorderly houses" (houses of prostitution) and public "indecency" threaten "public peace and order" because they make public that which should remain private. Public sale of sexual favors and display of sexual organs attack one of the moral foundations of stable marriage, namely, the conviction that sex should be shared privately by a married man and woman.

Founding-era laws criminalized "[t]hings which corrupt moral sentiment, as obscene actions, prints, and writings" (to quote a New York Supreme Court case). Such publications, said the court, "are punishable because they strike at the root of moral obligation, and weaken the security of the social ties."[57] In his *Principles of Politics*, Paley writes, "If fornication be criminal, all those incentives which led to it are accessories to the crime, as . . . wanton songs, pictures, books."[58]

---

[54] Jefferson, A Bill, in *Papers*, 2:497.

[55] Rogers M. Smith, *Civic Ideals: Conflicting Visions of Citizenship in U.S. History* (New Haven: Yale University Press, 1997), 37.

[56] Wilson, *Lectures on Law*, in *Collected Works*, 2:1159.

[57] Kent, *People v. Ruggles*, in *Founders' Constitution*, 5:101–2.

[58] Paley, *Principles*, 173.

In an 1815 prosecution for obscenity, the perpetrator had exhibited a "painting, representing a man in an obscene... and indecent posture with a woman." The judgment was based on the common law principle that "actions against public decency were always crimes, as tending to corrupt the public morals."[59] Geoffrey Stone is therefore incorrect when he writes that "the most striking fact about that era was the *absence* of any laws regulating" obscenity, from which he infers that "at the time the First Amendment was enacted, obscenity was treated completely differently from libel, blasphemy, and profanity." Joseph Slade provides a different explanation for the dearth of obscenity prosecutions: "polite communities simply ostracized the offenders."[60]

Legal historian Lawrence Friedman explains the early American view well. The laws regulating sex were strict, but they were hardly ever enforced except when misbehavior became "open and notorious": "The contrast with colonial law is extremely sharp," he writes. "The colonials make no distinction between just plain sin and open and notorious sin. If anything, they hated *concealed* sin more.... [After the founding,] the real crime was to act in such a way as to offend *public* morality. Hence vice won a certain grudging degree of toleration, or even acceptance – so long as it remained in the shadows."[61] Friedman cites an 1846 Michigan law that forbade "open and gross lewdness and lascivious behavior," but did not punish extramarital or adulterous sex if it were out of the public eye.[62] "State and local officials," writes Kann, "had the undisputed authority to regulate people's sex lives; but they rarely exercised that authority, and they almost never exercised it with a heavy hand."[63]

Was this nonintrusive attitude consistent with the rule of law? Should not laws approved by the people's representatives be enforced until modified or repealed? Clearly, the founders judged some crimes to be minimally injurious when the conduct was not "open and gross," such as unobtrusive prostitution and same-sex sex. There was therefore little

---

[59] PA Supreme Court, *Commonwealth v. Sharpless*, 1815, quoted in Morris L. Ernst and Alan U. Schwartz, *Censorship: The Search for the Obscene* (New York: Macmillan, 1964), 13.

[60] Geoffrey R. Stone, "Sex, Violence, and the First Amendment," *University of Chicago Law Review* 74 (2007): 1863. Joseph W. Slade, *Pornography and Sexual Representation: A Reference Guide* (Westport, CT: Greenwood Press, 2001), 40.

[61] Lawrence M. Friedman, *Crime and Punishment in American History* (New York: Basic Books, 1993), 130–1.

[62] Ibid., 130.   [63] Kann, *Taming Passion*, 168; also 72–5.

reason for government to focus law enforcement on these kinds of acts. They also believed that it is unreasonable to expect moral perfection in most people. Conduct that is not harmful if kept private could safely be ignored. Obviously, this category would not include crimes against person or property.

For the most part, this de facto "don't ask, don't tell" policy on sexual misconduct continued from the founding until what Friedman calls the "surge of interest in victimless crime, in vice, in sexual behavior, at the end of the nineteenth century." At that time Progressive ideology led to much more aggressive enforcement of sexual morals laws.[64] Progressives of that day adopted a view that the founders would have rejected as utopian. Political scientist John Burgess provides one of the more extreme but revealing statements of the Progressive vision: The "purpose of the state ... [is] the perfection of humanity; ... the perfect development of the human reason, and its attainment to universal command over individualism; the apotheosis of man. This end is wholly spiritual; and in it mankind, as spirit, triumphs over all fleshly weakness, error, and sin." Charles Merriam, explicitly repudiating the founders' political theory of natural rights and natural law, quotes from this passage to illustrate the new and improved political science of his time.[65] The spirit of law enforcement changed accordingly. A 1910 encyclopedia article on crime explains: "if commitments for minor offenses are ... on the increase, it is in almost every case due to the enactment of new laws, police regulations, etc., with the stricter enforcement of social and hygienic regulations – an indication, therefore, of social progress rather than of the reverse." Another article in the same encyclopedia is entitled "Prostitution or the Social Evil." In the founders' contrary approach, immoral conduct of this sort is of little interest to government as long as it stays behind closed doors. Aggressive prosecution of "vice" – homosexuality, prostitution, drug abuse, and the like – became and remained a feature of American law from about 1880 to 1960, during the heyday of moralistic Progressivism. A final example: in the founding, there were no laws against birth-control devices, and they were widely used in the first part of the nineteenth century. About fifteen years after the Civil War, legal bans began to be widely adopted

[64] Friedman, *Crime and Punishment*, 138.
[65] John W. Burgess, *Political Science and Comparative Constitutional Law* (Boston: Ginn & Co., 1893), 1:85; C. Edward Merriam, *A History of American Political Theories* (New York: Macmillan, 1903), 318.

and enforced.[66] After the Sexual Revolution of the 1960s, of course, everything changed.

Polygamy and Divorce

In addition to their policies on sex outside of marriage, the founders also criminalized having more than one spouse at a time. In the early republic, arguments against polygamy sometimes appealed to both reason and revelation, and sometimes to reason alone. Vermont's 1779 Act against Polygamy begins: "the violation of the marriage covenant is contrary to the command of God, and destructive to families."[67] More typical was Zephaniah Swift's strictly reason-based argument: "in the countries where the dreary religion of Mohamed has prevailed, polygamy has been introduced, the women have been treated as slaves, and considered as merely the objects of lust." In America, in "the highest point of improvement" in civilization, "they are considered as the equal companions and friends of the other sex."[68] Although Witherspoon was a Presbyterian minister, he too provides arguments grounded in mere reason. "Polygamy is condemned by nature," he writes, "for it is found that the males born are to the females as 13 to 12."[69] A generation later, Supreme Court Justice Joseph Story gives a fuller rational critique of polygamy, borrowed from Paley: it "divides the affections of parents. . . . It debases the female sex. . . . It weakens the motives to female chastity and to exclusive devotion to one husband. Besides, the very equality in point of numbers of the sexes seems to point out the law of God to be, that one woman shall be assigned to one man. And in point of fact, the countries where polygamy has been allowed have been uniformly debased, indolent, and enervated."[70] As with other founding-era policies, the argument is mainly based on natural-law reasoning, not Christianity.

Another sign of the founders' concern with public order and happiness, as opposed to the colonial preoccupation with moral purity, is seen in their

---

[66] "Crime," *New Encyclopedia of Social Reform*, ed. William Bliss and Rudolph Binder (New York: Funk & Wagnalls, 1910), 340, 978; D'Emilio and Freedman, *Intimate Matters*, 57–9; Andrea Tone, *Devices and Desires: A History of Contraceptives in America* (New York: Hill and Wang, 2001), 4–5.

[67] Act against Polygamy, February 19, 1779, in *Laws of Vermont*, ed. Soule, 39.

[68] Swift, *Laws of Connecticut*, 183.

[69] Witherspoon, *Lectures on Moral Philosophy*, Lecture 11, 195.

[70] Story, "Natural Law," 152–3 (apparently paraphrasing Paley, *Principles*, bk. 3, pt. 3, ch. 6).

attitude toward divorce. British colonial law banned divorce altogether in the 1770s. Shortly after 1776, every state except South Carolina legalized it under limited circumstances.[71] South Carolina did not officially permit divorce until 1868.[72]

For the founders, as we have seen, marriage is a contract. Just as any other contract can be legally cancelled when its terms are not met by one of the parties, so also divorce can be granted when one party violates the marriage contract. New Hampshire's 1791 statute was typical of several Northern states: divorce was permitted in cases of incest, bigamy, "for impotency, for adultery in either of the parties, or where either of the parties shall be absent for the space of three years . . . , [a]nd for the cause of extreme cruelty in either of the parties."[73] Impotency as a ground of divorce indicates the centrality of children to the founders' conception of marriage. The implication is that without the possibility of children, a marriage is not quite real because its primary purpose of bearing and raising children goes unfulfilled. New York, the strictest Northern state, allowed divorce only for adultery.[74] Pennsylvania states the single idea behind all these reasons for divorce in its 1785 law: "it is the design of marriage, and the wish of parties entering into that state, that it should continue during their joint lives; yet where the one party is under natural or legal incapacities of faithfully discharging the matrimonial vow, or is guilty of acts and deeds inconsistent with the nature thereof, the laws of every well-regulated society ought to give relief to the innocent and injured person."[75] Divorce is conceived of as a civil remedy for personal injury, marriage being an institution intended to benefit both spouses.

No-fault divorce was banned everywhere because, as James Wilson explains, "when divorces can be summoned to the aid of levity, of vanity, or of avarice, a state of marriage frequently becomes a state of war or stratagem." In 1830 James Kent agreed: "facility of separation" tends to

---

71 Friedman, *History of American Law*, 204–8 (the law of divorce in early America). Also Linda Kerber, *Women of the Republic: Intellect and Ideology in Revolutionary America* (Chapel Hill: University of North Carolina Press, 1980), 157–84.

72 Kellen Funksource, "'Let No Man Put Asunder': South Carolina's Law of Divorce, 1895–1950," *South Carolina Historical Magazine* 110, No. 3/4 (July–Oct. 2009): 134–53.

73 Act to . . . Regulate Divorces, February 17, 1791, in *Laws of New Hampshire*, 5:733.

74 Lawrence M. Friedman, *Private Lives: Families, Individuals, and the Law* (Cambridge: Harvard University Press, 2004), 29.

75 PA, Act concerning Divorces, in *Statutes at Large*, 12:94.

"destroy all mutual confidence, and to inflame every trifling dispute."[76] Falling out of love, fear of violence, small injuries, lack of civility, or other lesser inconveniences were insufficient grounds for divorce.

Rights and Duties of Husbands and Wives

In the common law of marriage that prevailed in every state (called *coverture*), the husband was the legal head of the family. A single woman or widow had many civil rights that were the same as men's: to own property, to sue, and to make wills and contracts. But when a woman got married, these rights were exercised by a husband alone on behalf of the whole family. Legally, all property, including his wife's wages, belonged to the husband. He had the right to determine where the family would live and how the children would be educated. The wife was legally obliged to care for her husband and "maintain" her children. In theory, the wife lost her distinct legal personality and became one person with her husband.[77] Perhaps the most important benefit to the husband was one that he is denied in contemporary American law: a legal guarantee that he would live together with his children (and their mother) while they were growing up. Only if he seriously misbehaved would his wife be permitted to divorce him and deny him his fatherly right to help raise their children.

The laws of coverture would not be tolerated today. But we misjudge coverture if we adopt the typical modern view, here stated by Kann, that "[w]omen did not have the authority to police men's behavior, sexual or otherwise."[78] As a matter of fact, a husband's rights came with corresponding duties, and in that regard women had a great deal of authority "to police men's behavior." The laws of the family were understood by both sexes to be protective of, not hostile to, women's rights. To appreciate this, we have to remember that marriage almost always meant children, and that resources for their support are always a matter of urgency. In the early republic, a single mother could expect little from the father or from government. But a married mother and her minor children had a lifetime "legal title to maintenance by the father."[79] In other words, the husband did not in fact own all of his own property

---

[76] Kent, *Commentaries on American Law*, 2:86. Wilson, "Of the Natural Rights of Individuals," pt. 2, ch. 12 of *Lectures on Law*, 2:1075.

[77] Reeve, *Law of Baron and Femme* (full account of coverture laws); Swift, *Laws of Connecticut*, 183–203. Modern summaries: Cott, *Public Vows*, 11–12; Grossberg, *Governing the Hearth*, 25.

[78] Kann, *Taming Passion*, 172.   [79] *Matchin v. Matchin*.

and that of his wife. She and their children had a legal title to part of it. He could not divorce a wife who wanted to remain married to him unless she violated the terms of the marriage contract, for example by sexual disloyalty. And in many states, if he were the adulterer or seriously abused his wife, she could divorce him and, as we will see, often get custody of the children. Did the founders' marriage laws maintain the integrity of the family at the expense of the wife's or husband's proper liberty to escape an unhappy marriage? That is the question we would ask them. The founders would ask us why a disgruntled but uninjured parent should have a legal right to make a child or an ex-spouse miserable by depriving the one of the company of a parent, and the other of a husband or wife.

After 1776 the laws of coverture were gradually revised, always with a view to the well-being of both sexes as well as children. Legal scholar Tom James writes, "American courts understood the doctrine of coverture as being intended for the protection of women, and therefore not something to be applied to their detriment."[80] Historian Linda Kerber explains: these laws were "interpreted flexibly and modified significantly." Although in theory a wife could not make a legally binding contract, in fact, writes Tapping Reeve in 1816, a husband "is bound to fulfill the contract of his wife, when it is such a one as wives, according to the usage of the country, commonly make [such as the purchase of household goods]."[81] In this case the husband was legally bound to fulfill contracts that he did not make. In England, Reeve reports, husbands at one time had the right to physically "chastise [a wife] moderately." But in Connecticut, "the right of chastising a wife is not...recognized by our law."[82] Of injuries committed by family members against each other, James Wilson writes, "whenever urgent emergencies arise; whenever any outrage is threatened or committed against the peace or safety of society,...the law will interpose its authority."[83] Wilson is referring to serious physical violence. In Pennsylvania, divorce could be obtained if a husband "by cruel and barbarous treatment endanger her [his wife's] life or offer such indignities to her person as to render her condition intolerable or life

---

[80] Tom James, *The History of Custody Law* (self-published, 2014), 108. James's useful research on this topic is also at http://tomjameslaw.com.

[81] Reeve, *Law of Baron and Femme*, 79.

[82] Ibid., 65; see also Hendrick Hartog, *Man and Wife in America: A History* (Cambridge: Harvard University Press, 2000), 105.

[83] Wilson, *Lectures on Law*, 2:1074.

burdensome." Violence of wives against husbands was not mentioned in this law.[84] Other states had similar provisions.

Under the law of coverture, married fathers were legal custodians of the children – on paper. But in divorce proceedings, writes Tom James, "most American courts ignored the coverture doctrine" whenever it was thought to conflict with the best interest of the child. James cites numerous early divorce cases showing that courts awarded "custody to the mother on the basis of her husband's misconduct." The tendency was to ignore the father's formal right and to grant custody to whichever divorced parent was not at fault.[85] In general, the laws of coverture were retained insofar as they reinforced the typical division of labor between husbands and wives within marriage, a division that both sexes mostly approved of; in other respects coverture laws were modified or abandoned.[86]

The legal rules governing the family were based on the belief that the natures of men and women differ in many ways, and that generating, supporting, and raising children works best when each sex specializes in those tasks for which it is by nature best suited and which it will therefore perform most happily and competently. Founding documents by John Adams and the town of Essex, Massachusetts, which were quoted in the earlier discussion of women's voting rights – in Chapter 6 – describe the sex differences in question.[87]

An additional difference is alluded to in an exchange between Abigail and John Adams. In her famous "Remember the ladies" letter to her husband, Abigail writes, "If particular care and attention is not paid to the ladies [in the laws of the new nation], we are determined to foment a

---

[84] Act concerning Divorces and Alimony, 1785, in *The Statutes at Large of Pennsylvania*, ed. James T. Mitchell and Henry Flanders (Harrisburg: Harrisburg Printing Co., 1906), 12:98.

[85] James, *History of Custody*, 99, 107–12; Mary Ann Mason, *From Father's Property to Children's Rights: The History of Child Custody in the United States* (New York: Columbia University Press, 1994), 54–5 (custody often granted to women); Hartog, *Man and Wife*, 193–6.

[86] The small minority of women who did complain of their lot is discussed in Janet Wilson James, *Changing Ideas about Women in the United States, 1776–1825* (New York: Garland Publishing, 1981), ch. 2.

[87] See also Noah Webster's bestselling textbook, *An American Selection of Lessons in Reading and Speaking . . . Being the Third Part of a Grammatical Institute of the English Language*, 3rd ed. (Boston: Isaiah Thomas and Ebenezer T. Andrews, 1793), 228–39 (moral and marital duties of men and women, based on the natural differences between the sexes).

rebellion, and will not hold ourselves bound by any laws in which we have no voice or representation." John responds with a serious jest: "Depend upon it, we know better than to repeal our masculine systems. Although they are in full force, you know they are little more than theory. We dare not exert our power in its full latitude. We are obliged to go fair, and softly, and in practice you know we are the subjects. We have only the name of masters, and rather than give up this, which would completely subject us to the despotism of the petticoat, I hope General Washington and all our brave heroes would fight."[88]

Adams is saying that women have great power over men in the whole realm of emotion and love, family and children, the realm celebrated by music and movies, often viewed by both sexes as more important than money and prestige. He implies that the greater legal status given to husbands keeps relations between the sexes more equal than they would otherwise be. Psychologist David Geary more or less makes Adams's point in the dry language of social science: women are superior in "processing of information related to the self, other individuals, and with respect to group dynamics" and in "manipulation of social relationships."[89] Here, perhaps, is another reason why so few women objected to coverture. At any rate, Abigail ends her letter in a conciliatory tone: "Regard us [women] then as beings placed by providence under your protection and in imitation of the Supreme Being make use of that power only for our happiness."[90] (Her reference to "the Supreme Being" alludes to the Bible, Ephesians 5.)

During and after the founding, the laws and customs on male–female relations changed. Historian Michael Grossberg calls this trend "the emergence of the republican family."[91] This development was a logical consequence of the natural right and natural law principles of the founding. Locke's *Two Treatises* had attacked patriarchalism in the name of equality and liberty. Americans applied these principles not only to political despotism, but to the patriarchal family of their colonial

---

[88] Abigail Adams to John Adams, March 31, 1776; John to Abigail, April 14, 1776, in *Adams Family Correspondence*, ed. L. H. Butterfield (Cambridge: Harvard University Press, 1963), 1:370, 382.

[89] David C. Geary, *Male, Female: The Evolution of Human Sex Differences*, 2nd ed. (Washington, DC: American Psychological Association, 2010), 380. Cf. H. L. Mencken, *In Defense of Women* (Garden City, NY: Garden City Publishing, 1922), 117 (the power of "feminine weapons").

[90] Abigail Adams to John, March 31, 1776, in *Adams Family Correspondence*, 1:370.

[91] Grossberg, *Governing the Hearth*, 4.

forebears.[92] After 1776, the American family was increasingly based on a new view of wives as equal partners with their husbands, although men and women were still expected to occupy partially separate spheres in life. Jan Lewis writes, "the Revolutionary generation found in the 'affectionate union' of marriage an alternative to the patriarchal model of political relationships."[93] Merril Smith provides an example: whereas a century earlier, children "were supposed to be guided by their parents" in choosing a spouse, by the late 1700s they "expected to choose their own spouses and married primarily for love."[94] Women's importance in forming the character of citizens – their children's and their husbands' – was frequently discussed and praised. A 1789 article in *Christian's Magazine* states, "it is... to the virtues of the fair... that society must be indebted for its moral, as well as its natural preservation."[95] This idea – equal importance but separate roles of men and women – was repeated again and again in the many women's magazines that flourished in the early republic. Historian Linda Kerber has called this new idea of women's role "republican motherhood."[96] The elevation of women's status is also illustrated by a striking fact reported by historian Jay Fliegelman: "Whereas before 1775 virtually all extant family portraits present the father standing above his seated family, after that date the vertical or hierarchical composition gives way to a horizontal or equalitarian composition in which all family members are shown on the same plane."[97]

Conclusion

Harvey Mansfield compares the founders' approach to sex differences with government's insistence today that male and female role differences should be blurred or abolished: "But in constructing the gender-neutral

---

[92] Jay Fliegelman, *Prodigals and Pilgrims: The American Revolution against Patriarchal Authority, 1750–1800* (Cambridge: Cambridge University Press, 1982); Wood, *Radicalism*, 145–68.

[93] Lewis, "Republican Wife," 689, referring to Fliegelman, *Prodigals and Pilgrims*, ch. 5.

[94] Merril D. Smith, *Breaking the Bonds: Marital Discord in Pennsylvania, 1730–1830* (New York: New York University Press, 1991), 5. Also Jan Lewis, "The Republican Wife: Virtue and Seduction in the Early Republic," *William and Mary Quarterly* 44 (1987): 689; Carl N. Degler, *At Odds: Women and the Family in America from the Revolution to the Present* (New York: Oxford University Press, 1980), 8–19, 26–30; Nancy F. Cott, *The Bonds of Womanhood: Women's Sphere in New England, 1780–1835* (New Haven: Yale University Press, 1976).

[95] Quoted by Lewis, "The Republican Wife," 700.

[96] Kerber, *Women of the Republic*, 285.   [97] Fliegelman, *Prodigals and Pilgrims*, 10.

society, it [modern America] has been... trying to impose the liberal state upon liberal society."[98] Mansfield implies that the founders' "liberal state" is gender-neutral while their "liberal society" tolerates or encourages practices and customs based on differences between men and women. He is right about the founders' "liberal society," but they did not embrace a "liberal state" in his sense. True, they aimed at a gender-neutral state in one important way: every person, male or female, is equally protected against injury by criminal and civil laws, as well as by impartially adjudicated trials when legal rights are in dispute. But starting with marriage law itself (requiring that marriage be between a man and a woman), the law was far from gender-neutral. Voting rights were generally limited to men, and women were mostly not eligible for government jobs. These practices were based on the view that the nature-based division of labor within the household would lead to the happiness of all concerned as much as possible. Their intention was to encourage stable marriages in which two loving parents would raise children to be good citizens, so that "the blessings of liberty" would be preserved for "our posterity."

In the 1960s, marriage was redefined. Law professor Alan Frank, writing in 1978, explains the new view: marriage "has become a vehicle for the maximizing of individual self-fulfillment and personal happiness."[99] Frank is partly right. The new conception of marriage indeed centers on "personal happiness" – but of only one person. Whenever one spouse no longer experiences "self-fulfillment and personal happiness," he or she may walk away. The fulfillment and happiness of the children or of the discarded spouse do not count. Another law professor, Helen Alvaré, remarks that in the legal discussions leading up to the institution of no-fault divorce in the 1970s, there was a "relatively greater amount of attention devoted to the interests of adults versus children in respecting marriage and divorce.... [C]harged, emotional language [was] used to express parents' desires for divorce, versus the clinical language used to express children's interests." Similarly, academics like Stephanie Coontz have little to say about the happiness of the ex-spouse or children. Judith Wallerstein, in contrast, writes that although the former marriage was "a dead issue" for half the ex-spouses she interviewed, the other half "were angry, bitter, and mired in conflict even fifteen years after the breakup.... My most troubling finding concerned the children.... Not

[98] Harvey C. Mansfield, *Manliness* (New Haven: Yale University Press, 2006), 243.
[99] Alan H. Frank et al., "No Fault Divorce and the Divorce Rate: The Nebraska Experience," *Nebraska Law Review* 58, No. 1 (1978): 29.

one considered it a dead issue.... They remembered the day that one parent left home with a vividness that took my breath away."[100]

After 1970, the law viewed children only as possible byproducts of marriage, but no longer central to it. Consequently, the older "marriage model" for raising and caring for children – adhered to by the founders as well as pre-1960s Progressives – was replaced by today's "child support model." By requiring child support whether or not the parents were ever married, together with the easy availability of divorce, the legal significance of marriage fades away. The wife gains power in the household because, as Coontz explains, she can now threaten divorce to get her way.[101] She knows that she will probably be awarded custody and child support.[102] If she is unmarried, the same rules apply. Enforcement of child support is draconian. In 2017 it was the only kind of debt for which a person can be – and often is – sent to prison.[103]

The older "marriage model" required the father to protect and provide for his wife and children, and to remain sexually loyal to her. It required the mother to remain sexually loyal to him, to perform appropriate household duties, and to allow her husband to take the lead in family affairs. The family was otherwise left mostly free of government supervision. After "love conquered marriage," in Coontz's phrase,[104] the "child support model" for raising children came to be perceived as superior to the "marriage model." The founders would have disagreed.

[100] Helen M. Alvaré, "The Turn toward the Self in the Law of Marriage and Family: Same-Sex Marriage and Its Predecessors," *Stanford Law and Policy Review* 16 (2005): 144; Stephanie Coontz, *Marriage, a History: How Love Conquered Marriage* (New York: Penguin Books, 2005), 305–6, 312–13; Judith S. Wallerstein and Sandra Blakeslee, *Second Chances: Men, Women and Children a Decade after Divorce* (New York: Houghton Mifflin, 1989), xiii.

[101] Coontz, *Marriage, a History*, 306.

[102] Margaret F. Brinig and Douglas W. Allen, "'These Boots Are Made for Walking': Why Most Divorce Filers Are Women," *American Law and Economics Review* 2, No. 1 (2000): 126–69 (women gain power within marriage because of a high likelihood of being awarded child support and custody).

[103] Elizabeth G. Patterson, "Civil Contempt and the Indigent Child Support Obligor: The Silent Return of Debtor's Prison," *Cornell Journal of Law and Public Policy* 18 (2008): 95–141.

[104] Coontz, *Marriage, a History: How Love Conquered Marriage.*

11

Cultivating Public Support for Liberty and Virtue

In Chapter 9, I explained that one of the founders' four kinds of moral law is the "law of fashion" or "law of opinion," and that government helps shape that "law" through schools, universities, and promotion of religion. This chapter will show how government shapes public opinion in other ways. Any group one happens to be part of always has its "law of fashion" – standards of morality and behavior enforced through praise and blame. Founder Edmund Randolph indicates the weakness of law if it does not have public opinion on its side: it "cannot, however, be denied that the vice [of excessive gambling] has not been extirpated [by Virginia's law].... [It] depends for correction on the censorship which the people possess over morals, on religion, and on the force of example and character."[1] In fact, the "law of fashion" is a more effective deterrent than the criminal law. "Public opinion sets bounds to every government," writes Madison, "and is the real sovereign in every free one."[2]

The law of fashion regulates little things, such as manner of dress, tastes in music, and what careers and universities are respectable. But it also touches more serious matters – including moral and political beliefs, and qualities of character – that receive the labels of right or wrong, noble

---

[1] "Edmund Randolph's Essay on the Revolutionary History of Virginia, 1774-1782," *Virginia Magazine of History and Biography* 44, No. 4 (Oct. 1936): 313.

[2] James Madison, "Public Opinion," 1791, in *Writings*, ed. Jack Rakove (New York: Library of America, 1999), 500. Colleen A. Sheehan, *James Madison and the Spirit of Republican Self-Government* (New York: Cambridge University Press, 2009); Sheehan, *The Mind of James Madison: The Legacy of Classical Republicanism* (New York: Cambridge University Press, 2015) (arguing that scholars have too often neglected Madison's concern with public opinion formation).

or disgraceful, honorable or dishonorable. The enforcers of this law of esteem today often make use of slang, such as cool, awesome, terrific, sweet, nerd, tool, or jerk. Heterodox opinions are supposedly protected by the First Amendment, but labels like racist, sexist, and homophobic indicate opinions that some Americans will not tolerate. Rejecting one's group's evaluations about cool or uncool, true or false, politically correct or incorrect, will lead to raised eyebrows, whispers behind one's back, negative comments on social media, and, in more serious cases, open ridicule, hatred, exclusion from the group, or termination of employment.

John Adams writes, "Wherever men, women, or children are to be found,... every individual is seen to be strongly actuated by a desire to be seen, heard, talked of, approved, and respected, by the people about him, and within his knowledge." The "desire of the esteem of others," he continues, "is as real a want of nature as hunger; and the neglect and contempt of the world... produces despair and a detestation of existence; [respect is] of equal importance to individuals, to families, to nations." This love of honor shapes people's moral sensibilities: "When children and youth hear their parents and neighbors, and all about them, applauding the love of country, of labor, of liberty, and all the virtues, habits, and faculties, which constitute a good citizen, that is, a *patriot* and a *hero*, those children endeavor to acquire those qualities, and a sensible and virtuous people will never fail to form multitudes of patriots and heroes."[3]

The law of opinion has its most powerful effect when it becomes a kind of second nature in the form of conscience or a sense of honor. This is nicely described by historian William Lecky: "It is the merit of the Anglo-Saxon race that beyond all others it has produced men of the stamp of a Washington...; who made the supreme majesty of moral rectitude the guiding principle of their lives, who proved in the most trying circumstances that no allurements of ambition, and no storms of passion, could cause them to deviate one hair's breadth from the course they believed to be their duty."[4]

Government cannot be indifferent to such a powerful force. Adams concludes, "It is a principal end of government to regulate this passion [for esteem], which in its turn becomes a principal means of government.

---

[3] John Adams, *Discourses on Davila*, 1790, ch. 2, in *Works of John Adams*, ed. Charles Francis Adams (Boston: Little, Brown, 1854), 6:232–4.

[4] William E. H. Lecky, *History of European Morals*, 3rd ed. (New York: Appleton, 1894), 1:153. Robert Middlekauf, *Washington's Revolution: The Making of America's First Leader* (New York: Knopf, 2015) (Washington's devotion to honor and honorableness).

It is the only adequate instrument of order and subordination in society, and alone commands effective obedience to laws, since without it neither human reason, nor standing armies, would ever produce that great effect."[5]

How Political Laws Form the Law of Opinion

Government's laws, firmly enforced, can change the law of opinion that prevails in times of chaos. In the violent state of nature, successful acts of violence are honorable. As Hobbes correctly remarks, "the two cardinal virtues" in that state are "force and fraud."[6] However, after government is established, criminals who are fined, sent to prison, or executed are thereby dishonored, no matter how much "force and fraud" they display in committing their thefts and murders and in fights with other criminals or with the police before they get arrested. Such punishment is humiliating because it exposes criminals as failures – overcome by superior force. Few will admire and praise them if the punishments are predictably quick and serious. Criminal law, then, affects moral conduct in two ways: directly through fear of physical punishment, and indirectly by making crime dishonorable in the eyes of one's friends, family, and associates. And, as we already noted, whatever is honored among the people we associate with insinuates itself into the heart.

The law of divine revelation can similarly inform the "law of private censure" when, in Adams's expression, "children and youth hear their parents and neighbors, and all about them, applauding" the same or similar religious opinions. As a common faith grows, the effectiveness of divine commandments will come more from what is honored in one's group. The faithful will be more mindful of the immediate threat of social disapproval or ostracism than of punishments threatened by God in the distant future. The power of religion over moral conduct in a society whose public tone is religious – as America was for a long time – comes more from social acceptance than truth.

Here too government laws can help by prohibiting public vilification of religion, by sponsoring prayer and religious teaching in schools, and by its own pronouncements of respect for and approval of the religious doctrines that it believes best suited to securing the rights of the people.

---

[5] Adams, *Discourses on Davila*, 6:234.
[6] Thomas Hobbes, *Leviathan*, 1651, ed. Edwin Curley (Indianapolis: Hackett, 1994), ch. 13, near the end.

Earlier we described how the founders involved government in teaching the natural law and religion in schools. I add here that schools were understood to be especially useful in forming the law of opinion. The Massachusetts Constitution states that public schools should "inculcate the principles of humanity and general benevolence, public and private charity, industry and frugality, honesty and punctuality in their dealings; sincerity, good humor, and all social affections, and generous sentiments among the people." Public schools "inculcate" these qualities by praising and honoring them in word and deed.

Speeches, Writings, and Awards of Public Officials – and Music

Government can also affect the law of private censure through speeches, writings, and honors bestowed by officials on exemplary individuals. Starting with the state constitutions, especially their bills of rights with their affirmations of republican virtue, honor was constantly given to qualities of good citizenship. To this end, statesmen also made good use of ceremonial occasions, state funerals, and the like. Washington's First Inaugural, quoted earlier, honors the kinds of moral and religious opinions that he thought were needed in a free society: "the propitious smiles of Heaven can never be expected on a nation that disregards the eternal rules of order and right which Heaven itself has ordained."[7] The Senate replied to Washington in these words: "We feel, sir, the force and acknowledge the justness of the observation that the foundations of our national policy should be laid in private morality.... It is therefore the duty of legislators to enforce, both by precept and example, the utility as well as the necessity of a strict adherence to the rules of distributive justice."[8]

Statesmen also help sustain a public sense of what is honorable by honoring those who perform outstanding deeds, such as soldiers, military leaders, and great statesmen. This sort of practice can be seen in decorations given by the military. Outstanding generals and common soldiers are honored in war memorials, including Civil War monuments still seen in cities and small towns all over the Eastern half of the nation. One may also recall the Washington Monument and the later memorials

[7] George Washington, First Inaugural Address, 1789, in *Writings*, ed. John Rhodehamel (New York: Library of America, 1997), 732–3.

[8] Address of the Senate to Washington, May 7, 1789, in *Messages and Papers of the Presidents*, ed. James D. Richardson (New York: Bureau of National Literature, 1897), 1:47.

built in honor of Lincoln and Jefferson. When Washington died, numerous politicians spoke in his praise. President Adams said, "His example is now complete, and it will teach wisdom and virtue to magistrates, citizens, and men, not only in the present age, but in future generations, as long as history shall be read."[9] The image of Washington as virtuous statesman was an important element in the education of Abraham Lincoln. He studied his biography as a child and aspired to emulate his example.[10]

American patriotic music, which began in the Revolutionary War, has also been a formative influence on morals. American leaders seem to have sensed, without ever articulating it explicitly, the insights of Plato. "[R]hythm and harmony," Socrates famously argues in the *Republic*, "insinuate themselves into the inmost part of the soul and most vigorously lay hold of it ... and they make a man graceful if he is correctly reared. ... [H]e would praise the noble things; and, taking pleasure in them and receiving them into his soul, he would be reared on them and become a noble and good man. He would blame and hate the ugly in the right way while he's still young." Music shapes the soul's perceptions of the world, of the heroic and the noble.[11]

Two leading founders composed songs that are still remembered. John Dickinson's "Liberty Song" was written in 1768, during the "No taxation without representation" controversy with Britain. It became so popular that the Tories composed a parody. This is Dickinson's first stanza and chorus:

> Come, join hand in hand, brave Americans all,
> And rouse your bold hearts at fair Liberty's call;
> No tyrannous acts shall suppress your just claim,
> Or stain with dishonor America's name.

Chorus:

> In Freedom we're born and in Freedom we'll live.
> Our purses are ready. Steady, friends, steady;
> Not as slaves, but as Freemen our money we'll give.[12]

---

9 Adams, reply to a message from the Senate, December 23, 1799, in ibid., 1:290.

10 Louis A. Warren, *Lincoln's Youth: Indiana Years, Seven to Twenty-One, 1816–1830* (New York: Appleton, Century, Crofts, 1959), 95.

11 *The Republic of Plato*, trans. Allan Bloom (New York: Basic Books, 1968), 401d-e (I have modified the translation slightly).

12 David Hackett Fischer, *Liberty and Freedom* (New York: Oxford University Press, 2005), 116–7.

In the first and fourth stanzas of James Warren's 1774 "Song of Liberty," America's rising greatness, based on the rule of law, is first contrasted with the two greatest nations hitherto, Athens and Rome, and then with the despotic governments of contemporary Europe:

> That seat of science, Athens, and earth's proud mistress, Rome,
> Where now are all their glories? We scarce can find their tomb.
> Then guard your rights, Americans, nor stoop to lawless sway,
> Oppose, oppose, oppose, oppose, for North America.
> Torn from a world of tyrants, beneath this western sky,
> We form'd a new dominion, a land of liberty:
> The world shall own we're freemen here, and such we'll ever be,
> Huzza, huzza, huzza, huzza, for love and liberty![13]

Government's flags, coins, and other symbols also contribute to forming public opinion. Historian David Hackett Fischer provides many examples that carry a teaching of liberty and resistance to tyranny in *Liberty and Freedom*.[14] Architecture too can inform the public view. Jefferson speaks of the importance of erecting "beautiful" and "noble" public buildings to "improve the taste of my countrymen" and as "models for their study and imitation."[15] Even the mere text of laws, apart from their enforcement, can also help, as Madison states regarding bills of rights: "The political truths declared in that solemn manner acquire by degrees the character of fundamental maxims of free government, and as they become incorporated within the national sentiment, counteract the impulses of interest and passion."[16]

The Great Seal of the United States

The Great Seal was approved by Congress in 1782 and is still printed on the dollar bill. It is a superb example of government's use of pictorial symbols to teach Americans how to understand the meaning of their country.

---

[13] Richard Frothingham, *Life and Times of Joseph Warren* (Boston: Little, Brown, 1865), 405, quoting *Massachusetts Spy*, May 26, 1774.

[14] Fischer, *Liberty and Freedom*, 19–84, 107–66. See also my discussion of the rattlesnake flag in Chapter 12.

[15] Jefferson to Madison, September 20, 1785, in *The Republic of Letters: The Correspondence between Thomas Jefferson and James Madison, 1776–1826* (New York: Norton, 1995), 1:384–5.

[16] Fischer, *Liberty and Freedom*, 32, 75–7, 154. Madison to Jefferson, October 17, 1788, in Madison, *Writings*, ed. Jack N. Rakove (New York: Library of America, 1999), 421–2.

The pyramid side of the Seal is a memorable representation of the theology of the Declaration of Independence – the relation between God and America – and of the highest aspiration of the founding. The Seal is often misunderstood, in part because its symbols are believed to be Masonic in origin. Gordon Wood writes, "Masonry create[d] enduring national icons (like the pyramid and the all-seeing eye of Providence on the Great Seal of the United States)."[17] In his book on early American freemasonry, historian Steven Bullock agrees: "Its symbols adorned . . . the nation's Great Seal."[18] However, neither Wood nor Bullock provides evidence for that claim.

On the contrary, the definitive history of the Seal – Richard Patterson and Richardson Dougall's *The Eagle and the Shield* – finds that the eye and pyramid symbolism had no connection to freemasonry at that time.[19] The providential eye in a triangle was established outside of Masonic circles long before the founding. Albert Potts reports: "On a medal of [English king] Charles II in 1660 and on another of William II struck in 1690, one finds the eye in triangle radiates very much as it appears on the great seal. This was reproduced on hundreds of coin dies engraved in the following century, especially in the cities of Germany."[20] Two eighteenth-century English medallions had the same providential rays of light surrounding a triangle.[21]

The best way to understand the Great Seal is to consult co-designer Charles Thomson's report, which accompanies the 1782 law.[22] Thomson explains, "The pyramid signifies strength and duration." On the base is inscribed MDCCLXXVI (1776) – the date, Thomson remarks, of the Declaration of Independence. The pyramid has thirteen rows of bricks, signifying the original states. The number of rows is not specified in

[17] Gordon S. Wood, *Empire of Liberty: A History of the Early Republic, 1789–1815* (New York: Oxford University Press, 2009), 50.

[18] Steven C. Bullock, *Revolutionary Brotherhood: Freemasonry and the Transformation of the American Social Order, 1730–1840* (Chapel Hill: University of North Carolina Press, 1996), 1.

[19] Richard S. Patterson and Richardson Dougall, *The Eagle and the Shield: A History of the Great Seal of the United States* (Washington: Government Printing Office, 1976), 529–32. Also Catherine L. Albanese, *Sons of the Fathers: The Civil Religion of the American Revolution* (Philadelphia: Temple University Press, 1976), 129–36.

[20] Albert M. Potts, *The World's Eye* (Lexington: University Press of Kentucky, 1982), 68–9.

[21] Edward Hawkins, *Medallic Illustrations of the History of Great Britain and Ireland to the Death of George II* (London: British Museum, 1885), 2:265, 647.

[22] Patterson and Dougall, *Eagle and the Shield*, 83–91 (quoting and discussing Thomson's report).

the law, but there are thirteen in co-designer William Barton's original drawing and on the 1778 fifty-dollar bill from which the pyramid idea was taken.[23] The pyramid is the United States, a strong and durable structure of freedom, built on the foundation of the Declaration. It is unfinished because America is still under construction, with more states to be added later.

"In the zenith" above the pyramid, the law calls for "an eye in a triangle, surrounded with a glory." The eye suggests that America is connected to the divine in three ways. First, Thomson explains, "The eye over it and the motto allude to the many signal interventions of providence in favor of the American cause." The motto, *annuit coeptis* ("He approves what has been started"), alludes to God's help in winning the War of Independence. The providential eye has its parallel in the Declaration of Independence, which expresses "a firm reliance on the protection of divine providence."

Second (and here I go beyond Thomson's report), the perfect triangle that represents God is a model for the imperfect triangular pyramid. The Declaration's "laws of nature and of nature's God" lay down a high and difficult standard of justice. In our imperfect earthly realm, we are never going to get beyond approximating it. America is therefore a work in progress in a deeper sense than its number of states. However many rows of bricks (new states) are added, America will always fall short of the triangular perfection of the Supreme Being at her "zenith." In the spirit of this view of America's relation to God, Lincoln once said: "It is said in one of the admonitions of the Lord, 'As your Father in Heaven is perfect, be ye also perfect.' The Savior, I suppose, did not expect that any human creature could be perfect as the Father in Heaven. . . . He set that up as a standard, and he who did most towards reaching that standard, attained the highest degree of moral perfection. So I say that in relation to the principle that all men are created equal, let it be as nearly reached as we can."[24]

Third, the divine eye is not only America's providential protector and model of perfection. God is also her judge. This is implied by the motto *annuit coeptis*, "He approves (or has approved) what has been started." Those words imply not only that God has approved of and therefore has helped America in its struggle for independence, but also that he

---

[23] Ibid., 66–8.
[24] Lincoln, speech at Chicago, July 10, 1858, in *The Collected Works of Abraham Lincoln*, ed. Roy T. Basler (New Brunswick: Rutgers University Press, 1953), 2:501.

will withdraw his approval if America strays too far from the right path. Similarly, the Declaration of Independence ends with an "appeal to the Supreme Judge of the world for the rectitude of our intentions." As America's judge, God will aid or abandon her, in accordance with her deeds. Jefferson spoke strongly of this possibility of divine judgment in connection with slavery, writing, "I tremble for my country when I reflect that God is just: that his justice cannot sleep forever."[25] In sum, America is a nation "under God" in three ways. God protects America, God is America's guide and goal, and God is America's judge. The same three themes can be found in Washington's Thanksgiving Proclamation, discussed in the previous chapter.

The Seal's two Latin mottoes are taken from the great Roman poet Virgil. The pyramid is labeled *novus ordo seclorum,* "a new order of the ages." Thomson explains, "the words under it signify the beginning of the New American Era, which commences from that date [1776]." The phrase is a variant of a line in Virgil's fourth *Eclogue*: "a great order of the ages is born anew."[26] This *Eclogue* describes the return of the golden age, an age of peace and plenty. The change of words is significant. America is a *novus ordo,* a "new order," not just the return of a *magnus ordo,* a "great order" that existed in the past. Virgil's golden age has come before and might come again, but nothing like the American founding has ever happened. No nation has ever grounded itself on a universal principle, discovered by reason, affirmed by God, and true for all human beings everywhere.

Literally translated, the words over the eye, *annuit coeptis,* mean: "he has nodded [or nods] to the things that have been started" – namely, the pyramid under construction, the "new order of the ages." These words are taken from book 11 of Virgil's *Aeneid.* Aeneas has led a remnant from conquered Troy to a land far to the west. After they arrive in Italy, the natives mount a ferocious attack against them. In the midst of the battle, Aeneas's son Ascanius prays to Jupiter, asking him to "nod to [i.e., approve] the daring things that have been started." Jupiter answers the prayer. Ascanius shoots, and his arrow pierces the enemy's head. The victory that follows enables the Trojan warriors to stay in Italy. Romulus, a descendant of Aeneas and Ascanius, will become the founder of Rome, the greatest empire in history.[27]

---

[25] Thomas Jefferson, *Notes on the State of Virginia,* Query 18, in *Writings,* ed. Merrill D. Peterson (New York: Library of America, 1984), 289.

[26] Virgil, *Eclogue* 4, line 5 (my translation).

[27] Virgil, *Aeneid,* bk. 9, line 625 (my translation). The same phrase also occurs in Vergil's *Georgics,* bk. 1, line 40.

The two Latin mottoes point to the founding of Rome (the *Aeneid*) and the golden age (*Eclogue* 4). Taken together, they suggest that America, with divine approval and support, will become a new Rome, combining the glory of the old imperial and military Rome with the freedom, prosperity, and peace of the golden age. America's foundation, like Rome's, had to be laid in violence. But unlike Rome, the New Order of the Ages will grow to greatness not through warfare and conquest, but through the arts of peace. On the front of the Great Seal, the eagle's head is pointed toward the olive branch in his right talon, not to the arrows of war in his left. As Washington writes in his letter to the Hebrew congregation (paraphrasing Micah 4:4), in America, if all goes as planned, "everyone shall sit in safety under his own vine and fig tree and there shall be none to make him afraid."[28] That was the original American dream. Still, although the eagle's head looks toward peace, his arrows show that he is prepared for war. The necessity of defending liberty – sometimes by violence – will never cease.

The Political Regime Itself as a Source of the Law of Fashion

Perhaps the most important way that government shapes the law of opinion is through the characteristic institutions of a free and republican political order.[29] These things, more than religion and educational institutions, or laws with penalties, invisibly shape popular opinion daily by means of their constant effect on behavior. There is much truth in Adams's observation that "the best republics will be virtuous, and have been so; but we may hazard a conjecture, that the virtues have been the effect of the well-ordered constitution, rather than the cause."[30] I will now consider how the distinctive features of the American regime generate a way of life that leads people to adopt standards of honor and dishonor that promote and sustain the moral law.

Early Marriages
The founders' doctrine of equality, together with the circumstances of a free society, changed the prevailing understanding of the family, as

---

[28] Washington to the Hebrew Congregation in Newport, RI, August 18, 1790, in *Writings*, 767.

[29] In support of my argument in this section: Lorraine Smith Pangle and Thomas L. Pangle, *The Learning of Liberty: The Educational Ideas of the American Founders* (Lawrence: University Press of Kansas, 1993), 205–13, "Law and the Governmental Process as Vehicles of Education."

[30] Adams, *Defence of the Constitutions*, 1787, in *Works of John Adams*, 6:219.

discussed in Chapter 10. In colonial America, there was a presumption that children – even grown-up children – should defer to their fathers in choice of marriage partners. This view was challenged by what Gordon Wood calls "the Revolution's assault on patriarchy."[31] Americans from the founding onward believed that there is a right to marry without parental interference and without consideration of family interests in regard to the spouse's class status.

This freedom promoted early marriage. Samuel Williams, a founding-era Vermont writer, celebrates this American custom: "The ease with which a family may be maintained, and the wishes of parents to see their children settled in ways of virtue, reputation, and felicity, are circumstances which also strongly invite to an early settlement in life. The virtuous affections are not corrupted nor retarded by the pride of families, the ambition of ostentation, or the idle notions of useless and dangerous distinctions, under the name of honor and titles. Neither parents nor children have any other prospects, than what are founded upon industry, economy, and virtue."[32] Franklin too remarks that "marriages in America are more general, and more generally early, than in Europe."[33] In the absence of laws sustaining aristocratic wealth and titles, what matters to a potential spouse, Williams implies, is not your family connections, but rather the sort of person you are and what you do. Early marriages based on affection result from a system of property rights that enable a hard-working, reasonably prudent young man to have a decent income at an early age; in support of that custom were laws and government-promoted norms discouraging sex outside of marriage and honoring marriage and families. Before they could do much youthful mischief, men settled down into responsible lives providing for wives and children. This is the way of life on which Alexis de Tocqueville lavished his praise.[34]

Political Freedoms

The institutions of political liberty were also significant yet largely invisible factors in forming the "law of opinion." Government guarantees

31 Gordon S. Wood, *The Radicalism of the American Revolution* (New York: Knopf, 1992), 147–51, 183–5 (quotation on 183).
32 Samuel Williams, *The Natural and Civil History of Vermont*, 1794, in *American Political Writing during the Founding Era*, ed. Charles S. Hyneman and Donald S. Lutz (Indianapolis: Liberty Press, 1983), 2:952.
33 Benjamin Franklin, "Observations Concerning the Increase of Mankind," in *Writings*, ed. J. A. Leo Lemay (New York: Library of America, 1987), 368.
34 Alexis de Tocqueville, *Democracy in America*, 1835, 1840, trans. Harvey C. Mansfield and Delba Winthrop (Chicago: University of Chicago Press, 2000), vol. 2, pt. 3, ch. 12, pp. 573–6.

the right to free elections, to assemble, to publish one's opinions on the political topics of the day, and to petition one's representatives. Many of these rights were explicitly named in the state and federal constitutions, and all of them were protected by law. The right to choose their own rulers encourages the people to pay attention to public affairs. It accustoms them to organize spontaneously with their fellow citizens to get things done, whether that means getting people elected to public office, or solving problems in the community. The explosive growth of private associations, later noticed by Tocqueville, is chronicled by historian Kevin Butterfield, who shows in detail "the importance of law in giving shape to early American civil society." These associations modeled themselves explicitly on the social compact basis of the nation, "creating formally organized, rule-bound, and wholly voluntary associations" that were distinctively American. There were "wide-ranging efforts ... to extend to private groups a set of principles already present in the early republic."[35] The law of opinion generated by the founding principles and early American law dominated the daily doings of private life.

In *Federalist* 57, Madison speaks of "the vigilant and manly spirit which actuates the people of America – a spirit which nourishes freedom, and in return is nourished by it."[36] Vigilance and manliness are "nourished" by a government under which a free people become accustomed to doing things for themselves, and who are therefore quick to respond strongly to threats to liberty. James Wilson adds, "the rights of suffrage, properly understood, properly valued, properly cultivated, and properly exercised, is a rich mine of intelligence and patriotism."[37]

As a young man, Madison had already understood the effect of a regime of liberty on character. In 1774, complaining about the recent jailing of Baptists for preaching without a license, he writes to a friend in Pennsylvania: "You are happy in dwelling in a land where ... the public has long felt the good effects of their religious as well as civil liberty. ... Industry and virtue have been promoted by mutual emulation and mutual inspection; commerce and the arts have flourished; and I

---

[35] Ibid., vol. 2, pt. 2, ch. 5–7, pp. 489–500; Kevin Butterfield, *The Making of Tocqueville's America: Law and Association in the Early United States* (Chicago: University of Chicago Press, 2015), 5, 8; Douglas Bradburn, *The Citizenship Revolution: Politics and the Creation of the American Union, 1774–1804* (Charlottesville: University of Virginia Press, 2009), 219 (after 1776 "the momentum of association proved overwhelming").

[36] Madison, *Federalist* 57, in Alexander Hamilton, James Madison, and John Jay, *The Federalist Papers*, ed. Clinton Rossiter (New York: Signet Classics, 2003), 350.

[37] James Wilson, Speech on Choosing the Members of the Senate by Electors, December 31, 1789, in the PA Ratification Convention, in *Collected Works of James Wilson*, ed. Kermit L. Hall and Mark David Hall (Indianapolis: Liberty Fund, 2007), 1:241.

cannot help attributing those continual exertions of genius which appear among you to the inspiration of liberty and that love of fame and knowledge which always accompany it. Religious bondage shackles and debilitates the mind and unfits it for every noble enterprise, every expanded prospect."[38]

In the founding and long afterwards, local governments brought the experience of political self-rule within the reach of many. Some believe Tocqueville was the first to notice the importance of local self-government in forming the American character, but John Adams had discussed it long before that. Adams argues that local government was one of the four main factors leading to the success of the American Revolution. The inhabitants of New England towns, he writes, "are invested with certain powers and privileges," including "the right to assemble" and "to choose their selectmen, constables, collectors of taxes, and above all, their representatives in the legislature." The right "to deliberate upon the public affairs of the town, or to give instructions to their representatives in the legislature" meant that the people "acquired from their infancy the habit of discussing, of deliberating, and of judging of public affairs."[39] Adams is explaining how the institutions of local self-government helped form an American "law of opinion": "The Revolution was in the minds and hearts of the people; a change in their religious sentiments of their duties and obligations.... This radical change in the principles, opinions, sentiments, and affections of the people, was the real American Revolution."[40]

The judiciary involves citizens in the administration of justice through jury service. It accustoms them to think that they are not passively victimized by circumstances outside their control, but instead belong to a confident, self-governing people. James Wilson, praising the beneficent effects of jury service, writes: "To promote an habitual courage, and dignity, and independence of sentiment and of actions in the citizens, should be the aim of every wise and good government. How much are these principles promoted, by this beautiful and sublime effect of our judicial system!"[41] An Anti-Federalist writer, the "Federal Farmer," writes that the jury, along with elected legislative bodies, "is the means by which the people are let into the knowledge of public affairs – are enabled to

---

[38] Madison to William Bradford, April 1, 1774, in *The Founders' Constitution*, ed. Philip B. Kurland and Ralph Lerner (Chicago: University of Chicago Press, 1987), 5:61.

[39] Adams to the Abbé de Mably, 1782, in *Works of John Adams*, 5:495.

[40] Adams to H. Niles, February 13, 1818, in ibid., 10:282–3.

[41] Wilson, "The Subject Continued. Of Juries," pt. 2, ch. 6 of *Lectures on Law*, in *Collected Works*, ed. Hall and Hall, 2:1009.

stand as the guardians of each other's rights."[42] In addition, as Ralph Lerner demonstrates, judges were expected to play a role in teaching a republican citizenry its rights and duties through their written opinions and their instructions to jurors. He argues that this educative function was performed best by the thoughtful opinions of the Supreme Court.[43]

Frequent elections, together with longer terms in some cases, foster good qualities not only in the citizens but also in their rulers. According to *The Federalist*, "the restraint of frequent elections" will provide "a habitual recollection of their dependence on the people." Elections make officials responsible to the people in the sense of being responsive to their opinions. But longer terms will make officials more responsible in a second sense: the people will be able to judge more accurately the worth of policies that take time to develop. "It will not be too strong to say that there will be a constant probability of seeing the station [the presidency] filled by characters preeminent for ability and virtue." The presidency, with its four-year term and the prospect of re-election, will attract men animated by "love of fame, the ruling passion of the noblest minds, which would prompt a man to plan and undertake extensive and arduous enterprises for the public benefit." When such men are honored, other ambitious politicians will aspire to imitate them.[44]

Finally, Hamilton notes that one reason a "free government [is] to be preferred to an absolute monarchy [is] . . . because of the tendency of the free government to interest the passions of the community in its favor, [which] beget public spirit and public confidence."[45] Hamilton argues that every parent, however wealthy and powerful, has an interest in a political regime of liberty because "if today I am among the favored few, my children, tomorrow, may be among the oppressed many."[46]

Equality under the Law, Property Rights, and the Law of Fashion

Above all else, the founders' laws protecting everyone's rights equally, combined with official disapproval of government-granted monopolies

---

[42] "Letters from the Federal Farmer," Letter 15, in *The Complete Anti-Federalist*, ed. Herbert J. Storing (Chicago: University of Chicago Press, 1981), 2:320.

[43] Ralph Lerner, *The Thinking Revolutionary: Principles and Practice in the New Republic* (Ithaca: Cornell University Press, 1987), 91–136.

[44] Madison, *Federalist* 57, p. 350; *Federalist* 63, pp. 381–2; Hamilton, *Federalist* 68, p. 412; *Federalist* 72, p. 436. See also my discussion of responsibility in Chapter 12.

[45] Hamilton's notes for a speech, June 6, 1787, in *The Records of the Federal Convention of 1787*, ed. Max Farrand (New Haven: Yale University Press, 1937), 1:145.

[46] Hamilton, speech of June 28, 1788, NY Ratifying Convention, in *The Papers of Alexander Hamilton*, ed. Harold C. Syrett (New York: Columbia University Press, 1961–79), 5:125.

and other special favors,[47] helped shape minds and hearts so as to create a nation of reasonably honest and hard workers. These workers acquired a strong sense of personal dignity, pride in their freedom, and habits of manly independence, making them hostile to both personal and political oppression. The goal of keeping government from granting special privileges was obviously not always attained in pre-Civil War America, but this standard was probably met more consistently then than in the last century,[48] which has seen a vast expansion of government favors and largesse.

In his "Information to Those Who Would Remove to America," Benjamin Franklin sums up the connection between the formation of a moral disposition (which then becomes part of the law of opinion) and the "good laws and liberty" that are the only aid that America then offered to immigrants. First, the laws provide equal protection of life, liberty, and property: "Strangers are welcome . . . ; the laws protect them sufficiently, so that they have no need of the patronage of great men; and everyone will enjoy securely the profits of his industry."[49]

Second, the laws not only "protect them" in their person and property but also make it possible to acquire the property they need by protecting freedom of market entry: "Tolerably good workmen in any of those mechanic arts are sure to find employ, and to be well paid for their work, there being no restraints preventing strangers from exercising any art they understand, nor any permission necessary. If they are poor, they begin first as servants or journeymen; and if they are sober, industrious, and frugal, they soon become masters, establish themselves in business, marry, raise families, and become respectable citizens."[50] Franklin has in mind the legal framework that secures the right to acquire property (explained in the chapters on property and economics below). It includes not only the right to enter any legal business on the same terms as others but also the other legal provisions that support free markets, such as the right to buy or sell property, to have contracts enforced in court, and to have a stable measure of money (gold and silver).

Third, Franklin notes that the first two points (protection of the laws and market freedom) will produce the right result only if government refuses to play favorites with some individuals, groups, or families.

---

[47] E.g., Bill of Rights of VA, 1776, §4; of MA, 1780, art. 6–7.

[48] Wood, *Radicalism*, 318–22.

[49] Franklin, "Information to Those Who Would Remove to America," 1784, in *Writings*, 977.

[50] Ibid., 978–9.

Franklin writes that if an immigrant "does not bring a fortune with him, he must work and be industrious to live.... America is the land of labor."[51] He quotes "[t]he 36th article of the constitution of Pennsylvania": "As every freeman, to preserve his independence, (if he has not a sufficient estate) ought to have some profession, calling, trade, or farm, whereby he may honestly subsist, there can be no necessity for, nor use in, establishing offices of profit; the usual effects of which are dependence and servility, unbecoming freemen, in the possessors and expectants; faction, contention, corruption, and disorder among the people."[52] Franklin could also have quoted this passage from the Massachusetts Constitution: "No man, nor corporation, or association of men, have any other title to obtain advantages, or particular and exclusive privileges, distinct from those of the community, than what arises from the consideration of services rendered to the public."[53] These two constitutional provisions are based on the equality principle. It is unjust for government to enable some people to live lazily by extracting the fruits of other people's labor by coercion (taxation). All able-bodied persons are expected to provide for themselves by getting a job or by having someone else provide for them voluntarily.

Franklin was aware that government could also create "dependence, and servility, unbecoming freemen" by means of what we would call welfare benefits. In England, he writes, there is "a heavy tax for the support of the poor.... [Yet] there is no country in the world in which the poor are more idle, dissolute, drunken, and insolent. The day you [Englishmen] passed that act, you took away from before their eyes the greatest of all inducements to industry, frugality, and sobriety, by giving them a dependence on somewhat else.... [Y]ou offered a premium for the encouragement of idleness, and you should not now wonder that it has had its effect in the increase of poverty."[54]

Equal protection of the laws, easy market entry, and the absence of patronage from aristocrats or government favors cause the people to adopt an industrious way of life. Franklin continues, "The almost general mediocrity of fortune that prevails in America obliging its people to follow some business for subsistence, those vices, that arise usually from idleness, are in a great measure prevented. Industry and constant employment are great preservatives of the morals and virtue of a nation."[55] The "morals

---

[51] Ibid., 977–8.   [52] Ibid., 976.   [53] MA Declaration of Rights, 1780, art. 6.
[54] Franklin, "On the Price of Corn, and Management of the Poor," 1766, in *Writings*, 587–8.

and virtue" that Franklin has in mind include self-reliance, assertiveness on behalf of one's just rights, self-restraint, frugality, and honesty. Because "industry" is necessary for survival and enables those who practice it to live independently and without servility, honor is given to work and the useful products of work, as Franklin writes:

Much less is it advisable for a person to go thither [to America], who has no other quality to recommend him but his birth. In Europe it has indeed its value; but it is a commodity that cannot be carried to a worse market than that of America, where people do not inquire concerning a stranger, "what is he?" but, "what can he DO?" If he has any useful art, he is welcome; and if he exercises it, and behaves well, *he will be respected* by all that know him; but a mere man of quality, who, on that account, wants to live upon the public, by some office or salary, *will be despised and disregarded.* The husbandman is *in honor there,* and even the mechanic, because their employments are useful. The people have a saying, that God almighty is himself a mechanic, the greatest in the universe; and *he is respected and admired* more for the variety, ingenuity, and utility of his handiworks, than for the antiquity of his family.[56]

Franklin's "Information," then, shows how the institutions and laws of a free government indirectly form the people's estimates of what is "welcome," "respected and admired," "in honor," and, conversely, what is "despised and disregarded." Franklin is describing here the older America, where competence and hard work were generally rewarded, while incompetence and laziness caused difficulties and poverty. Since the 1960s, in contrast, government's generosity has blurred this connection between the virtues prized by the founders and material well-being. When that happens, Franklin implies, people will grow increasingly dependent on government largesse and lose their capacity for frugality, industry, moderation, and self-reliance. The regime and laws will then tend to weaken, not strengthen, the character that Franklin and the founders thought necessary for free citizens.

Samuel Williams, quoted earlier, provides a Franklin-like account of how republican virtues are promoted by equal laws: "Depending upon their own industry, and having nothing to expect from speculation and gaming in public funds, . . . the views of the people are directed to their own employments and business. . . . The custom will not be to fall into scenes of expensive entertainments, amusement, and dissipation; but to provide for the calls and demands of nature, to preserve the health and vigor of the body, and to be able to raise up and support a family. And this will of course introduce a steady regard to economy." And when

---

[55] Franklin, "Information," 982.   [56] Ibid., 976–7 (my emphasis).

wealth is acquired without labor, in contrast, it makes men "degraded, effeminate, and unmanly."[57]

The conclusions of Franklin and Williams were shared by other founders. Adams's summary description of America recalls the argument made by Socrates in the *Republic*, book 8, according to which every political regime has a typical character that rules it and is produced by it. Adams writes, "a republic will produce strength, hardiness, activity, courage, fortitude, and manly, noble, and sublime qualities in human nature, in abundance.... It is the form of government which gives the decisive color to the manners of the people, more than any other thing."[58] Adams elaborates on this observation in his widely read *Thoughts on Government* (1776): "A constitution formed on these principles introduces knowledge among the people and inspires them with a conscious dignity becoming freemen; a general emulation takes place which causes good humor, sociability, good manners, and good morals to be general. That elevation of sentiment inspired by such a government makes the common people brave and enterprising. That ambition which is inspired by it makes them sober, industrious, and frugal. You will find among them some elegance, perhaps, but more solidity; a little pleasure, but a great deal of business; some politeness, but more civility."[59]

Aristotle anticipates Adams when he speaks of the qualities of a mixed regime or "polity" in his *Politics*, in which neither rich nor poor, but the moderate middle class predominates. The handsome, strong, well-born, and wealthy tend to be "arrogant and base on a grand scale," while the poor, weak, or dishonored are "malicious and base in petty ways," "consumed by envy," and "too humble." The middle class is respectful but not slavish toward their rulers. They wish neither to dominate nor to be dominated. They are not "slaves and masters" but "free."[60] This is the attitude praised by Washington in his First Annual Message to Congress: the people must "distinguish between oppression and the necessary exercise of lawful authority;... uniting a speedy but temperate vigilance against encroachments, with an inviolable respect to the laws."[61]

In *Democracy in America*, Tocqueville presents an extended contrast of the habits, attitudes, and manners of life produced by aristocracy and

---

[57] Williams, *Natural and Civil History of Vermont*, in *American Political Writing*, 2:953, 956.

[58] Adams to Mercy Warren, January 8, 1776, in *Founders' Constitution*, 1:669.

[59] Adams, *Thoughts on Government*, 1776, in *American Political Writing*, 1:408.

[60] Aristotle, *Politics*, trans. Carnes Lord, 2nd ed. (Chicago: University of Chicago Press, 2013), bk. 4, ch. 11.

[61] Washington, First Annual Message to Congress, 1790, in *Writings*, 750.

democracy. Franklin and Adams agree with Tocqueville about the difference between these ways of life, but Adams speaks of the aristocratic way without Tocqueville's old-world taste for its amenities: "A monarchy... would produce so much taste and politeness, so much elegance in dress, furniture, equipage, so much music and dancing, so much fencing and skating, so much cards and backgammon; so much horse racing and cockfighting, so many balls and assemblies, so many plays and concerts that the very imagination of them makes me feel vain, light, frivolous, and insignificant."[62] Adams' description corresponds to Franklin's observation on the American lack of interest in "paintings, statues, architecture, and the other works of art, that are more curious than useful."[63]

I quote an anonymous supporter of the Constitution who makes explicit a tie between laws enabling widespread ownership of land and the sense of independence and "dignity" (i.e., a sense of honor) that ownership fosters: "Our laws and customs, which divide great estates among all the children of the deceased owner; the way being open for industrious men, who are born to no inheritance, to acquire property; and the plenty and cheapness of land, will long cause property to be diffused among the people at large. The people do and will possess freeholds of their own; they can live comfortably and independently on their farms. Men in such a situation feel the dignity of human nature and scorn to be dependent on the will of a tyrant."[64] In the view of the writers cited in this section, a market economy promotes not only the self-restraining virtues, but also the "vigilant and manly spirit" praised by Madison in *Federalist* 57, quoted earlier.[65]

Gouverneur Morris, ambassador to France in the 1790s, recognized clearly the link between a nation of property owners and workers, and the kind of manly pride that makes Americans so courageous in time of war and so ready to resist oppression in peacetime. The following conversation began when a French nobleman told Morris that without a buildup of "fleets and armies to secure [America] against invasion," America was exposed to foreign conquest.

MORRIS: Nothing would be more difficult than to subdue a nation, every individual of which in the pride of freedom thinks himself equal to a king, and if, sir, you should look down on him would say: "I am a man, are you anything more?"

---

[62] Adams to Mercy Warren, 1:669.   [63] Franklin, "Information," 975–6.
[64] "The Republican: To the People," *Connecticut Courant*, January 7, 1788, in *Documentary History of the Constitution*, ed. Jensen, 3:529.
[65] *Federalist* 57, p. 350.

NOBLEMAN: All this is very well, but there must be a difference in ranks, and I should say to one of these people: "You, sir, who are equal to a king, make me a pair of shoes."

MORRIS: Our citizens, sir, have a manner of thinking peculiar to themselves. This shoemaker would reply: "Sir, I am very glad of the opportunity to make you a pair of shoes. It is my duty to make shoes and I love to do my duty. Does your king do his?"

In his diary, Morris entered this comment: "This manner of thinking and speaking however is too masculine for the climate I am now in." Few French commoners would have spoken to an aristocrat so bluntly. They had too little "pride of freedom." Morris thought that the French people were "so lately emancipated" that they were incapable of this kind of vigilant self-assertion.[66] He means that the attitude of "pride of freedom" is cultivated in part simply by living in an "emancipated" country that governs itself through elected representatives.

Constitutional Stability

One final consideration: Madison argues that public opinion can be shaped by the mere existence of the Constitution over time. Respect for the Constitution will grow, provided that it does not change very often. One reason a well-constructed government will be stable, Madison argues, is that each branch of government will have "the necessary constitutional means, and personal motives, to resist encroachments of the others." The government that can control itself from within will not need to be constantly reformed from without. A stable Constitution will acquire "that veneration, which time bestows on everything, and without which perhaps the wisest and freest governments would not possess the requisite stability." Given the weakness of human reason, "the most rational government will not find it a superfluous advantage, to have the prejudices of the community on its side."[67]

The Importance of Public Agreement on Fundamentals

Verbal acceptance of the founding principles was necessary to make Americans a single nation, but it was hardly sufficient. For those principles to be vital, lip service must be joined by trust and even friendship.

[66] Gouverneur Morris, *A Diary of the French Revolution*, ed. Beatrix C. Davenport (Boston: Houghton Mifflin, 1939), 1:2 (March 1, 1789).
[67] *Federalist* 49, pp. 311–12; *Federalist* 51, p. 319.

Citizenship, as Aristotle said and the founders agreed, cannot be constituted by a bare contract to refrain from mutual injury. Aristotle diagnosed
the problem in this way:

> Whoever takes thought for good governance, however, gives careful attention to
> political virtue and vice. It is thus evident that virtue must be a care for every city,
> or at least every one to which the term applies truly and not merely in a manner of
> speaking. For otherwise the community becomes an alliance which differs from
> others – from alliances of remote allies – only by location, and law becomes a
> compact and, as the sophist Lycophron said, a guarantor among one another of
> the just things [i.e., as Aristotle explains earlier, "that they should not act unjustly
> toward one another"], but not the sort of thing to make the citizens good and
> just.... This will not be possible, however, unless they inhabit one and the same
> location and make use of intermarriage. It was on this account that marriage
> connections arose in cities, as well as clans, [common religious] festivals, and
> the pastimes of living together. This sort of thing is the work of friendship; for
> friendship is the intentional choice of living together.[68]

At first it might seem that Aristotle is presenting a critique of America,
whose political theory maintains that the origin of government is a social
compact. Subscribing to this criticism, Paul Rahe quotes this same passage and asserts that the political community established in the founding
is "more like the 'alliance (*summachia*)' described by Lycophron" than
a regime "'able to make the citizens good and just.' As a consequence,"
Rahe continues, "ours is and almost always has been a remarkably unde-
manding polity which provides little in the way of clear, direct moral
guidance." In short, "the American founders established a regime lacking
a regimen."[69] For this reason, Rahe finds America's "regimen" wanting
in comparison with the harsh and invasive educational scheme of ancient
Sparta. The founders might have responded that a political order can
provide "clear, direct moral guidance" to its citizens (as well as effective
indirect guidance, as we have seen) without imposing on them a "Spartan" moral formation that requires the abolition of personal liberty.

The founders distinguished between the minimal criterion of just
government (namely, a voluntary social compact to establish a political
society to secure life, liberty, and property) and the sufficient conditions
of a community truly capable of securing those rights, in which citizens
would have a fair chance of attaining the happiness they pursue. The
founders would have agreed with Aristotle that a genuine community

---

[68] Aristotle, *Politics*, bk. 3, ch. 9 (I have changed the translation slightly).
[69] Paul A. Rahe, *Republics Ancient and Modern: Classical Republicanism and the American
Revolution* (Chapel Hill: University of North Carolina Press, 1992), 777.

must "make the citizens good and just," at least to some extent. It must provide for the formation of character not only by punishments but also by fostering a common sense of the noble and even the sacred by a common moral education, by ties of kinship and friendship, and, in general, by the formation of a consensus "law of private censure." Elizur Goodrich sums up the point in a 1787 sermon before the Connecticut legislature: "The safety and preservation of [America] depend, under God, on the friendly agreement of its citizens in all those things necessary for its honor and defense, happiness and glory."[70]

It is true that the founders would never have gone as far as Aristotle and Plato did in their prescriptions for promoting like-mindedness in the citizens. These ancient philosophers recommended, among other things, government-controlled literature and music, and the prohibition of religious freedom. By destroying liberty, these men aimed at "giving to every citizen the same opinions, the same passions, and the same interests" as much as possible – a policy that Madison rejected in *Federalist* 10 as "unwise," and a goal he rejected as "impracticable."[71] The founders promoted civic solidarity by effective but less drastic means, as we have seen.

Chapter 9 showed that the encouragement of like-mindedness was a leading purpose of the early interest in public schools. Thomas James writes: "The American common school of the nineteenth century was, first and foremost, an agency ... [for] projecting the ideal of unified civic conscience, a disciplined social imagination holding sway over a diverse population.... [C]ommon schools aimed to create a universal civic culture in support of republican political institutions."[72]

The founders sometimes made their concern for James's "universal civic culture" explicit, not only within each state, but throughout the nation. Adams writes, "[The proposed Constitution] seems to be admirably calculated to preserve the union, to increase affection, and to bring us all to the same mode of thinking."[73] The new Constitution would

---

70 Elizur Goodrich, *The Principles of Civil Union and Happiness*, 1787, in *Political Sermons of the American Founding Era, 1730–1805*, ed. Ellis Sandoz (Indianapolis: Liberty Press, 1991), 914.

71 Madison, *Federalist* 10, pp. 72–3.

72 Thomas James, "Rights of Conscience and State School Systems in Nineteenth-Century America," in *Toward a Usable Past: Liberty under State Constitutions*, ed. Paul Finkelman and Stephen E. Gottlieb (Athens: University of Georgia Press, 1991), 123–4.

73 Adams to Jefferson, November 10, 1787, in *The Adams-Jefferson Letters*, ed. Lester J. Cappon (New York: Simon and Schuster, Clarion Books, 1971), 210.

"increase affection" by making Americans think of themselves more as fellow citizens of a single country, and it would bring them "to the same mode of thinking" by setting up a strong national government which would be an authoritative example of responsible republicanism for the whole union.

Each of the first six presidents supported a national university. In his final message to Congress Washington emphasized its potential benefits in cultivating like-mindedness among Americans of all regions. He writes: "Amongst the motives to such an institution, the assimilation of the principles, opinions, and manners, of our countrymen, by the common education of a portion of our youth from every quarter, well deserves attention. The more homogeneous our citizens can be made in these particulars, the greater will be our prospect of permanent union." Congress never approved the national university; public education was left to the states.[74] But in other ways, just as Washington wanted, both state and federal governments did promote a shared civic identity, as we have seen throughout this and the last two chapters. The Revolutionary War itself contributed to that end, as Madison celebrates in *Federalist* 14: "the kindred blood which they have shed in defense of their sacred rights consecrate their Union and excite horror at the idea of their becoming aliens, rivals, enemies."[75]

The founders' views on criteria for immigration and naturalization belong to this discussion of a common civic culture. The nation's first naturalization law of 1790 states that "any alien being a free white person,... [after] two years, may be admitted to become a citizen, making proof... that he is a person of good character." The limitation of naturalization to whites continued until 1870, when "aliens of African nativity" and "persons of African descent" were added.[76] As for immigration, although no federal law regulated it until after the Civil War, individual states limited immigration in a variety of ways.[77] It is true that these

---

[74] Washington, Eighth Annual Message to Congress, 1796, in *Writings*, 982–3; George Thomas, *The Founders and the Idea of a National University: Constituting the American Mind* (New York: Cambridge University Press, 2015).

[75] Madison, *Federalist* 14, p. 99.

[76] Naturalization Act, March 26, 1790, *Public Statutes at Large*, ed. Richard Peters (Boston: Little and Brown, 1845), 1:108; Naturalization Act, July 14, 1870, *Statutes at Large*, ed. George P. Sanger (Boston: Little, Brown, 1871), 16:256. For an overview, see Reed Ueda, "Naturalization and Citizenship," *Harvard Encyclopedia of American Ethnic Groups*, ed. Stephan Thernstrom et al. (Cambridge: Harvard University Press, 1980), 739.

[77] Gerald L. Neuman, "The Lost Century of American Immigration Law, 1776–1875," *Columbia Law Review* 93, No. 8 (Dec. 1993): 1833–1901.

federal and state policies meant that European ancestry would continue to predominate in America. The point was to ensure that new citizens would be from nations that are not too different from the Anglo-Americans who made up most of the founders' America. Washington praised America's openness to immigrants "of all nations and religions," but he spoke for all when he clarified this generous sentiment in another letter: the Constitution will "render this country the asylum of pacific and industrious characters from all parts of *Europe*."[78] Washington especially favored the Dutch, who, he said, were known to be "friends to the rights of mankind." They would be "a valuable acquisition to our infant settlements."[79] The language of the Naturalization Act was racial ("free white person"), but Washington was obviously thinking not only of race but also of liberty and civilization when he made these remarks. Being of the same race as most Americans, white immigrants would obviously integrate more easily than nonwhites, but in addition, Europeans more than any other race shared with Americans a heritage of morality, Christianity, and a respect for reason and "the rights of mankind." That too made them preferred candidates for citizenship. A policy welcoming non-European immigrants would have been rejected by all.

Jefferson was even concerned about the difficulties of absorbing too many European immigrants at once: "It is for the happiness of those united in society to harmonize as much as possible in matters which they must of necessity transact together.... [Immigrants] will bring with them the principles of the governments they leave, imbibed in their early youth.... Suppose 20 millions of republican Americans thrown all of a sudden into France.... If it would be more turbulent, less happy, less strong, we may believe that the addition of half a million of foreigners to our present numbers would produce a similar effect here."[80]

It is true that blacks were citizens in some states during the founding. There was nothing in the founders' principles that required a one-race society. The Fourteenth Amendment, making blacks equal citizens, was always an option that was consistent with, but not required by, the founding principles. But even as late as 1965, few doubted that most Americans would and should be descendants of Europeans.[81]

---

[78] Washington to Joshua Holmes, December 2, 1783, in Founders Online, National Archives, http://founders.archives.gov; Washington to Jefferson, January 1, 1788, in ibid. (my emphasis).

[79] Washington to Van Der Kemp, May 28, 1788, in ibid.

[80] Jefferson, *Notes on the State of Virginia*, 1787, in *Writings*, ed. Merrill D. Peterson (New York: Library of America, 1984), Query 8, 211.

[81] For a fuller discussion, see Bradburn, *Citizenship Revolution*; James H. Kettner, *The Development of American Citizenship, 1608–1870* (Chapel Hill: University of North

Conclusion

We have now seen the remarkable extent of the founders' concern for morality and virtue. I will let Gouverneur Morris have the last word on its indispensability, which also happens to illustrate Jefferson's remarks on the French. Morris lived in Paris during the first years of the French Revolution. He quickly saw that it was destined to fail. In his estimation, the French character had been molded by a long history of rule by arrogant kings and aristocrats. The French were therefore deficient in the qualities of self-control: "Everybody agrees that there is an utter prostration of morals.... The great mass of the common people have no religion but their priests, no law but their superiors, no moral but their interest. These are the creatures who, led by drunken curates, are now in the high road *à la liberté*." A lack of self-restraint among the politicians made deliberation impossible in the French Assembly. "One half of the time is spent hallowing and bawling," while those who do try to speak are often shouted down by "a continual uproar till the orator leaves the pulpit." The other French defect, noted earlier in this chapter, was an absence of manliness among the common people.[82]

In this and the two preceding chapters I have detailed the multiple methods used by the founders to promote obedience to the moral laws of nature. Government made use of divine revelation, rational insight, laws with coercive force, and promotion of a healthy "law of private censure" in the minds of citizens. No one would claim that the means chosen by the founders to inculcate virtue were as strict, or as hostile to personal liberty, as one finds in classical political philosophers like Plato and Aristotle – to say nothing of American Puritans a century and a half earlier. Still, in light of the founders' far-reaching efforts, it is reasonable to question Thomas Pangle's claim that the founders' "framework makes very little provision for the inculcation, or fostering, or even preservation of these crucial excellences of character" that they believed necessary for a free society. One must also doubt Michael Walzer's statement that "liberalism did not create the self-control it required. The Lockean state ... rested on the assumed political virtue of its citizens." These remarks, which are all too typical, appear to have been made in ignorance of both Locke's

---

Carolina Press, 2005); Thomas G. West, *Vindicating the Founders: Race, Sex, Class, and Justice in the Origins of America* (Lanham, MD: Rowman & Littlefield, 1997), ch. 7.

[82] Morris, *A Diary*, 1:61 (to Washington, April 29, 1789); 1:382 (to Washington, January 24, 1790).

own unambiguous statements on the need for government-mandated moral rules, and of the founders' many actions undertaken for that end.[83]

[83] Thomas L. Pangle, "Republicanism and Rights," in *The Framers and Fundamental Rights*, ed. Robert A. Licht (Washington: AEI Press, 1991), 117; Michael Walzer, *The Revolution of the Saints: A Study in the Origins of Radical Politics* (Cambridge: Harvard University Press, 1965), 302.

12

What Virtues Should Government Promote?

In the previous four chapters, I showed that according to the founders, virtue is necessary for freedom, and that government cannot rely solely on private institutions such as families and churches to sustain it. I also sketched the founders' main policies for promoting virtue.

But it is not enough to know that the founders supported virtue and how they did so. Which virtues were deemed worthy of support? Did they have a clear view of the necessary qualities of mind and heart? Michael Zuckert suggests that they did not. As I noted at the beginning of Chapter 10, he correctly states that a natural rights republic needs a "'rights infrastructure' – the social institutions and traits of character that make rights-securing possible." To support his claim, Zuckert mentions Jefferson's "view that public education was a requisite to the rights infrastructure," but he says little about the moral content of that education.[1] He adds that the founders agreed on the need for limits on personal conduct – "prostitution can legitimately be seen as a threat to the health of the family" – but he also claims that "neither the founders nor we have arrived at a consensus" on what those limits should be.[2] Bernard Bailyn disagrees, asserting that "everyone agreed on the moral

---

[1] Michael P. Zuckert, "Founder of the Natural Rights Republic," in *Thomas Jefferson and the Politics of Nature*, ed. Thomas S. Engeman (Notre Dame, IN: University of Notre Dame Press, 2000), 22.

[2] Ibid., 23; Zuckert, *Launching Liberalism: On Lockean Political Philosophy* (Lawrence: University Press of Kansas, 2002), 228. Zuckert, *The Natural Rights Republic: Studies in the Foundation of the American Political Tradition* (Notre Dame, IN: University of Notre Dame Press, 1996), 27 (same argument).

qualities necessary to preserve a free government." Bailyn is correct, but even he does not tell us what those qualities are.[3]

The founders were not so reticent. This chapter will show that Zuckert is correct to argue that there are "traits of character that make rights-securing possible," and that Bailyn is correct regarding the founders' consensus on the "moral qualities necessary." But I will also show that the founders elucidated the virtues of citizenship much more fully than either Zuckert or Bailyn indicates.

The Social and Republican Virtues

The Constitution of 1787 sets up a division of labor between the federal and state governments. The federal government was responsible for foreign policy, ensuring a nationwide free market, inter-state harmony, and related matters. The states were to take care of everything else. The respective contributions of the federal and state governments were complementary and equally indispensable. Scholars such as James Q. Wilson should therefore stop reading significance into the fact that there is no mention of virtue, morality, education, and the like in the U.S. Constitution. American democracy, Wilson mistakenly claims, is based "on the novel belief that society could be held together by the natural affinities of free men." Wilson's evidence? "Under the U.S. Constitution, the federal government was to have no role in teaching or morally uplifting the people." By ignoring the states, Wilson confuses the founders' position with that of "politically engaged Americans" today who, says Wilson, "resist any but the mildest legal restraints on public speech and behavior."[4]

Almost every state published emphatic pronouncements on the importance of morality. I begin with the five early state constitutional provisions on virtue: Vermont, New Hampshire, Massachusetts, Pennsylvania, and Virginia.[5] Three of these five states were the most populous then existing, representing North, Middle, and South. Their provisions express the consensus of founding-era Americans, as may also be seen in the many quotations from other states in this and the preceding chapters. All five

---

[3] Bernard Bailyn, *The Ideological Origins of the American Revolution*, enlarged ed. (Cambridge: Harvard University Press, 1992), 46.

[4] James Q. Wilson, *The Moral Sense* (New York: Free Press, 1993), 244–50. See also my discussion of the same mistake made by Gertrude Himmelfarb and Mary Ann Glendon, at the end of Chapter 9.

[5] VA Declaration of Rights, 1776, §15; PA, 1776, art. 14; VT, 1777, art. 16; MA, 1780, art. 18; NH, 1784, art. 38.

constitutions affirm that "no free government, or the blessings of liberty, can be preserved" except by adhering to certain virtues, which are then listed.[6]

Most post-1784 state constitutions no longer included these statements on virtue. Perhaps it had become clear by then, as Hamilton writes in *Federalist* 84, that the "aphorisms which make the principal figure in several of our State bills of rights...would sound much better in a treatise of ethics than in a constitution of government."[7] However that may be, governmental concern for character formation was in no way diminished by these omissions. Historian Lawrence Cremin writes, "a degree of consensus [prevailed] during the early decades of the nineteenth century concerning what a broad public education in the arts of self-government might be. That education... [included] popular schooling, for the purpose of conveying literacy along with a certain common core of knowledge, morality, and patriotism."[8] This agenda is visible in my earlier discussions of sex and marriage laws, public education, promotion of religion, and government involvement with the formation of public opinion. The virtues articulated in the early state constitutions continued to be taught and promoted by government well into the twentieth century.

The five constitutional lists of virtues all include justice, moderation, temperance, industry, and frugality, except that Virginia omits "industry."[9] There are other minor variations among these five lists. Massachusetts adds piety, as does New Jersey in its instructions to its delegates in Congress.[10] New Hampshire adds "and all the social virtues." Virginia adds "virtue," as if "virtue" were a distinct virtue like justice, etc. We will return to these differences shortly.

The virtues that appear in these five constitutions can be summarized in the phrase used by New Hampshire, "the social virtues."[11] An

---

6 The quoted words are VA's; the other four are similar.

7 Alexander Hamilton, James Madison, and John Jay, *The Federalist Papers*, ed. Clinton Rossiter (New York: Signet Classics, 2003), *Federalist 84*, 512.

8 Lawrence A. Cremin, *American Education: The National Experience, 1783–1876* (New York: Harper Colophon, 1982), 104.

9 David Hackett Fischer, *Liberty and Freedom: A Visual History of America's Founding Ideas* (New York: Oxford University Press, 2005), 62–4.

10 New Jersey legislature, instruction to its delegates in Congress, December 4, 1777, in *Principles and Acts of the Revolution in America*, ed. Hezekiah Niles (1822; repr. New York: Burt Franklin, 1971), 461–2.

11 The term "social virtues" was in common use in the founding era, e.g., Abraham Williams, *An Election Sermon*, 1762, in *American Political Writing during the Founding Era, 1760–1805*, ed. Charles S. Hyneman and Donald S. Lutz (Indianapolis: Liberty Press, 1983), 8 ("without social virtues, society can't subsist").

anonymous 1790 magazine article on "Social Virtue" states: "To abstain from injuries – to deprive no man of the advantages he enjoys – to give to everyone what is due to him – to do good – to contribute to the happiness of others – and assist each other – this is being virtuous." The article continues, "Justice is the true basis of all the social virtues.... [It] remedies those evils that might arise from the inequality that nature has established among men; even makes it contribute to the general good – which secures to individuals their rights, their property, their persons, their liberty."[12] The social virtues are preeminently the virtues of peace, not war.

In these documents, there are five main social virtues:

First is *justice*, the disposition to obey the laws, but also to pay one's debts, and to respect and defend the rights of others – in general, "to give to everyone what is due to him."[13]

Second, *moderation* is the avoidance of extremes. South Carolina minister Thomas Reese, for example, speaks of "the moderation which Christianity enjoins in the pursuit of wealth," opposing "an immoderate desire of high and expensive living."[14]

Third, *temperance* is similar to moderation, but in the founding, its scope was generally more limited.[15] Temperance as a virtue means moderation in the realm of the desires, especially in regard to food and drink. Benjamin Franklin's *Autobiography* points to the difference. The precepts of temperance are "Eat not to dullness. Drink not to elevation." Moderation means: "Avoid extremes. Forbear resenting injuries so much as you think they deserve." John Witherspoon agrees with Franklin, describing temperance as "chiefly confined" to "being moderate in the use of meats and drink," whereas the word moderation has a wider scope; it includes guarding against "all the immoral passions" and against "an excessive indulgence in any passion."[16] In Franklin's formulation, moderation encompasses *civility*, a disposition to avoid unnecessary quarrels. This is probably

---

[12] Anonymous, "Social Virtues," in *The American Museum, or Repository*, vol. 8, July to Dec. 1790 (Philadelphia: Carey, Stewart, & Co., 1790), 168.
[13] Ibid.
[14] Thomas Reese, *An Essay on the Influence of Religion in Civil Society* (Charlestown, SC: Markland and M'Iver, 1788), 64, 69.
[15] However, in ibid., 60–70 (esp. 64), temperance and moderation are treated as identical.
[16] Benjamin Franklin, *Autobiography*, in *Writings*, ed. J. A. Leo Lemay (New York: Library of America, 1987), 1384–5. John Witherspoon, *Lectures on Moral Philosophy*, 1772–1794, Lecture 9, in *The Selected Writings of John Witherspoon*, ed. Thomas Miller (Carbondale: Southern Illinois University Press, 1990), 184.

related to the fact that in the founding, moderation appears to be
the preferred term for restraint of the passion to dominate others.
In *Federalist* 11, for instance, Hamilton says that America should
curb the "arrogant pretensions of the European" by limiting the
influence of Europe in the Western Hemisphere. Such a policy
would "teach that assuming brother moderation."[17] One should
not put too much weight on this distinction between temperance
and moderation, for in its adjectival form, temperance is not always
limited to food and drink. In his First Annual Message to Congress,
Washington speaks of "a speedy but temperate [i.e., nonexcessive]
vigilance."[18]

Fourth, *industry* is the habit of appropriately hard work. Its opposite is
laziness. People must be willing to work for a living and not expect
to be supported by the labor of others, as are the privileged classes
in an aristocracy.

Fifth, *frugality* is the habit of managing and spending one's earnings
carefully, so as to be able to provide for oneself and one's family in
the future (as opposed to relying on support from others).

Industry and frugality are not only social virtues – those which enable
people to live together peacefully without exploiting others – but also
republican virtues. No consent-based government can subsist unless the
bulk of the people possess what is today called the "work ethic." These
qualities were not considered virtues in aristocratic society, where work is
dishonored because the ideal is to be wealthy and to live at leisure, as we
see in Jane Austen's novels and in Aristotle's *Politics*.[19] Austen's novels,
"highly admired" by founder John Marshall,[20] belong to an English
literary movement that elevated the dignity of industry, frugality, and the
right to choose one's own spouse. These novels encouraged readers to
laugh at or despise aristocrats who prided themselves on their indolence
and their disdain for those who work for a living. The insufferable snob
Lady Catherine de Bourgh was immortalized in Austen's 1813 *Pride and
Prejudice*, and Samuel Richardson's portrayals of aristocratic cruelty

---

[17] Hamilton, *Federalist* 11, pp. 85–6.
[18] George Washington, First Annual Message to Congress, 1790, in *Writings*, ed. John
Rhodehamel (New York: Library of America, 1997), 750.
[19] Aristotle, *Politics*, trans. Carnes Lord, 2nd ed. (Chicago: University of Chicago Press,
2013), bk. 7, ch. 8–9.
[20] Eva Brann, "The Perfections of Jane Austen," in *The Past-Present: Selected Writings of
Eva Brann*, ed. Pamela Kraus (Annapolis: St. John's College Press, 1997), 23.

in *Pamela* (1740) and of paternal tyranny in *Clarissa* (1748) were well known in America.[21]

In the above list of five social and republican virtues, nothing explicit is said about the duties of family members. The founders would perhaps have considered marital fidelity, the respective duties of husbands and wives, parental care of children, children's respect for parents, and so on, as parts of justice. Witherspoon, at any rate, speaks of parents' duties to children as part of justice in his *Lectures on Moral Philosophy*,[22] and Pennsylvania regarded violation of the marriage contract as an injustice requiring legal restitution to the aggrieved spouse.[23]

Besides these five virtues, Massachusetts and New Hampshire add "piety and religion."[24] Although these are missing in the other constitutions, every state treated religion as an object of government support, as shown in Chapters 9 and 11. So too did the federal government: in the Northwest Ordinance, piety is "necessary for good government."[25] Washington's example in the Farewell Address was that justice requires honest testimony in court, which will be more likely if people believe that God forbids the sin of perjury.[26]

The Massachusetts and New Hampshire constitutions name additional virtues in their articles on government support of public education. Here is the Massachusetts version: "Wisdom, and knowledge, as well as virtue, ... [are] necessary for the preservation of their rights and liberties. ... [I]t shall be the duty of legislators ... to countenance and inculcate the principles of humanity and general benevolence, public and private charity, industry and frugality, honesty and punctuality in their dealings; sincerity, good humor, and all social affections, and generous sentiments among the people." New Hampshire's list is the same as that of Massachusetts, except that it replaces "good humor" with "sobriety." The Massachusetts list was composed by John Adams, who was perhaps a little less "Puritanical" than those who wrote the New Hampshire document.[27]

---

21 Jay Fliegelman, *Prodigals and Pilgrims: The American Revolution against Patriarchal Authority, 1750–1800* (Cambridge: Cambridge University Press, 1982), 27–9, 83–9.
22 Witherspoon, *Lectures on Moral Philosophy*, Lecture 8, 182.
23 The PA law is quoted in the section on divorce in Chapter 10.
24 MA Declaration of Rights, art. 3; NH Bill of Rights, 1784 and 1792, art. 6.
25 Northwest Ordinance, art. 3, in *Founders' Constitution*, 1:28.
26 Washington, Farewell Address, 1796, in *Writings*, 971.
27 MA Constitution, 1780, pt. II, ch. 5, §2; NH Constitution, 1784, and 1792, §83. David McCullough, *John Adams* (New York: Simon and Schuster, 2001), 220, 224 (Adams wrote the MA Constitution).

The additional virtues mentioned in these two constitutions – humanity, benevolence, charity, honesty, punctuality, sincerity, "generous sentiments" – have the same purpose as the other social virtues.[28] So also Virginia in its provision on religious liberty: "it is the mutual duty of all to practice Christian forbearance, love, and charity towards each other."[29] These virtues are not strictly mandatory, but qualities of this sort obviously enable people to live together more peacefully and harmoniously than they otherwise would. Humanity, charity, "generous sentiments," and love lead people to help each other in times of need. Trust among citizens will obviously be greater if they practice "honesty" and "sincerity," as opposed to habitually lying. Forbearance is another word for toleration, the virtue of putting up with actions or beliefs – even when one disapproves of them – as long as they are not harmful to others.

All five of our state constitutions speak of a need for "frequent recurrence to fundamental principles." Two of them mention knowledge and learning or wisdom. In a government based on the moral philosophy of the founding, it is not enough for the people to be obedient to the laws. They also must know what the laws are for, as shown in Chapter 9. Knowledge of one's rights and duties is one of the republican virtues. The people, and the rulers they elect, must have sound opinions about what the public good consists of, broadly speaking, so that government will pursue the right policies.

Two last virtues (or quasi-virtues) deserve comment: First, Virginia lists "virtue" among the several virtues that it praises. In the founding era, as with us, virtue was typically used as a term that includes several distinct qualities of mind and character, as we have seen. But the word virtue also sometimes referred to a specific quality or even a passion: public-spiritedness or devotion to the public good. This may be said to be a republican virtue. In a non-consensual government, it does not matter whether the people love the common good as long as they obey quietly and peaceably. But in a republic, in which rulers are chosen by popular elections, it matters that the people support the good of all. For John Adams, "public virtue is the only foundation of republics. There must be a positive passion for the public good."[30] In *The Spirit of the Laws* (1748), the French philosopher Montesquieu made famous this equation

---

[28] Besides MA and NH, humanity is also mentioned in the preambles of the constitutions of CT, 1776, and SC, 1776.

[29] VA Declaration of Rights, art. 16. See Chapter 13 (section on whether the founders' virtues are Christian).

[30] Adams to Mercy Warren, April 16, 1776, in *Founders' Constitution*, 1:670.

of virtue with love of country: "One can define this virtue [i.e., political virtue] as love of the laws and the homeland."[31] Virtue in this sense is especially needed in rulers, as Madison says: they ought to be "men who possess most wisdom to discern, and most virtue to pursue, the common good of the society."[32] The "wisdom to discern" without the "virtue to pursue" is useless.

Responsibility is our final republican quality – or virtue. Although that term does not appear in the founders' various lists of virtues, Charles Kesler calls it "the only virtue or quasi virtue that has entered our moral language from the American founding."[33] Other scholars agree with this assessment.[34] Harvey Mansfield observes that in *The Federalist*, the term responsibility "describes the correct behavior of a representative toward the people."[35] Most obviously, government officials are "responsible" to the people's "censure" and "punishment" through "frequency of elections."[36] In this sense responsibility is not a virtue but merely a minimal requirement of republican or consensual government. But in a second sense, *The Federalist* uses the term *responsible* as a synonym for *dutiful* or dedicated to performing the duties of the office. The responsibility of senators, Madison argues, will paradoxically be increased by their six-year term of office. It will give them "sufficient permanency to provide for such objects as require a continued attention, and a train of measures, [that] they may be justly and effectually answerable [i.e., responsible to the people's censure] for the attainment of those objects."[37] Responsibility in both senses sums up the job of public officials. They are to be both *responsible* to the people through elections, and faithful performers

---

[31] Montesquieu, *The Spirit of the Laws*, 1748, trans. Anne Cohler et al. (Cambridge: Cambridge University Press, 1989), bk. 4, ch. 5.

[32] Madison, *Federalist* 57, p. 348.

[33] Charles R. Kesler, "Responsibility in The Federalist," in *Educating the Prince: Essays in Honor of Harvey Mansfield*, ed. Mark Blitz and William Kristol (Lanham, MD: Rowman & Littlefield, 2000), 230.

[34] Harvey C. Mansfield, "Liberty and Virtue in the American Founding," in *Never a Matter of Indifference: Sustaining Virtue in a Free Republic*, ed. Peter Berkowitz (Stanford: Hoover Institution Press, 2003), 26–9; Mark Blitz, *Duty Bound: Responsibility and American Public Life* (Lanham, MD: Rowman & Littlefield, 2005), 1, 16–20. David F. Epstein, *The Political Theory of The Federalist* (Chicago: University of Chicago Press, 1984), 179–85, treats responsibility but does not call it a virtue; nor does Mansfield, *Taming the Prince: The Ambivalence of the Modern Executive Power* (New York: Free Press, 1989), 270–71.

[35] Mansfield, "Liberty and Virtue," 26.

[36] Hamilton, *Federalist* 70, p. 426; Madison, *Federalist* 63, p. 381.

[37] Madison, *Federalist* 63, p. 382.

of their official duty or *responsibility*. A responsible public official has "the inclination and the resolution to act his part well."[38] Kesler rightly adds that these two kinds of responsibility can conflict if terms of elected office are too short, because then the people have to make a short-term judgment on policies whose long-term effects are unknown. Responsibility to the people in the sense of being subject to frequent elections would stand in the way of their responsibility in performing their official duties. The U.S. Constitution tries to reconcile the twofold meaning of responsibility by providing for two-year terms for the House of Representatives and four- and six-year terms for president and senators.[39]

These observations of Mansfield and Kesler are perfectly sensible. But is it correct to say that responsibility is a new or distinct virtue in the founding? Insofar as it means electoral accountability to the people, it is nothing more than a restatement of the consent principle. And to the extent it is "the resolution to act his part well" in public office, it is hard to distinguish from the disposition to perform one's duty that had been associated with the term *responsible* long before the founding. A century earlier, Locke used the word as equivalent to *dutiful*. A man who is offered paper money by another, he says, cannot know whether "the bill or bond is true or legal, or that the man bound to me is honest or responsible."[40]

In that sense responsibility surely is a "virtue or quasi virtue." But we have seen that the founders' conception of virtue greatly exceeds Mansfield's modest example of responsibility: "voluntary assumption of a task, like changing diapers, that you might not choose for itself." Therefore Mansfield's suggestion that "responsibility is the virtue that makes possible the lack of virtue" cannot be accepted. Serious virtues, not merely responsibility in this narrow sense, are called for in a republic.[41]

Ralph Lerner's fine account of Jefferson's moral agenda in his 1778 proposed revision of Virginia's laws includes many of the qualities described above. Lerner concludes that for Jefferson, society "must be self-governed by truly free men." The goal of Jefferson's proposed domestic legislation was "that society be made worthy of free men and that individuals be made fit for free society.... A nation of private

---

[38] Hamilton, *Federalist* 72, p. 435.   [39] Kesler, "Responsibility," 219–30.

[40] Locke, "Some Considerations of the Lowering of Interest and Raising the Value of Money," 1691, in *The Works of John Locke in Ten Volumes* (London: J. Johnston et al., 1801), 22. Thanks to Will Morrisey for the reference.

[41] Mansfield, "Liberty and Virtue," 27–8.

calculators with short memories would forget the long-term consequences of not tending to the public business. More than anything else they needed to be instructed and confirmed in their present resolve not to be the wards of others."[42]

Nietzsche's Complaint: Herd Animal Morality

To clarify the founders' approach to virtue, I turn to philosopher Friedrich Nietzsche, a great critic of democracy. He calls the moral orientation that I have just described "herd animal morality." He associates it with the trend of European and American "degeneration and diminution of man into the perfect herd animal..., [the] animalization of man into the dwarf animal of equal rights and claims."[43] Nietzsche's view was hardly unique among educated Europeans. Allan Bloom rightly observes, "The new man of the new democratic political regime has been labeled bourgeois for more than two hundred years. This originally meant a diminished, egotistical, materialistic being without grandeur or beauty of soul."[44] In *Reconstructing America*, James Ceaser provides a multitude of examples – going back to the founding – of the European critique of America as insufferably bourgeois.[45]

This concern is not unreasonable. If a society honors only virtues that enable people to get along – to be timid and industrious worker bees – where is the opportunity, the encouragement, for human beings of rare talent and grand aspiration? Should people really be judged solely on how "nice" they are to one another?[46] Does not such a moral standard point mankind toward what Nietzsche scornfully calls "the universal green-pasture happiness of the herd, with security, lack of danger, comfort, and an easier life for everyone"?[47]

Scholars such as Thomas Pangle accept Nietzsche's critique, at least to some extent: "The goal [of education] was certainly not to make the

---

[42] Ralph Lerner, *The Thinking Revolutionary: Principle and Practice in the New Republic* (Ithaca: Cornell University Press, 1987), 89–90.

[43] Friedrich Nietzsche, *Beyond Good and Evil: Prelude to a Philosophy of the Future*, 1886, trans. Walter Kaufmann (New York: Vintage Books, 1989), §202–3.

[44] Allan Bloom, *The Closing of the American Mind* (New York: Simon and Schuster, 1987), 157.

[45] James W. Ceaser, *Reconstructing America: The Symbol of America in Modern Thought* (New Haven: Yale University Press, 1997).

[46] On "niceness" as a modern virtue: Mark Blitz, "Virtue, Modern and Ancient," in *Educating the Prince*, ed. Blitz, 3–17.

[47] Nietzsche, *Beyond Good and Evil*, §44.

chosen begin to conceive of themselves as an elite with a special or higher calling. . . . A productive life; a busy existence; a restless uneasiness whenever one finds oneself in idleness – this is the habit of soul at which the founders' education appears to aim." The spirit of American republicanism, Pangle adds, "is not a heroic spirit."[48] Harvey Mansfield seems to agree: "Franklin gives us the virtues enabling us to live in a free society; Publius gives us the virtues for governing it. . . . Nothing heroic is set forth [in *The Federalist*], much less required."[49]

The evidence that we have seen so far in this chapter would seem to support these complaints. But there is more to the story. Let us return to Nietzsche. On closer examination, he is not as hostile to "herd morality" as he at first appears. He admits that this kind of morality is necessary for the preservation of every community. But the "herd," the body politic, needs more than the "nice" virtues of self-restraint and hard work if it is to survive. It also needs the more assertive, more demanding virtues. Nietzsche writes, "There are certain strong and dangerous drives, such as enterprisingness, foolhardiness, revengefulness, craft, rapacity, ambition, which . . . – under different names, naturally, from those chosen here – . . . had to be trained and cultivated . . . because one constantly needed them to protect the community as a whole against the enemies of the community."[50] These qualities too belong to herd morality – "under different names," as Nietzsche rightly says.

What Nietzsche objects to, then, is not herd morality as such, for the community needs the self-restraining virtues in ordinary times and the strong virtues in times of danger. His concern is that in modern Europe and America, this tougher or manlier side of herd morality is disappearing: "High and independent spirituality, the will to stand alone, even a powerful reason are experienced as dangers; everything that elevates an individual above the herd and intimidates the neighbor is henceforth called *evil.* . . . Eventually, under very peaceful conditions, . . . any high and hard nobility and self-reliance is almost felt to be an insult and arouses mistrust."[51] In other words, in soft times, the "herd" forgets the need for the sterner virtues. We will see that the founders anticipated this problem and did their best to solve it.

---

[48] Thomas L. Pangle, *The Spirit of Modern Republicanism: The Moral Vision of the American Founders and the Philosophy of Locke* (Chicago: University of Chicago Press, 1988), 77, 260.

[49] Mansfield, "Liberty and Virtue," 24.

[50] Nietzsche, *Beyond Good and Evil*, §201.   [51] Ibid.

Nietzsche indicates one part of the remedy for this kind of degeneration into mediocrity, namely, internal or external danger. In *Twilight of the Idols*, he writes:

Liberal institutions . . . make men small, cowardly, and hedonistic. . . . These same institutions produce quite different effects while they are still being fought for; then they really promote freedom in a powerful way. On closer inspection it is war that produces these effects, the war *for* liberal institutions, which, as a war, permits *illiberal* instincts to continue. And war educates for freedom. For what is freedom? . . . That one becomes more indifferent to difficulties, hardships, privation, even to life itself. . . . Freedom means that the manly instincts which delight in war and victory dominate. . . . Danger alone acquaints us with our own resources, our virtues, our armor and weapons, our *spirit* – and *forces* us to be strong.[52]

Nietzsche is far from being the enemy of "herd morality," as long as the "herd" understands its need for the stronger and rarer virtues of hard-fighting soldiers and tough-minded law enforcers led by prudent statesmen and enterprising and crafty generals.

The Manly and Assertive Virtues

Pangle and Mansfield are far from being the only scholars who accept the "Nietzschean" view that the higher and rarer virtues are missing in the founding. Martin Diamond says that the founders promoted only the "less lofty" and "modest excellences" of the "bourgeois" and "republican virtues."[53] Gordon Wood argues that the founders' virtue "was soft and feminized, and capable of being expressed by women as well as men."[54] I provide more evidence than is strictly necessary in this section because this narrative of the founders' virtues as merely "bourgeois" is so widely believed.

In fact, the founders anticipated Nietzsche and other critics of the virtues of constitutional republicanism. "Herd morality" – or, to put it differently, the moral conditions of the preservation of society – requires not only cooperative and friendly qualities, but also dangerous and tough ones. For the founders, what Nietzsche called "illiberal instincts" are in

---

[52] Nietzsche, "Skirmishes of an Untimely Man," §38, in *Twilight of the Idols*, 1888, in *The Portable Nietzsche*, trans. Walter Kaufmann (New York: Viking, 1954), 541–2.

[53] Martin Diamond, *As Far as Republican Principles Will Admit*, ed. William A. Schambra (Washington: AEI Press, 1991), 361, 366.

[54] Gordon S. Wood, *The Radicalism of the American Revolution* (New York: Knopf, 1992), 216.

fact indispensable for liberty itself. Nietzsche's idea of "liberalism" simply does not describe the founders' America.

There are many examples of the founders' embrace of the hardy and warlike virtues. The Suffolk Resolves, adopted by Boston and then unanimously endorsed as the first official act of the Continental Congress in 1774, is typical of the manly eloquence of that day: "On the *fortitude*, on the *wisdom*, and on the *exertions* of this important day is suspended the fate of this new world and of unborn millions. If a boundless extent of continent... will tamely submit to live, move, and have their being at the arbitrary will of a licentious minister, they basely yield to voluntary slavery, and future generations shall load their memories with incessant execrations."[55] The virtues of fortitude (courage), wisdom (craft), and exertion (enterprise) were mentioned by Nietzsche in the passage quoted earlier – "under different names, naturally" – as necessary for the community to defeat its enemies.

Congress displays the same spirit in its memorable 1775 Declaration on Taking Up Arms: "We are reduced to the alternative of choosing an unconditional submission to the tyranny of irritated ministers, or resistance by force. The latter is our choice. We have counted the cost of this contest, and find nothing so dreadful as voluntary slavery. Honor, justice, and humanity forbid us tamely to surrender that freedom which we received from our gallant ancestors, and which our innocent posterity have a right to receive from us. We cannot endure the infamy and guilt of resigning succeeding generations to that wretchedness which inevitably awaits them, if we basely entail hereditary bondage upon them."[56]

These defiant proclamations express precisely the "heroic spirit" that Pangle, Mansfield, and others find lacking. Pangle does admit that a "high place... continues to be assigned to courage" in the founding. However, he goes on to claim that because "American 'manliness' is tied to... vigilant private interest" – to Jefferson's "precious principle of self-preservation" – it "cannot be expected to sustain a country in which citizens are frequently called upon to sacrifice themselves for the public good."[57] Yet in Congress's 1775 Declaration, nothing is said of the "private interest" or "self-preservation" of those now alive. Instead, the theme is "honor, justice, and humanity" and the "infamy and guilt"

[55] Suffolk Resolves, September 17, 1774, *Journals of the Continental Congress, 1774–89*, ed. Worthington C. Ford (Washington: Government Printing Office, 1904–37), 1:32.
[56] Declaration of the Causes of Taking up Arms, 217.
[57] Pangle, *Spirit of Modern Republicanism*, 96–7, 260.

that they will incur if they impose "wretchedness" and "hereditary bondage" on *future* generations. At the end of the Declaration of Independence, the signers "mutually pledge to each other our lives, our fortunes, and our sacred honor." They were prepared to risk their lives and fortunes in order to establish a government that would protect lives and fortunes. Clearly, the founders understood that there are occasions when appeals to mere self-interest are not enough – when nobler motives must come into play.

Charles Kesler writes, "As over against those present-day commentators who emphasize the lowness of 'unalienable rights,' reducing them to expressions of the most elemental passions – to the desperate liberty of doing anything to appease one's fear of violent death – Washington esteemed them as high and dignified principles."[58] We see this spirit in Washington's General Orders to the army on July 2, 1776: "The fate of unborn millions will now depend, under God, on the *courage* and *conduct* of this army. – Our cruel and unrelenting enemy leaves us no choice but a *brave* resistance, or the most abject submission. . . . – We have therefore to resolve to conquer or die: Our own country's honor, all call upon us for a *vigorous and manly exertion*, and if we now shamefully fail, we shall become infamous to the whole world."[59]

Nietzsche says that freedom means indifference to "difficulties, hardships, privation, even to life itself." That is exactly the "vigorous and manly exertion" affirmed by Congress and the "conquer or die" outlook to which Washington is exhorting his troops. In Congress's 1775 Declaration, death is preferable to slavery: "we will, in defiance of every hazard, with unabating firmness and perseverance, employ [our arms] for the preservation of our liberties; being with one mind resolved to die freemen rather than to live slaves."[60]

Unlike the state constitutions quoted earlier, which concentrated on the virtues of peace, in these wartime documents we hear of the virtues of strength: courage, "conduct" (meaning competent leadership), bravery, vigor, and manly exertion. Washington's praise of these virtues, and his

---

[58] Charles R. Kesler, "Civility and Citizenship in the American Founding," in *Civility and Citizenship in Liberal Democratic Societies*, ed. Edward C. Banfield (New York: Paragon Books, 1992), 62 (punctuation revised).

[59] George Washington, General Orders, July 2, 1776, in *Writings*, ed. John Rhodehamel (New York: Library of America, 1997), 225–6 (my emphasis).

[60] Declaration of the Causes and Necessity of Taking up Arms, July 6, 1775, in *The Papers of Thomas Jefferson*, ed. Julian P. Boyd et al. (Princeton: Princeton University Press, 1950–), 1:217.

disgust with "abject submission," expressed a general tide of opinion in Revolutionary America. David Hackett Fischer writes,

When the fighting began, they took up the common cry, "Liberty or Death." ... New Hampshire's General John Stark['s] ... advice to his countrymen was as simple as his life: "Live free or die – death is not the worse of evils." ... Isaiah Thomas proclaimed on the masthead of his *Massachusetts Spy,* "Americans! Liberty or Death! Join or Die!" The backcountry leader Patrick Henry made it into an individual idea: "As for *me,* give *me* liberty, or give *me* death." Foreign observers of the Revolution noted this fervor for "liberty or death" and were astonished to discover that Americans really meant it.[61]

Historian John Ferling adds, "the soldier was idealized, for he had come to embody the masculine and sacrificial virtues which Americans believed essential for maintenance of the new nation and its new republican freedoms."[62]

Other official documents contained similar sentiments. Charleston, South Carolina, published this statement on the eve of the war: "let us act like true patriots, and hold it out to the last, preferring one hour of virtuous liberty to a whole eternity of bondage.... Resolve rather to die the last of American freemen, than live the first of American slaves."[63] An address published by the New York legislature praises "those virtuous citizens who count temporary inconveniences as dust in the balance when weighed against their own freedom, and the happiness of posterity."[64]

Pangle states that the founders "look[ed] with some unease" upon the "glory of military valor."[65] He is undoubtedly correct with regard to men like Alexander the Great and Julius Caesar. Locke called them "the

---

[61] Fischer, *Liberty and Freedom,* 115–6. Some doubt that Henry actually spoke those words: Robert A. Ferguson, "The Dialectic of Liberty: Law and Religion in Revolutionary America," in *Liberty and American Experience in the Eighteenth Century,* ed. David Womersley (Indianapolis: Liberty Fund, 2006), 104. It hardly matters. The sentiment was expressed everywhere.

[62] John Ferling, "The New England Soldier: A Study in Changing Perceptions," *American Quarterly* 33, No. 1 (Spring 1981): 45. See also Nathan Tarcov, "The Spirit of Liberty and Early American Foreign Policy," in *Understanding the Political Spirit: Philosophical Investigations from Socrates to Nietzsche,* ed. Catherine H. Zuckert (New Haven: Yale University Press, 1988), 136–52, esp. 146.

[63] Resolution of Charlestown, SC, June 4, 1774, in *American Archives: Fourth Series,* ed. Peter Force (Washington: M. St. Clare Clarke, 1837–53), 1:383–4.

[64] An Address from the Legislature of New York to Their Constituents, March 13, 1781, in *Principles and Acts,* 129.

[65] Pangle, *Spirit of Modern Republicanism,* 86.

great butchers of mankind."[66] Pangle mentions that in *The Federalist* "military service" is not treated as "the crucial moral training ground for courage."[67] That too is true. But the context of this argument was the need to supplement the unreliable state militias with a more professional national military force. The educational role of military service was of subordinate concern to Hamilton in the context of the argument for a stronger national government. There really was a need for better military organization if America were to survive in future wars.[68]

In other contexts we find that the founders did appreciate the formative role of military service. Adams speaks of the institutions of local government, including mandatory militia service, as sources of "that *prudence* in council and that *military valor and ability* which have produced the American Revolution, and which I hope will be sacredly preserved as the foundations of the liberty, happiness, and prosperity of the people." Adams also writes, "wars, at times, are as necessary for the preservation and perfection, the prosperity, liberty, happiness, *virtue*, and independence of nations as gales of wind to the salubrity of the atmosphere, or the agitations of the ocean to prevent its stagnation and putrefaction."[69] David Ramsay's 1789 *History of the American Revolution* argues: "The American revolution, on the one hand, brought forth great vices; but on the other hand, it called forth many virtues, and gave occasion for the display of abilities which, but for that event, would have been lost to the world. When the war began, the Americans were a mass of husbandmen, merchants, mechanics and fishermen; but the necessities of the country gave a spring to the active powers of the inhabitants, and set them on thinking, speaking and acting, in a line far beyond that to which they had been accustomed."[70]

By way of contrast, Franklin Roosevelt's 1944 State of the Union speech famously argues that "true individual freedom cannot exist without economic security and independence. 'Necessitous men are not free men.' People who are hungry and out of a job are the stuff of which

---

[66] John Locke, *Some Thoughts Concerning Education*, 5th ed., 1705, ed. John W. and Jean S. Yolton (Oxford: Clarendon Press, 1989), §116.

[67] Pangle, *Spirit of Modern Republicanism*, 86.   [68] Hamilton, *Federalist* 25, p. 162.

[69] Adams to the Abbé de Mably, 1782, in *Works of John Adams*, ed. Charles Francis Adams (Boston: Little, Brown, 1854), 5:496 (my emphasis); Adams to Rush, July 7, 1812, in *The Spur of Fame: Dialogues of John Adams and Benjamin Rush, 1805–1813*, ed. John Schutz and Douglass Adair (San Marino, CA: Huntington Library, 1966), 228 (my emphasis).

[70] David Ramsay, *The History of the American Revolution*, 1789, ed. Lester H. Cohen (Indianapolis: Liberty Classics, 1990), ch. 26, Appendix 4, 2:629–30.

dictatorships are made." Roosevelt therefore proposed "a second bill of rights," guaranteeing "adequate . . . recreation," a "decent home," and much more.[71] Roosevelt was advocating a civil right to a comfortable existence that the founders would have rejected. It would undermine not only the virtues needed for a free society, but for the achievement of genuine excellence. Those virtues are bred in confronting and overcoming hardships, so there must be a real possibility of failure. Abigail Adams, in the midst of the Revolutionary War, wrote these strong words to her twelve-year-old son John Quincy, the future president: "The habits of a vigorous mind are formed in contending with difficulties. All history will convince you of this, and that wisdom and penetration are the fruits of experience, not the lessons of retirement and leisure. *Great necessities call out great virtues.* . . . [T]hen those qualities which would otherwise lay dormant wake into life, and form the character of the hero and the statesman."[72] For Abigail Adams and the founders, Roosevelt's dictum – "necessitous men are not free men" – is a recipe for enervation of mind and spirit, for dependency and the suffocation of real virtue. For her, *only* necessitous men can be free men. Only in "contending with difficulties" do the soul's strengths come to be cultivated and perfected.

The rattlesnake flag, labeled "Don't Tread on Me," became the quasi-official flag of the Navy during the Revolutionary War. Benjamin Franklin explains: "The rattlesnake . . . has no eyelids . . . [and] may therefore be esteemed an emblem of vigilance. She never begins an attack, nor, when once engaged, ever surrenders: she is therefore an emblem of magnanimity and true courage." Anticipating the view that a democracy is too preoccupied with self-interested pursuits to be capable of fighting, Franklin writes, "she appears to be a most defenseless animal; and even when those weapons [her teeth] are shown and extended for her defense, they appear weak and contemptible; but their wounds however small are decisive and fatal."[73]

Franklin mentions *vigilance* as one of the rattlesnake's characteristics. Madison praises "the vigilant and manly spirit which actuates the people of America, a spirit which nourishes freedom, and in return is nourished

---

[71] Franklin D. Roosevelt, State of the Union Message, January 11, 1944, in *Public Papers and Addresses*, ed. Samuel I. Rosenman (New York: Harper, 1938–50), 13:41.

[72] Abigail Adams to John Quincy Adams, January 19, 1780, in Founders Online, National Archives, http://founders.archives.gov (my emphasis).

[73] Fischer, *Liberty and Freedom*, 77–8; Benjamin Franklin, "The Rattle-Snake as a Symbol of America," Dec. 27, 1775, in *Writings*, 745.

by it." Vigilance is a republican virtue of self-assertion that enables the people to keep a wary eye on the doings of their elected officials, to "keep them virtuous whilst they continue to hold their public trust," in Madison's distrustful phrase.[74] Washington praises the same quality in his First Annual Message to Congress: citizens must be taught to combine "a speedy but temperate vigilance against encroachments, with an inviolable respect to the laws."[75] Vigilance is a virtue that is not quite as assertive as courage (because it requires only a wary watchfulness of government officials, not actual combat), and so it is a quality that can be acquired by many more citizens than the courage of soldiers. It is a kind of democratized courage, a milder form suitable to peacetime, but necessary for a free society that needs manly qualities even if not always in the full measure of risking life and limb.

The founders, like Nietzsche, were conscious of the dangers of ambition. But Washington spoke favorably of "that laudable kind [of ambition], which prompts a man to excel in whatever he takes in hand," and Hamilton praises "the love of fame, the ruling passion of the noblest minds, which would prompt a man to plan and undertake extensive and arduous enterprises for the public benefit."[76] James Wilson elaborates: "The love of honest and well-earned fame is deeply rooted in honest and susceptible minds. Can there be a stronger incentive to the energy of this passion than the hope of becoming the object of well-founded and distinguishing applause?"[77]

The manly qualities called for in official pronouncements were appreciated by the women of the American Revolution, at least if Abigail Adams (quoted above) and this Revolutionary War letter can be trusted: "I know this, that as free I can die but once, but as a slave I shall not be worthy of life. I have the pleasure to assure you that these are the sentiments of all my sister Americans. . . . If these are the sentiments of females, what must glow in the breasts of our husbands, brothers, and sons? They are as with one heart determined to die or be free."[78]

---

[74] Madison, *Federalist* 57, pp. 350, 348.
[75] Washington, First Annual Message to Congress, January 8, 1790, in *Writings*, 750.
[76] Washington to John Adams, September 25, 1798, in ibid., 1013; Hamilton, *Federalist* 72, p. 436.
[77] James Wilson, Speech on Choosing the Members of the Senate by Electors, at the PA convention for revising the state constitution, December 31, 1789, in *Collected Works*, 1:241.
[78] "Female Patriotism," in *Principles and Acts*, 305 ("a letter from a lady of Philadelphia to a British officer at Boston, written immediately after the battle of Lexington").

Against this evidence, Gordon Wood argues that "ancient classical virtue was martial and masculine" and that it was rejected by Americans in the founding era as "too forbidding, harsh, and austere." This older virtue was replaced by "modern virtue," which "was associated with affability and sociability, with love and benevolence." This "new virtue was soft and feminized."[79] I mentioned earlier that in Diamond's somewhat lukewarm case for the presence of virtue in America, he omits the martial virtues altogether.[80]

There are two errors in Wood's account. First, it is a mistake to think that the classics had no regard for the sociable virtues. Aristotle, for example, writes, "in finely-governed cities,...everyone has his own property, but he makes some of it useful to his friends, and some he uses as common things.... That the citizens become such as to use it in common – that is a task proper to the legislator."[81] There is a parallel in the Massachusetts Constitution: "it shall be the duty of legislators...to countenance and inculcate the principles of humanity and general benevolence, public and private charity,...and all social affections, and generous sentiments among the people."[82] Wood's second error is that he fails to report the founders' promotion of the spirited virtues of courage in battle, vigilance at home, and honorable devotion to the common good.

Wood is correct to this extent: the harsh, self-denying, almost brutal virtue of the Spartan or Roman warrior was rejected by the founders – as it was rejected by Plato and Aristotle, whose citizens were to be educated in poetry and music. Coriolanus was certainly good at killing the enemy, but his contempt for the social virtues made it impossible for him to get along with his fellow Romans.[83] For the ancient philosophers, civilization requires combining the virtues of self-restraint, such as moderation and justice, with those of self-assertion and manly strength (the theme of Plato's *Republic*, books 2 to 4). The founders believed this same combination was required in republican government, even if they were much more willing than Plato's Socrates to allow for broad personal freedom in matters of love and family, ownership of private property, and reading and publishing what one chooses.

---

[79] Gordon S. Wood, *The Radicalism of the American Revolution* (New York: Knopf, 1992), 216.

[80] Martin Diamond, "Ethics and Politics: The American Way," 1977, in *As Far as Republican Principles Will Admit* (Washington: AEI Press, 1991), 337–68.

[81] Aristotle, *Politics*, bk. 2, ch. 5 (my translation).

[82] MA Constitution, 1780, pt. 2, ch. 5, §2.

[83] Coriolanus is the subject of Shakespeare's play of the same name.

John Witherspoon argues that there is a connection between the virtues of industry and military valor in a 1776 sermon. "Habits of industry" breed toughness, while aristocratic leisure breeds weakness: "Industry brings up a firm and hardy race. He who is inured to the labor of the field, is prepared for the fatigues of a campaign. The active farmer who rises with the dawn and follows his team or plow, must in the end be an overmatch for those effeminate and delicate soldiers,... whose greatest exertion is in the important preparation for, and tedious attendance on, a masquerade, or midnight ball."[84]

Nietzsche worried that manly sentiments of this kind would disappear after a victorious fight for liberty. Likewise, Paul Rahe asserts that "the public-spirited rhetoric of 1776 quickly gave way to a tacit acknowledgment of the primacy of the private sphere." When Jefferson and Madison spoke of virtue after the war, they supposedly "almost always had independence, diligence, and frugality, not courage and martial vigor in mind. At the deepest level, the founders' concerns were private, not public."[85] Pangle too thinks that the martial spirit of 1776 quickly faded: "The Americans celebrated the Revolution's spirit of brotherhood in arms, sacrifice of life, and martial manliness, while creating a society in which commerce was to reign supreme, explicitly displacing old-fashioned heroic republicanism."[86] Thus one would expect later American history to show that as the founding principles took root, Americans' capacity for military valor diminished.

That did not happen. After the war, John Jay, Chief Justice of the Supreme Court, delivered a charge to a grand jury: "A just war is an evil, but it is not the greatest; oppression and disgrace are greater. War is not to be sought, but it is not to be fled from."[87] The celebration of the military virtues continued as a matter of official policy, as well as being honored in the law of fashion, well into the twentieth century. Rahe and Pangle are correct insofar as the private sphere has primacy in peacetime under the founders' principles. But American soldiers have been very effective

---

[84] John Witherspoon, *The Dominion of Providence over the Passions of Men: A Sermon, 1776*, in *Political Sermons of the American Founding Era, 1730–1805*, ed. Ellis Sandoz (Indianapolis: Liberty Press, 1991), 556.

[85] Paul A. Rahe, *Republics Ancient and Modern: Classical Republicanism and the American Revolution* (Chapel Hill: University of North Carolina Press, 1992), 1046, 858.

[86] Pangle, "Republicanism and Rights," in *The Framers and Fundamental Rights*, ed. Robert A. Licht (Washington: AEI Press, 1991), 117.

[87] John Jay, Charge to Grand Jury, Richmond, VA, May 22, 1793, in *The Correspondence and Public Papers of John Jay*, ed. Henry P. Johnston (New York: G.P. Putnam's Sons, 1891), 3:482.

at standing firm in battle, killing the enemy, and winning wars. From a merely quantitative point of view, the Civil War is the best example: about 140,000 Union men and 75,000 Confederates died in combat.[88] In battles like Antietam and Gettysburg, thousands of soldiers stood their ground in the heat of the conflict, sometimes firing at each other almost face to face. Towns and cities around the nation erected monuments to honor the valor of those who fought in the Civil War and in two world wars. Praise of military valor was a theme of American political rhetoric throughout the nineteenth century and beyond. The manly virtues have long been celebrated in Westerns, war movies, detective and police dramas, and stories of individual survivors who outwit and outfight their animal and human enemies. Victor Hanson argues, using examples ancient and modern, that consensually governed societies have consistently produced the best soldiers since the time of ancient Greece. Freedom, he says, breeds "a superior morale and greater incentive to kill the enemy."[89]

Overview of the Founders' Virtues

Let us sum up what we have seen so far concerning the virtues promoted by government in the founding. They fall into three classes.

First are the *social virtues* of self-restraint. These promote honest dealing, cooperation, mutual trust, stable families, and obedience to the laws. Those most frequently named in the state constitutions are justice, moderation, and temperance. "Virtue" in the sense of sincere pursuit of the public good is mentioned by Virginia and was supported by everyone. Piety and religion were everywhere regarded as *politically* valuable, not for the sake of the salvation of the soul (which exceeds the proper scope of politics), but as supports of the social virtues. We may add to the three basic virtues of self-restraint Virginia's "forbearance" and "love," and the Massachusetts and New Hampshire virtues of humanity, benevolence, charity, honesty, punctuality, sincerity, good humor or sobriety, and "all social affections and generous sentiments."

But the social virtues make people good citizens of any society, for even a dictatorship benefits from internal peace. *Republican virtues* – a second group – are needed to make people good citizens of a *free* society. The

---

[88] John W. Chambers II, ed., *The Oxford Companion to American Military History* (New York: Oxford University Press, 1999), 849.

[89] Victor Davis Hanson, *Carnage and Culture: Landmark Battles in the Rise of Western Power* (New York: Doubleday, 2001), 47.

republican virtues mentioned most frequently are industry and frugality. They are the virtues of self-reliant freemen who neither need nor crave the assistance of a wealthy patron.

The third class consists of *the virtues of self-assertion*. They are especially needed in war, but they are useful at all times in law enforcement or in self-protection when law enforcement is not ready at hand. The warlike virtues are prudence (sometimes called "conduct"), courage (fortitude, bravery), and exertion. Vigilance, a virtue of self-assertion, may also be considered a republican virtue. It is a spirited readiness to oppose government violations of the people's just rights. The assertive virtues are no less necessary than the social and republican virtues.

These three sets of virtues are not always in harmony. Many Americans today are law-abiding, and in fact quite docile. But do they have the kind of feisty public-spiritedness, the vigilant "don't tread on me" mentality, and the willingness to fight that the founders also thought indispensable? At the end of Plato's *Statesman*, the weaving or binding together of moderation and courage, proper self-restraint and proper self-assertion – virtues that are "dissimilar and contrarily diverging" – is one of the most important tasks of statesmanship.[90] In comparison with other nations, America seems to have been remarkably successful at uniting these qualities during its first two centuries and beyond. It will always be a task of statesmanship to encourage the continuation or, if need be, the revival of these virtues.

[90] Plato, *Statesman*, trans. Seth Benardete (Chicago: University of Chicago Press, 1986), 306a-311c (the quoted phrase is at 310a).

13

The Founders' Virtues

Questions and Clarifications

In this chapter we will consider questions and doubts that have been raised about the founders' virtues. These concerns typically arise out of a feeling that there is something defective or low in their conception of virtues and duties. First, were the founders' virtues Christian? Second, if the founders cared seriously about the manly virtues, why were they frequently omitted from early state constitutions and other documents? Does that omission reflect a typically modern, perhaps Hobbesian, denigration of the virtues of self-assertion? Third, to what extent were the founders' virtues a departure from those promoted in classical political philosophy? Finally, is it true, as some argue, that the founders' approach leads inexorably to an eclipse of the higher virtues?

Are the Founders' Virtues Christian?

Harvey Mansfield suggests that "the virtue of the majority of Americans at the time of the founding" was "more Christian and Protestant" than the virtues approved by the leading founders.[1] He implies that there is a difference between Christian virtues and the founders' virtues. A reading of the patriotic sermons of the Revolution quickly dispels this idea. The virtues praised by the preachers were mostly the same as those praised in the official documents. The Virginia Declaration of Rights calls for "Christian forbearance, love, and charity," but the meaning would be

---

[1] Harvey C. Mansfield, "Liberty and Virtue in the American Founding," in *Never a Matter of Indifference: Sustaining Virtue in a Free Republic*, ed. Peter Berkowitz (Stanford: Hoover Institution Press, 2003), 28.

no different if the word "Christian" had been omitted, for the social virtues named there were supported by Christians and non-Christians alike. Most founding-era Christians wanted government to do the same things as non-Christians did. The preachers attributed the fierce and vigilant American "Don't tread on me" attitude to the Bible itself. One can see it in this quasi-official sermon of Samuel Cooke: "[The faithful ruler] will not forget that he ruleth over men, – men who are of the same species with himself, and by nature equal, – men who are the offspring of God, and alike formed after his glorious image, –...men who are reasonable beings, and can be subjected to no human restrictions which are not founded in reason.... The people forfeit the rank they hold in God's creation when they silently yield this important point, and sordidly, like Issachar, crouch under every burden wantonly laid upon them."[2] The Bible compares Issachar, one of the children of the Israelite Joseph, to a donkey oppressed by a heavy load that he passively accepts.[3] Cooke takes Issachar to be a symbol of cowardly submissiveness to tyranny.

In a typical 1776 sermon, John Witherspoon mentions most of the social virtues listed in the state constitutions: "justice," "habits of industry," "frugality in your families, and every other article of expense," "[t]emperance in meals," "a restraint and moderation in all your desires," "liberality and charity to others." But he adds the warlike virtues of prudence and courage. Witherspoon quotes Scripture: "I would exhort you as Joab did the host of Israel, who... spoke like a prudent general and a pious man. 2 Sam. 10:12. 'Be of good courage, and let us behave ourselves valiantly for our people and for the cities of our God, and let the Lord do that which is good in his sight.'" In the same sermon, Witherspoon embraces the principles of the Revolution: "the cause in which

---

[2] Samuel Cooke, *A Sermon* (MA election sermon), 1770, in *The Pulpit of the American Revolution: Political Sermons of the Period of 1776*, ed. John Wingate Thornton (1860; repr. New York: Da Capo Press, 1970), 162–3. Another striking example of the spirited Christianity of the founders' generation is the Address of the Convention of the Representatives of the State of New York to their Constituents, 1776, authored by John Jay, in *The Correspondence and Public Papers of John Jay*, ed. Henry P. Johnston (New York: G.P. Putnam's Sons, 1891), 1:102–20. On the incorporation of manly virtue into American Protestantism: Thomas G. West, "The Transformation of Protestant Theology as a Condition of the American Revolution," in *Protestantism and the American Founding*, ed. Thomas S. Engeman and Michael P. Zuckert (Notre Dame, IN: University of Notre Dame Press, 2004), 187–223.

[3] Genesis 49:14–15.

America is now in arms, is the cause of justice, of liberty, and of human nature."[4]

It is true that some founders occasionally spoke of a possible conflict between Christian and republican virtue. John Adams writes, "it may be well questioned, whether love of the body politic is precisely moral or Christian virtue, which requires justice and benevolence to enemies as well as friends, and to other nations as well as our own."[5] But the sermons of the day do not betray any such hesitation concerning the propriety of patriotism for a Christian. Almost everyone, both Christians and "mere politicians," agreed with Washington's view that the promotion of "religion," i.e., for practical purposes Christianity, would support the morality needed in a free society.[6] Equally, most Christians believed that their religion is supportive of the morality of a well-ordered republic.

Why the Manly Virtues Are Omitted from the State Constitutions

In the previous chapter, I showed the founders' appreciation for the war-like, hard, and dominating virtues. Then why, one might ask, were the state constitutions silent on them? Four of the five early state constitutions discussed above were written during the War for Independence, so we cannot plausibly accuse their writers of being unaware of the virtues of war. Besides, few believed in what Hamilton called "the deceitful dream of a golden age . . . of perfect wisdom and perfect virtue." The U.S. Constitution provides for an army and navy, and the state constitutions refer to their militias and the right to own and carry firearms.

The word "manly" itself provides the clue to the omission of the warlike virtues from the state constitutions. These documents state foundational principles and fundamental law. Therefore they are addressed to every citizen. The virtues in the state constitutions are those which every citizen, male and female alike, can reasonably be expected to acquire, at least in some measure. All can be just (obedient to law), moderate and temperate (avoiding extreme or excessive behavior), industrious, and frugal. It is reasonable to limit the word *morality* to these social and

---

[4] John Witherspoon, *Dominion of Providence*, in *Political Sermons of the American Founding Era, 1730–1805*, ed. Ellis Sandoz (Indianapolis: Liberty Fund, 1990), 549, 556–7, 553.

[5] John Adams, *Defence of the Constitutions*, 1787, in *Works of John Adams*, ed. Charles Francis Adams (Boston: Little, Brown, 1854), 6:208.

[6] George Washington, Farewell Address, 1796, in *Writings*, ed. John Rhodehamel (New York: Library of America, 1997), 971.

republican virtues, if morality means obligations required of everyone. The harder, dominating virtues cannot be morally obligatory because they are rarer qualities that many citizens do not and cannot possess. Not even every male is capable of courage, for, as Hobbes correctly observes, there are some "men of feminine courage."[7] Prudence too, an intellectual virtue mostly omitted from the state constitutions, is obviously something that cannot be expected of everyone, for there are many fools in the world through no fault of their own.

We may speak, then, of two tiers of virtues in the founding. The first tier consists of those that may be called duties, moral qualities that every person should cultivate and acquire as best they can. The second-tier virtues of manly and intellectual excellence are also needed, but not everyone can be expected to have them. They cannot really be called "morality" at all, for moral obligations cannot reasonably exceed what most adults are capable of. It would be cruel to call timid people immoral if they should panic and run away during a battle. Nor would it be reasonable to say that an unusually stupid man who loses his money through foolish investments is morally deficient.

Within this second and rarer tier of virtues, some are more difficult to acquire than others. Most males can acquire enough courage to fight in battle, but few would have the qualities that make a capable statesman. John Adams remarks that the "tribe out of which proceeds your patriots and heroes, and most of the great benefactors of mankind"[8] does not consist of ordinary men with humdrum passions. Those lovers of fame who aspire to perform "extensive and arduous enterprises for the public benefit" are rare.[9] Hamilton writes of another rare kind of virtue, an unbending fidelity to one's obligations: "There are men who could neither be distressed nor worn into a sacrifice of their duty; but this stern virtue is the growth of few soils."[10]

Six state constitutions did mention some of the rarer virtues as qualities necessary in public officials as opposed to citizens in general. Pennsylvania and Vermont state, "The house of representatives...shall consist of persons most noted for wisdom and virtue."[11] Maryland and Kentucky

---

[7] Thomas Hobbes, *Leviathan*, 1651, ed. Edwin Curley (Indianapolis: Hackett, 1994), ch. 21, p. 142.

[8] Adams, *Discourses on Davila*, 1790, ch. 6, in *Works of John Adams*, 6:248.

[9] Hamilton, *Federalist* 72, in Alexander Hamilton, James Madison, and John Jay, *The Federalist Papers*, ed. Clinton Rossiter (New York: Signet Classics, 2003), 436.

[10] Hamilton, *Federalist* 73, p. 440.

[11] PA Constitution, 1776, ch. 2, §7; VT 1777, ch. 2, §7.

set up an indirect system of election for their state senators, stating that they should be "men of the most wisdom, experience, and virtue."[12] In Pennsylvania, Vermont, Massachusetts, and New Hampshire, "The people ought therefore to pay particular attention to these points [i.e., the named social and republican virtues] in the choice of officers and representatives, and have a right to exact a due and constant regard to them from their legislatures and magistrates."[13] In other words, political leaders should exceed others even in the ordinary moral virtues.

The talents of the best statesmen were widely recognized to be unusual and therefore especially worthy of cultivation by institutions of higher learning. A leading purpose of higher education, as presented in the official report of the Commissioners for the University of Virginia, is "to form the statesmen, legislators, and judges, on whom public prosperity and individual happiness are so much to depend." This is to be done by studies in "the principles and structure of government." "Political economy" is to be learned in order to promote the public industry. Students are also to be enlightened with "mathematical and physical sciences, which advance the arts, and administer to the health, the subsistence, and comforts of human life." Finally, the university is to "develop their reasoning faculties" and "enlarge their minds, cultivate their morals, and instill into them the precepts of virtue and order." All of this is in order "to form them to habits of reflection and correct actions, rendering them examples of virtue to others, and of happiness within themselves."[14]

The Bifurcation of Social and Manly Virtues in Machiavelli and Hobbes

To clarify the founders' two tiers of virtue, I will briefly show how some philosophers anticipated this distinction. Although the founders had little respect for the monarchist Hobbes, his *Leviathan* provides a helpful framework for analyzing their treatment of the virtues. Hobbes, who originated the modern natural law doctrine, did not reject the rare and manly virtues of the ancients, although it is generally believed that he did. It is true that Hobbes's natural law requires the peaceable social virtues, e.g., keep your contracts, treat others as if they were your equals, restrain

---

[12] Constitutions of MD, 1776, art. 15; KY, 1792, art. 1, §12.

[13] Declarations of Rights of PA, 1776, art. 14; VT, 1777, art. 16; MA, 1780, art. 18; NH, 1792, art. 83. (MA and NH change PA's "points" to "principles.")

[14] Thomas Jefferson, Report of the Commissioners for the University of Virginia, August 4, 1818, in *Writings*, ed. Merrill D. Peterson (New York: Library of America, 1984), 459–60.

your predatory appetites, and, in sum, "Do not that to another, which thou wouldst not have done to thyself."[15] Like the founders, Hobbes also includes temperance in the laws of nature: "There be other things tending to the destruction of particular men (as drunkenness, and all other parts of intemperance), which may therefore also be reckoned amongst those things which the law of nature hath forbidden."[16]

But Hobbes also has a place for the assertive virtues, even if scholars often fail to acknowledge it. Mansfield mistakenly suggests that Hobbes turns manliness into a vice: "In the *Leviathan* (1651), Hobbes pointedly omits courage, the virtue of manliness in premodern thought, from a list of the virtues."[17] Mansfield goes too far, just as Gordon Wood does in his assertion that virtue becomes feminized in the founding. Hobbes's "list of the virtues" that Mansfield refers to is in fact only a list of his peacetime virtues, just as the state constitutions list only the peacetime virtues. But since Hobbes defines virtue as something "that is valued for eminence," there are other virtues besides the social ones. "Magnanimity, liberality, hope, courage, confidence are honorable; for they proceed from the conscience [i.e., consciousness] of power." Courage, he says, is indeed a passion, but it is honorable, a sign of strength, and therefore a virtue. Further, "Magnanimity in danger of death or wounds [is] valor, fortitude."[18]

The warlike and peaceable virtues belong to Hobbes's first natural law, which is based on the "right of nature" to self-preservation. This law of nature has two branches. The first is "to seek peace and follow it." One should practice the social virtues as long as others are also willing to practice them. But no one is obliged to act peacefully if it would lead to his own destruction. So when one cannot obtain peace, one must follow the second branch of the first law of nature: "seek and use all helps and advantages of war." And: "Force and fraud are in war the two cardinal *virtues*."[19] "Under different names," to use Nietzsche's phrase, force and fraud might be called courage and prudence, the very virtues praised by the founders in the documents quoted in the last chapter. Hobbes is well aware of the value of courage for the commonwealth. Cowardice, he writes, "is naturally punished... with oppression."[20]

---

[15] Hobbes, *Leviathan*, ch. 14–15 (quotation in ch. 15, p. 99).
[16] Ibid., ch. 15, p. 99.
[17] Harvey C. Mansfield, *Manliness* (New Haven: Yale University Press, 2006), 166.
[18] Hobbes, *Leviathan*, ch. 10, pp. 53 and 55; ch. 6, p. 30; ch. 8, p. 38.
[19] Ibid., ch. 14, pp. 79–80; ch. 13, p. 78 (my emphasis).   [20] Ibid., ch. 31, p. 243.

Hobbes splits the virtues into two classes for the same reason that the founders implicitly distinguished between the social and republican virtues on the one hand (which most can acquire) and the more difficult virtues of war and statesmanship on the other. Hobbes says the natural laws "are called not only natural, but also moral laws; consisting in the moral virtues, as justice, equity, and all habits of the mind that conduce to peace, and charity." These social virtues are morally obligatory for all, at least when other people are willing to follow the same rules. But virtues like "force and fraud," and qualities expressive of personal strength or ability, being rare and difficult, cannot be moral obligations.[21]

Hobbes's bifurcation of the virtues is anticipated by Machiavelli. Leo Strauss writes: "Occasionally he [i.e., Machiavelli] makes a distinction between *virtù* and *bontà*. That distinction was in a way prepared by Cicero who says that men are called 'good' on account of their modesty, temperance, and above all, justice and keeping of faith, as distinguished from courage and wisdom. The Ciceronian distinction within the virtues in its turn reminds us of Plato's *Republic* in which temperance and justice are required of all, whereas courage and wisdom are required only of some.... [In Machiavelli,] while virtue is required of rulers and soldiers, goodness is required, or characteristic, of the populace engaged in peaceful occupations."[22] Machiavelli's separation of "virtue" (strength, prudence, and valor) from "goodness" (the social virtues) precedes the Hobbesian account just mentioned, which in turn anticipates the founders. I do not mean that the founders adopted Machiavelli's or Hobbes's analysis of virtue, for there is no evidence that they knew anything about it. Rather, the point is that the bifurcation in question is a venerable and reasonable one in both ancient and modern moral philosophy, and that the founders' approach is consonant with that tradition.

The Difference between the Founders and the Classical Philosophers on Virtue

The most thoughtful scholarly accounts of virtue in the founding tend to exaggerate the differences between the founders' conception and that

---

[21] Ibid., ch. 26, p. 185; ch. 8 and 10 (on the virtues or qualities of personal power); ch. 13, p. 78 (virtues of war).

[22] Leo Strauss, *Studies in Platonic Political Philosophy* (Chicago: University of Chicago Press, 1983), 215.

of the classical Greek and Roman philosophers.[23] Thomas Pangle, for example, argues that the founders' frequent appeals to virtue and honor indeed have "a genuine classical ring" and betray "a sense of indebtedness to the classics." However, he concludes that these "classical" appeals are in tension with the founders' "liberal" principles. His evidence: Madison speaks "in a more purely classical vein" when he states, "the people will have virtue and intelligence to select men of virtue and wisdom. Is there no virtue among us? To suppose that any form of government will secure liberty or happiness without any virtue in the people is a chimerical idea."[24] But why, one must ask, should we attribute a discordant "classical vein" to the founders if their conception of natural law logically and explicitly requires both the social and the assertive virtues – as we have seen that it does?

On the other hand, I do not mean to overstate the parallel between the classics and the founders. Although the virtues of the well-ordered community are roughly similar in Plato and the founding, it would be a mistake to equate the place of virtue in the political orders advocated by each. In Plato's *Republic*, virtue may be said to be the purpose of political life. Socrates' guardians are trained to love virtue as something supremely beautiful. They have no awareness of or concern with individual rights, which are completely contrary to the all-embracing communal spirit of Socrates' city. The guardians are unquestioningly obedient to their rulers.[25] The founders' citizens, in contrast, have the virtue of vigilance, a wary and spirited readiness to distrust their rulers – and, if they misbehave, to overthrow them. An additional difference lies in the

---

[23] I discuss Pangle in the text, but I also have in mind others, such as Wood, *Radicalism of the American Revolution*; Mansfield, "Liberty and Virtue"; Paul A. Rahe, *Republics Ancient and Modern: Classical Republicanism and the American Revolution* (Chapel Hill: University of North Carolina Press, 1992); Mark Blitz, "Virtue, Modern and Ancient," in *Educating the Prince: Essays in Honor of Harvey Mansfield*, ed. Mark Blitz and William Kristol (Lanham, MD: Rowman & Littlefield, 2000), 3–17; Richard Vetterli and Gary C. Bryner, *In Search of the Republic: Public Virtue and the Roots of American Government*, 2nd ed. (Lanham, MD: Rowman & Littlefield, 1996); John Patrick Diggins, *The Lost Soul of American Politics: Virtue, Self-Interest, and the Foundations of Liberalism* (New York: Basic Books, 1984).

[24] Thomas L. Pangle, *The Spirit of Modern Republicanism: The Moral Vision of the American Founders and the Philosophy of Locke* (Chicago: University of Chicago Press, 1988), 44–5, quoting Madison, speech in VA Ratifying Convention, June 20, 1788, in *Debates in the Several State Conventions*, ed. Jonathan Elliott (Philadelphia: J. B. Lippincott, 1907), 3:536–7.

[25] *The Republic of Plato*, trans. Allan Bloom (New York: Basic Books, 1968), 401d–402a, 389b–e.

founders' greater appreciation for the social virtues of civility, benevolence, charity, and humanity. This difference may reflect the founders' greater concern for the kind of friendly civic atmosphere they thought requisite for a successful republic – although, as we saw in Chapter 11, even Aristotle thought friendship and shared pastimes among citizens to be indispensable.

Humanity, discussed in Chapter 12, is one of the founders' social virtues. Pangle calls it "that unclassical virtue." Witherspoon agrees: "Humanity or benevolence you see is kept out of view [by the ancients], though a virtue of the first class."[26] However, here too one must be careful not to overstate the difference between the classics and the founders. Even among the ancients, some did appreciate this virtue, e.g., Plutarch, who praises humanity in the sense of kindness toward those in need. The title of Clifford Orwin's book, *The Humanity of Thucydides*, suggests that humanity (in the sense of avoidance of unnecessary cruelty and respect for civilization outside of one's own city) was a concern for this ancient historian.[27]

John Diggins rightly observes that the classical taste for aristocratic leisure stands opposed to the founders' view that "work itself could be a virtuous activity."[28] The classical disparagement of labor is most vividly stated in Aristotle's *Politics*, paraphrased by John Adams: "A city is constituted for felicity, ... [which] is reposed, according to the same philosopher, in the operations of virtue, and chiefly in the exertions of wisdom and prudence; those men, therefore, are not parts of a city, the operations of whom are not directed to those virtues; such are the husbandmen who are occupied, not in wisdom and prudence, but in laboring the earth; such are the artisans, who fatigue themselves night and day to gain a livelihood for themselves and their poor families; such, finally, are the merchants."[29]

In these respects the founders, in agreement with early modern philosophers like Locke, rejected the classical approach. The purpose of political

---

[26] Pangle, *Spirit of Modern Republicanism*, 72; John Witherspoon, *Lectures on Moral Philosophy*, 1772–94, in *The Selected Writings of John Witherspoon*, ed. Thomas Miller (Carbondale: Southern Illinois University Press, 1990), Lecture 9, p. 184.

[27] Plutarch, *Life of Cato*, trans. John Dryden, §9, http://oll.libertyfund.org; Clifford Orwin, *The Humanity of Thucydides* (Princeton: Princeton University Press, 1994).

[28] Diggins, *Lost Soul*, 14. Diggins is right about this and other differences between the classics and the founders, but, like many scholars, he overstates the contrast.

[29] John Adams, *Defence of the Constitutions of Government of the United States*, 1787, in *The Founders' Constitution*, ed. Philip B. Kurland and Ralph Lerner (Chicago: University of Chicago Press, 1987), 1:120; see Aristotle, *Politics*, bk. 7, ch. 9.

life is now security of natural rights, of the body, of life. Virtue is of concern to government not as an end in itself, but as a means to security and ultimately to happiness. This is clear from the language of many founding documents. In the Northwest Ordinance, morality is "necessary for good government and the happiness of mankind." Virginia's Declaration of Rights asserts that "no free government, or the blessings of liberty, can be preserved to any people, but by a firm adherence to...virtue." When virtue is treated as a means, it is understood in terms of what is useful to the community and the individual.

But we must not conclude that because they declined to make virtue the end of political life, the founders had a stunted or degraded understanding of human life as a whole in comparison with the supposedly nobler vision of the classics. For Locke and the founders, there is a difference between the purpose of politics (security of person and property) and the purpose of life (happiness, understood as inseparable from virtue, honor, and, for believers, salvation of the soul). This distinction is the basis of limited, constitutional government. The separation of church and state in the founders' sense – perhaps the most important instance of their separation of the public from the private sphere – means that the highest things will no longer be a concern of the government, except insofar as they aid or oppose securing natural rights.

However, some scholars fail to acknowledge the distinction just mentioned between the purpose of politics and the purpose of life, at least with regard to Locke and the founders. Harvey Mansfield writes, "Liberalism is unmanly in setting down self-preservation as the end of man, as do Hobbes and Locke."[30] On the contrary, both Hobbes and Locke set down happiness, not self-preservation, as the end of man.[31] In fact, it is precisely because self-preservation is not "the end of man" that Hobbes's state of nature is so violent. "[M]an, whose joy consisteth in comparing himself with other men, can relish nothing but what is eminent," says Hobbes. Not self-preservation but happiness ("joy") is man's end, and honor is a necessary ingredient.[32]

My analysis so far has taken for granted that the classics held that virtue, understood as citizen virtue, is the purpose of political life. That is not quite true. The classical Greek philosophers indeed begin with the perspective of the citizen, but they do not stay within that perspective.

---

[30] Mansfield, *Manliness*, 185.
[31] Hobbes, *Leviathan*, ch. 11, and Locke, *Essay*, bk. 2, ch. 21, §41–51.
[32] Hobbes, *Leviathan*, ch. 17.

The citizen thinks of virtue as noble or good in itself, as well as useful. But the philosopher sees that insofar as virtue is a concern of the political community, the definition of virtue will in fact be determined largely by what is useful to preserve the community. Virtue will be defined as "political virtue," i.e., virtue as understood by the citizens, as opposed to genuine virtue.[33] Tocqueville sagely remarks, "I doubt that men were more virtuous in aristocratic centuries than in others, but it is certain that the beauties of virtue were constantly spoken of then; only in secret did they study the side on which it is useful."[34] Tocqueville exaggerates here, as one may see in Cicero's *On Duties*, where virtue is examined from the point of view of "the beauties of virtue" (which Cicero calls *honestum* – noble, honorable) *and* of the usefulness of virtue (called *utile*). The gap between the classical and modern conception of virtue is not as great as it first appears to be.

The classical philosophers' analysis of virtue points in two directions. In one way, virtue consists in those qualities of character and mind which the moral man regards as good in themselves. In a second way, these qualities prove on closer examination to be what is useful. In Aristotle's *Ethics*, courage is praised as being "for the sake of the noble," but nothing is said of its usefulness.[35] But in the *Rhetoric*, "the greatest virtues are those most useful to others.... Because of this, they honor most those who are just and courageous, for the latter are useful to others in war, the former also in peace."[36] The philosopher sees that from the point of view of the moral man, virtue is understood as noble, as something right and good in itself. But citizen virtues such as justice and courage are ultimately honored as noble because they are "useful to others."

Eclipse of the Higher Virtues?

Ultimately, from the philosophic point of view, the truest or highest virtue consists of those qualities that are useful for the cultivation of the

---

[33] Plato and Aristotle both speak of "political" or "citizen" courage as a deficient form: *Republic*, 430c, 500d; and Aristotle, *Nicomachean Ethics*, trans. Robert C. Bartlett and Susan D. Collins (Chicago: University of Chicago Press, 2011), bk. 3, ch. 8.

[34] Alexis de Tocqueville, *Democracy in America*, trans. Harvey C. Mansfield and Delba Winthrop (Chicago: University of Chicago Press, 2000), vol. 2, pt. 2, ch. 8, p. 501.

[35] Aristotle, *Nicomachean Ethics*, bk. 3, ch. 7.

[36] Aristotle, *Rhetoric*, bk. 1, ch. 9 (my translation).

understanding.[37] There is a place for that kind of genuine virtue in the founding. But Pangle denies it, arguing that there is an "eclipse" of the higher virtues. In his telling, the founders did not appreciate the philosophic life, and their view of religion was too cool and calculating to encourage the kind of sincere religious devotion characteristic of an earlier age. Pangle also notes that when the founders spoke of science, they typically had in mind the useful sciences rather than the non-utilitarian insight of the thinker who finds bliss in the pleasures of intellectual insight. He concludes that whatever appreciation there was for science, philosophy, and literature, it was "severely restricted by a relative narrow, shared moral horizon – the horizon of modern democracy."[38]

Pangle appears to fault the founders' view that public university education should be in the service of "national improvements" (such as scientific studies to advance agriculture and manufacturing) and the formation of able statesmen. He seems to think that the founders should have endorsed a different kind of higher education, one that leads the most gifted young people to transcend the moral and civic concerns of the politician and the citizen. In response, the founders would have asked how a government serving the common good could justly take money out of the pockets of hard-working citizens to fund "a noble leisure" for a privileged class of intellectuals. How could a government based on the social compact justify teaching its best and brightest to pursue "a life of study surrounded by books meant for rumination" while ignoring or despising the concerns of the supposed vulgarians who happen to be paying for their education?[39]

Is it so obvious that the classics would have disapproved of Jefferson's University of Virginia, as Pangle implies? That university, oriented toward producing future statesmen and other leaders, would certainly accommodate the chance philosopher in one niche or other of the curriculum, which included the study of ancient and modern languages, mathematics, physics, chemistry, ethics, rhetoric, "belles lettres" (literature), "the fine arts," as well as more practical instruction in things like medicine, architecture, and government.[40] Does it really make sense *for government* to attempt to go beyond this, to institutionalize an education to the philosophic life in a conventional academic setting? In the end, who

---

[37] Compare the philosopher's virtues in Plato, *Republic*, bk. 6, 485a–487a, with the guardians' virtues in bks. 3 and 4. Compare also virtue in bks. 3–5 versus bk. 10 of Aristotle, *Nicomachean Ethics*.

[38] Pangle, *Spirit of Modern Republicanism*, 74–8.   [39] Ibid., 76–7.

[40] Report of the Commissioners for the University of Virginia, August 4, 1818, in Jefferson, *Writings*, 462–3.

happens to be teaching, and who happens to be learning, will make all the difference. This cannot be planned or dictated by laws or educational administrators. If government tries to produce philosophers through its own ideas of proper instruction, is not the result more likely to be the production of frivolous intellectuals? The founders seem to have thought that it is better to set up the university with a view toward service to society. At its best, it would educate future statesmen in the principles and practice of republican government. In other ways it would train people in the sciences and in other arts to be useful to their society and to themselves. That is something that can be understood and done well by those who dwell far from the exalted heights of philosophy. As Rousseau reminds us in his *Discourse on the Sciences and Arts*, "Someone who his whole life long will remain a bad versifier or an inferior geometer, might perhaps have become a great clothier."[41]

Nevertheless, in their private capacity (as opposed to what they thought taxpayers should be forced to support), some of the founders did show their respect for the life of the mind independently of utilitarian considerations. Washington occasionally shows a statesman's appreciation for, and even a kind of deference toward, that life: "In a clouded state of existence, where so many things appear precarious to the bewildered research, it is here [in mathematics] that the rational faculties find a firm foundation to rest upon. From the high ground of mathematical and philosophical demonstration, we are insensibly led to far nobler speculations and sublimer meditations."[42]

John Adams shared Washington's sensibility. In a letter to a preacher he wrote, "Who would not wish to exchange the angry contentions of the former [i.e., of "those who tread the public stage"] for the peaceful contemplations of the closet? 'Where contemplation prunes her ruffled wings,/ And the free soul looks down to pity kings.'"[43] In a more famous later letter, Adams shows a similar respect from afar for a life that transcends the harsh dimension of politics and war: "It is not indeed the fine

---

[41] Jean-Jacques Rousseau, *Discourse on the Sciences and Arts*, 1750, in *The Discourses and Other Early Political Writings*, ed. Victor Gourevitch (New York: Cambridge University Press, 1997), 26.

[42] Washington to Nicholas Pike, June 20, 1788, in *Writings of George Washington*, ed. John C. Fitzpatrick (Washington: Government Printing Office, 1931–44), 30:2–3, discussed in Eugene F. Miller, "Washington's Patronage of Education," in *Law and Philosophy: The Practice of Theory: Essays in Honor of George Anastaplo*, ed. John Murley et al. (Athens: Ohio University Press, 1992), 712.

[43] Adams to Zabdiel Adams, June 21, 1776, in *Works of John Adams*, 9:400–1, quoting Alexander Pope, *Satires of John Donne Versified*, Satire 4, lines 186–7.

arts which our country requires. The useful, the mechanic arts, are those which we have occasion for in a young country. . . . I must study politics and war that my sons may have liberty to study mathematics and philosophy. My sons ought to study mathematics, and philosophy, geography, natural history, naval architecture, navigation, commerce, and agriculture, in order to give their children a right to study painting, poetry, music, architecture, statuary, tapestry, and porcelain."[44] Adams emphasizes the cultivation of useful studies for the sake of ultimately transcending the whole dimension of the practical for the sake of contemplating that which is beautiful but useless. One is reminded of Aristotle's dictum that the magnanimous man "is such as to possess beautiful and useless things more than useful and beneficial ones."[45]

Adams had already acquired as a young man something of his taste for philosophy: "If engagements to a party are necessary to make a fortune, I had rather make none at all; and spend the remainder of my days like my favorite author, that ancient and immortal husbandman, philosopher, politician, and general, Xenophon, in his retreat, considering kings and princes as shepherds, and their people and subjects like flocks and herds, or as mere objects of contemplation and parts of a curious machine in which I had no interest, than to wound my own mind by engaging in any party, and spreading prejudices, vices, or follies." Adams's reference to "herds" anticipates Nietzsche's use of the term. Adams is remembering Xenophon's comparison of political communities to animal herds in *The Education of Cyrus*.[46]

Finally, we should not neglect James Wilson's striking remark at the 1787 Convention: "he could not agree that property was the sole or the primary object of government and society. The cultivation and improvement of the human mind was the most noble object."[47] Pangle remarks that this statement "betrays no awareness of any possible tension or gulf between the philosophic and the political life, and bespeaks no classical notion of the superiority of the former to the latter."[48] This is correct

---

[44] Adams to Abigail Adams, May 1780, *Adams Family Correspondence*, vol. 3, ed. L. H. Butterfield (Cambridge: Harvard University Press, 1988), 342.

[45] Aristotle, *Nicomachean Ethics*, bk. 4, ch. 3.

[46] Adams, "On Self-Delusion," 1763, in *Works of John Adams*, 3:433; Xenophon, *The Education of Cyrus*, trans. Wayne Ambler (Ithaca: Cornell University Press, 2001), ch. 1, §1.

[47] James Wilson, speech on July 13, in *Records of the Federal Convention of 1787*, ed. Max Farrand (New Haven: Yale University Press, 1937), 1:605.

[48] Pangle, *Spirit of Modern Republicanism*, 75.

with regard to Wilson's admittedly vague remark, but the statements of Washington and Adams just quoted do in fact express something of what Pangle calls a "classical notion," namely, the ultimate superiority of the contemplative life to that of the citizen or statesman, and the gulf between the two ways of life. Kevin Slack makes a convincing case that Franklin possessed the genuine spirit of philosophic inquiry to a greater degree than any other founder. The "happiness of a rational creature," writes Franklin, involves "a faculty of reasoning justly and truly in searching after [and] discovering such truths as relate to my happiness."[49]

I would not claim that all the founders shared Washington's, Adams's, Wilson's, and Franklin's respect for contemplative activity. For example, Jean Yarbrough argues that Jefferson's respect for science was always tied to its usefulness for mankind.[50] For most founders, the philosophic or contemplative life was something they were perhaps aware of, but of which, in their own lives, they had limited experience and understanding. They were statesmen and gentlemen, admiring from afar, just as Aristotle's gentleman looks up to the philosopher in the *Ethics*, and Plato's Glaucon learns to admire philosophy in the *Republic*. Political life cannot and should not attempt to produce philosophers or poets, but a well-governed polity can provide a place for the life of the mind as something beyond its ken but which can still be an object of respect.

---

[49] Franklin, Proposals and Queries to be Asked the Junto, 1732, in *Writings*, 210; discussed in Kevin Slack, "Benjamin Franklin's Metaphysical Essays and the Virtue of Humility," *American Political Thought* 2, No. 1 (Spring 2013): 52. See also Slack, *Benjamin Franklin, Natural Right, and the Art of Virtue* (Rochester: University of Rochester Press, 2017).

[50] Jean M. Yarbrough, *American Virtues: Thomas Jefferson on the Character of a Free People* (Lawrence: University Press of Kansas, 1998), 159–65.

PART III

PROPERTY AND ECONOMICS

I4

The Founders' Understanding of Property Rights

Although there are many scholarly treatments of the founders' under-standing of property and economics – some of them to be discussed in the next few chapters – few present an overview of the principles and policies they agreed on. Even the fact that there *was* a consensus is often denied. Scholars tend to focus on the founders' differences rather than their agreements. It is true that there were bitter disputes in the 1790s over particular policies, such as how to pay down the national debt, the existence of a national bank, and whether to subsidize domestic manufac-tures. Chapter 18 will consider these quarrels more fully. By concentrating on them, however, one can easily fail to see the founders' broad agree-ment on the three main policies that provide the necessary protection of property rights. These are, first, the legal right to own and use property in land and other goods; second, the right to sell or give property to others on terms of one's own choosing (market freedom); and third, government support of sound money. The founders' battles were fought over the best means to those ends – and over such subordinate questions as whether and how large-scale manufacturing should be encouraged.

The founders' more recent critics generally misunderstand their approach to property and economics. Richard Rorty asserts that the founders' "moral and social order" eventually became "an economic sys-tem which starves and mutilates the great majority of the population." Such is the "selfishness" of an "unreformed capitalist economy." There is "a constant need for new laws and new bureaucratic initiatives which would redistribute the wealth produced by the capitalist system."[1]

[1] Richard Rorty, *Achieving Our Country: Leftist Thought in Twentieth-Century America* (Cambridge: Harvard University Press, 1998), 47 (quoting with approval Herbert Croly's

Another criticism holds that the founders' view of economics is obsolete. It may have been reasonable to protect property rights and free markets in a simpler time with vast tracts of available land, but these policies, we are told, cannot address the problems of the poor in today's complex industrial society. William Brennan, the Supreme Court's leading liberal during the second half of the twentieth century, writes: "Until the end of the nineteenth century, freedom and dignity in our country found meaningful protection in the institution of real property. . . . To a growing extent economic existence now depends on less certain relationships with government – licenses, employment, contracts, subsidies, unemployment benefits, tax exemptions, welfare and the like. . . . [B]efore this century, . . . a man's answer to economic oppression or difficulty was to move two hundred miles west. Now hundreds of thousands of Americans live entire lives without any real prospect of the dignity and autonomy that ownership of real property could confer."[2] Another argument against the founders' "obsolete" approach is that in modern times free markets are subject to "market failure," the inability to produce an adequate and reliable supply of some goods and services.[3] These views assume that current knowledge of economics and production is unquestionably superior to that of the long-dead amateurs who founded the American regime.

But America is the wealthiest nation in world history. Even those Americans classified as poor often enjoy goods that were out of the reach of everyone two or three centuries ago: inexpensive fresh meat, fresh fruits and vegetables all year, housing with refrigerators, indoor plumbing, and central air conditioning and heating. This is to say nothing of cell phones, televisions, recordings of top-quality music, and the easy availability, in paperback and on the Internet, of many of the greatest books ever written. All this took place in a nation still governed, somewhat, by the founders' idea of respect for private property.

1909 critique of capitalism), 76. Richard Hofstadter, *The American Political Tradition and the Men Who Made It* (1948; repr. New York: Vintage, 1989), 20–21, presents a similar critique. Jennifer Nedelsky, *Private Property and the Limits of American Constitutionalism: The Madisonian Framework and Its Limits* (Chicago: University of Chicago Press, 1990), 261–3, 272–3, agrees.

[2] William Brennan, "To the Text and Teaching Symposium," October 15, 1985, Federalist Society website, www.fed-soc.org.

[3] Francis M. Bator, "The Anatomy of Market Failure," *Quarterly Journal of Economics* 72, No. 3 (Aug. 1958): 351.

This undeniable prosperity raises yet another doubt: has it been bought at the price of spiritual dehumanization? Has America's growth in prosperity proceeded in tandem with a moral and intellectual degradation? That is the gist of critics such as historian Gertrude Himmelfarb. She quotes Joseph Schumpeter, who argues that "capitalism creates a critical frame of mind which, after having destroyed the moral authority of so many other institutions, in the end turns against its own."[4] Leo Strauss, even more radically, asserts that John Locke, looking for "an immoral or amoral substitute for morality," decided that "that substitute is acquisitiveness. Here we have an utterly selfish passion whose satisfaction does not require the spilling of any blood and whose effect is the improvement of the lot of all."[5]

I have explained in the chapters on the moral conditions of freedom how the founders would have responded to some of these claims. In the five chapters of Part III we will see that it is a gross caricature to claim that the founders built their understanding of property and economics on a legitimation of selfish, exploitative passions. Instead, they earnestly attempted to articulate a theory of economics – and to implement it in practice – that would provide a greater degree of justice than any other economic order can achieve or has achieved.

In this light, the founders might have regarded moralistic disgust with property and markets as a sign of intellectual and spiritual shortcomings. They might have said, as Strauss himself also writes, "we are in the habit of expecting too much" from politics.[6] As for the founders' supposedly primitive understanding of economics, their views were not only sophisticated but perhaps even superior to the dominant views of our day. They provide principles and policies by which even the most complex economic order can be governed.

Two Reasons for Property Rights: Justice and Utility

In the founding era, defenses of property rights proceeded along two main lines: justice and utility. The former treats property as a fundamental right that would be morally wrong to infringe, regardless of whether it

---

[4] Gertrude Himmelfarb, *One Nation, Two Cultures* (New York: Vintage Books, 2001), 12–13.
[5] Leo Strauss, *What Is Political Philosophy? And Other Studies* (Glencoe, IL: Free Press, 1959), 49–50.
[6] Ibid., 107.

serves a useful purpose. The Continental Congress declared in 1774, for example, that "by the immutable laws of nature," the people "are entitled to... property." In the Virginia Declaration of Rights (1776), property is an "inherent" right. Massachusetts (1780) called it a right "natural, essential, and inalienable." Four other states used similar language and all the states agreed with it.[7]

Over the past two centuries, writes Greg Forster, "the moral argument for capitalism became less prominent. The case for capitalism was more often made on efficiency grounds alone." The most effective defenders of property rights – "from Aquinas to Locke to our own time – have successfully availed themselves of both approaches."[8] Yuval Levin observes that today's proponents of capitalism, in contrast with Adam Smith, tend not to provide it with a moral defense. Yet capitalism, he observes, is more vulnerable to a moral critique than an economic one. "There is not today, and perhaps there never has been, a serious economic critique of the fundamental tenets of capitalism. There are only moral critiques."[9]

The founders' argument from justice rests ultimately on the claim that "all men are by nature equally free and independent, and have certain inherent rights," one of which is "the means of acquiring and possessing property." In this understanding, all are born free, meaning that they own their own minds and bodies and may freely use their talents to acquire and use property. The use of force to prevent people from acquiring property or from transferring property to others deprives them of the fruits of their labor. From the point of view of justice, deprivation of property rights is immoral. Jefferson describes criminals who "commit violations on the... property of others" as "wicked and dissolute men."[10]

This last remark helps us to understand why none of the leading founders defended the essential rightness of slavery, and why most looked forward to its eventual abolition. Property rights in the founders' sense, far from favoring slavery (as some scholars[11] say), are in fact

---

[7] Declarations of Rights of VA, 1776, art. 1; PA, 1776, art. 1; VT, 1777, art. 1; MA, 1780, art. 1; NH, 1784, art. 2. DE Constitution, 1792, Preamble.

[8] Greg Forster, "Sacred Enterprise," *Claremont Review of Books* 9, No. 3 (Summer 2009): 40.

[9] Yuval Levin, "Recovering the Case for Capitalism," *National Affairs* 3 (2010): 128.

[10] VA Declaration of Rights, 1776, §1; Thomas Jefferson, A Bill for Proportioning Crimes and Punishments, 1778, in *The Founders' Constitution*, ed. Philip B. Kurland and Ralph Lerner (Chicago: University of Chicago Press, 1987), 5:374.

[11] James L. Huston, *Calculating the Value of the Union: Slavery, Property Rights, and the Economic Origins of the Civil War* (Chapel Hill: University of North Carolina Press, 2003), 16 ("property rights constituted the frontline [Southern] defense" of slavery).

opposed to slavery. In *Federalist* 54 Madison indeed admits that in the laws of the South, "the slave may appear to be degraded from the human rank, and classed with those irrational animals, which fall under the legal denomination of property." But he immediately qualifies this admission by noting that "if the laws were to restore the rights which have been taken away" – their natural rights to liberty and property – "the Negroes could no longer be refused an equal share of representation with the other inhabitants."[12]

The founders also understood and defended property rights in terms of their *usefulness* to life and society, independently of the question of justice. New York's General Assembly asserted in 1764 that property, a "natural right of mankind," is one of the "rights, the deprivation of which will dispirit the people, abate their industry, discourage trade, introduce discord, poverty, and slavery; or, by depopulating the colonies, turn a vast, fertile, prosperous region into a dreary wilderness."[13] But besides the loss of material prosperity, it is also good to remember, writes Gordon Wood, that Hamilton's "goal was as much political as economic" in his economic policy recommendations of the 1790s.[14] The same is true of the other founders. The purpose of government is "to secure the existence of the body-politic [and] to protect it," because that is the condition of providing "the individuals who compose it with the power of enjoying... their natural rights."[15] Economic policies that promote prosperity are an important means to that end, while policies that impoverish a nation leave it vulnerable to conquest or destruction.

But property is also necessary for something higher – for liberty and happiness. In his widely read *Letters from a Farmer* (1768), John Dickinson writes "that we cannot be happy, without being free – that we cannot

Forrest McDonald, *Novus Ordo Seclorum: The Intellectual Origins of the Constitution* (Lawrence: University Press of Kansas, 1985), 268 ("the [Constitution's] prohibition against interference in the slave trade before 1808" concerned "property rights").

[12] Madison, *Federalist* 54, in Alexander Hamilton, James Madison, and John Jay, *The Federalist Papers*, ed. Clinton Rossiter (New York: Signet Classics, 2003), 334–5.

[13] New York Petition to the House of Commons, October 18, 1764, In *Prologue to Revolution: Sources and Documents on the Stamp Act Crisis, 1764–1766*, ed. Edmund S. Morgan (New York: Norton, 1959), 9, 13.

[14] Gordon S. Wood, *Empire of Liberty: A History of the Early Republic, 1789–1815* (New York: Oxford University Press, 2009), 103. Also Karl-Friedrich Walling, *Republican Empire: Alexander Hamilton on War and Free Government* (Lawrence: University Press of Kansas, 1999) (Hamilton's policies all served the same end: securing liberty, with an eye to the problems of war).

[15] Preamble, MA Constitution, 1780.

be free, without being secure in our property."[16] To sum up its vision of political happiness, the 1776 New York Convention said – paraphrasing Micah 4:4 – that during most of the state's colonial history, "every man sat under his own vine and fig tree, and there was none to make him afraid." The Continental Congress, George Washington, and many others used the same memorable biblical image of security for life and property.[17] James Wilson speaks of the nobler purposes of property as well: it is "highly important to . . . the elegancies, to the refinements, and to some of the virtues of civilized life."[18] Everyone needs food, clothing, and shelter, and therefore has a right to acquire and possess these goods – not only for the sake of mere life, but also for the good life.

Defenders of property rights today generally neglect the first way of treating property – as a matter of justice – and turn instead to the second way, expedience or utility. However, the utility of private property is typically described in our time in terms of material abundance, as opposed to life, freedom, and happiness. For example, Senator Ted Cruz writes, "Thanks to America's free market system, the average poor American has more living space than the typical non-poor person in Sweden, France, or the United Kingdom. In 1970, . . . only 36 percent of the U.S. population enjoyed air conditioning. Today, 80 percent of poor households in America have air conditioning."[19] When the usefulness of market freedom is defined in merely material terms, capitalism comes to be seen as low. In our time, capitalism is widely believed to be ignoble, in part because of the arguments of its defenders.

Accepting this view, historian Martin Malia, a critic of socialism, writes, "Masses of humanity could once surge through Red Square

[16] *Letters from a Farmer*, Letter 12, in *The Political Writings of John Dickinson, 1764–1774*, ed. Paul L. Ford (1895; repr. New York: Da Capo, 1970), 400.

[17] Address of the Convention of the Representatives of the State of New York to their Constituents, 1776, authored by John Jay, in *The Correspondence and Public Papers of John Jay, 1763–1781*, ed. Henry P. Johnston (New York: G.P. Putnam's Sons, 1891), 1:104. Congress, Address to the Inhabitants of the United States, May 13, 1777, in *Journals of the Continental Congress, 1774–89*, ed. Worthington C. Ford (Washington: Government Printing Office, 1904–37), 8:401. Washington to the Hebrew Congregation in Newport, RI, August 18, 1790, in Washington, *Writings*, ed. John Rhodehamel (New York: Library of America, 1997), 767. Dickinson uses the image in *Letters from a Farmer*, Letter 5, in *Political Writings*, 338; also Mason to Washington, in *The Papers of George Mason, 1725–1792*, ed. Robert A. Rutland (Chapel Hill: University of North Carolina Press, 1970), 1:267.

[18] James Wilson, "On the History of Property," in *Collected Works of James Wilson*, ed. Kermit L. Hall and Mark David Hall (Indianapolis: Liberty Fund, 2007), 1:305.

[19] Senator Ted Cruz, "The Miracle of Freedom," *Imprimis*, May–June 2013, 4.

chanting 'forward to the victory of socialism!' but it is quite inconceivable that shareholders should march down Wall Street mouthing such rousing slogans about capitalism." Malia thinks of socialism, but not capitalism, as idealistic. He forgets the many passionate demonstrations in favor of property rights during the American Revolution, some in the form of mobs. Malia says that socialism may be described as "a secular religion," but he denies that capitalism could generate religious passion. He muses that a "capitalist manifesto" would be based on boring "growth statistics."[20] But the founders, using language at once idealistic and religious, pledged to each other "our lives, our fortunes, and our sacred honor" in their fight for the God-given rights of life, liberty, and property. True, the Declaration of Independence does not mention property, but as we saw earlier, many leading founding documents speak of life, liberty, and property in their statements of basic principles.

The early modern philosophic proponents of property rights – men like John Locke – defended their position in the same twofold manner. Locke in particular knew that most people are unable to think clearly about what promotes both their own good and the common good. Human reason can lead us to truth, but there are so many obstacles: lack of time for study, reluctance to disagree with one's peers, strong passions that get in the way, to say nothing of ordinary stupidity.[21] In the absence of genuine insight, it helps greatly if there are principles of justice that bring us to the same goal. In the view of Locke and other philosophers of his persuasion, the human problem is not that people follow their own self-interest too much, but that they follow it too little because they are so prone to misunderstand it. Hamilton makes this point in *Federalist* 6: "momentary passions and immediate interests have a more active and imperious control over human conduct than general or remote considerations of policy, utility, or justice."[22] The easily understood doctrine of natural rights is a sound practical substitute for a complex chain of reasoning showing that property rights are indispensable for human well-being.

A resolution of Charleston, South Carolina, illustrates the founders' typical blend of arguments from justice and interest: "the man who demands my money with a pistol at my breast is commonly called a robber, and . . . no proposition in Euclid is more capable of demonstration,

[20] Martin Malia, *The Soviet Tragedy: A History of Socialism in Russia, 1917–1991* (New York: Free Press, 1994), 24.
[21] John Locke, *An Essay concerning Human Understanding*, 4th ed., 1700, ed. Peter H. Nidditch (Oxford: Clarendon Press, 1975), bk. 4, ch. 20, "On Error."
[22] Hamilton, *Federalist* 6, p. 51.

than that such a man has as good a right to the money in my pocket as the House of Commons to tax us without our consent." That statement is an indignant appeal to what Charleston calls "the justice of their cause." But the same resolution appeals also to the condition of misery that will ensue if Americans fail to defend their just rights: "soon would desolation frown over the uncultivated earth. Suns would in vain arise, and in vain would showers descend; for who would be industrious when others would reap the fruit of his labor?"[23] Justice and usefulness – these are the two grounds of the right to property.

The Twofold Right to Property: Possession and Acquisition

So far I have spoken of property rights as though the meaning of that phrase is obvious. At a minimum it means that government should permit private ownership and protect owners against robbery and theft. But government must do much more than that.

To begin, we must dispose of the most common misconception. For the founders, property rights are not merely about possession of what one already has. Falling into this error, law professor Kenneth Karst writes that "the protection of property and economic liberty" is something that matters only "to people at the top of the heap."[24] Karst is thinking of property as something that the rich possess and the poor lack. But this is to conceive of property as static rather than dynamic, as if one person's ownership is another's deprivation. Other scholars make the same mistake. Political theorist Eric Voegelin writes, "Throughout [Locke's *Second*] *Treatise* runs the iron principle that men may be unequal in every conceivable respect, but that they are equal in the protection that they receive for the inequality. The government will preserve with divine impartiality the poverty of the poor and the wealth of the rich." He then paraphrases Anatole France's well-known cynical remark: "the majestic equality of the laws... forbids rich and poor alike to sleep under the bridges, to beg in the streets, and to steal their bread."[25] Voegelin seems to have been unaware of Locke's argument (which is also the founders'

---

[23] Resolution of Charlestown, SC, June 4, 1774, in *American Archives: Fourth Series*, ed. Peter Force (Washington: M. St. Clare Clarke, 1837–53), 1:383–4.

[24] Kenneth L. Karst, *Belonging to America: Equal Citizenship and the Constitution* (New Haven: Yale University Press, 1989), 179.

[25] Eric Voegelin, *The New Order and Last Orientation* (Columbia: University of Missouri Press, 1997), 150–51; Anatole France, *The Red Lily*, trans. Winifred Stephens (New York: John Lane, 1910), 95.

argument) that private ownership, by creating strong incentives to produce things useful for life, leads to greater wealth for everyone.[26]

The founders anticipated this criticism by insisting that the right to property includes not only possession of what one has but also acquisition of what one needs. The Virginia Declaration of Rights states, "all men... have certain inherent rights," including "the enjoyment of life and liberty, with the means of acquiring and possessing property." Six other early declarations echo this language.[27] If the right includes both *acquiring* and *possessing* property, then it is not enough to be allowed to keep and protect what you currently own. Such a right would benefit only those who already have what they need. There must also be some "means of acquiring" more than one has, so that the poor as well as the rich can benefit from property rights.

In the founding, the right to acquire property precedes the right to possess because you have to acquire it before possessing it. Besides, acquisition of property is inherent in the natural right to liberty itself. James Madison's *Federalist* 10 explains: there is a "diversity in the faculties of men, from which the rights of property originate.... The protection of these faculties is the first object of government." The *first* object of government is to protect a person's "faculties" (talents) because they are the means of *acquiring* property, as Madison says: "From the protection of different and unequal faculties of acquiring property, the possession... of property immediately results."[28]

Nathaniel Chipman, writing in 1793, explains the founders' understanding. He speaks of "primary rights," among which is "the right which men have of using their powers and faculties, under certain reciprocal modifications, for their own convenience and happiness.... [An instance of this right is] the right of acquisition. To the security of this right,

---

[26] John Locke, *Two Treatises of Government*, 1690, ed. Peter Laslett (Cambridge: Cambridge University Press, 1960), *Second Treatise*, §37, §41.

[27] Declarations of Rights of VA, 1776, art. 1; PA, 1776, art. 1; VT, 1777, art. 1; MA, 1780, art. 1; NH, 1784, art. 2; OH, 1802, art. 1; also DE Constitution, Preamble, 1792. Locke too grounds the right to possess on the more fundamental right to acquire "those things, that were necessary and useful to his being" (*First Treatise*, §86).

[28] *Federalist* 10, p. 73. The primacy of the right to acquire is rightly stressed by James W. Ely, *The Guardian of Every Other Right: A Constitutional History of Property Rights* (New York: Oxford University Press, 1992), 29; by Thomas L. Pangle, *The Spirit of Modern Republicanism: The Moral Vision of the American Founders and the Philosophy of Locke* (Chicago: University of Chicago Press, 1988), 97; and especially by Paul A. Rahe, *Republics Ancient and Modern: Classical Republicanism and the American Revolution* (Chapel Hill: University of North Carolina Press, 1992), 559–61.

certain regulations as to the modes and conditions of enjoying the secondary rights, or in other words, of holding property, are necessary"[29]
The "security of this right [to acquire]" is primary, but the "secondary"
right of possessing or "holding" property must also be protected. As
Charleston asked in 1774, "who would be industrious when others
would reap the fruit of his labor?" Government protects the possessions
of the rich in order to guarantee the right of the rich and poor alike to
acquire what they need "for their own convenience and happiness."

Is There a Conflict between Possession and Acquisition?

At the end of Chapter 1, I mentioned that natural rights can sometimes
conflict with each other. This can also be seen in the case of property
rights. If everyone has a right to acquire *and* to possess property, a conflict
between the haves and have-nots *in which both sides are right* will be
unavoidable in a condition of extreme scarcity. Unless the possessors
voluntarily choose to spread their wealth around, those who are starving
will have no way of getting what they need except by theft or violence.
One might argue that there is no conflict of rights here, because, as John
Locke writes, "it would always be a sin, in any man of estate, to let his
brother perish for want of affording him relief out of his plenty."[30] But
in this remark Locke supposes a state where some property owners have
"plenty." What happens when the possessors do not have "plenty," but
only barely enough to subsist? Then one party or the other must starve.
The non-owners will have a right to acquire, and the owners will have a
right to defend their possessions. It will be a war of all against all, where,
as Hobbes says of the state of nature, "one *by right* invades, and the other
by right resists."[31]

Some might wonder whether this is a problem that afflicts the modern
natural rights doctrine (such as that of the founders) because of its
supposedly selfish foundation. But the difficulty under consideration is
not unique to the moderns. The problem arises from reality itself. There
are multiple human goods. Sometimes one good can be obtained only at
the expense of another. The killing or torturing of an innocent person,

---

[29] Nathaniel Chipman, *Sketches of the Principles of Government*, 1793, in *Founders'
Constitution*, 1:557.

[30] Locke, *First Treatise*, §42.

[31] Thomas Hobbes, *De Cive* ("On the Citizen"), in *Opera Philosophica quae Latine Scrip-
sit*, ed. William Molesworth (London: Bohn, 1839), 2:166, ch. 1, §12 (my translation;
italics in the original).

or the destruction of his property, is forbidden by the natural law, but in time of war, an innocent person might have to suffer in order to save the community from destruction. In this case, the intention of the law of nature, which is to preserve life, will be partially unfulfilled. Leo Strauss argues that this is also a problem inherent in the Aristotelian approach: the usual rules of natural right may need to be violated in emergencies.[32]

This potential and sometimes actual conflict between natural rights was also acknowledged during the founding era. In his *Full Vindication*, Alexander Hamilton writes, "Self-preservation is the first principle of our nature. When our lives and properties are at stake, it would be foolish and unnatural to refrain from such measures as might preserve them, because they would be detrimental to others."[33] Hamilton is referring to the 1774 American embargo against British goods, which was harmful to British manufacturers excluded from the American market.

Jefferson addressed the potential tension between the right to acquire and the right to possess when he was American ambassador to France in the 1780s. He observed that there were vast tracts of land there left untouched "for the sake of game," that is, for the wealthy to use as hunting grounds. "Whenever there are in any country uncultivated lands and unemployed poor, it is clear that the laws of property have been so far extended as to violate natural right.... If for the encouragement of industry we allow [land] to be appropriated, we must take care that other employment be provided to those excluded from the appropriation. If we do not, the fundamental right to labor the earth returns to the unemployed."[34] The laws protecting property can "violate natural right" if they prevent the exercise of the primary right to acquire. That happened in France, Jefferson argues, because so few owners possessed so much property that they had no incentive to develop it. Consequently, the poor could not find enough opportunities to labor. Jefferson implies that the French poor had a right to seize the land of the wealthy by force, if there were no other way to acquire the property they needed to live.

---

[32] Leo Strauss, *Natural Right and History* (Chicago: University of Chicago Press, 1953), 160–61.

[33] Hamilton, *A Full Vindication of the Rights of Congress*, 1774, in *The Papers of Alexander Hamilton*, ed. Harold C. Syrett (New York: Columbia University Press, 1961–79), 1:51.

[34] Jefferson to Madison, October 28, 1785, in *Writings*, ed. Merrill D. Peterson (New York: Library of America, 1984), 841–2.

Could the founders' principles lead to the conclusion, then, that socialism or some other scheme of government redistribution of income could
be the most just economic order? Using government coercion to redistribute property certainly violates the natural right to *possess* property.
But what if this policy is the best way to enable everyone to exercise their
right to *acquire* it? Would that not be in greater conformity with natural
right than the starvation or deprivation of the poor?

That conclusion would follow only if there is no way to reconcile the
right to acquire and the right to possess. The founders' natural rights
principles therefore require the analysis of an empirical question: What
government policies most effectively enable owners to keep their property
while enabling everyone else to acquire property of their own? The answer
requires an understanding of how wealth is generated. Economics – the
study of what leads to a greater or lesser production of goods – thus
becomes an indispensable part of the practical application of natural law
and natural rights.

Someone might object that an analysis of the facts of economic production has nothing to do with the laws of nature. Does not this analysis
exceed, and therefore expose, the limits of the natural rights theory?
But this objection misunderstands the idea of natural right. The natural
rights theory provides only the basic principles of moral and political
order. It does not lead self-evidently to a complete legal code. Consider
the question of governmental structure. The founders' principles require
government by consent of the governed. They also require government to
secure the natural rights of the governed. But those two statements do not
tell us that government needs a legislative, executive, and judicial branch,
whether the legislative body should have two houses, how often elections
should take place, or what the duties and virtues of the executive should
be. Such things had to be decided by the practical wisdom of those
who wrote the state and federal constitutions. They are "inventions of
prudence," to use Madison's expression in *Federalist* 51. Yet without
these "inventions," the two governmental requirements of the founders'
natural rights argument – consent of the governed and security of
individual rights – cannot both be realized. The Constitution's particular
arrangement of offices is not required by the natural rights theory. Perhaps a parliamentary form would work just as well or even better. What
is indispensable, as *Federalist* 51 says, is that "you must first enable the
government to control the governed [i.e., to prevent them from violating
each other's natural rights]; and in the next place, oblige it to control

itself [so that it does not oppress them]."[35] Finding policies that reconcile the right to possess with the right to acquire property is no less necessary and no less difficult than inventing a structure of government that promotes security of rights on the basis of consent. That is what I will now explain.

Elements of Economic Theory in the Founding

In Jefferson's report on the proposed University of Virginia, one of its purposes was "by well-informed views of political economy to give a free scope to the public industry."[36] Nowhere in the writings or laws of the founders are the elements of their "political economy" set forth with clarity and completeness. We have to reconstruct their position by gathering into a coherent whole the relevant constitutional provisions, laws, and official reports, supplemented by remarks of individual founders when they help to explain these documents. Many of the founders' laws on this and other topics were inherited from colonial days. Without that foundation, it is unlikely that they would have been able to set up the requisite system. But the founders also changed those colonial laws in important ways, always with a view to making them conform more closely to the requirements of the natural rights theory – to "give a free scope to the public industry."

In this area, as in almost all areas of domestic policy, we will be looking mainly at the policies adopted and explained at the level of state government. As Madison writes in *Federalist* 45: "The powers reserved to the several States will extend to all the objects which, in the ordinary course of affairs, concern the lives, liberties, and properties of the people."[37] Still, we will also see that there was an important federal role in securing property rights.

The beginning of economic wisdom, for the founders as for all serious economists, is the need for labor. The uncultivated earth does not provide sufficient food, clothing, and shelter. Human beings must work for the things they need. But the real source of wealth is not mere labor, but intelligent labor. The division of labor among people who have the right

---

[35] Madison, *Federalist* 51, p. 319.
[36] Report of the Commissioners for the University of Virginia, August 4, 1818, in Jefferson, *Writings*, 460.
[37] Madison, *Federalist* 45, p. 289.

skills is what makes efficient and plentiful production possible. This was well known to the founders, of whom I quote Hamilton, Madison, and James Wilson.

Hamilton explicates this idea in his Report on Manufactures, written in his capacity as treasury secretary. He deploys two arguments. First, the division of labor enables each person to make the best use of his peculiar nature: "When all the different kinds of industry obtain in a community, each individual can find his proper element, and can call into activity the whole vigor of his nature." Second, Hamilton notes that the division of labor makes possible the "greater skill and dexterity naturally resulting from a constant and undivided application to a single object." This "has the effect of augmenting the productive powers of labor, and with them, the total mass of the produce or revenue of a country."[38] The more developed the division of labor is, and the more "natural" it is (suited to the experience, ability, and inclinations of each), the greater the fruits of their labor – to the benefit of all.

Madison shared Hamilton's appreciation for the division of labor: "we should find no advantage in saying, that every man should be obliged to furnish himself by his own labor with those accommodations which depend upon the mechanic arts, instead of employing his neighbor, who could do it for him on better terms. It would be of no advantage to the shoemaker to make his own clothes to save the expense of the tailor's bill, nor of the tailor to make his own shoes to save the expense of procuring them from the shoemaker. It would be better policy to suffer each to employ his talent in his own way."[39] Madison, like Hamilton, is explaining how specialization leads to greater production for all. Shoes and clothing are produced "on better terms" – the quality and quantity are greater – when each "employ[s] his talent" on that which he knows best. James Wilson agrees: "The full effects of industry cannot be obtained without distinct professions and the division of labor."[40]

But how best to encourage this division of labor? In this and the following chapters, we will see how far the founders were from the view that government's sole duty in regard to property is to get out of the way. The founders rejected the doctrines of both contemporary libertarians (who call for little or no government involvement) and contemporary liberals

---

[38] Hamilton, Report on Manufactures, 1791, in *Papers*, 10:255, 249.
[39] Madison, Speech of April 9, 1789, First Federal Congress, in *Founders' Constitution*, 2:442.
[40] Wilson, "On the History of Property," 1:306.

(who champion massive government involvement, including extensive redistribution of income). Government has an extensive set of responsibilities that it must fulfill in order to enable people to exercise their right to acquire and possess property. There are three main founding-era economic policy principles that enable sufficient production, for rich and poor alike, of the goods needed for life and the pursuit of happiness.

The first principle is private ownership. Government must define who owns what, allow property to be used as each owner deems best, encourage widespread ownership among citizens, and protect property against infringements by others, including unjust infringement by government itself.

Market freedom is the second principle. With a few exceptions, everyone must be free to sell anything to anyone at any time or place at any mutually agreeable price. Government must define and enforce contracts. Means of transportation must be available to all on the same terms.

The third principle is reliable money. To facilitate market transactions, there must be a medium of exchange whose value is reasonably constant and certain.

My treatment of the founders on property and economics deliberately avoids the question of where they got their economic ideas. I aim to describe the founders' consensus and to show that it was coherent and intelligent. Their basic approach is certainly more or less in agreement with the free market teachings of classical economists like John Locke and Adam Smith. But many other students of economics, ancient and modern, have shared their approach. Legal historian Adam Mossoff shows the broad agreement among political philosophers and legal writers, from Aristotle to Cicero to Locke and Blackstone, on the conception of property as the right to acquire, use, and dispose of a thing.[41] In book 2 of the *Republic*, Socrates outlines the features of a minimal political community, including the need for specialization of labor on the basis of expertise, private property, a free market, and money for a stable medium of exchange.[42] More recent economists often emphasize these same policies. Anders Aslund's study of the post-Soviet economies of Eastern Europe and Russia devotes separate chapters to "privatization" (private ownership), "liberalization" (freedom to acquire and trade), and "financial stability" (money with stable value). In a popular summary,

[41] Adam Mossoff, "What Is Property? Putting the Pieces Back Together," *Arizona Law Review* 45 (2003): 372–443.

[42] *The Republic of Plato*, trans. Allan Bloom (New York: Basic Books, 1968), 369b–372e.

William Röpke stresses the same three.[43] What is distinctive about the founders is not so much their shared understanding of how goods and services are best produced, but that they justified this understanding in terms of natural rights and then consciously shaped their laws to embody these basic insights.

[43] Anders Aslund, *How Capitalism Was Built: The Transformation of Central and Eastern Europe, Russia, and Central Asia* (New York: Cambridge University Press, 2007), ch. 4–6; William Röpke, "Free Economy and Social Order," *The Freeman*, January 11, 1954, http://mises.org/story/3715.

15

Private Ownership

To protect property rights, government must first establish the right to possess and use property. The following were the main features of founding-era policies on property and economics:

1. Government must define ownership.
2. Restrictions on the use of property must be few and must contribute to securing natural rights.
3. Government must promote widespread ownership.
4. Government must protect owners against damages to their property by fellow citizens or foreign nations.
5. Government must protect owners against harm to property by government itself.

Government Must Define Ownership

Government cannot protect the right to property unless it establishes clear legal rules determining who owns what. These legal procedures for designating ownership are so old that Americans today hardly notice them. In the founding, however, they were not always taken for granted. Pennsylvania's 1776 Constitution, for example, requires that "an office for the recording of deeds, shall be kept in each city and county."[1] Five other early state constitutions specifically mention the office of register or recorder of deeds.[2] All states have maintained such offices up to the present.

---

[1] PA Constitution, 1776, ch. 2, §34.
[2] NH, 1784; VT, 1777, §31; MA, 1780, ch. 6, §2; DE, 1776, art. 14. MD, 1776, art. 4 mentions "Recorder," presumably of deeds.

Today, all land in America is officially surveyed, and records of the surveys and owners are kept in one place in each county (or equivalent). In the early days of the republic, much of the nation was uncharted wilderness, occupied sporadically by Indians and settlers. An early federal law, the Land Ordinance of 1785, provided for the surveying and recording of land in the Northwest Territory so that ownership could be firmly established.[3] The Northwest Ordinance of 1787 required these property titles to be sustained in the transition from territory to statehood: "The legislatures of those districts or new States shall never interfere with the primary disposal of the soil by the United States in Congress assembled, nor with any regulations Congress may find necessary for securing the title in such soil to the bona fide purchasers."[4] Although it is true that this concern for establishing clear title does not appear in the federal Constitution, the Northwest Ordinance has quasi-constitutional status. It was intended to be, and became, the authoritative pattern by which future states were to be admitted. Along with the Declaration of Independence, Articles of Confederation, and U.S. Constitution, this ordinance was listed by Congress in 1878 as one of the four organic laws of the nation.[5]

The founders' general policy – to establish, as quickly as possible, unquestioned title to private ownership of land – was not always attained. In sparsely populated areas of the early American South, people often let their livestock run free without regard to land ownership.[6] On the frontier, land purchased by absentee owners was sometimes settled by squatters. In Maine, the presence of squatters led to government "withholding clear title for many years," thus hindering development.[7] The squatters often received titles to the land because they elected friendly state legislators who granted ownership to actual settlers rather than absentee owners. Few are aware that the 1823 Supreme Court case *Green v. Biddle* declared these state laws unconstitutional – a decision that was

[3] Ordinance for the Sale of Western Lands, May 20, 1785, in *The Documentary History of the Ratification of the Constitution*, ed. Merrill Jensen (Madison: State Historical Society of Wisconsin, 1976), 1:157–60.

[4] Northwest Ordinance, 1787, art. 4, in ibid., 173.

[5] Richard Cox, *Four Pillars of Constitutionalism: The Organic Laws of the United States* (Buffalo: Prometheus Books, 1998), 31–4.

[6] Forrest McDonald, *Novus Ordo Seclorum: The Intellectual Origins of the Constitution* (Lawrence: University Press of Kansas, 1985), 30–31.

[7] Oscar and Mary Handlin, *Commonwealth: A Study of the Role of Government in the American Economy: Massachusetts, 1774–1861*, rev. ed. (Cambridge: Belknap Press of Harvard University Press, 1969), 84–6.

widely ignored.[8] In spite of these early anomalies, American property law always aimed at, and usually provided, reliable records of ownership.

Economist Hernando de Soto argues that without knowledge of ownership, it is very difficult for wealth to be produced. A major reason that most of the world's nations are so poor is this absence of titles. Outside of Western nations, ownership is unclear for the great majority. De Soto writes, "Imagine a country where nobody can identify who owns what.... You have just put yourself into the life of a developing country or former communist nation; more precisely, you have imagined life for 80 percent of its population, which is marked off...sharply from its Westernized elite."[9] Another economist writes, "Despite decades of attempts to register land titles, during both the colonial and independence eras, today only about 1 percent of land in Africa is registered under the formal system."[10]

This point was well understood in the founding, as Zephaniah Swift's 1795 legal treatise testifies: "Every person has a clear title to the property he acquires.... In some of the most fertile countries of Asia and Africa, where the spontaneous productions of nature furnish the inhabitants with all the luxuries and elegancies of life, the despotism of government has rendered them completely wretched and miserable. The title to their property is dependent on the arbitrary will of the master, and all the wealth they can accumulate is perpetually exposed to be taken from them by the hands of the rapacious vultures that govern them. Under such a government, genius droops, industry languishes, woe and misery reign triumphant, and happiness is banished from the land."[11] Without clear title, markets cannot function efficiently. Economic production is discouraged. Buyers cannot count on being able to keep their purchased property. Banks will not make loans if property cannot be reliably used as collateral.

It is true, in a sense, that property in land belongs also to "the collective body of the people," and not only to private owners. North Carolina's 1776 Declaration of Rights makes that explicit: "The property of the soil,

---

[8] *Green v. Biddle*, 8 Wheaton 1 (1823), discussed in Hernando de Soto, *The Mystery of Capital: Why Capitalism Triumphs in the West and Fails Everywhere Else* (New York: Basic Books, 2000), 130–35.

[9] Ibid., 15.

[10] William Easterly, "Can the West Save Africa?" NBER Working Paper 14363, National Bureau of Economic Research, Sept. 2008, p. 94, http://www.nber.org/papers/w14363.

[11] Zephaniah Swift, *A System of the Laws of the State of Connecticut* (Windham, CT: John Byrne, 1795), 182–3.

in a free government, being one of the essential rights of the collective body of the people, it is necessary, in order to avoid future disputes [e.g., with South Carolina], that the limits of the State should be ascertained with precision."[12] This collective right of the people of the state over its land is not the same as full ownership, for neither the state nor federal government has a right to interfere arbitrarily with privately owned property (although it may certainly use its own property, such as courthouses and military bases, as it chooses). It simply means that when it comes to government regulation and protection of property, as well as exclusion of illegal immigrants or other invaders, it is necessary to establish the scope of the relevant political jurisdiction.

Presumption in Favor of Free Use and Early American Regulation

Clear title is only the first step. Second, government must give maximum leeway to the owner in the use of property. Since production depends on skilled labor, the owner should be the one who determines how the property is to be used. The owner alone – and no one else, especially not government officials claiming to be experts – is most likely to have either the necessary skill for using property productively or financial interest in hiring or renting to someone with skill. Jefferson writes, "Were we directed from Washington when to sow and when to reap, we should soon want bread." Madison elaborates: "if industry and labor are left to take their own course, they will generally be directed to those objects which are the most productive, and this in a more certain and direct manner than the wisdom of the most enlightened legislature could point out."[13]

Still, the founders did accept the need for some regulations to be placed on the use of property. They did not consider property to be an absolute right, although some scholars have contended they did. David Schultz writes, "in their political discourse they generally described property in absolutist terms.... [O]ur Founders in one breath were defending the absolutism of property while also supporting legal limits on property rights." Schultz also incorrectly attributes the "absolutist" view of property to Locke, who of course famously justifies taxation (government taking of private property) if approved by the people.[14]

---

[12] NC Declaration of Rights, art. 25.

[13] Jefferson, *Autobiography*, 1821, in *Founders' Constitution*, 1:297; Madison, Speech of April 9, 1789, in First Federal Congress, ibid., 2:442.

[14] David Schultz, "Political Theory and Legal History: Conflicting Depictions of Property in the American Founding," *American Journal of Legal History* 37 (1993): 491, 493;

John Witherspoon stated the general view: "Whatever is a person's property, he has a right to do with it as he pleases, with this single exception, . . . that he may not use it to the injury of others."[15] Zephaniah Swift agrees: "The original right to property is founded in the nature of things. It consists in the power of using and disposing of it, without control. But in a state of society, it became necessary, for the mutual convenience of mankind, that this natural right should be laid under certain restrictions and limitations. . . . Every man in the exercise of common reason is capable to acquire property, to use and improve it in such manner as he thinks fit, if he injures no other person, and to convey, transfer, and dispose of it as he pleases, in conformity to certain rules and regulations prescribed by law."[16] This limit on free use was later labeled one of government's "police powers," protecting "the peace, good order, morals, and health of the community."[17]

One may compare property rights to other natural rights such as freedom of the press or the right to keep and bear arms. Those freedoms too have limits. The Massachusetts Supreme Court explains: "The liberty of the press was to be unrestrained, but he who used it was to be responsible in case of its abuse; like the right to keep firearms, which does not protect him who uses them for annoyance or destruction."[18] Negligent use of property, for example of an automobile or a gun, can lead to fatal accidents.

Those whose negligent or malicious use of speech, firearms, or property led to their neighbors' harm could be sued or prosecuted. An example of an early regulation is an 1823 New York City law restricting the right to bury the dead in residential neighborhoods. The law was challenged in court by churches claiming abridgment of their right to free use. The city argued that cemeteries in heavily populated areas constitute a public nuisance because of the greater prevalence of disease around burial sites. The New York court agreed: the city has the "power so to order the use of private property in the city as to prevent its proving pernicious

---

John Locke, *Second Treatise*, §140, in *Two Treatises of Government*, 1690, ed. Peter Laslett (Cambridge: Cambridge University Press, 1960).

[15] John Witherspoon, *Lectures on Moral Philosophy*, 1772–94, in *The Selected Writings of John Witherspoon*, ed. Thomas Miller (Carbondale: Southern Illinois University Press, 1990), Lecture 10, 194.

[16] Swift, *A System*, 182.

[17] Justice Stephen Field's dissent, *Munn v. Illinois*, 94 U.S. 113 (1876), 145.

[18] Chief Justice Isaac Parker, opinion of the Massachusetts Supreme Court, *Commonwealth v. Blanding*, 20 Mass. 304, 314 (Mass. 1825), in *Founders' Constitution*, 5:177.

to the citizens generally.... [T]he suspension of the rights in question"
is justified because citizens' rights to free use of property "always are
[properly suspended] when one of their number is forbidden to continue
a nuisance."[19] Legal historian Eric Claeys explains: "According to the
law of nature, property may not be used in a manner that threatens
others' rights to health or safety.... [S]elf-preservation takes precedence
over the acquisition of property. Every owner benefits equally from a
moral command barring all her neighbors from using property to inflict
serious health or safety risks on their neighbors."[20]

Some scholars, such as William Novak, take the founders' approval
of property regulation as indicating that they did not follow the natural
rights doctrine at all. Novak criticizes as "mythology" the view that
"nineteenth-century political ideology . . . was quintessentially Lockean."
He denies that "early Americans clung to an absolutist faith in the private
legal mechanics of property and contract to carry out the necessary social
negotiations among otherwise isolated, autonomous individuals."[21]
But Novak's view of early American "Lockean" political ideology
is no less a caricature than David Schultz's, quoted earlier. Claeys
responds: "Novak sets out to prove that there was an 'overwhelming
presence of regulatory governance' in American life during the early
nineteenth century. The examples Novak gives, however, closely track
a conception of the police powers . . . [limited to regulation of] health
and safety, . . . public morals, . . . and laws regulating the use of public
commons [such as navigable waterways]."[22]

The presumption in favor of free use affected the development of state
property law. In the first few decades after the founding, writes Howard
Gillman, "property law was shifting away from its feudal preoccupation with safeguarding a person's undisturbed dominion over his land to
accommodate . . . the greater interest in efficient resource development."[23]
An 1818 New York case, *Platt v. Johnson*, illustrates Gillman's point. The
court ruled in favor of an upstream property owner whose dam, built to

---

[19] *Coates v. City of New York*, 7 Cow. 585 (N.Y. Sup. Ct. 1827), quoted in Eric R. Claeys,
   "Takings, Regulation, and Natural Property Rights," *Cornell Law Review* 88, No. 6
   (Sept. 2003): 1578.
[20] Ibid.
[21] William J. Novak, *The People's Welfare: Law and Regulation in Nineteenth-Century
   America* (Chapel Hill: University of North Carolina Press, 1996), 6.
[22] Claeys, "Takings," 1562–3, quoting ibid.
[23] Howard Gillman, *The Constitution Besieged: The Rise and Demise of Lochner Era
   Police Powers Jurisprudence* (Durham: Duke University Press, 1993), 49.

power a mill, occasionally interfered with the water flow downstream. Following the common law maxim *sic utere tuo ut alienum non laedas* ("use your own property such that it does not harm another"), the court stated that property rights "must be taken and construed with an eye to the natural rights of all."[24] The court was saying that law has to be interpreted in a way that enables everyone to use his own property as freely as possible, even if there is some interference with the property of another.[25] What Gillman calls "resource development" is what the court calls "natural rights," i.e., the right to acquire, which must be interpreted legally in such a way as to benefit as many owners as possible.

Novak is correct to say that legal limits on injurious use of property were common in the founding and after. But laws limiting use were subjected to scrutiny in state courts. "By mid-century," Claeys writes, "litigants and courts throughout the several states understood *Platt* as a precedent for the principle that a legislature unconstitutionally invaded private rights if a state law arbitrarily restrained the free use of private property."[26] The question asked was whether the legal restriction was reasonably related to the protection of the general public or whether it aimed at the benefit of a particular class or individual.

Property misuse was also controlled by laws limiting harm in ways other than physical injury. In his *Lectures on Law*, James Wilson writes that *nuisances* are "crimes and offenses which attack several of those natural rights [of individuals]. . . . To keep hogs in any city or market town is a common nuisance."[27] The general principle that one should be able to use one's property for any purpose must be limited by the principle that one should use it in such a way that it does not injure others. Vile odors can destroy the enjoyment of one's home no less than trespassing or arson.

As long as Americans continued to follow the founders' understanding of natural law – until about 1900 – the police power tended to be

---

[24] *Platt v. Johnson*, 15 Johns. 213, 218 (N.Y. 1818), quoted in Morton Horwitz, *The Transformation of American Law, 1780–1860* (Cambridge: Harvard University Press, 1977), 37.

[25] See also Joseph Postell, "Regulation, Administration, and the Rule of Law in the Early Republic," in *Freedom and the Rule of Law*, ed. Anthony A. Peacock (Lanham, MD: Lexington Books, 2010), 41–70; Postell, "Regulation during the American Founding: Achieving Liberalism and Republicanism," *American Political Thought* 5 (Winter 2016): 85–8 (examples of founding-era regulations).

[26] Claeys, "Takings," 1592.

[27] James Wilson, *Lectures on Law*, 1791, in *Collected Works of James Wilson*, ed. Kermit L. Hall and Mark David Hall (Indianapolis: Liberty Fund, 2007), 2:1157, 1159.

exercised compatibly with broad economic freedom. Legal historian Jeff Lewin writes, "In the early years of the twentieth century, legal positivism superseded natural rights as the dominant philosophy in American jurisprudence, particularly with respect to property rights." The legal community's Restatement of Torts in 1939 cut off nuisance law "from its natural rights origins, substituting a positivist right determined according to utilitarian criteria of cost and benefit." This approach treats government limitations on the right to use one's own property "as a pure question of policy," no longer as a possible violation of individual rights.[28] The political theory of early Progressivism, followed in this respect by post-1960s liberalism, made use of this new unbounded conception of state power to justify government encroachments on property rights – encroachments previously considered unjust.

Government Must Encourage Widespread Ownership

Besides defining property and allowing its free use, it also must encourage wide ownership. To prevent the emergence of a hereditary aristocracy of extreme wealth, and to provide the greatest opportunity for citizens to acquire property by their own efforts, government must make sure that the bulk of the nation's wealth, including land, is privately owned and in many hands. But because of the natural right to possess property, it must do so without taking property from current owners.

One such policy was reform of inheritance law. Entail limited the right of an owner to sell or divide his estate, and primogeniture favored the first-born son in inheritance. All states that had primogeniture and entail abolished them during the Revolution.[29] The Northwest Ordinance of 1787 also included an anti-entail provision.[30] Maryland's legislature stated in a 1786 law: "the law of descents, which originated with the feudal system and military tenures, is contrary to justice." Maryland property would henceforth be treated as legally owned "in fee-simple" and, if the owner dies intestate (without making a will), it would descend

---

[28] Jeff L. Lewin, "*Boomer* and the American Law of Nuisance: Past, Present, and Future," *Albany Law Review* 54 (1990): 210. See also Robert G. Bone, "Normative Theory and Legal Doctrine in American Nuisance Law: 1850 to 1920," *Southern California Law Review* 59 (1986): 1224.

[29] Gordon S. Wood, *The Radicalism of the American Revolution* (New York: Knopf, 1992), 183. Examples: PA Constitution, 1776, §37; NC, 1776, §43; VT, 1777, §34. GA, 1777, art. 51.

[30] Northwest Ordinance, 1787, §2, in *Founders' Constitution*, 1:27.

"to the kindred, male and female,... first to the children and their descendants."[31]

Primogeniture and entail are "contrary to justice" for two reasons. The first may be seen in a 1784 North Carolina law: "it will tend to promote that equality of property, which is of the spirit and principle of a genuine republic, that the real estates of persons dying intestate should undergo a more general and equal distribution than has hitherto prevailed in this state.... [E]ntails of estates tend only to raise the wealth and importance of particular families and individuals, giving them an unequal and undue influence in a republic, and prove in manifold instances the source of great contention and injustice."[32] Historian Stanley Katz quotes the same argument from a 1794 Delaware statute: "it is the duty and policy of every republican government to preserve equality amongst its citizens, by maintaining the balance of property as far as it is consistent with the rights of individuals."[33] Jefferson makes the same point in his *Autobiography*: "The transmission of this property from generation to generation in the same name raised up a distinct set of families who, being privileged in the law in the perpetuation of their wealth, were thus formed into a Patrician order." Jefferson continues: "To annul this privilege... was deemed essential to a well ordered republic."[34] (On this topic, Holly Brewer refutes the erroneous view of some historians by demonstrating that "Jefferson was right when he claimed that abolishing entail and primogeniture undercut aristocracy in Virginia.... [M]ost of Virginia's real estate was entailed by the time of the Revolution, not only in the tidewater but also in the piedmont and even along the frontier."[35])

Jefferson's observations in France, quoted in the previous chapter, show that the absence of wide ownership "violate[s] natural right" for a second reason: property was "concentered in a very few hands," with the consequence that "the enormous wealth of the proprietors... places them above attention to the increase of their revenues by permitting these

---

[31] An Act to Direct Descents, January 20, 1786, *Laws of Maryland, 1785–1791*, Maryland State Archives, 204:184, http://aomol.msa.maryland.gov.

[32] An Act... To Do Away Entails," 1784, in *Laws of the State of North Carolina*, ed. Henry Potter (Raleigh: J. Gales, 1821), 465, 467.

[33] Stanley N. Katz, "Republicanism and the Law of Inheritance in the American Revolutionary Era," *Michigan Law Review* 76, No. 1 (Nov. 1977): 14.

[34] *Autobiography*, in Jefferson, *Writings*, 32.

[35] Holly Brewer, "Entailing Aristocracy in Colonial Virginia: 'Ancient Feudal Restraints' and Revolutionary Reform," *William and Mary Quarterly* 54, No. 2 (Apr. 1997): 311, 323.

lands to be labored."[36] Poor people consequently had fewer opportunities to acquire property by farming.

The founders were careful not to adopt any policy that would intrude on the property rights of existing owners. There would be no "land reform" (forcible redistribution of property). Instead, as we have seen, the solution adopted everywhere was to divide property equally among the children of the landowner, unless the owner had made a will to the contrary. As Jefferson writes, "no violence was necessary, no deprivation of natural right, but rather an enlargement of it by a repeal of the law. For this would authorize the present holder to divide the property among his children equally, as his affections were divided; and would place them, by natural generation, on the level of their fellow citizens."[37]

Under colonial law, other legal limits on the use of property could be imposed by previous owners. Some of these are still found in property law today, such as bequests or trusts that must be used indefinitely for a purpose designated by a dead donor. In the founding, any such limit on future property use was inherently suspect, as North Carolina's Bill of Rights states: "perpetuities and monopolies are contrary to the genius of a free State, and ought not to be allowed."[38]

A second instance of early American interest in broadening the right to ownership can be seen in the development of corporation law. Oscar and Mary Handlin write that incorporation was a "privilege originally conceived as selective and exclusive." At first, therefore, corporations were chartered through individual acts of state legislatures. But that meant people with political connections were most likely to be able to form such companies. So in the 1790s and early 1800s, "democratic unwillingness to confine the corporation to a favored few had dispersed it among many holders" in Massachusetts.[39] Beginning with New York in 1811, states passed general incorporation laws, which opened to every citizen, however poor, the legal right to incorporate under equal conditions.[40]

---

[36] Jefferson to James Madison, October 28, 1785, in *Writings*, 841–2 (my emphasis).

[37] *Autobiography*, in Jefferson, *Writings*, 32–3.

[38] NC Bill of Rights, 1776, §23. See also Jefferson to Madison, September 6, 1789, in ibid., 963–4 (critique of perpetuities).

[39] Handlin, *Commonwealth*, 133, 161.

[40] L. Ray Gunn, *The Decline of Authority: Public Economic Policy and Political Development in New York, 1800–1860* (Ithaca: Cornell University Press, 1988), 226; Gordon S. Wood, *The Radicalism of the American Revolution* (New York: Knopf, 1992), 321. An excellent treatment of the emerging law of corporations and other private associations and its connection to founding principles is Kevin Butterfield, *The Making*

We see the same concern for wide ownership in a third area, land policy. After the treaty of 1783, which ended the Revolutionary War, the federal government held vast tracts of land. The Land Ordinance of 1785, mentioned earlier in connection with property titles, set the pattern for the next century. A substantial number of lots small enough for individuals to buy were made available, and almost all the land was designated for future private ownership.[41] From the founding to about 1900, "the most significant aspect of federal land policy was the creation and nurturing of a great land market through which the public domain passed into private ownership."[42]

Since 1900, this earlier presumption in favor of private ownership has been reversed. Private owners came to be viewed with growing suspicion as threats to the environment or exploiters of the poor. For Theodore Roosevelt, "the national government must bear a most important part" in the management of public lands because otherwise our "natural resources" will be "monopolized for the benefit of the few."[43] Government agencies tasked with land management were presumed to know better than individuals or corporations how land should be used. One consequence is that in the Western states, which were settled last, the federal government owns about 50 percent of the land. In the Northeast, settled earliest, federal land amounts to only 3 percent.[44]

of Tocqueville's America: Law and Association in the Early United States (Chicago: University of Chicago Press, 2015).

[41] Ordinance for the Sale of Western Lands, May 20, 1785, in *Documentary History of the Ratification*, 1:156–63.

[42] Sidney Ratner, James H. Soltow, and Richard Sylla, *The Evolution of the American Economy: Growth, Welfare, and Decision Making* (New York: Basic Books, 1979), 137. Additional sources: Farley Grubb, "U.S. Land Policy: Founding Choices and Outcomes, 1781–1802," in *Founding Choices: American Economic Policy in the 1790s*, ed. Douglas A. Irwin and Richard Sylla (Chicago: University of Chicago Press, 2011), 259–87; Payson Jackson Treat, *The National Land System, 1785–1820* (New York: E. B. Treat & Co., 1910); Benjamin H. Hibbard, *A History of the Public Land Policies* (New York: Macmillan, 1924); Jeremy Atack et al., "Northern Agriculture and the Westward Movement," in *The Cambridge Economic History of the United States*, vol. 2: *The Long Nineteenth Century*, ed. Stanley L. Engerman and Robert E. Gallman (Cambridge: Cambridge University Press, 2000), 285–328.

[43] Theodore Roosevelt, "The New Nationalism," 1910, in *American Progressivism: A Reader*, ed. Ronald J. Pestritto and William J. Atto (Lanham, MD: Lexington Books, 2008), 219.

[44] U.S. Bureau of the Census, *Statistical Abstract of the United States: 1997* (Washington: Government Printing Office, 1997), Table 369 (Total Federally Owned Land), 228; Niraj Chokshi, "More Than Half the West Is Federally Owned," *Washington Post*, http://washingtonpost.com, October 15, 2013.

Protection of Property through Criminal and Civil Law

Protection of property against theft and violence is the fourth condition of property ownership. As we saw in Chapter 7, without a strong national defense and effective criminal law, none of the other measures discussed in this and the next two chapters will suffice. Government secures natural rights against foreign violence by maintaining strong armed forces and using them against those who would subordinate the nation to their will. It protects rights against domestic violence by the criminal laws (providing for government prosecutions) and civil laws (providing for private lawsuits). Massachusetts' Declaration of Rights explains: "Each individual of the society has a right to be protected by it in the enjoyment of his life, liberty and property, according to standing laws." This provision refers to criminal law against serious harm to person or property. Another provision refers to the right to sue for recovery of damages to property: "Every subject of the Commonwealth ought to find a certain remedy, by having recourse to the laws, for all injuries or wrongs which he may receive in his person, property, or character."[45] These two principles, while not always made explicit as in Massachusetts, animated the criminal and civil laws of every state.

Protection of Property Owners against Government Itself

Fifth and finally, government itself must be limited if private property is to be secure. Government is a potential source of danger to property rights because in order to punish criminals and protect the nation against foreign enemies, it must necessarily have extensive powers. Those powers can be abused. Government officials, no less than private persons, can infringe the rights of individuals. They can deprive citizens of property just as effectively as "wicked and dissolute" – to use Jefferson's phrase – fellow citizens or foreign nations.

The founders' remedy to the problem of government abuse is in most cases to allow government to take property only by laws formally enacted, so as to ensure that takings are not based on arbitrary edicts of government officials. There are four kinds of laws by which government can legitimately take property: criminal and civil laws intended to punish or compensate actions that injure others, taxation, eminent domain (takings of private property for public use), and regulatory takings (limits on

---

[45] MA Declaration of Rights, 1780, art. 10 and 11. See also Chapter 7 of this book.

property use to prevent injury to public health, safety, or morals). We will discuss each in turn.

Due Process of Law

Early state constitutions often included "due process" or "law of the land" clauses, as well as various safeguards for person and property, such as the right of habeas corpus and trial procedures designed to protect the innocent. For example, the Pennsylvania Declaration of Rights says: "That in all prosecutions for criminal offences, a man hath a right to be heard by himself and his counsel, to demand the cause and nature of his accusation, to be confronted with the witnesses, to call for evidence in his favor, and a speedy public trial, by an impartial jury of the country, without the unanimous consent of which jury he cannot be found guilty; nor can he be compelled to give evidence against himself; nor can any man be justly deprived of his liberty except by the laws of the land, or the judgment of his peers."[46]

Today, government is given a wide leeway to seize property without having to prove in court that a law has been violated. The Internal Revenue Service, for example, routinely freezes the bank accounts of people who are only suspected of violating the tax laws, or, in some cases, merely to put pressure on them to reveal information about other people's tax violations. Drug laws allow government officials to seize cars and money, without first having to put their owners on trial.[47]

Complementing its due process clause in the Fifth Amendment, the U.S. Constitution also banned bills of attainder. St. George Tucker, an early American legal writer, explains: "Bills of Attainder are legislative acts passed for the special purpose of attainting particular individuals of treason, or felony.... They are state-engines of oppression.... [They are] a legislative declaration of the guilt of the party, without trial, without a hearing, and often without the examination of witnesses, and subjecting...his estate to confiscation."[48] Several states had passed attainders against British loyalists during the Revolution when passions were high.

---

[46] PA Declaration of Rights, 1776, §9. The constitutions of seven other states included "due process" or "law of the land" clauses: See the Declarations of Rights of MD, 1776, art. 21; PA, 1776, art. 9; NC, 1776, art. 12; MA, 1780, art. 12; NH, 1784, art. 15. Also in the SC Constitution, 1776, art. 41; and DE, 1792, art. 1, §7.

[47] E.g., *United States v. $124,700 in U.S. Currency*, 8th Cir. 2006; Leonard W. Levy, *A License to Steal: The Forfeiture of Property* (Chapel Hill: University of North Carolina Press, 1996).

[48] St. George Tucker, *Blackstone's Commentaries*, 1803, in *Founders' Constitution*, 3:348.

The prohibition of attainders meant that government could seize private property as a punishment only after judicial trial.

Taxation

Government may also intrude on private property by levying taxes. The founders thought of holding political office as "public service"[49] because it provides a service to the people by securing their natural rights. It must therefore be viewed in the same light as any other "producer" who asks for compensation for providing something of value to the consumer. Government in this light may be viewed as a hired hand who is serving his "employer," the people. In its 1772 Rights of the Colonists, the town of Boston makes that analogy explicit: "In the state of nature men may, as the patriarchs did, employ hired servants for the defense of their lives, liberty and property: and they should pay them reasonable wages. Government was instituted for the purposes of common defense; and those who hold the reins of government have an equitable natural right to an honorable support from the same principle 'that the laborer is worthy of his hire'; but then the same community which they serve, ought to be assessors of their pay."[50] A government dedicated to securing natural rights must be strong and energetic in its appointed sphere, but it must not exceed that sphere.

But how should taxes be apportioned? There are two dangers to be avoided: first, taxes should be no higher than needed for government to perform its essential tasks. Pennsylvania's 1776 constitution states the principle: "before any law be made for raising it, the purpose for which any tax is to be raised, ought to appear clearly to the legislature to be of more service to the community than the money would be, if not collected, which being well observed, taxes can never be burdens."[51] In this statement, the burden of proof is on government when it wants to raise taxes. The presumption is that property is "of more service to the community" when owned and used privately.

The second danger is that taxes may be imposed unfairly. Madison writes, "A just security to property is not afforded by that government, under which unequal taxes oppress one species of property and reward another species: where arbitrary taxes invade the domestic sanctuaries of

---

[49] James Madison to Henry Lee, November 23, 1786, in *The Papers of James Madison*, ed. Robert A. Rutland et al. (Chicago: University of Chicago Press, 1975), 9:176.

[50] Boston, Rights of the Colonists, 1772, in *The Writings of Samuel Adams*, ed. Harry A. Cushing (1904–08; repr. New York: Octagon Books, 1968), 2:354.

[51] PA Constitution, 1776, §41, repeated in VT 1777, §37 (also VT 1786 and 1793).

the rich, and excessive taxes grind the faces of the poor."[52] In agreement
with Madison, the Massachusetts Bill of Rights states that "each individual...is obliged...to contribute his share to the expense of this protection," i.e., government's protection of "the enjoyment of his life, liberty
and property."[53] But Massachusetts prohibits "particular and exclusive
privileges," and that would mean that no class of people may be exempted
from paying "his share."

The practical question, which much vexed politicians of the founding
era, is what taxes are "unequal" and "excessive," and what is the individual's fair "share"? One meaning of "equal" is for every man to pay
the same amount. This was the poll tax, which "required all adult white
men to pay the same amount regardless of their wealth or income."[54] In
the early republic, poll taxes were a significant source of revenue in many
states, especially in New England. The constitutions of Massachusetts
and New Hampshire both mandated poll taxes.[55]

But these taxes were especially burdensome to the poor. Maryland's
1776 constitution denounced this kind of taxation: "levying taxes by
the poll is grievous and oppressive, and ought to be abolished;...[but
everyone] ought to contribute his proportion of public taxes, for the support of government, according to his actual worth, in real or personal
property."[56] Maryland's preferred tax, the ad valorem property tax, was
assessed in proportion to the value of one's property. It became the major
source of revenue in most states.[57] It satisfied the general sense, as the New
York Assembly stated in 1779, that taxation should be according to the
"ability of each respective person to pay taxes collectively considered."[58]
In addition to the poll tax, the constitutions of Massachusetts and New
Hampshire provided for taxes to be "assessed on...estates...; in order
that such assessments may be made with equality, there shall be a val-
uation of estates within the Commonwealth taken anew once in every

---

52 Madison, "Property," March 29, 1792, in *Founders' Constitution*, 1:598.
53 MA Declaration of Rights, 1780, art. 10. Similar taxation provisions are in the Declaration of Rights of PA, 1776, art. 8; MD, 1776, art. 13; VT, 1777, art. 9; NH, 1792,
   art. 12.
54 Robert A. Becker, *Revolution, Reform, and the Politics of American Taxation, 1763–
   1783* (Baton Rouge: Louisiana State University Press, 1980), 6.
55 MA, 1780, ch. 1, §1, art. 4; NH, 1784.
56 MD, Declaration of Rights, 1776, art. 13. Echoed in OH Bill of Rights, 1803, art. 8,
   §23.
57 Becker, *Revolution*, 193, 200, 210 (NC, VA, and SC adopted ad valorem property tax
   in place of poll tax).
58 Ibid., 113–218, tells the story state by state. The NY quotation is on 159.

ten years at least." In this passage, "equality" means proportioned to the taxpayer's ability to pay.[59]

Some states also imposed a rudimentary income tax (called a "faculty tax") on those who owned little or no physical property. Robert Becker explains: "faculty taxes... ('faculty' meaning a man's skill or ability) [were] a way of taxing non-farmers. Connecticut assessors [in the 1770s], for example, estimated the annual 'gains and returns' of craftsmen and tavern keepers as best they could. Massachusetts' faculty tax was the most extensive. It taxed 'the incomes or profits which any person or persons... do or shall receive from any trade, faculty, business, or employment whatsoever, and all profits which shall or may arise by money or commissions of profit, in their improvement.'"[60] However, faculty taxes were never a major revenue source.[61] Although higher tax rates on the wealthy were occasionally proposed in several states, this kind of redistributive tax policy made little headway in the founding era and long afterwards.

As for the federal government, it relied almost entirely on tariffs until about 1914. The Constitution does permit a federal "capitation" tax (poll tax), but Congress has never levied one.[62] In 1791 Congress instituted an "excise tax" – a sales tax – on liquor, but it occasioned widespread resistance (the "Whiskey Rebellion") and was repealed when Jefferson became president in 1801.[63]

Government Takings of Private Property

Government sometimes takes property from private owners (a practice known as *eminent domain*) for roads, canals, forts, public parks, public buildings, and the like. Vermont's 1777 Declaration of Rights states, "private property ought to be subservient to public uses, when necessity requires it; nevertheless, whenever any particular man's property is taken for the use of the public, the owner ought to receive an equivalent in money."[64] Four other early state constitutions, the federal Northwest

---

[59] Constitutions of MA, 1780, ch. 1, §1, art. 4; NH, 1784 and 1792.

[60] MA, PA, CT, and DE laws imposing faculty taxes are quoted in *Maryland v. Wynne*, 575 U.S. ___ (2015), note 1.

[61] Becker, *Revolution*, 11.   [62] U.S. Constitution, art. 1, §9.

[63] Stanley Elkins and Eric McKitrick, *The Age of Federalism* (New York: Oxford University Press, 1993), 462.

[64] VT, Declaration of Rights, 1777, art. 2. Colonial practice is described by Forrest McDonald, *Novus Ordo Seclorum*, 22–4.

Ordinance, and the Fifth Amendment of the U.S. Constitution had similar compensation clauses.[65] These provisions for "reasonable" or "just" compensation were meant to remedy colonial practices under which governments would seize private lands for roads without payment to the owners.

James Ely suggests that Vermont's takings clause reveals an inconsistency in the founding. Ely believes there is a conflict between "republican theory" (concerned with the public good) and property rights (concerned with private rights). In support of this claim, Ely quotes only the first part of Vermont's clause (up to "when necessity requires it") and omits the requirement that the owner receive "an equivalent in money." With this crucial addition, Vermont recognizes that although government must have the right to take property for public use, the individual owner's property right must be acknowledged by monetary compensation.[66] For the founders, there was no conflict between "republican theory" and individual rights because republican theory as they understood it was based on the principle that government's purpose is "to secure these rights" on the basis of consent of the governed.

Vermont mentions three limitations on government takings. First, it must be for "the use of the public," meaning that it cannot be for private use. Second, property may be taken only "when necessity requires it": it must be needed to secure the natural rights of all. To that end, public use of some people's property will sometimes be required. The Northwest Ordinance defines the "necessity" in question explicitly in terms of the natural right to life: the taking must be "for the common preservation." The third limit is that "the owner ought to receive an equivalent in money."

In the early republic, "public use" was limited to things the general public or the government would actually use. There must be a connection to security of natural rights: military bases are needed for the armed forces that deter foreign aggression; courthouses and prisons are places where those who violate the rights of others are judged and punished; roads facilitate travel and commerce. Public parks can be justified as a legitimate "public use," but that is a harder case because parks for

---

[65] MA Declaration of Rights, 1780, art. 10; PA Constitution, 1790, art. 9, §10; DE Constitution, 1792, art. 1, §8; TN, 1796, art. 11, §21; Northwest Ordinance, art. 2, in *Founders' Constitution*, 1:28.

[66] James W. Ely, *The Guardian of Every Other Right: A Constitutional History of Property Rights* (New York: Oxford University Press, 1992), 33.

recreation have no clear connection to security of natural rights. That may explain why hardly any public parks existed in America until the 1880s,[67] when the founders' political theory was beginning to be widely questioned.

In the founding era and afterwards, it was generally considered a violation of both natural and constitutional right for government to take property from one private owner and give it to another.[68] Supreme Court Justice William Paterson states in a 1795 case: "The constitution [of Pennsylvania] expressly declares that the right of acquiring, possessing and protecting property is natural, inherent, and inalienable.... Where is the security, where the inviolability of property, if the legislature, by a private act, affecting particular persons only, can take land from one citizen, who acquired it legally, and vest it in another?"[69] In this case, although the Pennsylvania Constitution lacked an explicit takings clause, the court ruled unconstitutional a transfer of property from one private party to another. According to Claeys, this was common in state courts prior to the Civil War: "courts sometimes treated takings and due process guarantees interchangeably," he writes. "Before the 1840s, state courts sometimes relied on the Contracts Clause, on the theory that states could not use their police powers to strip owners of the substance of property rights."[70]

By contrast, in contemporary American law, government often takes private property for use by a different private owner that government officials prefer for economic development, improvement of a neighborhood's appearance, or increasing the local tax base. In 2005, the U.S. Supreme Court approved a plan of the city of New London, Connecticut, to take the home of Susette Kelo and transfer ownership to a private company.[71] Historian Leonard Levy observes that in 1984, the Supreme Court "unanimously held that the state could do the very thing that

---

[67] Ney C. Landrum, *The State Park Movement in America: A Critical Review* (Columbia: University of Missouri Press, 2004), 29–30.

[68] Claeys, "Takings," 1575.

[69] *Vanhorne's Lessee v. Dorrance*, 2 Dall. 304, Circuit Court, District of PA, 1795, in *Founders' Constitution*, 1:599–600.

[70] Claeys, "Takings," 1575.

[71] *Kelo v. New London*, 545 U.S. 469 (2005); James W. Ely, Jr., "'Poor Relation' Once More: The Supreme Court and the Vanishing Rights of Property Owners," in *Cato Supreme Court Review, 2004–2005*, ed. Mark Moller (Washington: Cato Institute, 2005), 39–69 (the Supreme Court's abandonment of the earlier understanding of takings over the past century).

Justice Paterson had said it could not do – take property from one citizen, even at a just compensation, and give it to another at that price."[72]

It is true that "at the time of the founding," as Justice Clarence Thomas writes in his *Kelo* dissent, "many States . . . authorized the owners of grist mills operated by water power to flood upstream lands with the payment of compensation to the upstream landowner. Those early grist mills 'were regulated by law and compelled to serve the public for a stipulated toll and in regular order,' and therefore . . . the public could legally use and benefit from them equally."[73] In these limited circumstances, the founders' principles would allow for transfer of private property from one owner to another. Modern examples of this kind of taking would be using eminent domain to enable the building of a privately owned freeway or an oil pipeline.

Limits on "Regulatory Takings"

Government regulations that limit the free use of property but do not actually take the ownership title away are known as "regulatory takings." These are common in our time, especially in environmental policy. These takings are generally not compensated. Confirming the constitutionality of this practice in 2002, the U.S. Supreme Court approved a multiyear government ban on construction of homes on Lake Tahoe lots that had been previously zoned and approved for residential housing.[74]

The founders favored environmental regulations, but they insisted that they have a real connection to the protection of free use of property. Polluting the air with unusual amounts of smoke or loud noise causes actual harm to other people's innocent enjoyment of their own property. That sort of thing used to be dealt with legally by means of private nuisance lawsuits. The founders would have had two objections to the Lake Tahoe regulation. First, the ban on new housing was not related to public health, safety, or morals. Second, there was no "public use" at stake, so even if the regulatory taking had been compensated (which it was not), it would still have been an injustice. For the founders, ownership of property was not some sort of arbitrary "bundle" of rights changeable

---

[72] Leonard W. Levy, *Seasoned Judgments: The American Constitution, Rights, and History* (New Brunswick, NJ: Transaction, 1995), 23, referring to *Hawaii Housing Authority v. Midkiff*, 467 U.S. 229 (1984).

[73] Dissent of Clarence Thomas, *Kelo v. New London*.

[74] *Tahoe-Sierra Preservation Council v. Tahoe Regional Planning Agency*, 535 U.S. 302 (2002).

at whim by government, but involved full control of its use, limited only by rules to protect others in the free use of their property.[75]

Zephaniah Swift again states the founders' consensus: All have "an indisputable right to do every act which they please, in the pursuit of their own happiness, that does not contravene the moral law, nor injure any of their fellow creatures.... The original right to property...consists in the power of using and disposing of it, without control." The limits to this right can be clearly stated: "in a state of society, it became necessary, for the mutual convenience of mankind, that this natural right should be laid under certain restrictions and limitations" in order to prevent injury and to sustain the moral law. No other restrictions on property are compatible with natural right.[76]

Property in Slaves as a Denial of Slaves' Property Rights

The states did a tolerably successful job of protecting property rights in the decades following the founding. There was one great and nearly fatal exception: slavery, which was a total denial of property rights for a large portion of the population. Jefferson's rough draft of the Declaration of Independence says that selling free persons into slavery violates their "sacred rights of life and liberty." Madison called American slavery "the most oppressive dominion ever exercised by man over man."[77] Although these quotations do not address property rights explicitly, the right to liberty includes the freedom to use one's own faculties to produce things for oneself or for the market, as shown earlier. Political theorist John Wettergreen writes, "there is nothing more contrary to the rules of commerce than slave-commerce" because the slave is not free to engage in commerce.[78] The contradiction between slavery and the natural right to property was recognized by Chief Justice John Marshall, a Virginian, in an 1825 Supreme Court case: "That [slavery] is contrary to the law of

---

[75] Claeys, "Takings" (an analysis of regulatory takings in light of the founders' approach). On the "bundle" theory of property, widely accepted today, see Eric Claeys, "Property 101: Is Property a Thing or a Bundle?" *Seattle University Law Review* 32, No. 3 (Spring 2009): 617–50.

[76] Swift, *A System*, 10, 182.

[77] Jefferson, rough draft of the Declaration, in *Writings*, 22. Madison, speech of June 7, in *The Records of the Federal Convention of 1787*, ed. Max Farrand (New Haven: Yale University Press, 1937), 1:135.

[78] John Adams Wettergreen, "Capitalism, Socialism, and Constitutionalism," in *To Secure the Blessings of Liberty: First Principles of the Constitution*, ed. Sarah Baumgartner Thurow (Lanham, MD: University Press of America, 1988), 258.

nature will scarcely be denied. That every man has a natural right to the fruits of his own labor is generally admitted; and that no other person can rightfully deprive him of those fruits, and appropriate them against his will, seems to be the necessary result of this admission."[79]

The Fourteenth Amendment extended federal protection to the main legal rights of a state's own citizens. This amendment was passed after the Civil War to counter the Southern states' policy of refusing to protect basic civil rights of former slaves, including property rights.

I conclude that the founders held protecting private ownership to be a necessary component of securing natural rights. Policy and judicial decisions at both the state and federal level support this conclusion. The next two chapters will show that the founders also adopted policies on market freedom and money that complement their policies on owning and using property.

[79] *The Antelope*, 10 Wheat. 66 (1825), in *Founders' Constitution*, 3:304.

16

Free Markets

The founders' understanding of property rights includes the rights not only of owners but also of non-owners – or rather, future owners. The natural right to liberty includes a right to possess, but more fundamentally, also a right to acquire property. The previous chapter concerned the right to possess and use property. But that is only one part of government's role. What about those who own little more than their own bodies and minds, such as young adults when they set out on their own? They too must have a chance to acquire and own property. That can be done only if they are free to buy and sell property, even if the "property" they sell is nothing more than the temporary use of their talents in exchange for wages. To protect the natural right to acquire and possess, government must permit and protect the free exchange of goods and services. The founders all held the freedom to trade to be a natural right. Occasionally they named it as such, as Jefferson did in his *Summary View*: "the exercise of a free trade with all parts of the world [is] possessed by the American colonists as of natural right."[1] Freedom of trade is a natural right of individuals in the state of nature, and through the social compact, this right carries over into civil society collectively in its dealings with other nations. (Of course freedom to trade is also freedom not to trade, so trade policy has always been a part of American foreign policy.) "Life, liberty, property, *and the disposal of that property* with our own consent, are natural rights," asserts the Massachusetts Council in

[1] Thomas Jefferson, *A Summary View of the Rights of British America*, 1774, in *Writings*, ed. Merrill D. Peterson (New York: Library of America, 1984), 108.

1773.[2] In his description of America written for potential immigrants, Benjamin Franklin writes, "there [are] no restraints preventing strangers from exercising any art they understand, nor any permission necessary."[3]

In Chapter 14, I mentioned the need for division of labor because labor is most skillfully employed when applied to tasks that fit the experience, talents, and inclinations of the laborers. "But labor cannot be divided," writes founder James Wilson, "nor can distinct professions be pursued, unless the productions of one profession and of one kind of labor can be exchanged for those of another."[4] To this end, the laws must permit and protect markets. James Madison sets forth the basic rationale in the same way: "I own myself the friend to a very free system of commerce.... [The shoemaker and the tailor are] each capable of making particular articles in sufficient abundance to supply the other – thus all are benefitted by exchange, and the less this exchange is cramped by government, the greater are the proportions of benefit to each."[5]

For the founders, free markets were secured by three main policies, which were affirmed in state and federal constitutions and in other important documents.

First, at least in general, everyone must be allowed to sell anything to anyone at any price. No one may be excluded from buying or selling in any market, with few exceptions. Entry must be open to all on the same basis and with minimal government-created obstacles or expense.

Second, contracts must be permitted. Government must define what constitutes a legal contract, and there must be easy access to courts for enforcement. Neither government nor private persons may interfere with contracts once they are agreed to. The only exception would be contracts injurious to life, liberty, property, or the moral conditions of freedom.

Third, government must make sure that everyone enjoys access to the means of transportation and travel on the same terms as everyone else. If a river or highway is available to the boats or trucks of some citizens, it must be made available to the use of others on the same terms.

[2] Answer of the Council of Massachusetts to Governor Thomas Hutchinson, 1773, in *The Briefs of the American Revolution*, ed. John P. Reid (New York: New York University Press, 1981), 35 (my emphasis).

[3] Benjamin Franklin, "Information to Those Who Would Remove to America," 1784, in *Writings*, ed. J. A. Leo Lemay (New York: Library of America, 1987), 978–9.

[4] James Wilson, "On the History of Property," in *Collected Works of James Wilson*, ed. Kermit L. Hall and Mark David Hall (Indianapolis: Liberty Fund, 2007), 1:306.

[5] Madison, speech of April 9, 1789, in First Federal Congress, in *The Founders' Constitution*, ed. Philip B. Kurland and Ralph Lerner (Chicago: University of Chicago Press, 1987), 2:442.

Freedom to Buy and Sell

The founders adopted several kinds of policies to ensure the maximum freedom of commerce that was consistent with securing the equal rights of all. Madison asserts that "the less [commerce] is cramped by government," the greater the "benefit to each." Government cramps commerce whenever it interferes with free exchanges of property between consenting parties. Exceptions to protect public health, safety, or morals are acceptable, such as Pennsylvania's 1787 law establishing minimal safety conditions for chimney sweepers[6] or laws banning murder-for-hire and prostitution. In all other respects, the whole nation must be a free-trade area. Broad freedom to buy and sell must be open to all.

Prohibition of Monopolies

Monopolies are one limitation on the right to buy and sell. Today a monopoly is often understood as a private company that dominates a particular market, such as Microsoft in computer software in the early 2000s. The New York ratifying convention of 1788 defined monopoly as a government grant of "exclusive advantages of commerce" to particular persons.[7] The term monopoly was occasionally used in our sense, but the monopolies prohibited in official documents are the ones set up by government. For example, in 1773, the British government gave the East India Tea Company a quasi-monopoly on the tea trade in the American colonies. In American cities today, governments typically establish a monopoly in the operation of buses and taxis, and the provision of water, electricity, and natural gas. Four state constitutions – Maryland, North Carolina, Tennessee, and Massachusetts – prohibited monopolies explicitly. Maryland provides this explanation: "monopolies are odious, contrary to the spirit of a free government, and the principles of commerce; and ought not to be suffered."[8] The constitutions of North Carolina and Tennessee prohibited monopolies as "contrary to the genius of a free State."[9] The "spirit of a free government" or "genius [i.e., character] of

---

[6] An Act to Regulate Chimney Sweepers, September 29, 1787, in *The Statutes at Large of Pennsylvania, 1682 to 1801* (n.p.: Wm. Stanley Ray, State Printer of Pennsylvania, 1902), 12:573–6.

[7] Proposed amendment to the U.S. Constitution, NY ratifying convention, July 26, 1788, in *Documents Illustrative of the Formation of the Union of the American States*, ed. Charles C. Tansill (Washington: Government Printing Office, 1927), 1040.

[8] MD Declaration of Rights, 1776, art. 39.

[9] NC Declaration of Rights, 1776, art. 23; TN Constitution, 1796, art. 11, §23.

a free state" is incompatible with favoritism. Equal rights for all; special privileges for none.

When Maryland says that monopolies are "contrary to . . . the principles of commerce," it implies that commerce – the exchange of goods and services – has "principles," namely, freedom of access to markets for all persons or associations on the same minimally burdened terms. Monopolies arbitrarily exclude some citizens from particular trades or professional pursuits, or arbitrarily advantage some persons or businesses over others, thus imposing an unwarranted obstacle to the natural right to acquire property.

The ratifying conventions of four states recommended that the U.S. Constitution be amended to prohibit monopolies, using this or similar language: "That Congress erect no company of merchants with exclusive advantages of commerce."[10]

Jefferson complained of the injustice of monopolistic policies imposed on the colonies by Britain. In one law, "an American subject is forbidden to make a hat for himself of the fur which he has taken perhaps on his own soil." Jefferson called this "an instance of despotism." Another law established a monopoly for British iron manufacturers and forbade Americans to manufacture objects out of iron.[11] Historian Bernhard Knollenberg details numerous additional British restrictions on American manufacturing and commerce.[12]

In Madison's essay "Property," monopolies deny free use of one's faculties. They are therefore a denial of the natural right to acquire property: "That is not a just government, nor is property secure under it, where arbitrary restrictions, exemptions, and monopolies deny to part of its citizens that free use of their faculties, and free choice of their occupations, which not only constitute their property in the general sense of the word; but are the means of acquiring property strictly so called."[13] Madison ties security of property not only to actual possession and use (as discussed in the previous chapter) but also to the freedom to sell what one

---

[10] The language quoted was proposed by MA, February 7, 1788. The other states are NH (June 21, 1788), NY (July 26, 1788), and NC (August 1, 1788). In *Documents*, ed. Tansill, 1019, 1025, 1040, 1051.

[11] Jefferson, *Summary View of the Rights of British America*, 1774, in *Founders' Constitution*, 1:437.

[12] Bernhard Knollenberg, *Origin of the American Revolution: 1759–1766*, ed. Bernard W. Sheehan (Indianapolis: Liberty Fund, 2002), 157–73.

[13] Madison, "Property," Mar. 29, 1792, in *Founders' Constitution*, 1:598.

produces with it. Here Madison explicitly mentions the right of "acquiring property," the fundamental property right. He gives this example of a monopoly: "What must be the spirit of legislation where a manufacturer of linen cloth is forbidden to bury his own child in a linen shroud, in order to favor his neighbor who manufactures woolen cloth; where the manufacturer and wearer of woolen cloth are again forbidden the economical use of buttons of that material, in favor of the manufacturer of buttons of other materials!"[14] In agreement with Madison, Nathaniel Chipman writes: "To give to any individual, or class of men, a monopoly, an exclusive right of acquisition . . . is an exclusion of the rights of others. It is a violation of the equal rights of man."[15]

Today it is customary for government to establish quasi-monopolies through licensing requirements that limit market entry in a variety of areas, from air conditioning repair to public transportation to cosmetology. Supporters of licensing argue that government must protect the public by officially certifying that those who provide goods and services meet minimal legal requirements. In practice, according to Milton Friedman, the result of licensing "is invariably control over entry by members of the occupation itself and hence the establishment of a monopoly position."[16] "Today," writes Clark Neily, "about one quarter of American workers must obtain a government-issued license to do their job, up from less than five percent in the 1950s."[17]

In American pre-Civil War state court cases, government licensing was generally considered invidious, unless the license was reasonably related to protecting public health, safety, or morals. A law requiring physicians to have a license was upheld by the Massachusetts Supreme Court in 1835, but only because the law was evaluated as both sincerely intended and likely in terms of its content "to guard the public against ignorance, negligence, and carelessness in the members of one of the most useful professions."[18] Because of the presumption against it, licensing of this kind was infrequent prior to the Civil War. During that period, almost

---

[14] Ibid.

[15] Nathaniel Chipman, *Sketches of the Principles of Government* (Rutland, VT: J. Lyon, 1793), 178.

[16] Milton Friedman, *Capitalism and Freedom* (Chicago: University of Chicago Press, 1962), 148.

[17] Clark Neily, "Beating Rubber-Stamps into Gavels: A Fresh Look at Occupational Freedom," *Yale Law Journal* 126 (2016): 304.

[18] *Hewitt v. Charier*, 16 Pick. (33 Mass.) 353 (1835), 354–6, in Howard Gillman, *The Constitution Besieged: The Rise and Demise of Lochner Era Police Powers Jurisprudence* (Durham: Duke University Press, 1993), 52.

every state had adopted some variant of the Virginia Bill of Rights anti-monopoly provision stating "That no man, or set of men, are entitled to exclusive or separate emoluments or privileges from the community, but in consideration of public services."[19]

What about the federal government? First, "The citizens of each state shall be entitled to all privileges and immunities of citizens in the several states."[20] Some legal historians argue that this clause is an equality provision "intended to guarantee Americans traveling or temporarily residing in another state, or doing business or owning property outside their home states, that they would be treated exactly like the local people."[21] The second view of privileges and immunities is given in a 1797 Maryland case, *Campbell v. Morris*, which argues that the clause "invest[s] the citizens of the different states with the general rights of citizenship." These include "any civil right which a man as a member of civil society must enjoy." Specifically, "one of the great objects [of the clause was] enabling the citizens of the several States to acquire and hold real property in any of the States."[22] Either reading of the clause guarantees to out-of-state citizens the same commercial and property rights as the local residents have. No state can set up rules monopolizing commercial rights by limiting them to its own citizens. Legal historian Michael Greve writes, "Whatever exactly may be embraced under 'privileges and immunities,'... the commercial core is unmistakable." The clause "embodies a fiercely competitive principle."[23]

Intellectual Property and Temporary Monopolies
The founders did allow for temporary monopolies in what we call intellectual property. In the U.S. Constitution, Congress may make laws "to promote the progress of science and useful arts, by securing for

[19] Gillman, *Constitution Besieged*, 55, citing Michael Les Benedict, "Laissez Faire and Liberty: A Re-Evaluation of the Meaning and Origins of Laissez-Faire Constitutionalism," *Law and History Review* 3 (1985): 321–2; VA Bill of Rights, 1776, §4.

[20] U.S. Constitution, art. 4, §2.

[21] Stewart Jay, "Origins of the Privileges and Immunities of State Citizenship under Article IV," *Loyola University Chicago Law Journal* 45 (2013): 1.

[22] Samuel Chase's opinion, *Campbell v. Morris*, 3 H. & McH. 535, 553–54 (Md. 1797), in *Founders' Constitution*, 4:490. See also *Corfield v. Coryell*, 6 F. Cas. 546, 551–52 (C.C.E.D. Pa. 1823), ibid., 4:503. David R. Upham, "*Corfield v. Coryell* and the Privileges and Immunities of American Citizenship," *Texas Law Review* 83 (2005): 1492, 1502 (supporting the same reading).

[23] Michael S. Greve, *The Upside-Down Constitution* (Cambridge: Harvard University Press, 2012), 114.

limited times to authors and inventors the exclusive right to their respective writings and discoveries."[24] Madison explains in *Federalist* 43: "The
copyright of authors... [is already] a right at common law. The right to
useful inventions seems with equal reason to belong to the inventors."[25]
The British common law protected the copyright of authors but did not
protect the copyright (patents) of inventors. When Madison argues that
both should be protected "with equal reason," he means that both inventors and writers ought to be able to establish a property right in things
that they make with their intellectual labor. Again, the origin of the right
to property is one's natural property in oneself – in one's own mind
and body. The 1783 copyright laws of three states make this connection
between property rights and labor explicit: "there [is] no property more
peculiarly a man's own than that which is produced by the labor of his
mind."[26] Madison also writes, "The public good fully coincides in [this
case] with the claims of individuals."[27] The "public good" in question is
"the progress of science and useful arts" encouraged by patents and copyrights. People will have a financial incentive to produce inventions and
writings that will benefit the community. As for the "claims of individuals" mentioned by Madison, they are grounded in the right to property
in the fruits of one's labor.

However, since the protection of intellectual property creates a
monopoly, the founders thought the right should not be protected indefinitely. Therefore patents and copyrights must be "for limited times," as
the Constitution says. In a letter to Jefferson written in the same year as
The Federalist, Madison speaks of patents and copyrights as government
grants of "monopolies," which he defends as socially useful – in contrast
with all other monopolies.[28] In a letter written some years later, Jefferson
emphatically agrees: "If nature has made any one thing less susceptible
than all others of exclusive property, it is the action of the thinking power
called an idea, which an individual may exclusively possess as long as he
keeps it to himself; but the moment it is divulged, it forces itself into the
possession of every one, and the receiver cannot dispossess himself of

---

[24] U.S. Constitution, art. 1, §8.   [25] Madison, *Federalist* 43, p. 268.

[26] Thorvald Solberg, ed., *Copyright Enactments of the United States, 1783–1906* (Washington: Government Printing Office, 1900), 14, 18–19, quoted in Adam Mossoff, "Who
Cares What Thomas Jefferson Thought about Patents? Reevaluating the Patent 'Privilege' in Historical Context," *Cornell Law Review* 92 (2007): 982.

[27] Madison, *Federalist* 43, p. 268.

[28] Madison to Jefferson, October 17, 1788, in *Writings*, ed. Jack N. Rakove (New York:
Library of America, 1999), 423.

it.... Inventions then cannot, in nature, be a subject of property. Society may give an exclusive right to the profits arising from them, as an encouragement to men to pursue ideas which may produce utility."[29]

Evidently the founders thought of copyrights and patents as partly justified from the point of view of natural right (to the fruits of one's labor), but they worried about the anti–natural rights implication of following the logic of that right rigidly (permanent monopolies). The apparent conflict between the right to enjoy the fruit of one's labor and the right of everyone to acquire property by entering the market freely was resolved in the idea of a temporary monopoly.

In accord with the founders' understanding, the Copyright Act of 1790 provided for a relatively brief 28-year maximum protection of published works. In contrast, the 1998 Copyright Term Extension Act, passed after intense lobbying by Disney and other Hollywood corporations, covers publications for up to 120 years.[30]

Although some states set up monopolies after independence, few of them violated the principles of commerce under discussion here. They were established only for limited terms, anticipating the spirit of the patent clause of the U.S. Constitution. Massachusetts, for example, gave Paul Revere and an associate "a fifteen-year monopoly on the manufacture of iron with the use of steam power."[31] However, after 1776, restrictions on market entry were rare, as Franklin noted in the passage quoted earlier: no one is prevented "from exercising any art they understand."[32]

Constitutional Curbs on State Government Restrictions of Free Trade
The principles sketched in this chapter were not always observed during the Revolutionary War. Several states interfered with free markets by outlawing practices such as engrossing (buying goods to be resold at a higher price in the same place) and forestalling (buying up all of a particular product in order to raise its price). Some states, following Congress's 1777 advice "to regulate the prices of labor, manufacturing, [and] internal produce," tried to establish maximum wages and prices in response to the inflation caused by the government's own printing of paper money.

[29] Jefferson to Isaac McPherson, August 13, 1813, in *Writings*, 1291–2.
[30] Chris Sprigman, "The Mouse That Ate the Public Domain: Disney, the Copyright Term Extension Act, and *Eldred v. Ashcroft*," March 5, 2002, http://findlaw.com.
[31] Forrest McDonald, *Novus Ordo Seclorum: The Intellectual Origins of the Constitution* (Lawrence: University Press of Kansas, 1985), 102.
[32] Franklin, "Information to Those Who Would Remove to America," in *Writings*, 979.

These laws violated the "principles of commerce," which require freedom of trade. Gordon Wood asserts that these "numerous attempts in the early years of the war to suppress prices, control wages, . . . [were] in no way inconsistent with the spirit of '76. . . . [R]epublicanism was essentially anti-capitalistic." In fact, all of these wartime laws interfering with free markets failed and were soon largely abandoned. No one denied the general principle, stated by the Massachusetts Assembly in 1768, that it is "an unalterable law in nature that a man should have the free use and sole disposal of the fruit of his honest industry, subject to no control."[33] Defined in this way, capitalism is required by the law of nature.

More serious obstacles to free trade were imposed by state governments under the Articles of Confederation. Forrest McDonald explains: "New York and Pennsylvania, through which neighboring states did most of their importing, collected sizable revenues from import duties that were ultimately paid by consumers in New Jersey, Delaware, and Connecticut."[34] The U.S. Constitution banned these and similar practices. First, "No State shall, without the consent of the Congress, lay any imposts or duties on imports or exports, except what may be absolutely necessary for executing its inspection laws." States were also forbidden to require ships to pay fees for the use of a port ("lay any duty of tonnage"), or to require passing ships to use their ports.[35] The Constitution set similar limits on Congress's ability to interfere with freedom of commerce: "No tax or duty shall be laid on articles exported from any state. No preference shall be given by any regulation of commerce or revenue to the ports of one State over those of another; nor shall vessels bound to, or from, one state, be obliged to enter, clear, or pay duties in another."[36]

Other provisions promoting a national free market include Congress's power to create uniform bankruptcy laws; its power to grant patents and copyrights, thereby relieving inventors "from the trouble of securing

---

[33] Joseph G. Rayback, *A History of American Labor*, expanded ed. (New York: Macmillan, 1966), 40–2; McDonald, *Novus Ordo*, 111; Harry M. Ward, *The War for Independence and the Transformation of American Society* (New York: Routledge, 2000), 153–4; William W. Crosskey, *Politics and the Constitution in the History of the United States* (Chicago: University of Chicago Press, 1953, 1980), 3:12; Gordon S. Wood, *The Creation of the American Republic, 1776–1787* (New York: Norton, 1969), 64, 418; MA House of Representatives to Henry Conway, February 13, 1768, in *The Writings of Samuel Adams*, ed. Harry A. Cushing (New York: Octagon, 1968), 1:190.

[34] McDonald, *Novus Ordo*, 102–6; Crosskey, *Politics and the Constitution*, 3:12.

[35] U.S. Constitution, art. 1, §10.   [36] Ibid., art. 1, §9.

thirteen separate patents, without which their inventions might be pirated in some state or states"[37]; and its powers to standardize weights and measures, to set up a national postal system, and to establish a uniform rule of naturalization to clarify who will enjoy citizen rights.

These provisions, together with the commercial and citizenship clauses, and the monetary clauses to be explained in the next chapter, were meant to establish a nationwide free market. Michael Greve's *Upside-Down Constitution* is an extended demonstration of the many ways by which the Constitution was meant to set up an institutional framework that would guarantee nationwide freedom of trade. Edward Countryman agrees: "the Constitution created a legal environment far more favorable to entrepreneurial values than anything America had known."[38] The framers of the new Constitution, writes economic historian Curtis Nettels, sought "the establishment of a single trading area to which every American producer would have free access; the abolition of the confusing currencies, commercial codes, and tariffs of thirteen individual states would so simplify and facilitate business as to give a vigorous spur to enterprise." Nettels explains: "The exclusive power of Congress to regulate commerce among the states assured merchants that all shipments in interstate trade would be subject to a single set of uniform rules, while the grant of taxing power required that all federal duties, imposts, and excises should be uniform throughout the United States."[39] The *only* purpose of the commerce clause mentioned by Madison in *The Federalist* was to make sure the states were restrained from burdening each other's commerce.[40] It is characteristic of our time that the Constitution's commerce clause, originally intended to promote a nationwide free market, has so often been used to justify today's massive apparatus of state and federal regulations of businesses and commerce. Many of these have the effect, often intended, of curtailing freedom of trade. Greve notes that in the past century, Congress and the federal courts have mostly abandoned earlier efforts to prohibit state governments from interfering with a national freedom of trade. States impose detailed regulations that differ from one state to another. Greve argues convincingly that this

---

[37] Curtis P. Nettels, *The Emergence of a National Economy, 1775–1815* (New York: Holt, Rinehart, and Winston, 1962), 101.
[38] Greve, *Upside-Down Constitution*; he sums up the significance of the relevant constitutional provisions on 58–62; Edward Countryman, "Of Republicanism, Capitalism, and the 'American Mind,'" *William and Mary Quarterly* 44, No. 3 (July 1987): 560.
[39] Nettels, *Emergence*, 91–2, 100–101.   [40] Madison, *Federalist* 42, pp. 263–5.

congressional and judicial inaction seriously frustrates one of the main original purposes of the Constitution.[41]

Legitimate Limits on Freedom of Commerce

Just as the free use of property was limited by law when it led to harm, similar limits were also imposed on freedom of exchange. Selling sexual favors or hiring someone to murder a personal enemy was prohibited. The same considerations treated in the previous chapter in regard to government restrictions of property use apply equally to commerce that harms public health, safety, and morals.

Government Must Define and Enforce Contracts

In addition to the freedom to engage in commerce discussed in the previous section, freedom of exchange requires, secondly, clear legal definitions as well as impartial enforcement of contracts, i.e., of voluntary agreements to exchange property. Everyone must be able to know at what point a promise becomes legally binding. The law must distinguish between casual remarks, such as "I would trade my car for yours in a heartbeat," and formal written promises, as "I hereby agree to pay $10,000 for your car." Contracts often involve on one side an immediate receipt of goods or money, and on the other a promise to pay or do something of value later. In a credit card transaction, one receives groceries on the spot, but payment is made only after the bill arrives. Efficient production of goods and services – a condition of the natural right to possess and acquire property – cannot exist unless these promises to pay are enforced by courts of law. That is why the right "to institute and maintain actions of any kind in the courts of the state" was considered a privilege of citizenship.[42] Access to civil courts as a privilege of citizens is implied in Maryland's 1776 constitution: "every freeman, for any injury . . . ought to have remedy, by the course of the law of the land."[43]

A corollary to this is the provision in the U.S. Constitution providing that "No state shall . . . pass any . . . law impairing the obligation of contracts." The Northwest Ordinance, anticipating this constitutional

---

[41] Greve, *Upside-Down Constitution*, 91–111, 343–4, and throughout.

[42] The quotation is from *Corfield v. Coryell*.

[43] Declaration of Rights of MD, 1776, art. 17. Similar provisions in bills of rights of MA, 1780, art. 11; of NH, 1792, art. 14; of DE, 1792, art. 1, §9; of PA, 1790, art. 9, §11; of KY, 1792, art. 12, §13; and of TN, 1796, art. 11, §17.

provision, explicitly links its contracts clause with security of property rights: "And, in the just preservation of rights and property,... no law ought ever to be made... that shall, in any manner whatever, interfere with or affect private contracts."[44]

Four early state constitutions also contained contract clauses, of which three were put in place only after 1787.[45] South Carolina's 1776 constitution was the only one to include a pre-1787 prohibition on government "impairing the obligation of contracts," although it dropped that provision two years later in its constitution of 1778. By 1787, leading founders had become alarmed by a disturbing trend that began during the economic troubles of the 1780s. Several states passed "stay laws," enabling debtors to postpone or escape paying some of their debts. In South Carolina, "Stay laws of 1782, 1783, and 1784 suspended suits for debts antedating Feb. 26, 1782, until 1786, when [only] one-fourth of the amount became suable." The same state's Pine Barren Act of 1785 "permitted debtors to tender distant property or worthless pineland in discharge of their obligations."[46] Laws of this kind were forbidden by the Contract Clause of the U.S. Constitution, by the Northwest Ordinance, and by a growing number of state governments. Laws allowing people to avoid paying their debts came back into fashion in the 1930s during the Great Depression.[47]

In the founding, a voluntary contract between persons or associations was understood to be a sign of the equality between them. Gordon Wood writes, "Contracts came to be thought of as positive bargains deliberately and freely entered into between two parties who were presumed to be equal and not entirely trustful of each other."[48] Each side agrees to give up some of its own property in exchange for property that it values more than his or her present possession. In Madison's example, quoted earlier, the shoemaker and tailor are "each capable of making particular articles in sufficient abundance to supply the other – thus all are benefitted by

---

[44] Northwest Ordinance, 1787, art. 2, in *Founders' Constitution*, 1:28.

[45] SC Constitution, 1776, art. 9, §2; PA, 1790, art. 9, §17; KY, 1792, art. 12, §18; TN, 1796, art. 11, §20.

[46] David D. Wallace, *The Life of Henry Laurens* (New York: G.P. Putnam's, 1915), 428 (stay laws). James W. Ely, *The Guardian of Every Other Right: A Constitutional History of Property Rights* (New York: Oxford University Press, 1992), 37 (Pine Barren Act).

[47] U.S. Supreme Court, *Home Building & Loan v. Blaisdell*, 290 U.S. 398 (refusing to enforce the Contract Clause on the ground of "emergency").

[48] Wood, *Radicalism*, 162.

exchange."[49] The shoemaker values the tailor's clothing more than the shoes that he has made, while the tailor values the other's shoes more than his own clothing. The same happens in an employer–employee relation. Each side has property. The owner has money, while the workers have, to quote Madison, "free use of their faculties, and free choice of their occupations, which ... constitute their property in the general sense of the word." The worker prefers to give up the "free use of [his] faculties" for several hours per day in exchange for money. The employer prefers to exchange money for the worker's labor. Each equally believes that he will benefit from the exchange, at least in comparison with the available alternatives. As a voluntary agreement between equals, a contract is an expression of the principle that no one is born the slave or master of another.[50]

The free-labor principle also means that if workers want to form a union and quit their jobs simultaneously to put pressure on their employer for better wages or working conditions, there is no injustice in that. But workers cannot violate the natural right principle of freedom of association and establish a "closed shop" that legally bars nonunion workers from being hired – as became routine in the twentieth century.[51] Historians Christopher Tomlins and Kevin Butterfield have found that in the early republic, American law permitted labor unions ("journeymen's societies"), but only as long as they did not attempt to dictate the terms of labor for workers who were not members.[52] In a free society, when a group of workers goes on strike, the employer has two choices. If they demand more than he is able or willing to give, he can go through the inconvenience of hiring and training other workers. Or he can negotiate with the workers on strike and come to a voluntary agreement with them.

On the eve of the Civil War, Lincoln summed up the founders' understanding of the link between liberty of contract, opposition to slavery, and the right to strike. "I am glad to see that a system of labor prevails in New England under which laborers *can* strike when they want to, where

---

[49] Madison, Speech of April 9, 1789, in First Federal Congress, in *Founders' Constitution*, 2:442.

[50] Madison, "Property," Mar. 29, 1792, in *Founders' Constitution*, 1:598.

[51] F. A. Hayek, *The Constitution of Liberty* (1960; repr. Chicago: University of Chicago Press, 2011), 384–404.

[52] Christopher L. Tomlins, *Law, Labor, and Ideology in the Early American Republic* (New York: Cambridge University Press, 1993), 107–27; Kevin Butterfield, *The Making of Tocqueville's America: Law and Association in the Early United States* (Chicago: University of Chicago Press, 2015), 201–18.

they . . . are not tied down and obliged to work whether you pay them or not! I *like* the system which lets a man quit when he wants to, and wish it might prevail everywhere. One of the reasons I am opposed to slavery is just here."[53] This idea of the basic equality between employer and employee was later used by other opponents of slavery to explain the difference between a slave and a free worker. Historian William Forbath writes, "abolitionists talked about the freedom of the Northern worker in terms of self-ownership, that is, simply not being a slave, being free to sell his own labor."[54]

A sign of the new American view of contracts was a change in the vocabulary of employers and employees. In colonial America, the employer was the superior. He was called *master*, and his employees were *servants*. After the Revolution, those who offered jobs for wages were no longer called "master" but "boss," as a sign of the voluntary nature and therefore mutual equality of the employer–employee relation. Hired hands in hotels insisted on being called "help" or "waiters," to distance themselves from the condition of inferiority implied in the name of servant.[55]

There was one exception to the normal rule that all are legally obliged to fulfill their contractual obligations. In colonial America and even after the founding, when a person could not pay, he could be sent to debtors' prison. Recognizing that inability to pay debts is not always due to a moral fault, states began to adopt bankruptcy laws. The U.S. Constitution gave Congress the power to make "uniform laws on the subject of bankruptcies." In bankruptcy, a debtor's assets are divided among his creditors, so that each can get partial payment. "It cannot be denied," admitted the Pennsylvania Supreme Court in 1816, "that . . . contracts are impaired by a bankrupt law." Why then should bankruptcies be permitted? The court explains: "such are the hazards to which those who engage in trade and commerce are unavoidably exposed that, I believe, it has been found necessary in all commercial countries to relieve the

53 Lincoln, Speech at New Haven, March 6, 1860, in *Collected Works of Abraham Lincoln*, ed. Roy T. Basler (New Brunswick: Rutgers University Press, 1953), 4:24.
54 William E. Forbath, "The Ambiguities of Free Labor: Labor and the Law in the Gilded Age," *Wisconsin Law Review* 4 (1985): 783, summarizing Eric Foner, *Politics and Ideology in the Age of the Civil War* (New York: Oxford University Press, 1980), 73.
55 Wood, *Radicalism*, 184–5. See also Morton J. Horwitz, *The Transformation of American Law, 1780–1860* (Cambridge: Harvard University Press, 1977), ch. 6, esp. 164–5 (opposing my interpretation of the founders on contracts); Philip A. Hamburger, "The Development of the Nineteenth-Century Consensus Theory of Contract," *Law and History Review* 7, No. 2 (Fall 1989): 241–329 (answering Horwitz).

unfortunate from the burden of their debts, upon the surrender of all their property."[56] In bankruptcy we have a conflict of natural rights: the right of the creditor to have the debt paid, and the right of the debtor not to have his right to liberty taken away because of circumstances that may have been outside his control. The founders judged the liberty of the debtor to outweigh the contractual rights of the creditor. That presumption has been abandoned in modern American law in at least one instance: debtors are now routinely imprisoned for inability to pay child support.[57]

Freedom of contract is viewed with suspicion today. Many believe that such freedom leads to exploitation and oppression of workers by employers. America now limits freedom of contract in many ways: for example, by minimum wage laws, laws allowing unions to monopolize the supply of labor, and affirmative action and disability laws that deny employers the right to hire and fire as they choose.

Equal Access to Transportation

A third element of market freedom is the right of physical movement and communication. The general privileges of citizenship protected by both the state and federal governments included the right to travel, to do business in any state on the same terms as others, and to have equal access to *common carriers* (coaches, ships, and railroads) and *public accommodations* (such as restaurants and hotels where alternative accommodations are not readily available). Founding-era documents mostly take for granted that these citizen privileges may be suitably regulated by government to secure access on equal and reasonable terms. The Northwest Ordinance explicitly guarantees access to the public waterways and highways that were used to transport goods to market: "The navigable waters leading into the Mississippi and St. Lawrence, and the carrying places between the same, shall be common highways and forever free."[58]

Access to markets is made easier by better opportunities for transportation, as Hamilton pointed out (quoting Adam Smith) in his Report on

---

[56] *Farmers & Mechanics' Bank v. Smith*, 3 Serg. & Rawle 63 (Pa. 1816), in *Founders' Constitution*, 2:628.

[57] Elizabeth G. Patterson, "Civil Contempt and the Indigent Child Support Obligor: The Silent Return of Debtor's Prison," *Cornell Journal of Law and Public Policy* 18 (2008): 95–141.

[58] Northwest Ordinance, 1787, art. 4, in *Founders' Constitution*, 1:29.

Manufactures.⁵⁹ State governments therefore promoted and often funded the building of roads and canals, and the U.S. Constitution gives Congress the power to "establish . . . post roads" over which the mail can be delivered to every state and locality. These provisions are of course a departure from the general principle that goods and services are to be provided by the private market. The difficulty of acquiring through voluntary purchase long stretches of contiguous land required for roads or canals, and the considerable financial barriers to market entry for would-be builders, were thought to justify the exception. It must be immediately added that state canal-building proved to be frequently corrupt, as state legislatures awarded contracts and grants to their friends and supporters. In practice, consequently, government involvement in roads and canals sometimes proved to be a violation of the founders' principle that "no man, or set of men, are entitled to exclusive or separate emoluments or privileges from the community, but in consideration of public services."⁶⁰ Many of the canals and railroads built on the basis of government grants and subsidies went bankrupt, as often happens when government dispenses large sums of money to its favorites. The English poet William Wordsworth famously lamented the loss of his investments in Pennsylvania state bonds, and the young Whig Abraham Lincoln energetically but imprudently pushed Illinois to invest in canal and railroad schemes that collapsed soon afterwards.⁶¹ On the other hand, the state and federal highway system helped to bring about the desired result – promotion of a national commercial market.

---

⁵⁹ Alexander Hamilton, Report on Manufactures, 1791, in *The Papers of Alexander Hamilton*, ed. Harold C. Syrett (New York: Columbia University Press, 1961–79), 10:310–11.
⁶⁰ VA Bill of Rights, 1776, §4.
⁶¹ William Wordsworth, "To the Pennsylvanians," 1845, in *The Poetical Works of William Wordsworth*, ed. William Knight (London: Macmillan, 1896), 8:179–80; Gabor S. Boritt, *Lincoln and the Economics of the American Dream* (Urbana: University of Illinois Press, 1978), ch. 1 and 3.

17

Sound Money

Today's approach to property and economics departs most obviously from the founders' in its view of money. A National Public Radio broadcast sums up the conventional wisdom: "Almost all economists agree, the system we have today is better than the gold standard. Not perfect, but much better."[1] Prevailing opinion today, conservative and liberal alike, not only opposes but ridicules the founders' idea of a gold and silver standard. Therefore we should reacquaint ourselves with the founders' reasons for their view of money.

Besides private property and free markets, the founders were convinced that there is a third major requisite for the protection of the right to possess and acquire property: money with a reasonably stable value. The U.S. Constitution affirms a precious-metals monetary standard, which remained the basis of American monetary policy well into the twentieth century.

The main argument made in the founding is this: if money is devalued by government emissions of paper bills, debts and investments will be reduced or cancelled by government through inflation. Property will be taken in effect by manipulating the supply of money. The founders – at least the ones who prevailed at the Constitutional Convention – called this policy "wicked" and "pernicious."[2] Contracts paid with inflated paper-money currency, says founding-era writer Pelatiah Webster, will require

---

[1] David Kesterbaum, "Why We Left the Gold Standard," on *All Things Considered*, National Public Radio, April 21, 2011, www.npr.org.

[2] Alexander Hamilton, James Madison, and John Jay, *The Federalist Papers*, ed. Clinton Rossiter (New York: Signet Classics, 2003): Madison, *Federalist* 10, p. 79; Hamilton, *Federalist* 85, p. 521.

a creditor "to receive a less valuable thing in full payment of a more valuable one" – a violation of "laws grounded in the nature of human rights."[3]

The Experiment with Paper Money, 1776–1789

The American Revolution almost failed for want of money. Congress, lacking the power to tax (except by passing unenforceable requisitions on the state governments), issued "bills of credit," paper money known as "Continentals." They were supposed to be promissory notes, eventually redeemable in gold or silver coin. But Congress had no access to coins, and the states failed to raise enough taxes to pay for the federal bills of credit. Just as Congress did, every state issued paper money for the next several years. By 1780, these federal and state bills had lost almost all their face value. The 400 million now worthless federal and state paper dollars mostly disappeared from circulation, and the expression "not worth a Continental" was commonly heard.[4]

Congress and the states also financed the war by borrowing money from American and European lenders. The American lenders were given loan certificates. These did not depreciate as much as the paper money. The holders were promised that they would someday be paid back the face value of the loan certificates in gold or silver – as they eventually were, after Congress adopted Hamilton's debt policies in the 1790s.[5]

The use of inflated paper money as a back-door method of financing the Revolutionary War leads Forrest McDonald to conclude that "Americans were not as secure in their property rights between 1776 and 1787 as they had been during the colonial period.... Congress... engineered a massive expropriation of private property through a

---

[3] Pelatiah Webster, "Strictures on Tenure Acts," 1780, in *Political Essays* (Philadelphia: n.p., 1791), 130.

[4] Richard Sylla, "The Political Economy of Early U.S. Financial Development," in *Political Institutions and Financial Development*, ed. Stephen Haber, Douglass C. North, and Barry R. Weingast (Stanford: Stanford University Press, 2008), 63–4; E. James Ferguson, *The Power of the Purse: A History of American Public Finance, 1776–1790* (Chapel Hill: University of North Carolina Press, 1961), 25–35, 44–7, 57–9, 64–9; Curtis P. Nettels, *The Emergence of a National Economy, 1775–1815* (New York: Holt, Rinehart, and Winston, 1962), 23–9; Margaret G. Myers, *A Financial History of the United States* (New York: Columbia University Press, 1970), 24–30.

[5] Ferguson, *Power of the Purse*, 35–42, 59–69; Nettels, *Emergence*, 29–34; Myers, *Financial History*, 32–6.

calculated policy of inflation."[6] McDonald's description of what happened is correct, but he fails to acknowledge that such a desperate measure was believed necessary precisely to secure the people's natural rights. Only by achieving independence could the United States government effectively put a stop to British violations of the consent principle and of the rights to life, liberty, and property. That urgent necessity had to be solved before the Americans could establish their own institutions to protect their rights. For the founders, the "duty of self-preservation" is "the first law of nature."[7]

The national government under the Articles of Confederation lacked the power to tax. Some other means had to be found to pay for the war, without which the Revolution would have failed. James Madison explains: "Being engaged in a necessary war without specie [gold or silver] to defray the expense, or to support paper emissions for that purpose redeemable on demand, and being at the same time unable to borrow, no recourse was left, but to emit bills of credit to be redeemed in future."[8] Madison's explanation is the same as Jefferson's justification of military seizures of private property in the war for independence: in an emergency, property rights have to be sacrificed to "the unwritten laws of necessity, of self-preservation, and of the public safety."[9]

With the inflation of the 1770s, this mass of paper money lost its value and disappeared. There was a resumption in the use of specie and a consequent deflation in the 1780s. Many who had borrowed money in cheap paper dollars now found themselves unable to pay their taxes and other debts, as everyone got less money for their crops, products, and services. Under popular pressure, seven states again issued paper money.[10] This intentional re-inflation of the currency complemented the "stay laws" mentioned in Chapter 16, which freed debtors from part of the obligation to pay back their loans. All this led to further turmoil

---

[6] Forrest McDonald, *Novus Ordo Seclorum: The Intellectual Origins of the Constitution* (Lawrence: University Press of Kansas, 1985), 154.

[7] Boston, Rights of the Colonists, 1772, in *The Writings of Samuel Adams*, ed. Harry A. Cushing (1904–08; repr. New York: Octagon Books, 1968), 2:351.

[8] Madison, "Money," 1791, in *The Papers of James Madison*, ed. William T. Hutchinson and William M. E. Rachal (Chicago: University of Chicago Press, 1962), 1:305.

[9] Jefferson to John B. Colvin, September 20, 1810, in *The Founders' Constitution*, ed. Philip B. Kurland and Ralph Lerner (Chicago: University of Chicago Press, 1987), 4:127.

[10] Nettels, *Emergence*, 81–8. Myers, *Financial History*, 28; William W. Crosskey, *Politics and the Constitution in the History of the United States* (Chicago: University of Chicago Press, 1953, 1980), 3:329 (the paper-money states: RI, NY, NJ, PA, NC, SC, and GA).

as some states passed tender laws requiring merchants and creditors to accept inflated paper currency at face value in payment of debts. Curtis Nettels explains the situation in North Carolina: "In 1787–1788 the specie value of the paper had shrunk by more than fifty percent. Coin vanished, and since the paper had practically no value outside the state, merchants could not use it to pay debts they owed abroad; hence they suffered severe losses when they had to accept it at inflated values in the settlement of local debts."[11]

However necessary these policies may have been as measures of desperation, they are singled out for harsh criticism in *The Federalist*. Madison condemned a "rage for paper money" as an example of an "improper or wicked project." Hamilton lamented the "practices on the part of the state governments, which have undermined the foundations of property and credit, have planted mutual distrust in the breasts of all classes of citizens, and have occasioned an almost universal prostration of morals."[12]

The Constitution's Prohibition of Paper Money

By the time the Constitution was written in 1787, most prominent Americans agreed that government-issued paper money should stop. George Washington expressed the consensus: "Paper money has had the effect in your State [Rhode Island] that it ever will have, to ruin commerce, oppress the honest, and open a door to every species of fraud and injustice."[13] The remedy was a constitutional ban on any state involvement in monetary policy, along with a mandate for the federal government to limit money to gold and silver coins. This was an exception to the general constitutional design of allowing the states to take care of domestic policy relating to property rights. The Constitution's framers thought the states had misbehaved so badly in their monetary policies that nothing less than a federal takeover was sufficient.

The Constitution also restrained Congress, for it too had proved untrustworthy in this area. The power to "emit bills on the credit of the United States" – paper money – which Congress had under the Articles of Confederation,[14] was deliberately omitted from the Constitution. In the Constitutional Convention, a proposal was discussed to continue

---

[11] Nettels, *Emergence*, 82.

[12] Madison, *Federalist* 10, p. 79; Hamilton, *Federalist* 85, p. 521.

[13] Washington to Jabez Bowen, January 9, 1787, in *Writings of George Washington*, ed. John C. Fitzpatrick (Washington: Government Printing Office, 1931–44), 29:139.

[14] Articles of Confederation, art. 9.

to allow Congress this same power, but it was easily voted down. Oliver Ellsworth spoke for the majority when he said he "thought this a favorable moment to shut and bar the door against paper money." James Wilson agreed: "It will have a most salutary influence on the credit of the United States to remove the possibility of paper money." In Madison's notes on the Convention debates, he explains in a footnote that he wanted the government to be able to issue "public notes as far as they could be safe and proper," but that meant the Constitution had to "cut off the pretext for a paper currency and particularly for making the bills a tender either for public or private debts." (In contrast, these exact words appear on paper money today.) Madison seems to mean that government should be permitted to borrow money and issue promissory notes (bonds) to pay the debt incurred. That at any rate seems to be what delegate Nathaniel Ghorum had in mind when he pointed out that "the power, as far as it will be necessary or safe, is involved in that of borrowing."[15] Madison and Ghorum seem to have expected that government bonds would circulate in the market and be used as an informal substitute for money. That is actually what happened, starting in the 1790s. But there was no intention of allowing Congress to mandate that government bonds be accepted as legal tender for private debts.

Some scholars, such as Nettels, argue that the Constitution does permit Congress to issue paper money: "if Congress should deem it necessary and proper to issue bills of credit . . . in order to borrow money or to give effect to any other power vested in the federal government, such action would obviously be with the authority conferred by the Constitution."[16] But Nettels seems to be conflating loan certificates and government bonds with "bills of credit." Properly speaking, bills of credit are paper money not redeemable in gold or silver. In fact, Nettels seems to admit this. He writes that because of their opposition to "the pestilent effects of paper money," the framers of the Constitution "intended to create a national

---

[15] Madison's notes on August 16, in *The Records of the Federal Convention of 1787*, ed. Max Farrand (New Haven: Yale University Press, 1937), 2:309–10. Hamilton was absent when this debate occurred; perhaps that is why he later incorrectly implied that the federal government has the power to issue paper money, in Report on a National Bank, 1790, in *The Papers of Alexander Hamilton*, ed. Harold C. Syrett (New York: Columbia University Press, 1961–79), 7:321–2, discussed in Sylla, "Political Economy," 74.

[16] Nettels, *Emergence*, 99–100. Hugh Rockoff agrees: "Banking and Finance, 1789–1914," in *The Cambridge Economic History of the United States*, vol. 2: *The Long Nineteenth Century*, ed. Stanley L. Engerman and Robert E. Gallman (Cambridge: Cambridge University Press, 2000), 644.

currency based on coin."[17] Congress was given the power to "borrow money on the credit of the United States," a very different thing from issuing paper money. This allows for the creation of loan certificates or bonds redeemable for coin, presumably bearing interest, on a date certain.

The lack of an enumerated constitutional power to issue paper money is clarified by four constitutional clauses. First, Congress is given the power to "coin money."[18] This phrase was understood literally by everyone in the eighteenth century. It meant coining coins, issuing pieces of metal marked with their monetary value. To show that the founders equated "coin money" with "issue coins," I quote Jefferson's 1785 *Propositions respecting Coinage*, which begins: "First. The value of silver compared with gold. Second. The weight or size of the several pieces of money that are to be made."[19] The Constitution specifies the name of the "coin" then commonly in use, the dollar (in Article 1, section 9, and in the Seventh Amendment). Jefferson explains that the "Spanish Dollar...is a known coin, and the most familiar of all to the minds of the people. It is already adopted from South to North." The "Spanish dollar" was minted in Mexico and other Spanish colonies.[20]

The second constitutional provision is Congress's power to "regulate the value thereof, and of foreign coin."[21] The "value" of coined money

---

[17] Nettels, *Emergence*, 99–100. Most scholars conclude that the Constitution forbids both federal and state governments from issuing paper money: Bray Hammond, *Banks and Politics in America: From the Revolution to the Civil War* (Princeton: Princeton University Press, 1957), 92 ("by striking it out, the convention purposed prohibiting it"). Richard H. Timberlake, *Monetary Policy in the United States: An Intellectual and Institutional History* (Chicago: University of Chicago Press, 1993), 4 ("Congress [was limited] to setting the legal tender value of the monetary metal"). Farley Grubb, "Creating the U.S. Dollar Currency Union, 1748–1811: A Quest for Monetary Stability or a Usurpation of State Sovereignty for Personal Gain?" *American Economic Review* 93, No. 5 (Dec. 2003): 1778n1 ("the Constitution also forbade the federal government from issuing paper money"). Edwin Vieira, Jr., "The Forgotten Role of the Constitution in Monetary Law," *Texas Review of Law and Politics* 2, No. 1 (1997): 77–116 (constitutional money is gold and silver coin). Vieira's article is based on his 1,722-page study *Pieces of Eight: The Monetary Powers and Disabilities of the United States Constitution*, 2nd ed. (Fredericksburg, VA: Sheridan Books, 2002). See also Timberlake, *Constitutional Money: A Review of the Supreme Court's Monetary Decisions* (New York: Cambridge University Press, 2013) (supporting Vieira).

[18] U.S. Constitution, art. 1, §10, §8.

[19] Jefferson, Propositions respecting Coinage, May 13, 1785, *Founders' Constitution*, 3:7. Also Robert Morris to President of Congress, January 15, 1782, in ibid., 3:2–5 (proposing a mint "to coin money," i.e., silver and gold coins).

[20] Jefferson, Notes on Coinage, Mar.-May 1784, in *The Papers of Thomas Jefferson*, ed. Julian P. Boyd et al. (Princeton: Princeton University Press, 1950–), 7:175, 177.

[21] U.S. Constitution, art. 1, §8.

is the weight of metal that makes a unit of coin. The Coinage Act of 1792 followed Jefferson's advice, repeated by Hamilton as secretary of the treasury in his Report on a Mint. Congress "regulate[d] the value" of the dollar by defining it as the "Spanish milled dollar," containing "371 4/16 grains of pure ... silver." Congress provided for a mint to "coin" these dollars. The Coinage Act also states the weight of gold "eagles" to be minted, "each to be of the value of ten dollars."[22] Thus the United States was originally on a silver standard, the dollar being defined in terms of silver dollars, not gold.[23] In spite of these facts, people today often assume, incorrectly, that "to coin money" means "to print currency," i.e., paper money. That is precisely what the Constitution prohibits.

This original plan for bimetallic (silver and gold) coins failed because Congress did not "regulate the value" of gold eagles to take account of their changing market value. When Mexico increased its silver production, gold coins gained in value compared with silver. Gold disappeared from circulation, because it became advantageous to sell gold coins abroad for more than their Congress-defined "value" in silver dollars. In 1834, Congress finally adjusted the silver–gold ratio, but this time it overvalued gold, especially after the discoveries of gold in California and elsewhere in the 1840s. The consequence was that America in effect shifted from a silver to a gold standard, which it retained until its gradual abandonment in the twentieth century.

Congress acted on its power to "regulate the value ... of foreign coin" in 1793, declaring that the "foreign gold and silver coins [of Britain, France, Portugal, and Spain] shall pass current as money ..., and be a legal tender for the payment of all debts," at rates specified in the act.[24]

In a third constitutional provision, Congress is given the power to "provide for the punishment of counterfeiting the securities and current coin of the United States." "Securities" are loan certificates, and "current coin" means coins in circulation. Nothing is said about counterfeiting paper money, of course, because Congress has no power to issue it.

Fourth, the Constitution's limits on state governments make it even clearer that the only constitutional money permitted is gold or silver. The

---

[22] Hamilton, Report on the Establishment of a Mint, January 28, 1791, in *Papers*, 7:570–607. Coinage Act, April 2, 1792, §9, in *Public Statutes at Large*, ed. Richard Peters (Boston: Little and Brown, 1845), 1:248.

[23] Vieira, "Forgotten Role," 108.

[24] An Act Regulating Foreign Coins, February 9, 1793, in *Public Statutes at Large*, 1:300; Vieira, "Forgotten Role," 114–15 (other federal laws regulating the value of foreign coin).

states are forbidden to "coin money; emit bills of credit; make any thing but gold and silver coin a tender in payment of debts." Commenting on this provision, Roger Sherman summed up the Constitutional Convention's agenda: "this [is] a favorable crisis for crushing paper money." There was hardly any debate on this provision; only one state opposed it.[25]

The insistence on "gold and silver coin" as the sole legal tender that the states were permitted to require again makes clear that the "money" to be "coin[ed]" by Congress is gold and silver, and that the "value thereof" is the amount of gold or silver in a coin of a particular denomination.

The point of all these provisions was to establish a reliable medium of exchange that could not be stripped of its value by arbitrary government creation of paper money. Bray Hammond sums up the framers' concern: "in the 18th century . . . it was stipulated that money should comprise gold (and silver), so much were the precious metals esteemed above the word of political authority. But in the twentieth century money has become a creature of government, political authority having supplanted, in the domestic sphere, the place the precious metals primitively held."[26] One of the fundamental conditions for security of property rights – sound money – was thereby placed by the founders, to the best of their ability, beyond the control of "political authority." The Constitution, writes economic historian Richard Timberlake, "took monetary manipulation out of the range of political discretion – or so the Founding Fathers believed."[27]

Madison summarizes the founders' arguments against paper money in *Federalist* 44, where he characteristically blends the twin themes of justice and utility ("public prosperity"): "The extension of the prohibition to bills of credit must give pleasure to every citizen in proportion to his love of justice, and his knowledge of the true springs of public prosperity. . . . [S]ince the peace, [America has suffered] from the pestilent effects of paper money, on the necessary confidence between man and man; on the necessary confidence in the public councils; on the industry and morals of the people, and on the character of republican government."[28] The fierceness of Madison's opposition to paper money here and, as previously noted, in *Federalist* 10 (where he calls it "wicked") is striking. He proceeds to defend the other monetary provisions of the Constitution in this way: "Had every state a right to regulate the value of its coin,

---

[25] Debate on August 28, 1787, in Farrand, *Records of the Federal Convention*, 2:439.
[26] Hammond, *Banks and Politics in America*, 110.
[27] Timberlake, *Monetary Policy*, 4. [28] *Federalist* 44, p. 278.

there might be as many different currencies [i.e., coins in circulation] as states; and thus the intercourse among them would be impeded; retrospective alterations in its value might be made, and thus the citizens of other states be injured; and animosities be kindled among the states themselves.... The power to make any thing but gold and silver a tender in payment of debts is withdrawn from the states on the same principle with that of issuing of paper currency." Madison's point is that money must be stable and reliable so that people's property rights will be secured against the injury created by government-induced inflation, and so that commerce among the states will be properly encouraged.

The establishment of a national precious metals standard, and the prohibition of paper money, received little criticism from the opponents of the Constitution. "Anti-Federalists advanced numerous complaints," writes James Ely, "but they rarely attacked the specific provisions related to property interests."[29] Hammond agrees: "On the whole, the monetary clauses of the Constitution seem to have won exceptional favor, offering what was objectionable to the fewest people and what was commendable to the most."[30] Most of the Anti-Federalist references to government-issued paper money agree that it is a bad thing. For example, the "Federal Farmer" admits that "several legislatures, by making tender, suspension, and paper money laws, have given just cause of uneasiness to creditors.... [This conduct] has prepared many honest men for changes in government."[31]

Banks, Private and Public

The Constitution does not allow government to issue paper money, but it says nothing against privately owned banks doing so. This would include both the banks incorporated by state governments, and the First and Second Banks of the United States, incorporated by federal law but

[29] James W. Ely, *The Guardian of Every Other Right: A Constitutional History of Property Rights* (New York: Oxford University Press, 1992), 51.

[30] Hammond, *Banks and Politics*, 103; Pauline Maier, *Ratification: The People Debate the Constitution, 1787–1788* (New York: Simon & Schuster, 2011), 224 (paper money was of little interest to Anti-Federalists except in RI, which was strongly committed to paper money).

[31] "Letters from the Federal Farmer to the Republican," Letter 1, October 8, 1787, in *The Complete Anti-Federalist*, ed. Herbert J. Storing (Chicago: University of Chicago Press, 1981), 2:226–7.

predominantly private. (The federal government owned one-fifth of the First Bank.)[32]

Although it is true that private banks issued bank notes long after the founding, it is also true that as private businesses they were liable to the same market constraints as other businesses. Bank notes could never be "money" or "tender in payment of debts" in the constitutional sense because although bank notes were claims on the bank's gold and silver coin, they were not themselves gold or silver. Bank notes were accepted as a proxy for real, metallic money by private persons only as long as they believed the bank could redeem the notes in gold or silver coin. The same was true of the First Bank of the United States, established on Hamilton's recommendation, which issued bank notes redeemable in specie.

Today, writes Timberlake, "the central bank proper has become the recognized agency for controlling the community's stock of money."[33] In contrast, the founders rejected "the belief that deliberate control over the money and banking system could be undertaken by delegated authority in order to provide a more rational monetary structure." He continues: "the dominant monetary institution during the period I examine [the early American republic] was the self-regulatory specie standard.... Since central banking institutions [such as the First and Second Bank of the United States] had to operate within these formal frameworks, their scope for action was limited. Only in the twentieth century did specie standards fade away."[34]

Private banks in the states faced the same constraints. No bank was protected against bankruptcy, which could occur if a "run on the bank" revealed that the bank did not have enough coin to redeem its notes. During economic "panics" or recessions, state governments sometimes postponed the bankruptcy threat by permitting banks to suspend specie payments temporarily. But in the long run, no bank could stay in business if its paper notes could not be paid in gold or silver.[35]

---

[32] John Jay Knox, *A History of Banking in the United States* (New York: Bradford Rhodes, 1903), 36 (summarizing the law authorizing the First Bank of the U.S.).

[33] Timberlake, *Monetary Policy*, 1.

[34] Richard H. Timberlake, *The Origins of Central Banking in the United States* (Cambridge: Harvard University Press, 1978), vii–viii.

[35] Murray N. Rothbard, *A History of Money and Banking in the United States* (Auburn, AL: Ludwig von Mises Institute, 2002), 72–132 (showing how this process worked in several nineteenth-century recessions).

The Abandonment of Constitutional Money

No feature of the founders' consensus on economics and property has been more thoroughly repudiated than the Constitution's provisions on money. Most people today, including those who call themselves "constitutional conservatives," ignore what they consider this embarrassing part of the Constitution. At least Bray Hammond has the honesty to admit that the current monetary regime, which he defends, contradicts the Constitution: "Economic change in time made the use of paper money indispensable, and the Constitution had to be accommodated to that fact."[36] Most contemporary economists agree that the gold or silver standard would not work in a modern economy. And we have seen with our own eyes that a modern, productive economy can survive and even thrive on the basis of paper or fiat money. However, there are still some who advocate a return to constitutional money.[37] They argue that America experienced rapid economic growth – perhaps its most rapid – during the period when there was no national bank and a specie standard prevailed. Robert Gallman writes, "No European economy grew so fast for so long as did that of the United States before World War I."[38]

The purpose of this chapter has been to describe the Constitution's original silver-gold standard, not to defend it. That exceeds the scope of this book, to say nothing of the limits of my own expertise. I mention the current debate only to show that the founders' approach continues to be defended by thoughtful scholars.

[36] Hammond, *Banks and Politics*, 108.
[37] They include Timberlake, Rothbard, and Vieira, cited earlier.
[38] Robert E. Gallman, "Economic Growth and Structural Change in the Long Nineteenth Century," in *Cambridge Economic History*, 2:22, 5.

18

The Hamilton–Jefferson Quarrel

We must at last confront an obvious objection to the analysis of the previous four chapters. It is widely believed that the founders were divided by two opposed visions, and that it is therefore incorrect to speak of a "founders' view" of property and economics. Historian Drew McCoy, for example, asserts that Jefferson and Madison believed that America's best hope was to remain "a virtuous agrarian republic" – a republic that would only be corrupted by "commerce and industry." In contrast, "Hamilton's vision of the future was not clouded by the traditional republican fears that continued to plague Madison and much of agrarian America. He simply accepted social inequality, propertyless dependence, and virtually unbridled avarice as the necessary and inevitable concomitants of a powerful and prosperous modern society."[1] In McCoy's account, Hamilton (the bad guy) stands for the "unbridled avarice" of free-market selfishness, while (good guys) Madison and Jefferson sought agrarian virtue and the common good.

The same contrast is presented by political scientist James Q. Wilson from a pro-Hamilton viewpoint: "on the role of business and commerce, the framers were divided. Alexander Hamilton wanted a national commercial regime, while . . . Jefferson opposed it. In the long run Alexander Hamilton succeeded, and the country has been, I think, made greater by

---

[1] Drew R. McCoy, *The Elusive Republic: Political Economy in Jeffersonian America* (New York: Norton, 1980), 133–4.

this: we have a sound currency, free enterprise, and encouragement for entrepreneurship."[2]

If these descriptions were accurate, one would indeed have to conclude that America's founders had no consensus view of economic policy and property rights. But in fact, these pictures are gross exaggerations. Jefferson and Madison, no less than Hamilton, strongly affirmed the need for the "sound currency, free enterprise, and encouragement for entrepreneurship" praised by Wilson. All agreed on full payment of government debts. All were "capitalists," if we define capitalism as the legal order protecting property rights. The three leaders (four, if we include Hamilton's boss, President Washington) were really fighting over means, not ends. As historian Lance Banning writes, "Madison's and Hamilton's agreements were extensive and profound. Both of them believed that proper governments originate in the consent of the society they serve and are intended to secure the people's happiness and rights."[3]

Jefferson's preferences for agriculture, for state governments, and for France were tactical. He thought this path better for American liberty. Hamilton's preference for England, for manufacturing, for federal payment of state government debts, and for a national bank were also judgments about the best means to create a nation that could secure and protect liberty. Both Jefferson and Hamilton embraced the principles of the founding, including the right to acquire and possess property, the moral authority of natural law, and government by consent of the governed. The "first principle of association," writes Jefferson, is "the guarantee to everyone of a free exercise of his industry, and the fruits acquired by it." In almost identical language, Hamilton agrees that true liberty "protect[s] the exertions of talent and industry and secur[es] to them their justly acquired fruits."[4]

---

[2] James Q. Wilson, "Did Tocqueville and the American Founders Disagree?" in *Alexis de Tocqueville and the Challenges of American Society*, ed. Murray Bessette (lulu.com, 2008), 16. See also Thomas K. McCraw, *The Founders and Finance: How Hamilton, Gallatin, and Other Immigrants Forged a New Economy* (Cambridge: Harvard University Press, 2012), 365 (in praise of Hamilton).

[3] Lance Banning, "Political Economy and the Creation of the Federal Republic," in *Devising Liberty: Preserving and Creating Freedom in the New American Republic*, ed. David Thomas Konig (Stanford: Stanford University Press, 1995), 39.

[4] Thomas Jefferson to Joseph Milligan, April 6, 1816, in *The Founders' Constitution*, ed. Philip B. Kurland and Ralph Lerner (Chicago: University of Chicago Press, 1987), 1:573. Hamilton, "The Defence of the Funding System," 1795, in *The Papers of Alexander Hamilton*, ed. Harold C. Syrett (New York: Columbia University Press, 1961–79), 19:52. Hamilton explains the content of natural law in *The Farmer Refuted*, 1775, in ibid., 1:86–8.

Three main economic policy questions divided Hamilton from Jefferson and Madison in the 1790s: how to pay government debts incurred in the Revolutionary War, whether to establish a national bank, and whether taxpayers should subsidize selected industries. Hamilton, as secretary of the treasury, laid out his proposals on these topics in three long papers. (Hamilton's fourth major report, on the Mint, was uncontroversial. Almost everyone favored a currency of gold and silver coin, as shown in the previous chapter.[5])

Federal Payment of State and National Debt

In his 1790 Report on Public Credit, Hamilton argues that full payment of government debts incurred during the Revolutionary War will establish the credit of the United States government. Credit, the ability to borrow money, is proportionate to people's belief that the money will be paid back. Credit is vital to government, Hamilton explains, because it will "add to . . . security against foreign attack" by enabling the government to borrow money more easily in time of war.[6] This part of his argument was not controversial. In Jefferson's First Inaugural, he remarks in passing that one of the "essential principles of our government" is "the honest payment of our debts and sacred preservation of the public faith."[7]

But three features of Hamilton's debt plan alarmed Jefferson and Madison. First, Hamilton wanted the federal government to assume responsibility for the remaining debts of the state governments. This, he said, would tie the interest of the wealthy to the success of the new and still weak federal government. "If all the public creditors receive their dues from one source, . . . their interests will be the same. Having the same interests, they will unite in support of the fiscal arrangements of government."[8] Jefferson and Madison saw this as a dangerous scheme to create a class of wealthy insiders whose support would make the government independent of public opinion. Congress approved this part of the plan, but only after the Southerners who opposed it were promised that

---

[5] Alexander Hamilton, Report on the Establishment of a Mint, Jan. 28, 1791, in *Papers*, 7:570–607. Forrest McDonald, *Alexander Hamilton: A Biography* (New York: Norton, 1982), 198 (the Report "elicited no serious controversy").

[6] Hamilton, Report on Public Credit, 1790, in *Papers*, 6:67, 70.

[7] Thomas Jefferson, First Inaugural Address, 1801, in *Writings*, ed. Merrill D. Peterson (New York: Library of America, 1984), 495.

[8] Hamilton, Report on Public Credit, 80.

the national capital would be located on the Potomac River and not in New York or Philadelphia.

Second, in Hamilton's plan government bonds would pay interest, but there would be no definite date on which the bond would be paid off. The point was to enable bonds to "answer most of the purposes of money" by remaining in circulation indefinitely and being trusted as "equivalent to payments in specie."[9] Jefferson and Madison were concerned that these bonds would become objects of speculation – in effect, gambling by wealthy investors – diverting people's energies away from productive labor.

Third, Hamilton proposed that the new interest-bearing bonds would go entirely to those who currently held debt certificates, many of whom happened to be wealthy speculators, rather than to those who had originally loaned their money to the government and who had sold their certificates to speculators at a loss. For Hamilton, this was a simple matter of property rights. "It is inconsistent with justice" not to pay those who currently hold the certificates, "because, in the first place, it is a breach of contract – a violation of the rights of a fair purchaser."[10]

Madison said he too respected "the great and fundamental principles of justice."[11] "No logic," he said, "no magic, in my opinion, can diminish the force of the obligation. The only point on which we can deliberate is, to whom the payment is really due." Madison thought it unjust to enrich speculators and leave the original purchasers uncompensated. So he proposed to pay the present holders of government debt "the highest price which has prevailed in the market; and let the residue belong to the original sufferers."[12] Congress rejected Madison's advice. They easily approved full payment to current certificate holders, mainly because Madison's plan was seen, writes Banning, "as such a violent breach of preexisting contracts as to absolutely wreck the nation's credit."[13]

Hamilton's plan had the advantage that the market value of federal bonds quickly became the same as their face value. The goal of establishing the credit of the government was wholly successful. The plan had the disadvantage of enriching a small class of clever speculators, some

---

[9] Ibid., 70.   [10] Ibid., 73.

[11] James Madison, Speech in the House of Representatives, Feb. 18, 1790, in *The Papers of James Madison*, ed. William T. Hutchinson et al. (Chicago: University of Chicago Press, 1962-), 13:48–9.

[12] Madison, speech in the House of Representatives, Feb. 11, 1790, in ibid., 13:35, 37.

[13] Lance Banning, *Conceived in Liberty: The Struggle to Define the New Republic, 1789–1793* (Lanham, MD: Rowman & Littlefield, 2004), 11.

of whom had learned of the plan through leaks (unknown to Hamilton) from William Duer, Hamilton's corrupt assistant in the Treasury Department.[14] Jefferson and Madison came to believe that Hamilton's credit scheme was part of a devious attempt to take government out of the hands of the people and replace them with a moneyed elite. Hamilton saw it as a sensible measure to strengthen the new and weak federal government with the support of the wealthy.[15]

To sum up: the disagreement over paying the government debt was over the relatively narrow questions of how to determine fairly who the real debtors were, how rapidly to retire the debt, and whether the federal government should pay the state debts.

Leaving aside the uncontroversial Coinage Act, the federal assumption of state debts and the funding of the debt by means of long-term bonds were arguably the most successful part of Hamilton's financial plan. The public, and foreign lenders, were convinced (correctly) that the government would pay back every dollar borrowed during the Revolution. Historian Max Edling notes that "the funding act introduced policies and institutions of debt management that outlived the [1790s].... Though the Virginia dynasty presided over the liquidation of the revolutionary debt, Jefferson, Madison, and James Monroe actually administrated a Federalist repayment plan."[16]

The Bank of the United States

The second great quarrel between Hamilton and Jefferson concerned the national bank. The experience of Britain and four other nations with privately owned national banks had convinced Hamilton that such an institution was necessary for American economic development. It would serve as a source of loans for government as well as private business, and as a convenient depository for taxes. Hamilton argued that the Bank of the

[14] Stanley Elkins and Eric McKitrick, *The Age of Federalism* (New York: Oxford University Press, 1993), 138–9.

[15] Standard treatments of the debt controversy are E. James Ferguson, *The Power of the Purse: A History of American Public Finance, 1776–1790* (Chapel Hill: University of North Carolina Press, 1961), 289–325; Lance Banning, *The Sacred Fire of Liberty: James Madison and the Founding of the Federal Republic* (Ithaca, NY: Cornell University Press, 1995), 309–25; McDonald, *Alexander Hamilton: A Biography*, 163–87; Elkins and McKitrick, *Age of Federalism*, 136–53; McCraw, *Founders and Finance*, 97–109.

[16] Max M. Edling, "'So Immense a Power in the Affairs of War': Alexander Hamilton and the Restoration of Public Credit," *William and Mary Quarterly* 64, No. 2 (Apr. 2007): 325.

United States would establish responsible privately issued bank notes that would avoid "an inflated and artificial state of things, incompatible with the regular and prosperous course of the political economy." Congress authorized the Bank to issue paper bills in excess of the amount of gold and silver in their possession, but it was required to redeem the bills in gold or silver on demand.[17]

One must admit immediately that any bank given unique privileges by law violates the anti-monopoly principles of the founding. However, those principles did permit government to grant special privileges in exchange for public services. The Massachusetts Bill of Rights states: "No...corporation...ha[s] any other title to obtain...exclusive priv- ileges...than what arises from the consideration of services rendered to the public." Hamilton claimed that the Bank would indeed provide services to the public that private banks could not. For example, the Bank enabled the government to have quick access to short-term loans. This was probably its most important contribution to the public good. Economist Richard Sylla explains: "once he [Hamilton] had decided to fund all federal and state debts at par, revenue shortfalls gave him no choice other than to borrow a lot from the Bank, which is why he fought so hard for its establishment."[18]

Madison and Jefferson strongly opposed the Bank. They saw it, like the debt plan, as another way by which Hamilton would enrich support- ers of the Federalist-dominated government. Hamilton had admitted this all along, but he considered it a benefit. As early as 1781 he wrote that a national bank, "by uniting the influence and interest of the moneyed men with the resources of government, can alone give it that durable and extensive credit of which it stands in need."[19] Those wealthy enough to purchase stock in the Bank saw the value of that stock go up, although excessive speculation later led the price of the Bank's stock to fall. Madi- son and Jefferson were disgusted at the spectacle of what they regarded, with some justice, as wild gambling on the price of the stock.

In spite of their initial passionate opposition, both Jefferson and Madi- son quietly accepted the Bank during their own presidencies. Madison signed the 1816 law chartering a Second Bank of the United States.

---

[17] Alexander Hamilton, Report on a National Bank, 1790, in *Papers*, 7:306–9, 315, 322.
[18] Richard Sylla, "Financial Foundations: Public Credit, the National Bank, and Securities Markets," in *Founding Choices: American Economic Policy in the 1790s*, ed. Douglas A. Irwin and Richard Sylla (Chicago: University of Chicago Press, 2011), 78.
[19] Hamilton, *The Continentalist*, No. IV, 1781, in *The Revolutionary Writings of Alexan- der Hamilton*, ed. Richard B. Vernier (Indianapolis: Liberty Fund, 2008), 186.

Jefferson and Madison also initially opposed the Bank on constitutional grounds. I omit discussion of this question here. A reasonable case can be made either way, as Banning argues convincingly. Besides, government-chartered corporations, including banks, were regarded as constitutional at the state level, so federal power to do the same thing has no connection with the principles of natural right. The most important and successful part of Hamilton's financial plan – the federal assumption of state debts and its issuing of interest-paying bonds on the national debt – could have been done with or without a bank.[20]

Did the Bank of the United States really serve the public good? Did it make the right to acquire and possess property more secure? Scholars continue to debate these questions, and there is no need to resolve them here.[21] In the short term, writes Richard Sylla, "Given the precariousness of the nation's finances, the Treasury needed to draw on the credit of a large bank as soon as it could . . . . In 1792 and 1793, the Treasury did in fact receive four loans from the BUS [Bank of the United States] totaling $1 million. The BUS became for the Treasury a reliable source of short-term credit, a depositary for public revenues, and a mover of government funds through its nationwide branch network to where they were needed.

---

[20] On the bank controversy: Elkins and McKitrick, *Age of Federalism*, 223–44; Banning, *Sacred Fire of Liberty*, 325–33; McDonald, *Alexander Hamilton*, 189–210; Colleen A. Sheehan, *James Madison and the Spirit of Republican Self-Government* (New York: Cambridge University Press, 2009), 109–11 (Madison's view of the constitutional question); James H. Read, *Power versus Liberty: Madison, Hamilton, Wilson, and Jefferson* (Charlottesville: University Press of Virginia, 2000), 35–42 (correcting the anti-Madison bias of Elkins and McKitrick).

[21] Forrest McDonald defends Hamilton's economic policies, in *Novus Ordo Seclorum: The Intellectual Origins of the Constitution* (Lawrence: University Press of Kansas, 1985), 140, and in *Alexander Hamilton: A Biography*. Other Hamilton admirers include Peter McNamara, *Political Economy and Statesmanship: Smith, Hamilton, and the Foundation of the Commercial Republic* (DeKalb: Northern Illinois Press, 1998), 95–151; Karl-Friedrich Walling, *Republican Empire: Alexander Hamilton on War and Free Government* (Lawrence: University Press of Kansas, 1999), 175–208; Carson Holloway, *Hamilton versus Jefferson in the Washington Administration: Completing the Founding or Betraying the Founding?* (New York: Cambridge University Press, 2015); Bray Hammond, *Banks and Politics in America: From the Revolution to the Civil War* (Princeton: Princeton University Press, 1957), 114–43; McCraw, *Founders and Finance*, 87–136. Hamilton critics include Murray N. Rothbard, *A History of Money and Banking in the United States: The Colonial Era to World War II* (Auburn, AL: Ludwig von Mises Institute, 2002), 68–72; and Hans Eicholz, review of McCraw, *Founders and Finance*, www .libertylawsite.org/author/hans-eicholz, Feb.–Mar. 2013, under these titles: "Alexander Hamilton and the Politics of Impatience"; "Alexander Hamilton: Switzerland or the Caribbean, Anyone?"; "The Bank of the United States and Mr. Hamilton's Surprise!"; "Alexander Hamilton's Legacy in Banking and Finance."

It issued convertible bank notes used throughout the country."[22] But in the long run, Sylla admits, the United States would have thrived with or without a federally chartered national bank: "One need not speculate on the alterative [to a national bank] because subsequent U.S. history gives examples.... The absence of a central bank [from 1836 to 1914] did not prevent the U.S. economy from growing to become the world's largest in the long interim."[23] Far more important than the Bank was Hamilton's successful push for federal assumption of the Revolutionary War debt. On the basis of the government's record of paying this debt, it was able to borrow large sums of money during the War of 1812, the Mexican War, and the Civil War. Loans also financed the purchase of Louisiana.[24] The Bank of the United States probably had less effect on the economy, for good or ill, than its proponents or detractors had anticipated.

Federal Subsidies of Selected Industries and Protective Tariffs

The third policy dispute of the 1790s concerned government subsidies of industry. Hamilton's 1791 Report on Manufactures rejects "the proposition, that industry, if left to itself, will naturally find its way to the most useful and profitable employment." Government must therefore provide "bounties, premiums, and other artificial encouragements." Hamilton argues, first, that ingrained habits are a natural obstacle to new means of production. People are too stubborn to turn away from the familiar. Second, bounties (subsidies of selected businesses) were supposedly needed to counteract European subsidies commonly given "to enable their own workmen to undersell and supplant all competitors in the countries to which those commodities are sent."[25]

Targeted subsidies of government-approved businesses obviously violate the founders' general principle that free markets are the best way to determine what goods and services should be produced. In this case, Hamilton followed the contrary advice of economic writers respected in Europe such as Jacques Necker and James Steuart. Although Hamilton paraphrases Adam Smith's *Wealth of Nations* extensively in his Report on Manufactures, he rejects Smith's free-market arguments against

---

[22] Sylla, "Political Economy," in *Political Institutions*, ed. Haber, 73.
[23] Sylla, "Financial Foundations," in *Founding Choices*, ed. Irwin and Sylla, 84–5.
[24] Edling, "'So Immense a Power,'" 326.
[25] Alexander Hamilton, "Report on Manufactures, 1791," in *The Papers of Alexander Hamilton*, ed. Harold C. Syrett (New York: Columbia University Press, 1961–79), 10:266.

bounties.[26] Madison opposed Hamilton's bounty proposal, as one might expect of a man who famously denounced monopolies in writing.[27] But even Madison had inconsistently written three years earlier in *Federalist* 41 that there would eventually be a need for bounties to promote American exports.[28]

Congress refused to approve bounties. However, Hamilton and others persuaded the state of New Jersey to subsidize the Society for Establishing Useful Manufactures (SEUM) in 1791. Hamilton alludes to the Society in his Report on Manufactures as an example of the kind of bounties for industry that he wanted Congress to approve.[29] SEUM was set up by Hamilton and some trusted associates to manufacture a variety of products (including paper, clothing, and metal wire) using the most advanced machinery imported from Europe. New Jersey gave the corporation all sorts of monopoly privileges, including exemption of all employees, and of the corporation itself, from taxation.[30]

But, as is not uncommon in government-subsidized enterprises, everything went wrong. SEUM went bankrupt and closed in 1795. Hamilton had imprudently recommended William Duer to head the SEUM, a man who knew nothing about the actual manufacture of goods, but who had made a fortune speculating wildly in government securities with his own and with other people's money. By 1792, Duer lost his personal fortune and contributed to the financial ruin of many others. He "remained in jail, hopelessly insolvent, for the rest of his days."[31]

The whole episode shows the difficulty, underappreciated by Hamilton, of politicians making hiring and investment decisions in particular industries. Perhaps Hamilton should have stuck with his general position that government's most important role is to provide reliable protection for property owners, enforcement of contracts in impartial courts, a stable gold and silver standard, and encouragement of American industry through moderate tariffs. Even in the Report on Manufactures, the background assumption is that free enterprise is generally best: all

---

[26] For Hamilton's debts to these and other writers, see the editor's footnotes in his Report on Manufactures, in ibid., 10:230–340; also Elkins and McKitrick, *Age of Federalism*, 107–12 (discussing the Report on Manufactures).

[27] Madison, "Property," March 29, 1792, in *Founders' Constitution*, 1:598, discussed in the section on monopolies in Chapter 15 above.

[28] Madison, *Federalist* 41, p. 258.   [29] Hamilton, Report on Manufactures, 328.

[30] Joseph Stancliffe Davis, *Essays in the Earlier History of American Corporations* (Cambridge: Harvard University Press, 1917), 1:384, 387.

[31] Elkins and McKitrick, *Age of Federalism*, 262–3, 272–8.

property, including that which receives bounties, is to be privately owned, and most producers, whether farmers, merchants, or manufacturers, will receive no targeted government support. Historian Forrest McDonald writes, "While rejecting *laissez faire*, however, Hamilton was emphatic [in his Report on Manufactures] in his commitment to private enterprise and to a market economy."[32] In *Federalist* 12, Hamilton defends free markets with familiar arguments that continue to be heard today from advocates of free enterprise: money, the object "of human avarice and enterprise,... serves to vivify all the channels of industry and to make them flow with greater activity."[33] One of Hamilton's maxims, quoted near the beginning of this chapter, is that true liberty "protect[s] the exertions of talent and industry and secur[es] to them their justly acquired fruits."[34] But he tended to forget this natural rights principle (shared by almost all founders) when his mind turned to grandiose dreams of government-subsidized manufacturing.

Contrary to Hamilton's predictions, the first successful large-scale manufacturing enterprise in America was established without government subsidy by a group of private investors, the Boston Associates, who set up profitable cotton mills in Lowell, Massachusetts, in the 1820s.[35] Gordon Wood writes, sensibly, that Hamilton "was incapable of foreseeing that the actual source of America's manufacturing would come from below, from the ambitions, productivity, and investments of thousands upon thousands of middling artisans and craftsmen who eventually became America's businessmen."[36] I would modify Wood's verdict by noting that outside of the Report on Manufactures and related schemes, Hamilton was always ready to acknowledge the capacity of America's "thousands of middling artisans and craftsmen" to contribute to an economy of wealth.

Just as one purpose of the original 1789 Tariff Act was "the encouragement and protection of manufactures," so too Hamilton's Report on Manufactures advocates "protecting duties" to the same end.[37] His actual

---

[32] McDonald, *Alexander Hamilton*, 235.   [33] Hamilton, *Federalist* 12, p. 86.

[34] Hamilton, "Defence of the Funding System," 52.

[35] Elkins and McKitrick, *Age of Federalism*, 280; John Michael Cudd, *The Chicopee Manufacturing Company, 1823–1915* (Wilmington, DE: Scholarly Resources, 1974), 13–15.

[36] Gordon S. Wood, *Empire of Liberty: A History of the Early Republic, 1789–1815* (New York: Oxford University Press, 2009), 102–3.

[37] An Act for Laying a Duty on Goods, July 4, 1789, in *Public Statutes at Large*, ed. Richard Peters (Boston: Little and Brown, 1845), 1:24; Hamilton, Report on Manufactures, 296.

proposed tariff rates, however, were limited, observes Richard Irwin, to "raising some duties on imported manufactures and lowering some duties on imported raw materials."[38] Irwin elaborates: "Although the report is often associated with protectionist trade policies, Hamilton's proposed tariffs were quite modest, particularly in light of later experience. This reflected his emphasis on using tariffs to generate fiscal revenue to fund the public debt; indeed, the country's finances were his top priority, not discouraging imports for the sake of domestic manufacturers."[39] Elkins and McKitrick correctly add that it is "misleading to connect Hamilton too closely with the protective tariff theorists of the early nineteenth century, much as they may have looked to him for inspiration."[40] However, it is also true that Congress from the start had in mind at least some protective purpose; in the debate on the tariff of 1789, which preceded Hamilton's proposal, protectionism was a significant part of the congressional discussion. It was not Hamilton but rather Jefferson and Madison who wanted high tariffs – not for the sake of promoting domestic manufactures, but (they hoped) to force Britain into more favorable terms of trade with America.[41] In the end, Congress adopted most of Hamilton's tariff proposal.[42]

I mention the tariff here only to show that although it became highly contentious later, it was not particularly controversial at the time of the founding. Most agreed that some protection of American commerce was proper, and that the tariff was the best way to raise federal revenue. Use of the tariff to limit international trade was not a matter of principle. What was essential was that the market at home be free. The terms of trade with other nations was a matter to be determined by considerations of interest – above all, the preservation of the American nation, the first duty of government according to the social compact theory. In the Report's first paragraph, Hamilton writes that the main purpose of encouraging manufactures is "to render the United States independent on foreign nations for military and other essential supplies" – a goal

---

[38] Douglas A. Irwin, "The Aftermath of Hamilton's 'Report on Manufactures,'" *Journal of Economic History* 64, No. 3 (Sept. 2004): 820.

[39] Irwin, "Aftermath," 801; Irwin, "Revenue or Reciprocity? Founding Feuds over Early U.S. Trade Policy," in *Founding Choices*, 89–120.

[40] Elkins and McKitrick, *Age of Federalism*, 261.

[41] Irwin, "Aftermath," 801; William Hill, "Protective Purpose of the Tariff Act of 1789," *Journal of Political Economy* 2, No. 1 (Dec. 1893): 54–76.

[42] Elkins and McKitrick, *Age of Federalism*, 271 (the "Report on Manufactures was not acted upon at all"); refuted by Irwin, "Aftermath," 800–1.

agreed to by all.[43] In this important respect, all founders agreed with Hamilton's goal of combining "economic nationalism and economic liberalism."[44] No one believed in laissez-faire economics at the expense of American prosperity or national defense.

Objections by Madison and Jefferson

Madison and Jefferson had a short-term and a long-term objection to Hamilton's policies. For the immediate future, they were alarmed that all three of Hamilton's proposals (on the debt, the Bank, and subsidies) would put a lot of money into the pockets of financiers from the Northeast. Political theorist Colleen Sheehan summarizes Madison's agitated complaint: "the Federalist initiatives of the 1790s constituted an agenda clearly intended to undermine republican principles and practices .... [T]he Federalists supported ... a system that promoted inequality of property by governmental fiat and tied the interests of the favored opulent class to the national government.... [They were] intent on severing the government from the will of the people."[45] Hamilton denied the charge that he meant to cut government off from popular will, but he thought that will was insufficient by itself. He believed that self-interest would tie the wealthy, who would benefit financially from his policies, to the new and weak federal government. He did not believe that the bond between these men and the government would undermine America's commitment to government by the people. On the contrary, Hamilton thought that republican government at the national level would have its best chance of success if the powerful men in each state transferred some of their personal attachments from the state governments to the federal. Besides, Hamilton had also become convinced that productive investments would come only from this class of men. They, he wrote, will have "greater means for enterprise" than ordinary farmers, artisans, and workers.[46]

Jefferson and Madison feared and despised precisely these money men, who, in their view, were more interested in pursuing private gain by

---

[43] Hamilton, Report on Manufactures, 230.

[44] Holloway, *Hamilton versus Jefferson*, 120, quoting Christine Margerum Harlen, "A Reappraisal of Classical Economic Nationalism and Economic Liberalism," *International Studies Quarterly* 43, No. 4 (Dec. 1999): 733.

[45] Sheehan, *James Madison*, 119, 121.

[46] Hamilton, Report on Public Credit, 71. Elkins and McKitrick, *Age of Federalism*, 109–19, 777.

buying and selling securities than by doing something useful for the public. They worried that Hamilton's plans would give wealthy investors a disproportionate influence on federal policy at the expense of the public good. Jefferson told Washington that Hamilton's plan "flowed from principles adverse to liberty and was calculated to undermine and demolish the republic."[47]

These accusations were exaggerations. But let us keep in mind the common ground. Neither Madison nor Jefferson objected to paying the debt. They objected to the Bank, but neither tried to get rid of it during his own presidency. As for subsidies of private businesses, Madison himself had written in support of them in *The Federalist*. It was the way Hamilton proposed to do these things, and the anti-popular end that he seemed to aim at, that led Madison and Jefferson into their unrelenting, almost frantic, opposition. Hamilton had no such nefarious purpose, but it is easy to understand why his political enemies objected to a policy that appealed so obviously to the selfish interest of the business elite.

Contemporary scholars sometimes get caught up in the partisan hyperbole typical of the 1790s. Peter NcNamara writes, "Hamilton's conservative and libertarian critics see him as a 'big government conservative' indistinguishable for the most part from the progressive advocates of the contemporary administrative state. Hamilton's critics' case has been helped by the embrace of Hamilton by liberal writers such as Michael Lind."[48] I would add Gordon Wood, who grossly exaggerates when he writes, "Hamilton would be right at home in our present-day United States and our present-day world. He would love our government's vast federal bureaucracy, its huge public debt, its taxes beyond any he could have hoped for."[49] Wood's claims, if true, would make Hamilton a proto-liberal of the Franklin Roosevelt or Bill Clinton type. But Wood is rehashing a Progressive-Era myth originally invented to create a precedent for the Progressive departure from the founders' natural-rights and limited-government consensus.[50] The opposite bias, directed against Jefferson,

---

[47] Jefferson to Washington, Sept. 9, 1792, in *Writings*, 994.

[48] Peter McNamara, review of Federici, *Political Philosophy of Alexander Hamilton*, Dec. 26, 2012, Liberty Fund's Library of Law and Liberty website, http://libertylawsite.org,. McNamara refers to Michael Lind, *Hamilton's Republic: Readings in the American Democratic Nationalist Tradition* (New York: Free Press, 1997).

[49] Gordon S. Wood, "The Statist," *New Republic*, October 15, 2001, 48; see also Wood, *Empire of Liberty*, 104.

[50] An example of the Progressive-Era caricature of Hamilton is Herbert Croly, *The Promise of American Life*, 1909 (Boston: Northeastern University Press, 1989), ch. 2.

is often found among pro-Hamilton scholars. On the first page of this chapter, I quoted James Q. Wilson's caricature of Jefferson, who, Wilson implies, promoted policies that opposed Hamilton's interest in "a sound currency, free enterprise, and encouragement for entrepreneurship." As if Jefferson favored inflation and opposed free enterprise and entrepreneurship!

The long-term objection of Madison and Jefferson was that Hamilton's plan for industrialization would succeed. They worried that large-scale manufacturing would inevitably bring with it a large class of poor workers without attachment to property rights. In a nightmare vision of what he regarded as a likely American future, Madison thought that as population grows and farmland runs out, "the great majority of the people will not only be without landed, but any other sort of property." He foresaw a class struggle "between the great capitalists in manufactures and commerce and the members employed by them" – "indigent laborers."[51] At that point, when workers will be "without the means or hope of acquiring it, what is to secure the rights of property"? It was precisely Madison's concern for free enterprise and entrepreneurship that led him to fear Hamilton's plans.[52]

Jefferson shared Madison's fear. He denounced domestic manufacturing in his *Notes on the State of Virginia* on the ground that manufacturing brings with it "mobs" in "great cities." Jefferson elaborated his concern two decades later: "I had under my eye, when writing [*Notes on Virginia*], the manufacturers of the great cities in the old countries, at the time present, with whom the want of food and clothing necessary to sustain life has begotten a depravity of morals.... My expressions looked forward to the time when our own great cities would get into the same state."[53] Madison and Jefferson therefore supported territorial expansion because they thought it would postpone the evil day when the frontier would close and people would be compelled to take up

---

[51] Madison, Speech at the Constitutional Convention, Aug. 7, in *The Records of the Federal Convention of 1787*, ed. Max Farrand (New Haven: Yale University Press, 1937), 2:203–4.

[52] James Madison, Note to His Speech on the Right of Suffrage in the Constitutional Convention, 1821, in *Founders' Constitution*, 1:601.

[53] Jefferson, *Notes on the State of Virginia*, 1787, Query 19, in *Writings*, 291. Jefferson to Lithgow, Jan. 4, 1805, in *The Works of Thomas Jefferson*, ed. Paul Leicester Ford (New York: G.P. Putnam's Sons, 1904), 4:86–7.

manufacturing instead of farming.[54] Drew McCoy is not exaggerating much when he writes, with regard to large-scale manufacturing, "what Hamilton applauded as positive growth and development, Madison shunned as corruption and decay."[55]

Jefferson and Madison occasionally spoke of farmers, quite unrealistically, as if they were self-sufficient and not dependent on the market. Farmers, wrote Jefferson, "look up to heaven, to their own soil and industry, . . . for their subsistence, [while others] depend for it on the casualties and caprice of customers." Madison agreed: farmers "provide at once their own food and their own raiment, [and] may be viewed as the most truly independent and happy."[56] Yet both men knew well that most Americans, farmers included, relied on the market. Tobacco farmers were quite dependent on "the casualties and caprice of customers" overseas. Madison and Jefferson were eager to open up the Mississippi River to agricultural products destined for international trade.[57] "All the world is becoming commercial," Jefferson wrote in 1784. "Our citizens have had too full a taste of the comforts furnished by the arts and manufactures to be debarred the use of them."[58]

After the War of 1812 had demonstrated the need for America to be economically independent of Europe, Jefferson abandoned his earlier flirtation with a utopian dream of America as a nation of farmers. He now became a strong advocate of manufacturing: "He, therefore, who is now against domestic manufacture, must be for reducing us either to dependence on . . . foreign nations, or to be clothed in skins, and to live like wild beasts in dens and caverns. I am not one of these; experience has taught me that manufactures are now as necessary to our independence as to our comfort."[59] Madison's views similarly became much

---

[54] Paul A. Rahe, *Republics Ancient and Modern: Classical Republicanism and the American Revolution* (Chapel Hill: University of North Carolina Press, 1992), 734; McCoy, *Elusive Republic*, 155.

[55] McCoy, *Elusive Republic*, 155.

[56] Jefferson, *Notes on the State of Virginia*, 1787, in *Writings*, 290. Madison, "Republican Distribution of Citizens," 1792, in *Writings*, ed. Jack Rakove (New York: Library of America, 1999), 512.

[57] Rahe, *Republics Ancient and Modern*, 734.

[58] Jefferson to Washington, Mar. 15, 1784, in *Writings*, 787. On Jefferson's essentially capitalistic or free-market orientation, see also Joyce Appleby, *Capitalism and a New Social Order: The Republican Vision of the 1790s* (New York: New York University Press, 1984); Luigi Marco Bassani, *Liberty, State, and Union: The Political Theory of Thomas Jefferson* (Macon, GA: Mercer University Press, 2010).

[59] Jefferson to Benjamin Austin, Jan. 9, 1816, in *Writings*, 1371.

friendlier toward commerce and manufacturing than McCoy and others admit.

The notion that the development of industrial manufacturing necessarily produces a decline in wages – a view that Karl Marx later made famous – was not unusual among economic theorists of that day. Eighteenth-century British mercantilist writers often argued, writes Drew McCoy, that an economy of refined manufactures "could be sustained only by a dense population with a large pool of 'pauper' laborers who worked for extremely low wages."[60] Michael Sandel rightly notes that "Jefferson's objection was not to manufacturing as such, but to enterprises that would concentrate men and machines in cities and erode the political economy of citizenship." Benjamin Franklin shared Jefferson and Madison's concern: "Great establishments of manufacture require great numbers of poor to do the work for small wages; these poor are to be found in Europe, but will not be found in America, till the lands are all taken up and cultivated, and the excess of people, who cannot get land, want employment."[61] Franklin opposes subsidies for manufacturing in the same paragraph. Yet the same Franklin anticipated the dramatic growth of production based on technological innovation that proved to be a major achievement of America's economy: "The rapid progress true science now makes occasions my regretting sometimes that I was born so soon. It is impossible to imagine the height to which may be carried in a 1000 years the power of man over matter. We may perhaps learn to deprive large masses of their gravity and give them absolute levity, for the sake of easy transport. Agriculture may diminish its labor and double its produce. All diseases may by sure means be prevented or cured, not excepting even that of old age."[62]

Paradoxically, the anti-subsidy policy favored by Franklin and the Southerners, together with the entrepreneurial spirit of Americans and legal protections for property and markets, promoted the very development of "great establishments of manufacture" that worried these men. But their fears proved to be misplaced. As the later history of America demonstrates, wages for factory work, instead of declining, generally went up – except for periods of mass immigration. Industrial workers

---

[60] McCoy, *Elusive Republic*, 53–5. Michael J. Sandel, *Democracy's Discontent: America in Search of a Public Philosophy* (Cambridge: Harvard University Press, 1996), 144.

[61] Benjamin Franklin, "Information to Those Who Would Remove to America," 1784, in *Writings*, ed. J. A. Leo Lemay (New York: Library of America, 1987), 981. See also McCoy, *Elusive Republic*, 56.

[62] Franklin to Joseph Priestly, Feb. 8, 1780, in *Writings*, 1017.

did not become, as Madison feared they would, enemies of private property rights. Instead, the "hope of acquiring property," which Madison worried was fading, continued to animate the poor and wealthy alike. Hamilton's vision of an industrial America was realized, but mostly on the basis of the Jefferson–Franklin policy of leaving individual businesses and investors alone to fend for themselves.

One must add, of course, that the Southerners' commitment to market freedom had one massive exception. Jefferson and Madison were fully aware that slavery totally contradicts what the Maryland Constitution calls the "principles of commerce" by denying to the slaves the right to own or acquire property.[63]

Conclusion

Looking backward, we see that both sides erred. Jefferson and Madison "blundered," Paul Rahe writes, when they concluded that "the spread of large-scale manufacturing would inevitably pose a grave threat to the maintenance of republican liberty."[64] They were also wrong to oppose the payment of the federal debt to the existing bondholders. Their policy would have greatly weakened the credit of the United States. If Madison's debt-payment proposal had passed, writes Richard Sylla, "holders of U.S. debt would have learned that they could not trust the new government . . . to live up to its contracts . . . . In that case, the overall plan for financial reform, if not stillborn, would have suffered a drastic setback."[65]

But Rahe should have added that Hamilton also blundered. He was wrong to believe that rapid economic development would not occur without subsidies. He may also have been mistaken about the importance of a national bank, judging by the long post-Bank period of rapid American economic growth in the nineteenth century. And he seems to have over-estimated the importance of the financial elites' self-interest and under-estimated the warmth of the American people's attachment to a political order that protects their natural rights.

In retrospect, we can say that Hamilton should have paid more attention to the implications of his own observation in *The Federalist* that there is an "adventurous spirit, which distinguishes the commercial character of America." Hamilton had observed that by holding forth the hope of

---

[63] See the discussion at the end of Chapter 14 above.

[64] Rahe, *Republics Ancient and Modern*, 738.   [65] Sylla, "Political Economy," 69.

profits to the "assiduous merchant, the laborious husbandman, the active mechanic, and the industrious manufacturer," free markets would "invigorate all the channels of industry."[66] Everyone agreed that there was, as Washington said, a "spirit of trade which pervades these states."[67] Subsidies and other special privileges proved to be unnecessary. If they had been widely adopted, they would likely have been as wasteful as was New Jersey's investment in Hamilton's Society for Establishing Useful Manufactures or Abraham Lincoln's canal-building scheme in Illinois.

Southerners like Virginia congressman William Branch Giles seem to have understood this aspect of economics better than Hamilton. In terms that anticipate not only the Jacksonians, but also today's defenders of market freedom, Giles argued that "bounties, in all countries and at all times, have been the effect of favoritism; they have only served to direct the current of industry from its natural channel, into one less advantageous or productive; and in fact, they are nothing more than governmental thefts committed upon the rights of one part of the community, and an unmerited governmental munificence to the other."[68] It was on the basis of Giles's understanding that Hamilton's hoped-for industrialization was eventually realized. For the great majority of citizens, America arguably did become a nation in which, as Hamilton wrote, "each individual can find his proper element, and can call into activity the whole vigor of his nature," where "[e]very new scene, which is opened to the busy nature of man to rouse and exert itself, is the addition of a new energy to the general stock of effort."[69]

The differences between Hamilton and Jefferson seemed tremendously important in the 1790s. Today, however, the danger is that by concentrating on these and other founding-era quarrels, we fail to see – as the founders themselves often failed to see – the areas of agreement that were far broader and deeper. Historian John Nelson's verdict on the 1790s is sound: "when the causes of the slow dissolution of consensus among America's ruling elites after ratification of the Constitution are detailed, the evidence points to *specific* disagreements over programmatic issues and not fundamental schisms over the essential role of

---

[66] Hamilton, *Federalist* 11, p. 79; *Federalist* 12, p. 86.

[67] Washington to James Warren, Oct. 7, 1785, in Washington, *Writings*, ed. John Rhodehamel (New York: Library of America, 1997), 592.

[68] *Annals of Congress* (Washington: Gales and Seaton, 1845), Second Congress, 1st Session, Feb. 8, 1792, 399.

[69] Hamilton, Report on Manufactures, 255–6, discussed in Sheehan, *James Madison*, 54.

government."[70] Banning adds, "the views of both colliding parties were legitimate expressions of the highest aspirations of the Revolution.... Sometimes they came very close to losing sight entirely of the fundamentals neither challenged."[71] Political scientist Carson Holloway agrees: "the protagonists, despite their important disagreements, really were reasoning within the context of a shared set of principles."[72] Even Hamilton saw bounties as "temporary," designed to get industries started until such time as they could thrive on their own. "It would be misleading," write Elkins and McKitrick, "to picture Hamilton as conjuring up a kind of 'neo-mercantilism.' Mercantilism was a conscious policy of controlling the economy for purposes of state; Hamilton's purpose was a temporary stimulant of key sectors in an effort to mobilize the energies of the entire community."[73] Forrest McDonald argues persuasively that Hamilton's lifelong goal was to promote "a modern, dynamic market economy [to] replace the static, fixed economy that had been rooted in feudalism."[74] Jefferson also favored a market economy to replace the static feudal one, as his critique of entail made clear: "To annul this privilege, and... to make an opening for... virtue and talent, which nature has wisely provided for the direction of the interests of society, and scattered with an equal hand through all its conditions, was deemed essential to a well-ordered republic."[75] In this fundamental respect, the founders thought and spoke as one.

Government today has strayed far from the founders' approach to economics and property. However, many of the older policies are still in force. We still have freedom of transportation, recorders of deeds, enforcement of contracts in court, a considerable degree of competition in many markets, and more. It is true that America has abandoned the founders' views on the gold and silver standard, prohibition of monopolies, the presumption of freedom to use property as one likes, and requiring government to limit its regulation of property to the protection of health, safety, and the moral foundations of freedom. Still, in comparison with many other nations, America continues to offer a considerable degree of protection to the natural right to acquire and possess property, in the founders' sense of that right.

[70] John R. Nelson, Jr., *Liberty and Property: Political Economy and Policymaking in the New Nation, 1789–1812* (Baltimore: Johns Hopkins University Press, 1987), 77.

[71] Banning, *Conceived in Liberty*, 3.   [72] Holloway, *Hamilton versus Jefferson*, 329.

[73] Hamilton, Report on Manufactures, 302; Elkins and McKitrick, *Age of Federalism*, 261.

[74] McDonald, *Alexander Hamilton*, 312.

[75] Jefferson, *Autobiography, 1743–1790*, in *Writings*, 32.

Conclusion

Justice, Nobility, and the Politics of Natural Rights

In conclusion, I will answer four questions that have been raised about the founders' political theory:

1. Is there a place in the founders' natural rights theory for welfare policy?
2. Did the founders reject socialism because the natural rights theory is selfish at bottom?
3. Does the natural rights theory aim at a commercial republic whose purpose is "private gratification and physical comfort"?
4. Why did the founders regard the classical "politics of virtue" as morally inferior to their own "politics of freedom"?

Natural Rights, Poverty, and Welfare Policy

In earlier chapters I showed how policies securing natural rights, which sought to establish a market economy and stable marriages, enabled the great majority to prosper – or, if not always to prosper, to acquire enough property to avoid destitution. But there will always be some – the poorest of the poor – who are unable or unwilling to obtain even this minimal sustenance. After reading the last few chapters, one might come away with the impression that the founders made no provisions for such people. Not so. Although "acquiring and possessing property" is usually achieved by one's own labor or by uncoerced dealings with others (family, friends, or the market), sometimes people cannot do that for themselves due to temporary economic conditions, disability, death of one's parents, and the like. Continuing a tradition established in colonial times, the founders passed laws providing for the poor – at the state and local level, of course, not the federal (whose scope was limited mostly to foreign and property policy). Although it is true that the founders partly relied on churches, families, and other private associations to take care of the poor, historian Michael Katz writes, correctly, that the "golden age of charity when neighbors took care of each other without the help of government remains pure myth."[1]

Normally, it was expected (sometimes mandated) that families would take care of their own dependents, be they children, disabled, or unemployed. Massachusetts required "the kindred of any such poor person, if any he shall have, in the line or degree of father or grandfather, mother or grandmother, their children or grandchildren,... living within this Commonwealth, of sufficient ability," to care for the indigent person.[2] If families were unable or unwilling, other private associations would often step in. But government everywhere assumed the obligation to provide a "safety net" of last resort. A natural rights republic must have laws providing for the poor.

Every state recognized and to a considerable extent met this obligation.[3] Massachusetts' 1794 law is typical: "every town and district... shall be holden to relieve and support all poor and indigent persons, lawfully settled therein; and... see that they are suitably relieved, supported, and employed, either in a work house, or in such other way and manner as they... shall direct."[4]

A libertarian might object that this sort of policy violates natural right. In a passage previously quoted, Jefferson says, "the first principle of

---

[1] Michael B. Katz, *In the Shadow of the Poorhouse: A Social History of Welfare in America* (New York: Basic Books, 1986), xv, 4–22; Walter I. Trattner, "The Era of the American Revolution," *From Poor Law to Welfare State: A History of Social Welfare in America*, 6th ed. (New York: Free Press, 1999), ch. 3. Katz and Trattner seem to rely substantially on Benjamin Joseph Klebaner, *Public Poor Relief in America, 1790–1860* (New York: Arno Press, 1976). See also Thomas G. West, *Vindicating the Founders: Race, Sex, Class, and Justice in the Origins of America* (Lanham, MD: Rowman & Littlefield, 1997), ch. 6.

[2] An Act Providing for the... Poor, February 26, 1794, in *The Perpetual Laws of the Commonwealth of Massachusetts, 1780–1800* (Boston: I. Thomas and E. T. Andrews, 1801), 2:220. See also Edward Warren Capen, *The Historical Development of the Poor Law of Connecticut* (New York: Columbia University Press, 1905), 116 (same policy as MA).

[3] Klebaner, *Public Poor Relief* (state-by-state descriptions of poor laws in the early republic). See also William P. Quigley, "Reluctant Charity: Poor Laws in the Original Thirteen States," *University of Richmond Law Review* 31, No. 1 (Jan. 1997): 111–78. Although my footnotes refer mostly to laws in Northern states, Klebaner and Quigley show that these policies existed throughout the nation.

[4] An Act for the Poor, in *Perpetual Laws of Massachusetts*, 2:220.

association" – i.e., of the social compact – "[is] the guarantee to everyone the free exercise of his industry and the fruits acquired by it." How then could it be just to take from the producer, who has a right to the fruits of his labor, and give it to the needy, who have no right to it? Is that not a violation of "the first principle of association"?

I have found nothing in the founding that explicitly links the natural rights theory with government responsibility for the poor. However, the logic that justifies all government policies, including welfare policy, is given in the *Essex Result*: "When men form themselves into society,... [e]ach individual ... surrenders the power of controlling his natural alienable rights, only when the good of the whole requires it.... [T]he equivalent every man receives, as a consideration for the rights he has surrendered, ... consists primarily in the security of his person and property."[5] We saw earlier in this book that government provides for "security of person" in domestic policy by laws against such crimes as murder and robbery, and by civil laws establishing clear rules for property ownership and use, buying and selling, and the like. But we must add that government also provides for "security of person," in the opinion of the founders, by giving limited support to people who cannot or will not provide for themselves through their own labor or through the voluntary support of family or neighbors. Essex emphasizes that the "good of the whole" requires that there be "equal benefit" for "every member." These are the terms in which the founders thought of poor laws (what we call welfare policy). If government comes to your assistance when your life is endangered by extreme poverty, you benefit. But everyone benefits equally from that policy, because poverty or disability can happen to anyone at any time, just as auto insurance can be worth having even if car accidents are rare.

However, a policy which allows able-bodied people to live off the labor of others no longer serves "the good of the whole." It serves the good of the idle poor at the expense of working people. To that extent, government is treating the productive part of the populace as slaves. In Abraham Lincoln's pithy formulation, slavery "is the same tyrannical principle. It is ... the same spirit that says, 'You work and toil and earn bread, and I'll eat it.'"[6] Jefferson sums up the founders' solution: "Vagabonds, without

---

[5] *The Essex Result*, 1778, in *American Political Writing during the Founding Era, 1760–1805*, ed. Charles S. Hyneman and Donald S. Lutz (Indianapolis: Liberty Press, 1983), 1:487, 489.

[6] Seventh Lincoln–Douglas debate, October 15, 1858, in *Collected Works of Abraham Lincoln*, ed. Roy T. Basler (New Brunswick: Rutgers University Press, 1953), 3:315.

visible property or vocation, are placed in workhouses, where they are well clothed, fed, lodged, and made to labor."[7] Thus a Massachusetts poor law of 1789 called for "erecting houses for the employment of idle persons who neglect and refuse to exercise any lawful calling or business to support themselves and families, and for the poor and indigent that want means to employ themselves."[8]

To clarify the founders' approach, one might compare philosophy professor John Rawls, whose *Theory of Justice* (1971) provides an influential justification of the kind of welfare policy that is widely accepted today. Rawls argues that "since inequalities of birth and natural endowments are undeserved, these inequalities are to be somehow compensated for." "[N]atural talents" are therefore to be viewed "as a common asset" to be shared with the less talented, not as the rightful possession of the talented individual.[9]

Rawls's approach is the opposite of the founders', for whom self-ownership is the original natural right ("born equally free and independent," i.e., no one's slave) from which all the other natural rights may be said to flow. In *Federalist* 10, "the protection of different and unequal faculties of acquiring property" "from which the rights of property originate... is the first object of government."[10] Therefore, welfare policy may intrude on the fruits of one's labor only as far as it is compatible with securing the basic rights to life and liberty – including the liberty to acquire property – for everyone.

For Rawls, the founders' definition of justice – security of natural rights – is fundamentally unjust. Rawls explains: "to provide genuine equality of opportunity, society must give more attention to those with fewer native assets and to those born into the less favorable social positions.... [G]reater resources might [therefore] be spent on the education of the less rather than the more intelligent."[11] For the founders, welfare is a social insurance policy for hard times or unusual circumstances. For Rawls, its purpose is to take wealth and social status away from those who have more than others and give them instead to people who have less.

7 Thomas Jefferson, *Notes on the State of Virginia*, 1787, Query 14, in Jefferson, *Writings*, ed. Merrill D. Peterson (New York: Library of America, 1984), 259.
8 An Act for Erecting Work Houses for the Reception and Employment of the Idle and Indigent, January 10, 1789, in *Perpetual Laws of Massachusetts*, 2:25.
9 John Rawls, *A Theory of Justice* (Cambridge: Harvard University Press, 1971), 100–1.
10 Madison, *Federalist* 10, in Alexander Hamilton, Madison, and John Jay, *The Federalist Papers*, ed. Clinton Rossiter (New York: Signet Classics, 2003), 73.
11 Rawls, *Theory of Justice*, 101.

The goal is to equalize as much as possible the distribution of "primary goods," i.e., "things that every rational man is presumed to want."[12] The founders' minimal safety net would then be replaced by such things as a comfortable home of one's own, food of one's own choice, top-quality medical care, and special advantages for the less "advantaged" in education and in the job market.

For the founders, it was a concern that the safety net not be so generous that it would entice people to prefer government benefits to marriage or gainful employment. At first the founders tended to rely on what scholars call "outdoor relief" – government payments directly to welfare recipients or to the private persons taking care of them. This kind of relief was administered locally, where public officials would hopefully be acquainted with the recipients of public support. This was more or less the policy that prevailed before independence in 1776. Jefferson explains how this system worked in Virginia in the 1780s: "[The overseers of the poor] are usually the most discreet farmers, so distributed through their parish, that every part of it may be under the immediate eye of some one of them. . . . The poor who have neither property, friends, nor strength to labor, are boarded in the houses of good farmers, to whom a stipulated sum is annually paid. To those who are able to help themselves a little, or have friends from whom they derive some succors, inadequate however to their full maintenance, supplementary aids are given, which enable them to live comfortably in their own houses, or in the houses of their friends." Vermont's 1779 Act for Supporting the Poor is also typical of this initial outdoor-relief approach: "each town in this state shall take care of, support, and maintain their own poor[,] . . . supplying them, or any of them, with victuals, clothing, firewood, or any other thing necessary for their support or subsistence."[13]

The lazy and the dishonest easily took advantage of outdoor relief. State after state shifted its policy from outdoor to "indoor relief" – workhouses or almshouses. Political scientist Joseph Klebaner writes, "Poorhouses may be said to have become the fashion in public welfare during the nineteenth century. By 1860 few populous communities were without them."[14] The poorhouse of the late eighteenth and early nineteenth century is what we today might call a group home with

---

[12] Ibid., 62.
[13] Act for Maintaining and Supporting the Poor, 1779, in *Laws of Vermont, 1777–1780*, ed. Allen Soule, vol. 12 of *State Papers of Vermont* (Montpelier: Secretary of State, 1964), 158.
[14] Klebaner, *Public Poor Relief*, 103.

work requirements. This approach had been recommended by Jefferson in his 1778 proposed Virginia Bill for the Support of the Poor and his Bill Concerning Apprentices.[15] A Maryland law explains: "the necessity, number, and continual increase of the poor ... is very great and exceedingly burdensome, which might be greatly lessened by a due regulation and employment of them."[16] North Carolina authorized the building of poorhouses starting in 1785. Its law mentioned that these almshouses were also intended to help the mentally disabled who are "incapable of self-preservation" – one of the natural rights that government is supposed to secure.[17] In these poorhouses or almshouses, people were usually required to work to the extent of their ability in exchange for room, board, and minimal medical care.

Massachusetts too saw the workhouse as a superior alternative to Vermont's early policy of giving benefits to the poor to enable them to live in their own homes. Its 1793 poor law mandates, "Every town ... shall be holden to relieve and support all poor and indigent persons ... and shall see that they are suitably relieved, supported, and employed, either in the work-house or other tenements belonging to such towns or districts, or in such other way and manner as they, at any legal meeting, shall direct."[18] In a 1795 ordinance of the Northwest Territory, based on a Pennsylvania law, outdoor relief was explicitly forbidden. Poorhouses were to be established, and "if any poor person shall refuse to be lodged, kept, maintained, and employed in such house or houses, he or she shall not be entitled to receive relief from the overseers during such refusal."[19] The provisions of this law were duplicated by Ohio, Michigan, Wisconsin, and other states.[20] In his chapter on "The Trend toward Indoor Relief," Walter Trattner tends to assume that the turn to poorhouses was

---

[15] Jefferson, A Bill for Support of the Poor and A Bill Concerning ... Apprentices, 1778, in *The Papers of Thomas Jefferson*, ed. Julian P. Boyd et al. (Princeton: Princeton University Press, 1950–), 2:422, 487.

[16] Preamble to a 1768 MD law, repeated in five MD poor laws passed in the 1770s and 1780s, in Klebaner, *Public Poor Relief*, 104.

[17] Roy M. Brown, *Public Poor Relief in North Carolina* (Chapel Hill: University of North Carolina Press, 1928), 28.

[18] An Act Providing for the Relief and Support ... of the Poor, February 26, 1794, in *Perpetual Laws of Massachusetts*, 2:220.

[19] A Law for the Relief of the Poor, June 19, 1795, in *The Statutes of Ohio and the Northwestern Territory, 1788–1833*, ed. Salmon P. Chase (Cincinnati: Corey & Fairbank, 1833), 1:176.

[20] Trattner, *From Poor Law to Welfare State*, 40–1.

a nineteenth-century development. In fact, poorhouses were already being widely built in the 1780s and '90s – i.e., soon after the political theory of natural rights had begun to influence the direction of public policy and the reshaping of colonial laws.[21]

The practical consequence of the founders' approach to poverty – providing aid, but minimally and with work requirements – was that most people who found themselves in need of the poorhouse quickly found a way to get out of it, often by getting a job and becoming self-supporting. The experience of Albemarle County in Virginia was typical: when the county stopped funding outdoor relief, it "found the number of its paupers reduced from an average of eighty (from 1800 to 1808) to a maximum of thirty." The poor list of Virginia's Essex County "was reduced by two-thirds; . . . these now lived by their own efforts, or with the help of private charity."[22]

The poorhouse was also expected to provide moral improvement. One of Philadelphia's almshouses was popularly known as a "bettering house," according to Klebaner. He explains: "The lazy were expected to become industrious; sots, abstainers; and the vicious, virtuous." To this end religious instruction was often a part of life in the poorhouse. It was hoped, as an 1810 Pennsylvania newspaper article reports, that "many of them [namely, drunken paupers] might by degrees become so far reformed as to be favored with the blessing of repentance and a happy amendment of life."[23]

While the adult poor were sent to workhouses, orphans and other children in need of support would often be placed with private families as apprentices or workers, where they would presumably learn useful skills. This policy was part of the Vermont law just quoted: "[I]f there be any poor children . . . that live idly, or are exposed to want and distress, and there are none to take care of them, it shall and may be lawful . . . to bind [them] out . . . to be apprentices, or servants."[24] In the Northwest Territory, the overseers of the poor were instructed "to put out, as apprentices, all such poor children, whose parents are dead, or shall be by the said justices found unable to maintain them, males till the age of twenty-one, and females till the age of eighteen years."[25] Private

---

[21] Ibid., 47–76, and Brown, *Public Poor Relief*, 28.

[22] Klebaner, *Public Poor Relief*, 112.   [23] Ibid., 110–11.

[24] Vermont, Act for Maintaining and Supporting the Poor, 158. For CT: Capen, *Historical Development of the Poor Law*.

[25] Law for the Relief of the Poor, in *Statutes of Ohio*, 1:177.

orphanages, often partly subsidized by the state governments, soon supplemented and increasingly replaced the practice of "binding out" children as apprentices or servants.[26]

In contrast to the sketch provided here, Trattner writes, in his standard history of American welfare, "by the late eighteenth and early nineteenth century, Americans began to believe that poverty could, and should, be obliterated – in part, by allowing the poor to perish."[27] Trattner's claim is untrue, as he himself should have acknowledged on the basis of his own evidence. His book details many of the features of early American welfare policy that I have described here. In practice, of course, the poorhouse system was open to abuses from inadequate funding or poor management. Still, historian Robert Cray's verdict is more accurate than Trattner's: "Local communities attempted as best they could to assist their destitute neighbors, balancing compassion with economy, benevolence with discipline."[28] The rights to life, liberty, and acquiring property were protected for all.

Natural Rights and Socialism

Just as one might have doubts about the justice of the founders' market economy toward the poor, so also the socialist alternative to free markets might be considered more just. Why did the founders reject socialism?

President Dwight Eisenhower once told a story that illustrates this doubt – and exposed his ignorance of the natural rights theory. At the end of World War II, Eisenhower commanded the armed forces of America and its Western allies, while Georgy Zhukov commanded the Soviet forces. After the war, Eisenhower toured the Soviet Union with Zhukov. Eisenhower later reported: "one evening we had a three-hour conversation. We tried, each to explain to the other just what our systems meant, our two systems meant, to the individual, and I was very hard put to it when he insisted that their system appealed to the idealistic, and we completely to the materialistic. And I had a very tough time trying to defend our position, because he said: 'You tell a person he can do as he

---

[26] Marvin Olasky, *The Tragedy of American Compassion* (Washington: Regnery Gateway, 1992), 14.

[27] Trattner, *From Poor Law to Welfare State*, 54.

[28] Robert E. Cray, *Paupers and Poor Relief in New York City and Its Rural Environs, 1700–1830* (Philadelphia: Temple University Press, 1988), 199.

pleases, he can act as he pleases, he can do anything. Everything that is selfish in man you appeal to.'"[29]

Eisenhower, who had served America honorably during the war, had a "very tough time" defending America's system of self-government and free enterprise against the verbal attack of a high-ranking official in an oppressive, communist system led by Joseph Stalin, one of history's greatest mass murderers.[30] Clearly, Eisenhower not only failed to embrace but knew nothing about the view of the founders, for whom, as was often said in the founding era, liberty "is totally different from licentiousness. Many have no other idea of liberty, but for everyone to do as he pleases – to be as honest as he pleases – to be as knavish as he pleases.... Such a liberty... ought to be done away with."[31] New York's 1777 Constitution makes the same distinction: "the liberty of conscience hereby granted shall not be so construed as to excuse acts of licentiousness."[32] We saw in Part II that a free society requires people to control their predatory and self-indulgent passions, to serve their country, and to fulfill their contracts, whether commercial or marital. The founders would not have hesitated to repudiate a claim of "idealism" raised by Zhukov, a man whom they would have judged a minion of a bloody tyrant. If "idealistic" policies are those that enable the poor to escape poverty and allow all to live in temperate liberty, then the most idealistic order is one that secures the natural right to acquire and possess property.

The history of communism in colonial America taught the founders a valuable lesson. James Wilson tells the story of two early American colonies – Plymouth, Massachusetts, settled in 1620, and Jamestown, Virginia, in 1607 – that started off with what we today would call socialism or communism. In Plymouth, Wilson writes, the colonists agreed that "the produce of their joint industry should be deposited in a common magazine, and that from this common magazine, everyone should be supplied under the direction of the council." The result was disastrous: "happy was he that could slip from his labor, or slubber over his work in any manner.... Even the most honest and industrious would scarcely

---

[29] Dwight D. Eisenhower, Presidential News Conference, July 15, 1957, American Presidency Project, University of California at Santa Barbara, www.presidency.ucsb.edu.

[30] Stephane Courtois et al., *The Black Book of Communism: Crimes, Terror, Repression* (Cambridge: Harvard University Press, 1999), pt. I–III.

[31] "A Freeman: To the People of Connecticut," *Connecticut Courant*, Dec. 31, 1787, in *The Documentary History of the Ratification of the Constitution*, ed. Merrill Jensen (Madison: State Historical Society of Wisconsin, 1976-), 3:519.

[32] NY Constitution, 1777, art. 38.

take so much pains in a week, as they would have done for themselves in a day." The introduction of private ownership, Wilson continues, "immediately produced the most comfortable change in the colony, by engaging the affections and invigorating the pursuits of its inhabitants."[33]

Wilson's summary is confirmed by William Bradford's seventeenth-century account of how Plymouth was able to overcome the "hunger and famine" of its first years: "So they began to think how they might raise as much corn as they could, and obtain a better crop than they had done, that they might not still thus languish in misery.... [The governor] assigned to every family a parcel of land, according to the proportion of their number.... This had very good success, for it made all hands very industrious, so as much more corn was planted than otherwise would have been..., and gave far better content. The women now went willingly into the field, and took their little ones with them to set corn; which before would allege weakness and inability; whom to have compelled would have been thought great tyranny and oppression."[34]

Communism was also tried in early Jamestown. Just as in Plymouth, "the colonists were sometimes in danger of starvation." The authorities there resorted to "severe whipping, which was often administered to promote labor, [but] was only productive of constant and general discontent."[35] Jamestown thereby anticipated the policy of the late Soviet Union. A Soviet poster of 1931, labeled "We Smite the Lazy Workers," pictures a man who is still in bed at 9:07 a.m. having his head smashed by a sledgehammer.[36] Wilson's narration implies that the logic of socialism leads to both increasingly harsh punishments and the impoverishment of the great majority.

It is true that the founders' economic order leads to inequality in the distribution of property. In *Federalist* 10, Madison writes, "From the protection of different and unequal faculties of acquiring property, the possession of different degrees and kinds of property immediately results." People with more talent and ambition will generally acquire

---

[33] James Wilson, "History of Property," in *Collected Works*, ed. Hall and Hall, 1:305, citing George Chalmers, *Political Annals of the Present United Colonies from Their Settlement to the Peace of 1763* (London, 1780), 89, 90.

[34] William Bradford, *Of Plymouth Plantations, 1620–1647* (orig. written about 1650; New York: Modern Library, 1981), 160, 132–3.

[35] Wilson, "History of Property," 305, quoting William Stith, *History of the First Discovery and Settlement of Virginia* (Williamsburg, VA: W. Parks, 1747), 39.

[36] See the paperback cover of Martin Malia, *The Soviet Tragedy: A History of Socialism in Russia, 1917–1991* (New York: Free Press, 1994). Also at www.columbia.edu/itc/sipa/U8150/communism/77.html.

greater wealth. Can that be just? The founders' answer was "yes," for two reasons.

First is an argument from principle. No adult can justly be compelled to submit to the will of another. Whatever differences in wealth may emerge, property rights benefit all classes equally insofar as they protect the body and mind of every individual from exploitation or enslavement by others. Whenever government uses compulsion to redistribute wealth for the purpose of equalization, it violates the "first principle of association": the right to liberty, the right to the free exercise of one's own mind and body. Jefferson writes, "To take from one, because it is thought his own industry and that of his fathers has acquired too much, in order to spare to others, who, or whose fathers, have not exercised equal industry and skill, is to violate arbitrarily the first principle of association, the guarantee to everyone the free exercise of his industry and the fruits acquired by it."[37]

The founders' second argument justifying unequal distribution of property is based not on principle but on utility. James Wilson explains: "The right of private property seems to be founded in the nature of men and of things. . . . Exclusive property multiplies the productions of the earth, and the means of subsistence. Who would cultivate the soil, and sow the grain, if he had no peculiar interests in the harvest?"[38] An economic order in which some acquire more than others is the condition of greater prosperity for all.

Natural Rights and the Justice and Nobility of the Commercial Republic

Zhukov's remarks in his conversation with Eisenhower reminds one of Ralph Lerner, who argues that the commercial republic produced by the founders' natural law principles is built on "the common passions for private gratification and physical comfort."[39] Lerner admits the founders knew that a commercial society is not an unambiguous good, that its very success can have harmful consequences. "From the conclusion of this war," wrote Jefferson in 1781, "we will be going down hill." The

---

37 Jefferson to Joseph Milligan, April 6, 1816, in *The Founders' Constitution*, ed. Philip B. Kurland and Ralph Lerner (Chicago: University of Chicago Press, 1987), 1:573.

38 Wilson, "History of Property," 305–6.

39 Ralph Lerner, *The Thinking Revolutionary: Principle and Practice in the New Republic* (Ithaca: Cornell University Press, 1987), 201. In the passage quoted, Lerner is discussing European thinkers. But later in the chapter he implies that the founders were broadly in agreement with their program.

people "will forget themselves, but in the sole faculty of making money." John Adams worried that "without virtue, there can be no political liberty.... Will you tell me how to prevent riches from being the effects of temperance and industry?... Will you tell me how to prevent luxury from producing effeminacy, intoxication, extravagance, vice, and folly?" Hamilton agreed: "True liberty, by protecting the exertions and talents of industry, and securing to them their justly acquired fruits, tends more powerfully than any other cause to augment the mass of national wealth and to produce the mischiefs of opulence." However, after acknowledging the difficulty, Hamilton then posed this sensible question: "Shall we therefore on this account proscribe liberty also?... Tis the portion of man assigned to him by the eternal allotment of Providence that every good he enjoys shall be alloyed with ills... except virtue alone."[40]

Lerner quotes Hume's "Of Commerce": since it is "too difficult to support" the "passion for the public good" that was expected of citizens of the ancient city, "it is requisite to govern men by other passions, and animate them with a spirit of avarice and industry, art, and luxury." Lerner continues: although the founders "did not promote this new policy with quite the breezy equanimity of Hume,... neither did the leading Americans reject Hume's premises."

Lerner is correct to claim that the founders rejected a reliance on virtue alone, but he and Hume go too far when they suggest that the alternative to unrealistic expectations from virtue is the unleashing of "avarice," as if moral standards can be dispensed with.[41] The founders allowed and encouraged people to pursue their private interest within the limits of moderation and justice, while promoting and requiring the submission of one's private interest to the requirements of the common good. The Naturalization Oath still includes the promise "that I will bear arms on behalf of the United States when required by the law" or perform some other legally approved service.[42] The Massachusetts Bill

---

[40] Jefferson, *Notes on Virginia*, Query 17, in *Writings*, ed. Peterson, 287. Adams to Jefferson, December 21, 1819, in *The Adams-Jefferson Letters*, ed. Lester J. Cappon (New York: Simon & Schuster, 1959), 551. Hamilton, Defence of the Funding System, July 1795, in *The Papers of Alexander Hamilton*, ed. Harold C. Syrett (New York: Columbia University Press, 1961–79), 19:32. Also Washington to James Warren, October 7, 1785, in *Writings*, ed. John Rhodehamel (New York: Library of America, 1997), 592; Jay to Washington, June 27, 1786, in *The Correspondence and Public Papers of John Jay*, ed. Henry P. Johnston (New York: G.P. Putnam's Sons, 1891), 3:204.

[41] Lerner, *Thinking Revolutionary*, 206.

[42] Oath of renunciation and allegiance, United States Code, Title 8, ch. 12, Subchapter III, Part II, §1448, www4.law.cornell.edu/uscode/8/1448.html.

of Rights similarly states that "each individual of the society has a right to be protected by it in the enjoyment of his life, liberty and property, according to standing laws. He is obliged, consequently, to contribute his share to the expense of this protection; to give his personal service, or an equivalent, when necessary."[43] Government protects rights, but citizens also have duties.

In Part II of this book we explored the founders' policies that would help to sustain a society where public spirit and self-restraint would not be overwhelmed by the wealth and money-making spirit unleashed by freedom. One element of that is the very market economy that is presumed to degrade and lower the tone of society. When free markets are established and sustained by the policies sketched in Part III, they subordinate greed and avarice to the requirements of self-restraint and justice. Self-restraint is required because success requires savings and investment, i.e., postponement of gratification. Justice is required because for enduring commercial success, one must fulfill one's contracts, deal honestly with fellow citizens, and refrain from violence and thievery.

Whatever dangers may arise from security of property rights, the alternative was believed to be far worse. At the end of the Declaration of Independence, the founders pledged to each other "our lives, our fortunes, and our sacred honor." They did not think they were striving for an unheroic goal. They were prepared to give up life and property in the noble fight to establish a nation based on the true principles of justice: a nation that would protect the lives and property of their families and descendants. Such a nation was judged worthy of their devotion because they believed that justice is the purpose of civil society. If all went well, America would become the most just nation ever created. The opposite of life, liberty, property, and the pursuit of happiness is not some sort of transcendent political perfection. It is death, slavery, destitution, and misery.

The Politics of Freedom versus the Politics of Virtue

I conclude with a very brief remark on one of the most influential alternatives to the founders: Plato's case against a free society as presented in his *Republic*. The root of the difference lies in the juridical status of the individual. For the founders, all men are created equal. No one is by nature the owner or ruler of anyone else. Therefore, as the Massachusetts House

---

[43] MA Declaration of Rights, 1780, art. 10.

of Representatives declares, "a man should have the free use and sole disposal of the fruit of his honest industry."[44] Plato's Socrates, however, never speaks of equality or individual rights. That is because Socrates makes the problem of human knowledge and ignorance the central consideration. There are very few people, he argues, who are sufficiently sound-minded to be entrusted with political power. In the opening pages of the *Republic*, Socrates makes a compelling case against the right of anyone "of unsound mind" to own property,[45] including, we can easily infer, property in his own person. Anyone who lacks sufficient understanding to keep from harming himself or others can hardly be said to have a right to any sort of property. The founders agreed with Socrates up to a point. With John Locke, they thought that a child "has not understanding to direct his will," so that "he that understands for him, must will for him too." Locke might even be said to agree with Socrates when he writes, "we are born free, as we are born rational."[46] Locke and the founders argue, however, in apparent disagreement with Socrates, that most adults may be presumed to be rational enough to be capable of self-ownership and self-government – as opposed to being owned and governed by others – and therefore capable of owning other forms of property as well.

The great strength of the Platonic approach is that it does not allow us to make the mistake of thinking that human life has no higher concern than providing for the needs of our bodies or for our paltry whims and desires. Socrates never forgets the importance of aspiring to something purer and nobler than mere survival. Zhukov's complaint quoted earlier ("You tell a person he can do as he pleases, he can act as he pleases, he can do anything") echoes Socrates's criticisms of democracy in *Republic* book 8.[47] In Plato, the purpose of government is not only to provide for the body but also for the soul. After Socrates finishes describing the education of the guardians, virtue proves to be the purpose of political life. The incipient capitalism of the "healthy city" is checked by Socrates's "purge" of luxury and license from the city. Although there is still a place

---

[44] Massachusetts House of Representatives to Henry Seymour, February 13, 1768, in *Writings of Samuel Adams*, ed. Harry A. Cushing (1904–08; repr. New York: Octagon, 1968), 1:190.

[45] Plato, *Republic*, 331c-e.

[46] John Locke, *Two Treatises of Government*, 1690, ed. Peter Laslett (Cambridge: Cambridge University Press, 1960), *Second Treatise*, §58, §61. See the discussion of children at the end of Chapter 3 above.

[47] Karl Marx, *On the Jewish Question*, 1843, in *The Marx-Engels Reader*, ed. Robert C. Tucker, 2nd ed. (New York: Norton, 1978), 26–46; Plato, *Republic*, 557a–558c.

for market freedom for the lower classes, the use and exchange of property will be strictly regulated with a view to what the rulers consider to be beneficial, non-corrupting goods and services.[48]

But Plato's politics of virtue, the cultivation of self-denying devotion to the common good, carries with it its own dangers. Karl Marx's promise that communism would end human selfishness was cited to excuse murderous oppression in the Soviet Union. The founders, following the lead of philosophers like Locke, thought that it was better to teach people not to expect too much from politics. In their view, political life cannot deliver the kind of perfection longed for by those who are attracted by the "beautiful city" of the *Republic*.[49] The founders made a distinction between the purpose of politics (security of life, liberty, and property) and the purpose of human life (happiness). Property and personal freedom are not the highest things. They are not ends. They are means for the pursuit of happiness. That is why Allan Bloom's statement that the founders' natural rights are "life, liberty, and the pursuit of property" – as if they equated property with happiness – is so profoundly misleading.[50]

The higher things were expected to be found not in public but in private life. Some founders acknowledged that explicitly, e.g., James Wilson in his *Lectures on Law*: "government is the scaffolding of society: and if society could be built and kept entire without government, the scaffolding might be thrown down, without the least inconvenience or cause of regret."[51] The true home of religion and philosophy and science, of revelation and reason, of the family and domestic happiness, is in private society.

By abstaining from defining and compelling a particular vision of the highest life, government paradoxically enables that life to flourish. Freedom of religion meant, as the Virginia Declaration of Rights makes clear, that government no longer stands in the way of "the duty which we owe to our Creator."[52] Government is no longer in the business of defining the one true religion. It also meant that individuals are free to live their lives independently of religious faith. Harry Jaffa argues that the regime established in the founding, at least "in its principles," is "the best regime of Western civilization" because it refrains from using the coercive power of government to resolve the unresolvable dispute between the claims of

---

[48] Plato, *Republic*, 372e–417b.   [49] Ibid., 527c.

[50] Allan Bloom, *The Closing of the American Mind* (New York: Simon and Schuster, 1987), 287.

[51] Wilson, *Lectures on Law*, 1791, in *Collected Works of James Wilson*, ed. Kermit L. Hall and Mark David Hall (Indianapolis: Liberty Fund, 2007), 1:452.

[52] VA Declaration of Rights, 1776, art. 16.

faith and the claims of mere reason as the best guide to life. A government that protects religious liberty, "defusing the tension between reason and revelation," thereby "provided for the coexistence of the claims of reason and of revelation in all their forms, without requiring or permitting any political decisions concerning them. It refused to make unassisted human reason the arbiter of the claims of revelation, and it refused to make revelation the judge of the claims of reason."[53]

The founders' regime aims at securing the conditions of happiness and the right to pursue happiness but does not attempt to define the content of happiness. It is true that the founders sometimes spoke of "public happiness" as the end of government. To them that meant public prosperity and security of individual rights, a condition in which, in Washington's words quoted from the Bible, "every one shall sit in safety under his own vine and fig tree, and there shall be none to make him afraid."[54] Public happiness is not necessarily individual happiness. That depends on how each person lives his or her own life. Only if government stops trying to dictate the best way of life for everyone can it provide for public happiness and thereby set the stage for private happiness.

The nobility of the founding consists in its realism about the self-interested nature of man, combined with its idealism about building a government that serves the common good by enabling people to acquire enough property to live, while making it possible for people in their private lives to serve God in the way they believed best and to cultivate their minds without being tormented by persecution.

Plato's regime of perfect virtue depends on the rule of philosopher-kings. But Plato himself might well accept Madison's epitaph on that dream: "the philosophical race of kings wished for by Plato" does not exist.[55] In their absence, rulers claiming the mantle of wisdom would be the unworthy pretenders so vividly disparaged in *Republic* book 6. Instead of the hoped-for virtuous community, it would be a bleak despotism. In his First Inaugural, Jefferson says: "Sometimes it is said that man cannot be trusted with the government of himself. Can he, then, be trusted with the government of others? Or have we found angels in the forms of kings to govern him? Let history answer this question."[56]

---

[53] Harry V. Jaffa, "The American Founding as the Best Regime," 2002, Claremont Institute, www.claremont.org.

[54] Washington to the Hebrew Congregation in Newport, RI, August 18, 1790, in *Writings*, 767.

[55] Madison, *Federalist* 49, p. 312.

[56] Jefferson, First Inaugural Address, 1801, in *Writings*, 494.

The Founders' Political Theory Today

The state of nature is the basis of the founders' understanding of politics. If human beings are born free and equal in a natural state, subject only to the laws of nature, then government is a product of human making to secure the equal natural rights of the citizens. Thomas Paine explains: "as nature knows ... not [kings], they know not her, and although they [kings] are beings of our own creating, they know not us, and are become the gods of their creators."[57] Nature knows nothing of kings because political rule comes not from nature but rather from "our own creating." Kings do not know nature because by being elevated above the people, they fall into the delusion of being gods. Once equality in the state of nature is understood, no one can be expected to submit blindly to any merely human claim of authority. John Adams complains that in the Middle Ages, it was "stipulated between them, that the temporal grandees [kings and aristocrats] should contribute everything in their power to maintain the ascendency of the priesthood, and that the spiritual grandees, in their turn, should employ their ascendency over the consciences of the people, in impressing on their minds a blind, implicit obedience to civil magistracy."[58] That kind of politics is impossible under the natural rights doctrine.

This tendency of human beings to "blind, implicit obedience" is not limited to medieval times. Leo Strauss observes that Martin Heidegger, a leading German thinker of the past century, "welcome[d], as a dispensation of fate," the rise of Hitler to power. Heidegger's example teaches us, Strauss concludes, "that man cannot abandon the question of the good society, and that he cannot free himself from the responsibility for answering it by deferring to History or to any other power different from his own reason."[59] Everyone must use his or her own judgment in the face of any human claim to authority. That means no one is obliged to submit blindly to anyone who claims to rule him rightfully without his consent. In this limited but important sense, almost all philosophers have agreed that "all men are created equal."

The founders would maintain that the natural rights doctrine will be politically relevant as long as there are people who claim the right to rule

---

[57] Appendix to *Common Sense*, 1776, in *Writings of Thomas Paine*, ed. Conway, 1:112–13.

[58] John Adams, *Dissertation on the Canon and Feudal Law*, 1765, in *Works of John Adams*, ed. Charles Francis Adams (Boston: Little, Brown, 1865), 3:450.

[59] Leo Strauss, *What Is Political Philosophy? And Other Studies* (Glencoe, IL: Free Press, 1959), 27.

not by consent but because they belong to a class anointed by God, by History, by moral credentials earned by serving the disadvantaged, or by Harvard and Yale. In other words, they would regard it as relevant at all times. At the beginning of World War II, Strauss remarked that the re-emergence of a religious "totalitarian country" that punishes doubts about "the holy book or books of the ruling class" might be "not so remote from reality as it might first seem."[60] In the face of atheistic Nazism and atheistic Communism, which in 1941 were the two most pressing threats to liberty and civilization, Strauss's strange worry about a future religious despotism may have been unique. Yet in the twenty-first century, the growing number of religiously inspired governments hostile to reason suggests that Strauss's concern might not have been misplaced. The founders' doctrine that all men are by nature equally free and independent – that all political societies are produced by human beings, not by God or nature or an inexorable historical process – might continue to prove useful. It might even be true.

---

[60] Leo Strauss, "Persecution and the Art of Writing," *Social Research* 8, No. 4 (Nov. 1941): 490–1.

Index

411